ROUTLEDGE HANDB
COMPARATIVE CONSTI⎯ ⎯ ⎯⎯⎯⎯⎯⎯
CHANGE

Comparative constitutional change has recently emerged as a distinct field in the study of constitutional law. It is the study of the way constitutions change through formal and informal mechanisms, including amendment, replacement, total and partial revision, adaptation, interpretation, disuse and revolution. The shift of focus from constitution-making to constitutional change makes sense, since amendment power is the means used to refurbish constitutions in established democracies, enhance their adaptation capacity and boost their efficacy. Adversely, constitutional change is also the basic apparatus used to orchestrate constitutional backslide as the erosion of liberal democracies and democratic regression is increasingly affected through legal channels of constitutional change.

Routledge Handbook of Comparative Constitutional Change provides a comprehensive reference tool for all those working in the field and a thorough landscape of all theoretical and practical aspects of the topic. Coherence from this aspect does not suggest a common view, as the chapters address different topics, but reinforces the establishment of comparative constitutional change as a distinct field. The book brings together the most respected scholars working in the field, and presents a genuine contribution to comparative constitutional studies, comparative public law, political science and constitutional history.

Xenophon Contiades is Professor of Public Law, Panteion University and President of the Centre for European Constitutional Law, Athens, Greece.

Alkmene Fotiadou is a Research Fellow at the Centre for European Constitutional Law, Athens, Greece.

ROUTLEDGE HANDBOOK OF COMPARATIVE CONSTITUTIONAL CHANGE

Edited by Xenophon Contiades and Alkmene Fotiadou

Routledge
Taylor & Francis Group

LONDON AND NEW YORK

First published 2021
by Routledge
2 Park Square, Milton Park, Abingdon, Oxon OX14 4RN

and by Routledge
52 Vanderbilt Avenue, New York, NY 10017

Routledge is an imprint of the Taylor & Francis Group, an informa business

British Library Cataloguing-in-Publication Data
A catalogue record for this book is available from the British Library

Library of Congress Cataloging-in-Publication Data
Names: Kontiadēs, Xenophōn I., editor. | Phōtiadou, Alkmēnē, editor.
Title: Routledge handbook of comparative constitutional change / edited by Xenophon Contiades and Alkmene Fotiadou.
Description: Abingdon, Oxon ; New York, NY : Routledge, 2020. |
Includes bibliographical references and index.
Identifiers: LCCN 2020004475 (print) | LCCN 2020004476 (ebook) | ISBN 9781138496644 (hardback) |
ISBN 9781351020985 (ebook)
Subjects: LCSH: Constitutional amendments. | Constitutional law. | Law reform.
Classification: LCC K3168 .R68 2020 (print) | LCC K3168 (ebook) | DDC 342.03–dc23
LC record available at https://lccn.loc.gov/2020004475
LC ebook record available at https://lccn.loc.gov/2020004476

ISBN: 978-1-138-49664-4 (hbk)
ISBN: 978-0-367-50085-6 (pbk)
ISBN: 978-1-351-02098-5 (ebk)

Typeset in Bembo
by Swales & Willis, Exeter, Devon, UK

CONTENTS

CONTRIBUTORS

Richard Albert is William Stamps Farish Professor in Law and Professor of Government, The University of Texas at Austin

Elisa Arcioni is Associate Professor, University of Sydney Law School

Nathalie Behnke is Professor, Institute of Political Science, Technical University of Darmstadt

Juliano Zaiden Benvindo is Professor of Constitutional Law, University of Brasília; CNPq Research Fellow

Arthur Benz is Professor, Institute of Political Science, Technical University of Darmstadt

Robert Blackburn QC is Professor of Constitutional Law, Kings College London

Paul Blokker is Associate Professor, Department of Sociology and Business Law, University of Bologna

Eoin Carolan is Full Professor, Centre for Constitutional Studies, University College Dublin

Joel I. Colón-Ríos is Professor of Law, Victoria University of Wellington

Xenophon Contiades is Professor of Public Law, Panteion University; President of the Centre for European Constitutional Law, Athens, Greece

Giacomo Delledonne is Postdoctoral Researcher in Comparative Public Law, Istituto di diritto, politica e sviluppo (Dirpolis), Scuola superiore Sant'Anna, Pisa, Italy

Oran Doyle is Professor in Law, Trinity College Dublin

David Feldman is Emeritus Rouse Ball Professor of English Law; Emeritus Fellow of Downing College, University of Cambridge

Alkmene Fotiadou is Research Fellow, Centre for European Constitutional Law

James Fowkes is Professor of Foreign and International Law, University of Münster

Tom Ginsburg is Leo Spitz Professor of International Law and Professor of Political Science, University of Chicago

Marco Goldoni is Senior Lecturer, School of Law, Glasgow University

Yasuo Hasebe is Professor of Law, Waseda Law School

Jaakko Husa is Professor in Law and Globalisation, University of Helsinki

Tomasz Tadeusz Koncewicz is Professor of Law, Director of the Department of European and Comparative Law, University of Gdańsk

Helle Krunke is Professor of Constitutional Law, Faculty of Law, University of Copenhagen

David S. Law is Sir Y.K. Pao Chair in Public Law, University of Hong Kong; Professor, University of California, Irvine School of Law; Visiting Professor, University of Pennsylvania Law School

Zoran Oklopcic is Professor, Department of Law and Legal Studies, Carleton University, Ottawa

Tarik Olcay is Lecturer in Law at the University of Dundee

Yaniv Roznai is Associate Professor, Harry Radzyner Law School, Interdisciplinary Center Herzliya

Manfred Stelzer is Professor, University of Vienna

Adrienne Stone is Redmond Barry Distinguished Professor, Kathleen Fitzpatrick Australian Laureate Fellow, Melbourne Law School

Silvia Suteu is Lecturer in Public Law, Faculty of Laws, University College London

Chris Thornhill is Professor in Law, University of Manchester

Mark Tushnet is William Nelson Cromwell Professor of Law, Harvard Law School

Ryan Whalen is Assistant Professor, University of Hong Kong Faculty of Law

ACKNOWLEDGEMENTS

We knew that the time for *The Routledge Handbook of Comparative Constitutional Change* had come, when it became apparent that this newly established academic field had begun to mature. Organizing a workshop to exchange ideas and comments on the chapters was our next step. The workshop was held in Aegina island, Greece on 4–7 September 2018 and gave us the chance to discuss the future of the field.

We offer our profound thanks to our fellow contributors whose brilliant work has taken the study of comparative constitutional change one step further.

We owe special thanks to the Centre for European Constitutional Law – Themistocles and Dimitris Tsatsos Foundation for the financial and institutional support to the workshop.

We especially want to thank our friend and colleague Prof. Richard Albert with whom we have been working to establish the field. The Routledge Series on Comparative Constitutional Change which we co-edit was a major step in this direction. The invaluable support of Prof. Thomas Fleiner has been of great importance.

We are deeply indebted to Routledge for the fruitful co-operation over the years and for the opportunity to edit this Handbook. Our editor Alison Kirk's encouragement and support toward launching the Comparative Constitutional Change Book Series and publishing the Handbook has been immense. We owe her a lot. Emmy Summers's support toward the completion of the Handbook has been valuable.

This Handbook is dedicated to comparative constitutional studies scholars worldwide, whose work on constitutional change has formed the field.

The editors

1

INTRODUCTION

Comparative constitutional change: a new academic field

Xenophon Contiades and Alkmene Fotiadou

The study of comparative constitutional change

A novel field of study

Constitutions change. Once enacted, constitutions function in an ever-changing environment and are themselves, as a rule, subject to formal and informal change. Comparative constitutional change (CCC) is the study of how, when, why and by whom constitutions change formally or informally.[1] Constitutional change includes alteration, revision, evolution, interpretation, replacement and revolution through formal and informal channels.[2] CCC uses comparative methodology to examine how constituted amending power is organized and exercised, as well as how it is complemented or substituted by other constitutional change mechanisms.

Comparison in the field of constitutional change is simultaneously vertical and horizontal, combining cross-time and cross-country analysis. Time is important: time with regard to constitutional change progresses at different speeds. Time moves fast with regard to *events*, slows down in constitutional *episodes* and is slow in the realm of constitutional *culture*. Changing time density explains the difference between incremental updates and episodic shifts in constitutional continuance which, when intermingled, produce constitutional change. Formal and informal amendment move at different speeds, and through their interrelation constitutions evolve.

Constitutional change and stability are not mutually preclusive: constitutions and societies alike have some stable fundamental features, which not only are crucial for understanding change but are potentially interdependent with change. For change to happen some stable points of reference are necessary and for constitutional stability to be achieved evolution is also necessary. Absence of change is also important: the question whether a constitution can or should be change-proof is a question about the nature of constitutions.

---

1 X. Contiades and A. Fotiadou, 'Models of Constitutional Change' in X. Contiades (ed), *Engineering Constitutional Change: A Comparative Perspective on Europe, Canada and the USA* (Routledge 2013) 417–468, 418.
2 R. Albert, 'Introduction: The State of the Art in Constitutional Amendment' in R. Albert, X. Contiades and A. Fotiadou (eds), *The Foundations and Traditions of Comparative Constitutional Amendment* (Hart Publishing 2017) 1–19.

The field of CCC approaches constitutions through the way they change with the use of various methodological tools, encompassing and revealing different perceptions of the constitution. The components of CCC are in themselves subject to multiple approaches. Comparison, constitutions and change are multi-dimensional concepts that can be approached through a variety of ways. Comparative research is a world of its own. Distinct methodological dilemmas have surfaced as comparative constitutional law has been challenged by the growth of comparative constitutional studies, which appears to have taken comparative constitutional law dilemmas one step further,[3] whereas focus on change sets novel challenges.

The concept of *constitution*, that is, defining what a constitution is, remains open to perpetual discussion from numerous perspectives including constitutional law, history and political thought. *Change*, that is, to become different, has many facets. With regard to constitutions, evolution, incremental change, abrupt change, endurance, resilience and backslide are different forms of change. The study of change is a unique conceptual lens: when Western missionaries introduced modern chemistry to China in the 1860s, they called this discipline *hua-hsueh*, literally, 'the study of change'.[4] Similarly, the study of constitutional change can be described as capturing the essence of what a constitution is.

Focus on constitutional change does not undermine the value of constitution-making, which remains as important as ever. Conversely, it provides constitution-writing with a valuable new toolkit as it has become obvious that the future of novel constitutions depends on their amendability. Thus, the drafting of formal amendment rules acquires particular importance, as it is during moments of transformational change that constitutions develop their full-fledged functions. Even in the case of the constitutions perceived as imposed, it is the manner in which they change that determines ownership.[5]

CCC examines the operation of constitutional change mechanisms and the way they interact in different environments. CCC, the younger child of comparative constitutional law, and its interdisciplinary counterpart comparative constitutional studies, is growing rapidly through the work of numerous constitutional scholars and political scientists, comparatists and historians. A novel conceptual lens for approaching constitutions and constitutional orders is thus available for all whose work relates to the study of constitutions.

The novel field of study of CCC relates to the broader discipline of comparative constitutional studies. CCC qualifies as a distinct disciplinary field, since it has a particular object of research (constitutions shared with comparative constitutional studies and comparative constitutional law, with a focus on change), it has theories and concepts to organize the accumulated knowledge, it uses specific terminologies, a specific language adjusted to its research object, and has developed specific research methods tailored to its specific research requirements.[6]

In 2014, during the International Association of Constitutional Law World Congress held in Oslo, the research Group on Constitution-making and Constitutional Change was convened by Xenophon Contiades to encourage the comparative study of constituent and

---

3 R. Hirschl, *Comparative Matters: The Renaissance of Comparative Constitutional Law* (Oxford University Press 2014); G. Frankenberg, *Comparative Constitutional Studies between Magic and Deceit* (Edward Elgar Publishing 2018).

4 J. Reardon Anderson, *The Study of Change: Chemistry in China, 1840–1949* (Cambridge University Press 2003).

5 See R. Albert, X. Contiades and A. Fotiadou (eds), *The Law and Legitimacy of Imposed Constitutions* (Routledge 2018).

6 See A. Krishnan, 'What are Academic Disciplines? Some Observations on the Disciplinarity vs. Interdisciplinarity Debate', ESRC National Centre for Research Methods, Working paper 03/09. Available at: http://eprints. ncrm.ac.uk/783/1/what_are_academic_disciplines.pdf.

constituted power and to bring together the scholars working in this field (https://constitutional-change.com). It is also worth mentioning that a thematic-specific book series on CCC exists: the Routledge Series on Comparative Constitutional Change edited by R. Albert, X. Contiades, Th. Fleiner and A. Fotiadou.

Already the study of CCC is an integral part of the syllabus of comparative constitutional law classes, while new modules that focus exclusively on CCC have started to be taught. Thematic-specific tables on CCC are parts of the programme of the most prestigious international conferences. A specific jargon is in the making: amendability, unamendability, endurance, resilience, rigidity, rigidities, constitutional flexibility, adaptation, constitutional design, incremental change, revision, replacement, ownership-imposition, flexible-rigid, difficulty of change, formal amendment rules, formula, revision, amendment, replacement, desuetude, total revision, eternity clauses, procedural-material limits, etc.

The language of CCC develops through comparative routes: the input of distinct legal cultures, the translation of words from language to language (and inevitably from and to English) is a process of language construction. This language allows comparative constitutional scholars from around the world to communicate on the same level of comprehension and further their research. For example, writing about constitutional law in country X is written differently when addressed to an exclusively domestic audience than when it is expected to be read by international readers. To follow up on the example, pinning down a constitutional moment in legal order X entails connotations about the drivers of constitutional change, which are subsequently integrated in a novel context (and also impacted by this process). Constitutional comparison is also a language, a code of communication.

Fundamental concepts are scrutinized. The rigid/flexible and the formal/informal change dipoles, viewed through a comparative lens, emerge not as much as opposites but as guides to understand constitutional change. The rigidity/flexibility scheme translates to levels of rigidity. The formal/informal dipole, also described as explicit/implicit, indicates the distinctions between changes to the text of the constitution and changes in its meaning through interpretation and practice.[7]

The pioneers

The journey of CCC started with pioneering work that began addressing the complexity of constitutional design, rigidity and change: B.E. Rasch in 'Rigidity in Constitutional Amendment Procedures',[8] B.E. Rasch and R. Congleton in 'Amendment Procedures and Constitutional Stability',[9] D.S. Lutz in 'Principles of Constitutional Design'[10] and I. Lorenz, 'How to Measure Constitutional Rigidity: Four Concepts and Two Alternatives'[11] set out to explain aspects of constitutional change that were (perhaps) taken for granted by constitutional scholars. Contemporary writing on constitutional change owes a great deal to debate.

---

7 Contiades and Fotiadou (n 1) 459.
8 E. Smith (ed), *The Constitution as an Instrument of Change* (Forlag 2003) 77.
9 R. Congleton and B. Swedenborg (eds), *Democratic Constitutional Design and Public Policy: Analysis and Design* (The MIT Press 2006) 319.
10 D.S. Lutz, *Principles of Constitutional Design* (Cambridge University Press 2006).
11 I. Lorenz, 'How to Measure Constitutional Rigidity: Four Concepts and Two Alternatives' (2005) 17 *Journal of Theoretical Politics* 339.

In a parallel world, Sanford Levinson had edited a volume where top US scholars probe amendment as a response to imperfection.[12] These works mark the beginning of a dialogue focused on rigidity, amendment process and the use of empirical methodology. It is a safe bet that all around the world constitutional scholars have worked in their native languages on the topic. This work slowly infiltrates CCC theory through the work of comparatists who write in English.

Work addressing the concept of constitutional time can be viewed as foundational of the new discipline. The seminal concept of constitutional moments reveals the ideal type of episodic change. Work on Bruce Ackerman including critique by S. Choudhry, M. Tushnet and A. Sajo, deals with time but also with the metaphor of time.[13] As the field of CCC grows, the importance of time becomes more and more apparent. Recently Gary Jeffrey Jacobsohn and Yaniv Roznai set out to explore constitutional revolutions and their duration, renewing interest in the concept.[14] On the particularity of constitutional change in federal systems, extensive work has been done by A. Benz and N. Behnke.[15] An early US discussion on the relevance of constitutional amendments, questioning the importance of formal change, is still a point of reference for the modern dialogue on the interrelation between formal and informal change.[16]

A distinct moment in the study of constitutional time is the work by Z. Elkins, T. Ginsburg and J. Melton on the endurance of national constitutions.[17] Through this seminal ground-breaking work, the importance of understanding change and what impacts constitutional life through empirical methodology came to light and influenced the shaping of the field.

The present and future of CCC scholarship

There are three major edited volumes that delineate the field. These mark the beginning of consciousness: scholars becoming aware that a new field is being formed. The first volume is edited by Dawn Oliver and Carlo Fusaro and the second by Xenophon Contiades.[18]

---

12 S. Levinson (ed), *Responding to Imperfection* (Princeton University Press 1995).

13 Constitutional moments, see B. Ackerman, *We the People: Foundations* (Harvard University Press 1991) vol. I; Id., *We the People: Transformations* (Harvard University Press 2000) vol. 2; Id., '2006 Oliver Wendell Holmes Lectures: The Living Constitution' (2007) 120 *Harvard Law Review* 1737ff.; S. Choudhry, 'Ackerman's Higher Lawmaking in Comparative Constitutional Perspective: Constitutional Moments as Constitutional Failures?' (2008) 6(2) *International Journal of Constitutional Law* 193–230; S. Levinson, 'Transitions' (1999) 108 *Yale Law Journal* 2215ff.; A. Sajo, 'Constitution without the Constitutional Moment: A View from the New Member States' (2005) 3 *International Journal of Constitutional Law* 243ff.; M. Tushnet, 'Misleading Metaphors in Comparative Constitutionalism: Moments and Enthusiasm' (2005) 3 *International Journal of Constitutional Law* 262ff.

14 G.J. Jacobsohn and Y. Roznai, *Constitutional Revolution* (Yale University Press 2020).

15 A. Benz, 'Dimensions and Dynamics of Federal Regimes' in Arthur Benz and Jörg Broschek (eds), *Federal Dynamics: Continuity Change and the Varieties of Federalism* (Oxford University Press 2013) 70–90; N. Behnke and A. Benz, 'The Politics of Constitutional Change between Reform and Evolution' (2009) 39 *Publius: The Journal of Federalism* 213–240.

16 D. Strauss, 'The Irrelevance of Constitutional Amendments' (2001) 114 *Harvard Law Review* 1457, 1487; B.P. Denning and J.R. Vile, 'The Relevance of Constitutional Amendments: A Response to David Strauss' (2002) 77 *Tulane Law Review* 247.

17 Z. Elkins, T. Ginsburg and J. Melton, *The Endurance of National Constitutions* (Cambridge University Press 2009). See also A.C. Hutchinson and J. Colon-Rios, 'Democracy and Constitutional Change' (2010) 6(II) Osgoode CPLE Research Paper Series, Research Paper No. 48.

18 D. Oliver and C. Fusaro (eds), *How Constitutions Change: A Comparative Study* (Hart Publishing 2011); X. Contiades (ed), *Engineering Constitutional Change: A Comparative Perspective on Europe, Canada and the USA* (Routledge 2013).

Both volumes describe constitutional change in specific jurisdictions. The second volume, *Engineering Constitutional Change*, offers a typology of constitutional change. A more recent volume, *The Foundations and Traditions of Constitutional Amendment*, edited by Albert, Contiades and Fotiadou, examines the foundations and traditions of constitutional change, recognizing the birth of a new discipline.[19] Gathering a variety of aspects, this volume reflects the new work done in the field, with more emphasis on innovative work. The volume aims to pave the way toward further elaboration of the newly established discipline.

Special mention must be made here to R. Albert's work on constitutional amendment and formal amendment rules. His contribution to the development of the discipline through articles and edited volumes is immense and culminated with the publication of his book *Constitutional Amendments, Making, Breaking, and Changing Constitutions*.[20]

The question of what impacts constitutional life is addressed by the work triggered by the global financial crisis. The edited volume *Constitutions in the Global Financial Crisis* by Xenophon Contiades, tracing how constitutions reacted to the financial crisis, was published in 2013, shortly after the onset of the crisis, when it became apparent that crises impact constitutions. The volume examined constitutional reactions toward the crisis in real time. The volume edited by Tom Ginsburg, Mark Rosen and Georg Vanberg, *Constitutions in Times of Financial Crisis*,[21] published in 2019, offers a mature evaluation of constitutional change in the face of crisis. Focus on the impact of crises on constitutional change led to establishing the concept of constitutional resilience. Contiades and Fotiadou suggest that constitutional resilience can be defined as the ability of a constitution to respond to severe crises without normativity loss, enabling democracy and the rule of law to also demonstrate resilience.[22]

A unique tool to follow constitutional change is the The I·CONnect-Clough Center Global Review of Constitutional Law, published by the Clough Center for the Study of Constitutional Democracy.[23] These reports feature constitutional developments on a yearly basis in an impressive number of countries. As the publication continues it provides a way to follow and compare constitutional change, both formal and informal, in the constitutional orders analysed. A future meta-analysis of these reports could possibly illuminate trends of constitutional change.

The new wave of work on CCC boasts books that explore constitutional change with regard to specific topics or in particular geographical areas through a comparative lens. R. Albert, C. Barnal and J.Z. Benvido's *Constitutional Change and Transformation in Latin*

---

19 R. Albert, X. Contiades and A. Fotiadou (eds), *The Foundations and Traditions of Constitutional Amendment* (Hart Publishing 2017).

20 R. Albert, *Constitutional Amendments: Making, Breaking, and Changing Constitutions* (Oxford University Press 2019).

21 T. Ginsburg, M. Rosen and G. Vanberg, 'Introduction' in T. Ginsburg, M. Rosen and G. Vanberg (eds), *Constitutions in Times of Financial Crisis* (Cambridge University Press 2019) 21; Elkins, Ginsburg and Melton (n 17).

22 X. Contiades and A. Fotiadou, 'On Resilience of Constitutions: What Makes Constitutions Resistant to External Shocks?' (2015) 3 *International Constitutional Law Journal* 3–26; R. Albert and M. Pal, 'The Democratic Resilience of the Canadian Constitution' in M. Graber, S. Levinson and M. Tushnet (eds), *Constitutional Democracy in Crisis?* (Oxford University Press 2018) 117–138.

23 R. Albert, D. Landau, P. Faraguna and S. Drugda, *The I·CONnect-Clough Center 2016 Global Review of Constitutional Law* (August 3, 2017). Available at SSRN: https://ssrn.com/abstract=3014378; R. Albert, D. Landau, P. Faraguna and S. Drugda, *The I·CONnect-Clough Center 2017 Global Review of Constitutional Law* (July 19, 2018). Available at SSRN: https://ssrn.com/abstract=3215613; R. Albert, D. Landau, P. Faraguna and S. Drugda, *The I·CONnect-Clough Center 2018 Global Review of Constitutional Law* (October 18, 2019). Available at SSRN: https://ssrn.com/abstract=3471638.

America is an excellent example. Y. Roznai's work on unamendability has triggered a vivid discussion on the subject.[24] Extensive work on entrenchment clauses is currently being done by M. Hein.[25] A unique example of the way new scholarship questions traditional concepts is M. Vesteeg and E. Zackin's, 'Constitutions Un-entrenched: Toward an Alternative Theory of Constitutional Design',[26] where alternative ways of entrenchment are sought in the language of the constitution rather than in formal amendment rules.[27]

All the above areas of work can be correlated to the crucial question of culture. What does it mean for constitutional change to be culture dependent? Contiades and Fotiadou have argued that the dynamics of constitutional change depend on the rapport between *institutional* or *factual* impediments to change (rigidities). Institutional rigidities are institutionally embedded ways of increasing the difficulty level of constitutional change (formal amendment rules, system of government, constitutional review system). Factual rigidities are sources of impediments to constitutional change situated in the practices, attitudes and behaviour patterns of different actors, which emerge through the application of institutional requirements, or address areas that fall outside the scope of institutional regulation, or stem directly from the political, legal or social culture and constitutional ethos. What matters is the compatibility between the institutional arrangements and the constitutional culture: in case of mismatch, multiple dysfunctionalities emerge.[28]

Ginsburg and Melton discern the idea of 'an amendment culture at the level of a constitutional system'. They describe amendment culture as the set of shared attitudes about the desirability of amendment, independent of the substantive issue under consideration and the degree of pressure for change. In other words, there is a baseline level of resistance to formal constitutional change in any particular system; as this baseline level increases, the viscosity of the constitutional amendment process decreases even under identical institutional arrangements.[29]

The parallel development of empirical methodologies in conjunction with culture-based approaches allows a glimpse into the future of CCC studies, a future full of possibilities. Through the language of change, this new bulk of literature allows a deeper understanding of constitutions.

---

24 Albert, C. Bernal and J. Z. Benvindo (eds) *Constitutional Change and Transformation in Latin America*. (Hart Publishing 2019); Y. Roznai, *Unconstitutional Constitutional Amendments: The Limits of Amendment Powers* (Oxford University Press 2017). See also (2019) 3 *European Journal of Law Reform*. Available at: www.elevenjournals.com/tijdschrift/ejlr/2019/3

25 M. Hein, 'Do Constitutional Entrenchment Clauses Matter? Constitutional Review of Constitutional Amendments in Europe' (2019) 17 *International Journal of Constitutional Law*.

26 M. Vesteeg and E. Zackin, 'Constitutions Un-entrenched: Toward an Alternative Theory of Constitutional Design' (2016) 110(4) *American Political Science Review* 657, accessed September 1, 2016.

27 On the matter of constitutional length, see also G. Tsebelis and D.J. Nardi, 'A Long Constitution is a (Positively) Bad Constitution: Evidence from OECD Countries' (2016) 46(2) *British Journal of Political Science* 457–478; X. Contiades and A. Fotiadou, 'Amendment-Metrics: The Good, the Bad and the Frequently Amended Constitution' in R. Albert, X. Contiades and A. Fotiadou (eds), *The Foundations and Traditions of Constitutional Amendment* (Hart Publishing 2017) 219; J.E. Fleming, 'Comment on Amendment-Metrics: The Good, the Bad and the Frequently Amended Constitution' in R. Albert, X. Contiades and A. Fotiadou (eds), *The Foundations and Traditions of Constitutional Amendment* (Hart Publishing 2017) 241.

28 Contiades and Fotiadou (n 1).

29 T. Ginsburg and J. Melton, 'Does the Constitutional Amendment Rule Matter at All? Amendment Cultures and the Challenges of Measuring Amendment Difficulty' (2015) 13(3) *International Journal of Constitutional Law* 686–713, 712.

Why and how to change a constitution: the amendment checklist

Factors of constitutional change

Constitutions are amended in order to endure operating in an ever-changing environment, adapt in order to demonstrate resilience in the face of crises or erode and retrogress abused by autocrats. All these are forms of constitutional change. Mechanisms of constitutional change are important for endurance and resilience. The exercise of constituted, amending power has surfaced as equally or even more important than the much-discussed primordial constituent power. Constituted power plus includes both formal and alternative channels of change: focus on informal change necessitates the interrelated study of the routes constitutional change may follow.

Constitution-making itself benefits from the input of CCC: more knowledge is now available on the functions and consequences (either intended or unintended) of formal amendment rules and on how such rules impact the overall performance of constitutions. Constitutional change has also proved to be the basic apparatus used to orchestrate constitutional backslide. The erosion of liberal democracies and democratic backsliding is effected through the legal channels of constitutional change. Constitutions have revealed that they can be vulnerable. Constitutional vulnerability and the way resilience mechanisms can be built within a constitution to render it resilient have surfaced as important aspects of constitutional design. Whatever the reason for change, it is engineered through constitutional change mechanisms. Understanding why and how constitutions change entails understanding how these mechanisms work.

Constitutional change occurs through the operation of mechanisms consisting of actors, formal amendment rules and other constitutional arrangements that interact in various combinations and work complementarily or competitively to channel change intentionally or as a side effect.[30] The actors involved and the means employed to effect change connect to form a mechanism. Mechanisms can be simple or elaborate, and operate simultaneously, alternatively or complementarily. Antagonism between actors and between mechanisms is a driver of constitutional change. Mechanisms of constitutional change are subject to a series of parameters that determine their modus operandi, the way they relate to each other, and their 'market dominance'. This happens because these parameters shape the role and status of the actors involved, and account for the specific features of the means used by the actors to induce changes.

Tradition and polity, state structure, ethnic, linguistic and religious composition, party system and patterns of democracy, polarization and consent, constitutional ethos and the judicial review system in conjunction with the requirements of the amending formula determine in what way mechanisms of constitutional change are set up and how and when they operate. Formal amendment rules are catalysts for change, whether it happens in accordance to their requirements or not.[31] Mechanisms of change function within specific constitutional and political cultures that influence their operation, and shape them. Transformations of the political party system or the system of judicial review, and changes in electoral laws often have the power to implicitly reshape formal amendment rules, which are not as change-proof and stable as they appear to be.

Mapping out the way the multiple actors who drive constitutional change interact is possible through the study of constitutional change mechanisms. This leads to abandoning

---

30 Contiades and Fotiadou (n 1).
31 Contiades and Fotiadou (n 1) 441.

the use of the dyads rigid/flexible and formal/informal as the basic comprehension tool, to turn toward studying multiple factors that affect change. Such factors are institutional or factual: either institutionally embedded ways that increase the difficulty level of constitutional change or fetters to constitutional change situated in the behaviour patterns of different actors. Understanding the factors of constitutional change dictates looking at the application of institutional requirements in the context of the political and constitutional culture in place. What determines constitutional change is the rapport and equilibrium between the factors affecting it, which are in turn dependent on the compatibility between institutional arrangements and political and constitutional culture.

Constitutional resilience and constitutional endurance

Mechanisms of change are major factors that determine the endurance as well as the resilience of constitutions. Constitutional endurance is important. 'Without endurance, constitutions cannot provide a stable basis of politics and cannot constitute a people out of diverse elements'.[32] Inclusion, flexibility and specificity appear to account for endurance.[33]

Constitutions are designed to last. Constitutional resilience is endurance plus. Resilience is about experiencing shocks and surviving them, which suggests the ability to absorb shocks. Resilience does not have to do with time, nor is it measurable with relation to time: what is important is the continuance in performing the necessary functions in the face of crises. Resilience has to do with shock resistance and not with time endurance. The recent financial crisis and the way it was experienced in distinct constitutional orders triggered the development of constitutional resilience theory.[34]

Scholarly work on the financial crises brings forth crisis-response as a major parameter of constitutional change. The bulk of work on how rule-of-law guarantees can be dismantled shows that the analysis of backward-looking constitutional change is also crucial.[35] The experience of constitutional backslide is particularly important for building constitutional resilience mechanisms. Resilience is defined as

> the ability of a system and its component parts to anticipate, absorb, accommodate, or recover from the effects of a potentially hazardous event in a timely and efficient manner, including through ensuring the preservation, restoration, or improvement of its essential basic structures and functions.[36]

At the heart of this reasoning lies the 'adapting capacity, the ability to adapt to changing circumstances while fulfilling one's core purpose'.[37]

---

32 T. Ginsburg, 'Constitutional Endurance', Chapter 4 in this volume.

33 See Elkins, Ginsburg and Melton (n 17).

34 On the first definition of the notion of 'constitutional resilience' see Contiades and Fotiadou (n 22); X. Contiades and A. Fotiadou, 'The Resilient Constitution: Lessons from the Financial Crisis' in A. Herwig and M. Simoncini (eds), *Law and the Management of Disasters. The Challenge of Resilience* (Routledge 2016) 189.

35 T. Koncewicz, 'The Democratic Backsliding in the European Union and the Challenge of Constitutional Design', Chapter 19 in this volume.

36 C.B. Field, V. Barros, T.F. Stocker and Q. Dahe (eds), *Managing the Risks of Extreme Events and Disasters to Advance Climate Change Adaptation* (Cambridge University Press 2012) 33.

37 A. Zolli and A.M. Healy, *Resilience: Why Things Bounce Back* (Free Press 2012) 8.

A constitution's resilience depends on its adaptability. Constitutional resilience and constitutional change are closely interrelated: constitutional resilience theory is a constitutional change theory.

> A 'resilient constitution can respond to severe crises without losing its normativity, enabling also democracy and the rule of law to demonstrate resilience'.[38] This two-pronged definition entails, on the one hand, the ability of a constitution to withstand shocks and, on the other, its capacity to enable the legal order, whose ground rules it sets out, to seek recovery within the constraints of these ground rules. Formal amendment rules are multifunctional and determine the relationship between constitutions and time, which appears to accelerate in times of crisis. Adaptability within constraints and maintenance of core constitutional functions are crucial for constitutional resilience against shocks.[39]

The essence of constitutional resilience is that core constitutional values persist throughout a crisis. Resilience-building at the constitutional level aims at ensuring that the core purposes of the constitution are accomplishable under any conditions. The ability to continue setting the basic rules of the game is important. Resilience-building at the constitutional level aims at finding ways to render the core purposes of the constitution accomplishable under the stress of a severe crisis. The fundamental rules of democracy and the rule of law must be able to withstand the shock of crises. In liberal democracies, the rule-of-law guarantees are inevitably part of the core of the constitution.[40]

The core of a constitution is not a fixed concept. Two notions of the core of a constitution can be detected: a core that every constitution contains and a core that distinguishes this constitution from other constitutions. Under this rationale, a constitution that does not provide for the rule of law does not even qualify as a constitution.[41] This is important for the definition of resilience: a resilient constitution does not merely withstand a severe crisis itself but it also makes it possible for the rule-of-law guarantees to be operational in crisis conditions. Still, the rule of law itself appears to have become a more flexible notion. It is possible that it is the very type of rule of law guaranteed by a constitution that gives a constitution its identity. In that sense understanding varieties of constitutionalism is the route to understanding distinct constitutional identities. Furthermore, applying the 'good enough' standard might prove helpful for allowing room for adaptability at the face of crises.[42]

---

38 Contiades and Fotiadou (n 22); see also X. Contiades and A. Fotiadou, 'Constitutional Resilience and Unamendability: Amendment Powers as Mechanisms of Constitutional Resilience' (2019) 21(3) *European Journal of Law Reform* 243–258.

39 Contiades and Fotiadou (n 22).

40 For a further elaboration of the concept of constitutional resilience and its connection to democracy, see Albert and Pal (n 22).

41 A. Stone, 'Unconstitutional Constitutional Amendments: Between Contradiction and Necessity', University of Melbourne Legal Studies, Research Paper No. 786. Available at: https://ssrn.com/abstract=3216896; R. Dixon and A. Stone, 'Constitutional Amendment: A Comparative and Philosophical Reflection' in D. Dyzenhaus and M. Thorburn (eds), *Philosophical Foundations of Constitutionalism* (Oxford University Press 2016) 95–115.

42 For an analysis of the 'good enough' standard see M. Tushnet, 'Varieties of Liberal Constitutionalism', Chapter 6 in this volume.

Thus, the more elusive part of resilience is the core that is distinct in each constitution. That part is culture dependent. Constitutional cultures reflect common understandings and attitudes toward the constitution.[43] Constitutions emerge and are enacted within a specific legal culture and also operate, are enforced, interpreted and developed within and through that legal culture.[44] Emphasis put in constitutional culture as an ever-evolving project allows room for adaptation: sameness is maintained through evolution.

The constitutional amendment checklist: how to change a constitution

Constitutional change reflexivity with regard to constitutional design entails a process of constant review and reassessment of various variables related to the functioning of constitutional institutions in a given legal, political and social environment, which is itself subject to unpredictable changes and transformations. It is in this exact context that the question of balance between participatory and technocratic constitutional design arises. Constitutional change in pluralist democracies must be characterized by the involvement of civil society, consultation and consensus. The challenge for modern democracies is to achieve a successful correlation between legitimacy of constitutional change stemming from participation with workability achieved through 'technocratic' rational constitutional design. The ultimate question is how necessary is a contemplated change to the constitutional text, which translates into how persuasive is the argumentation in favour of a specific amendment. Argumentation matters and can be structured by responding to ten interrelated questions.

1. What is the aim of the constitutional provision undergoing formal change; can this aim be fulfilled by the specific choices made by the constitutional designer? Awareness of the aim and the conscious choice of the means to achieve it matter.
2. How will changes to constitutional institutions or provisions fit into the constitutional order and how are they expected to interact with other institutions and provisions?
3. What are the conditions that will ensure the effective implementation of a specific constitutional dictate and what public policies are needed to make it relevant?
4. How does an amendment fit in the framework of the legislation in place, the administrative structure and the case law? Changes with regard to a specific constitutional theme might aim to introduce a new constitutional dictate, confirm an established practice by way of constitutional enshrinement, respond to judicial interpretation, or fix a malpractice. Confirming pre-existing conditions, improving them or, by contrast, bringing about radical change, require context awareness.
5. If already part of the constitutional text, how did constitutional dictates under reform work in practice? An assessment of prior implementation.
6. What does an amendment to the constitutional text add to the constitutional order? What would the removal of a constitutional provision mean for the legislature or the judiciary?
7. The amendment cost: How can consensus on the content of the amendment be achieved without sacrifices with regard to word economy, effectiveness and rationality of a constitutional provision under construction or refurbishment?

---

43 J. Mazzone, 'The Creation of a Constitutional Culture' (2004) 40(4) *Tulsa Law Review* 671–698.
44 See H. Vorländer, 'What Is "Constitutional Culture"?' in S. Hensel, U. Bock, K. Dircksen and H.-U. Thamer (eds), *Constitutional Cultures* (Cambridge Scholars Publishing 2012) 21.

8. Are amendments compatible with international and supranational commitments and with the jurisprudence of international and supranational courts (for example, in EU member states with the jurisprudence of the European Court of Human Rights and the Court of Justice of the European Union)? Would the existence of a compatibility requirement suggest implicit constitutional imposition?
9. Is a specific amendment compatible with the constitutional culture in place? Assessment of the proposed amendment through a comparative lens. The growth of CCC has provided knowledge on the uses and misuses of borrowing and on the importance of constitutional culture and identity.
10. Difficulty level of future change. How difficult will it be to change again a proposed change? Amendability matters with regard to the range of choices. Incremental change or experimenting by introducing innovations in the constitutional text depend on the available ways of changing it again, if necessary.

The checklist is neither a list of aims to be reached nor a wishlist. It is a tool that can be used to facilitate reflective constitutional design through an assessment of the aims, cost and possible repercussions of constitutional change. The CCC checklist allows the application of the 'good enough standard' in the context of constitutional change.[45]

The field of CCC enhances constitutional self-awareness and reflexivity. This results from accepting that the object of study is in flux: CCC studies through a variety of methodologies constitutions that change within changing environments, as they evolve in different political and constitutional cultures. Constitutions are *mobilis in mobili*, just like Captain Nemo's Nautilus from the Jules Verne novel *Twenty Thousand Leagues Under the Sea*: they are moving within the moving element, changing in the changes. Better amendment rules and better design through amendment is the optimal result. Awareness of malfunctions in the operation of such rules and possessing a toolkit for assessing constitutional change is a realistic expectation.

The big issues in comparative constitutional change

Which are the big issues in CCC? The study of constitutional change includes a reflexive approach to the theoretical background and the methodologies used. Formal change has multiple aspects that stem from formal amendment rules: amending formulas create different levels of constitutional rigidity, enhancing or relaxing institutional and factual determinants of constitutional change. Inescapably interrelated with the mechanisms of formal change are the various channels of informal change, which is the counterpart of formal change. In scholarly writings, formal and informal change were often seen as rivals, which culminated in the harsh characterization of formal change as irrelevant.[46] The comparative study of constitutional change has shed light on the interrelationship between the two and on the multiplicity of factors that influence their balance.

The direction toward which constitutions change reveals the contemporary challenges in CCC. Change is about the passage of time, which continuously produces new challenges. The theory and practice of constitutional change must face this perpetual procession of

---

45 Tushnet (n 42).
46 Strauss (n 16) 1487; Denning and Vile (n 16); R. Albert, 'The Structure of Constitutional Amendment Rules' (2014) 49 *Wake Forest Law Review* 913.

issues to be addressed. Country-specific case studies reveal specific profiles of constitutional change. Each case study produces or illuminates a constitutional change profile. Case studies that focus on a specific legal order, or on examples of more than one legal order that share common features, bring forth the particularities in the manner of constitutional change that are useful from a comparative aspect and the characteristics that are possibly shared with other legal orders. This serves as a reminder that case studies are indispensable for understanding constitutions from a comparative aspect.

Reading the case studies along with the analysis of typologies and modelizations demonstrates how case studies written through a comparative conceptual lens enrich the field of CCC.[47] Likewise, comparative and empirical methodology issues, and endurance and resilience issues, read in conjunction with the case studies, reveal the potential of combined methodologies that are state of the art in CCC.[48] Characteristic of the progress in CCC is that the choice of paradigms can be made from a wider portfolio of countries. As the field develops, important knowledge stems from the analysis of constitutional orders that were not the focus of attention in the past.

The *Routledge Handbook of Comparative Constitutional Change*, following the big issues, is structured in five parts: Part I is a comprehensive guide to the theory and methodology of CCC; Part II focuses on formal constitutional change, that is, the constitutionally prescribed way of changing the constitution following formal amendment rules; Part III explains informal constitutional change; Part IV deals with contemporary challenges faced by the theory and practice of constitutional change; and Part V consists of representative case studies. Chapters cover the most fundamental knowledge on each topic, but also present contested and challenging aspects of each big issue, taking research one step further. A common thread runs through the chapters: recurring themes presented from different angles introduce readers to the universe of CCC.

Theoretical and methodological big issues

Methodology

Distinct methodological issues are raised as the field of CCC continues to grow and old dilemmas take new form. Methodologies in comparative constitutional law have reached a degree of sophistication that differentiates them from the general issues and doctrines used in comparative law. The rise of comparative constitutional studies suggests the necessity of a more interdisciplinary approach to the comparative study of constitutions.

The development of CCC is a trigger for new methodological approaches. The comparative method is applied in the field of CCC in a distinct way. Is the nature of the study of CCC about knowing more rather than persuasion? Are the empirical tools suitable for understanding constitutions, and if so, are they compatible or rival to more traditional normative approaches? All the above not only impact but are also influenced themselves by the birth and growth of CCC.

---

47 O. Doyle, 'Order from Chaos? Typologies and Models of Constitutional Change', Chapter 3 in this volume.

48 J. Husa, 'Comparative Methodology and Constitutional Change', Chapter 2 in this volume; T. Ginsburg (n 32); D.S. Law and R. Whalen, 'Constitutional Amendment versus Constitutional Replacement: An Empirical Comparison', Chapter 5 in this volume.

A three-pronged approach of the methodology of comparative law, the purposes of comparative constitutional law, and the purposes of studying constitutional change touches on the variety of longstanding and newborn challenges in the study of CCC: universalism and culturalism, the potential relevance of legal families, legal transplants, qualitative and quantitative research. The comparative study of constitutional change allows different intellectual styles and innovates the comparative toolkit to render such approaches feasible.[49]

Typologies

Models and ideal types of constitutional change are based on the detection of constitutional amendment patterns. Such typologies require a certain level of abstraction, necessary to build models, and do not preclude degrees of differentiation between countries that share similar characteristics. What are the criteria for building models and how does modelization impact our knowledge of constitutional change? Typologies and models of constitutional change themselves can be subject to assessment with regard to their utility, both for constitutional designers and within comparative constitutional scholarship. Formal change mechanisms are numerous and can be combined with one another and/or subjected to limitations in a bewildering number of ways. Comparative constitutional scholars seek to develop typologies and models of constitutional change that give order to the diversity of constitutional practices.[50]

Endurance

The length of constitutional life, constitutional endurance, longevity and the factors that impact the lifespan of constitutions lie at the heart of an open-ended discussion about constitutional change.[51] This discussion has heavily influenced the current debate about what matters in constitutional change. The landmark book on the length of constitutional life, *The Endurance of National Constitutions* by Z. Elkins, T. Ginsburg and J. Melton, has triggered various ongoing debates about the connection of constitutional durability with quality and the factors that influence them.[52] The notion of endurance is revisited through new data on constitutional change, furthering the understanding of the formal/informal distinction with regard to constitutions, institutions and change, which becomes even more complex placed across geographical and temporal contexts.[53]

Semantics and empirical methods

How can the empirical tools serve understanding constitutions? Are they compatible or rival to more traditional normative approaches? Exploring the potential of empirical methodology in understanding language and terminology is important. It can be used to clarify 'what we talk about when we talk about'[54] constitutional change. As the field of CCC grows and

---

49 Husa (n 48).
50 Doyle (n 47).
51 Elkins, Ginsburg and Melton (n 17).
52 Elkins, Ginsburg and Melton (n 17).
53 Ginsburg (n 32).
54 R. Carver, *What We Talk About When We Talk About Love* (Vintage Publishing 2009).

comparatists from all over the world participate in an open dialogue, the meaning of words becomes less obvious. The differences between amendment, revision, replacement, change, etc. are not as yet clear across constitutional jurisdictions. The everyday distinction between constitutional 'amendments' and constitutional 'replacements' can be illuminated through the use of empirical research. Labels can be misleading: a so-called 'amendment' may amount to a constitutional replacement in all but name, while an ostensibly 'new' constitution may be merely a clone of its predecessor.

Yet it is also difficult to empirically evaluate how reliable these labels happen to be, for the simple reason that constitutional change is difficult to quantify. A semantic measure of constitutional change that relies on automated text analysis techniques shows the potential of empirical research. Looking into the meaning of words, exploring the semantics of CCC terminology through the use of empirical methods not only is an excellent example of the use of empirical methodology in the field of CCC, but also shows the innovation that is currently unfolding in the field.[55]

Variations of constitutionalism

New conceptualizations of constitutionalism impact the study of CCC. A variety of 'constitutionalisms' is gradually becoming acceptable, leading to novel taxonomies and rendering reference to one exclusive notion of constitutionalism with a fixed content difficult, if not impossible.[56] Words matter in the comparative universe. Comparing paths of constitutional change often involves departure from what is understood as constitutionalism, which has become a point of reference for change. Scholarly accounts of constitutionalism offer either maximalist or minimalist accounts of liberal constitutionalism, however other varieties of liberal constitutionalism exist.

A new vocabulary is necessary for discussing change within liberal constitutionalism. That vocabulary is helpful in allowing us to distinguish reforms or alterations of liberal constitutionalism from abusive constitutionalism. The strongly liberal constitutionalist regimes do not provide a yardstick against which the other systems can be measured. Rather, that liberal constitutional systems are or are not 'good enough' is the only truly workable normative standard available. Introducing the 'good enough' standard might prove as valuable to CCC as it is to parenting, freeing comparison from an air of implicit competitiveness toward self-awareness and self-acceptance.[57]

Big issues in formal change

Formal amendment rules

The beginning and the end of understanding constitutional change are formal amendment rules, which are the central axis of all constitutional change. Even where informal change is the primary route of change, it is inescapably correlated to the formal channels of change. Amendment formulas consist of a variety of rules that set procedural and often material limits to constitutional amendment. Such rules perform multiple functions and monitor or

---

55 Law and Whalen (n 48).
56 M. Tushnet, 'Varieties of Constitutionalism' (2016) 14 *International Journal of Constitutional Law* 1.
57 Tushnet (n 42).

influence the rigidity level of the constitution. Notwithstanding whether or not such rules fulfil their intended purposes, they greatly impact constitutional change. The design of formal amendment rules is one of the most challenging tasks performed by constitutional legislators. The study of formal amendment rules has made a comeback and these rules are recognized as the axis around which constitutions evolve. Mapping the scholarly understanding of formal amendment rules allows better appreciation of their various forms and functions. An agenda for further research into the structure, purposes and uses of formal amendment is generated.[58]

Constitutional design

What do changing, modifying or altering a constitution have to do with the design of provisions, institutions, etc.? How related is constitutional change to the amelioration of constitutional design? Is constitutional change the route toward a better, more efficient constitution? Design through the use of constituted power is distinct from design during the phase of constitution-making. Consensus and legitimacy work differently. Improving, reforming or making a different choice with regard to existing constitutional provisions is a unique constitution-rewriting process. Constitutions are 'designed' when their features are arranged according to a plan rather than 'constructed' or 'patched up'. How designers choose constitutional features through cognitive assumptions is important.[59]

Unamendability

Constitutional restraints, eternity clauses and, most importantly, the possibility of judicial control has recently surfaced as a distinct puzzle with regard to formal change. Recent work on unconstitutional constitutional amendments has updated questions about the violation of amendment rules. The imposition of restrictions on the formal constitutional amendment power, that is, unamendability, has various uses. It can be used as a 'stop sign'; a 'speed bump'; a 'warning sign'; and a 'billboard'. Recent abuses of unamendability by courts either captured by executives or acting in judicial self-dealing indicate it is a useful (but also potentially dangerous) mechanism.[60]

Federalism

Examining how constitutions change in federal systems as well as questions of devolution is an important part of CCC. What are the features of constitutional change that interact with federalism? In federal systems constitutional change depends on a matrix of parameters that render it a multi-level game for a variety of players. Formal amendment rules have more players to tame while there also exist multiple actors who generate informal change through their interaction.

Constitutions need to respond to the dynamic nature of federations. In case of a federal constitution that divides powers of central and sub-central governments, either by general principles or by specific rules, irrespective of how powers are defined and whether they are

---

58 R. Albert, 'Formal Amendment Rules: Functions and Design', Chapter 7 in this volume.
59 M. Stelzer, 'Constitutional Design through Amendment', Chapter 8 in this volume.
60 Y. Roznai, 'The Uses and Abuses of Constitutional Unamendability', Chapter 9 in this volume.

separated or shared, they are contested and have to be adjusted to changing tasks. As central and sub-central governments engage in intergovernmental relations to coordinate their policies, the function of formal amendment rules as monitors of constitutional change is challenged and change often happens implicitly, driven by political parties or courts.[61]

Referendums

The assets and risks of citizen involvement in amending constitutions, especially at times when populism thrives, are central to the approach of CCC. Citizen-led constitutional change is a particular type of formal change effected mainly through referendums often accompanied by deliberative participatory procedures. How do these channels of change work? What are their dangers? We seem to have entered an age of referendums, with major and often unexpected consequences for constitutional orders.[62]

Big issues in informal change

Political practice

Are constitutions as flexible as the actors who operate them? Besides case law, constitutional and political practices may reshape the constitution. Political and constitutional culture is particularly important in the comprehension of such paths of constitutional change. Political practice can change constitutions in two ways: first, as part of a formal process for constitutional amendments; second, changing political practice informally produces constitutional change. Political, legal and administrative practices interact bringing about constitutional change.[63]

Judge-made change

Judges induce constitutional change, while in certain jurisdictions they take the lead in constitutional change. Dialogical models are also a possibility: the constitution evolves through the dialogical exchange between lawmaker and judge. Metaphors such as 'the living tree constitution' express this important path of constitutional change, which has even triggered debates about the irrelevance of formal change. Judge-made change is defined as instances in which judicial action (or inaction) leads to informal or formal changes in a constitutional order. The following categories, which may sometimes overlap with each other, can be discerned: (1) changes through interpretation; (2) changes in review standards; (3) changes in the relationship between the branches of government; (4) attribution of a new status to certain norms; (5) recognition of new rights; and (6) judicially triggered constitutional change.[64]

---

61 N. Behnke and A. Benz, 'Federalism and Constitutional Change', Chapter 10 in this volume.
62 E. Carolan, 'Participatory Constitutional Change: Constitutional Referendums', Chapter 11 in this volume.
63 D. Feldman, 'Political Practice and Constitutional Change', Chapter 12 in this volume.
64 J.I. Colón-Ríos, 'Judge-made Constitutional Change', Chapter 13 in this volume.

Global values

Constitutional change does not happen in a vacuum. International principles that have been formed as part of the evolution of global constitutionalism seem to govern to a great extent constitutional design and thus are a great part of CCC. How do those principles influence constitutional evolution? Is there a road toward some sort of homogeneity? It is crucial to explore whether and how international values and principles guide constitutional change through quantitative and qualitative methodology.[65]

Crises

Constitutional change can be triggered by crises. In recent years we have witnessed how liberal democratic constitutions react toward severe and unexpected crises. The global financial crisis and the threat of terrorist attacks have put a strain on constitutional orders. How do emergencies impact constitutional change and how does the notion of a state of emergency evolve in the face of contemporary risks? Understanding the interplay between three umbrella concepts demands covering a wide variety of situations: crises, emergency regimes, and constitutional change through a comparative, diachronic analysis. Ways that allow constitutions to respond to crises are central in the study of CCC.[66]

The material study

The approach of informal paths of constitutional change triggers novel methodological approaches, characteristic of the pace of development of the new field of CCC. Along with legal constitutionalism, political constitutionalism – an alternative way to approach political practices as a means of constitutional change – has surfaced in the material study of constitutional orders. This approach entails an integrated view on constitutional change which is defined as 'material' and relates constitutional change to the formation and development of the undergirding social order.[67]

Contemporary big issues

European constitutionalism and constituent power

CCC is about constituted power, which is inescapably correlated to constituent power. What happens, however, when preconceived notions of constituent power are questioned? The critical analysis of theories of constituent power produces new questions. It can be argued that the normative model of constitutionalism that ascribes the legitimacy of a constitution to the exercise of national constituent power cannot be applied to any factual constitution-making process in contemporary European societies. Could it be that the theory of constituent power falsely extracts a model of democratic constituent power from national societies? Departure from preconceived notions of constituent power is necessary to understand the focus placed on constitutional change rather than in constitution-making. Fetishized notions of constituent power provide a poor beginning for the study of constituted power.[68]

---

65 H. Krunke, 'Global Values, International Organizations and Constitutional Change', Chapter 14 in this volume.
66 G. Delledonne, 'Crises, Emergencies and Constitutional Change', Chapter 15 in this volume.
67 M. Goldoni and T. Olcay, 'The Material Study of Constitutional Change', Chapter 16 in this volume.
68 C. Thornhill, 'Constituent Power and European Constitutionalism', Chapter 17 in this volume.

Populism

Constitutional reform is often the target of populism. Populism, by setting out to impact constitutional arrangements, becomes a phenomenon relevant not only to political theory but also to comparative constitutional studies, that address constitutional change. Must the populist approach toward constitutionalism, often understood as such, be reduced to an entirely negative, abusive or destructive force? Populist constitutionalism could be understood as an alternative constitutional project, rallying against existing injustice and inequality which are attributed to the institutions and workings of liberal constitutional democracy. Depending on its specific manifestation, the populist counterconstitutional project reveals and addresses important shortcomings in existing constitutional systems. At the same time, however, it tends to pose a great menace for pluralistic, inclusive projects of constitutional democracy.[69]

Constitutional backslide

The recent phenomenon of constitutional backslide is backward change and can be characterized as unconstitutional constitutional change. Backsliding in the context of the EU entails systemic challenges and changes to the European legal order. The liberal democracy, rule of law and human rights, which serve as the axiological triad of the EU, are at stake. Given the interconnectedness and the interdependence of the member states and the highly integrated nature of the legal order of the EU, backsliding in one state affects the foundations and values of the community as a whole and, as such, critically tests the assumptions and the viability of the post-war European constitutional design.[70]

Self-determination

Self-determination, or rather the aspiration of notions of self-determination, seems to have become a motive for constitutional change. Questions about secession, indivisibility of the state, devolution, etc. are increasingly becoming issues of constitutional change that pose difficult comparative questions. Two concepts (and the way we imagine them) are at play: 'constitution' and 'self-determination'. Those speak to a remarkably similar, if not identical set of actions, aspirations, situations and institutional manifestations. Although their relationship appears as politically complementary, if not conceptually co-constitutive, it can be argued that once we decide to approach these terms from the perspective of a particular theory (or with the help of a more specialized disciplinary vocabulary) the conceptual differences between 'constitution' and 'self-determination' start to become clear.[71]

Gender

Gender issues, identity and sexual orientation are expressions of subtle culture wars posing crucial constitutional questions that have to be resolved through formal or informal constitutional change. The constitutional aspects of gender equality, gender identity and sexual orientation mark our era. The way constitutions adapt to accommodate equality is

---

69 P. Blokker, 'Populism and Constitutional Change', Chapter 18 in this volume.
70 Koncewicz (n 35).
71 Z. Oklopcic, 'Constitution and Self-determination', Chapter 20 in this volume.

a key issue in CCC. The starting point is inclusive definition of gender. Areas of recent intense constitutional activity exist in the field of gender equality and non-discrimination, as the formal and informal mechanisms are used for bringing about reform: the continued fight for women's rights, especially access to abortion and gender quotas, gender and sexual minority rights, in particular marriage equality and the recognition of a non-binary conception of gender. The framing of these debates will be very important, as will the promotion of a change in societal attitudes alongside any constitutional and legislative change.[72]

Big issues in constitutional change profiles

The UK

The UK is an inescapable point of reference for comparative constitutional scholars. The absence of formal amendment rules has long tested preconceptions of difficulty of constitutional change, sources of rigidity and impediments to change. The challenge has become even trickier as constitutional change faces the stress test of the continuing Brexit process. The UK is facing unprecedented challenges to its constitutional law and practices, arising from the effects of radical social and technological changes impacting on its traditional forms and processes of government. Many of the constitutional problems and reform proposals arising relate to questions of democratic accountability, political representation and national identity. Substantial research and planning will be needed for tailoring the legal options for future reform of the UK constitution in order to modernize its ancient institutions and structure while retaining the positive elements in its working and culture. The resolution of these matters will be tantamount to a new constitutional settlement for the UK.[73]

Australia

The written Constitution is rigid and exists within a tradition of judicial legalism. however, several forces call into question the significance of the constitution's textual rigidity. judicial legalism has been deployed in ways that call into question the claim that it has stymied constitutional development. the constitution's narrowness facilitates political change, some of which constitutes informal constitutional change. the social role of the constitution is slowly, subtly shifting, which indicates a disruption of the orthodox view of the constitution and which may provide impetus for future constitutional change.[74]

Latin America: Chile and Brazil

The stakes of constitutional change in the Latin American example are related to democratic resilience. Latin America has become more democratic over the years despite persisting instabilities in some countries. Yet this positive outcome has proven interestingly adaptive to

---

72 S. Suteu, 'Gender in Comparative Constitutional Change', Chapter 21 in this volume.

73 R. Blackburn, 'The Future of UK Constitutional Law', Chapter 22 in this volume.

74 E. Arcioni and A. Stone, 'Constitutional Change in Australia: The Paradox of the Frozen Continent', Chapter 23 in this volume.

practices that are far from ideal for a democratic environment. Could practices, as preservationist strategies of political elites, be interpreted as a second-best solution for democratic stability? By focusing on how such strategies apply to constitutional change as they have taken place in Chile and Brazil, the main argument is that such preservationist constitutional changes, though helping democracy to be more resilient, may paradoxically challenge this very democracy by the legitimacy gap they foster.[75]

South Africa

Profiling South Africa provides a compelling case study that probes the formal/informal dipole. At first glance, and indeed perhaps at second, post-apartheid South Africa presents quite an ordinary picture of constitutional change. Partly because these formal channels of constitutional change are demonstrably not blocked, South Africa might appear an unlikely site for a discussion of informal constitutional change. This in itself has something to tell us about informal constitutional change. But if we press further, we will find that looking for informal constitutional change in an apparently unpromising case such as South Africa can be revealing and matters to understand parts of South Africa's emerging constitutionalism.[76]

Japan

The case of Japan presents a conundrum for comparatists. Preconceptions about imposition, longevity and change are tested. Could it be that the supposedly archetypal imposed constitution was never really imposed? Modern Japan has experienced two radical constitutional changes: the enactment of the Constitution of the Empire of Japan of 1889 and the creation of the Constitution of Japan of 1946. The former constitution was based on the monarchical principle that Japan borrowed from the 19th-century southern German states; the latter, imposed by the American occupying forces, is based on the popular sovereignty principle and regarded as moderately pacifist. Modern Japan has faced various predicaments in trying to realize constitutional ideals in this imperfect world.[77]

Conclusion

As constitutional comparison develops, alongside the explicit attempt 'to disengage from the national constitutional framework'[78] and juxtaposing with focus on similarities and differences, a communicative dimension also develops, which entails CCC scholars participating in an open dialogue. This impacts the way constitutional comparatists use methodology and the way they write: they look at constitutions through a comparative lens and when they do not produce comparative work per se, they write in such ways that their work can be used for comparative purposes.

---

75 J.Z. Benvindo, 'Preservationist Constitutional Change in Latin America: The Cases of Chile and Brazil', Chapter 24 in this volume.

76 J. Fowkes, 'Informal Constitutional Change in Unlikely Places: The Case of South Africa', Chapter 25 in this volume.

77 Y. Hasebe, 'Constitutional Changes in Japan', Chapter 26 in this volume.

78 J. Husa, 'Comparison' in D.S. Law and M. Langford (eds), *Research Methods in Constitutional Law: A Handbook* (Edward Elgar Publishing 2020 forthcoming).

Use of the internationalized CCC terminology is important for that task. CCC is a culture of reading and a culture of writing about constitutions. A new form of awareness is being formed. This impacts the use of comparison in the actual practice of constitutional change. Clumsy constitutional borrowing can be avoided, whereas culture-conscious examination of possibilities through the use of the available comparative knowledge is used.

Constitutions are defined by the way they change. Constitutional orders are defined by the way constitutions change. The study of constitutions through a comparative approach of constitutional change is important because it offers new insight on the nature of constitutions and on the various forms of constitutionalism.

It has currently become apparent that focus on how, why and toward which direction constitutions change is a distinct and rapidly growing field. The shift of focus from constitution-making to constitutional change makes sense, as amendment power is the means used to refurbish constitutions in established democracies, enhance their adaptation capacity, and boost their efficacy.

PART I

The study of comparative constitutional change

Theoretical and methodological aspects

2

COMPARATIVE METHODOLOGY AND CONSTITUTIONAL CHANGE

Jaakko Husa

Introduction

Researching constitutional change by using the comparative approach lies at the heart of comparative constitutional law and interdisciplinary comparative constitutional studies. It is about concentrating on constitutional change as a substantive matter by abandoning a country-bound approach and drawing comparisons between different systems.[1] Whether it is a question of formal or informal change is of no consequence, i.e. comparing differences and similarities and trying to find explanations for them is a core technique when we are studying constitutional change. There is more to it because the novel research field of comparative constitutional change makes the comparative approach its methodological centrepiece. As a result, researching constitutional change comparatively cannot be parochial; it expands over the traditional epistemic boundaries of constitutional law scholarship and deepens our understanding of constitutional change.

The emergence of the new field has taken shape under two major developments. First, comparative constitutional law has freed itself from the paradigmatic grip of a private law-oriented comparative study of law.[2] This has brought new approaches and an openness toward various methods not familiar from doctrinal comparisons.[3] In short, the suffocating epistemic embrace of private law-focused legal doctrine has all but died out.[4] Second, many constitutional scholars have conceived that research of such things as amendments, replacements, revisions, adaptations, interpretation, disuse, and even revolution is not only a single area of study but, rather, a distinct field that combines comparative constitutional law and constitutional studies under a united thematic banner.[5] Studying constitutional change comparatively is essentially a multidisciplinary

---

1 See, e.g., Oliver and Fusaro (2011).
2 See, e.g., Ginsburg and Dixon (2012) and Rosenfeld and Sajó (2012b).
3 Empirical study of constitutional narratives is a good example of an approach not familiar from private law comparisons, see Law. Typically, new approaches rely on empirical and quantitative approaches such as Ginsburg and Versteeg (2014).
4 It is argued that comparative constitutional law 'has now moved front and center', Rosenfeld and Sajó (2012a: 1).
5 See, e.g., Contiades (2013) and Albert, Contiades, and Fotiadou (2017).

endeavour. Constitutional change is both a legal and political phenomenon that fuses the normative and factual together so that narrow views such as 'law' or 'politics' become virtually untenable because of the subject matter itself.[6] The legal dimensions of constitutions are intertwined with the political when constitutions or their smaller components transform.[7]

This chapter addresses comparative methodology in studying constitutional change. The chapter, while written from the point of view of comparative constitutional law, is based on a theoretically and methodologically broad and flexible view shunning a narrow legal perspective. In articulating key issues of comparative methodology, the following section of this chapter discusses the methodology of comparative law. The third section deals with the purposes of comparative constitutional law and this is followed by a discussion of the purposes of studying constitutional change comparatively. The chapter then addresses specific issues by discussing universalism and culturalism, the potential relevance of legal families, and legal transplants. The concluding section draws out the key points and rounds off the discussion. In addition, questions that concern case selection and choice of method are discussed throughout this chapter because they are interlinked to nearly everything this chapter deals with.

Method and methodology

In a comparative study of law, method refers to a particular way in which a series of research steps are taken in a predetermined manner. This includes processes, tools, and techniques by means of which a research topic is addressed. Methodology, on the other hand - the theme in this chapter - deals in a general way with the principles that guide research practices and operations.[8] Comparing constitutions opens possibilities for many kinds of research techniques. In principle we can apply any method as long as it helps to find answers to research questions. In essence, answering becomes possible through understanding the constitutional material under scrutiny. An element of qualitative approach is involved, stressing the role of understanding underlying the comparative approach. This is not to say that quantitative approaches would not enter the question. On the contrary, numerical data is useful but underused in a comparative study of law. Numerical approaches fit well with comparative constitutional law. Moreover, there are no reasons to limit the scope of comparative constitutional law as it leads to overtly jurisprudential or, at worst, legalistically narrow comparisons that needlessly shy away from quantitative or interdisciplinary methods.[9]

Without a shadow of doubt, quantitative methods have their place in the study of constitutional change. As Meuwese and Versteeg say,

---

6 Accordingly, to study constitutional engineering as a phenomenon of constitutional change cannot rely on a narrow approach but has to take multi-faceted parameters into account (e.g. party systems, the role of civil society and constitutional experts, and informal constitutional change). See Albert, Contiades, and Fotiadou (2017).

7 One example of this fusion is that constitutional changes have become more citizen-led as we have seen the growth of popular participation. See Contiades and Fotiadou (2017).

8 Adams, Husa, and Oderkerk (2017: xi).

9 'The proliferation of constitutional courts, judicial review, and constitutional rights jurisprudence worldwide, indeed the rise of the human rights discourse more generally, turned the comparative study of constitutionalism into a predominantly legalistic enterprise that is heavily influenced by the prevalent case-law method of instruction', Hirschl (2013: 6).

[w]ell-executed research designs, relying on the quantitative analysis of legal or semi-legal texts or using survey- or indicator-based data, either as the lead method in large cooperative projects or in a clearly defined support role, are good candidates to offer ... help to comparative law.[10]

Accordingly, comparative study of constitutional law is not about disciplinary boundaries or differences between qualitative and quantitative approaches but about suitable research designs. In practice, this means that comparative study of constitutional change can combine doctrinal-legal and empirical approaches. Moreover, research may rely on an interpretative-legal approach but it may also utilise avant-garde computational techniques. Importantly, the approach should be chosen according to the research design, not according to disciplinary boundaries.[11] The key factor is that there is no such thing as a one-size-fits-all method in comparative research of constitutional change.

The methodological choices of comparative research can be roughly divided into two categories. These are, on the one hand, choices of a technical nature (e.g. what kind of constitutional change is being studied), and on the other hand, theoretical choices having to do with different schools of thought, such as choosing between culturalism and universalism. Choices are not exclusive but take turns during the research process: how many cases and what kind of constitutional changes are included may depend on time, resources, and linguistic reach. Undoubtedly, a great number of methods are available to be applied in the comparative study of constitutional change. As such, this is a strength, not a weakness, because comparisons are not similar and do not have identical purposes.[12] For example, analysing one case of constitutional transplantation is sure to differ from a text-oriented computational analysis looking for a longer time-series in numerous constitutional systems. Yet the object of study is the same: constitutional change in its various forms and manifestations.

Importantly, the attempt to compare constitutional change concerns rejection of constitutional ethnocentrism, pushing away the implicit thought pattern according to which national solutions are considered usual and what lawyers inherently expect. In the world of constitutional law we can learn from others; we can see ourselves in the foreign mirror. None of this is to say, however, that comparative constitutional change would necessarily require a commitment to universalistic assumptions.[13] Comparisons are of significant importance because studying constitutional change is a specialised thematic field that does not focus on any specific country or group of countries but on a certain issue or problem related to the change of constitutions in general. Importantly – and this is a key factor – only comparison can reveal the details and complexities of constitutional change worldwide, thus rendering them understandable in a larger context.

In fact, the larger context is the bread and butter of comparative constitutional law, pushing beyond judicial comparativism and a narrow legal framework. For the study of constitutional change this is an important feature because a narrow legal point of view seldom yields satisfactory answers to the research question 'how', which can be found on the basis of 'Large N' (looking for patterns in a large number of cases) studies enabled by

---

10 Meuwese and Versteeg (2013).
11 See Tushnet (2017).
12 Cf. Rosenfeld and Sajó (2012a: 8).
13 See, e.g. Teitel (2004).

new information technology. What is more, unlike judges – who are bound to their normative framework – scholars enjoy a greater degree of epistemic freedom in their attempt to describe, analyse, and ultimately understand constitutional change.[14] Importantly, national constitutions were not born – or have not grown – in isolation.[15] Scholarly work in constitutional change renounces the idea according to which constitutions are inherently national products and instead demonstrates the importance of border-crossing constitutional diffusion, as we shall see later in this chapter.[16] In essence, only a comparative approach can properly highlight this phenomenon and produce general knowledge on the subject exceeding the national framework.

Domestic constitutions have adopted far more from others than doctrinalists comprehend: constitutional ideas and doctrines are migrating; for example, the separation of powers, constitutional judicial review, and constitutional rights. Nevertheless, constitution-drafters and other constitutionally relevant actors are not distinctly aware of the layers of loans, borrowings, and all sorts of constitutional plagiarism that their own constitution accommodates. In contrast, comparative constitutional scholars are well aware that national systems consist of patchworks of migration alongside domestic ideas. However, this is certainly not to say that constitutional transfers would be problem-free.[17] Ideas and doctrines move beyond borders whether we admit it or not, and whether they work in the ways intended or not.[18] Comparative constitutional change is an illustration of how everything that is not bolted down can be copied to elsewhere.[19] Moreover, it should go without saying that nothing is bolted down in the world of constitutional ideas; indeed, the world of constitutional law is a world of migration.

Purposes and approaches

In a broad view, the purposes of studying constitutional change are rather similar to the purposes of comparative study of constitutional law in general. A comparative approach to the study of constitutional change might benefit from many possible uses and involve multiple goals. Generally speaking, we can distinguish two basic purposes. These are description and analysis. Be that as it may, these aims cannot be separated from the aims of comparative law in general. The underlying idea, namely that comparative study of law needs a specific aim, is a crucial one; comparison is undertaken for a purpose and not merely to decorate a nationally oriented study of law as some kind of supplementary nicety. Before addressing description and analysis, however, we need to briefly discuss the purposes of comparative law more generally.

14 For a more detailed discussion on 'Large N' and 'Small N' studies, see Ginsburg (2016).
15 See Versteeg and Goderis (2014). They argue that even though constitutions are normally regarded as purely domestic products, shaped by national ideas and politics, they are in fact much more transnational.
16 See Ginsburg, Foti, and Rockmore (2014).
17 'Read ten constitutions and you know them all, at least you know the most common varieties of constitutional construction. Such will be the implicit message of the hasty traveller', Frankenberg (2010: 563).
18 See for more detailed discussion, Spector (2008) (speaking mostly about the Argentinian experience).
19 However, transplants are difficult to control: 'Once grafted onto a different constitutional system, transplants can grow, evolve, or atrophy', Rosenfeld and Sajó (2012a: 15).

General aims

One key aim of comparing laws (in a broad sense) has been to use comparison as an instrument of learning. By and large, this has meant expanding knowledge as a means of understanding law better. For example, French constitutional law textbooks have typically also contained comparative parts.[20] Albeit these lightweight comparisons have not been rigorously comparative, nevertheless they have provided a larger comparative context for reaching a better understanding of the French system. We can characterise this kind of lightweight comparison as contextual because it provides a comparative context for the study of a single system. However, it is not genuinely comparative in the sense that it does not look at differences and similarities in a balanced way but, rather, focuses on a certain system which it hopes to better explain by using foreign examples and illustrations. At best, lightweight comparison might provide concepts and tools for understanding constitutional change within a single system.

Another key aim has been to use comparative law as an instrument of evolutionary and taxonomic science. Taxonomic comparatists have tried to mimic sciences in which classification has enjoyed a long and successful history, even though no truly scientific global classification of legal systems has ever emerged, as we shall see later in this chapter. Yet another category of key aims has included various utilitarian and pragmatic aims, such as improving national legislation or using foreign legal ideas in judicial problem-solving.[21] Whereas legislatures are motivated by political or economic considerations, courts might look elsewhere to draw inspiration when no domestic rule is available or the domestic rule is unclear and needs interpretation.[22] No doubt, these aims are familiar from the comparative study of constitutional law, too. However, comparative constitutional scholarship has stepped out of the methodological and epistemological boundaries of general comparative law. This transformation has opened new areas for interdisciplinarily flavoured comparative constitutional law research such as comparative constitutional change.

Stepping out of the old boundaries has been facilitated and enhanced by growing interest in the international diffusion of constitutional ideas. One of the key consequences has been a shift away from a mere description of differences and similarities and outdated taxonomy-building to genuinely seeking to explain comparative findings. Notwithstanding that this is not necessarily a shared view or the paradigmatic position of all comparatists, yet the effort to move the focus toward a more explanation-oriented study and use of non-doctrinal approaches has gained in popularity. In any case, in the comparative study of constitutional change it is useful to distinguish the two basic purposes mentioned above, i.e. description and analysis.

Describing and analysing

Describing constitutional change plays an important role in the comparative endeavour. Without reliable description it is not possible to move on to analysis. Disciplined descriptions of national systems, and the ways they change, provide crucial data for comparative study. One of the key outcomes of these kinds of non-doctrinal descriptions is that they highlight the role of change taking place outside the official amendment procedures. For example, Strauss has demonstrated and

---

20 See, e.g., Duhamel and Tusseau (2013). A classic example is Duverger (1960).
21 Glenn (2012: 66–70).
22 See Smits (2006).

described how many changes in the US Constitution have come about without changing formal constitutional law. His study demonstrates how American constitutional law is not simply a matter of legal concern but, rather, the result of a complex evolutionary process and not merely a result of political acts by a sovereign people.[23] We can also analyse the gradual change within a shorter period within a single system by analysing key judgments without textual change taking place.[24] A further example is Albert's study of quasi-constitutional amendments (especially highlighting the Canadian case), which analytically describes sub-constitutional changes that achieve constitutional status over time because of their constitutional substance.[25] These kinds of case-oriented studies provide a thick description of a certain constitutional system (or a group of systems) without aiming at establishing generalised relationships between a great number of variables. Case-oriented studies provide comprehension of complex units (constitutional systems) following a different logic of research, that is, other than variable-oriented approaches.[26]

Besides descriptions, the comparative study of constitutional change needs to analyse its results and draw conclusions. Whereas describing the actual working of a certain system seeks to characterise the constitutional reality in its complexity, analysis seeks to understand the nature of what is being described in order to determine its essential features against a larger comparative framework. In the field of comparative constitutional change, analysis can produce new knowledge and challenge our previous understanding of the phenomenon. For instance, Ginsburg, Elkins, and Melton relied on cross-national historical data and produced interesting results on constitutional mortality. They demonstrated that – against commonplace expectations – constitutions actually last only 19 years.[27] To take a further example, Law's research on constitutional archetypes is an illustration of a study that uses an empirical text-based approach to analyse constitutional narratives. On the basis of his research, Law finds a combination of three basic archetypes, which he labels as a liberal archetype, a statist archetype, and a universalistic archetype. The study finds evidence of these archetypes in constitutional preambles. Law's applied computational linguistic analysis also points out a growing interdependence between constitutional law and international law because the language used in universalistic preambles mirrors the language of leading international human rights instruments.[28]

On the basis of description and analysis it is possible to move to interpretation and evaluation. For example, theory building or judging whether or not a constitutional transplant has been a success becomes possible only after the research object's relevant features have been described and analysed. For comparative methodology in the study of constitutional change, the key conclusion seems clear: even though we may distinguish between approaches using a large number of cases and those concentrating on a few cases in depth, this distinction is not decisive. In short, the choice of comparative approach arises from the interests of the researcher, the research problem, and the availability of data. A particularly relevant topic in this context is the question concerning the distinction between the quantitative and qualitative approaches.

---

23 'forms of popular rule that are less romantic than the idea of the People speaking with one voice to amend the Constitution … these forms of popular rule may be less congenial to lawyers because they do not provide a canonical text to be scrutinized and interpreted', Strauss (2001: 1505).
24 For example, Hong Kong's system has been changed – without textual amendments to the Basic Law – by the authoritative interpretations of the Standing Committee of the National People's Congress. See, e.g., Husa (2017).
25 Albert (2016).
26 See, e.g., Pap (2017; analyses the Hungarian system and describes its slide toward illiberalism).
27 Ginsburg, Elkins, and Melton (2008).
28 Law (2017).

Quantifying data or the empirical approach

In the above, description and analysis were discussed. However, another methodologically important basic distinction exists between constitutional data: qualitative and quantitative. Traditional jurisprudentially oriented approaches are typically qualitative in nature. Essentially, a qualitative approach is a specific form of empirical research where data are not in numerical form. Commonplace, qualitative approaches assume an interpretive – or even an almost naturalistic – approach to their subject matter, relying typically on legal doctrine or a judicial framework.[29] Because this approach is so typical and widespread, it is not meaningful to discuss it here.[30] The traditional law-focused approaches differ from quantitative approaches because the latter follow the more general model of empirical social sciences.

In essence, the quantitative approach is based on an idea according to which it quantifies the research problem by way of generating data that can be transformed into utilisable statistics. Quantitative research is particularly interested in collecting numerical data and generalising it across groups of variables or to explain a specific phenomenon such as, in this case, constitutional change. Importantly, statistics make it possible to turn quantitative constitutional data into useful information. Then, statistics can be used to summarise data and to describe patterns, relationships, and connections between constitutionally relevant factors. When quantitative data are used descriptively, it enables the researcher to summarise data and, in doing so, compress information on a particular subject. Then again, if we use quantified data inferentially we can identify relevant differences between variables and between groups of data. A crucial benefit of quantitative research is that it uses measurable data to formulate facts and uncover patterns not visible in the qualitative framework. In other words, relying on quantitative data means that research is more structured than if relying on qualitative data and accompanying interpretative or naturalistic approaches.[31]

An example of the use of the quantitative approach is the study by Law and Versteeg on sham constitutions.[32] They first match their quantified data on the rights-related content of the world's constitutions concerning human rights performance, and then they calculate numerical scores. These scores represent the extent to which countries violate the rights pledged in their constitutions or how they uphold more rights than their constitution seems to contain. Scores are also used to rank countries according to their constitutional performance (under-performance or over-performance). Statistical analysis is finally deployed to identify a number of variables that seem to be able to predict the degree to which countries perform in relation to their codified constitutional guarantees.

In the discussion on methodology of comparative constitutional law, quantitative methods have met resistance because they are so different from jurisprudential approaches. However, several reasons have been proposed as to why empirical methods – or, in a slightly broader sense social science-based approaches – are needed. One reason is that extra-judicial factors play an important role in constitutional court decision-making patterns. This means that even though constitutional courts and judges use the language of legal doctrine, their real decision-making patterns are correlated with such things as policy preferences and ideological factors. A second reason is that constitutional law as such, i.e. as a normative phenomenon, has rather limited

---

29 See, e.g., de Visser (2013).

30 'Quantitative research is empirical research where the data are in the form of numbers. Qualitative research is empirical research where the data are not in the form of numbers' (Punch 1995: 4).

31 See Brannen (2005; underlines contextualisation, particularly in cross-national research).

32 'Our goal is to measure the extent to which constitutional rights are actually realized', Law and Versteeg (2013: 879).

capability to cause real, on-the-ground change, independently. In other words, legal rules alone do not suffice but other things are needed in order to turn such values as constitutional rights into reality. A third reason comes from the methodology of comparative constitutional law, a methodology that can be described in a critical tone as 'fuzzy and amorphous at best'. This argument basically claims that comparative study of constitutional law simply lags behind the social sciences and does not perform controlled comparisons or seek to trace causal links.[33]

However, we do not need to go this far in order to see a justified place for empirical approaches in the study of constitutional change. Other scholars have pointed out that accepting empirical approaches as a part of our methodology does not alter the fact that various conceptual, philosophical, analytical, and even classical jurisprudential questions remain relevant in the comparative study of constitutional law.[34] Finally, if more traditional approaches to constitutional law involve a risk of becoming overtly jurisprudential, then that risk is matched by another: of overemphasising empirical and other formal approaches, too. As noted by Hirsch, large-N studies could open up new kinds of possibilities for scholarship and 'constitutional drafting, notably the possibility of a "scientific", "planned", or perhaps even computerized process of constitutional design'.[35] This kind of focus on a formal computational approach might be a step too far in terms of comparative study of constitutional change. As Jackson points out, 'Law cannot be a science in the way some other disciplines can – especially in our field, of comparative constitutional law'.[36] Moreover, we know from the general methodology of social sciences that quantitative approaches have been typically more directed at theory verification whereas qualitative approaches are typically more concerned with theory generation.[37] Quantitative approaches are arguably more objective than qualitative approaches, but then again, because constitutional change is a multidimensional and cultural phenomenon it would be a mistake to rely only on quantitative approaches.

Comparing constitutional change

It would be wrong to claim that interest in constitutional change is a novelty. As the classic distinction between rigid and flexible constitutions demonstrates, constitutional change has been in the focus of constitutional theory for quite some time.[38] However, what does tell the old and the present interests apart is the fact that our recent interest in constitutional change is guided by methodological self-consciousness based on the comparative nature of the attempt to understand constitutional change beyond the national level. As a result, the field of comparative constitutional change today holds a keen interest in research design and methodology.

How does one start planning a comparative research design when focusing on constitutional change? The methodological toolbox of comparative constitutional law (broadly understood) does not provide an exact methodology but, instead, contains a number of useful rules of thumb. Due to the variety of legal cultures and the differing

---

33 Hirschl (2013: 7–9).
34 Möllers and Birkenkötter (2014: 621).
35 Hirschl (2014: 272).
36 Jackson (2016: 1374).
37 Punch and Oancea (2014: 23).
38 See, e.g., Bryce (1905: 3–94).

interests of comparatists, the methodology of comparative constitutional law is, generally speaking, heuristic. This, however, does not mean that justifiable methods for comparative constitutional law could not be found. And, to be sure, research design does not need to be qualitative/case-oriented merely because it has been the tradition in comparative law. As pointed out in the introduction to this chapter, studying constitutional change requires both legal and non-legal factors to be taken into account. Indeed, as also noted in the above section, both case-oriented and variable-oriented approaches can be used. To address these issues in more detail, we need to discuss illustrative examples in what follows.

Evidence is available that quantitative approaches form a natural part of the comparative study of constitutional law, i.e. systematic empirical approaches have been shown to be able to provide constitutionally interesting findings. For example, Law and Versteeg provide empirical and systematic information about the extent to which the US Constitution has influenced the revision and adoption of formal constitutions in other countries. Their key conclusion is that the USA is not leading the way in terms of global constitutionalism because the US Constitution appears to be losing its appeal as a global model for constitutional drafters.[39] In other words, the US model does not inspire constitution-drafters in terms of changing constitutions worldwide. What is more, the choice of approach is, of course, connected to selection of research data: one needs quantitative techniques seeking to explain when there are many cases, whereas hard cases can also be studied by a more traditional jurisprudential (i.e. case-oriented) approach that can highlight detailed legal questions and provide thick descriptions in the shape of offering legal-cultural context and meaning so that a scholar outside a given system is able the better to comprehend.[40]

With many cases it makes sense to apply statistical or computational methods and produce generalised results whereas with a few difficult cases it makes sense to underline a thick description and an understanding of the cases qualitatively.[41] Illustrative cases, on the other hand, can be used in order to show the range of scenarios that may occur concerning a particular research subject, such as distinguishing different models of judicial review (for example, centralised vs. decentralised, constitutional court vs. no constitutional court, abstract norm control vs. concrete case-bound control).[42] Crucially, as already noted, the research question has a decisive role for the choice of method, not the disciplinary banner under which research takes place. For such a thematic field as comparative constitutional change this is methodologically a crucial factor.

An important point needs to be made here. Instead of methodological relativism we need look to the direction of heuristics as suggested above. Heuristics concerns an approximation method by the use of which it is usually possible to get sufficiently close to what is deemed a satisfactory result.[43] Typical heuristic methods include rules of thumb that are based on a limited but sufficient amount of information. In the context of the research process, this means that the constitutional comparatist need not consider available approaches in a methodological vacuum. Example approaches as to how comparative research can be carried out are available. Previous studies are a store of methods from which

---

39 See, e.g., Law and Versteeg (2012).
40 See also, presenting different classification of approaches, Hirschl (2005).
41 See, e.g., Versteeg and Goderis (2014).
42 See, e.g., Husa (2000).
43 'Heuristic contains "sign-posts", while methodology tells us, even if provisionally, whether we are going in the right direction', Kiss (2006: 317).

the constitutional comparatist can learn without minutely following a particular approach. Accordingly, the methodology of comparative constitutional change can be defined as a heuristic compilation of rules of thumb on exposure and discovery. Much, if not all, depends on the purpose of the research: aiming at generalisation requires a variable-oriented approach, whereas aiming to explain complexity (and to generalise only in a very limited manner) requires a case-oriented approach.

For the comparative study of constitutional change this relative methodological freedom is a welcome facet because it helps to focus on suitable comparative approaches instead of fixating on one type of method only. The downside of this is, of course, that the comparative study of constitutional change offers no exact methodology (in the sense of a cookbook: offering straight directions). Importantly, practical methodological literature is available that highlights case selection, as Hirschl's useful proposition shows. He distinguishes five basic principles of case selection: (1) the most similar cases logic, (2) the most different cases logic, (3) the prototypical cases principle, (4) the most difficult cases principle, and (5) the outlier cases principle.[44] None of these is a method in a technical sense (research technique), yet they provide guidance and conceptual tools in relation to the interests of the researcher. In practice, we can see that these kinds of methodological choices are intertwined.[45] Of course, other methodological frameworks are also provided by recent methodological scholarship in comparative constitutional law.[46] In any case, we will next discuss specific issues of methodological significance.

Specific methodological issues

As already stated above, comparative constitutional change is a broad field of study; hence, it is not possible to deal with all relevant issues on its methodology in a single chapter of a handbook. Moreover, the heuristic nature of methodology and broad variety of methods prevent addressing all the possible questions in a thorough manner. Consequently, instead of trying to cover all relevant methodological questions, this section addresses three select themes of methodological importance. These analyses are heuristic instances that help make important methodological questions clear, even though they are not designed to offer methods in a technical sense. The specific issues chosen deal with universalism and culturalism, the role of legal families, and legal transplants. All these issues are familiar from comparative law scholarship but, crucially, they play a different role and lead to different implications for the comparative study of constitutional change.

Universalism and culturalism

The debate between universalists and culturalists (or particularists) is a well-known issue in comparative law scholarship.[47] However, to address or rehearse that abundant debate here

---

44 See Hirschl (2005).
45 See, e.g., Bilchitz and Landau (2018; studies the change of separation of powers from a comparative perspective and shows how it has developed in the countries of the global South.)
46 See, e.g., Tourkochoriti (2017). Distinguishes three approaches: (1) focusing on the social and political context in an attempt to explain differences or similarities, (2) a philosophical analysis informed by the study of differences or similarities in the regulation of rights, and (3) a combination of these two approaches aiming at challenging existing philosophical and socio-political frames.
47 See Husa (2006).

would not make much sense. Instead, we discuss the juxtaposition of universalism and culturalism in the area of constitutional law, where it is a key underlying factor in so-called global constitutionalism.

Global constitutionalism is related to the broader notion of global law. Global constitutionalism consists of various strands.[48] The state of current debate on global constitutionalism has been described as 'a constitutional cacophony'.[49] One strand argues that constitutionalism is moving beyond the nation state into the transnational sphere and the private sector. It is argued that even transnational corporations are obliged to respect human rights.[50] Another strand underlines that globalisation has placed states and domestic constitutions under strain. This strand holds that states have transferred certain previously government-held functions to non-state actors. What is more, it is argued that governance is exercised beyond the traditional confines of nation states.[51] The third strand assumes that a new international order is being developed following the principles and values of Western constitutionalism. In effect, this strand maintains that various scattered international legal texts form a body of international constitutional law that is a specific subset of the international legal order.[52] These strands are all universalist; however, there is also a cultural counter-argument. Because global ideas are so sweeping, they face difficulties when they meet the realities of what constitutional law globally actually is.

The project of global constitutionalism is especially appealing to universalist public international lawyers.[53] Notwithstanding, international law is a minimalist and fragmented body of law which is mostly subject to the will of states still holding on to their sovereignty.[54] Regardless of globalisation, the Westphalian order refuses to become merely a shadow of the past and international law holds no supremacy over other law, such as written national constitutions.[55] Essentially, global constitutionalism is built on national ideas and national constitutions, in turn, are based on certain preconditions of which one of the most important is the common political community creating a base for a constitutional order.[56] According to the Western view, the constitutional chain of legitimacy starts from the people and is channelled into a constitution.[57] But, in the case of substantive-wise constitutionalised and seemingly universal international law, there is no such community, no such polity or democratic way to channel the political will to the international law sphere.[58] Instead, we have a rich plurality of cultures, languages, and accompanying ideas about the constitution. Global constitutionalism undoubtedly changes constitutions but the overall picture is less than clear.

There is a gap between universal and cultural notions of constitutionalism. Saunders points out that constitutional differences still matter and we need to 'bridge the gap between the universalist assumptions of international law and the realities of constitutional difference'.[59]

---

48 Peters (2015).
49 Mac Amhlaigh (2016: 176).
50 Peters (2015).
51 Ibid.
52 Ibid.
53 See Schwöbel (2012).
54 See Koskenniemi and Leino (2002).
55 Peters (2015).
56 Basically, this is the same critique that is known as the 'no demos thesis' in connection with the question of the so-called European constitution. See Weiler (1995).
57 Mac Amhlaigh (2016) interprets constitutionalism as a specific form of constitutional legitimacy.
58 However, see Habermas (2001).
59 Saunders (2009: 38).

The keyword here is 'difference' – constitutional globalists are essentially universalists and they seek to homogenise, setting aside the concerns of comparative study of constitutional law, showing great differences between systems. For the study of constitutional change, this is a relevant observation because it addresses the choice between universalism and particularism.

In essence, global constitutionalism contains an inherent component of universalism. At the same time, constitutionalism is the theory and practice of government and law, which is a product of modern Western civilisation.[60] Like most globalising legalities, global constitutionalism is quintessentially a Western construct seeking universal acceptance. Yet, as Koskenniemi points out, 'constitutionalism is not necessarily tied to any definite institutional project, European or otherwise', by which he means to say that constitutionalism may also be grasped as a political and moral mind-set.[61] Then again, the growth of the global legal universe does not mean that this would lead to a unified constitutional space.[62] The comparative approach has specific value here because it enables one to 'appreciate the diverse capacities of human societies in the domain of constitutionalism'.[63] Comparative appreciation might require us to unlearn what we have learned from our domestic constitutions and domestic forms of constitutionalism.[64]

The quintessential problem is that theoretically or normatively focused constitutional universalism disregards the fact that constitutional assumptions are not epistemologically universal but are based on one or a set of constitutional systems.[65] To govern constitutional change globally is practically not possible. Consequently, strong universalism might not be the best epistemological assumption guiding the choice of method in the study of constitutional change. Be that as it may, assuming an over-strong cultural and relativist view underlining the singularity of each constitutional system is a step too far; it would deny variable-oriented approaches, which does not make sense in the comparative study of constitutional change. In the end, both nomothetic and ideographic dimensions exist in constitutional change and they both need to be taken into account: sometimes an interpretative jurisprudential approach might work, and at other times empirical or computational approaches might work better. In principle, the impulses for constitutional change may be domestic, foreign, or sometimes transnational. Some changes might be national, some regional, and some even global. In any case, the research problem should play a decisive role for the choice of comparative method. Consequently, researching constitutional change comparatively requires taking into account both universalist and cultural factors depending on the purpose of the study at hand. Whether one chooses to underline universalism or particularism is not essentially a methodological but a philosophical or political choice.

Relevance of legal families

Comparative law scholars have traditionally constructed such macro-concepts as legal families, legal cultures, and legal traditions. Even though differences between them do exist, their contents are in fact very similar.[66] Of these notions, the notion of 'legal family' is the

---

60 Chen (2010: 650).
61 Koskenniemi (2007: 18).
62 For more in-depth discussion, see Kuo (2010).
63 Harding and Son Bui (2016: 170).
64 Cf. Schwöbel (2012: 21).
65 See Dixon and Stone (2016).
66 Husa (2016).

most widespread and discussed; but what does it mean for the methodology of comparative study of constitutional change?

As an academic field, comparative law can be divided into two main areas of research, albeit this division is flexible as to its nature. Customarily, micro-comparison deals with specific legal rules, cases, and institutions, whereas macro-comparison normally focuses on larger-scale themes and questions. Systematisation, grouping, and classification of the legal systems of the world lie at the heart of macro-comparative law: it deals with comparison between entire legal systems, not specific small-scale problems of a legal nature.[67] The assumption has been that a limited number of different typical key questions relate to the classification of legal systems: can legal systems or legal cultures of the world be classified into entities belonging to only a few large groups? Which are the large legal families of the world? According to what criteria can inclusion of an individual legal system in a specific legal family be decided? What is the relevance of these issues for the methodology of comparative constitutional change? To begin with, one should realise that comparative law's macro-constructs are, to a great extent, overlapping although the comparatists who created these constructs might emphasise the differences between macro-constructs. On closer inspection each of these classifications resembles the other.

In their classic work on Roman, Germanic, and Nordic laws, Zweigert and Kötz listed the common law and the Far Eastern systems, Islamic systems, and Hindu law. Their work has conveyed to the twenty-first century this epistemological tradition that is based on the theoretical and conceptual foundation of European legal history. Moreover, in the French tradition the phrase '*familles de droit*' has been, and still is, used when referring to the so-called grand modern legal systems (*grands systèmes de droit contemporains*). In short, family has been a metaphor favoured by many a macro-comparatist. In the classic work by David, Romano-Germanic law, common law, and socialist law were presented. Like other non-Western legal systems David mentioned Islamic, Hindu, and Jewish law and the laws of the Far East, Africa, and Madagascar.[68]

A significant change in macro-classifications has been the fact that socialist law has been dropped since the early 1990s. It seems to have been replaced by Islamic law as the Other law (the main form of non-Western law; representing legal otherness) and not only in a limited sense. Islamic law also appears in the form of different mixed law combinations with secular law in various systems in which the aim is to observe Islamic teachings. A more recent example of classification that concentrates on legal families features in the work on 'grand' legal systems by Cuniberti. He distinguishes between Western law, Eastern/Oriental law, and African law. Cuniberti's macro-comparison is based on David's work in terms of everything that is essential although his classification differs in its contents from the (outdated) classifications by David.[69] It makes sense to point out that all of these classifications are compiled by private law-oriented scholars for private law-oriented scholars.

Now, we need to ask: what is the value of legal families for the comparative study of constitutional change? To begin with, seemingly no equivalent classifications exist in comparative constitutional law. Nevertheless, this is perhaps a misleading view because constitutional law has for a long time had other types of ways to classify constitutions. The purpose of these classifications has been to offer knowledge of the structure and scope of

---

67 See Zweigert and Kötz (1998: 4–5).
68 *Les grands systèmes de droit contemporains* was first published in 1964.
69 Cuniberti (2011).

constitutions. As a result of comparison, among other reasons, the following classifications of constitution have been recognised: written/unwritten; coherent/dispersed; rigid/flexible; monarchic/republican; and federal/unitary.[70] In fact, it is a question of basic alternatives that concern the constitutional model of governance. The basic models mentioned offer a conceptual framework by means of which it is easier for the comparatist to approach constitutions and constitutional laws that form part of foreign legal and political structures. To take another example, it is possible to compare the controlling organs of constitutionality in many respects: nature of norm control, controlling organ, organisational control, effect of control, and so on. It is also possible to distinguish different legal-cultural features in the supervision of the constitutionality of laws.[71]

Altogether, the classification of legal families does not offer too much for the comparative study of constitutional change. However, it might provide useful information on context and explain general legal-cultural factors of a constitutional system. For instance, the fact that the UK does not have a codified constitution but Germany does can be broadly explained by the differences between common law and civil law legal families. Accordingly, the specific ways in which constitutional change takes place are influenced by the plain fact of which legal family the system belongs to. But in terms of more detailed research questions, either in the form of variables or ideographic detail, the explanatory force of the legal family diminishes quickly. So far, no equivalent has been found to legal families in the comparative study of constitutional law, although the idea of specific 'public law families' is not unheard of.[72] Notwithstanding, constitutional scholars and political scientists tend to inadvertently distinguish between democratic and non-democratic or constitutionalism-abiding and unconstitutional systems. However, these can hardly be characterised as constitutional families in the sense of a legal family.

Legal transplantation

One key theme in comparative study of constitutional change is the use of legal transplants. This is a contested notion that Watson introduced in 1974.[73] Originally it was important for a legal transplant to have a historical connection between the formal laws of the systems concerned. What was essential was the 'relationship of one legal system and its rules with another'.[74] What takes place is a movement of law (broadly understood) between states.[75] Study on borrowings and legal transplants breaks the idea of the nationality of law and its bond to a particular system by pointing out the reciprocal relations that cross national restrictions. This is precisely why transplantation is so relevant a theme for comparative study of constitutional change. Yet it is a contested concept.

Criticism of the transplant theory was severe from the very beginning. Kahn-Freund presented an influential early criticism.[76] He underlined the significance of the social context of law. According to critique, the whole concept of transplant was out of place in the world

---

70 See, e.g., the classic work by Wheare (1966).
71 See, e.g., Husa (2000).
72 See Venter (2000: 41).
73 Watson (1993).
74 Ibid 6.
75 See Van Hoecke (2016).
76 'Requires a knowledge not only of the foreign law, but also of its social, and above all its political, context', Kahn-Freund (1974: 27).

of law, although it was possible to metaphorically refer with it to a surgical operation in which a kidney from one individual was transplanted to another person. Notwithstanding, 'we cannot take for granted that rules or institutions are transplantable'.[77] Accordingly, it would be essential to observe the societal context of law, or the result could be transplant rejection in the new system.[78]

Discussion has continued over the years, and various replacements have been proposed for the concept of legal transplant, with one of the best known being the proposal by Teubner. He emphasised that the result of transplantation can be anything. Therefore, we should not speak of a transplant but of an irritant.[79] Teubner stressed that when some element is transferred from one foreign legal culture to another, something happens - but not what is expected: it is not transplanted into another organism; rather, it works as a fundamental irritant that triggers a whole series of new and unexpected events. In other words, what follows transplantation is an evolutionary legal dynamic, the consequences of which are very difficult, if not impossible, to fully predict. Other critiques include Legrand who presented a culturalist and relativistic view of the sheer absurdity of (private law) legal transplants.[80] At present, concepts such as legal translation, legal transformation, and legal transposition are also used.[81] However, the majority of comparatists continue to use the notion of legal transplantation either solely or in parallel with other conceptualisations. Constitutional comparatists are no exception to this: it seems to be a part of our comparative constitutional law vocabulary, whether we like it or not.

To be sure, legal diffusion, copying or transplanting does take place in the world of constitutional law – but how well it actually works and whether it leads to the desired results or not, are different questions altogether.[82] Notwithstanding, it remains a fact that migration of constitutional law is taking place everywhere or, as one scholar puts it: 'Legal rules are extracted from one context, transferred and implanted in another context, or migrate across sometimes fluid borders and so on'.[83] One needs only to read constitutional documents around the world for the migration of constitutional ideas and doctrines to become crystal clear, as pointed out above when discussing Law's study on constitutional archetypes.[84] Altogether, it seems that a belief in legal transplants still forms part of comparative law scholarship and, more importantly, part of national legal practices, and there are scholars trying to outline a methodology for successful legal transplants.[85]

Typically, comparative study of constitutional transplants concentrates on and starts with a constitutional text. Numerous examples show that constitutional transplantation has taken place. But, as noted above in this chapter, the study of constitutional change cannot focus only on constitutional provisions. This is because constitutional rules are interrelated with other rules, principles, doctrines, and larger institutional structures. Many kinds of

---

77 Kahn-Freund (1974: 9).
78 See, e.g., Nichols (1997); Alshorbagy (2012).
79 See Teubner (1998).
80 See Legrand (1997).
81 See, e.g., Örücü (2002); Langer (2004); Xu (2004); Chen-Wishart (2013).
82 'Constitutional borrowing and transplantation of constitutional norms, structures, doctrines, and institutions is a fact of life regardless of ideological or theoretical objections to these practices', Rosenfeld and Sajó (2012a: 13).
83 Tohipur (2013: 33).
84 Law (2017).
85 See Peerenbom (2013).

constitutional ideas can migrate and this includes ideas that are not based on written constitutional norms, such as constitutional doctrines and methods. One area of globally significant migration is the expansion of judicial review. This, in turn, is flanked by the growing significance of constitutional rights.[86] This has changed systems that did not previously have constitutional judicial review as a part of their constitutions.[87] Perhaps, nonetheless, the most noteworthy example of constitutional transplant in the area of methods is proportionality. Originally it migrated from Prussian administrative law to many present-day national and supranational judicial organs around the world.[88]

The proportionality principle is basically a set of rules that determines the conditions for a limitation of constitutionally protected rights. Today it is widespread not only in Western democracies but also worldwide.[89] It has been argued that by 'the end of the 1990s, virtually every system of constitutional justice in the world, with the partial exception of the United States, had embraced the main tenets of proportionality analysis ... [It has become] a foundational element of global constitutionalism'.[90] The speed and width of the migration of proportionality has been such that it may be labelled as the 'most successful legal transplant of the twentieth century'.[91] However, it would be a mistake to regard constitutional transplants as only a relatively recent phenomenon, as indeed the example of the Nordic institution of Ombudsman clearly shows.[92] On the whole, constitutional borrowing is a historical fact: constitution-drafters and developers copy, adapt, and recycle constitutional ideas.[93] In other words, constitutional transplanting (broadly understood) takes place and is an important way to change a constitution.[94]

At the same time, we need to tread carefully when we speak of comparative methodology and transplants. For the comparative study of constitutional change, legal transplantation is not a method as such. However, it is a way to conceptualise the migration of constitutional ideas as a means of constitutional change. Crucially, legal transplantation cannot dictate the choice of method or case selection: case-oriented or variable-oriented and jurisprudential or non-legal approaches are all possible in terms of studying constitutional change through legal transplants. To repeat a point, research interest plays a key role in choice of method(s) even when studying constitutional transplants.

Conclusion

From the above, it should be reasonably clear that comparative constitutional change is a distinct field of scholarship with an interwoven link to comparative methodology. Constitutional change is conceived not at a national level but in a broader comparative framework. Quintessentially, it is a comparative endeavour seeking to provide a broad

---

86 See Horwitz (2009).
87 For a broader discussion, see Gyorfi (2016; argues against strong constitutional review).
88 See Perju (2012: 1314–1316).
89 See Bendor and Sela (2015).
90 Stone Sweet and Mathews (2008: 74).
91 Kumm (2003: 595).
92 See, e.g., Gregory and Giddings (2000).
93 For example, the Canadian Charter of Rights and Freedoms (1982) influenced constitution making in South Africa, New Zealand, Hong Kong, Israel, and many members of the Council of Europe. See Oliver, Macklen, and Rosiers (2017: 5–6).
94 See Tebbe and Tsai (2010).

framework through which changing constitutions and constitutionalism can be conceived, freed from the epistemic boundaries created by national borders. Constitutional change goes beyond studying formal constitutional amendments and reaches out to fields outside the scope of legal disciplines.

As a distinct field, comparative constitutional change is methodologically open and flexible because it encompasses all sorts of comparisons, ranging from the study of formal amendment procedures to analysing more subtle mechanisms of change. Accordingly, comparative approaches in this field can be ideographic when seeking to describe and analyse contingent and unique cases such as use of transplants as a means of constitutional change. Crucially, in terms of constitutional change it is necessary to bear in mind that non-measurable aspects that impact how constitutions change might, indeed, be involved. However, comparative approaches can also be nomothetic in the sense that they may seek to explain and derive general rules of constitutional change worldwide and in longer time-series. In other words, both case-oriented and variable-oriented approaches are possible. The key factor in the choice of approach is the research interest of the researcher. Accordingly, comparative methodology of comparative constitutional change is necessarily of a heuristic nature flanked by a rejection of one-size-fits-all methodology. Consequently, qualitative and quantitative research methods that are often juxtaposed as representing different epistemic views can both be used in the study of constitutional change; i.e. comparative study of constitutional change allows different intellectual styles in terms of research methods.

However, the heuristic nature of methodology does not mean that there would not be some sort of general methodological guidelines. Crucially, the comparative study of constitutional change needs to follow shared guidelines even though it needs also to allow use of diverse tools. In practice, when planning research design one needs to look carefully at what kinds of previous research and data are available. In principle, certain types of existing good practices (some of them mentioned in this chapter) should be followed, albeit allowing the use of diverse techniques and constitutional data. Identifying a research topic and problem holds imperative significance for the choice of a particular approach. Finally, it is beyond any shadow of doubt that studying constitutional change comparatively places methodological questions at the forefront and obliges researchers to pay close attention to methods in relation to their particular research interests and research designs.

References

Adams M., Husa J. and Oderkerk M., 'Method and Methodology of Comparative Law: Introductory Remarks' in Adams M., Husa J. and Oderkerk M. (eds), *Method and Methodology of Comparative Law* (Edward Elgar Publishing 2017) xi–xxxvii.

Albert R., 'Quasi-Constitutional Amendment' (2016) 65 *Buffalo Law Review* 739.

Albert R., Contiades X. and Fotiadou A. (eds), *The Foundations and Traditions of Constitutional Amendment* (Hart Publishing 2017).

Alshorbagy A., 'On the Failure of a Legal Transplant: The Case of Egyptian Takeover Law' (2012) 22 *Indiana International & Comparative Law Review* 237.

Bendor A. and Sela T., 'How Proportional is Proportionality?' (2015) 13 *International Journal of Constitutional Law* 530.

Bilchitz D. and Landau D. (eds), *The Evolution of the Separation of Powers* (Edward Elgar Publishing 2018).

Brannen J., 'Mixing Methods: The Entry of Qualitative and Quantitative Approaches into the Research Process' (2005) 8 *International Journal of Social Research Methodology* 173.

Bryce J., *Constitutions* (Oxford University Press 1905).

Chen A., 'A Tale of Two Islands: Comparative Reflections on Constitutionalism in Hong Kong and Taiwan' (2010) 37 *Hong Kong Law Journal* 647.

Chen-Wishart M., 'Legal Transplant and Undue Influence: Lost in Translation of a Working Misunderstanding' (2013) 62 *International and Comparative Law Quarterly* 1.

Contiades X. (ed), *Engineering Constitutional Change: A Comparative Perspective on Europe, Canada and the USA* (Routledge 2013).

Contiades X. and Fotiadou A. (eds), *Participatory Constitutional Change* (Routledge 2017).

Cuniberti G., *Grands systèmes de droit contemporain* (LGDJ 2nd ed. 2011).

David R., *Les grands systèmes de droit contemporains* (Dalloz 1964).

de Visser M., *Constitutional Review in Europe: A Comparative Analysis* (Hart Publishing 2013).

Dixon R. and Stone A., 'Constitutional Amendment and Political Constitutionalism: A Philosophical and Comparative Reflection' in Dyzenhaus D. and Thorburn M. (eds), *Philosophical Foundations of Constitutional Law* (Oxford University Press 2016) 103.

Duhamel O. and Tusseau G., *Droit constitutionnel et politique* (Le Seuil 2013).

Duverger M., *Institutions politiques et droit constitutionnel* (Presses Universitaire De France 1960).

Frankenberg G., 'Constitutional Transfer: The IKEA Theory Revisited' (2010) 8 *International Journal of Constitutional Law* 563.

Ginsburg T., 'How To Study Constitution-Making: Hirschl, Elster, and The Seventh Inning Problem' (2016) 96 *Boston University Law Review* 1347.

Ginsburg T. and Dixon R. (eds), *Comparative Constitutional Law* (Edward Elgar Publishing 2012).

Ginsburg T., Elkins Z. and Melton J., *The Endurance of National Constitutions* (Cambridge University Press 2008).

Ginsburg T., Foti N. and Rockmore D., '"We the Peoples": The Global Origins of Constitutional Preambles' (2014) 46 *George Washington International Law Review* 305.

Ginsburg T. and Versteeg M., 'Why Do Countries Adopt Constitutional Review?' (2014) 30 *Journal of Law, Economics, and Organization* 587.

Glenn HP., 'The Aims of Comparative Law' In: Smits J. (ed), *Elgar Encyclopedia of Comparative Law* (Edward Elgar Publishing 2nd ed. 2012) 65.

Gregory R. and Giddings J., *Righting Wrongs: The Ombudsman in Six Continents* (IOS Press 2000).

Gyorfi T., *Against New Constitutionalism* (Edward Elgar Publishing 2016).

Habermas J., *The Postnational Constellation: Political Essays* (MIT Press 2001).

Harding A. and Son Bui N., 'Recent Work in Asian Constitutional Studies: A Review Essay' (2016) 11 *Asian Journal of Comparative Law* 163.

Hirschl R., 'The Question of Case Selection in Comparative Constitutional Law' (2005) 53 *American Journal of Comparative Law* 125.

Hirschl R., 'From Comparative Constitutional Law to Comparative Constitutional Studies' (2013) 11 *International Journal of Constitutional Law* 1.

Hirschl R., *Comparative Matters: The Renaissance of Comparative Constitutional Law* (Oxford University Press 2014).

Horwitz M.J., 'Constitutional Transplants' (2009) 10 *Theoretical Inquiries in Law* 535.

Husa J., 'Guarding the Constitutionality of Laws in the Nordic Countries: A Comparative Perspective' (2000) 48 *American Journal of Comparative Law* 345.

Husa J., 'Methodology of Comparative Law Today: From Paradoxes to Flexibility?' (2006) 58 *Revue internationale de droit comparé* 1095.

Husa J., 'The Future of Legal Families' in *Oxford Handbooks Online* (2016) www.oxfordhandbooks.com/view/10.1093/oxfordhb/9780199935352.001.0001/oxfordhb-9780199935352-e-26

Husa J., '"Accurately, Completely, Solemnly": One Country, Two Systems and an Uneven Constitutional Equilibrium' (2017) 5 *Chinese Journal of Comparative Law* 231.

Jackson V., 'Comparative Constitutional Law, Legal Realism, and Empirical Legal Science' (2016) 96 *Boston University Law Review* 1359.

Kahn-Freund O., 'On Use and Misuse of Comparative Law' (1974) 37 *Modern Law Review* 1.

Kiss O., 'Heuristic, Methodology or Logic of Discovery? Lakatos on Patterns of Thinking' (2006) 14 *Perspectives on Science* 302.

Koskenniemi M., 'Constitutionalism as Mindset: Reflections on Kantian Themes about International Law and Globalization' (2007) 8 *Theoretical Inquiries in Law* 9.

Koskenniemi M. and Leino P., 'Fragmentation of International Law? Postmodern Anxieties' (2002) 15 *Leiden Journal of International Law* 553.

Kumm M., 'Constitutional Rights as Principles: On the Structure and Domain of Constitutional Justice' (2003) 2 *International Journal of Constitutional Law* 574.

Kuo M-S., 'The End of Constitutionalism as We Know It? Boundaries and the State of Global Constitutional (Dis)Ordering' (2010) 1 *Transnational Legal Theory* 329.

Langer M., 'From Legal Transplants to Legal Translations' (2004) 45 *Harvard International Law Journal* 1.

Law D., 'Constitutional Archetypes' (2017) 95 *Texas Law Review* 153.

Law D. and Versteeg M., 'The Declining Influence of the United States Constitution' (2012) 87 *New York University Law Review* 762.

Law D. and Versteeg M., 'Sham Constitutions' (2013) 101 *California Law Review* 863.

Legrand P., 'The Impossibility of Legal Transplants' (1997) 4 *Maastricht Journal of European and Comparative Law* 111.

Mac Amhlaigh C., 'Harmonising Global Constitutionalism' (2016) 5 *Global Constitutionalism* 173.

Meuwese A. and Versteeg M., 'Quantitative Methods for Comparative Constitutional Law' in Adams M. and Bomhoff J. (eds), *Practice and Theory in Comparative Law* (Cambridge University Press 2013) 230.

Möllers C. and Birkenkötter H., 'Towards a New Conceptualism in Comparative Constitutional Law, or Reviving the German Tradition of the Lehrbuch' (2014) 12 *International Journal of Constitutional Law* 603.

Nichols P.M., 'The Viability of Transplanted Law: Kazakhstani Reception of a Transplanted Foreign Investment Code' (1997) 18 *University of Pennsylvania Journal of International Law* 1235.

Oliver D. and Fusaro C. (eds), *How Constitutions Change: A Comparative Study* (Hart Publishing 2011).

Oliver P., Macklen P. and Rosiers N., 'Introduction' in Oliver P., Macklen P. and Rosiers N. (eds), *The Oxford Handbook of the Canadian Constitution* (Oxford University Press 2017) 1.

Örücü Ö., 'Law as Transposition' (2002) 51 *International and Comparative Law Quarterly* 205.

Pap A., *Democratic Decline in Hungary* (Routledge 2017).

Peerenbom R., 'Toward a Methodology for Successful Legal Transplants' (2013) 1 *Chinese Journal of Comparative Law* 4.

Perju V., 'Constitutional Transplants, Borrowing, and Migrations' in Rosenfeld M. and Sajó A. (eds), *The Oxford Handbook of Comparative Constitutional Law* (Oxford University Press 2012) 1304.

Peters A., 'Global Constitutionalism' in Gibbons MT. (ed), *The Encyclopedia of Political Thought* (Wiley-Blackwell 2015) 1484.

Punch K., *Introduction to Social Research: Quantitative and Qualitative Approaches* (Sage 1995).

Punch K. and Oancea A., *Introduction to Research Methods in Education* (Sage 2nd ed. 2014).

Rosenfeld M. and Sajó A., 'Introduction' in Rosenfeld M. and Sajó A. (eds), *The Oxford Handbook of Comparative Constitutional Law* (Oxford University Press 2012a) 1.

Rosenfeld M. and Sajó A. (eds), *The Oxford Handbook of Comparative Constitutional Law* (Oxford University Press 2012b).

Saunders C., 'Towards a Global Constitutional Gene Pool' (2009) 4 *National Taiwan University Law Review* 1.

Schwöbel C., 'The Appeal of the Project of Global Constitutionalism to Public International Lawyers' (2012) 13 *German Law Journal* 1.

Smits J., 'Comparative Law and its Influence on National Legal Systems' in Reimann M. and Zimmermann R. (eds), *The Oxford Handbook of Comparative Law* (Oxford University Press 2006) 477.

Spector H., 'Constitutional Transplants and the Mutation Effect' (2008) 83 *Chicago-Kent Law Review* 129.

Stone Sweet A. and Mathews J., 'Proportionality Balancing and Global Constitutionalism' (2008) 47 *Columbia Journal of Transnational Law* 72.

Strauss D., 'The Irrelevance of Constitutional Amendments' (2001) 114 *Harvard Law Review* 1457.

Tebbe N. and Tsai R., 'Constitutional Borrowing' (2010) 108 *Michigan Law Review* 459.

Teitel R., 'Comparative Constitutional Law in a Global Age' (2004) 117 *Harvard Law Review* 2570.

Teubner G., 'Legal Irritants: Good Faith in British Law or How Unifying Law Ends Up in New Divergences' (1998) 61 *Modern Law Review* 11.

Tohipur T., 'Comparative Constitutional Studies and the Discourse of Legal Transfer' in Frankenberg G. (ed), *Order from Transfer: Comparative Constitutional Design and Legal Culture* (Edward Elgar Publishing 2013) 29.

Tourkochoriti I., 'Comparative Rights Jurisprudence: An Essay on Methodologies' (2017) 8 *Law and Method* 10.5553/REM/.000030

Tushnet M., 'The Boundaries of Comparative Law' (2017) 13 *European Constitutional Law Review* 13.

Van Hoecke M., 'Legal Culture and Legal Transplants' in Nobles R. and Schiff D. (eds), *Law, Society and Community* (Routledge 2016) 273.

Venter F., *Constitutional Comparison: Japan, Germany, Canada and South Africa as Constitutional States* (Martinus Nijhoff 2000).

Versteeg M. and Goderis B., 'The Diffusion of Constitutional Rights' (2014) 39 *International Review of Law and Economics* 1–19.

Watson A., *Legal Transplants: An Approach to Comparative Law* (University of Georgia Press 2nd ed. 1993).

Weiler J.H.H., 'Does Europe Need a Constitution? Demos, Telos and the German Maastricht Decision' (1995) 1 *European Law Journal* 219.

Wheare K.C., *Modern Constitutions* (Oxford University Press 2nd ed. 1966).

Xu Z., 'Western Law in China: Transplantation or Transformation' (2004) 25 *Social Sciences in China* 3.

Zweigert K. and Kötz H., *An Introduction to Comparative Law* (Oxford University Press 2nd ed. 1998).

3

ORDER FROM CHAOS?

Typologies and models of constitutional change

Oran Doyle[*]

Introduction

Constitutions change. Sometimes they are replaced. Sometimes constitutional actors utilise a textually prescribed mechanism to change the text of the constitutional document. Sometimes the operation of the constitution informally changes without any formal alteration of the constitutional text. Each of these methods of constitutional change has its own sub-varieties. Constitutional replacement can occur through violent revolution or consensual processes. Formal change mechanisms are numerous and can be combined with one another and/or subjected to limitations in a bewildering number of ways. Informal constitutional change is a label applied to very different practices that achieve the substance of constitutional change without following the forms. Replacement, formal change and informal change also interact with one another. The availability of one method of change makes the utilisation of other methods less likely, and vice versa.

The field of comparative constitutional change, in short, presents in a state of confusion and complexity. Faced with such chaos, it is unsurprising that comparative constitutional scholars have sought to develop typologies and models of constitutional change that impose order on the diversity of constitutional practices, providing a conceptual map to the field.[1] Maps can be aesthetically beautiful, but their utility is always relative to a particular purpose. The mapmaker must decide what sort of information the map will present: is it a street-map or a topographical map? What scale is appropriate? Is the map intended to help a pedestrian navigate a city or an airline pilot to navigate a continent? In order to be useful, a map must omit information. This is also true of conceptual maps, typologies and models.[2] It therefore

---

[*] I am grateful to the editors and to Richard Albert and Juliano Zaiden Benvindo for their helpful comments on an earlier draft.

1 On conceptual maps, see Arend Lijphart, *Patterns of Democracy: Government Forms and Performance in Thirty-Six Countries* (Yale University Press 2nd ed. 2012) xv.

2 For a helpful account of typologies in relation to constitutions generally, see Dieter Grimm, 'Types of Constitutions' in Michel Rosenfeld and Andras Sajó (eds), *The Oxford Handbook of Comparative Constitutional Law* (Oxford University Press 2012) 98. Although Grimm's project is far more ambitious than that undertaken in this chapter, his comments about the limits and uses of typologies apply equally here.

makes no sense to criticise a typology or model on the basis that it omits detail. A good typology or model coherently provides the right type of information at a sufficient level of detail (but no more than that) in order to serve some useful purpose.

In this chapter, I analyse typologies and models of constitutional change, critically assessing their utility both for constitutional designers and within comparative constitutional scholarship. In the next section, I introduce the concept of a master-text constitution and formal change, before exploring the abstract function performed by formal change mechanisms and defining the parameters of the discussion. I present typologies of formal change mechanisms that have been advanced in the academic literature. I draw out a distinction between typologies that seek to compare the difficulty levels of formal change mechanisms and typologies that identify differences in the way that formal change mechanisms distribute power among constitutional actors. Next, I show how typologies grapple with these different dimensions (difficulty level and distribution of power) in relation to different components of formal change mechanisms: initiation, ratification and constraints. I argue that typologies that seek to compare difficulty levels across jurisdictions face probably insuperable obstacles. I then present models of constitutional change that seek to account for formal and informal constitutional change alongside political culture. Although these provide a good basis for a theory of constitutional change, they cannot simultaneously account *both* for the difficulty of constitutional change *and* the distribution of constitutional power.

Master-text constitutions, formal change and informal change

We can think of a constitution both as the set of rules and principles that constitute the governance system of a state and as a canonical written text that claims to be the highest law in a legal system, codifying the most important constitutional rules—in other words, the master-text constitution.[3] The master-text constitution is the highest posited law within the legal system. Among other things, it establishes the procedures for changing other laws in the legal system, what we might call the standard legal change mechanism. Typically the standard legal change mechanism involves a majority in each house of the legislature. For a master-text constitution to be amenable to formal change, it must contain a provision that allows for and regulates its own change.[4] If the master-text constitution were changeable only in accordance with a provision laid down in another document, this would undercut its status as the constitutional master-text.

It is not technically impossible for a master-text constitution to allow for its own change in accordance with that standard legal change mechanism. However, such an approach would prevent a constitution from performing a number of functions that are commonly attributed to constitutions, such as the protection of minority rights and majoritarian procedures from the self-interested actions of the current electoral majority. If a parliamentary majority can

---

3 On master-text constitutions, see John Gardner, *Law as a Leap of Faith* (Oxford University Press 2011) 90.

4 In Canada prior to 1982, the constitution could only lawfully be changed by a constitutional actor in another legal system, the Westminster Parliament. However, this apparent exception is one that proves the rule: this process for amendment of the British North America Act cast doubt on whether Canada had its own autochthonous legal system, a doubt that was only fully resolved by patriation in 1982. For discussion of these issues, see Brian Slattery, 'The Independence of Canada' (1983) 5 *Supreme Court Review* 369 and Peter Oliver, *The Constitution of Independence: The Development of Constitutional Theory in Australia, Canada, and New Zealand* (Oxford University Press 2005) Chapter 6. For a view that emphasises changes to the identity of the legislator, see Geoffrey Marshall, *Constitutional Conventions: The Rules and Forms of Political Accountability* (Clarendon Press 1984) 207–208.

rewrite the constitution, constitutional restraints on its powers become legally meaningless. I do not here take a position on whether these constitutional functions are necessary features of constitutions. But nearly all master-text constitutions perform these functions insofar as they make constitutional change more difficult than the standard legal change mechanism. This approach might be taken because of a high-minded devotion to the values of constitutionalism or a more self-interested desire to entrench a transient partisan advantage against easy change in the future. Either way, formal constitutional change tends to be more difficult than legal change in general. As well as retarding constitutional change, formal change mechanisms make an important political choice in their distribution of the power of constitutional change between constitutional actors. Constitutional change mechanisms can therefore be assessed along two dimensions: the extent to which they retard constitutional change and the way in which they distribute constitutional power. These dimensions are reflected in the typologies that we will consider in the next section.

Much ink has been spilt in an attempt to demonstrate that formal constitutional change mechanisms are necessarily limited and never authorise major changes that fundamentally alter the constitution. Some have argued that any such purported change is conceptually impossible, and hence legally invalid.[5] For others, there is an analytical distinction between amendment and more fundamental change, labelled by Richard Albert as dismemberment.[6] I am not persuaded by the conceptual basis for these types of claim.[7] Furthermore, I share Strum's view that general distinctions between minor amendments and major amendments are 'conceptually slippery, impossible to operationalize, and therefore generally useless'.[8] Particular constitutions may, of course, prescribe more onerous formal change mechanisms for more significant types of constitutional change, but this is a contingent legal distinction not a conceptually necessary distinction. We need not resolve these disagreements for present purposes, however. Our focus is on formal constitutional change mechanisms, which includes all constitutional provisions for the constitution's own change, whether that change is labelled as amendment, reform, revision or replacement. This not only avoids pre-emptively removing subject-matter from the field but also escapes the difficulty of assessing at what point a particular change is so large as to be excluded from our purview. Quantifying all constitutional changes would be close to impossible; relying on the terminology in constitutional texts would be inappropriate where we are necessarily working with translations.

Typologies of formal constitutional change mechanisms

When one surveys formal constitutional change mechanisms, what immediately stands out is the sheer variety. Core requirements tend to recur across constitutions, but often with very

---

5 This is the position of Carl Schmitt and contemporary theories that build on his work in different ways. For a presentation of this argument, see Po Jen Yap, 'The Conundrum of Unconstitutional Constitutional Amendments' (2015) 4 *Global Constitutionalism* 114, 116 and Yaniv Roznai, 'Unconstitutional Constitutional Amendments: The Migration and Success of a Constitutional Idea' (2013) 61 *American Journal of Comparative Law* 657, 690–693.

6 Richard Albert, 'Constitutional Amendment and Dismemberment' (2018) 43(1) *Yale Journal of International Law* 1.

7 See Oran Doyle, 'Constraints on Constitutional Amendment Powers' in Richard Albert, Xenophon Contiades and Alkmene Fotiadou (eds), *The Foundations and Traditions of Constitutional Amendment* (Hart 2017).

8 Albert L Strum, *Thirty Years of State Constitution-Making: 1938–1968* (National Municipal League 1970), quoted in Donald S Lutz, *Principles of Constitutional Design* (Cambridge University Press 2006) 152.

slight variations. These requirements can be combined together in a number of different ways. Moreover, any one constitution can prescribe multiple change processes: whether by allowing constitutional actors to choose between alternatives or requiring different processes for different levels of change or for change initiated by different constitutional actors. Typologies seek to reduce this complexity by making sound decisions about what differences are important and unimportant, reducing the wide variety of mechanisms to a small number of types, thereby providing a conceptual map that provides a simplified view of the field.

Dawn Oliver and Carlos Fusaro present a simple typology that essentially distinguishes between a super-majority in parliament and extra-parliamentary participation, including both referendums and intervening elections.[9] The core distinction between parliamentary and non-parliamentary mechanisms is significant, but there is considerable scope for differentiating further among non-parliamentary mechanisms. Other theorists have provided more detail in this regard.

In his seminal work of constitutional theory, *Ulysses Unbound*, Jon Elster identifies six main hurdles for constitutional amendment:

- Absolute entrenchment;
- Adoption by a super-majority in parliament;
- Requirement of a higher quorum than for ordinary legislation;
- Delays;
- State ratification (in federal systems);
- Ratification by referendum.[10]

The characterisation of the formal change mechanisms as 'hurdles' is telling. The purpose of Elster's typology is to assist an exploration of the extent to which constitutions can usefully be understood as societal pre-commitments. This claim gains plausibility if there are 'hurdles' to constitutional change. Elster quickly notes that there is greater variety than is captured by this typology: there can be constraints on the adoption of constitutional change; there can also be significant differences between the level of super-majority required in parliament; delay mechanisms can function in very different ways.[11] The omission of these details does not establish that Elster's typology is flawed. Recall that we should think of typologies as navigational maps for a particular purpose. Elster's typology maps the domain in a way that is adequate for his broad theoretical inquiry into constitutions as pre-commitment devices. Although Elster's theoretical concern is with amendment difficulty, his types do not attempt to mark out different levels of amendment difficulty. Rather, the typology shows how formal constitutional change mechanisms can retard constitutional change by effecting different distributions of constitutional power. We could inquire whether the distribution of constitutional power is consistent with other features of the constitutional system, e.g. federalism or popular control. But this is not Elster's purpose and

---

9 Dawn Oliver and Carlo Fusaro, 'Changing Constitutions: Comparative Analysis' in Dawn Oliver and Carlos Fusaro (eds), *How Constitutions Change* (Hart 2011) 395. In this context, Oliver and Fusaro also mentioned intra-parliamentary protections, terminological provisions, and states of exception, but these do not seem as relevant to our concern, formal constitutional change mechanisms.

10 Jon Elster, *Ulysses Unbound: Studies in Rationality, Precommitment, and Constraints* (Cambridge University Press 2000) 100.

11 Ibid 101–103.

he does not seek to theorise the differences between different hurdles. In sum, Elster's typology is a rather basic one but a good one in the sense that it is useful for his purpose of showing that very different formal change mechanisms can all retard constitutional change.

In a similar vein, Jan Erik Lane provides a typology of constitutional change mechanisms that is designed to support an argument about constitutional inertia. He identifies at least six types:

- No change;
- Referendums;
- Delay;
- Confirmation by a second decision;
- Qualified majorities;
- Confirmation by sub-national government.[12]

This differs from Elster in not listing quorum requirements while treating delays as a separate category from confirmation by a second decision. His typology, like that of Elster, illustrates how ideologically different distributions of the constitutional change power can each cause constitutional inertia. It provides a useful conceptual map to these differences, although again it does not offer a theoretical account of the differences.

Lane's typology does not account for all differences and in some circumstances one might seek a more detailed exposition. Having used Lane's conceptual map to orient oneself to a consideration of countries that use referendums as part of their constitutional change mechanism, one might perceive an important difference between a referendum with a simple majority requirement (50% + 1 of those voting) and a referendum with an absolute majority requirement (50% + 1 of those registered to vote). The absolute majority requirement values definitive popular approval for any constitutional change. The simple majority requirement, in contrast, simply enables electors to have their say in the constitutional change process if they wish. But it is not a criticism of Lane's typology that it does not capture this level of detail. The typology provides a conceptual map at a particular scale that adequately serves Lane's purpose. If one needs more detail for a particular purpose, one could develop a sub-typology in much the same way as one might consult a larger scale map. But if Lane were to provide all this level of detail at the outset, it would be far more difficult to find what one is looking for, undermining the whole purpose of the conceptual map.

Arend Lijphart identifies four basic types of change procedure:

- The standard legal change procedure (an ordinary majority);
- Approval by a two-thirds majority;
- Approval by a less than two-thirds majority but greater than 50% (e.g. a 60% majority or combination of a legislative majority and a referendum);
- Approval by more than a two-thirds majority (e.g. a 75% majority or a combination of a two-thirds majority and approval by sub-national legislatures).[13]

Lijphart's typology is more parsimonious than that of Elster, and directly addresses the degree of change difficulty. The same basic type can accommodate very different

---

12 Jan Erik Lane, *Constitutions and Political Theory* (Manchester University Press 2nd ed. 2011) 41.
13 Lijphart (n 1) 207.

distributions of constitutional power: approval by referendum is equated with a 60% super-majority in parliament; approval by sub-national legislatures is equated with a 75% super-majority in parliament. Lijphart's indifference to these differences is not a flaw in his typology. To re-emphasise, a typology is a navigational map for a particular purpose. Lijphart's purpose is not an ideological characterisation of formal change mechanisms; rather his typology attempts a classificatory scheme that forms part of a wider endeavour to place constitutional democracies along a spectrum from majoritarian to consensual.[14] The easier it is to amend a constitution, the fewer constitutional actors need to agree to that change and the more majoritarian the political system. In this regard, Lijphart (correctly in my view) treats a referendum requirement as a delaying (and hence consensual) device rather than a majoritarian device.[15] This contradicts a general view of referendums as crude majoritarian devices. Where a referendum is required in addition to a legislative majority, as distinct from where it is used to circumvent standard representative democracy, it serves to delay change and prompt consensus building.

Unlike Elster and Lane, who sought to explore a general conceptual claim about constitutions, Lijphart seeks to compare constitutions. In this regard, a more sound challenge to his typology might be that the four types do not reliably capture differences in amendment difficulty. Lijphart's equation of a referendum with a 60% parliamentary super-majority and his equation of sub-national approval with a 75% parliamentary super-majority are both questionable. In any one country, it will be difficult to assess how onerous a referendum requirement is against the counter-factual of a particular legislative super-majority. It is even more heroic to postulate that the correlations of referendums and sub-national approval with legislative super-majorities will be the same in all countries. Nonetheless, Lijphart might reasonably respond that some simplification is required or we will get nowhere.

Finally, Lijphart's typology draws into sharp focus a problem with attributing a difficulty level to formal constitutional change *in a particular country*. Many countries have alternative formal change mechanisms. Which one is to be counted? Lijphart suggests two ways of dealing with this problem. When alternative methods can be used, he counts the least restraining method. When different rules apply to different parts of constitutions, he counts the rule pertaining to amendments of the most basic articles of the constitution.[16] While the first manoeuvre is sound, the second is more problematic. Article 148 of the Lithuanian Constitution, for example, adopts three amendment processes. Most provisions can be amended by two votes, separated by at least three months, with a two-thirds majority in the Seimas. The provisions of the First Chapter (the State of Lithuania) and the Fourteenth Chapter (Amendment) can only be amended by referendum. Finally, the provision of Article 1 that provides 'the State of Lithuania shall be an independent democratic republic' may only be altered by referendum if not less than three-quarters of the citizens of Lithuania with the electoral right vote in favour thereof. This provision is tantamount to making the provision unamendable; indeed the subject-matter is often made unamendable in other constitutions. It arguably distorts the level of amendment difficulty in Lithuania (both in absolute terms and as a comparison with other countries) to focus on this clearly exceptional amendment procedure.

14 Ibid 1–2.
15 Ibid 219–221.
16 Ibid 252.

Donald Lutz provides a far more detailed typology designed to capture amendment difficulty. As we noted at the outset, the variety in formal constitutional change mechanisms derives considerably from the different ways in which the same basic mechanisms can be combined with one another. If we were to faithfully account for each possible combination of change mechanisms, we would end up with an absurd number of types, making the typology useless. Lutz provides a way around this problem.[17] He exhaustively assigns a score to each requirement that the approval of a particular constitutional actor is needed for a formal constitutional change. Those scores can then be added together where the approval of two or more constitutional actors is needed. He identifies 30 variations on how an amendment proposal can be initiated and 38 variations on how an amendment proposal can be approved. He attributes a score to each variation. For instance, if an election is required between two votes in order to initiate a proposal, this has a score of 0.25. If an absolute majority is required at a referendum in order to ratify an amendment proposal, this has a score of 1.75. One can then add up all the requirements in a particular amendment process to assign it a level of difficulty. This, in turn, allows Lutz to rank the countries under examination in terms of amendment difficulty, without simplifying them into a limited number of types.

Lutz's project is to develop and test a number of propositions about the relationship between amendment difficulty and other constitutional features. For instance, he wishes to test whether a more difficult change mechanism correlates with a lower amendment rate. This in turn supports a normative project of arguing for a constitutional design that allows for a moderate amendment rate.[18] Lutz's typology is finely honed to allow a comparison of amendment difficulty in different countries in a way that will test his propositions. However, the apparent comprehensiveness and mathematical certainty of his approach should not blind us to certain issues. First, everything turns on the initial factor of difficulty identified by Lutz. These are obviously contestable. To take one example: Lutz attributes a score of 1.5 to a popular referendum with a simple majority requirement (50% plus one of those voting) and, as we just saw, a score of 1.75 to a popular referendum with an absolute majority requirement (50% plus one of those registered to vote). It seems questionable to me whether this adequately captures the difference in difficulty levels. For instance, in Ireland from 1937 to 2019, 30 amendments have passed the simple referendum requirement but only two of these passed by an absolute majority.[19] Contrastingly, 25 of the amendments exceeded a 60% threshold, to which Lutz attributes a weighting of 2, i.e. a higher difficulty rating than he attaches to an absolute majority requirement. Now it could be that Ireland is an outlier in this regard, but this reveals a further problem. While it might be possible to identify that in a particular constitutional system, mechanism A is a specific amount more difficult than mechanism B, it is highly unlikely that this degree of difference will hold constant across all constitutional systems.

Second, Lutz also faces the difficulty, where a country has more than one constitutional change mechanism, of deciding which procedure's score should be attributed to that country. In this regard, Lutz essentially takes the opposite approach to that taken by Lijphart.[20] He weights the score for each amendment path according to the percentage of

---

17 Lutz (n 8) 167–168.
18 He states that a successful constitution is an old one with a moderate rate of amendment. Ibid 155.
19 The amendment in 1972 to allow Ireland to become a member of the European Communities and the amend-
    ment in 1998 to allow Ireland to ratify the Northern Ireland peace settlement and make consequential changes.
20 Lutz (n 8) 169.

amendments passed by means of it during the relevant time period. But this is problematic in a different direction. Part V of the Canadian Constitution establishes different change mechanisms for different issues, with the most difficult change mechanism reserved for matters related to core features of the state and the balance between federal and provincial powers. This is seen as one of the most onerous amendment provisions in the world, leading some to contend that on those matters the Canadian Constitution is *de facto* unamendable.[21] In this regard, the fact that a change mechanism has not been used might itself be an indication of amendment difficulty. Lutz does not categorise Canada but it well illustrates why it is problematic to discount an amendment mechanism because it is too difficult to use if what you are trying to do is assess the level of amendment difficulty.[22] In short, Lutz's approach to the problem of alternative procedures raises the opposite problems from Lijphart's. For accurate comparison, we should neither assume that the most difficult mechanism is always used nor that the non-use of a more difficult mechanism renders it irrelevant. Ideally, to compare amendment difficulty in different countries, we should contrast how the levels of difficulty on the same topic differ. However, this would require further levels of categorisation that might render the typology too convoluted to serve as a useful conceptual map.

Based on a survey of 101 world constitutions, Edward Schneier provides a wider typology, identifying 18 methods of constitutional amendment and ascribing each one to a number of countries:

- Legislative amendment by simple majority vote +

  - No further action;
  - Referendum;
  - Intervening election or referendum;
  - Referendum or two-thirds vote plus president;
  - Approval by Provincial Legislatures or Constitutional Convention.

- Legislative Amendment by three-fifths vote +

  - Referendum or different majority;
  - One month to one year delay;
  - Constitutional convention.

- Legislature by 65% vote +

  - Three readings and presidential assent;

- Legislature by two-thirds vote +

  - No further action;
  - Executive approval;
  - Referendum;

---

21 Richard Albert, 'Constructive Unamendability in Canada and the United States' (2014) 67 *Supreme Court Law Review* 181.

22 The same logic would suggest that Japan's Constitution should be accorded an amendment difficulty rate of 0 because the amendment process has never been used.

- ○ Majority of provinces;
- ○ Two-thirds of provinces;
- ○ Three-quarters of states.

- Legislature by three-quarters vote +

  - ○ No further action (or by majority vote plus referendum);
  - ○ Majority of provinces;
  - ○ Four-fifths majority after one year.[23]

This typology accounts for a wider range of change mechanisms than Elster and Lijphart, without engaging in the comparative ranking of Lutz. However, its rather open-ended character renders it a less than useful typology. We might question whether it is really necessary to distinguish between a legislative two-thirds majority combined with either two-thirds of provinces or three-quarters of states. These are clearly different, but if our conceptual map is to be useful, we would surely be justified in eliding these differences. Conversely, the reduction to 18 types is achieved by a number of questionable judgments and simplifications. For instance, no account is taken of different majority thresholds for referendums, and it is not clear why constitutional amendment by a simple majority with approval by provincial legislatures should be categorised the same as a constitutional amendment by a simple majority with approval by a constitutional convention. These reflect very ideologically different distributions of power. The point here is not to criticise Schneier's failure to be comprehensive. However, his typology falls between two stools: too large to be immediately helpful but still beset with unjustified and sometimes misleading categorisation choices.

Schneier provides a further way of addressing the problem that many constitutions provide alternative methods: he ascribes to each country the change mechanism that he believes to be the common practice of the method most frequently used.[24] However, this leads to a repeat of the Canada problem discussed above in relation to Lutz. Schneier identifies Canada as a country where a legislative amendment by simple majority combined with approval by provincial legislatures is required. But if this is the most common practice in Canada, it perhaps simply reflects that other amendment processes are too difficult to use. That is a highly salient fact that is obscured by Schneier's typology.

The typologies considered thus far have focused on the basic process through which constitutional changes must be approved. While some of the authors refer to the fact that there might be categorical restrictions on constitutional change, they make little effort to include those restrictions within their typologies. For some authors, this might be because this would multiply the problem of alternative procedures. How do we compare the difficulty of formal constitutional change in country X with country Y, if in country X the republican character of the state is amendable while in country Y the republican character of the state is not amendable? A further complicating factor is that many restrictions of this type derive not from the constitutional text but rather from judicial action.[25]

---

23 Edward Schneier, *Crafting Constitutional Democracies: The Politics of Institutional Design* (Rowman & Littlefield 2006) 224–225.
24 Ibid 225.
25 See Yaniv Roznai, 'Unconstitutional Constitutional Amendments: The Migration and Success of a Constitutional Idea' (2013) 61 *American Journal of Comparative Law* 690.

In 2017, I published a chapter that provided a stand-alone typology of constraints on constitutional change powers. I argued that constraints on powers of constitutional amendment could be conceptualised in terms of three cross-cutting distinctions:

- Process v. content;
- Rule v. standard;
- Legislator-created v. court-created.[26]

Similar to the typologies above, I used these three distinctions to map how a particular constraint makes the constitution more difficult to amend, by moving power away from current electoral majorities toward either the past generation or the current courts or both. This was a much more intuitive and impressionistic presentation of change difficulty than that attempted by Lijphart or Lutz. It was designed to sharpen a political and moral inquiry into whether such constraints on the amendment power could be justified. The other side of the equation was an ideological categorisation of the constraints in terms of whether they served foundational values (such as territorial integrity), majoritarian values (such as a fair electoral process), or counter-majoritarian values (such as human dignity). We could then inquire whether particular moral values justified decisions to move the change power away from a contemporary electoral majority.

Xenophon Contiades and Alkmene Fotiadou have presented a typology of constitutional change mechanisms that is alert to the ideological stakes in both the formal change process and the constraints that can be imposed on the powers of change. They ask the following questions:

- Whether the amending formula is an attempted simulation of the constituent moment endeavouring to imitate the exercise of *pouvoir constituent*;
- Whether the formula includes eternity clauses;
- If and to what extent the amending formula includes popular participation;
- Whether revision is concluded in one parliamentary term or more than one after a general election;
- Whether the amending formula provides for super-majorities or enhanced majorities;
- Whether, as well as the Parliament, the Head of State or Cabinet has a role in constitutional revision;
- As well as central state, whether organs of constituent or peripheral states participate;
- Whether there is a mandatory lapse of time between the conclusion of the amending process and initiation of the new one.[27]

This typology is perhaps less closely defined than some of the others we have considered, but this is because it serves a different purpose of establishing broad models of constitutional change, to which I shall return below.

Reflections on typologies of constitutional change mechanisms

We have seen how two concerns animate the typologies in the academic literature: comparing the level of amendment difficulty and identifying different constitutional

---

26 Doyle (n 7).
27 Xenophon Contiades and Alkmene Fotiadou, 'Models of Constitutional Change' in Xenophon Contiades (ed), *Engineering Constitutional Change: A Comparative Perspective on Europe, Canada and the USA* (Routledge 2013) 431.

Table 3.1 Schema of typologies

Typologies of change difficulty	Lutz	Lutz Lijphart Schneier?	Doyle
Change process	Initiation →	Ratification →	Constraints
Typologies of power distribution	Contiades and Fotiadou	Oliver and Fusaro Elster Lane Contiades and Fotiadou	Doyle

distributions of constitutional power. The typologies in turn focus on three discrete, though related, aspects of a constitutional change mechanism: initiation, ratification and constraints. Adopting this schema, we can present the typologies as shown in Table 3.1.

If I can flog the map analogy for a while longer, this schema is akin to the contents page of an atlas, directing the reader to where more detailed conceptual maps, oriented to different purposes, focusing on each aspect of the constitutional change mechanism, can be found.

The distinction between initiation and ratification, while important legally in particular jurisdictions, is of limited (but real) conceptual significance. For instance, in Ireland a proposal to amend the constitution must be introduced by a member of the lower house (the Dáil). However, as the approval of a majority of the Dáil is also necessary for the proposal to pass, the method of initiation adds nothing to our understanding of either the difficulty level or the distribution of constitutional power. In terms of assessing difficulty level, there is little to be gained by distinguishing (as Lutz does) between initiation and ratification: we can simply take cognisance of all constitutional actors whose approval is necessary (at whatever stage) for a formal constitutional change to be made. Sometimes, however, constitutions grant alternative rights of initiation. This does not affect the difficulty level of formal constitutional change as it merely opens up another way to commence the process without reducing the threshold for ultimate approval. But it does affect the constitutional distribution of power by granting (or perhaps formalising) a role for another constitutional actor.

In this regard, I would suggest that the most important types of alternative initiation rights are popular and presidential initiation.[28] The Baltic Republics, Switzerland and Venezuela, for example, all allow for popular initiation. These countries can make a much better claim to instantiate popular sovereignty in their change processes than can the (far more numerous) countries that merely provide for a referendum as part of the approval process. Popular sovereignty is not established by merely allowing the people to vote on changes approved by elected representatives. Presidential initiation is commonplace in Latin America, practised for example in Brazil, Chile, Ecuador and Paraguay. In many situations this might not make a practical difference, given that the president might well have the support of the majority in the legislature. Nevertheless, it is always important symbolically and at least enhances the status of the president vis-à-vis her co-partisans if she formally holds that role. It is a very relevant factor in assessing whether the constitution feeds hyper-presidentialism.[29]

28 Guatemala allows for initiation by the Constitutional Court, but this is an outlier.
29 I am grateful to Juliano Zaidan-Benvindo for these insights.

Table 3.2 Distributions of constitutional power

Consensus	Legislative super-majorities	France, Spain
Deliberation	Delays, intervening elections, constitutional assemblies	Belgium, Norway, Russia, Argentina
Popular	Referendums	Switzerland, Ireland
Federal	Sub-unit approval	USA, Canada

Much greater consideration is given in the typologies to the distribution of constitutional power in the ratification stage. For Elster and Lane, this is essentially an elaboration of how constitutional change mechanisms retard the pace of constitutional change—a fundamental feature of constitutions that they then seek to theorise. For Oliver and Fusaro and for Contiades and Fotiadou, the diversity of power distributions is explored in order to allow a characterisation of constitutional change rather than being immediately put in service of a broader theoretical claim about constitutions. Nevertheless, all of these typologies use terminology that departs little from a description of the change mechanism. I suggest that we could usefully abstract somewhat to allow a more theoretical characterisation of these different distributions of constitutional power (see Table 3.2).

This ideological characterisation of the distribution of constitutional power in relation to formal constitutional change allows a characterisation of constitutional change that can also feed into a broader characterisation of the constitution as a whole. For instance, it is important that some countries (for instance India) that are federal in some respects do not adopt a federal approach to constitutional change. This might allow us to distinguish between a bottom-up federalism and a top-down federalism and inquire which is more vulnerable to centrifugal secessionist forces. Furthermore, if we see a constitution combine a number of different distributions of power reflecting very different ideological approaches, we might conclude that the formal change mechanism is not based on a clear ideological vision of which constitutional actors should hold the power but rather is designed just to make formal change very difficult. For instance, the Additional Articles to the Constitution of Taiwan in 2005 introduced a new change process that requires a legislative super-majority (75%), a delay period (six months), and a referendum (absolute majority), thereby simultaneously following a consensus, deliberation and popular approach. The combined effect of these is to make the constitutional settlement of Taiwan's democratisation virtually unamendable. That unamendability, rather than an ideological commitment to consensus, deliberation or popular control, was probably the point.

Finally, the typologies of difficulty have been shown to be less than satisfactory. There is no convincing solution to the problem of how to ascribe one level of amendment difficulty to a country when there are alternative mechanisms of formal constitutional change. Moreover, any categorical assigning of difficulty levels to particular change processes fails to account for how other political rules (e.g. electoral systems) and background political culture determine how those processes will operate. Lijphart's typology is less problematic in this regard since the ease of amendment difficulty is but one factor in assessing whether a democracy is majoritarian or consensual in character. But if our focus is narrowly on constitutional change, it is highly questionable whether we can assume that the change-difficulty differential between methods will be a constant across all countries that adopt those methods.

Lutz's typology promises an answer to an intriguing question: how difficult is it formally to change the constitution in each country? Given the difficulties just explored, however, it might simply be impossible to answer this question. Indeed, Ginsberg and Melton have argued that the choice of amendment rule is not so important in measuring amendment difficulty; amendment culture (measured as the rate of amendment in the immediately preceding constitution) is a much more important predictor of constitutional change.[30] Lutz's typology, or some variation thereof, might help constitutional designers assess which constitutional change mechanism would be more difficult within their own system (thereby holding other factors steady). Even there, however, the constitutional designers are likely to have better insight into their own system and not need the typology in the first place.

I have distinguished between difficulty typologies and distribution of power typologies. However, we must recognise that making change more difficult can itself serve ideological purposes. On the one hand, it can lock in a political compromise so that those who fear losing power under the new constitutional dispensation can protect their own interests. On the other hand, it can serve the value of constitutionalism by making it more difficult for a transient majority (other than the founding generation) to interfere with minority rights or the fairness of majoritarian processes. Even without assuming that the founding generation had a stronger commitment to constitutionalism than the current generation (who might choose to amend the constitution so that it better protects minority rights or majoritarian processes), the value of constitutionalism is still generally served by slowing down democratic politics. This involves a cost to democracy but potentially a cost worth paying. In principle, the ideological choice about who should have the power formally to change the constitution is separate from the ideological choice about how difficult formal change should be. Ideally, those designing formal change mechanisms should consider both issues in tandem. However, it is possible that one concern could dominate the other as arguably is the case with the change provisions in the Constitution of Taiwan, considered above.

This discussion hopefully demonstrates that typologies have a genuine but limited use in our analysis of comparative constitutional change. They provide conceptual maps to discrete aspects of formal change mechanisms. These maps allow us better to understand the choices, both concerning the distribution of constitutional power and the difficulty of formal change, that are reflected in particular mechanisms. This may provide some assistance to constitutional designers, at least providing a menu of options that could give effect to the values of their own political community. The conceptual maps are also of assistance to comparative constitutional scholars, in terms of reducing the complexity of the field. They only serve this function, however, where they make coherent and plausible distinctions, reducing the number of types to an easily manageable level. In this regard, no typology can be comprehensive, nor should we desire this. Instead, we should adopt a typology that serves our own purpose. If one does not exist, we can develop one. No typology, however, provides a convincing account of change difficulty across constitutions.

Models of constitutional change

The typologies of formal change mechanisms that we have considered are, perhaps counter-intuitively, rather unconcerned with constitutional change. The typologies of Elster and

---

30 Tom Ginsburg and James Melton, 'Does the Constitutional Amendment Rule Matter at All? Amendment Cultures and the Challenges of Measuring Amendment Difficulty' (2015) 13(3) *International Journal of Constitutional Law* 686.

Lane are oriented toward a characterisation of constitutions as retarding political change. Lutz's typology, while attempting to facilitate comparative analysis of formal change difficulty in constitutions, is again oriented to high-level claims about the purposes of constitutions. Those typologies that focus on the distribution of constitutional power make relatively little attempt to theorise different types of formal change, largely describing different approaches rather than articulating the values that lie behind them. Of course, the typologies are not unconcerned with constitutional change but for the most part it is not seen as a discrete phenomenon within comparative constitutional law that warrants theorisation. In this, they are reflective of the priorities of comparative constitutional law in general. It is striking that the *Oxford Handbook of Comparative Constitutional Law*, published in 2012, did not contain a discrete chapter on constitutional amendment, let alone a section on constitutional change.[31] This comment is in no way a criticism of that excellent publication but instead is intended to illustrate how it is largely in the last five to ten years that comparative constitutional change has become such a significant focus of scholarship. This increasing concern with constitutional change is also reflected in a desire to move beyond typologies of formal constitutional change mechanisms and develop models of constitutional change more broadly.

Before considering the models, it is necessary to say a brief word about informal constitutional change. Informal constitutional change occurs where the constitution in some sense changes even though there has been no formal change through the stipulated constitutional change process. This requires us to conceptualise both what this constitution is and how it can be changed. As this is more directly the focus of the contributions in Part III of this volume, I shall not consider it in detail here. However, since the models that I shall explore below incorporate both formal and informal change, it is necessary to give the topic some consideration.[32] On occasion, the political elite may bypass the amending formula, as happened with President de Gaulle's use of a referendum to amend the French Constitution in 1962. Informal change can also occur through political practice; this will be particularly apparent in constitutional systems in which constitutional conventions play an important role. The legislator may legislate on issues of constitutional significance that are not directly regulated by the master-text constitution. Informal change might also occur through judicial interpretation and judicial review. This category depends on some conception of when interpretation is so significant as to amount to change, itself a rather contested matter. Sub-national entities may prompt informal change at the national level by altering their regional constitutions or legislation. Actions by supranational legislators and courts, particularly but not exclusively in Europe, might prompt informal change at the national level.

With this outline of informal change in mind, we can now consider the five models of constitutional change presented by Contiades and Fotiadou. These aim to give a far deeper insight into the way in which constitutional change occurs in a country, but still through the approach of defining types. Their models are as follows:

- *Elastic model*: an unentrenched constitution may be changed simply through the law-making process with no procedural limits or eternity clauses.

---

31 Rosenfeld and Sajó (n 2).
32 This discussion draws partly on Contiades and Fotiadou (n 27) 436–440.

- *Evolutionary model*: where formal change is difficult, there is dynamic evolution through informal change.
- *Pragmatic model*: formal change works efficiently either because the formula itself is not overly onerous or because a consensual political culture allows an ostensibly onerous procedure to be followed.
- *Distrust model*: this combines demanding and complex amending formulas with an oppositional political culture that makes compromise on constitutional issues difficult.
- *Direct-democratic model*: the people have the final say on constitutional change as well as being able to initiate constitutional change.[33]

These models provide a much more detailed picture of constitutional change than do the typologies considered in the previous section. The first four models are focused on the difficulty of constitutional change. They are more sophisticated than the typologies considered above (in the section headed 'Typologies of formal constitutional change mechanisms') in that they recognise (a) that change difficulty is a factor of other constitutional rules and political culture as well as the formal change mechanism and (b) that difficulty in formal change might sometimes push political actors toward informal change.[34] They lack the simplicity of a typology but they provide us with a considerably richer and broadly convincing account of constitutional change, thereby providing a good basis for developing a theory of constitutional change. The fifth model, in contrast, focuses on the distribution of constitutional power. As such, it seems to cut across the other models rather than offering a discrete category on the same dimension. A particular country could be an example of the direct-democratic model and yet also be an example of the evolutionary model if it is difficult to secure constitutional change (as is arguably the case with Japan[35]), of the pragmatic model if the referendum hurdle can relatively easily be passed (as is arguably the case with Ireland[36]), or of the distrust model if the referendum model forms part of a political culture in which compromise is difficult (as is arguably the case with Italy[37]).

What this suggests is that even when one develops sophisticated models rather than simplistic typologies, it might not be possible simultaneously to explain change difficulty and distribution of constitutional power. Models of constitutional change can still assist in developing a theory of constitutional change but they do not of themselves provide a theory of constitutional change. They help to reduce the diversity of constitutional practices to a manageable number of models, but they do not provide a comprehensive spectrum of constitutional change practices. One final word should be said about models. A strength of Contiades and Fotiadou's approach is that it shows the extent to which constitutional change practice is not deliberately designed. Political culture is as important as the precise amendment formula; overly difficult amendment rules might prompt a turn to informal change in its stead. But we can safely assume, I suggest, that few constitutional drafters

---

33 Ibid 442–454.
34 Oliver and Fusaro share this insight, but are less sanguine than Contiades and Fotiadou, counselling that this can lead to a lack of constitutional legitimacy. Oliver and Fusaro (n 9).
35 Satoshi Yokodaido, 'Constitutional Stability in Japan Not Due to Popular Approval' (2019) 20(2) *German Law Journal* 263.
36 Oran Doyle, *The Constitution of Ireland: A Contextual Analysis* (Hart 2018) Chapter 10.
37 Tania Groppi, 'Constitutional Revision in Italy: A Marginal Instrument for Constitutional Change' in Contiades and Fotiadou (n 27) 203.

adopt difficult formal change rules in order to encourage informal constitutional change. An important lesson must be drawn from this. Because the models are not deliberately produced, they cannot serve as examples for others to follow. They aid our understanding of comparative constitutional change by plausibly dividing countries' constitutional change practices into four categories, in a way that is much richer than the typologies of formal change mechanisms. But they serve the interests of constitutional scholarship rather than constitutional design.

Conclusions

In this chapter, I have explored a number of typologies and models of constitutional change presented in the academic literature. I have drawn attention to how these models and typologies are animated by two competing concerns: the difficulty of constitutional change and the distribution of constitutional power among constitutional actors. There is no model or typology that can simultaneously present an account of these two concerns. We have seen the limited, but real, way in which typologies can help us understand the different components of formal change mechanisms. They can provide us with an overview of the components of mechanisms (initiation, ratification and constraints); they can also provide a somewhat simplified (and therefore manageable) account of either the difficulty level or the power distribution associated with particular formal change mechanisms. All of this can assist us in mapping and theorising the field of constitutional change. However, there seems little prospect that a typology of formal change mechanisms will ever allow us to compare the difficulty of formally changing constitutions.

4

CONSTITUTIONAL ENDURANCE

Tom Ginsburg

Introduction

Most drafters of constitutions act as if their handiwork should last a long time (Kay 2000: 33), and constitutional scholars since Aristotle have generally assumed that endurance is a good idea. Indeed, it is safe to say that virtually every normative constitutional theory presumes that constitutions survive over a relatively extended period of time. Without endurance, constitutions cannot provide a stable basis of politics and cannot constitute a people out of diverse elements. The assumption of endurance is thus built into the very idea of a constitution (Raz 1998: 153).[1]

But national constitutions, it turns out, do not last very long. As my colleagues and I at the Comparative Constitutions Project (CCP) documented in a 2009 book (Elkins et al. 2009), the expected lifespan of a national constitution, for all such documents promulgated since 1789, is only nineteen years. For some regions of the world, the life expectancy is even lower: the average constitution will last a mere eight years in Latin America and Eastern Europe. This fact raises all kinds of positive and normative questions, which we will survey in this chapter.

Some terminological matters should be clarified first. What exactly is constitutional replacement? We generally define a 'new' constitution in nominal terms. That is, if those promulgating the constitution declare it to be a 'new' document, we believe them. If the actors claim to be amending the constitution, we believe them. This is regardless of whether there is legal continuity with a prior constitution, such as by following the old amendment formula. The Japanese Constitution of 1946 is viewed as a new constitution by virtually everyone who writes about it, and even more importantly by the current Japanese government, which has followed the 'revisionist' policy of seeking a replacement. But it was scrupulously adopted using the amendment formula of the previous document of 1889. Still, we call it a 'new' document. Andrew Arato's (2013) useful distinction between continuity in its legal and legitimacy senses is helpful to think about this problem, and it is probably the case that many new constitutions are adopted in moments when there is either a break in legal or legitimacy continuity. But clearly this is not always the case. Some constitutional

---

1 Raz (1998: 153) places endurance among the central features that define a constitution: 'it is, and is meant to be, of long duration'.

replacements – I like to use the example of Sweden in 1974 – are adopted for more or less technical reasons, without major political or legal rupture.

This point raises the question of why we should care. After all, many amendments of constitutions can replace large and significant amounts of the text, while replacements might preserve much of the earlier document. These points are correct, but we show that, on average, replacements change more of the text than do amendments. Amendments tend to change very small amounts of text while replacements are more significant. Ginsburg and Melton (2015) report levels of similarity that are well above 95% for the average amendment, while replacements correlate at 80% or less on average. This makes sense given that constitutional replacements are *costly*: there are more items to be negotiated, more issues to coordinate and more complications. The process too, can be thorny, particularly if the public must be involved somehow.

Constitutional replacement may be seen as symbolically more significant than constitutional amendment. Beginning in the mid-1990s, for example, Taiwan underwent four rounds of constitutional amendments to streamline a governmental system that had originally been designed to govern all of China. This involved eliminating a National Assembly, the Provincial Government of Taiwan, and reorganizing executive-legislative relations. When President Chen Shui-bian proposed drafting an entirely new constitution, however, China strenuously objected, and this was sufficient to cool Taiwan's population to the proposal. This was a case in which a set of amendments substituted for replacement for political reasons.

Some facts

Let us turn to a few facts, updating the 2009 volume. Since we wrote the book on constitutional endurance, the list of countries that have adopted 'new' constitutions includes Cuba, Côte d'Ivoire, Egypt, Fiji, Guinea, Hungary, Kenya, Kyrgyzstan, Libya, Madagascar, Morocco, Nepal, Somalia, St. Vincent and the Grenadines, Syria, Tunisia, and Zimbabwe. South Sudan appeared on the world stage with its own 'Provisional' text. The Dominican Republic, Egypt, Fiji, Niger, and Tunisia have each promulgated multiple texts during that period. This rate of new production might actually be slowing down from the historical average: in total we count 846 'new' and 'interim' constitutions over just over 200 years of constitutional history, suggesting that in some years we have experienced more than the two a year of the last decade. Figure 4.1, which is adapted from our book, provides the time trends in terms of number of constitutions adopted in any given year (the bars), as well as the overall trend toward adopting written constitutions as a form. The bars, it will be easily seen, tend to come in waves following great global conflict: the Springtime of Nations, World Wars I and II and the end of the Cold War are each accompanied by double digits of new constitutions within a very short timespan.

It will be surmised that many of these new documents involve the creation of new countries from the breakup of empires, and that is surely part of the story. As the number of countries has expanded, it has usually led to the end of a prior constitutional order, as states have broken apart. But this is not the only story. Constitutions in some countries are exceptionally short lived: the Dominican Republic has now promulgated over 30 constitutions since it first emerged as an independent state in 1844. The United States Constitution, on the other hand, is 230 years old (though many would say it is showing its age). I will return to these national patterns, explored in our 2009 book, later in this chapter.

Another factual point worth mentioning is that most constitutions die young. Figure 4.2 provides a histogram for the percentage of constitutions that survive to a particular age, with the

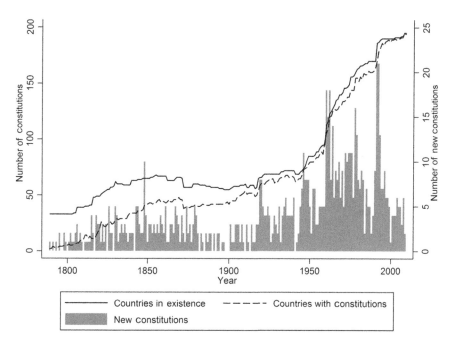

Figure 4.1 New constitutions by year

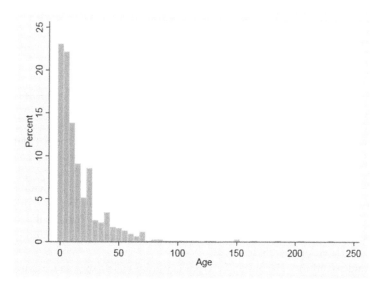

Figure 4.2 Percentage of all constitutions to survive to a given age

bars representing five-year brackets. The single highest percentage die within the first five years, and nearly 50% are dead by age ten. Only a handful – fifteen in history – have survived to age 100 (see Table 4.1). Furthermore, as Table 4.2 indicates, the average lifespan for constitutions is actually getting shorter as time progresses, in contrast with the human lifespan.

Table 4.1 Constitutions aged over 100 years

Rank	Country	Years	Lifespan (years)
1	United States	1789–	231
2	Norway	1814–	206
2	Netherlands	1814–	206
4	Belgium	1831–	189
5	Sweden	1809–1974	168
6	Canada	1867–	153
7	Luxembourg	1868–	152
8	Argentina	1853–1966; 1983–	c.148
9	Tonga	1875–	145
10	Liberia	1847–1980	136
11	Switzerland	1874–2000	128
12	Australia	1901	119
13	Colombia	1886–1991	108
14	Mexico	1917–	103
14	Liechtenstein	1921–	99

Table 4.2 Ages of expiration over time

Promulgation date	Mean age of expired constitution (n)	Mean age of all constitutions (including alive in 2018)
<1900	16.9 (195)	21 (200)
1900–1945	11.2 (113)	14.7 (118)
1946–89	10.5 (230)	17.7 (289)
1990–	6.1 (51)	13.4 (151)
TOTAL	12.4	17.2

One of the distinctions we make is between constitutional change and regime change. That is, constitutional change is not simply a product of switches between democracy and dictatorship. We do note that a history of volatility in democracy scores (the standard deviation of a country's historical Polity score) is moderately correlated with a country's frequency of constitutional replacement (r = 0.54). Roughly one in five of transitions from or to democracy are accompanied by constitutional replacements.[2] And of all constitutional replacements, one in five come into force within one year of a transition. The two phenomena are related but hardly identical.

One can understand the relationship between constitutional change and regime change by examining trends in the level of democracy and the incidence of new constitutions within individual countries. Elkins et al. (2009) ask whether shifts in democracy correspond to constitutional changes. Japan's history has been one of punctuated equilibrium, with each of

2 Transitions are defined as a move from three or more points on the 20-point Polity scale. By this measure, constitutional replacement occurs in 19% of cases of democratic transition and 27% of cases of authoritarian transition.

its two constitutions marking sharp increases in a democratic direction. French history also shows a close relationship between constitutional change and democracy, as its new constitutions tend to correspond with shifts between republic and empire. But there are other countries in which the relationship is not so clear. Chile's 1980 Constitution, commissioned by General Augusto Pinochet, institutionalized the authoritarian practices initiated by the coup in 1973 and laid out a path for transition to democratic rule. The constitution remains in force today in a democratic era, albeit with significant amendments. Colombia is even more pronounced in this regard, in that it experienced multiple regime transitions under a single constitutional regime from 1886. In contrast, in the Dominican Republic, regime change is rare but constitutional change is frequent: the country has had roughly 29 different constitutions in its history, but has until recently not had a sustained period of democracy. And some countries, such as Greece and Uruguay, are unstable in both realms: Greece has had, by our count, thirteen constitutional changes and thirteen regime changes, while Uruguay has had seven of each.

One might think that these patterns are simply driven by country characteristics, with some national soils being more or less amenable to enduring constitutions. But there is sufficient variation *within* countries to suggest that this is not the case. In some countries, such as Mexico, the early years of statehood were accompanied by great constitutional instability but eventually institutions stabilized and more enduring constitutions were adopted: the 1857 and 1917 documents are among the longer-lasting in world history. Uruguay represents the opposite pattern, as it enjoyed an early stable constitution followed by breakdown and a struggle to find enduring institutions. Panama represents another pattern that we might label Jeffersonian, in light of his preference for constitutional replacement: Panama has experienced periodic renewal of the constitution, every generation or so.

Finally, one might object to the whole inquiry to argue that constitutional replacement is not the important phenomenon of interest. If a formal constitution is replaced but many of the prior institutions remain in place, then it hardly should matter in reality. This is a sound objection – for most theories of endurance, it is institutions, not constitutions, that actually matter. But my colleagues and I investigated this point, and found that while constitutions on average do correlate relatively highly with their predecessors on measures of content, they also do tend to introduce more change than do, say, constitutional amendments. And the process of making a new constitution can be costly and disruptive. In short, we find that on average, constitutional change involves institutional change.

Theories of endurance

What might make constitutions endure? There is a small amount of theory in a rational choice vein addressing this question. The dominant current view draws on the literature on self-enforcing institutions. Constitutions, as Hardin (1989), Niskanen (1990), Przeworski (1991) and Ordeshook (1992) pointed out, do not have an external enforcer who can ensure that the terms of the constitution are enforced. While courts purport to enforce the constitution through the power of judicial review, one must still develop an account as to why powerful actors obey the courts. Constitutions must, therefore, be self-enforcing, meaning that it is in the interest of all powerful factions to abide by the provisions of the constitution. A constitution will endure so long as parties believe they are better off within the bargain than in risking new constitutional negotiations. A well-designed constitution becomes an equilibrium, so that no one with the power to defect has the interest to do so.

Weingast (1997) generalizes this idea to explain that constitutions represent coordination devices that allow citizens and elites to develop shared understanding of the limits of government, and to enforce those limits. In democracies, enforcement of these constitutional limitations ultimately relies on citizens. If they can coordinate, citizens can prevent the government from imposing costs on them and violating the political bargain. If they cannot coordinate, democracy might not be stable, as the government will continuously adjust the bargain in its favor with political acquiescence. The coordination problem is that citizens, having disparate interests, will be unlikely to reach agreement on their own as to what is considered to be a violation of the constitution, and on when and how to enforce the bargain. A willingness to stand against the government requires a belief that others will join the citizen; otherwise the potential protestor will fear ending up in jail while oppression continues. When all citizens coordinate their expectations that others will join in the protest, however, the expectations become self-fulfilling and government will refrain from violating the bargain. Written constitutions may be useful instruments to help citizens overcome the coordination problem, because texts define violations and thus increase the probability of coordination (Carey 2000). We might also expect that constitutions adopted with widespread participation would be more widely known and hence more likely to be self-enforcing.

In later work, Weingast (2006, 2018) explores how to design stable constitutions. He argues that majoritarian conceptions of democracy, while responsive to changing preferences among the people, also create risks to constitutional stability. Because majorities can threaten minoritarian interests, they raise the stakes of politics, which can lead to destabilizing conflict. Instead, Weingast argues, constitutions should adopt some counter-majoritarian institutions so as to reduce the stakes of politics, which in turn can prevent those with power to disrupt the constitutional order from doing so. Counter-majoritarian institutions increase self-enforcement, even if they decrease responsiveness. And sometimes political payoffs to interest groups are required to keep the bargain stable.

If endurance results from self-enforcement, we still cannot have confidence that enduring constitutions are always good constitutions. It might be the case that it is better to 'live fast and die young', to quote the title of James Dean's biography (Dean died at the age of 24 in 1955). Sutter (1997, 2003) derives conditions under which durability will facilitate the general interest rather than rent-seeking. He argues that constitutions that make rents transferable and that require rent-seekers to turn over periodically can dis-incentivize interest groups from rent-seeking. Because any rents acquired early on will potentially be taken away in later stages by new coalitions, such constitutions reduce the value of rents. Sutter suggests that democracy, by requiring periodic turnover, approximates the second condition. On the other hand, if interest groups have already secured advantage in the current system, autocracy might provide a mechanism for breaking through rent-seeking equilibria.

Sutter's argument builds on other work by scholars who are skeptical about constitutional provisions that are too detailed. As stated by Przeworski (1991: 36): 'Constitutions that are observed and last for a long time are those that … define the scope of government and establish rules of competition, leaving substantive outcomes open to the political interplay'. This position is echoed in the literature on constitutional political economy, which has developed normative arguments in favor of endurance and opposed to special interest provisions in constitutions (e.g. Gwartney and Wagner 1988). The literature has tended to assume that these two things go together.

My co-authors and I (Elkins et al. 2009) build on self-enforcement theory to argue for three specific design features that will help constitutions to endure. We follow what is now the conventional approach of conceiving of constitutions as bargains among major groups that must remain supportive of the constitution for it to endure. We argue that the primary threat to bargains among these groups lies in 'shocks' that affect costs and benefits flowing from the constitution. Such change can be exogenous or endogenous: it might consist of a global financial crisis, or a change in the relative power of the groups produced by constitutional terms. Either way, a shock will put pressure on a constitutional bargain and render it less likely to survive. We argue that flexible constitutions that are easy to amend will be able to adjust when new social and political circumstances arise. We also argue that inclusion – greater public involvement in the creation of the constitution – will render it more likely to be enforced. Inclusion refers to the involvement of important groups in society – broadly speaking, the more groups with a stake in the constitution, the more likely it is to endure. Finally, we argue that more specific constitutions are likely to survive because they will represent greater levels of investment on the part of the drafters.

As noted above, some constitutions can endure through frequent amendment. There is an increasingly voluminous literature on amendment, to which many of the contributors to this volume have made important contributions themselves. I want to limit myself to a couple of points. First of all amendment frequency seems to be increasing, as Figure 4.3 indicates. The first panel reproduces in modified form Figure 4.1 above; the second examines amendments (drawn from Ginsburg and Melton 2015). To some degree amendment *can* operate as a substitute for replacement, and it is in theory a better way to go about constitutional change as it is incremental and less costly. But it is also the case that countries differ dramatically in their attitudes to amendment. In some countries, such as Japan, constitutional amendment has never been utilized. In others, such as the United States, it is rare, but the courts play an important role in keeping the constitutional order up to date. In countries such as Norway, Brazil or Mexico, constitutional amendment is frequent and common, being used for relatively minor matters as well as major ones. Thus we observe what seem to be different attitudes about the appropriateness of constitutional amendment in different contexts.

With what consequences?

Does constitutional replacement matter, in any meaningful sense? This has been a question since the adoption of the U.S. Constitution, when both Thomas Jefferson and James Madison offered their views. Jefferson, who was partial to radical democracy and supportive of the French Revolution, proposed that constitutions should be replaced every generation (nineteen years in one of his calculations, based on European life expectancies at the time); Madison argued that his handiwork should be preserved so as to provide stability. There are surely good theoretical arguments for either side. The benefits of constitutional replacement include, at least in the case of the American Constitution, better fit with changing social norms, which might lead to more effective representation, and upgrades to suboptimal or outmoded institutions. Jefferson considered constitutions a kind of technology that should evolve with the times. With my co-author Aziz Z. Huq, I have recently argued that the U.S. Constitution is particularly poorly designed for our era of democratic backsliding, and renders us susceptible to democratic erosion (Ginsburg and Huq 2018). But there are good arguments on Madison's side: stable constitutions can allow institutions to function better, and can play a symbolic role in creating national identity in a diverse society. They also can

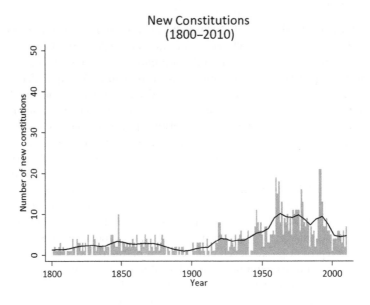

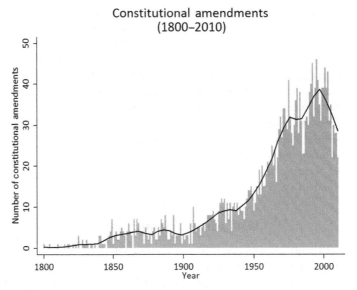

Figure 4.3 Amendment and replacement

potentially facilitate investment and economic activity. And constitutional change itself is costly, upsetting settled expectations and creating potentially destabilizing political conflict (Landau 2013). The perennial tension between flexibility and commitment is at the core of this debate, and there is rarely any one-size-fits-all resolution; answers will depend upon the context, and the characteristics of each constitution. Some of these arguments are testable, however, and it is useful to summarize what we know of the empirical evidence.

Let us start with the Jeffersonian claim about the benefits of technological updating, allowing the replacement of institutions deemed to be outdated or suboptimal. For a variety of reasons, one would expect that replacements could bring improvements in design, as drafters and citizens can identify poor institutions, and learn from the experience of other countries. In this view, institutions are subject to progressive evolution, and constitutions might continuously improve over time in their adoption of new technologies of governance. But when we examine the histories of some countries, we see that replacement does not always bring improvement. My co-authors and I identify two other patterns (Elkins et al. 2009). One is what we might term institutional *churn*, in which states replace their constitutions frequently, but remain anchored to the same institutional choices. Socialist countries such as China reflect this model, as did the Dominican Republic under the Trujillo dictatorship and other periods in its history. Venezuela, whose nineteenth-century constitutions rarely endured longer than six or seven years and differed very little from one another, seems also to have exhibited this pattern. Another plausible pattern is *cycling*, in which a country caught in the grip of two competing and irreconcilable groups will bounce back and forth between constitutions according to which group is in power. Again, we can turn to nineteenth-century Latin America, where a number of countries seem to have experienced this roller coaster, with constitutions marking the rise and fall of groups on opposite sides of issues such as the degree of centralization, the structure of executive-legislative relations, or ideology. Haiti's liberal constitution of 1843, for example, was overturned in 1849 but served as the basis for the constitutions of 1867 and 1879. Similarly, the 1854 and 1858 constitutions of the Dominican Republic would be the touchstone for authoritarians and liberals for much of the remainder of the nineteenth century. In these environments, constitutional transitions reflect a transfer of power from one set of elites to another, and largely parallel ordinary turnover in democratic polities. Such constitutions may simply map policy and internal regime organization, without any long-term stabilizing function and without the progress that the Jeffersonian argument envisions.

One can gain some understanding of these effects by exploring patterns in the similarity of constitutions over time. One pattern, which we describe in some detail in our book, is a gradual drift of Latin American constitutions away from the U.S. model that had been so influential to early Latin American constitutional drafters. It seems quite plausible that, in this drift, Latin American drafters have moved away from some of the suboptimal elements of the U.S. document, and perhaps tailored their institutions more carefully to the local environment. It could also be, however, that these countries have chased new institutional fashions that do not necessarily represent advances.

Consider first bicameralism.[3] The four federal countries in Latin America – Mexico, Venezuela, Argentina, and Brazil – all adopted in their early constitutions a bicameral legislature, in which the upper house used an American-style scheme with equal representation for each sub-unit. This system has come under severe attack in the United States as fundamentally undemocratic. Each of the Latin American countries has since replaced their constitution several times in the interim period, and of the four federalisms, only Argentina and Brazil have retained an upper house apportionment with a fixed number of senators per state, while Venezuela recently adopted a unicameral legislature and Mexico has moved (through a constitutional amendment, not replacement) to a mixed system for the upper house, in which some senators are elected at large and some from the states. We see, then, two cases in which multiple constitutional replacements have not overturned an

---

3 Thanks to Zach Elkins for the following observations.

allegedly suboptimal apportionment scheme, one that has, and one that made the improvement without recourse to a constitutional replacement.

Nevertheless, other aspects of the U.S. model in Latin American constitutions have been 'modernized' through a steady process of replacement. Rights such as those to bear arms and the non-quartering of soldiers – protections that many drafters of contemporary constitutions probably now see as anachronistic, if not suboptimal – have been eliminated. At its peak in the 1860s nearly 30% of constitutions – almost all of them in Latin America – provided for a right to bear arms. This began to drop as the number of countries in the world expanded in the twentieth century and by 2000, the United States, Mexico, and Guatemala were alone in providing this right.[4] Consider another controversial provision of the U.S. Constitution, life tenure for federal judges. That provision, also once a mainstay of Latin American constitutions, is increasingly rare among modern constitutions across the world, including those in Latin America (Ginsburg 2003). Modern constitutions tend to adopt long fixed terms or maximum age limits to avoid the problem of geriatric judges. True life tenure might have made sense when the life expectancy was 45, as it was in the late eighteenth century, but hardly does in an era where a judge could potentially serve on a high court for four decades or more. In short, the U.S. model of upper house representation, the right to bear arms, and true life tenure have gone out of style, probably because these do not fit modern conditions.

Technological innovation works by addition as well as subtraction. Besides rejecting outmoded institutions, constitutions can add new ones that are discovered. A constitution written today is likely to have an array of 'fourth branch' accountability institutions, such as counter-corruption commissions, ombudsmen, and auditors, whose task is to ensure that other branches of government do their job. Rights, too, have seen a massive expansion, so that the average constitution today includes a whole array of positive rights, to health, education, and welfare, that were not widespread in the nineteenth century.

A close look at the institutional trajectory of countries undergoing periodic constitutional replacement (in particular, those in Latin America) yields mixed results. Some countries clearly experience mere churn or cycling, rather than updating. But over time, there seems to be a good deal of updating that has occurred, especially in the post-World War II era. Whether the benefits of these institutional improvements outweigh the costs associated with institutional instability is a more complex question. It is hard to assess the benefits of wholesale constitutional amendment as opposed to constant and frequent amendment, as countries such as Mexico, Brazil, and India seem to undertake.

Let us now turn to the Madisonian arguments, and begin with the symbolic, or constitutive, function of constitutions. The claim is that a stable, and consequently venerated, constitution will help to unify an otherwise fragmented society. This has certainly been the American experience, but this might be rather exceptional. Elkins and Sides (2007) examine whether certain institutional arrangements are more or less successful in creating a national identity among minorities in multi-ethnic states. They find that while particular institutions such as federalism, proportional representation electoral systems, and democracy itself – powersharing institutions that are thought to incorporate minorities – have little bearing on a minority citizen's pride in the state, the duration of some of these arrangements matter. For example, an accumulated history of stable democracy tends to increase the national attachment of both minorities and majorities, while contemporary

---

4 Haiti has a provision allowing the bearing of arms to defend the home.

levels of democracy matter little. There is some reason to believe that constitutional endurance works in the same way.

Next, consider the claim that enduring constitutions will promote increasing fit between the text and the actual practice. The idea here is that new constitutions involve institutional change, and so it might take some time for implementation to actually occur. This is especially true for aspirational constitutions that seek transformative change, which can take generations. From this point of view, we might see increasing convergence between the constitution on paper and the constitution in practice. On the other hand, enduring constitutions can give rise to informal understandings that diverge from the formal text. Interpretations of the constitution by judges and political actors might lead to new constitutional rules for which the formal text might have only a loose semiotic relationship (Strauss 1996). If so, any measure of the congruence between the formal text and de facto practice may show divergence over time.

In analyses that we report in our book, my co-authors and I compare the fit of constitutions over time in two domains: the level of parliamentary power and the protection of civil liberties. Rather than increased fit over time, what we see is that legislatures assume more power as the constitution ages and that respect for rights outstrips their provision in the constitution. To the extent that one believes that alignment between the de facto and de jure constitution is a good thing, the observed gap might be troubling. But it is noteworthy that the divergence seems to be in the direction of greater protection of civil liberties, and greater levels of parliamentary power. Constitutions may, in general, be floors but not ceilings on the provision of rights or power. This finding provides some support for Strauss's (1996) conjecture.

Finally, consider some of the instrumental benefits of longevity. My co-authors and I have noted that endurance is positively associated with GDP per capita, democracy, and political stability and negatively associated with political crises. On average, countries are richer, more democratic, more politically stable, and experience fewer crises, as their constitution ages. There does seem to be a fair amount of variation in the relationship between each of these variables and age in young constitutions, but over the longer term, enduring constitutions tend to be associated with these desirable features. Of course, the number of such constitutions is small, and we recognize that the relationship is likely reciprocal: as wealth and democracy deepen, they reinforce commitment to the existing constitution, reducing the chance of early death.

Conclusion

A standard critique of our inquiry is that formal institutions do not matter. The proper response is that this is itself an empirical question. For example, Elster (2013) critiques our study for including 'sham' constitutions, but we now know that dictatorships vary in terms of their use of constitutions to legitimate their rule, from systems such as Chile under Pinochet which took constitutions somewhat seriously (Barros 2002) to those like the former Soviet Union in which the constitutions provided at best a symbolic document (Solomon 1996). So constitutional efficacy is a discrete phenomenon from regime change, though in many cases they might be linked.

It is of course, possible to shift analytic focus to non-constitutional institutions that play constitutional functions, but this leads to two methodological concerns. The first is to define in a rigorous way all institutions that are 'constitutional' but not found in the formal constitution. Different scholars have offered different examples of statutes, political statements, court decisions, and unwritten norms that might be considered to fulfill a constitutional function. While these sources of norms are quite properly considered constitutional for many purposes, it is tricky to come up with a precise definition that works across geographic and temporal contexts. Thus shifting to the informal constitution makes it difficult to be comparative even as it increases one's understanding of what is 'constitutional'.

The second methodological issue is that, by shifting to informal institutions, analysts sometimes make an implicit assumption that formal institutions are less important. This move raises a puzzle. If the written constitution is of relatively low stakes, why do states spend so much energy in drafting written texts and negotiating institutional choices embodied in them? And why do others resist attempts at formal constitutional change through amendment or redrafting processes? The puzzle suggests that writing does matter, though we are only beginning to rigorously theorize the ways that it does (Breslin 2009).

References

Arato, Andrew, *Post Sovereign Constitution Making: Learning and Legitimacy* (Cambridge University Press 2013).

Barros, Robert, *Constitutionalism and Dictatorship: Pinochet, the Junta, and the 1980 Constitution* (Cambridge University Press 2002).

Breslin, Beau, *From Words to Worlds* (Johns Hopkins University Press 2009).

Carey, John, 'Parchment, Equilibria, and Institutions' (2000) 33 *Comparative Political Studies* 735–61.

Elkins, Zachary, Ginsburg, Tom and Melton, James, *The Endurance of National Constitutions* (Cambridge University Press 2009).

Elkins, Zachary and Sides, John, 'Can Institutions Build Unity in Multiethnic States?' (2007) 101 *American Political Science Review* 693–708.

Elster, Jon, *Securities Against Misrule: Juries, Assemblies, Elections* (Cambridge University Press 2013).

Ginsburg, Tom, *Judicial Review in New Democracies* (Cambridge University Press 2003).

Ginsburg, Tom and Huq, Aziz Z., *How to Save a Constitutional Democracy* (Chicago: University of Chicago Press 2018).

Ginsburg, Tom and Melton, James, 'Does the Constitutional Amendment Rule Matter At All? Amendment Cultures and the Challenge of Measuring Amendment Difficulty' (2015) 13 *International Journal of Constitutional Law* 686–713.

Gwartney, James D. and Wagner, Richard E. (eds), *Public Choice and Constitutional Economics* (JAI Press 1988).

Hardin, Russell, 'Why a Constitution?' in Bernard Grofman and Donald Wittman (eds), *The Federalist Papers and the New Institutionalism* (New York: Agathon Press 1989) 100–20.

Kay, Richard, 'Constitutional Chronomony' (2000) 13(1) *Ratio Juris* 31–48.

Landau, David, 'Constitution-Making Gone Wrong' (2013) 64 *Alabama Law Review* 923–80.

Niskanen, William, 'Conditions Affecting the Survival of Constitutional Rules' (1990) 1(2) *Constitutional Political Economy* 53–62.

Ordeshook, Peter C., 'Constitutional Stability' (1992) 3(2) *Constitutional Political Economy* 137–75.

Przeworski, Adam, *Democracy and the Market* (Cambridge University Press 1991).

Raz, Joseph, 'On the Authority and Interpretation of Constitutions: Some Preliminaries' in Larry Alexander (ed), *Constitutionalism Philosophical Foundations* (Cambridge University Press 1998) 152–70.

Solomon, Peter, *Soviet Criminal Justice under Stalin* (Cambridge University Press 1996).

Strauss, David, 'Common Law Constitutional Interpretation' (1996) 63 *University of Chicago Law Review* 877–935.

Sutter, Daniel, 'Enforcing Constitutional Constraints' (1997) 8 *Constitutional Political Economy* 139–50.

Sutter, Daniel, 'Durable Constitutional Rules and Rent Seeking' (2003) 31(4) *Public Finance Review* 413–28.

Weingast, Barry, 'The Political Foundations of Democracy and the Rule of Law' (1997) 91(2) *American Political Science Review* 245–63.

Weingast, Barry, 'Designing Constitutional Stability' in Roger Congleton and Birgitta Swedborg (eds), *Democratic Constitutional Design and Public Policy* (MIT Press 2006) 319–42.

Weingast, Barry, 'From High to Low Stakes Politics: Should Majoritarians Embrace Countermajoritarian Constitutional Provisions?' Manuscript (2018). Available at https://papers.ssrn.com/sol3/papers.cfm?abstract_id=3178278 (accessed October 1, 2018).

5

CONSTITUTIONAL AMENDMENT VERSUS CONSTITUTIONAL REPLACEMENT

An empirical comparison

David S. Law[*] and Ryan Whalen[**]

The field of comparative constitutional law has been transformed in recent years by groundbreaking research – often of a quantitative and empirical variety – on the creation, content, and longevity of constitutions.[1] Some of this literature necessarily presupposes a distinction between constitutions that are new and constitutions that have merely been amended. At the same time, however, the distinction between amendments and replacements is known to be problematic. Even at a conceptual level, it is not clear how to distinguish between these two supposedly distinct categories of constitutional change without engaging in a certain degree of potentially arbitrary or subjective line-drawing. Practical implementation of the distinction for purposes of empirical analysis is harder still.

A common and convenient approach is simply to look to whether these changes are formally labeled as 'amendments' or 'replacements'. Unfortunately, these formal labels may themselves be arbitrary or idiosyncratic and do not necessarily correspond to the actual importance or magnitude of the changes in question. The resulting methodological challenge is to find some objective way of evaluating how reliable – or unreliable – these labels happen to be. In this chapter, we employ text analysis techniques to investigate empirically the difference between changes that are labeled 'amendments' and those that are labeled 'replacements'. We find that so-called 'amendments' tend on average to involve changes of a lesser magnitude than so-called 'replacements', measured in

[*] This chapter was made possible by a General Research Fund grant awarded by the Research Grants Council of Hong Kong (project number 17610717). Felicia Cao, Yulin Cheng, Desmond Chu, Marisa Sylvester, Jacob Walker, and Wilson Yuen provided invaluable assistance in collecting and reconstructing the corpus of amended constitutions analyzed in this chapter. Earlier versions of this chapter were presented at the Conference on Constitutional Change held in Aegina in September 2018, and at Academia Sinica and the Conference on Empirical Legal Studies in 2019. We are grateful to all participants on both occasions for their suggestions and feedback, including Yun-Chien Chang, Jimmy Chia-Hsin Hsu, Ryan Hubert, Po-Sheng Lee, Chien-Chih Lin, and Yen-Tu Su; and last but not least to Tom Ginsburg and the Comparative Constitutions Project for their generous cooperation and support in sharing their collection of historical constitutions.

1 For an introduction to this literature, see the chapters by Tom Ginsburg and Jaakko Husa in this volume.

terms of the proportion of the text that changes. It is also clear, however, that the 'amendment' and 'replacement' labels are often misleading as to the actual magnitude of change and cannot be used to reliably distinguish major changes from minor changes. On occasion, amendments can be massive and amount in substance to stealth replacements. More often, replacements can be inconsequential and amount in substance to overblown amendments. Indeed, most changes – regardless of how they are labeled – are relatively minor in magnitude.

Our analysis also yields empirical evidence of a relationship between the magnitude of constitutional change and the passage of time. The more time that elapses between constitutional changes, the bigger that changes tend to be. Countries exhibit patterns of constitutional change over time that tend to fall along a continuum ranging from incremental and frequent tinkering to periodic bursts of major revision. This finding suggests that the need or demand for constitutional change accumulates over time and tends as a result to lead to periodic major changes if it is not instead satisfied by smaller, more frequent adjustments.

Two approaches to the amendment–replacement distinction

A recurring concept in the study and practice of constitutional change is the distinction between constitutional *amendments* and constitutional *replacements*. A number of constitutions prescribe different procedural requirements for amendments, on the one hand, and comprehensive or fundamental reform, on the other hand.[2] Likewise, a growing number of courts distinguish between mere amendments (which in their view are permissible pursuant to the ordinary procedures for amendment) and constitutional 'substitutions' or alterations of the constitution's 'basic structure' (which are not permissible pursuant to amendment procedures).[3]

The amendment–replacement distinction also pervades the scholarly literature.[4] For example, it is common for scholars to treat constitution-making as distinct from mere tinkering, and to prescribe more elaborate procedures for the former than the latter. Likewise, much of the quantitative empirical literature on formal or 'large-C' constitutions presupposes that it is possible to distinguish between new constitutions and versions of an existing constitution. Without such a distinction, the object of study becomes impossible to define or unjustifiably broad. One cannot study 'constitutions' without first defining the universe of 'constitutions', and one cannot define the universe of 'constitutions' without some way of determining what counts as the 'same' constitution and what counts as a 'different' constitution.

Notwithstanding its ubiquity, the amendment–replacement distinction is widely acknowledged to be problematic and potentially misleading. On the one hand, many so-called replacements involve only small or incremental changes, as seen in the case of many supposedly new Latin American constitutions in the nineteenth century. On the other hand, it is widely known that

---

2 Rosalind Dixon and David Landau, 'Tiered Constitutional Design' (2018) 86 *George Washington Law Review* 438, 448–49 (discussing examples of constitutions that prescribe procedural requirements of varying stringency for amendment, 'partial reform', and 'total reform').

3 David Landau, 'Constitutional Backsliding: Colombia' in David S. Law (ed), *Constitutionalism in Context* (forthcoming 2020) (describing the Colombian Constitutional Court's 'substitution of the constitution' doctrine); David S. Law and Hsiang-Yang Hsieh, 'Judicial Review of Constitutional Amendments: Taiwan' in *Constitutionalism in Context*, supra.

4 See, e.g., Donald Lutz, 'Toward a Theory of Constitutional Amendment' (1994) 88 *American Political Science Review* 355, 356–57; George Tsebelis and Dominic Nardi, 'A Long Constitution Is a (Positively) Bad Constitution: Evidence from OECD Countries' (2016) 46 *British Journal of Political Science* 457, 464–67; Zachary Elkins et al., *The Endurance of National Constitutions* (Cambridge University Press 2009) 55–59.

some so-called amendments are, in reality, so great in magnitude that they amount in substance to replacements. For example, South Korea and Taiwan made considerable changes to their constitutions when they transitioned from authoritarianism to democracy in the late 1980s, yet these changes were labeled amendments rather than replacements. To this day, fear of interference or retaliation by mainland China is one factor that has prevented Taiwan from adopting a new constitution that reflects and acknowledges the reality of Taiwan's separation and independence from mainland China.[5]

Some scholars use blanket terms such as 'constitutional revision', or simply 'constitutional change', to avoid having to define or employ this admittedly problematic distinction. Another strategy, available to scholars working in a qualitative or 'small-n' vein, is to acknowledge that some 'amendments' are tantamount in practical terms to 'replacements' (and vice versa), then limit the analysis to a handful of cases that do not raise borderline definitional challenges. But that strategy is largely unavailable to scholars working in a quantitative or 'large-n' empirical vein, who by definition study large numbers of cases and thus must quantify or classify even the most difficult cases in consistent and unambiguous ways. A quantitative empirical approach to the study of constitutional 'amendments' or 'replacements', or to the study of 'constitutions' more generally, leaves little scope for definitional uncertainty or evasion of borderline cases.

The challenges involved in distinguishing between amendments and replacements are both conceptual and empirical. At a conceptual level, it is not clear how the distinction should be drawn or defined. Broadly speaking, there are two possible approaches, which we might call the *formalistic approach* and the *objective approach*. The formalistic approach is to accept the formal label affixed by those responsible for making the change: if the drafters deem their handiwork an 'amendment' rather than a 'replacement', or vice versa, that is the end of the inquiry. By contrast, the objective approach asks whether the change is, in some objective sense, big enough or important enough that it ought to count as a replacement rather than an amendment, regardless of how it is labeled by its drafters. Both approaches have advantages and disadvantages.

The objective approach

In principle, the objective approach is highly appealing. It seems intuitive that any amendment–replacement distinction ought to turn on the actual degree of change rather than the potentially arbitrary label applied by the drafters. In practice, however, the objective approach might be prohibitively difficult to implement. The first challenge is definitional: we must decide what criteria should be used to distinguish between amendments and replacements. The second challenge is to operationalize the definition: we must find some way of measuring whether the criteria have been satisfied.

The good news is that these challenges are not unique to the amendment–replacement distinction. Most concepts of interest to legal scholars and political scientists – such as 'democracy', or 'rule of law', or 'judicial independence', or 'judicial ideology' – pose similar conceptual and practical challenges.[6] The bad news is that the challenges surrounding the

---

5 Law and Hsieh (n 3).

6 See, e.g., Joshua B. Fischman and David S. Law, 'What Is Judicial Ideology, and How Should We Measure It?' (2009) 29 *Washington University Journal of Law & Policy* 133; Julio Ríos-Figueroa and Jeffrey K. Staton, 'An Evaluation of Cross-National Measures of Judicial Independence' (2014) 30 *Journal of Law, Economics, and Organization* 104; Svend-Erik Skaaning, 'Measuring the Rule of Law' (2010) 63 *Political Research Quarterly* 449; Shawn Treier and Simon Jackman, 'Democracy as a Latent Variable' (2008) 52 *American Journal of Political Science* 201.

definition and measurement of those other concepts have tied scholars in knots for decades, and it is not clear why the amendment–replacement distinction would be much easier to handle.

First, it is not self-evident what objective criteria should be used to distinguish between amendments and replacements. There is more than one way of defining constitutional change, and thus of drawing the line between amendment and replacement. When people speak of 'constitutional change', they may be referring to changes in the *text* of the constitution, or the *meaning* of the constitution, or both. Textual and substantive change are both plausible benchmarks for distinguishing between amendments and replacements. Should the test of replacement be the proportion of the text that is changed, or should it be the substantive importance of the changes? Or some combination of both?

For example, if a so-called 'amendment' is so extensive that it doubles the length of the constitution, should we say that it is in fact a 'replacement'? Would we reach a different conclusion if the new material merely amounts to codification of existing practice? In other words, what if the change is in some literal sense large in magnitude, but relatively inconsequential in practice? Conversely, how should we classify a so-called 'amendment' that is only one sentence long, but the sentence in question renounces the monarchy or gives international law or EU law supremacy over national law?

Second, some ostensibly objective criteria may not lend themselves to objective application, much less quantification. This is likely to be a problem if we decide that the amendment–replacement distinction should turn solely on the substantive importance of the change. There is no obvious way of reliably and consistently measuring whether a given constitutional change is, in some objective and substantive sense, more important than some other change. Even the most expert readers will have to employ a substantial element of judgment (or subjectivity), and will disagree with each other, as to whether a given change is so important that it ought to count as a replacement rather than an amendment. The result is not so much the introduction of an objectively grounded amendment–replacement distinction as the substitution of one form of subjectivity for another: the subjective evaluation of the reader replaces the subjective label applied by the drafter.

Efforts to rank constitutional changes on the basis of their substantive importance or impact face the further problem that constitutions are polydimensional and changes on different dimensions are incommensurable with each other. Anyone attempting to rank constitutional changes in order of substantive magnitude is likely to face an endless succession of apples-and-oranges comparisons between, say, the elimination of life tenure for judges, the introduction of an executive veto, and the adoption of a right to human dignity. Who is to say which change is objectively bigger or smaller, and on what basis?

Moreover, even if it were somehow possible to overcome these problems and rank all possible changes in order of substantive importance, we would then face the question of whether the importance of a particular constitutional change might vary depending upon the context and, if so, how the ranking could be adjusted to reflect this. Is it possible, for example, that the introduction of judicial review might be viewed in one country as revolutionary and in another as inconsequential, depending upon each country's political, historical, institutional, or constitutional baseline?

Finally, even if there were some way for human readers to reliably and consistently rank constitutional changes in order of magnitude or importance, there is no natural dividing line between amendments and replacements. In reality, the difference between an amendment and a replacement is one of degree, not of kind. The amendment–replacement distinction is binary and thus requires us to sort constitutional changes into two categories, but actual constitutional changes fall along a continuous spectrum. Consequently, any bright–line rule for categorizing 'amendments' and 'replacements' is bound to be at least somewhat arbitrary.

In sum, efforts to distinguish between amendments and replacements by evaluating and ranking the substantive importance of various constitutional changes run the risk of yielding an amendment–replacement distinction that is arbitrary, poorly defined, and variable from one person to the next. From a measurement perspective, this is the worst of all worlds. If amendments and replacements are to be distinguished in practice, rather than only in theory, there is much to be said for an approach that does not depend on widely differing subjective evaluations. One possibility is to adopt objective criteria that do not depend on the evaluation of substantive importance, such as measuring the proportion of the text that changes. Another possibility is simply to rely on formal labels.

The formalistic approach

It should by now be evident why the formalistic approach looks attractive compared to the objective approach, especially for purposes of empirical work. Relying on formal labels has important practical and methodological advantages of clarity, ease, and replicability. It is convenient and yields unambiguous classifications: one only needs to look at the label attached to the document by its authors. A formalistic approach also makes it unnecessary to engage in time-intensive and subjective assessments of the substantive magnitude or importance of particular changes.[7] There is even a conceptual argument to be made in favor of the formalistic approach. Insofar as a constitution is a formal legal document, then form inherently matters. If the question of whether a given document counts as a 'constitution' is a matter of form, then surely the question of whether a given document counts as an 'amended' constitution as opposed to a 'replacement' constitution should also be a matter of form.

The drawbacks of the formalistic approach, however, are also serious. Although this approach saves scholars from having to draw arbitrary distinctions, it does so by relying on the potentially arbitrary or idiosyncratic distinctions drawn by the constitutional drafters. Because drafters in different countries have different standards and criteria, the very same change might be labeled an 'amendment' in country A but a 'replacement' in country B. Moreover, the reasons that constitutional drafters have for labeling a constitutional change an 'amendment' rather than a 'replacement' may have little or nothing to do with anything that we are interested in measuring or studying.[8] Above all, the fact that a particular change is formally labeled an 'amendment' rather than a 'replacement' does not necessarily tell us anything about the intrinsic magnitude or significance of the change. Any attempt to compare formally labeled 'amendments' with formally labeled 'replacements' will merely be a comparison of what certain drafters chose to label as 'amendments' with what other drafters chose to label as 'replacements'.

As a result, scholarship that relies on the formal distinction between 'new' and 'amended' constitutions rests on unstable ground. On the one hand, it cannot be assumed that supposedly 'new' constitutions represent more of a departure from the status quo than constitutions that have merely been 'amended'. Some so-called constitutional 'replacements' change very little and might be more accurately described as *overblown amendments*. On the

---

7 Thus, for example, Elkins, Ginsburg, and Melton treat a constitution as continuing to endure if it is merely amended, whereas a constitution that has been replaced is deemed to have been perished. See Elkins et al. (n 4) 55.

8 See *supra* text accompanying note 5 (citing the example of Taiwan).

Table 5.1 Typology of amendments and replacements

	Minor change	*Major change*
Change labeled 'amendment'	True amendment	Stealth replacement
Change labeled 'replacement'	Overblown amendment	True replacement

other hand, a constitution that has merely been 'amended' may in fact represent a greater departure from the status quo than a constitution that has supposedly been 'replaced'. In other words, some so-called constitutional 'amendments' might amount in substance to replacements: we might call these *stealth replacements*. Depending upon whether the formal label is aligned with the actual magnitude of the change, constitutional changes can be divided into the four categories in Table 5.1: true amendments, true replacements, overblown amendments, and stealth replacements.

Two empirical approaches to the measurement of constitutional change

To quantify or not to quantify?

Ideally, it would be possible to distinguish between amendments and replacements in a way that combines the best of both the objective and formalistic approaches. The amendment–replacement distinction should not depend upon potentially arbitrary or misleading formal labels. Nor, however, should it turn on purely subjective impressions of importance that vary freely from one observer to the next. What is needed, instead, is a clear, consistent, and transparent way of measuring the magnitude of constitutional changes, which can then provide the basis for distinguishing amendments from replacements.

The existing empirical literature on constitutions suggests two possible candidates. The first might be called a *coding similarity approach*, while the second is a *semantic similarity approach*. A coding similarity approach relies on coded data, meaning that researchers must evaluate the substance of each constitution, record their evaluations in numerical form, then measure change by comparing the numerical evaluations or 'codes' attached to different constitutions. This type of approach aims to minimize measurement inconsistency and definitional uncertainty by adopting explicit, detailed rules (set forth in the form of a 'codebook') as to how particular words or provisions should be quantified. A semantic similarity approach, by contrast, involves simply measuring the extent to which constitutions are semantically (linguistically) similar.

Once similarity has been quantified using either approach, it is straightforward to distinguish between amendments and replacements by stipulating some threshold or cutpoint above which a change counts as a replacement rather than an amendment. For example, we might say that any change in similarity score of 10% or more ought to count as a replacement, whereas any change below that threshold ought to count as an amendment, regardless of how it is labeled.

Any numerical threshold or cutpoint of this type suffers from the obvious problem of being at least somewhat arbitrary. However, this problem is not unique to quantitative empirical approaches. Any scholar seeking to apply a binary amendment–replacement distinction will also have to engage in arbitrary line-drawing. The real difference is that we may be unable to observe how the line is being drawn, or even if the line is being drawn consistently. The use of an exact and unambiguous numerical threshold does not introduce arbitrariness into the line-drawing exercise; it merely makes the arbitrariness obvious, which is an advantage rather than a disadvantage of the quantitative empirical approach. A bright-line numerical distinction is much more transparent, and much easier to apply consistently across the entire corpus, than an individual expert's subjective evaluation of whether a particular change ought to be described as an 'amendment' or 'replacement' in substantive terms.

The opacity of scholarly judgment may enable us to entertain the belief that human line-drawing is less arbitrary as well as more nuanced and more accurate. But in reality, it may mean simply that we cannot see what combination of arbitrariness, imprecision, and inconsistency underlies the line-drawing exercise. In other words, the relief it brings may be nothing more than the bliss of ignorance.

The coding similarity approach

A version of the coding similarity approach is illustrated by Ginsburg, Elkins, and Melton in their groundbreaking 2009 book, *The Endurance of National Constitutions*.[9] A key finding of the book is that the longevity of constitutions depends in part upon how difficult they are to amend. The amendment–replacement distinction is thus central to their analysis: one cannot study the effect of constitutional amendment on the likelihood of constitutional replacement unless one can distinguish between amended constitutions and replacement constitutions. The authors draw this distinction on the basis of how the documents are formally labeled, but they do not blindly assume that these labels correspond to the actual magnitude of change. Instead, they use their own hand-coded data to confirm that formal 'replacements' actually involve more change than formal 'amendments'.

Using a 'similarity index' that is intended to capture the similarity between constitutions, they muster empirical evidence that the formal 'amendment' and 'replacement' labels affixed by constitutional drafters are in fact correlated with the magnitude of the actual change. Their 'similarity index' is a 'measure of inventory similarity' that captures the extent to which two constitutions 'address the same issues'.[10] The authors note several examples of so-called 'amendments' that are, even by this measure, bigger than so-called 'replacements'. They find, however, that formal 'amendments' are, on average, smaller in substantive magnitude than formal 'replacements'.[11]

The overall approach of using some objective measure of constitutional similarity to test whether the formal labels are misleading is extremely sensible. However, inventory similarity in particular is not a very discriminating measure of constitutional similarity. For example, if two constitutions address the same topic (say, the domestic status of international law) but take diametrically opposite approaches to the topic (for example, one constitution explicitly makes international law superior to ordinary legislation, whereas the other constitution explicitly does the opposite), an inventory-similarity approach treats the two constitutions as identical for purposes of that topic. At the extreme, this approach would treat two constitutions with completely opposite approaches to the same set of topics as indistinguishable.

---

9 Elkins et al. (n 4).
10 Ibid at 24, 56.
11 Ibid at 59.

A more refined approach would be to employ a similarity index that takes into account not only the extent to which two constitutions address the same issues, but also the extent to which they address those issues in the same way. Even this measurement approach, however, would still suffer from another methodological vulnerability common to nearly all of the growing body of scholarship that involves the computer-assisted analysis of constitutional content. In most work of this variety, the computer cannot analyze the text directly. Instead, the text must first be converted or 'coded' into numerical form that is then susceptible to the same range of statistical techniques as any other body of numerical data. Specifically, scholars must devise a coding scheme, or a set of rules for determining what attributes of a document should be converted or 'coded' in numeric form and in what manner. Human readers ('coders') must then go through each document in the corpus and apply the coding scheme to each document.

To give a simplified example, a coding scheme might stipulate that any constitution that renders international law superior to ordinary legislation should be assigned a numeric code of 2, whereas a constitution that renders international law inferior to ordinary legislation should be coded as a 1. A constitution that does not address the status of international law at all might be coded as a 0. Such a coding scheme would require the coder to read each constitution and to decide, in each case, whether the constitution should be coded a 0, 1, or 2.

The use of coded data, although standard practice, is far from a foolproof approach to the study of legal texts. There is, of course, the obvious and well-known problem of 'coding error': the actual application of the coding scheme by the coders may be unreliable or inconsistent. When the object to be studied is something as subtle as a linguistic pattern, the problem is aggravated and might be better described as one of coding impossibility rather than mere coding error: certain aspects of a text are inherently difficult for human coders to detect, much less measure. A related problem is that coding can, especially in difficult or borderline cases, involve an element of subjective judgment that is difficult to eliminate entirely. In other words, a coding-based approach to implementing an 'objective' amendment–replacement distinction may not be entirely objective.

Other problems stem not from the act of coding, but from the coding scheme itself. Coding schemes are prone to oversimplification and imprecision insofar as they aim to quantify complex phenomena (such as the substantive importance of a constitutional revision) that are inherently difficult to quantify.[12] Another problem is that the coding scheme may be incomplete. Data captured pursuant to a coding scheme will, at best, only capture what is in the coding scheme. With coded data, we cannot find what we do not set out to find from the very beginning. Coders cannot and will not code what you do not ask them to code. The only dimensions along which constitutional similarity is measured are those incorporated in the coding scheme. If the developers of the coding scheme have not fully and correctly ascertained at the outset everything that ought to be coded, it will not be coded. The more complex or nuanced the source material that we are attempting to code, the greater the risk of an inaccurate or incomplete coding scheme. And needless to say, constitutions can be very complex and nuanced.

---

12 See, e.g., David S. Law, 'Constitutional Archetypes' (2016) 95 *Texas Law Review* 153, 188–90 (discussing the inherent difficulty of coding constitutional preambles); David S. Law, 'Constitutional Dialects: The Language of Transnational Legal Orders' in Greg Shaffer et al. (eds), *Constitution-Making as Transnational Practice* (Cambridge University Press 2019) 110, 111 (noting the difficulty of coding 'subtle or complex linguistic patterns' that might be indicative of various influences on constitution-making.

The semantic similarity approach

Advances in technology and computational power combined with an explosion in the quantity and variety of digital information that can double as data – also known as the trend toward 'big data' – have made possible a family of alternative approaches to the analysis of legal texts. These approaches go by a variety of names, including natural language processing (NLP), corpus linguistics, or automated content analysis (ACA), but they share two important characteristics. First, they eliminate the need for coding because they treat the text itself as the data. Second, they excel at identifying and quantifying subtle verbal patterns. The same techniques used to determine that a particular play was authored by Christopher Marlowe rather than William Shakespeare, for example, can also be used to analyze legal texts.[13] Some research using these methods has even begun to focus on the language of constitutions.[14]

These methods offer several advantages over both coding-based approaches and unassisted human reading. As compared to coding-based approaches, they liberate us from having to analyze legal texts (such as constitutions) exclusively through the prism of potentially flawed or incomplete coding schemes. Nor is there any possibility of coding error, or flawed execution of the coding scheme. They are also better at capturing and measuring subtle linguistic and wording differences across large numbers of documents.

Suppose, for example, that we are interested in how constitutions differ in their handling of executive immunity. With a coding-based approach, it is relatively easy to generate a measure of *inventory similarity* that indicates which constitutions contain provisions relating to executive immunity, but that is, again, a relatively crude measure of similarity. A more discriminating approach might attempt to capture the substantive bottom-line result in each case, or what we might call *outcome similarity*: namely, does the constitution in question confer or reject executive immunity? However, coding more textured data increases both the effort required and the likelihood of inaccurately or incompletely coded data. Overly complicated or nuanced evaluations are difficult to reduce to numerical form. Consequently, there is a tradeoff between the sensitivity and the accuracy of coded data: the more complex or nuanced the information that one attempts to quantify, the harder it becomes to quantify the information consistently and correctly. For these kinds of reasons, outcome coding of this type is a frequent target of criticism, even among quantitative empirical scholars themselves.[15]

Measurements of *semantic similarity*, by contrast, can differentiate at the linguistic level between different ways of addressing the same topic or even reaching the same outcome. It

13 See Christopher D. Shea, 'Dream Team of Writers: Shakespeare-Marlowe?' (Oct. 25, 2016) *New York Times* at C3 (describing how scholars have used the 'latest tools in text analysis' to investigate the authorship of certain plays by seizing upon telltale verbal patterns such as 'frequent use of certain articles, and certain words commonly occurring in a row, or being close to each other in the text').

14 See Law, 'Constitutional Archetypes' (n 12) (using an unsupervised form of automated content analysis called topic modeling to analyze the content of constitutions and treaties); David S. Law, 'The Global Language of Human Rights: A Computational Linguistic Analysis' (2018) 12 *Law & Ethics of Human Rights* 111 (same); Law, 'Constitutional Dialects' (n 12) (same). See generally Ryan Whalen (ed), *Computational Legal Studies: The Promise and Challenge of Data-Driven Research* (forthcoming 2020); Brandon Stewart, 'Automated Content Analysis' in David S. Law and Malcolm Langford (eds), *Research Methods in Constitutional Law: A Handbook* (forthcoming 2020).

15 See, e.g., William M. Landes and Richard A. Posner, 'Rational Judicial Behavior: A Statistical Study' (2009) 1 *Journal of Legal Analysis* 775 (criticizing the coding of Supreme Court decisions as 'liberal' or 'conservative' in the United States Supreme Court Judicial Database); Anna Harvey, *What Makes a Judgment 'Liberal'? Coding Bias in the United States Supreme Court Judicial Database*, SSRN (June 15, 2008), http://dx.doi.org/10.2139/ssrn.1120970 (March 13, 2020).

is helpful to know whether two constitutions both contain provisions addressing executive immunity (inventory similarity), and more helpful to know whether both constitutions confer or reject executive immunity (outcome similarity). Even better, however, is to know whether two constitutions reach these outcomes using similar or dissimilar language (semantic similarity).

One might object at this point that old-fashioned human reading surely yields the most nuanced evaluations of all – in which case, why bother with computers? To be sure, human readers possess powers of interpretation, judgment, and expertise that computers cannot match (at least for now). Even as compared to old-fashioned reading by a knowledgeable scholar, however, current ACA methods still boast considerable advantages. The most obvious advantage is that they save time: a text corpus that might take a human reader months or even years to absorb can be analyzed by a computer in a matter of seconds. But computers are not merely faster than humans; they are also better at certain things. ACA methods are capable of consistently and reliably detecting and measuring subtle and complex linguistic patterns that elude the naked eye. Given the limits of human cognition, not even the most knowledgeable scholar can hope to identify subtle patterns of verbal similarity and dissimilarity in a systematic and objective fashion across a vast text corpus.

Perhaps the biggest advantage of the semantic similarity approach, however, is that it embodies two measures of constitutional change for the price of one. First, it captures textual change perfectly. Even if we use translated documents, the degree of textual change in the English translation will still correlate with the degree of textual change in the original language. We can also minimize the risk that textual change will reflect a change in translations by consistently using the same translation source over time whenever possible. Furthermore, as explained below in the section entitled 'Data and methods', the ACA technique that we use is designed to measure similarity and change between documents even if they do not use precisely the same terminology to refer to the same concept.[16] Thus, our implementation of the semantic similarity approach is inherently robust against minor differences in wording that result from translation discrepancies.

Second, semantic change is also likely to be a reasonable proxy for substantive change. Of course, there is no good way of evaluating how precisely semantic change tracks substantive change for the simple reason that there is no good way of quantifying substantive change in the first place. The problem with using substantive change as the benchmark is that the benchmark itself cannot be measured. It seems safe to assume that the correlation between semantic change and substantive change will be imperfect. On average, however, replacing 30% of the text of a constitution is probably going to entail more substantive change than replacing 5% of the text.

The basic reason why semantic change will not be a perfect proxy for substantive change is that some words matter more than others. To some degree, constitutional changes will inevitably vary in what we might call their *semantic efficiency*, meaning that some changes pack more substantive change into fewer words. The crucial question is whether we can expect the error to be systematic rather than random. Our expectation was that a semantic measure would be less likely to blow small substantive changes out of proportion than to overlook major substantive changes. On the one hand, it appears to be rare (if not also

---

16 See Law, 'Constitutional Archetypes' (n 12) 229–31 (explaining why topic modeling is inherently robust against minor translation error).

inherently difficult) for a country to change a lot of constitutional language without also changing the substance of the constitution significantly.

On the other hand, it seems more common (if not also easier) for countries to pack fairly meaningful substantive changes into relatively small verbal packages. In other words, we might say that the use of semantic change to capture substantive change seems unlikely to yield false positives (meaning that it is unlikely to exaggerate or overstate the degree of substantive change) and may be more prone instead to false negatives (meaning that it may understate the degree of substantive change).[17] Our admittedly subjective impression of the results is that these expectations are essentially correct: major semantic change appears to be a reliable indicator of major substantive change, but minor semantic change may on occasion be the vehicle for relatively important substantive change.[18]

A precise proxy for substantive change may be unnecessary, however, insofar as the goal is simply to sort changes into two broad categories, 'amendments' and 'replacements'. Crude categories do not demand precise measurement. At the extreme, it is theoretically possible that we might encounter textually major changes that amount in substance to mere amendments or, conversely, textually minor changes that amount in substance to constitutional replacement. In practice, however, neither scenario is likely to be common. It is hard to imagine how a major textual overhaul of a constitution could fail to have a significant substantive impact. Likewise, although textually minor changes can certainly have significant substantive impact, it is difficult to think of actual examples of minor textual changes that could fairly be described as wholesale *replacement* of the constitution.

An empirical analysis of the amendment–replacement distinction

Natural language-processing techniques excel at quantifying semantic similarity between documents and are thus well suited to exploring the difference in magnitude between so-called 'amendments' and 'replacements'. We find that, on average, changes labeled as 'amendments' are indeed of lesser magnitude than changes labeled as 'replacements'. However, it is also clear that the formal labels attached to constitutional changes are misleading in more ways than one. First, most so-called 'replacement' constitutions change relatively little and might more accurately be described as overblown amendments. Second, some so-called 'amendments' involve a high degree of semantic change. In other words, stealth replacements are a real phenomenon, although they are not nearly as common as overblown amendments.

We also find evidence of an empirical relationship between the *frequency* and the *magnitude* of constitutional change. Frequency of change and magnitude of change are inversely correlated: the more time that elapses between changes, the bigger the changes tend to be. Conversely, the more frequently a constitution changes, the smaller the changes tend to be. In other words, constitutional change exhibits a temporal pattern of either incremental tinkering or periodic bursts.

17 In the language of classification theory, we might say that our semantic measure of substantive change is *sensitive*, but not *specific*.
18 See sections entitled 'True amendments versus stealth replacements' and 'True replacements versus overblown amendments' below.

Data and methods

Our text corpus consists of a combination of new and amended constitutions. It includes the full text of virtually every new (or replacement) national constitution since 1791 as well as every version of every constitution amended over the 15-year period from 2003 through 2017, inclusive.[19] The resulting text corpus consists of 1,028 documents, each of which is the full text of a constitution or a version thereof. The corpus includes 304 new constitutions, 413 so-called 'replacement' constitutions and 311 so-called 'amended' constitutions, which allows us to calculate 724 difference scores between successive versions of constitutions.

For certain purposes, it is helpful that the data on new and replacement constitutions extends back further in time than the data on amended constitutions. Formal replacements are much less frequent than formal amendments: from 2003 through 2017, there were a total of 311 cases in which a constitution was formally amended, but only 47 cases in which a constitution was formally replaced. The entire text corpus is used to estimate the latent semantic analysis model described below, but for certain purposes, our analysis is necessarily limited to constitutions from 2003 onward because those are the only years for which we have collected or reconstructed all versions of all constitutions.

To measure the textual similarity between constitutional versions, we use latent semantic analysis, a well-established technique in computer science for performing a type of automated content analysis known as topic modeling.[20] We first perform a fairly minimal and standard set of automated preprocessing steps to prepare the text for analysis, such as stemming and the removal of punctuation and stopwords.[21] The software then transforms the entire corpus of documents into a 'document-term matrix'. In this matrix, each row represents a document (in the present case, a constitution or version thereof), and each column represents a term that appears somewhere in the corpus (e.g., gender, monarchy, vote, etc.). The resulting matrix is very large: the number of rows equals the number of documents (1,028), and the number of columns equals the size of the corpus vocabulary, meaning the number of unique terms that appear anywhere in the entire corpus (in this case, 27,894). The value in each cell of the matrix corresponds to the frequency of a particular term's usage in a particular document.

The software next breaks down the text corpus into semantic patterns known as 'topics'. In this context, 'topic' is a term of art: it refers to a weighted vocabulary of words that tend to co-occur with certain frequency. Each word is weighted according to the frequency of its appearance within the topic.[22] For example, a hypothetical and highly simplified 'topic'

---

19 The new and replacement constitutions dating back to 1791 were collected by the Comparative Constitutions Project and graciously provided with the disclaimer that the collection might not be entirely complete. To the best of our knowledge, the collection appears to be relatively comprehensive and free of systematic omissions. We are grateful to Tom Ginsburg for his cooperation and support. The amended constitutions from 2003 through 2017 were collected (or, where necessary, reconstructed) by the authors and their research assistants.

20 See Scott C. Deerwester et al., 'Indexing by Latent Semantic Analysis' (1990) 41 *Journal of the Association for Information Science and Technology* 391.

21 Stop words are common words that provide little insight into meaning (such as 'the', 'is', 'at', 'of', and so forth). Stemming involves reducing variants of the same word to their common stem. Thus, for example, the words 'constitution' and 'constitutional' are both stemmed to 'constitut'. 'Stemming is helpful from a methodological perspective because it reduces the complexity of the model to be estimated, but it also has the substantive benefit of ensuring that variations of the same word are not misidentified and overcounted as entirely different words'. Law, 'Constitutional Archetypes' (n 12) 198. Words that appear only once in the entire corpus are also discarded. See Law, 'The Global Language of Human Rights' (n 14) 121–22.

22 When weighting the terms, it is standard practice in LSA to use 'term frequency-inverse document frequency' (tf-idf) values rather than the raw frequency with which the terms appear. Tf-idf scores capture the frequency

might consist of the words 'federal', 'limit', and 'power', with the numerical weightings 0.1, 0.3, and 0.5, respectively. These weightings would indicate that 'power' appears more frequently in connection with the topic than either 'federal' or 'limit'. Words like 'power' or 'limit' are common and will appear across multiple topics, but their weighting will vary across to reflect the fact that the word appears more frequently in connection with certain topics than others.

As a practical matter, the 'topics' identified by LSA and other versions of topic modeling tend to correspond to 'topics' in the lay sense of substantive topics (such as federalism, or executive power). However, they may also capture recurring verbal patterns that are more indicative of a particular genre or style of writing, than a 'topic' in the conventional sense. Previous work suggests, in fact, that a considerable proportion of constitutional text consists of language that is associated more with a particular genre or 'dialect' of constitution-writing than with a substantive topic in the conventional sense.[23]

The major model specification choice that LSA requires the user to make is to specify the number of 'topics' into which the text corpus (and each document therein) will be decomposed. Based on both the guidance in the literature for analyzing corpora of this size and our own diagnostic tests, we estimate a model that decomposes the text corpus into 50 topics. As a robustness check, we also implemented 100-topic and 30-topic models to ensure that our results are not being driven by the number of topics chosen. Varying the number of topics in this way had no meaningful impact on our substantive findings.

Like some other forms of topic modeling, LSA breaks the text corpus down into topics by decomposing the document-term matrix into (1) a document-topic matrix, which identifies the mix of topics that makes up each document, and (2) a term-topic matrix, which identifies the weighted mix of terms that make up each topic. Each row in the document-topic matrix corresponds to a particular constitution and contains 50 values, one for each topic. This vector represents a particular constitution's location in 'constitutional topic-space' and can be used to compute its semantic distance from (or similarity to) any other constitution – whether it be an amended version of the same constitution, or a replacement constitution, or the constitution of an entirely different country.

We then calculate each constitution's similarity to every other constitution in the corpus by comparing the mix of 'topics' (or semantic patterns) that the documents discuss.[24] The result is that, for every possible pairing of constitutions, we have a measure of the similarity between the two documents. This numerical measure takes the form of a *similarity score* that captures the extent to which any two documents contain a similar selection and concentration of topics. It theoretically ranges from −1 to 1, where a score of −1 indicates that two constitutions contain a completely opposite selection of topics, whereas +1 indicates that they discuss the same topics in the same proportions. A score of 0 means that two documents are orthogonal, or neither similar nor dissimilar. Generally speaking, the similarity score can be interpreted in much the same manner as a correlation coefficient.

---

with which terms appear within a particular document while also adjusting for the frequency with which those terms appear in other documents. The result is a weighting that reflects not only how frequently a term appears in a particular document, but also how distinctive that term is to that particular document. Robustness checks using both tf–idf and raw counts reveal substantially similar results.

23 See Law, 'Constitutional Dialects' (n 12) 122.

24 Specifically, we measure the similarity between any two documents in the corpus by calculating the cosine similarity between their respective vectors.

A topic-modeling approach to measuring document similarity is obviously more complicated than an approach that simply compares raw vocabulary and word frequency. A major advantage of such methods, however, is that the results tend not to be swayed by minor and random differences in terminology. If two documents use slightly different vocabulary to discuss the same topic, LSA is still likely to identify both discussions as concerning the same topic. This is an especially important advantage if (as in the present case) terminology is prone to minor variations because some of the documents are translations and the same concept may have been translated in different ways. Topic modeling is robust against this kind of variation because the topics themselves are inferred from patterns of word co-occurrence:

> Because a topic consists of a set of words that appear in conjunction with each other, any words that share similar neighboring words in common will tend to be sorted into the same topic. Thus, it makes little difference if the same word is translated in a multitude of ways (splitting error): as long as both the original and the translated word are used in similar verbal contexts, they will be (correctly) sorted into the same topic. Likewise, no harm is done if different concepts are mis-translated into the same word (lumping error), as long as the original words are used in sufficiently similar verbal contexts that they would have been sorted into the same topic anyway.[25]

By contrast, an approach that merely compares the differences in raw vocabulary between documents is more likely to be confounded by slight differences in wording and to erroneously distinguish between two translations of the same substantive material.

A disadvantage of using LSA to measure semantic similarity is that the measure does not lend itself to straightforward or intuitive interpretation. The dimensions or 'topics' detected and measured by LSA are a function of the statistical co-occurrence of terms and their distribution across documents in the corpus, which renders them difficult to interpret in substantive terms. It is not the case, for example, that a similarity score between two documents of 0.8 means that the two documents share a 0.8 proportion (or 80%) of their verbal content in common.

Fortunately, our LSA-based semantic similarity scores are highly correlated with a more intuitive measure of textual similarity – namely, the degree to which different documents share the same raw vocabulary. A 'Jaccard index' simply measures the extent to which two documents use the same vocabulary.[26] The Jaccard index ranges from 0 to 1, where 0 represents a total lack of vocabulary overlap and 1 represents identical vocabularies. Consider for example two constitutional version-pairs, one representing a major semantic change (the replacement of Iraq's constitution of 1925 in 2005), and another representing a minor semantic change (the 2011 amendment of the Irish constitution). As seen in Table 5.3, the LSA model identifies Iraq's constitutional replacement as one of the ten

---

25 Law, 'Constitutional Archetypes' (n 12) 229.
26 For example, if the entire vocabulary of one document consists of 'cat', 'dog', 'ball', and 'house', whereas the entire vocabulary of another document consists of 'cat', 'bird', 'hoop', and 'stick', the Jaccard index would be 0.25. This Jaccard index is calculated by first doing similar text pre-processing as for the LSA model – i.e. stop word removal – then taking the set of words used in each document and calculating the Jaccard index (intersection/union) of those two sets.

biggest semantic shifts in the entire data set, with a similarity score between the two constitutional texts of only 0.03. Consistent with this finding, the Jaccard index is 0.23, meaning that the old and new versions share less than a quarter of their vocabulary in common. On the other hand, the Irish constitutional amendment of 2011 changed very little of the document. In this case, the LSA-based similarity score of 0.99 and the Jaccard index of 0.97 paint the same picture of minimal change.

National versus cross-national differences

At the semantic level, constitutions vary enormously from country to country, but countries rarely make drastic changes to their own constitutions. In other words, constitutions tend to be heterogeneous at the international level but homogeneous at the national level. On the one hand, if we calculate the pairwise distance between randomly selected constitutions from anywhere in the world, at any point in time, they are likely to exhibit very low similarity. The dotted-line histogram in Figure 5.1 depicts the distribution of similarity scores across all pairings of all constitutions in our dataset. The modal (or most common) pairwise similarity score is less than 0.2.

On the other hand, when countries change their own constitutions – whether by 'amendment' or by 'replacement' – the initial and subsequent documents tend to be highly similar to one another. The solid-line histogram in Figure 5.1 depicts the distribution of similarity scores for these 'before' and 'after' documents. In over 70% of these cases, the similarity score exceeds 0.9. In substantive terms, this distribution tells us that it is rare for a country to make drastic changes to a constitution, even when it is purporting to replace the constitution instead of merely amending it.

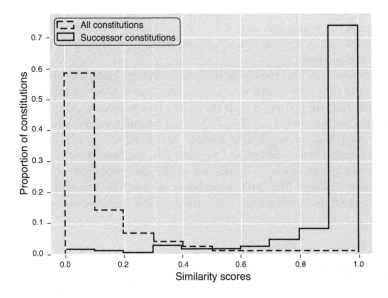

Figure 5.1 Distribution of semantic similarity scores for (a) randomly paired constitutional documents (dotted line) and (b) changed constitutions (whether 'amended' or 'replaced').

Temporal patterns

Analysis of the full text corpus spanning over two centuries reveals an inverse correlation between *how frequently* countries change their constitutions and *how much* they change their constitutions. This inverse correlation manifests itself in the dominance of two general patterns of constitutional change, which we might call the *incremental tinkering* pattern and the *periodic burst* pattern. On average, countries that change their constitutions more frequently tend to make smaller changes each time ('incremental tinkering'). By contrast, when countries wait a longer time between changes, the changes themselves tend to be bigger ('periodic bursts').

These patterns are evident from Figure 5.2, which graphs semantic similarity between constitutional versions against time elapsed between constitutional versions. The downward-sloping trend line means that, as the time between versions increases, the similarity between versions decreases. This inverse correlation between the frequency of change and the magnitude of change is statistically significant.[27] Figure 5.2 depicts the trend for both replacements and amendments together, which introduces the unwelcome complication of combining data with different time frames. However, even if both amendments are wholly excluded from the analysis and only replacements are considered, the inverse correlation still holds and remains

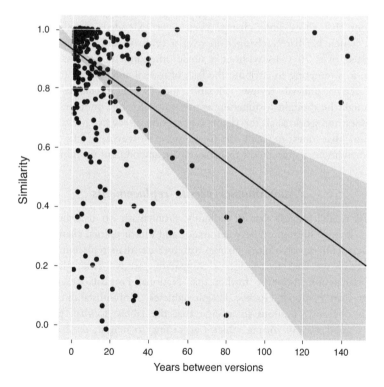

Figure 5.2 The relationship between (a) the time elapsed between constitutional versions and (b) the degree of semantic change between versions.

27 Pearson's r = −0.39, p < 0.0001.

statistically significant.[28] Likewise, even if we limit the analysis to the period from 2003 onward for which we have comprehensive data on both replacements and amendments – thus discarding the vast majority of our data – the correlation is still negative and statistically significant.[29] In short, the incremental tinkering and periodic burst patterns are robust findings no matter how we slice and dice the data.

It is not difficult to see why these patterns might exist. An obvious explanation would be that the need or demand for constitutional change naturally accumulates over time. All other things being equal, the passage of time can be expected to render a static constitution increasingly out of sync with changing needs and circumstances. The resulting need for constitutional adaptation can presumably be satisfied either through smaller, more frequent changes or bigger, less frequent changes. In the absence of regular and incremental change, the pent-up demand for change translates into more drastic changes at longer intervals. The modes of constitutional change thus resemble those of biological evolution: constitutions, like organisms, can evolve through either gradualism (meaning slow and steady adaptation) or punctuated equilibrium (meaning long periods of stasis interrupted by spurts of drastic change). These modes of evolution operate, moreover, as substitutes for each other: reliance on one obviates reliance on the other.

Although these patterns are statistically significant, they are merely overall tendencies rather than universal rules, and there are many exceptions. Prominent and extreme examples of constitutions that show little change even over extended periods include the U.S. Constitution, which has barely changed in over a century, and the Japanese Constitution, which has lasted over 70 years without a single amendment. At least in the case of the United States, it is tempting to attribute the lack of formal amendment to the country's long tradition of active judicial review. Flexible judicial interpretation and constitutional amendment might be thought to function as substitutes for one another. Unfortunately, this explanation does not work at all for Japan, where judicial review is essentially moribund.[30] An explanation that does fit both of these cases, however, is the existence of fairly demanding amendment requirements that may make amendment prohibitively difficult.[31]

'Amendments' versus 'replacements'

Our empirical results suggest that it is highly problematic to use the 'amendment' and 'replacement' labels to distinguish between major and minor textual changes. This is so even though 'replacements' involve more change, on average, than replacements. To understand why, suppose that we wish to conduct a comparative study of the physical endurance of short versus tall people. Suppose further that National Football League athletes are, on average, taller than National Hockey League athletes. Notwithstanding this difference in averages, it is obviously perilous to assume that the labels 'football player' and 'hockey player' offer a good way of sorting athletes according to height, or that we can study tall athletes by focusing on football players and ignoring hockey players. Although the 'hockey

---

28 Pearson's $r = -0.16$, $p < 0.001$.
29 Pearson's $r = -0.15$, $p < 0.01$, based on a truncated data set of $n = 319$ (311 amendments and 8 replacements).
30 David S. Law, 'Why Has Judicial Review Failed in Japan?' (2011) 88 *Washington University Law Review* 1425; David S. Law, 'The Anatomy of a Conservative Court: Judicial Review in Japan' (2009) 87 *Texas Law Review* 1545.
31 Lutz (n 4).

player' and 'football player' labels convey some information about average height, they are obviously not synonymous with 'short' and 'tall'. Hockey players are not 'short' in absolute terms, and indeed, even relative to football players, many hockey players are taller than many football players. Moreover, even when football players are taller, the difference in height will often be insignificant.

Now suppose instead that it is our goal to study major changes that in some objective sense deserve to be called constitutional replacements. Suppose further that changes labeled as 'replacements' are on average greater in magnitude than changes labeled as 'amendments'. The problem is, of course, that even a statistically significant correlation between the formal label and the degree of change is ultimately just a correlation. It does not tell us that there is a substantively meaningful or important difference in magnitude between amendments and replacements. And it certainly does not tell us that the 'replacement' and 'amendment' labels can be used to reliably distinguish between major and minor constitutional changes.

Not surprisingly, statistical analysis confirms that changes labeled as 'replacements' are, on average, greater in semantic magnitude than changes labeled as 'amendments'. Table 5.2 reports the results of an ordinary least squares regression model in which the dependent variable is the semantic similarity score, and the predictor variables are (1) a binary indicator of whether the change in question was labeled an 'amendment' as opposed to a 'replacement', and (2) the number of years elapsed between the initial and subsequent constitutional versions. Both variables are statistically significant predictors of semantic similarity: the 'amendment' label is associated with higher similarity, whereas a longer time between versions is correlated with lower similarity.[32] The regression coefficients indicate that an 'amendment' yields a similarity score that is 0.21 higher on average than a 'replacement', controlling for years between constitutional versions. (Conversely, the same coefficients tell us that magnitude of change is positively correlated with time elapsed between versions, controlling for whether the change is labeled a 'replacement' or an 'amendment'.)

Another way of comparing 'replacements' with 'amendments' is to calculate the likelihood that a randomly chosen 'replacement' involves more semantic change than a randomly chosen 'amendment'. Computer simulation techniques can be used to perform this kind of random comparison a very large number of times – say, one million times – and the result, it turns out, is that the 'amendment' involves more change than the 'replacement' 10% of the time.[33] In other words, we might say that the assumption is wrong 10% of the time. Whether this is an acceptably high level of accuracy – or an appropriate benchmark of accuracy – is partly in the eye of the beholder but also depends heavily on the context. An assumption that holds true 90% of the time might make for a useful rule of thumb in everyday life, but it is more troubling to say that 10% of the data used in a statistical analysis were mislabeled or miscoded.

To truly understand why the 'replacement' and 'amendment' labels cannot be used to distinguish between major and minor changes, however, we must probe further. The fact that the average 'replacement' involves more change than the average 'amendment' tells us nothing about how big the difference tends to be, or whether the 'replacement' and 'amendment'

32 The 'amendment' dummy variable is statistically significant at the $p < 0.001$ level, while the years–elapsed variable is significant at the $p < 0.01$ level.

33 Specifically, we simulated 1,000,000 random draws of 'amendments' and 'replacements' from our text corpus. The similarity score associated with the 'replacement' was higher (meaning less change) than the similarity score associated with the random 'amendment' approximately 10% of the time.

Table 5.2 OLS regression analysis

	Model 1 DV = Similarity	Model 2 DV = Similarity
Amendment	0.25***	0.21***
	(0.021)	(0.026)
Years elapsed		−0.002**
		(0.001)
	adj. r² = 0.29	adj. r² = 0.31

n = 355; ** = p < 0.01; *** = p < 0.001

labels correspond to different magnitudes of change. How big is this difference? Is it big enough to allow for meaningful sorting of major and minor changes? To what extent do the 'replacement' and 'amendment' labels refer to changes of similar magnitude?

First, most changes – regardless of how they are labeled – are low in magnitude. Large changes are likely to be labeled as 'replacements', but that does *not* mean that 'replacements' tend to be large changes. Thus, even if a random 'replacement' involves more change than a random 'amendment', the difference is likely to be minor. Second, there is just as much variation among replacements as there is between amendments and replacements. Many amendments are bigger than many replacements (and, equivalently, many replacements are smaller than many amendments). In other words, 'replacements' and 'amendments' are overlapping rather than distinct categories of constitutional change. Indeed, were we to draw a Venn diagram of 'replacements' and 'amendments', we would see not only that the two categories of change overlap, but that the so-called 'amendments' are a *subset* of the so-called 'replacements'.

To understand the extent to which 'amendments' and 'replacements' are overlapping rather than distinct categories of change, consider the distribution of similarity scores for both types of changes. Figure 5.3 shows the distribution of similarity scores for all formal 'amendments' since 2004, while Figure 5.4 shows the distribution for all formal 'replacements' since 1980.[34] Figure 5.5 overlays the two distributions to facilitate comparison of their overall shape.

Unsurprisingly, the two distributions are different in statistically significant ways.[35] The 'replacement' distribution has a noticeably thicker left tail than the 'amendment' distribution, which means that 'replacements' are more likely than 'amendments' to involve significant change. However, it is also obvious that the two distributions overlap substantially and broadly resemble each other in shape. Both distributions are heavily skewed toward the right, with the amendment distribution being more lopsided than the replacement distribution. In substantive terms, the rightward skew of both distributions means that most 'replacements' as well as most 'amendments' involve little semantic change.

---

34 The distribution of 'amendment' similarity scores in Figure 5.3 only extends back to constitutions amended after 2003 because that is the earliest year for which we have comprehensive data on amendments. Figure 5.4 and Figure 5.5 report the distribution of 'replacement' similarity scores over an expanded timeframe (since 1980) because the relatively low number of post-2003 replacements makes for a noisier histogram. However, expanding or contracting the timeframe in this way makes little difference to the shape of the distribution.

35 The difference between the two distributions is statistically significant, with a Komogorov-Smirnov test statistic of 0.48 (p < 0.0001) and a difference in means of T = 7.6 (p < 0.0001).

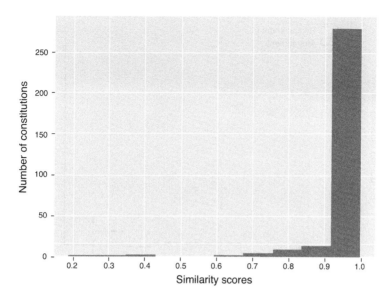

Figure 5.3 Distribution of similarity scores for 'amended' constitutions (2004 onward).

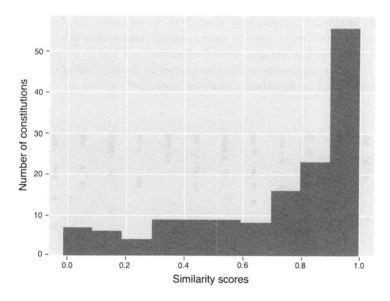

Figure 5.4 Distribution of similarity scores for 'replacement' constitutions (1980 onward).

On the relatively rare occasions that major semantic shifts do occur, they are more likely to be labeled 'replacements' than 'amendments'. Nevertheless, major changes do sometimes take the form of 'amendments'. In other words, what we have dubbed *stealth replacements* – major constitutional shifts that are labeled as amendments – are a rare but real phenomenon.

The failure of the 'amendment' and 'replacement' labels to track any distinction between major and minor change can be seen in Figure 5.6, which plots the similarity scores for all

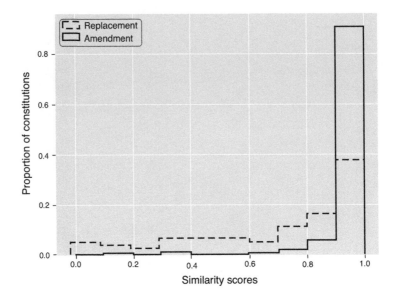

Figure 5.5 Distribution of similarity scores for 'amendments' (solid line) and 'replacements' (dotted line).

constitutional versions on a yearly basis since 2004. Constitutions that have been formally 'amended' are represented in the graph by squares, whereas constitutions that have been formally 'replaced' are represented by triangles. Both the 'amendments' and the 'replacements' exhibit high variability but are disproportionately clustered toward the high end of the similarity scale. The 'amendments' and 'replacements' cannot be partitioned off and are instead thoroughly

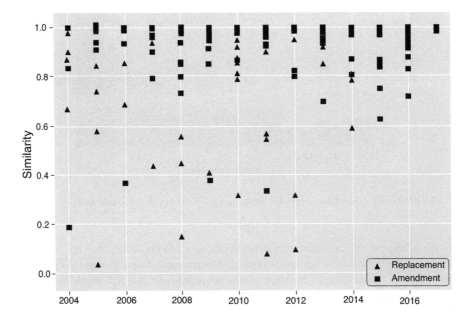

Figure 5.6 The magnitude of replacements and amendments since 2004.

intermingled. Any threshold (or horizontal line) that one might choose for distinguishing between major and minor changes is bound to group together substantial numbers of 'amendments' and 'replacements'.

In sum, the 'amendment' and 'replacement' labels do not provide an accurate or reliable way of distinguishing between minor and major changes. First, both 'amendments' and 'replacements' usually make changes that are relatively minor in semantic terms. Second, both 'amendments' and 'replacements' exhibit wide variability. On those occasions when major semantic shifts do occur, the change can take the form of either an amendment or a replacement. The most extreme semantic shifts are more likely to take the form of replacements, but major shifts do often take the form of amendments.

Insofar as scholars wish to study constitutional changes that are major or deserve to be called replacements, a data set that consists exclusively of formal 'replacements' and excludes all formal 'amendments' will be both underinclusive and overinclusive. It will be underinclusive, in the sense that it will fail to capture some major changes. But it will also be highly overinclusive, in the sense that it will consist primarily of minor changes that are similar in magnitude to the excluded 'amendments'. To analyze formal 'replacements' is not to focus on major changes or substantive replacements, but rather to analyze a relatively small number of major changes combined with a large and nonrandom sample of minor changes.

True amendments versus stealth replacements

The results of the LSA model highlight the enormous variation in semantic magnitude among constitutional changes labeled as 'amendments'. They also provide an objective and empirical basis for identifying the most extreme cases of mislabeling, in which the label attached to a change understates or overstates the actual magnitude of the change. At one end of the spectrum are what we might call 'true amendments', which change relatively little and are thus accurately labeled as 'amendments'. At the opposite end are the 'stealth replacements', which involve major change notwithstanding the fact that they are labeled as 'replacements'.

The most extreme examples in both directions are listed below in Tables 5.3 and 5.4.[36] Table 5.3 lists the 'amendments' in our text corpus that involved the least semantic change: these are all clear examples of 'true amendments'. An example would be the Indian constitutional amendment of 2015 that formalized a land boundary agreement with Bangladesh. Table 5.4 lists the 'amendments' that involved the most semantic change. Based on the results of the LSA model, these are the clearest examples of what we have called 'stealth replacements'. By any measure, these so-called 'amendments' involve a high degree of change: the first six listed in this table rank among the top 15% of all changes in terms of semantic magnitude.[37]

The LSA model's identification of these amendments as involving highly substantial changes is borne out in practice. For instance, the United Arab Emirate's constitutional amendments of 2009 made a variety of substantive changes to rights and powers that are reflected in the relatively major semantic change between documents. Among other things,

---

36 Unlike the general findings in the preceding sections about the relative magnitude of amendments and replacements, the document-specific findings reported in these tables should be taken with a grain of salt because they depend on the comprehensiveness of the text corpus, which cannot easily be guaranteed. See *supra* note 19 (discussing the collection and scope of the text corpus). At the very least, however, these lists offer a representative sampling of the most and least consequential constitutional 'amendments' in recent years.

37 The 15th percentile similarity score is 0.76. The top 15% of all changes therefore refers to those changes resulting in a similarity score of less than 0.76.

Table 5.3 True amendments: constitutional amendments that involved the least semantic change (since 2003)

Country	Old version	New version	Semantic similarity
Chile	2009	2011	1
India	2014	2015	1
Papua New Guinea	2012	2013	1
Malaysia	2007	2010	1
Papua New Guinea	2010	2011	1
Turkey	2005	2006	1
Malawi	2010	2012	1
Kosovo	2012	2013	1
Italy	2003	2007	1
Malawi	2012	2017	1

Table 5.4 Stealth replacements: constitutional amendments that involved the most semantic change

Country	Old version	New version	Semantic similarity
United Arab Emirates	2004	2009	0.375913
Costa Rica	2003	2015	0.62653
Hungary	2011	2013	0.698122
Mexico	2015	2016	0.718864
Brazil	2007	2008	0.733104
Burkina Faso	2013	2015	0.749007
Nicaragua	2005	2007	0.792416
North Korea	2009	2012	0.796579
Burkina Faso	2009	2012	0.796996
Senegal	2007	2008	0.80037

these amendments redefined the office and role of the deputy prime minister, changed legislative term limits, and altered the timing and duration of legislative sessions. Similarly, the changes to Hungary's constitution in 2013 were formally billed as amendments but in reality made sweeping changes to the country's constitutional order by (inter alia) undermining the constitutional court, reducing media freedom, and curtailing civil liberties. Regardless of how they were labeled, these changes amounted to a wholesale transformation of the constitutional order.[38] Burkina Faso's 2012 amendments, which modified no fewer than 62 of the constitution's 173 articles, involved such major reforms as the creation of an upper legislative chamber and a shift toward semi-presidentialism.[39]

---

38 See Yaniv Roznai, 'Constitutional Transformation' in David S. Law (ed), *Constitutionalism in Context* (forthcoming 2020) (discussing the fourth and fifth amendments to Hungary's Fundamental Law of 2011).

39 Révision de la Loi Fondamentale Burkinabé: Le quitus du Conseil constitutionnel, Lefaso.net, July 10, 2012, http://lefaso.net/spip.php?article49048 (accessed March 13, 2020).

The geographical diversity of the countries listed in Table 5.4 illustrates that 'stealth replacements' are not specific to any particular region but are instead a worldwide phenomenon. The nine countries on this list hail from almost every continent: the Middle East, South America, Europe, North America, Africa, and East Asia are all represented.

True replacements versus overblown amendments

Just like constitutional amendments, constitutional replacements run the gamut: some truly amount to a major overhaul or fresh start, while others change very little. Table 5.5 lists the constitutional 'replacements' in the text corpus that involved the most semantic change and thus live up to their billing in an objective sense. Unsurprisingly, a number of the most momentous replacements from a semantic perspective have occurred in the context of war, military occupation, regime change, or even replacement of the state itself. For example, Iraq's 2005 constitution is a high-profile case of constitution-making under conditions of post-conflict occupation,[40] while Libya's 2011 constitution was adopted following the overthrow of longtime dictator Muammar Qaddafi. Yemen's 'replacement' constitution of 1991 was, in fact, the constitution of a successor state: that was the year in which the Yemen Arab Republic (North Yemen) merged with the People's Democratic Republic of Yemen (South Yemen) to form the Yemen of today.

The majority of so-called constitutional 'replacements', however, involve relatively little change and are thus more akin to amendments from a semantic perspective. Since

Table 5.5 True replacements: constitutional replacements that involved the most semantic change

Country	Old version	New version	Semantic similarity
Ukraine	1978	1996	−0.0135
Russia	1977	1993	0.014336
Iraq	1925	2005	0.033535
Laos	1947	1991	0.040669
Moldova	1978	1994	0.063883
Libya	1951	2011	0.074537
Ethiopia	1955	1987	0.083652
Somalia	1979	2012	0.097655
Yemen Arab Republic	1970	1991	0.120255
Cambodia	1989	1993	0.129182

40 Zachary Elkins et al., 'Baghdad, Tokyo, Kabul …: Constitution Making in Occupied States' (2008) 49 *William & Mary Law Review* 1139.

Table 5.6 Overblown amendments: constitutional replacements that involved the least semantic change (since 1980)

Country	Old version		New version	Semantic similarity
Dominican Republic	1994		2002	0.99998
Lithuania	1938		1992	0.999587
Sierra Leone	1978		1991	0.999452
Azerbaijan	1991		1995	0.999357
Nigeria	1989		1999	0.996718
Burundi	2004		2005	0.991906
China	1978		1982	0.990262
Switzerland	1874		1999	0.990237
Azerbaijan	1995		2009	0.988938
Nigeria	1978		1989	0.988605

1980, a total of 33 so-called 'replacements' have involved changes of below-average semantic magnitude.[41] Table 5.6 lists the 'replacements' that involved the least semantic change. From a semantic perspective, these so-called 'replacements' can fairly be described as 'overblown amendments'. Indeed, some might not even amount to 'amendments' in any meaningful sense. Burundi's 'replacement' of its interim constitution in 2005 is a case in point: in that case, a draft of the final constitution doubled as the interim constitution until a referendum could be held.[42]

In other cases, one might argue that the 'replacements' were more consequential from a substantive perspective than the semantic similarity scores might suggest. For example, China's 1982 constitution is objectively one of the least noteworthy 'replacements' in our text corpus, at least from a semantic perspective. Whether the 1982 Chinese constitution amounts merely to an 'overblown amendment' from a substantive perspective, however, is open to debate. On the one hand, the 1982 constitution did not represent a radical break from its 1978 predecessor but instead continued and extended the 1978 constitution's turn away from the excesses of the Cultural Revolution era. On the other hand, the 1982 constitution made more than cosmetic changes and is widely viewed as a symbol of China's reform era.[43] Semantic change is bound to be an imperfect proxy for substantive change, but the Chinese example is at least consistent with our initial expectation that a semantic measure of constitutional change is more prone to understate than overstate the degree of substantive change. Examples of the opposite phenomenon – namely, constitutions that undergo a high degree of semantic change but a low degree of substantive change – are much harder to identify or imagine.

41 In this context, 'below average' means that the level of semantic similarity between the initial and 'replacement constitutions' is above the median similarity level for all constitutional changes in the text corpus. The post-1980 subset of the data includes 147 formal 'replacements' and 311 formal 'amendments'. Use of the median rather than the mean as the threshold is preferable because the skewed nature of the data deflates the mean: most similarity scores are quite high, with a median of 0.96 but a mean of only 0.84.

42 Burundi: New interim constitution ushers optimism, Nov. 3, 2004, https://reliefweb.int/report/burundi/burundi-new-interim-constitution-ushers-optimism (accessed March 13, 2020).

43 Qianfan Zhang, *The Constitution of China: A Contextual Analysis* (Hart Publishing 2012) 47–52.

Conclusion

The study of constitutional change poses a serious challenge for empirical scholars because constitutional change is inherently difficult to quantify. This is so for a variety of reasons. It is multifaceted and can take different forms; scholars can and do disagree over the magnitude of specific changes; and so on. But progress can and should be made. A natural first step is to carve out a relatively concrete and narrow yet also undeniably central aspect of constitutional change for analysis – namely, formal constitutional revision. Fortunately, natural language-processing techniques drawn from computer and information science lend themselves to this task: they provide a rapid, reliable, and objective means of measuring the extent to which texts differ semantically from each other, and thus of gauging the semantic magnitude of constitutional changes.

Application of these techniques to a large text corpus of constitutional texts yields empirical findings that ought to be of interest to constitutional scholars generally but also have important methodological implications for the empirical study of constitutional change in particular. The analysis confirms that the 'amendment' and 'replacement' labels are correlated with the magnitude of semantic change. However, our results also show that these labels cannot be used to distinguish reliably between major revisions and minor changes. First, there exist a significant number of what might be called overblown amendments (so-called 'replacements' that change relatively little) and stealth replacements (so-called 'amendments' that actually involve major change). Second, most changes – regardless of how they are labeled – tend to be minor in degree. Consequently, overblown amendments – meaning small changes that have been mislabeled as 'replacements' – are especially common.

From a methodological perspective, these findings mean that it is no easy task for scholars interested in studying only major (or minor) constitutional changes to correctly identify the population of interest. On the one hand, scholars cannot study 'new' constitutions or major changes by focusing on formal 'replacements' because the population of 'replacements' is, in fact, heavily skewed toward minor changes. On the other hand, the population of formal 'amendments' is laced with some major changes that objectively deserve to be called replacements. Automated content analysis techniques of the type used in this chapter potentially offer a more accurate and objective (as well as faster) means of sorting constitutional changes on the basis of magnitude than either reliance on formal labels or manually coded data.

Our automated content analysis also yields empirical insight into the relationship between the magnitude of change and the passage of time. On average, when countries change their constitutions more frequently, the changes themselves tend to be smaller. Conversely, when more time elapses between changes, the changes themselves tend to be larger. These findings support the view that the need for constitutional change builds over time and can be accommodated via incremental tinkering, periodic bursts of activity, or some intermediate pattern of change. To borrow the language of biological evolution, constitutional evolution runs the gamut from gradualism (meaning slow and steady adaptation) to punctuated equilibrium (meaning long periods of stasis interrupted by spurts of drastic change).

These findings merely begin to demonstrate how natural language-processing techniques can advance the empirical study of constitutional change. One promising avenue for further research concerns the relationship between the formal legal rules governing constitutional change and the actual magnitude of change. For instance, some countries have tiered amendment procedures, wherein the stringency of the procedural framework for changing the constitution is supposed to vary according to the substance or magnitude of the change.[44] The existence of tiered amendment procedures raises the empirical question of whether the more stringent or demanding tiers are, in fact, used to adopt bigger changes, or if major changes are instead smuggled through less demanding procedures.

The relationship between linguistic change and substantive change is also ripe for exploration. For example, it might be the case that particular words or phrases are associated with greater or lesser degrees of substantive change. Identification of such highly predictive terms would enhance our ability to measure substantive change using ACA techniques.

Best of all, natural language-processing techniques are highly complementary to more traditional qualitative or hermeneutic approaches in a variety of ways. First, they can enrich the scholarly agenda by unearthing and highlighting research questions that are well suited to qualitative research methods. For example, the identification of certain words or phrases that are telltale indicators of major semantic change raises the question of whether and why certain ideas and concepts might be associated with constitutional transformation – a question that can fruitfully be explored via in-depth analysis of specific episodes and countries.

Second, ACA is a boon for traditional scholarship when it comes to the crucial task of case selection. Whereas quantitative or 'large-n' research struggles sometimes with the quantification of complex phenomena, the type of small-n qualitative research traditionally favored by comparative legal scholars has its own Achilles heel – namely, case selection. The fact that such research focuses in depth on a very small number of cases makes it imperative to select the most relevant or significant cases for analysis.[45] Semantic analysis can assist qualitative scholars by placing a bull's-eye over cases that are especially suitable or deserving of study.

Third, natural language processing techniques can be applied in conjunction with traditional legal research methods to gain traction on the thorniest of research questions. A well-known advantage of mixed-methods research is the potential for validation: when different methods yield the same answers to the same questions, each method has the effect of validating the other and justifiably bolstering our confidence in the results.[46] Perhaps even more valuable, however, are the learning opportunities that arise when the results obtained via different methods do *not* coincide. Consider, for example, those cases in which semantic measures of constitutional change diverge from subjective impressions or even the most careful of qualitative assessment. Divergence of this type signals that certain cases demand further investigation, and it can prompt reflection and improvement upon the methods themselves. But such divergence is also a vehicle for conceptual refinement and theory-building: it forces us to scrutinize and elaborate our understanding of what makes a particular change major or minor, important or unimportant.

A phenomenon as complex and diverse as constitutional change presents us with a vast quantity of heterogeneous data that does not lend itself to one single research method, to the exclusion of all others. The best approach is likely to be a combination of approaches – old and new, qualitative and quantitative, time-tested and cutting-edge alike.

---

44 Dixon and Landau (n 2) 444–50.

45 Ran Hirschl, 'The Question of Case Selection in Comparative Constitutional Law' (2005) 53 *American Journal of Comparative Law* 125, 133.

46 Malcolm Langford, 'Methodological Pluralism' in David S. Law and Malcolm Langford (eds), *Research Methods in Constitutional Law: A Handbook* (forthcoming 2020).

6

VARIETIES OF LIBERAL CONSTITUTIONALISM

Mark Tushnet

Introduction

Discussing and rejecting the claim that recent developments in central and eastern Europe show that some nations in that region have a distinctive form of constitutionalism, Matej Avbelj argues that '[p]rivileging the already dominant religion; closing down channels of communication; clamping down on NGOs and sanctioning non-compliant universities; undermining judicial independence', and other actions are 'the denial' of constitutionalism.[1] I want to take this as suggesting a *maximalist* definition of liberal constitutionalism. Under such a definition, liberal constitutionalism requires compliance with a rather long list of specifically defined criteria, typically including compliance with a list of fundamental rights.

Unsurprisingly, there are *minimalist* definitions of liberal constitutionalism as well. Under a minimalist definition, liberal constitutionalism requires only that the government be constrained by a principle of non-arbitrariness: Every action it takes must be justifiable (or perhaps actually justified) by reasons stated in general terms. The requirement of generality is a weak though not toothless one. Minimalist definitions can also be described as requiring compliance with the rule of law but nothing more.

When we look at political orders that most people would describe as liberal constitutional ones, though, we rarely observe systems that satisfy *any* maximalist definition of liberal constitutionalism. Nor do we observe systems that we unhesitatingly describe as liberal constitutionalist but whose only real characteristic is non-arbitrariness.[2]

This suggests that there might be some value in developing an analysis of *varieties* of liberal constitutionalism, filling in the space between maximalist and minimalist ones. Doing so might provide more than conceptual clarity. Consider a common phenomenon, hinted at

---

1 Matej Avbelj, 'There Is No Such Thing as a Particular "Center and Eastern European Constitutionalism"', Verf-Blog, 2018/5/18, https://verfassungsblog.de/there-is-no-such-thing-as-a-particular-center-and-eastern-euro pean-constitutionalism/.

2 For discussions of some systems of that sort, see the instructively titled Tom Ginsburg and Alberto Simpser (eds), *Constitutions in Authoritarian Regimes* (Cambridge University Press 2014). For a discussion of the possibility of illiberal constitutionalism, see Mark Tushnet, 'The Possibility of Illiberal Constitutionalism' (2017) 69 *Florida Law Review* 1367–84.

in Abvelj's statement, whereby a regime that we comfortably describe as liberal constitutionalist modifies a large number of important rights-related matters. As Abvelj's comment suggests, we might want to say that the regime is no longer a liberal constitutional one. But, suppose that the regime modifies only one or two of those rights: After having adopted a regulation of hate speech, it repeals the regulation; it moves from a system of appointing judges to the highest court in which judges alone choose their successors to using a standard judicial nominating commission; it imposes regulations for the accreditation of universities to ensure that fly-by-night operators do not defraud its citizens. Having a vocabulary that accommodates varieties of liberal constitutionalism would allow us to discuss and criticize such changes without having to insist that the changes have pushed the regime out of the domain of liberal constitutionalism altogether.

This chapter attempts to develop such a vocabulary.[3] As just observed, that vocabulary might help us understand and analyze some kinds of constitutional change. Such a vocabulary might well be essential in understanding what constitutional changes amount to 'abuses' of liberal constitutionalism rather than reforms or alterations within it.[4] Here the vocabulary might assist in external evaluations of constitutional systems and changes in them.

Similarly, the vocabulary might be helpful in understanding some aspects of the 'basic structure' doctrine according to which constitutional amendments that alter the basic structure of a nation's constitution might be unconstitutional. Consider again the shift from a system of judicial appointments controlled by the courts to one with a standard judicial nominating commission. Does the shift compromise judicial independence as part of a basic structure? In some circumstances it would not, but in others it might. The vocabulary might be helpful in prising out the conditions under which the change might be unconstitutional. Here the vocabulary might be helpful for analysis of constitutional doctrine by directing attention to the ways in which particular changes fit into an overall or aggregated notion of constitutionalism.[5]

In addition to diachronic uses, the vocabulary can have synchronic value, allowing us to treat existing liberal constitutional orders as variations on a theme. For example, some nations have laws banning hate speech, and most observers treat these nations as liberal constitutionalist (subject of course to satisfaction of other requirements of liberal constitutionalism), whereas other nations lack such laws and even – as in the United States – treat many of them as unconstitutional, and yet many observers are willing to describe them as liberal constitutionalist nonetheless. This chapter is an initial effort to identify some ideas that can help us understand both change over time within a liberal constitutional regime and differences among liberal constitutional regimes.

A final preliminary: Liberal constitutionalism is a normative enterprise. One might see it as a subcategory – probably today the largest subcategory – within a broader descriptive concept, 'constitutionalism'. That broader category would also encompass forms of constitutionalism that simply lay out the powers of government and its component institutions – constitutionalism as a power map, as some have put it, rather than as a set of institutions that limit the exercise of government power.

---

3 For a similar exercise, see David Collier and Steven Levitsky, 'Democracy with Adjectives: Conceptual innovation in Comparative Research' (1997) 49 *World Politics* 430–51.

4 For the work that initiated the concept of abusive constitutionalism, see David Landau, 'Abusive Constitutionalism' (2013) 47 *University of California – Davis Law Review* 189–260.

5 As noted below, analysts must pay attention to local circumstances when using the vocabulary in this way.

Here are the components on which my discussion will focus.[13] First, public policy is made either through representatives elected for reasonably short terms, with the six-year terms for United States senators at or beyond the outer limit, or through direct public participation in referenda and initiatives. Second, all citizens are civically equal. Formal exclusions rest on narrow definitions of incapacity designed primarily to ensure that exclusion of very young people from the franchise does not make the system non-liberal, and informal exclusions based upon material circumstances are a matter of concern and of public policy aimed at reducing such exclusions.

Third, the right of free expression, including the rights of assembly and association, is quite robust.[14] The right covers not merely speech about public policy but expression on matters that help form public attitudes about such policy (including fiction and the arts).[15] Acknowledging that expression can cause harm, the system authorizes some restrictions on expression, but those restrictions must be justified by compelling reasons. In general, free expression requires a tight causal connection between speech and the harm that it is said to cause, and requires that, again in general, liability for harm be placed on the person who directly imposes the harm rather than on speakers who persuade that person to act. The shorthand here is that the U.S. free expression law as developed by the late twentieth century provides the best model for a maximalist definition.[16]

Notably, most maximalist definitions are relatively insensitive to many institutional problems with which many modern constitutional systems are concerned. They are indifferent to the choice between parliamentary, semi-presidential, and full separation-of-powers systems, for example, and to the choice between a fully centralized government and a federal system, and within federal systems to the precise design of federalism.[17] Maximalism's only structural requirement is that there be a system of independent courts with some substantial power to ensure that primary and secondary legislation conform to the constitution's rights-based components. A truly maximalist definition would require that these courts have (and exercise) the power to set aside in general, and disapply in individual cases, primary legislation that the courts conclude is inconsistent with the constitution.

That final requirement provides a useful transition to this chapter's next section. Including that requirement in the maximalist definition implies that neither the United Kingdom nor New Zealand are liberal constitutionalist regimes. It suggests as well that Canada is within the definition only because the Canadian parliament's power to make primary legislation effective notwithstanding its inconsistency with judicial interpretations of the constitution has been rendered empty by Canadian constitutional practice. And yet there seems something askew in saying that these three nations are not liberal constitutionalist regimes. The next section explores

---

13 Other authors might add other components or refine mine. I believe that nothing important in the subsequent analysis turns on the precise definition of maximalism.

14 The scoring system used by Freedom House to develop its reports on 'Freedom in the World' illustrates a maximalist approach. According to the scoring system, that the media is not 'excessively partisan' counts in favor of freedom, and the 'improper editorial control' of private media by their owners counts against freedom.

15 Again, the Freedom House scoring system asks, 'Are works of literature, art, music, or other forms of cultural expression censored or banned for political purposes?'

16 I include the temporal qualification to exclude from the maximalist definition relatively recent developments in the U.S. law of free expression that quite controversially expand its scope beyond the rather broad scope achieved by the end of the twentieth century.

17 See, e.g., Aziz Huq and Tom Ginsburg, 'How to Lose a Constitutional Democracy' (2018) 65 *UCLA Law Review* 78–169, 91 (liberal democracy 'can be accomplished through centralized or federalized governance, parliamentary or executive-led administrations').

the value of distinguishing among minimalist, modest, and maximalist definitions by examining why one might want to use a maximalist definition even with its implications for the categorization of the United Kingdom, New Zealand, and Canada.

The value of distinguishing varieties of liberal constitutionalism

No real-world constitutional regime satisfies what a maximalist account requires. They all fall short on one or more components in the account. And, perhaps more important, there are often alternative reasonable specifications of individual components, each of which might plausibly be defended as sufficiently robust. The most obvious example is hate speech regulation: On one account of what a robust system of free expression contains (in a society committed to equality, another component of the maximalist account), regulation of hate speech is impermissible, whereas on other (equally robust) accounts regulation of hate speech in such societies is permissible or even required. Is the United States, which generally bans hate speech regulation, not a constitutionalist system? Are most other nations in the global North, which allow such regulation, not constitutionalist?

Another example: What test does the system of free expression require to justify the imposition of liability for making statements that increase the risk that illegal acts will occur? We can agree that the test must require a reasonably close causal connection between the speech and the illegal action, but must the system require that the illegal action be 'imminent', as in U.S. constitutional law today, or is it sufficient that the danger be reasonably clear and present, as U.S. law was some generations ago?

And a third example: Some systems of free expression allow regulation only of expression that either causes social harm narrowly defined as law-breaking or violates some other person's constitutional rights, while other systems allow regulation in the service of public order more broadly defined or of vindication of private non-constitutional rights. Both versions – and of course variants within each – are defensible specifications of the general principle of free expression.

The availability of reasonable alternative specifications means that the definition of constitutionalism is parasitic upon choices among controversial accounts of liberalism's requirements. We can, of course, engage in reasoned discussion of which is the best account of liberalism with respect to various elements such as free expression and equality. I doubt that we gain much by escalating those discussions into the domain of disagreements about what constitutionalism requires.[18]

In light of the inevitability of shortfalls and the availability of reasonable alternative specifications, what do we gain by defining constitutionalism in maximalist terms? A simple and obvious answer is that such a definition sets out an ideal, departures from which can provide the basis for criticism or a standard for determining when there is a shortfall. Maximalist definitions conduce to what Kim Lane Scheppele calls 'checklist' constitutionalism.[19] The definitions provide a checklist of matters that liberal constitutionalism is said to require. Identifying

---

18 Similarly, I doubt the value of discussing in detail which of the maximalist definitions of liberal constitutional-ism is (generally) better; which is better will depend upon the particular purposes of the inquiry, and those purposes will ordinarily be served by focusing on which definition of some component of the maximalist defin-itions is better.

19 Kim Lane Scheppele, 'The Rule of Law and the Frankenstate: Why Governance Checklists Do Not Work' (2013) 26 *Governance* 559–62.

shortfalls with respect to one or more items can serve a useful reform function, suggesting to political actors that they would do well to revise their systems 'upward', that is, in the direction of the maximal requirement for each item.

Yet, we might wonder why an ideal of *constitutionalism* is needed, rather than an ideal with respect to each of its components. That is, suppose we observe some departure from the ideal version of free expression. That provides a basis for criticizing the system with respect to free expression. But, it is not obvious that it provides a basis for criticizing the system on the ground that it falls short of an ideal of constitutionalism. Suppose, for example, that system A fully satisfies the maximal definition of constitutionalism with respect to equality, but falls short with respect to free expression, and that system B exhibits the departures in reverse: falling short on equality but fully satisfying free expression. Criticisms based on shortfalls on each dimension make sense; criticism that both systems are defective from the point of view of constitutionalism seems to me more questionable.

Another problem with maximalist definitions arises in connection with systems that fall short, to a modest degree, with respect to many components: some exclusions from the franchise that are not justifiable according to maximalism's requirements; a requirement that speech that has a strong tendency to cause illegal action rather than a requirement of imminence or 'presentness'; and the like. Because each shortfall is modest, it seems to me wrong to say that the systems are not even constitutionalist. A richer vocabulary seems desirable.

One possibility is simple: Make 'constitutionalism' itself a dimensional idea. We could have strongly constitutionalist systems, modestly constitutionalist ones, and weak constitutionalist ones. We would place systems in the appropriate categories by making a judgment about where on each component of constitutionalism the system lies (strong on the free expression dimension, weaker on the equality dimension, and the like), assigning weights to the components (free expression getting more weight than equality, or the reverse), and then aggregating those judgments. The important point here is that the terms 'strong', 'modest', and 'weak', are descriptive, not normative. That is, weak constitutionalist systems are not inferior, qua constitutional systems, to stronger ones because each system's version of each component instantiates a reasonable specification of the component's content (again, free expression, equality, and the like).[20]

With these ideas in hand, I return to Avbelj's list of departures from maximalist constitutionalism: '[p]rivileging the already dominant religion; closing down channels of communication; clamping down on NGOs and sanctioning non-compliant universities; [and] undermining judicial independence'.[21] Whether these departures remove the system from the domain of liberal constitutionalism or simply create a modestly or weakly constitutionalist system depends – at this point in the analysis – almost entirely upon the precise content of the departures.

Most obviously, does 'undermining judicial independence' consist of creating a system for evaluating judicial performance and competence similar to those used in unquestionably

---

20 One might go on to provide an account of why one system is weak, another modest, and the like. Such an account might invoke aspects of the nation's history (weak constitutional review in nations with a Commonwealth background, strong constitutional review in other nations), or its culture (different accommodations between equality and freedom of religion depending upon the relative role of majority and minority religions in shaping the nation's self-understanding).

21 Avbelj (n 1).

liberal systems, shifting from a judicial nomination and appointment process strongly dominated by judges to one in which political actors have a larger role (neither of which necessarily removes the system of the domain of liberal constitutionalism), or does the undermining take the form of direct and uncontrolled political appointment and removal of judges?

Similarly, we would have to know the grounds for 'closing down channels of communication', and the mechanisms for doing so. In some settings, withdrawing government subsidies for publications would enhance the system of free expression whereas in others it would damage the system. In some (highly fraught) settings, closing down a newspaper that publishes reasoned arguments that are likely to exacerbate communal tensions might be consistent with liberal premises, whereas in others we might require a showing that the publications' content was presented in an incendiary way.

My interim conclusion is that we should have a language of constitutionalism capable of treating all systems that incorporate reasonable specifications of each component of liberal constitutionalism as liberal constitutional systems *tout court*. But, of course, there is more to be said.

How to use the idea of varieties of constitutionalism: abusive constitutionalism

Suppose that each item on Abvelj's list as actually implemented could be, in appropriate circumstances, a reasonable specification of the components of liberal constitutionalism. Still, one might worry that the checklist approach makes it difficult to identify what we might call constitutional systems at risk. This concern has been set out by Scheppele as well. Her argument is best captured by beginning with the observation that sometimes we can rank alternatives along a single dimension, as the terminology of shortfalls suggests. The earlier examples of causal connection and public-order restrictions on free expression are of that sort: We can describe one causal connection ('imminence', for example) as tighter or more stringent than another ('clear and present'); one system can recognize more public-order justifications for regulation than another. Now suppose that we find a system where the specifications of a large number of matters fall near the low end of the ranking dimension. Although each specification is consistent with the principles animating liberal constitutionalism (though not with the maximalist specification of those principles), we might be concerned that the system is, cumulatively, not truly a liberal constitutionalist one.[22]

Pinning down this concern is analytically difficult. There is one easy way out, which in my view pervades the literature on abusive constitutionalism. The analyst observes that political leaders in the system have moved away from the maximalist definition by shifting many items from high on each dimension to low on each. She then asks, 'Why have these changes been instituted?' And, typically, she imputes to the political leaders an overarching scheme to move from a liberal constitutional order to a non-liberal (authoritarian) one – rather than imputing to them a considered judgment that the 'low-end' specifications are more suitable than high-end ones, for reasons specific to their recent national experience. This, it seems to me, is what underlies Abvelj's judgment – made about Hungary and

---

22 Scheppele calls this a 'Frankenstate', a regime assembled from principles each of which can be found in some liberal constitutional system, but which in the aggregate is monstrous. Scheppele (n 19).

Poland – and, as the examples indicate, sometimes this imputation will be accurate. But not always: Sometimes it is a simple political judgment offered by critics who disagree with the direction the political leaders have taken the nation. And, again, it seems to me that such political judgments are better framed as criticisms of the leaders' policy choices than in terms of departures from constitutionalism.

Another possibility is that the items on the checklist interact: The chance that the current holders of political power will be displaced is greater if many items are high on their dimensions, and that chance is lower if many are at the low end. The thought, not well spelled out in any works of which I am aware, is something like this.[23] Consider a system with several features. The transparency of government decisions is relatively low, but still consistent with liberalism's basic principles (for example, the system makes opaque decisions dealing with national security quite broadly defined, and with matters of personal privacy also broadly defined). Terms of office are relatively long and electoral units have significant population disparities, justified with reference to 'communities of interest' (but the disparities are not so large as to give any community general veto power over public decisions). A new system of judicial appointments is instituted, replacing an older one in which judges dominated the choice of those who serve on the highest courts with a judicial appointment commission in which the government in place has a substantial though not automatically dominant role.

We can add other 'low-end' features, but the idea should be clear: When all these features are combined, it becomes quite difficult for the political opposition to push the government out of office. The intuition behind this approach is clear. Renata Uitz describes it well:

> Unusually long terms of appointment to key constitutional posts may easily be dismissed as occasional departures from more common solutions, especially when each institution is viewed in isolation. Yet, the practical significance of these new institutional arrangements cannot be fully appreciated until we have analyzed the transformation of these particular constitutional solutions. This analysis can be achieved only if we keep in mind the political context in which these changes took place (i.e., a political majority with exclusive and unfettered access to constitution-making powers).[24]

Here the analysis is both aggregated – operating at the level of the constitutional system as a whole – and dynamic, concerned with how the system with a new element will operate over time. Unfortunately, the mechanisms of interaction are quite difficult to spell out in detail. Why exactly do relatively (but permissibly) opaque decisions make it harder to displace officeholders with long terms but not short ones? As to the latter, the idea must be that the opposition can make opacity a political issue, a reason for voting against the government. Why is that more difficult when terms of office are long? I can imagine a speculative argument cast in terms of the shortness of voters' memories, and similar

---

23 For a short statement asserting that interactions are a matter of concern, see Huq and Ginsburg (n 17) 90 ('there can be a robust equilibrium (i.e., constitutional liberal democracy) that emerges as a system-level consequence of the interaction between these different elements').

24 Renata Uitz, 'Can You Tell When an Illiberal Democracy Is in the Making? An Appeal to Comparative Constitutional Scholarship from Hungary' (2015) 13 *International Journal of Constitutional Law* 279–300.

speculative arguments about other sorts of interactions among 'low-end' specifications. And, against these speculations is the brute fact that each specification is reasonable (though low-end) with respect to liberalism's principles.

The foregoing argument suggests how the idea that there are varieties of liberal constitutionalism can help us understand the concept of abusive constitutionalism. Abusive constitutionalism has several elements. First, it occurs when political leaders shift numerous components from higher on the relevant dimensions to lower, while ensuring that each component is a reasonable specification as evidenced by its presence in some constitutional systems that are unquestionably liberal constitutional ones.[25] Second, though, the specific political context in which the changes occur enables interactions among the constitution's components that, in turn, pose a substantial risk that the system will convert into a non-liberal constitutional one, or into an authoritarian one. Third, the general mechanism by which this occurs is that the changes cumulatively weaken the political opposition in ways that will vary depending on both the precise changes and the political context.[26]

More generally, the analysis of 'mere' shifts from strongly liberal constitutionalist systems to more modest ones should generate an inquiry into whether the shift is only from one variety of liberal constitutionalism to another. Sometimes the inquiry will lead us to conclude that we are seeing an example of abusive constitutionalism, but sometimes not. This inquiry is difficult without the idea that there are varieties of liberal constitutionalism.

How to use the idea of varieties of constitutionalism: the basic structure doctrine

As the discussion of interactions suggests, one technique of dealing with low-end specifications, and the 'Frankenstate' concern in particular, is to assert that each low-end specification is tolerable – keeps the system within the category *liberal constitutionalism* – because of *other* features of the constitutional system. Perhaps a low-end specification of free expression is offset by a high-end specification of equality, for example because the latter supports a highly pluralist political system that makes it difficult to enact and enforce troublingly restrictive regulations of expression even if, once enacted, those regulations are constitutionally permissible under the domestic constitution.[27]

More interesting, and I think more important, low-end specifications are tolerable because of features of the constitutional system *not* included in the checklist. Here the hate speech example is instructive. As noted, in the United States hate speech regulation is generally unconstitutional, yet such regulation is widely adopted in other nations that count as liberal constitutional systems. One way of accounting for the difference is institutional in a relatively simple sense. Nearly everyone who discusses hate speech regulation acknowledges that such regulation poses risks of enforcement abuse: 'Mere' political disagreement, which principles of free expression protect, can sometimes plausibly but

---

25 This was an explicit strategy in Hungary, where the Orban government solicited a letter from legal experts from France and Norway explaining that most elements of a controversial set of constitutional amendments could be found in the constitutions of other European nations. See Uitz (n 24).

26 For example, in some political settings a ban on aisle crossing – breaches of party discipline by parliamentarians – can weaken the political opposition, while in other settings it can strengthen the opposition. The example is discussed in a bit more detail below.

27 Something similar might be said about guarantees of material security, sometimes under the heading of a right to private property and sometimes under the heading of constitutionally guaranteed economic rights.

erroneously be described as hate speech.[28] That risk may be realized to a troublingly large extent in legal systems where many enforcement authorities have the power to impose sanctions on hate speech, whereas the risk might be contained in systems where enforcement is quite centralized. And, finally, the U.S. federal system has quite a large number of decentralized enforcement authorities, while in many nations with hate speech regulations the power to impose sanctions for hate speech is substantially more centralized.

The example shows how institutional features that cannot be components of a checklist for constitutionalism matter a great deal in understanding why, and whether, a system can or should use one rather than another reasonable alternative specification of specific components of liberal constitutionalism.[29] Is this an isolated example, though, or one that illustrates a more general phenomenon?

I believe that it is an illustration, and that quite a few additional illustrations could be added. Here is another: Some constitutions prohibit 'aisle crossing', which occurs when a member of parliament elected as a member of a specific party defects from that party's position (on a matter as to which the party's leaders have invoked party discipline). The rationale is that aisle crossing weakens political parties, holds out the possibility of corruption (when the defector's vote is 'bought' either for cash or for promises of future personal benefits), and breeds cynicism among the population, who as electors cannot know with assurance what they are actually getting when they vote for a candidate or a party. Other constitutional systems might prohibit political leaders from imposing party discipline on their parliamentarians. The rationale is that a well-functioning democracy works best when elected representatives exercise their best judgment on the issues of public policy that come before the legislature. Depending on circumstances, banning aisle crossing or banning the imposition of party discipline might better protect liberalism's principles.

A third example: Many U.S. scholars would claim, with the U.S. Supreme Court, that federalism and the separation of powers are important safeguards of individual liberty, and in some settings they are. Federalism, for example, allows people to sort themselves into jurisdictions that allow them to pursue their goals even if those goals lack majority support in the nation as a whole. Other theorists, though, would claim, with roughly equal warrant, that centralized power and parliamentary rule are important safeguards of liberty, and again in some settings they are. Centralization allows the nation as a whole to prevent petty local tyrants from exercising unconstitutionally coercive power, for example.

And a fourth: In various ways many liberal constitutions caution against the adoption of 'special interest' legislation. Their equality provisions impose a requirement of generality that special interest laws violate, for example (at least as the generality requirement is interpreted, a point relevant to the final example that follows). Or, they require that every piece of legislation deal with a single topic, which impedes legislators who might trade votes by putting two disparate policies into a single statute. Whether discouraging special interest legislation is a good idea depends on the overall structure of a nation's politics. Specifically,

---

28 For example, a colleague has suggested that the statements found to be constitutionally protected political dissent in *Brandenburg v. Ohio*, 395 U.S. 444 (1969), could plausibly be described as hate speech. The most pointed statement, made at a cross-burning by members of the Ku Klux Klan, was this: 'We're not a revengent organization, but if our President, our Congress, our Supreme Court, continues to suppress the white, Caucasian race, it's possible that there might have to be some revengeance taken'.

29 'Cannot be', because institutional details are at most quite remotely connected to liberalism's animating principles. Perhaps a checklist could include a box to check off if the government is effective in pursuing its goals, but I doubt that any other institutional components could be included on a checklist.

in a nation with a large number of relatively well-organized interest groups – a pluralist nation, in short – allowing special interest legislation might enable the legislature to adopt statutes that genuinely pursue the national interest, by buying off enough interest groups with minor concessions that induce them to vote for the larger package.[30] In a nation where a single political party dominates, in contrast, allowing special interest legislation might be an invitation to corruption.

Rather than proliferate examples, I conclude this discussion by noting a central feature of constitutional doctrine (everywhere, I believe). The often abstract principles set out in liberal constitutions have to be brought to ground through practical applications. Often those applications take the form of constitutional doctrine. And we know that a central feature of constitutional doctrine – again, I believe, everywhere – is that doctrine must be administrable. That is, the decision-makers actually called upon to implement the constitution must be given tools, in constitutional doctrine, that they can use well enough. Whether a doctrine is administrable turns centrally upon institutional questions: Who are the people who are going to implement the doctrine? How competent are they in general? How facile are they in handling complex rules? To be more concrete: What sort of training do judges get? Do the selection mechanisms for judges guarantee that, in general, judges will be among the better lawyers in the nation?

Consider a nation with a large number of judges in the lower courts and a relatively small number on the constitutional court. The lower courts handle far more cases than the constitutional court does, and the judges on the latter court know that, because of their overall workload, they cannot effectively review every erroneous decision by a lower court. The judges on the constitutional court ask themselves, 'Should we adopt a general rule of proportionality or balancing, or should we use more categorical rules, knowing that the latter sometimes produce results at odds with what a fair balancing would yield?' They might reject proportionality and balancing because they believe that lower court judges lack the capacity to do balancing well (here meaning, reach the results that the judges of the highest court believe to be correct), and that well-crafted categorical rules, being easily administrable, would generate a better balance between correct and incorrect results. Here institutional questions are central to determining whether the system as a whole is a liberal constitutionalist one.

Whether a constitutional system is a liberal constitutionalist one, then, depends only in part upon constitutional provisions dealing directly with fundamental liberal principles. It also depends upon the overall set of institutional arrangements that implement those principles. A constitutional system with strong provisions on freedom of expression or equality, or judicial independence might actually be a weakly liberal constitutionalist regime, for example if there is a dominant political party. And one with weak provisions might actually be a strongly liberal one, for example if robust political competition among numerous parties limits the effective power of the government in place.

This analysis might help illuminate the 'basic structure' doctrine, according to which some constitutional amendments adopted in a procedurally regular manner are, nonetheless, substantive unconstitutional. In Colombia, for example, a constitutional amendment altering the terms of civil service tenure by giving political authorities more control over

---

30 I have laid out this argument in more detail in Mark Tushnet, 'Three Essays on Proportionality Doctrine' (August 4, 2016) *Harvard Public Law Working Paper* No. 16–43. Available at SSRN: https://ssrn.com/abstract=2818860 or http://dx.doi.org/10.2139/ssrn.2818860.

appointment and promotion was held unconstitutional.[31] Seen abstractly, the change seems like a reasonable alternative specification of the general principle that civil servants' tenure should be such that they are both adequately independent and adequately accountable. It might be, though, that in the specific setting of Colombia the specification posed too great a risk of political domination of routine bureaucratic decisions.[32]

We can understand in similar terms the Indian Supreme Court's decision holding unconstitutional the replacement of the existing system of judicial nominations to the Supreme Court, in which the choices were made by a 'plenum' of the most senior sitting Supreme Court justices, with a judicial nominating commission of a sort common in other constitutional systems.[33] The argument would be that in the context of the Indian political system, a judicial nominating commission would pose substantial risks to judicial independence even if similar commissions do not threaten judicial independence elsewhere.[34] A related example: In Canada the prime minister has legally unfettered power to choose members of the Supreme Court.[35] The actual choice is constrained by a strong set of norms, departure from which would impose substantial political costs on the prime minister. A legally constrained and purely political method of appointment does not threaten judicial independence in Canada because of those norms. Were the United States to adopt the Canadian system, the threat to judicial independence would be quite large because constraining norms are absent.

India, Canada, and the United States have dramatically different systems of judicial appointments, protected in India and perhaps in Canada by a 'basic structure' doctrine.[36] That doctrine can be understood as a way of articulating the proposition that liberal constitutionalism comes in many varieties, with the specifications of core liberal values permissible or impermissible depending upon features of the broader political system.

Conclusion

I draw the following conclusions from the foregoing discussion. First, if we pay attention to shortfalls and alternative reasonable specifications of liberal principles, we might be able to describe systems as 'strongly', 'modestly', or 'weakly' liberal constitutionalist. No finer distinctions can usefully be drawn. Those descriptions, though, would have little if any normative weight. In particular, the strongly liberal constitutionalist regimes do not provide a yardstick against which the other systems can be measured. Nor does the existence of one specification in a strongly liberal system provide a reason for changing the parallel

---

31 See Manuel Jose Cepeda Espinosa and David Landau, *Colombian Constitutional Law: Leading Cases* (Oxford University Press 2017).

32 I do not know enough about Colombia to endorse that argument, but use the example simply to show how the idea of varieties of constitutionalism can help understand the basic structure doctrine.

33 *Supreme Court Advocates-on-Record Association v. Union of India*, (2016) 4 SCC 1 (India). The nominating commission was not particularly well-designed, and flaws in design figured into the Supreme Court's decision, but I believe that the best reading of the opinion is that, in the Court's view, the Indian Constitution would allow only an extremely well-designed commission to replace the plenum method of appointment.

34 Again, as with the Colombia example, I do not know enough about the Indian political context to know whether this argument is correct. I use the example only for illustrative purposes.

35 Subject to a requirement that three members of the Court must be from Quebec. On the latter requirement, see Reference Re Supreme Court Act, ss 5 and 6, 2014 SCC 21 (2014) (Canada).

36 The Canadian Supreme Court's 2014 decision on who counts as a Quebec judge, contains hints that there might be a 'basic structure' limitation on the appointment power.

specification in a weakly liberal system; merely because of its presence in a strongly liberal system, the provision is not an ideal to which those working in a modestly or weakly liberal system should aspire.[37]

Second, and more broadly, we cannot determine whether a constitutional system is a liberal constitutional one simply by looking at the provisions most obviously connected to liberal principles; there is no checklist to be had.[38] Instead we must pay attention, often at a rather granular level, to the institutions of the political system as a whole. When we do, I believe, we will find ourselves quite puzzled about determining whether there is a single dimension of liberal constitutionalism along which systems can be arrayed. Rather than 'strong' or 'modest' or 'weak' liberal constitutionalism (as before in a descriptive, not normative, sense), we might find ourselves talking about 'good enough' liberal constitutionalism.[39] 'Good enough' is the only truly workable normative standard available to us.

Finally, and related to the preceding, the boundary between 'good enough' liberal constitutional systems and systems that are not good enough – illiberal systems – will always be fuzzy and contested in specific cases. Determining whether a system is good enough requires a complex judgment aggregating assessments of a large number of institutional components and then attending to dynamic interactions among those components. The latter, in particular, are likely to be heavily dependent upon quite local circumstances, as the examples offered above about judicial selection mechanisms suggest.

The recent spate of democratic elections that have produced governments with programs including movements away from maximalist definitions of particular components of liberal constitutionalism, has led to great anxiety among those devoted to liberal constitutionalism, an anxiety about whether systems are in the process of movement from liberal to illiberal or authoritarian. Some, perhaps many, are, and with respect to them the anxiety is well placed. Yet, the possibility remains that some of the changes we have seen recently are occurring within liberal constitutionalism and will preserve it in a 'good enough' form. Having a vocabulary that accommodates varieties of liberal constitutionalism might help us better understand these recent developments.

---

37 It might be such an ideal because of rational arguments from liberalism's premises, not because of its presence in the strong system.

38 I emphasize that this conclusion is different from the one advanced by Scheppele, that those who use checklists overlook the possibility of bad interactions among provisions that are otherwise reasonable specifications of liberal principles.

39 I draw the term 'good enough' from a well-known book about parenting, D.W. Winnicott, *The Child, the Family, and the Outside World* (Penguin 1973).

PART II

Formal constitutional change

7

FORMAL AMENDMENT RULES

Functions and design

*Richard Albert**

Introduction: the importance of formal amendment rules

Formal constitutional amendment rules are the gatekeepers to the constitutional text. They detail the procedures for changing the written constitution,[1] specify what is subject to or immune from formal amendment,[2] promote deliberation about constitutional meaning,[3] distinguish the constitutional text from ordinary law,[4] and they also express constitutional values.[5] Formal amendment rules are often designed to channel popular will into institutional dialogue,[6] and they may also be deployed to check courts in their creation of informal constitutional amendments.[7] By their nature, formal amendment rules reflect both faith and distrust in political actors: they simultaneously authorize political actors to improve the constitution,[8] while limiting how and

---

* I benefited from comments on an earlier draft of this chapter presented at a conference hosted by the editors of the volume in Aegina, Greece, in September 2018. I thank the editors for their kind invitation to contribute to this important volume on the study of constitutional change. For a more elaborate explication of the ideas in this chapter, please see Richard Albert, Constitutional Amendments: Making, Breaking, and Changing Constitutions (Oxford University Press 2019).

1 Rosalind Dixon and Richard Holden, 'Constitutional Amendment Rules: The Denominator Problem' in Tom Ginsburg (ed), *Comparative Constitutional Design* (Cambridge University Press 2012) 195.

2 Jon Elster, 'Constitutionalism in Eastern Europe: An Introduction' (1991) 58 *University of Chicago Law Review* 447, 471.

3 Raymond Ku, 'Consensus of the Governed: The Legitimacy of Constitutional Change' (1995) 64 *Fordham Law Review* 535, 571.

4 András Sajó, *Limiting Government: An Introduction to Constitutionalism* (Central European University Press 1999) 39–40.

5 Richard Albert, 'The Expressive Function of Constitutional Amendment Rules' (2013) 59 *McGill Law Journal* 225, 236.

6 Walter Dellinger, 'The Legitimacy of Constitutional Change: Rethinking the Amendment Process' (1983) 97 *Harvard Law Review* 386, 431.

7 Rosalind Dixon, 'Constitutional Amendment Rules: A Comparative Perspective' in Tom Ginsburg and Rosalind Dixon (eds), *Comparative Constitutional Law* (Edward Elgar Publishing 2011) 96, 97.

8 Brannon P. Denning and John R. Vile, 'The Relevance of Constitutional Amendments: A Response to David Strauss' (2002) 77 *Tulane Law Review* 247, 275.

when political actors may do so.[9] Given the many essential functions formal amendment rules serve, we would expect constitutions to codify them, and indeed virtually all of them do.[10]

Yet the structure of formal amendment rules has received relatively little scholarly attention. Scholars have devoted more attention to informal amendment,[11] understood as 'the alteration of constitutional meaning in the absence of textual change'.[12] Though constitutions today commonly change less frequently via formal than informal amendment, and while constitutions both codified and uncodified deserve attention, constitutional designers must nonetheless understand the options available to them in order to structure their formal amendment rules. It is surprising, then, that constitutional designers have few academic resources to explain how to design the rules of formal amendment, which John Burgess described in 1890 'the most important part of a constitution',[13] and which Akhil Amar has more recently observed hold 'unsurpassed importance, for these rules define the conditions under which all other constitutional norms may be legally displaced'.[14]

In this chapter for the *Routledge Handbook on Comparative Constitutional Change*, I explain the functions we can attribute to formal amendment rules—not the functions of formal amendments but the functions of the rules by which codified constitutions are altered. I also critique existing classifications of formal amendment rules and suggest the beginnings of a more comprehensive account of their structure. I have two purposes in this chapter. My principal purpose is to map the scholarly understanding of formal amendment rules in order to better appreciate their various forms and functions. My second purpose is to help generate an agenda for further research into the structure, purposes, and uses of formal amendment. I identify patterns, similarities, and distinctions in order to encourage renewed interest in the study of formal amendment as a subject separate and distinct from informal amendment. This chapter is therefore both an inquiry and an invitation to further research.

The purposes of formal amendment rules

Formal constitutional amendment rules are largely corrective. Recognizing that a deficient constitution risks building error upon error until the only effective repair becomes legal or political revolution,[15] constitutional designers codify formal amendment rules that can be

---

9 Donald J. Boudreaux and A.C. Pritchard, 'Rewriting the Constitution: An Economic Analysis of the Constitutional Amendment Process' (1993) 62 *Fordham Law Review* 111, 123–24.
10 Bjørn Erik Rasch and Roger D. Congleton, 'Amendment Procedures and Constitutional Stability' in Roger D. Congleton and Birgitta Swedenborg (eds), *Democratic Constitutional Design and Public Policy* (MIT Press 2006) 319, 325; see generally Richard Albert 'Amending Constitutional Amendment Rules' (2015) 13 *International Journal of Constitutional Law* 655 (detailing purposes and explaining significance of amendment rules).
11 See, e.g., Bruce Ackerman, *We the People: Foundations* (Harvard University Press 1991) 266–94; Sanford Levinson (ed), *Responding to Imperfection: The Theory and Practice of Constitutional Amendment* (Princeton University Press 1995); Brannon P. Denning, 'Means to Amend: Theories of Constitutional Change' (1997) 65 *Tennessee Law Review* 155, 180–209; David A. Strauss, 'The Irrelevance of Constitutional Amendments' (2001) 114 *Harvard Law Review* 1457, 1469–86.
12 Heather K. Gerken, 'The Hydraulics of Constitutional Reform: A Skeptical Response to Our Undemocratic Constitution' (2007) 55 *Drake Law Review* 925, 929.
13 John Burgess, *Political Science and Comparative Constitutional Law* (Ginn 1890) Vol. I, 137.
14 Akhil Reed Amar, 'The Consent of the Governed: Constitutional Amendment Outside Article V' (1994) 94 *Columbia Law Review* 457, 461.
15 Karl Loewenstein, 'Reflections on the Value of Constitutions in Our Revolutionary Age' in Arnold J. Zurcher (ed), *Constitutions and Constitutional Trends Since World War II* (New York University Press 1951) 191, 215.

used to peacefully correct the constitution's design.[16] Fixing defects is, therefore, an essential function of formal amendment rules. We need not look any further than the word itself: formal amendment rules are used to 'amend' a constitution—from the Latin verb '*emendare*'—in order to 'free [it] from fault' or to 'put [it] right'[17]. As important as this corrective function is, formal amendment rules do more than light the path to perfect apparent imperfections in the codified constitution.

Why formal amendment rules?

First, as a basic matter, formal amendment rules distinguish the codified constitution from ordinary legislation. Ordinary law is commonly susceptible to repeal or amendment by a simple legislative majority but the higher law of a constitutional text is often subject to a more onerous threshold for alteration.[18] This higher threshold could be approval by a legislative or popular supermajority, or an altogether different configuration of consent.[19] More demanding procedures for formal amendment reflect both the higher significance afforded to constitutional over ordinary law and the view that ordinary law is derivative of constitutional law.[20]

Second, formal amendment rules structure the process by which political actors change the text and meaning of a constitution. Formal amendment rules provide a legal and transparent framework within which to alter the constitution,[21] whereas informal amendment occurs arguably pursuant to extralegal procedures.[22] To describe informal amendment procedures as 'extralegal' and formal amendment rules as 'legal' is only to highlight that informal amendment procedures are not specified in a constitutional text but the rules of formal amendment indeed are.

Third, formal amendment rules precommit future political actors to the entrenched choices of the constitution's authors. The strongest 'precommitment' device is a subject-matter restriction on formal amendment, which constitutional designers entrench to privilege something in the constitutional design by making it unamendable.[23] To borrow from Sanford Levinson, a formally unamendable constitution would reflect constitutional designers' 'inordinate confidence in their own political wisdom coupled perhaps with an equally inordinate lack of confidence in successor generations'.[24] Constitutional designers could well distrust political actors and consequently create formal amendment rules to limit their future choices.[25] Lawrence Sager makes plain this connection between precommitment and distrust, arguing that constitutional designers make constitutions difficult to amend because '[w]e trust ourselves, perhaps, but not those who will succeed us in stewardship of our political community'.[26]

16 Burgess (n 13) 137.

17 Bryan A. Garner, *Modern American Usage* (Oxford University Press 3rd ed. 2009) 41.

18 See Sajó (n 4); Carl Schmitt, *Constitutional Theory*, edited and translated by Jeffrey Seitzer (Duke University Press 2008) 71–72.

19 See Jan-Erik Lane, *Constitutions and Political Theory* (Manchester University Press 2nd ed. 2011) 41.

20 See Donald S. Lutz, 'Toward a Theory of Constitutional Amendment' in Levinson (n 11) 237, 240.

21 See Vivien Hart, 'Democratic Constitution Making' (2003) 107 *United States Institute of Peace Special Report* 1, 4.

22 See Dixon and Holden (n 1).

23 See Elster (n 2) 471.

24 Sanford Levinson, 'The Political Implications of Amending Clauses' (1996) 13 *Constitutional Commentary* 107, 112.

25 See Boudreaux and Pritchard (n 9) 123–24.

26 Lawrence G. Sager, 'The Birth Logic of a Democratic Constitution' in John Ferejohn, Jack N. Rakove and Jonathan Riley (eds), *Constitutional Culture and Democratic Rule* (Cambridge University Press 2001) 110, 124.

Fourth, formal amendment rules offer a way to improve the design of a constitution by correcting the faults that time and experience reveal.[27] Amendment procedures allow political actors to respond to the changing political, social, and economic needs of the political community[28]—needs that the governing constitution could inadequately serve, whether as a result of suboptimal constitutional design or new social circumstances.[29] Formal amendment rules therefore operate against the backdrop of human error and exist to redress shortcomings in the design of the constitution itself.[30]

Fifth, formal amendment rules also heighten public awareness and deliberation. They invite political actors to debate and negotiate publicly about what they believe best serves the common interest, and they 'ensure that society acts on well-founded and stable expectations about the consequences' of amending a constitution.[31] Formal amendment rules, which commonly require some form of supermajority action, 'promote careful consideration of the issues ... by forcing those in favor of a particular proposition to persuade a larger segment of the population'.[32] Therefore, for Donald Lutz, formal amendment rules are means '[t]o arrive at the best possible decisions in pursuit of the common good under a condition of popular sovereignty'.[33] The product of this public deliberation—a formal amendment inscribed in the text of a constitution— in turn makes possible the publication and reinforcement of constitutional norms. Formal amendment, write Denning and Vile, 'undeniably changes the Constitution in one significant respect: it adds language to the Constitution'.[34] As a result, '[t]he publicity accompanying the change may, in fact, increase public expectations that the change will be honored by the other branches [of government], raising the costs of evasion or under-enforcement'.[35]

Sixth, formal amendment rules also act as a check between branches of government. They give political actors a mechanism to revise the informal constitutional amendments made by courts of last resort in the course of constitutional interpretation,[36] or changes made by other actors in the regime. Rosalind Dixon observes that formal amendment rules allow political actors both to move courts toward new constitutional interpretations and to trump their constitutional judgments.[37]

Seventh, formal amendment rules have a democracy-promoting function. The right to amend a constitution is, above all, a right to democratic choice. Jed Rubenfeld has argued that '[t]he very principle that gives the [US] Constitution legitimate authority—the principle of self-government over time—requires that a nation be able to reject any part of a constitution whose commitments are no longer the people's own'.[38] Rubenfeld concludes

---

27 Denning and Vile (n 8) 275.
28 See Gabriel L. Negretto, 'Toward a Theory of Formal Constitutional Change: Mechanisms of Constitutional Adaptation in Latin America' in Detlef Nolte and Almut Schilling-Vacaflor (eds), *New Constitutionalism in Latin America: Promises and Practices* (Ashgate 2012) 51, 52.
29 See Ku (n 3) 542.
30 See Rasch and Congleton (n 10) 326.
31 Ibid 327.
32 Ku (n 3) 571.
33 Lutz (n 20) 239–40.
34 Denning and Vile (n 8) 279.
35 Ibid.
36 See Andrée Lajoie and Henry Quillinan, 'Emerging Constitutional Norms: Continuous Judicial Amendment of the Constitution—The Proportionality Test as a Moving Target' (1992) 55 *Law & Contemporary Problems* 285, 285.
37 Dixon (n 7) 98.
38 Jed Rubenfeld, *Freedom and Time: A Theory of Constitutional Self-Government* (Yale University Press 2001) 174.

that '[t]hus written constitutionalism requires a process not only of popular constitution-writing, but also of popular constitution-rewriting'.[39] In addition to promoting the majoritarian bases of democracy, formal amendment rules may also promote the substantive dimensions of democracy, namely its counter-majoritarian and minority-protecting purposes. As Roger Congleton explains, formal amendment rules 'support the rule of law insofar as constitutional stability is increased and/or minority protections are enhanced'.[40]

Eighth, formal amendment rules make possible sweeping but non-violent political transformations. This pacifying function is most clearly articulated by Walter Dellinger, who posits that the Article V amendment process in the United States Constitution 'represents a domestication of the right to revolution'.[41] Codifying the rules of formal amendment in a constitutional text provides a roadmap for effecting constitutional changes that range from modest to major, without having to write an entirely new constitution, or to resort to irregular methods of constitutional renewal, or to take up arms. In the United States at the Federal Convention of 1787, George Mason echoed this very point, recognizing that constitutional amendments would be inevitable but that 'it will be better to provide for them, in an easy, regular and Constitutional way than to trust to chance and violence'.[42]

An underappreciated purpose

Formal amendment rules have an additional yet underappreciated purpose: they express constitutional values. Formal amendment rules are one of many sites within a constitutional order for codifying values and communicating them both internally within the constitutional community and externally beyond its borders. Consider the South African constitution's escalating structure of three different formal amendments. Each may be used to amend a limited universe of constitutional provisions. Take the most demanding formal amendment procedure. It requires approval by three-quarters of South Africa's National Assembly and two-thirds of its National Council of Provinces, and it must be used for any formal amendment to the constitution's declaration of values and to this amendment formula.[43] The mid-level formula calls for a lower threshold—two-thirds approval in the National Assembly and two-thirds approval in the National Council of Provinces—and applies to any formal amendment to the Bill of Rights, the National Council of Provinces, and provincial matters.[44] The least demanding formula requires only two-thirds approval in the National Assembly and is to be used for formal amendments to all other constitutional matters.[45] What results from these escalating thresholds of formal amendment is a constitutional hierarchy, with South Africa's stated constitutional values and the formal amendment procedures at the top, the Bill of Rights and provincial matters in the middle, and all other constitutional provisions below.

We can likewise discern a constitutional hierarchy in subject-matter restrictions in the use of a constitution's formal amendment rules. When a constitutional text distinguishes one

---

39 Ibid.
40 Roger D. Congleton, *Perfecting Parliament: Constitutional Reform, Liberalism, and the Rise of Western Democracy* (Cambridge University Press 2011) 287.
41 Dellinger (n 6) 431.
42 Max Farrand (ed), *The Records of the Federal Convention of 1787* (Yale University Press rev ed 1966) vol I, 203.
43 Constitution of South Africa, s 74(1).
44 Ibid s 74(2).
45 Ibid s 74(3).

provision from another by expressly designating one of them as impervious to the formal amendment rules that apply to the other, one possible message both conveyed and perceived is that one of the two provisions is more highly valued. The degree to which a constitutional provision is insulated from formal amendment and also from the unpredictability of constitutional politics is, in this case, a proxy for preference. The stricter its entrenchment, the higher the constitutional worth of a given provision. Absolute entrenchment against formal amendment—what is called unamendability—is thus the strongest statement of a provision's value.[46]

To illustrate the point, consider a few examples of these subject-matter restrictions. The Cuban constitution absolutely entrenches socialism against formal amendment. The text states that socialism 'is irrevocable, and Cuba will never go back to capitalism'.[47] For Afghanistan, the highest constitutional value is Islam: the Afghan constitution declares that '[t]he principles of adherence to the tenets of the Holy religion of Islam as well as Islamic Republicanism shall not be amended'.[48] And in Brazil, federalism occupies the privileged position that socialism and religion occupy in Cuba and Afghanistan, respectively, insofar as its constitutional text states that '[n]o proposed constitutional amendment shall be considered that is aimed at abolishing ... the federalist form of the National Government'.[49] These content restrictions on the operation of formal amendment rules tell us just how much socialism, religion, and federalism matter in Cuba, Afghanistan, and Brazil, respectively. Constitutional designers believed these principles were important enough to make the choice to disable the formal amendment rules against them.

A constitutional hierarchy can also emerge concurrently from the combination of formal amendment rules and subject-matter restrictions. Consider the Ukrainian constitution, a text that codifies subject-matter restrictions alongside escalating tiers of formal amendment. The Ukrainian constitution's designers set apart three items from others—human rights and freedoms, national independence, and territorial integrity—by designating them as formally unamendable.[50] Visually, we can place these unamendable provisions at the summit of the constitutional hierarchy. At the intermediate level of the hierarchy of importance, we can place the Ukrainian constitution's statement of general principles, its rules for elections and referenda, and the formal amendment rules themselves, for which the constitution requires a proposal by either the president or two-thirds of the national legislature, adoption again by a two-thirds vote in the national legislature, and ratification via national referendum.[51] Finally, the remaining rules sit at the lowest level of Ukraine's constitutional hierarchy, for which formal amendment is possible by the lower of the two amendment thresholds: proposal by either the president or one-third of the national legislature, adoption by a majority of the national legislature, followed by a subsequent two-thirds vote in the national legislature.[52]

---

46 See Miriam Galston, 'Theocracy in America: Should Core First Amendment Values Be Permanent?' (2009) 37 *Hastings Constitutional Law Quarterly* 65, 115.
47 Constitution of the Republic of Cuba, s 3.
48 Constitution of Afghanistan, art 149.
49 Constitution of Brazil, art 60(4)(1).
50 See Constitution of Ukraine, art 157.
51 Ibid art 156.
52 Ibid art 155.

Formal amendment classifications

Existing formal amendment classifications have proven useful for limited purposes. Some focus principally on the voting thresholds that distinguish one constitution's formal amendment rules from another. These classifications are helpful in understanding how constitutions incorporate majoritarian or supermajoritarian procedures in formal amendment. Other classifications are attentive to both voting thresholds and nonvoting criteria in formal amendment rules, and accordingly illustrate how both may be used in combination to design formal amendment rules. Still others classify formal amendment rules in tandem with methods of informal amendment in an effort to demonstrate the relationship between the emergence and frequency of informal amendment and the flexibility or rigidity of formal amendment rules. Yet all three types of existing formal amendment classifications are incomplete. None can serve as a comprehensive guide for constitutional designers seeking to understand how formal amendment rules are structured.

Voting thresholds

Formal amendment rules can be classified according to the quantum of agreement needed to alter the constitutional text. All formal amendment rules in some way incorporate ordinary or extraordinary voting thresholds by representative assemblies or citizens. Arend Lijphart has classified formal amendment rules according to voting thresholds in thirty-six countries identified as democracies by Freedom House.[53] Lijphart identifies four categories of voting thresholds in his classification: approval by ordinary majority, two–thirds majority, less than two–thirds majority but more than an ordinary majority, and more than two–thirds majority.[54] Lijphart finds that a plurality of the countries in his sample—fifteen of the thirty-six countries—codify formal amendment rules requiring a two–thirds majority or its equivalent.[55] He finds that the next most popular thresholds are approval by supermajority greater than two–thirds and by supermajority greater than an ordinary majority but lower than two–thirds,[56] and that the least common voting threshold for formal amendment is approval by ordinary majority.[57]

Lijphart's classification is helpful to constitutional designers for three primary reasons. First, it classifies three dozen constitutions whose formal amendment rules vary in many ways. Second, it demonstrates how voting thresholds contribute to a constitution's flexibility and rigidity.[58] Lijphart contrasts how authorizing regular majorities to formally amend the constitution leads to constitutional flexibility, whereas limiting formal amendment to extraordinary majorities fosters constitutional rigidity.[59] Third, Lijphart also connects constitutional malleability with the strength of judicial review. He posits that 'judicial review can work effectively only if it is backed up by constitutional rigidity and vice versa',[60] meaning that a judicial ruling is more likely to be durable where the rules of formal

---

53 Arend Lijphart, *Patterns of Democracy: Government Forms and Performance in Thirty-Six Countries* (Yale University Press 2nd ed. 2012) 47–48.
54 Ibid 207.
55 Ibid 208.
56 Ibid.
57 Ibid.
58 Ibid 206–11.
59 Ibid 204.
60 Ibid 219.

amendment are difficult. He also uses his classification to suggest that 'completely flexible constitutions and the absence of judicial review permit unrestricted majority rule'.[61] His classification is instructive.

Nevertheless, Lijphart's classification cannot serve as a complete guide for constitutional designers designing their own formal amendment rules. It does not account for the complexity of formal amendment rules, and its generality misses important distinctions even within the various voting thresholds according to which he classifies formal amendment rules. For example, Lijphart's classification does not consider limits to formal amendment rules such as unamendable constitutional rules or periods of time during which the formal amendment rules are suspended—namely, in emergencies or other periods of pressure on the state. Constitutional designers cannot fully understand how to structure formal amendment rules without appreciating how these and other specifications fit within the amendment process.

Moreover, Lijphart acknowledges that his classification does not reflect nuances within particular voting thresholds. Specifically, Lijphart concedes that his classification does not account for different rules of formal amendment in the same constitution.[62] Lijphart has a two-part solution for this problem: 'first, when alternative methods can be used, the least constraining methods should be counted',[63] and 'second, when different rules apply to different parts of constitutions, the rule pertaining to amendments of the most basic articles of the constitution should be counted'.[64] Lijphart's classification therefore does not classify the multiple routes of formal amendment codified in a single constitution, nor does it classify the different formal amendment rules that apply to different sections of a constitution. Yet alternative methods of amendment and exclusive or specially assigned amendment rules are fundamental distinctions among formal amendment rules that must be reflected in any classification if the purpose of the classification is to serve as a complete guide for constitutional designers in designing formal amendment rules of their own. Lijphart's second solution—to apply the amendment rule for 'the most basic articles'— compounds the problem with either subjectivity or error. Sometimes formal amendment rules codify alternative, exclusive, or specially assigned amendment rules. That Lijphart does not classify these rules is problematic for identifying what he refers to as 'the most basic articles' of the constitutions in his classification.

Edward Schneier has developed a similar classification based on voting thresholds.[65] Schneier classifies 101 constitutions into five categories and a total of nineteen subcategories. His five main categories represent the voting thresholds pursuant to which the legislature may initiate a formal amendment: simple majority, sixty percent, sixty-five percent, two-thirds, and seventy-five percent.[66] Schneier divides each of these five categories into one of six subcategories that represent the methods and requirements for ratification (for instance, no further action, executive approval, or referendum).[67] His classification therefore allows us quickly to see that formal amendment in Argentina, for example, requires a legislative vote

---

61 Ibid.
62 Ibid 209.
63 Ibid.
64 Ibid.
65 Edward Schneier, *Crafting Constitutional Democracies: The Politics of Institutional Design* (Rowman & Littlefield 2006) 222–25.
66 Ibid 224–25.
67 Ibid.

by a two-thirds majority with no further action, or that Russia requires a legislative vote of sixty percent followed by a constitutional convention.[68]

Schneier's objective is both to summarize how constitutions may be formally amended and to identify patterns in formal amendment. His classification only partly achieves its objectives. Schneier concedes that his classification is limited because it 'glosses over important nuances' in formal amendment rules.[69] Although the classification does summarize methods of formal amendment, it is not complete. As Schneier acknowledges, his classification does not reflect the full range of formal amendment methods: 'many constitutions provide alternative methods including, most frequently, referendums. This table reflects what I believe to be common practice of the method most frequently used in each country'.[70] This raises a second limitation to Schneier's classification: it is time bound. That one method of formal amendment might today be common practice does not mean that it will remain common practice. Infrequently used methods might become more frequently used, just as more frequently used methods may lapse into disuse.[71] Relatedly, the implication of excluding infrequently used methods of formal amendment is to exclude certain formal amendment methods from his classification.

The consequence of abstracting from specific rules in search of larger patterns is sometimes to elide over important details. Schneier's classification is vulnerable to this criticism. For example, Schneier classifies the United States under the two-thirds category with ratification by three-quarters of states.[72] But this classification does not reflect Article V's prohibition on formal amendments to the Equal Suffrage Clause without the consent of the affected state.[73] Similarly, Schneier classifies Canada and South Africa under the simple majority vote and seventy-five percent categories, respectively, and under the subcategories of approval by provincial legislatures or constitutional convention and approval by majority of provinces, respectively.[74] Yet this classification does not reflect the escalating structure of both sets of formal amendment rules, whose intricate design distinguishes it from many other constitutions. In addition, Schneier includes sham constitutions in his classification.[75] Although sham constitutions codify formal amendment rules, those rules do not actually bind political actors, nor do citizens accept them as accurate and legitimate reflections of how power is actually exercised and constrained.[76]

Schneier's classification nevertheless identifies useful patterns in formal amendment. Schneier finds that most formal amendment procedures require a confirmatory vote, do not

---

68 Ibid.
69 Ibid 223.
70 Ibid 225.
71 See Richard Albert, 'Constitutional Amendment by Constitutional Desuetude' (2014) 62 *American Journal of Comparative Law* 641; Richard Albert, 'Constitutional Disuse or Desuetude: The Case of Article V' (2014) 94 *Boston University Law Review* 1029.
72 Schneier (n 65) 225.
73 Constitution of the United States, art V.
74 Schneier (n 65) 224–25.
75 Schneier includes countries such as Iran, Syria, Eritrea, Pakistan, and Sudan in his classification. See ibid 224–25. Some of the countries in Schneier's study qualify as 'competitive authoritarian regimes' where 'formal democratic institutions are widely viewed as the principal means of obtaining and exercising political authority', but '[i]ncumbents violate those rules so often and to such an extent, however, that the regime fails to meet conventional minimum standards for democracy'. Steven Levitsky and Lucan A. Way, 'Elections Without Democracy: The Rise of Competitive Authoritarianism' (2002) 13 *Journal of Democracy* 51, 52.
76 David S. Law and Mila Versteeg, 'Sham Constitutions' (2013) 101 *California Law Review* 863, 880.

involve the executive branch, and establish a modal legislative vote of two-thirds.[77] But he concludes that 'the most interesting pattern' from his analysis 'is that there are few discernible patterns'.[78] Schneier observes that '[c]ommonwealth countries excepted, the rules seem neither more nor less restrictive in parliamentary as opposed to presidential systems, in older as against newer democracies, or by regions of the world'.[79] Schneier's finding of few patterns of formal amendment design weakens the usefulness of his classification for constitutional designers seeking to structure their own rules of formal amendment.

Voting thresholds and nonvoting criteria

Formal amendment rules can also be classified under a combination of voting thresholds and nonvoting criteria. These classifications are more instructive to constitutional designers than those that classify formal amendment rules according only to voting thresholds because they offer a fuller view of amendment rules and illustrate the interrelations between voting thresholds and nonvoting criteria. In his classification of formal amendment rules, Jon Elster identifies what he calls six 'main hurdles' to formal amendment: absolute entrenchment, supermajority approval, higher quorum requirements, delays, subnational ratification, and referenda.[80] These six categories represent both voting thresholds, which include supermajority approval, higher quorum requirements, subnational ratification and referenda, as well as nonvoting criteria that include absolute entrenchment and delays. Elster's classification therefore differs from Lijphart and Schneier's respective classifications, neither of which uses a nonvoting criterion as a principal category in its classification of formal amendment rules.

Elster constructs his classification to demonstrate the features that make constitutions more difficult to change than ordinary laws.[81] Each of the six categories he identifies serves the function, either by design or effect, of controlling the pace of constitutional change. For instance, he points to the absolute entrenchment of rights or structures—their effect is to prohibit formal amendment.[82] Similarly, both supermajority approval and higher quorum requirements complicate formal amendment, although unlike absolute entrenchment they do not make it impossible.[83] Inserting delays in the process of formal amendment—for example, by requiring successive votes or imposing time limitations—likewise makes constitutions more difficult to formally amend than ordinary laws, as does requiring either subnational or referendal ratification.[84]

A similar effort to classify formal amendment rules is Jan-Erik Lane's six-part classification.[85] Five of Lane's six criteria overlap with Elster's criteria, the only exception being Lane's confirmatory votes in the place of Elster's higher quorum requirements.[86]

---

77 Schneier (n 65) 223.

78 Ibid.

79 Ibid.

80 Jon Elster, *Ulysses Unbound: Studies in Rationality, Precommitment, and Constraints* (Cambridge University Press 2000) 101.

81 Ibid 100–01.

82 Ibid 102.

83 Ibid.

84 Ibid 103.

85 Lane (n 19) 41.

86 Compare ibid with Elster (n 80) 102.

Lane's classification shows that the frequency of formal amendment is indirectly related to the textually specified mechanisms favoring constitutional inertia.[87] The more specific the rules of formal amendment and the more numerous the amendment mechanisms codified in the text, the greater the likelihood of constitutional inertia, argues Lane.[88] These mechanisms are the criteria according to which Lane classifies formal amendment rules: unamendable rules, referenda, delays, qualified majorities, subnational ratification, and confirmatory votes.[89]

Political scientist Donald Lutz has classified formal amendment rules in his larger effort to measure amendment difficulty in thirty-two countries.[90] Lutz identifies four general formal amendment strategies around which constitutional designers structure their formal amendment rules. The first, *legislative supremacy*, reflects 'unbridled dominance of the legislature by one legislative vote sufficient to amend the constitution'.[91] The second, which he calls *intervening election*, requires the national legislature to vote to approve a formal amendment in two separate sessions divided by an election.[92] The third, *legislative complexity*, is 'usually characterized by multiple paths for the amending process, which features the possibility of a referendum as a kind of threat to bypass the legislature'.[93] The fourth amendment strategy is *required referendum*, which is used in constitutional states that institutionalize a referendum as a method of formal amendment.[94]

Constitutional designers will find Elster's, Lane's, and Lutz's classifications moderately useful. Elster explains with examples how to combine those six categories to construct formal amendment rules.[95] He also advises designers that supermajority approval and delays are the most important categories for constitutional precommitment.[96] Lane's classification is a particularly useful resource for constitutional designers because it demonstrates how countries use multiple amendment mechanisms in many different combinations for different purposes, namely to protect minorities or to single out certain laws as special.[97] Lutz's classification evaluates formal amendment rules with an interest in understanding what contributes to amendment ease and difficulty, how to balance a written constitution's flexibility and stability, and the extent to which one amendment strategy affects the amendment rate.[98] Each of these classifications is a valuable resource for the design of formal amendment rules.

But all three classifications remain incomplete. Although they identify both voting thresholds and nonvoting criteria, they do not identify the larger structures around which formal amendment rules are built. Voting thresholds and nonvoting criteria are only part of the architecture of formal amendment rules insofar as they operate within deeper amendment foundations and frameworks that arise prior to the constraining effect that

---

87 Lane (n 85).
88 Ibid.
89 Ibid.
90 Donald S. Lutz, *Principles of Constitutional Design* 170 (Cambridge 2006).
91 Ibid 174.
92 Ibid 175.
93 Ibid 176.
94 Ibid 364.
95 Elster (n 80) 103.
96 Ibid 104.
97 See Lane (n 19) 41–43.
98 Lutz (n 90) 176–77.

voting thresholds and nonvoting criteria exert. Formal amendment rules, then, are anchored in underlying foundations and frameworks that Elster, Lane, and Lutz do not identify, and which would be helpful for constitutional designers to understand before setting out to design their formal amendment rules.

Conceptual categories

Scholars have also ventured beyond the formal rules of constitutional amendment to posit broader conceptual categories of constitutional change. Xenophon Contiades and Alkmene Fotiadou have developed a comprehensive conceptual classification of constitutional amendment comprising five models of constitutional change: elastic, evolutionary, pragmatic, distrust, and direct-democratic.[99] These models are descriptive, neither normative nor mutually exclusive, and reflect the basic features of amendment in constitutional regimes for the purpose of comparing their functional advantages and limitations.[100] As models, they are particularly useful in illustrating the interrelation between formal and informal amendment.

Contiades and Fotiadou describe the elastic model of constitutional change as 'operating under an unentrenched constitution, which may be altered through the normal lawmaking process, having no procedural limits and no eternity clauses'.[101] Anchored in parliamentary supremacy, the elastic model makes the legislative branch all-powerful because 'no obstacles to revision exist other than self-restraint flowing from legal culture, tradition, and political accountability'.[102] The United Kingdom's unwritten constitution is the paradigm of the elastic model.[103] In contrast, the evolutionary model is characterized by a strong judiciary, a high incidence of informal change, and rigid formal amendment rules.[104] Under this model, the difficulty of formal amendment prompts and legitimates informal methods of amendment ranging from constitutional revolutions to incremental alterations:

> Dynamic interpretation lies at the heart of that model, where constitutional change is meticulously construed through legal reasoning as befits judicial justification. Judge-made change may not be attributed exclusively to the judge; political elites or the people might be the driving force behind judicial constitutional evolution.[105]

Canada and the United States are two leading examples of this model.[106]

Constitutional regimes under the pragmatic model generally resort to formal amendment for constitutional change. Contiades and Fotiadou explain that '[t]he pragmatic model allows constitutional change to take place smoothly, with efficiency of formal change being the

---

99 Xenophon Contiades and Alkmene Fotiadou, 'Models of Constitutional Change' in Xenophon Contiades (ed), *Engineering Constitutional Change: A Comparative Perspective on Europe, Canada and the USA* (Routledge 2013) 417, 440–57.
100 Ibid 441.
101 Ibid.
102 Ibid.
103 Ibid 442.
104 Ibid 442–43.
105 Ibid 443.
106 Ibid.

most striking feature of the way the system works'.[107] Formal amendment rules are not usually difficult under this model. But even if they are stringent, the consensual political culture facilitates necessary formal amendments: 'The amending formula may be demanding, designed to secure constitutional stability; nevertheless, constant change is feasible due to a consensual constitutional ethos'.[108] Whereas the evolutionary model relies less on formal amendment than judicial interpretation to keep the constitution current, the pragmatic model relies less on the judiciary than formal amendment: 'A strong judiciary is a feature of this model; nevertheless, there is no need for constitutional review to operate as a substitute for formal amendment'.[109] In other words, '[J]udicial interpretation plays a complementary role and is not the primary vehicle of change',[110] conclude Contiades and Fotiadou. Germany illustrates this model.[111]

The distrust and direct-democratic models of constitutional change are opposites. The distrust model incorporates unamendable constitutional provisions, complicated formal amendment rules, and elite ratification into its procedures for constitutional change: 'Demanding and complex amending formulas, political elite-driven change, and difficulty in reaching compromises on constitutional issues are the basic ingredients of the distrust model'.[112] When situated within a polarized political culture, the distrust model exhibits conflict—and ultimately dysfunction—manifested by the near impossibility of formal amendment.[113] Contiades and Fotiadou ascribe this model to Belgium, Greece, Portugal, Spain, and the Netherlands.[114] The direct-democratic model differs in several ways: it grants citizens the power both to initiate and to have the last word on constitutional change; it makes constitutional referenda mandatory; it eschews un-amendability; and it privileges popular participation over elite decision making.[115] As Contiades and Fotiadou explain, 'The design and qualities of referendums are of great importance, while the role of political elites and courts is influenced by the fact that the ultimate amending power lies with the people'.[116] Switzerland is the leading example of this model.[117]

Contiades and Fotiadou are not alone in developing a classification of constitutional change. Carlo Fusaro and Dawn Oliver have advanced a theory of constitutional change that embraces both formal and informal amendment.[118] They categorize the drivers of constitutional change (the people, the people and the courts, legislative assemblies, the courts, governments and their leaders, and supranational institutions[119]), several legitimizing theories of constitutional change (sovereignty, parliamentary sovereignty, the constituting and constituted powers, representative versus direct democracy, *grundnorm* setting, and majoritarian and counter-majoritarian theories[120]), as well as the legal

107 Ibid 445.
108 Ibid 446.
109 Ibid.
110 Ibid.
111 Ibid 446–47.
112 Ibid 450.
113 Ibid 451–52.
114 Ibid 451–54.
115 Ibid 454.
116 Ibid.
117 Ibid 455.
118 See Carlo Fusaro and Dawn Oliver, 'Towards a Theory of Constitutional Change' in Dawn Oliver and Carlo Fusaro (eds), *How Constitutions Change: A Comparative Study* (Hart 2011) 405–33.
119 Ibid 414–16.
120 Ibid 416–21.

doctrines according to which we justify or approach constitutional change (positivism and neo-constitutionalism[121]). Their classification cuts across formal and informal amendment and provides useful abstractions about constitutional change. Yet they do not focus on the actual design of formal amendment rules.[122]

I have also developed elsewhere a classification of constitutional amendment accounting for both formal and informal methods of constitutional change. Drawing from codified democratic constitutions, I posited three models of constitutional change: the textual model, the political model, and the substantive model.[123] I classified Switzerland as an example of the textual model,[124] where 'the constitutional text enshrines the necessary and sufficient conditions for amending the constitution'.[125] The political model, represented by the United States,[126] recognizes that 'amendments may spring from expressions of popular will that manifest themselves in dialogic exchanges among the political branches and the citizenry' and that amendments therefore 'do not abide by the constitutionally enshrined procedures for amending the constitution'.[127] The substantive model, in contrast, 'chooses instead to elevate constitutional substance over political process, in so doing contemplating the possibility of invalidating constitutional amendments for departing from the spirit of the constitutional text—even if those amendments satisfy the textual requirements for constitutional entrenchment'.[128] I referred to India as a substantivist regime.[129] In retrospect, I would revise my classification, but not in material ways that would undermine my two conclusions: first, that formal amendment rules 'either conceal much about the actual practice of constitutional amendment or simply do not accurately reflect the political norms that shape and inform the practice of constitutional amendment',[130] and second, that 'the theory and practice of constitutionalism is at once rooted in constitutional texts, public institutions, judicial interpretation, political practice, extratextual customs, and citizens themselves'.[131] Nevertheless, my classification gave insufficient attention to the actual design of formal amendment rules in a way that could be used in constitutional design. As a consequence of their limitations, none of these three classifications—neither Contiades and Fotiadou's, Fusaro and Oliver's, nor mine—can serve as a complete guide for designers constructing formal amendment rules.

The three tiers of formal amendment rules

In this closing section, I explicate the structure of formal amendment rules by showing that formal amendment rules are structured around three tiers, with options within each of these

---

121 Ibid 421–23.

122 Fusaro and Oliver do, however, discuss some important details of formal amendment in an earlier chapter that is valuable and interesting, yet even this chapter does not explain how formal amendment rules are structured. See Dawn Oliver and Carlo Fusaro, 'Changing Constitutions: Comparative Analysis' in Oliver and Fusaro (n 118) 391–97.

123 Richard Albert, 'Nonconstitutional Amendments' (2009) 22 *Canadian Journal of Law & Jurisprudence* 5, 12–31.

124 Ibid 47.

125 Ibid 12.

126 Ibid 16.

127 Ibid 12.

128 Ibid 12–13.

129 Ibid 21.

130 Ibid 47.

131 Ibid.

tiers: one of two fundamental foundations, one of six operational frameworks, and a combination of supplementary specifications. This tripartite classification exposes the actual design of amendment rules in a way that designers can use to build their amendment rules and that scholars can interrogate. Much more detail is required to understand the structure of constitutional amendment rules but this exposition offers the beginnings of a basic understanding of their functioning.

The foundations of formal amendment

Formal amendment rules are anchored in the foundational distinction between amendment and dismemberment. The distinction holds that amendment alters the constitution within the existing framework of government while dismemberment amounts to a fundamental change that departs from the presuppositions of the constitution and could even reshape its framework.[132] As Thomas Cooley observed in the late nineteenth century,

> [an amendment m]ust be in harmony with the thing amended, so far at least as concerns its general spirit and purpose. It must not be something so entirely incongruous that, instead of amending or reforming it, it overthrows or revolutionizes it.[133]

More recently, John Rawls has defined an amendment as 'adjust[ing] basic constitutional values to changing political and social circumstances'[134] and 'adapt[ing] basic institutions in order to remove weaknesses that come to light in subsequent constitutional practice'.[135]

The Costa Rican constitution codifies the conceptual distinction between amendment and dismemberment. It distinguishes between a 'partial amendment' and a 'general amendment', the former referring to amendment and the latter to dismemberment. The constitution specifies that 'the Legislative Assembly may partially amend this Constitution complying strictly with the following provisions', going on to list eight requirements for effecting a partial amendment, including who may initiate a partial amendment and the requisite voting thresholds, as well as quorum requirements and time limits.[136] The constitution also outlines a special procedure for dismembering the constitution—a change that does more than merely fine tune the text. The dismemberment clause states as follows:

> A general amendment of this Constitution can only be made by a Constituent Assembly called for the purpose. A law calling such Assembly shall be passed by a vote of no less than two thirds of the total membership of the Legislative Assembly and does not require the approval of the Executive Branch.[137]

That the constitution sets strict requirements for partial amendment is consistent with the limited uses of amendment, as opposed to the more transformative changes possible with

---

132 See Richard Albert, 'Constitutional Amendment and Dismemberment' (2018) 43 *Yale Journal of International Law* 1.

133 Thomas M. Cooley, 'The Power to Amend the Federal Constitution' (1893) 2 *Michigan Law Journal* 109, 118.

134 John Rawls, *Political Liberalism* (Columbia University Press 2nd ed 2005) 238.

135 Ibid 239.

136 Constitution of Costa Rica, art 195.

137 Ibid art 196.

dismemberment, which may be authorized only by an extraordinary body or procedure, namely a Constituent Assembly in Costa Rica.

But most democratic constitutions leave unstated the distinction between amendment and dismemberment. These constitutions neither recognize nor imply that amendment and dismemberment entail different consequences and outcomes. The standard democratic design instead defines formal alteration exclusively with regard to amendment. Yet it does not follow from the non-codification of the distinction between amendment and dismemberment that the distinction does not exist or that its non-codification will foreclose its emergence from other sources. For example, the natural right of revolution is not usually codified in constitutions,[138] yet it remains an implicit restriction against which formal amendment rules and constitutions themselves are defenseless.[139] In cases where the distinction is left uncodified, courts (or less frequently legislatures) will sometimes enforce it in their creation and application of the basic structure doctrine or its equivalent, pursuant to which a procedurally perfect amendment may be nullified as unconstitutional.[140]

The frameworks of formal amendment

Codified constitutions generally embed one of six formal amendment frameworks into their formal amendment foundations. The frameworks of formal amendment vary according to the number of procedures available for formally amending the constitution and the range of the constitutional provisions open to formal amendment by those procedures. The first important observation about formal amendment frameworks is that formal amendment rules may codify either one or more procedures for formally amending the constitution. I divide these procedures into two categories: single-track, for formal amendment rules codifying only one procedure for formal amendment; and multi-track, for formal amendment rules codifying more than one procedure for formal amendment. Formal amendment procedures may differ with respect to the institutions authorized to initiate a formal amendment, to amend an amendment proposal, and to ratify an amendment.[141]

The second important observation about formal amendment frameworks is that formal amendment rules may also authorize the use of all, some, or one of these procedures of formal amendment to amend all, some, or one of the provisions codified in the constitution. I divide the range of constitutional provisions open to formal amendment into three categories: comprehensive, under which all amendable provisions are susceptible to amendment by all available procedures for formal amendment; restricted, pursuant to which each amendable provision is made amendable by a designated procedure for formal amendment; and exceptional, which creates an extraordinary procedure exclusively for one

---

138 Roughly twenty percent of the world's constitutions codify the right of revolution in some form. See Tom Ginsburg, Daniel Lansberg-Rodriguez, and Mila Versteeg, 'When to Overthrow Your Government: The Right to Resist in the World's Constitutions' (2013) 60 *UCLA Law Review* 1184, 1217–18.

139 John Locke, *Two Treatises of Government: The Second Treatise of Civil Government*, edited by Thomas Cook (Hafner 1947) (first published 1690) 246–47.

140 See, e.g., Yaniv Roznai, *Unconstitutional Constitutional Amendments: The Limits of Amendment Powers* (Oxford University Press 2017); Richard Albert, 'How a Court Becomes Supreme' (2017) 77 *Maryland Law Review* 181.

141 See Richard Albert, 'The Structure of Constitutional Amendment Rules' (2014) 49 *Wake Forest Law Review* 913.

Table 7.1 Formal amendment frameworks in constitutional democracies

	Single-track	Multi-track
Comprehensive	Comprehensive single-track (Germany)	Comprehensive multi-track (France)
Restricted	Restricted single-track (South Africa)	Restricted multi-track (Canada)
Exceptional	Exceptional single-track (Iceland)	Exceptional multi-track (United States)

constitutional provision or a set of related provisions. These criteria generate six possible combinations, depicted in Table 7.1.

The specifications of formal amendment

Formal amendment rules are, therefore, anchored in one of two foundations and structured around one of six frameworks. Yet these foundations and frameworks are neither self-executing nor do they provide the entire blueprint to formal amendment. They must be supplemented by specifications that set into motion their operation. These formal specifications are often codified in the constitution and expressly designed as operational restrictions on the formal amendment process that political actors must navigate to alter the constitution. Of the several types of formal specifications, five of them appear with relative frequency in written constitutions.

First, formal amendment rules codify thresholds specifying the quantum of agreement needed to use any of their procedures. Constitutional designers sometimes also specify quorum requirements that political actors must meet to validly deploy formal amendment rules. Where political actors do not achieve these quorum requirements, the formal amendment rules are effectively rendered inoperative. Constitutional designers have wide latitude to tailor these thresholds to the appropriate specifications in their jurisdictions.[142]

Second, constitutions often codify subject-matter restrictions on amendment. These unamendable rules preclude formal amendment to various features, including secularism,[143] theocracy,[144] republicanism,[145] unitarism,[146] republicanism,[147] monarchy,[148] or democracy.[149] In addition, they may prohibit formal amendments that suppress or diminish fundamental rights and freedoms[150] or violate principles of international law.[151] Note, importantly, that there is a deep

---

142 For a discussion of voting thresholds and their implications, see James M. Buchanan and Gordon Tulloch, *The Calculus of Consent* (University of Michigan Press 1962) Parts II–III.
143 See Constitution of Portugal, art 288(c).
144 See Constitution of Afghanistan, art 149.
145 See Constitution of France, art 89.
146 See Constitution of Indonesia, art 37.
147 See Constitution of Haiti, art 284.
148 See Constitution of Kuwait, art 175.
149 See Basic Law of Germany, art 79(3); ibid art 20.
150 See Constitution of Brazil, art 60.
151 See Constitution of Switzerland, art 194.

interconnection among unamendability, dismemberment, and the foundations of a constitution discussed above. Amending an unamendable rule would generally amount to a dismemberment.

Third, formal amendment specifications also limit amendments with respect to the timing of the various steps comprising the amendment process. We can identify two general types of these temporal limitations: *deliberation requirements*, of which there are two kinds (deliberation ceilings and deliberation floors)[152] and *safe harbor provisions*.[153] Temporal limitations of both varieties are commonly codified in written constitutions.[154] The Costa Rican constitution provides an instructive example of a deliberation ceiling.[155] The constitution requires a special commission to render advice on the proposed amendment within no more than twenty working days.[156] This is the upper limit for the commission to deliberate on the matter before the proposal proceeds through other steps. Conversely, the South Korean constitution offers an example of a deliberation floor.[157] A deliberation floor establishes a minimum period for deliberating on a proposal prior to a binding vote or action on the proposal.[158] Formal amendment rules are also sometimes temporally limited by a safe harbor. Whereas deliberation requirements compel political actors to consider the merits and demerits of an amendment proposal over the course of a defined period of time, safe harbors do the opposite: they prohibit political actors from making amendment proposals for a defined period of time. Safe harbors might, for example, foreclose political actors from reintroducing a defeated amendment proposal until the passage of a defined period.[159] Alternatively, safe harbors might ban amendment proposals for a fixed number of years beginning immediately upon the ratification of a new constitution.[160] Safe harbors might also prohibit subsequent formal amendments within a defined period of time after the successful formal amendment of the constitution.[161]

Fourth, constitutions also often impose electoral preconditions on amendment, requiring successive votes separated by an election. For instance, some prohibit the same voting body from both proposing and ratifying formal amendments without an intervening election to reconstitute the body before the second vote.[162]

Fifth, constitutional designers have also codified defense mechanisms within formal amendment rules. Spurred by fears that the amendment process could be hijacked by foreign or nefarious influences, rushed in the face of a national emergency, or compromised during times of war or instability, these defense mechanisms remove the power of formal amendment from

---

152 See Constitution of South Korea, art 129.
153 See Constitution of Estonia, s 168.
154 Constitutions commonly codify deliberation requirements. See Constitution of Australia, s 128; Constitution of Chile, art 129; Constitution of Costa Rica, art 195; Constitution of Italy, art 138; Constitution of Luxembourg, art 114; Constitution of Sweden, Regeringsformen 8, art 14. Safe harbors are also commonly codified. See, e.g., Constitution of Greece, art 110; Constitution of Uruguay, art 331.
155 Constitution of Costa Rica, art 195.
156 Ibid.
157 Constitution of South Korea, art 129.
158 See, e.g., ibid ('Proposed amendments to the Constitution shall be put before the public by the President for twenty days or more').
159 Constitution of Estonia, s 168 (stating that an amendment to the constitution regarding the same issue shall not be initiated within one year after the rejection of a corresponding bill by a referendum or by the *Riigikogu*).
160 Constitution of Cape Verde, art 309 (creating a five-year safe harbor).
161 Constitution of Greece, art 110 (establishing a five-year safe harbor); Constitution of Portugal, art 284 (same).
162 See Constitution of Belgium, art 195; Constitution of the Netherlands, art 137. Some constitutions establish this rule with exceptions. See, e.g., Constitution of Estonia, s 165.

political actors. It is not unusual for constitutional designers to disable the formal amendment process during a national emergency, martial law, or a state of siege or war.[163] Constitutions may also disable the formal amendment process during periods of regency or succession.[164]

Conclusion: an agenda for further research

An unamendable constitution is not an option for democratic constitutional design. It would lack the legitimacy of popular consent,[165] it would betray the self-assurance constitutional designers have in themselves and the distrust they bear for others,[166] and its rigidity would risk provoking revolution.[167] Yet hyper flexibility is as inadvisable as hyper rigidity because it erodes the distinction between a constitution and a statute. Constitutional designers must therefore take care when codifying amendment rules to design impermanent yet stable constitutions.

There is much more to be written about the structure of formal amendment, but this is a start to a better comprehensive understanding of its forms and functions. My corollary purpose has been to re-enliven the study of formal amendment rules. There are many empirical, historical, and normative questions to explore in the comparative study of formal amendment: whether democratic outcomes are more likely to follow from the codification of any of the foundations, frameworks, or specifications of formal amendment rules; whether any of the foundations, frameworks, or specifications are associated with constitutional mortality or endurance; and whether the ease or difficulty of amendment is influenced by the choice of amendment foundation, framework, or specification. My larger purpose has been to contribute to the understanding of formal amendment rules and to suggest that we would benefit from the revived study of formal amendment rules as a helpful complement to the continuing study of informal amendment.

---

163 See Constitution of Belgium, art 196; Constitution of Cape Verde, art 315; Constitution of Portugal, art 289.

164 See Constitution of Belgium, art 197; Constitution of Luxembourg, art 115.

165 Dellinger (n 6) 386–87.

166 See Sanford Levinson, 'The Political Implications of Amending Clauses' (1996) 13 *Constitutional Commentary* 107, 112–13.

167 Albert V. Dicey, *Introduction to the Study of the Law of the Constitution* (Liberty Fund 8th ed 1982) (1915) 66.

8

CONSTITUTIONAL DESIGN THROUGH AMENDMENT

Manfred Stelzer

Introduction

Many constitutional lawyers, even academic experts and especially those who work outside the English-speaking world would hardly be familiar with the term 'constitutional design'. This comes as no surprise, as this term relates to a research project that is mainly driven by political scientists and economists rather than constitutional lawyers. The overall aim of studies published within this research field is to improve the cognitive assumptions[1] on which constitutions may be drafted, highlighting, for instance, the socio-economic impact of particular constitutional arrangements.[2]

Thus, it is suggested that drafting a constitution involves an array of choices that can be made for different reasons – for example, historical or political ones. But these choices can also be informed by considerations resolved to pursue specific aims. If a constitution is purposefully drafted, or, in other words, there is a plan behind the arrangement of its features, then the constitution is 'designed'.

The interest in how constitutions are effectively made is driven by the observation that the average life span of constitutions worldwide amounts only to a mere nineteen years.[3] Therefore, constitution making occurs more frequently than probably assumed. It has been noted that it comes in waves:[4] one constitution often triggering several others, by and by spreading the constitutional project, originally developed in Western political philosophy during the Renaissance period[5] (with its roots in ancient Greece) and, one may add, the age of enlightenment. Therefore, drafters can take advantage (and they effectively do so) of the experience generated in other constitutional systems – of the present or the past – to write

---

1 Jon Elster, 'Forces and Mechanisms in the Constitution-Making Process' in Stefan Voigt (ed), *Design of Constitutions* Vol. 36 (Edward Elgar Publishing 2013) 68.

2 For an overview on the constitutional design project see e.g. Stefan Voigt (ed), *Design of Constitutions* Vol.36 (Edward Elgar Publishing 2013), Introduction, xi ff; Tom Ginsburg (ed), *Comparative Constitutional Design* (Cambridge University Press 2012) Introduction, 1 ff.

3 Voigt (ed) (n 2), xiii.

4 Elster (n 1) 71.

5 Donald S Lutz, *Principles of Constitutional Design* (Cambridge University Press 2006) 209.

a new constitution. Features of former or existing constitutions can be randomly picked (because, for instance, they look quite fashionable) or according to a plan, following specific aims. In the latter case, a constitution would be 'designed' while in the former it would be merely constructed.[6]

Although the constitutional design project focuses on the constitution-making process, it might be asked whether its findings can be relevant to analyse and understand the amendment process, the overall aim of this volume. Two strings of thought have to be brought together for this purpose: the predominant empirical studies of academics working on 'constitutional design' and the legal and/or philosophical reflections on constitutional amendments.

In doing so, this chapter will present the constitutional design project in more detail, reflect on the discussion about the scope of amendments and try to analyse in which way the theoretical approach of how constitutions may be designed can be related to constitutional amendments.

The constitutional design project

As already highlighted, the starting point of the constitutional design project is the idea or suggestion that arranging features of a constitution may follow a specific plan or purpose and thus the constitution can be designed. By following such a plan, constitutional designers choose between so-called 'design elements'[7]. On a more general level, choices are made, for instance, between a parliamentary or a presidential system, federalism or unitarism, various forms of constitutional review – if desired at all – a majoritarian system or proportional representation, the extent of involving the people in the law-making process, a bill of rights and others. On a more detailed level, choices are made to define the balance of powers and/ or the interaction between different institutions. The power of a constitutional court vis-à-vis the parliament, for instance, depends on the gateways to the court.[8] In that perspective, it can make a huge difference if individuals are entitled to ask the court to review a law or if only a certain number of members of parliament or a president can submit such a case to the court. Designers will further consider how the constitution may interact with society and what it probably takes to make the constitution 'successful' in terms of meeting the pursued aims.

At that point, empirical studies as performed under the constitutional design project can help to make such an assessment more convincing, as they analyse (especially) the economic and/or political effects and possible other consequences specific designs have already triggered in other countries. The parlance of 'constitutional design', therefore, has opened a wide field of research: it might be asked, for instance, whether bicameralism has had an influence on the amount of corruption,[9] or whether a more regular use of referenda has led to a lower budget deficit in countries embracing them than in countries where the political power is concentrated in a parliament.[10] In addition, the introduction of federal systems

---

6 Donald L Horowitz, 'Constitutional Design: Proposals Versus Processes' in Stefan Voigt (ed), *Design of Constitutions* Vol. 36 (Edward Elgar Publishing 2013) 21.

7 Voigt (ed) (n 2) xii.

8 See, e,g., the comparative study comparing the gateways to the Italian Constitutional Court with the French and the German model by John Ferejohn and Pasquale Pasquino, 'Constitutional Adjudication, Italian Style' in Tom Ginsburg (ed), *Comparative Constitutional Design* (Cambridge University Press 2012) 294 ff.

9 Cecilia Testa, 'Bicameralism and Corruption' (2010) 54(2) *European Economic Review* 181 ff.

10 Dennis Mueller, 'Constitutional Political Economy in the European Union' in Stefan Voigt (ed), *Design of Constitutions* Vol. 36 (Edward Elgar Publishing 2013) 3 (9).

may be discussed in the light of economic advantages or disadvantages or in which way 'individual preferences' should be best represented.[11]

Studies of that ilk will always involve comparative aspects. While constitution making is somehow construed as a process in which designers pick elements from a construction kit, it is rather obvious that these elements are derived from comparative studies and new constitutions are often designed comprising features of historical or contemporary constitutions. However, a manual on designing a constitution has not been developed and is probably not even possible.[12] Taking the philosophical foundations of empirical sciences seriously, their theories can only be disproven rather than proven. Predictions on what will work for a constitution under specific circumstances come with the caveat that reality might turn out differently.

Moreover, as many of the studies in question shape their theories on a statistical level, the rather complicated methodological issue arises of how to translate statistical evidence to an individual choice. Constitution making is, therefore, still understood as the art of finding a design that meets the needs and prerequisites of a society;[13] or as *Montesquieu* has already put it *'Les dogmes les plus vrais & les plus saints peuvent avoir de très-mauvaises consequences, lorsqu' on ne les lie pas avec les principes de la société'.*[14]

The best and most efficient judicial system, for instance, may have no impact at all when there is no appetite to litigate in a society, say for instance, for religious reasons.[15] What might prove to be beneficial for one society may prove to be a poor choice for another one. Therefore, it may still be difficult to advise drafters on the basis of empirical studies. But what these studies doubtlessly can achieve is destroying myths and helping to evaluate economic and/or political costs.

Constitutional doctrine or political science, quite often associate a specific design with a specific impact. For instance, in the debate that led to the introduction of a centralised constitutional review – contrary to a diffused system – it was held that a centralised system would add to legal certainty while a diffused system would only enhance legal uncertainty, at least in civil law systems.[16] This is based on the assumption that in a common law system the 'rule of *stare decisis*' leads to legal certainty as lower courts are 'automatically' bound by the decision of higher courts and, therefore, ultimately by the decision of the apex court.

In a civil law system, so it is argued, as no such formal rule exists, allowing all courts to scrutinise laws might therefore trigger a chaotic situation, leading to legal uncertainty. Empirical studies may try to support this argument[17] or identify it as a myth. They may show, on the one hand, that *stare decisis* cannot be enforced in common law systems, should a court deny the binding effect, other than by appealing the decision hoping that the higher

---

11 Ibid (2013) 10.

12 Voigt (ed) (n 2) xiii.

13 Lutz (n 5) 183 f: 'matching a government to a people'.

14 Charles Louis de Secondat de Montesquieu, *De l'esprit des lois* (1772), 24/19; ibid, The Spirit of Laws (1752), translated by Thomas Nugent, 477: 'The most true and holy doctrines may be attended with the very worst consequences when they are not connected with the principles of society'.

15 Andrew Harding and Peter Leyland, *The Constitutional System of Thailand: A Contextual Analysis* (Hart Publishing 2011) 220 f.

16 Hans Kelsen, 'Judicial Review of Legislation. A Comparative Study of the Austrian and the American Constitution' (1942) 4 *The Journal of Politics*, 183.

17 Alison Riley and Patricia Sours, *Common Law Legal English and Grammar: A Contextual Approach* (Internat. edn, Hart Publishing 2014) 314 f, express the arguable difference between the common law and the civil law system by using the terms 'binding effect' and 'persuasive effect'.

court may accept the binding effect of the relevant precedents. On the other hand, they may demonstrate that courts in civil law systems regard themselves to be bound by the case law of higher courts, in a similar way. Obviously, French courts have not caused havoc on the legal system when they used their power to set aside a domestic law, had it been found to violate the ECHR. Empirical studies may therefore, provide a more rational basis for future design choices.

The problem constitutional design faces, however, is that it is notoriously difficult, if not impossible, to prove if and how far design choices are based on a cognitive assessment. The reasons why specific arrangements occur are manifold.[18] They may be the result of a historic development that remains unchallenged. Further, they might be a compromise between different political or partisan ideologies (probably spoiling 'design' plans of political parties on all sides). Regarding the constitutional design project, it is probably irrelevant to what extent 'design' occurs, as long as it can be observed that cognitive assessments play a part in drafting a constitution. As long as this is the case, the studies carried out within this research field are a more or less valuable contribution to constitutional theory (rather than constitutional doctrine) and might advise drafters of a constitution who, ultimately, may become designers.

Because of this difficulty, it has already been suggested that the constitution making should be better understood as a process rather than an act of design,[19] especially with regard to democratic legitimacy that might be at risk if a designed constitution should be adopted without deliberations. But this would not make reflections on the design of a constitution meaningless.[20]

However, it may be asked if design choices only occur in the (original) drafting of a constitution or whether and to what extent constitutions may be designed or re-designed by an amendment. Before this question can be addressed, two further clarifications are necessary: for the sake of this chapter, it has to be determined, first, what is understood by the term 'amendment' and, second, by the term 'constitution'.

Usually, amendments are passed by the legislator (a body, the people) following procedures set out in a written document or accepted as part of a convention. More thorough studies,[21] however, reveal that a constitution can be changed in many ways, for instance, by reading it differently, especially if this involves a paradigm change in the jurisprudence of an apex court. One of the most prominent examples can be found in the case law of the Israeli High Court of Justice which not only created a bill of rights but also acknowledged its own power of scrutinising laws despite the absence of a written (and entrenched) constitution.[22]

Despite cases like that, the term 'amendment' will nevertheless have to be restricted to changes that occur through formal amendment procedures, as otherwise the discussion might get too complex and exceed the scope of this chapter.

---

18 Elster (n 1) 80 ff, lists the following: personal interest, group interest, institutional interest, passion and, finally, reason.
19 Horowitz (n 6) 20 ff (41).
20 Ibid 21.
21 See e.g., Xenophon Contiades and Alkmene Fotiadou, 'Models of Constitutional Change' in Xenophon Contiades (ed), *Engineering Constitutional Change: A Comparative Perspective on Europe, Canada, and the USA* (Routledge 2013) 417 ff.
22 Suzie Navot, *The Constitution of Israel: A Contextual Analysis* (Hart Publishing 2014) 196, 200.

The second point that requires some brief considerations ensues from the fact that the constitutional design project is focused on the formal, written constitution. That may prove highly unsatisfactory for comparative studies, especially when those studies are underpinned by a more functional approach. Some empirical studies analysing consequences of specific design elements and trying to assess whether they meet their intended or underlying purpose suggest that the results sometimes hinge on design elements usually implemented on a sub-constitutional level.[23]

For instance, the amount to which a proportional system shifts power from the people to political parties might depend on various stipulations usually enshrined in electoral laws. It, therefore, can be decisive if the party list is composed solely by the party or if the electorate has some influence on it, for example in changing the order of the candidates. The less influence the electorate has, the more the political career even of the elected member will depend on the goodwill of the party, consequently also affecting his or her behaviour in parliament.

Changing design elements on a sub-constitutional level is normally easier to facilitate and might, therefore, happen more frequently. In many cases, it would not even be noticed by the general public. Restricting 'constitutional design' to the formal constitutional level could thus miss important choices and, consequently, changes in other parts of the legal system that highly affect the 'success' of constitutional design in the sense of meeting its pursued aims. A more substantive understanding of constitution might therefore be desirable.

On the other hand, neither can it be observed that framers only make basic choices nor that they make all the choices one would expect them to do. Both issues differ from constitution to constitution, depending on the political and cultural background against which they were drafted.

For instance, Arts 55 and 56 of the Italian constitution, which provide for principles of the electoral law, leave it open whether a majoritarian or a proportional system should apply, possibly missing out on one of the basic design choices framers would typically make. Referring to another example, the Constitution of Thailand sets up a judicial system with a striking similarity to the Austrian and German systems,[24] but leaves the design of the gateway to the constitutional court to an organic law, while the Austrian and the German constitutions regulate these issues exhaustively.

Consequently, even fundamental changes to the electoral system in Italy or significant changes in the access to the constitutional court in Thailand, affecting the balance of powers between the court and other branches of government, would not need a formal constitutional amendment. Due to its strict limitation to the formal constitutional level, these changes would be of no significance from the constitutional design perspective.

'Constitutional design' does not offer a theory listing the fundamental choices designers have to make and how detailed these choices should be elaborated:[25] A constitution does not have to cover all fundamental choices that are necessary to make a system work and is not reduced to more basic choices like the one between a parliamentary and presidential system. How detailed a design is and which elements are enshrined in the constitution differ from constitution to constitution and result from the choices the framers have made. Even though one could distinguish 'major' from 'minor' design elements, constitutions would still be identified on formal grounds only.

---

23 Horowitz (n 6) 35.
24 Harding and Leyland (n 15) 161.
25 Some constitutions may, therefore, have a 'looser' design than others: Horowitz (n 6) 41.

History and scope of amendment clauses

Today, amendment rules are fairly common in (codified) constitutions. It is, therefore, interesting to know that the drafters and framers of earlier constitutions were not entirely convinced that their constitutions should contain amendment provisions. In the 1789 US Constitutional Convention as well as in the 1789–91 French Constituent Assembly, providing for amendment rules was highly contentious.[26] Concerns were raised that frequent amendments might lead to political instability and jeopardise the acceptance of the document. Especially the French believed that amendment rules could never infringe on the right of the people – 'the only legitimate fountain of power' according to Madison[27] – to design a new constitution. In some quarters, it was held that changes to the constitution had to be assigned to different bodies than the ordinary legislature as they would need more thorough consideration which should be unaffected by daily political skirmishes.

Finally, in both assemblies the argument prevailed that it was preferable to have an avenue to deal with possible imperfections. At no point, however, was the right of the people to overthrow the constitution and to draft a new one denied – for such a 'revolutionary act' the constitution could not provide for procedures as that would limit the power of the 'sovereign'.

Thus, at an early stage in the history of modern constitutions a dichotomy was established between an amendment of the constitution and the drafting of a new constitution, in other words that of an evolutionary and a revolutionary change. The only issue that has been contentious until today is whether the borderline between amendment and a new constitution is to be drawn along formal criteria (only) or whether there are also substantive issues to be taken into account.[28]

While this should not be exaggerated, it is probably still worth noting that the terms 'amendment' and 'revision' as used in the US and French constitutions, respectively, still somehow reflect the original idea of dealing with imperfections. The term 'amendment' suggests that the respective act improves or at least heals something that has been broken (and therefore needs to be mended). The term 'revision' suggests that something has to be scrutinised against flaws or imperfections that have to be eradicated. Although, for comparative reasons, the term amendment nowadays is used ubiquitously, it might still be of some relevance that some constitutions, such as the German and the Austrian, use the (German) term '*Änderung*' (of the *Grundgesetz*, Art 79 GG) or '*Verfassungsänderung*' (Art 44 B-VG) respectively, which literally translates to (constitutional) change leaving it open in which direction such a change may happen. The Swiss constitution uses the term 'revision' in its French version and sticks to it also in its German version ('Revision', Arts 138 and 139 BV). The framers of the Czech constitution clearly distinguished between three different terms in Art 9 allowing for 'supplementing (*dopiňována*)' or 'amending (*měněna*)' the constitution and prohibiting 'changes (*změna*)' in the essential requirements of democracy or the rule of law. The use of different terms and different phrasing may inform the national debate in a way that might be lost on a comparative level where the terms 'amendment', 'revision' and 'change' are used without the precise reference to a specific

---

26 See the detailed account given by Mark Tushnet, 'Amendment Theory and Constituent Power' in Gary Jacobsohn and Miguel Schor (eds), *Comparative Constitutional Theory* (Edward Elgar Publishing 2018) 317 ff.

27 James Madison, Alexander Hamilton and John Jay, 'Federalist Paper no XLIX' in Isaac Kramnick (ed), *The Federalist Papers* (Penguin 1987) 313.

28 Gary J Jacobsohn, 'Theorizing the Constitutional Revolution' (2014) 2(1) *Journal of Law and Courts* 10 ff.

constitutional document and quite often synonymously. Nevertheless, the use of different language may play a part in drawing the line between 'amendment' and 'revolution' if both terms are understood in a more substantive sense.

The design of the amendment rules vary from constitution to constitution and cannot be analysed here. For the purpose of this chapter, it has to suffice that regulating the amendment procedure has become a given part of a constitution. Some constitutions entrench certain parts deeper by providing for separate amending procedures, other constitutions even exclude certain parts from being changed.

What these rules have in common is establishing more demanding or cumbersome procedures to amend constitutional laws than to amend ordinary laws, often by providing for a super-majority vote in parliament. These rules may also be analysed under the perspective of 'constitutional design', possibly advising drafters of how to design amendment rules and/or procedures depending on the desired degree of rigidity or flexibility.[29]

Constitutional design and amendments

To start with, it is a rather trivial proposition that drafters of an amendment would find themselves in a different situation from drafters of a new constitution. While it can be construed (at least theoretically) that a new constitution can be drafted from scratch according to a plan based on cognitive assumptions,[30] an amendment will almost always relate to an existing constitution and thus to its original design. (*Strictu sensu*, this can only apply to constitutions that are 'designed' rather than 'constructed' or 'patched up'.) Only in the case of amendment powers being limitless, may drafters be put into a similar position to designers of a new constitution.

In general, amendments will relate to the original design of the constitution they aim to revise. Basically, it may be suggested, amendments can fall under five categories: they can be design-enhancing, design-adjusting, design-neutral, design-completing or design-changing. To what extent especially design-changing amendments are legally possible depends on the scope of the amendment powers. Establishing them involves legal arguments that are usually not aligned with the constitutional design theory.

Design-enhancing and design-adjusting amendments

As already outlined above,[31] the framers of the US constitution and the first French constitution were only convinced to include amendment clauses in their constitutions as such rules would open an avenue to deal with imperfections of the constitution discovered at a later stage. In parlance of the constitutional design theory, amendments were, therefore, meant to target flaws in the original design of the constitution. They would help to improve the constitution, but obviously within the design chosen by the framers. Empirical

---

29 See, e.g., Rosalind Dixon and Richard Holden, 'Constitutional Amendment Rules: The Denominator Problem' in Tom Ginsburg (ed), *Comparative Constitutional Design* (Cambridge University Press 2012) 195; they prove that, on the state constitutional level in the US, a larger house of representatives leads to a significantly lower probability of constitutional amendment. Although these conclusions are highly interesting, they are drawn against a rather uniform political system and one might wonder if they can so easily be transferred to political systems that are informed by a strong party hierarchy and/or a strong party discipline.

30 Although it might be questioned if that ever happens in reality: see Horowitz (n 6) 41.

31 See above, section entitled 'History and scope of amendment clauses'.

studies as carried out within the constitutional design project can help to detect imperfections and reveal which design elements of a constitution are not successful in terms of fulfilling their aims and, moreover, may also inform their repair. To what extent these studies are effectively used depends on the amendment procedures provided for by the constitution and the degree of influence of political parties. Partisan strategies will ultimately decide on the involvement of experts and chances are high that the more they support party interests the more they are welcome.

In many cases, however, amendments are not due to initial flaws in the design of a constitution but might be demanded by a change of circumstances. When the Germans, for instance, reorganised their federal system by redistributing the powers between the federation and the states at the beginning of the new millennium, they did so in order to modernise the system.[32] It was not held that it had initial flaws or shortcomings that had to be mended, but that time begged for a change to make the system effective again. This amendment, one might argue, although modifying it, merely adjusted the original design to changed circumstances.

Although it looks likely to be the case, only a huge and broadly designed empirical study can reveal if most amendments that are actually passed may fall under these two categories.

Design-neutral and design-completing amendments

Apart from amendments that enhance or adjust the original design by erasing flaws and/or make it more effective in the light of a changing world, design-neutral amendments, although they might be rare, are nevertheless conceivable. Such amendments would add something to the constitution or change a detail without influencing the design. In a 1982 amendment,[33] for instance, a right to freedom of arts was added to the Austrian bill of fundamental rights. Until then, this right was protected by the freedom of expression as enshrined in Austria's domestic bill of rights (Art 13) as well as the ECHR (Art 10), which Austria had already adopted in the rank of a constitutional law. The only difference between the right to freedom of arts and the right to freedom of expression lay in the latter being qualified and the former being unqualified. As this difference had only marginal practical implications, it can hardly be argued that it changed or influenced the constitutional design, for instance, in the sense of altering the balance or relationship between design elements or institutions.

More fundamental changes to a bill of rights or its introduction, like the first ten amendments to the US constitution, clearly have an impact on the constitutional design as they might rebalance the power between parliament and a constitutional court. But it is debatable whether these amendments were actually design-changing (see below). Insofar as a bill of rights might already have been envisaged by the framers of the constitution[34] and thus been part of the original design, it might be argued that its introduction did not change the original design (plan) of the constitution but merely completed it. It sometimes happens

---

32 Cf. Andreas Haratsch in Helge Sodan (ed), *Grundgesetz* (3rd edn), Art 70 Rn 2: '*das erklärte Ziel war in erster Linie die Modernisierung der bundesstaatlichen Ordnung*', which translates roughly to: 'the manifested aim was primarily to modernise the federal system'.
33 BGBl 262/1982.
34 Cf. an account of the debate on the bill of rights given by Melvin I Urofsky, *A March of Liberty: A Constitutional History of the United States* (Knopf 2nd ed 2002) 123 ff.

that parts of a constitution are not enacted simultaneously but delayed for further, more detailed consideration or deliberation. The 1920 Austrian constitution, for instance, did not finally divide the powers between the federation and the states. The relevant clauses were only enacted in 1925[35] when the design of the constitution, one might argue, was completed.

Design-changing amendments

As the understanding of the term 'amendment' has evolved, and as constitutions drafted in languages other than English use different terms, it seems clear that constitutional amendments may eventually change – partly or profoundly – the original design of a constitution, thus interfering with or even tearing into the original 'plan' according to which its features had been arranged. The French constitution, for instance, has strengthened the judiciary, foremost by expanding the power of the constitutional court ('*conseil constitutionnel*') and therefore rebalanced the powers of parliament and the judiciary.[36] The UK – albeit in the absence of a codified and entrenched constitution – has introduced regional parliaments by way of 'devolution' and a Human Rights Bill that allows courts to scrutinise laws passed by parliament and to enter into a 'dialogue' with the legislator.[37] This has changed the constitution to an extent that it might even be regarded as a 'revolution' (in a substantive reading of that term).[38] Again, constitutional amendments that eventually design or redesign the constitution may be supported by empirical studies, providing for changes on a more rational basis. In that respect an amendment might re-arrange design features according to a (new) plan and thus be 'designed'.

Limiting design changes

Design changes, however, may be restricted to the limits of amendment powers. Limits may occur by interpreting amendment powers in a restrictive way, sticking to the more historical reading of the term 'amendment' or, more prominently, by specific clauses enshrined in the constitution. As already mentioned, some constitutions protect some parts (or design elements, as they may be called) against changes either by stipulating higher procedural thresholds or by excluding them completely from change. In these cases, drafters of amendments are explicitly bound to original design choices.

Which parts are specifically protected depends on the particular constitution and does not fit a predefined terminology of 'major' or 'minor' design elements. Two (spectacular, albeit rare) examples may illustrate that: One example relates to the Austrian constitution where specific principles (the democratic principle, the Federal State and the principle of '*Rechtsstaat*', according to the constitutional court) are more deeply entrenched than other parts of the constitution. Changing these principles would have to be backed by a (mandatory) referendum.[39] The other example is taken from the Spanish constitution

---

35 BGBl 268/1925.

36 Sophie Boyron, *The Constitution of France: A Contextual Analysis* (Hart Publishing 2013) 173 ff.

37 Peter Leyland, *The Constitution of the United Kingdom: A Contextual Analysis* (Hart Publishing 3rd ed 2016) 195, 246 ff; Alison L Young, *Parliamentary Sovereignty and the Human Rights Act* (Hart Publishing 2009) 127 ff.

38 Jacobsohn (n 28) 15.

39 Art 44 B-VG; see Manfred Stelzer, *The Constitution of the Republic of Austria: A Contextual Analysis* (Hart Publishing 2011) 32.

where certain parts – among others: basic principles, some fundamental rights and the section governing the Crown – can only be changed after achieving a two-thirds majority in both houses, the election of a new parliament that has to ratify the decision to initiate the reform, another two-thirds majority in both houses, followed by a referendum.[40]

The first observation that can be made is that albeit both constitutions offer a path to change the whole design of the constitution, the procedure may be so burdensome that some design elements are effectively excluded from change. This leads to a very peculiar situation in Spain, as not only is the monarchy as such specifically protected by the constitution, but the whole section of the constitution relating to the Crown. Consequently, introducing an equal right to succession for females would require going through the cumbersome procedures outlined above. So far, this has not been done.[41] It might be debatable whether protecting that specific design element from an easier change was really the aim of the framers or if this problem was just overlooked as it was not addressed in the relevant debates. However, it shows that it is entirely up to the framers to decide which parts or elements of a constitution they wish to entrench more deeply than others and this is not necessarily informed by a possible distinction between major or minor design elements.

As long as specific clauses enjoy a special protection, it is easy to identify an amendment that tries to change them. With regard to principles, it is considerably more difficult to assess the limits they might set for design-changing amendments. According to the Austrian doctrine as well as the case law of the constitutional court, the democratic principle of the constitution first and foremost protects the representative democracy and, as such, the power of parliament.[42] Strikingly, this has the consequence that a Swiss-style referendum that would allow the people to pass a law without the consent of parliament, could not be introduced by a simple amendment but would require a referendum. In contrast – although this was contentious[43] – the 1929 amendment that added decisive features of a presidential system to the constitution by shifting powers from parliament to the federal president was officially not seen as a violation of the democratic principle and was therefore passed on a two-thirds majority in parliament only, without submitting the amendment to a referendum.

In both Austrian cases – notwithstanding the result – a referendum would have been or might be conceivable with politicians campaigning in favour of the respective amendment. In another, albeit single, case, decided by the constitutional court,[44] it can hardly be seen that a referendum would ever be held, thus effectively ruling out the particular amendment. To protect all state laws on public procurement from constitutional review for a transitional period, the federal parliament passed a constitutional law declaring those laws as 'constitutional'. (Such a move seemed to be preferable as all federal and state laws on public procurement had similar flaws and the court was due to rescind the relevant provisions one after the other. As a general reorganisation of the whole field of law was envisaged, also involving the distribution of responsibilities between the federation and the states, upholding

---

40 Cf. Victor Ferreres Comella, *The Constitution of Spain: A Contextual Analysis* (Hart Publishing 2013) 57 f.
41 Cf. ibid 85 ff.
42 Stelzer (n 39) 33.
43 Hans Kelsen, 'Die Verfassungsreform' 1929 JBl 450 ff, for instance advocated the view that this amendment represented a total revision of the constitution and would therefore have required a referendum.
44 VfSlg (the Official Compilation of the Austrian Constitutional Court's rulings and decisions) 16.327/2001.

the legal situation for a transitional period seemed to be desirable.) Nevertheless, the constitutional court held that such a law that exempts a whole field of legislation from scrutiny would violate the '*Rechtsstaat*' principle, and therefore it rescinded the constitutional law. On a strictly legal level, the court did not completely rule out such an amendment – it only required it to be backed by a referendum. But it seems to be a rather preposterous idea that politicians might campaign for supporting such an amendment in the run up to a referendum arguing the need to infringe on the principle of '*Rechtsstaat*' because they needed time to reorganise the whole field of public procurement law to erase unconstitutionalities that were not considered in the first place. Besides, as this amendment was only meant for a transitional period, preparing for and holding a referendum would probably have taken too much time anyway and, moreover, would have proved to be too costly.

Thus, the design of '*Rechtsstaat*' under the Austrian constitution as read by the constitutional court effectively limits the shift of power from the court to parliament (this is what the amendment effectively had done) and therefore restricts the options of changing the design of the constitution even beyond the obvious: abolishing the whole principle and/ or its institutional set-up (which in that case would be, foremost, the arrangement of independent courts).

While the Austrian and the Spanish constitutions – at least according to their wording – offer a path for amending even the more deeply entrenched parts, the German constitution establishes a so-called 'eternity clause'. Art 79 para 3 rules out any changes of the Basic Law ('*Grundgesetz*') that touch on the federal structure, the participation of the states in the federal legislation or the principles as laid down in Art 1 and 20 of the Basic Law. These articles cover among others the principles of human dignity, democracy, the social welfare state, the division of powers and popular sovereignty. Again, Art 79 para 3 not only protects the provisions that lay down these principles from being changed or abolished but also the core elements of these principles which are established by the constitutional court and the constitutional doctrine. It is, therefore, their task to define the limits of amendment powers and the design options they might have.[45]

The German example has been followed, for instance, partly by the Czech constitution, as already mentioned, which rules out any changes in the essential requirements of democracy and the rule of law. More interestingly, the Supreme Court of India has developed a doctrine, influenced by the German debate, according to which amendment powers are limited. They must not extend to the basic features or the basic structure of the constitution which, therefore, cannot be changed by an amendment. The crucial point is that this 'firewall' was erected by the constitutional court without the explicit support of the wording of the constitution, basically by restricting the scope of 'amendment'. In the parlance of 'constitutional design' it might be noted that according to this doctrine an amendment has to respect the constitutional identity[46] or the basic features of the constitutional design. Clearly, the findings of the court are highly contentious in Indian constitutional doctrine and would probably be in any other constitutional doctrine as well.[47]

---

45 Haratsch (n 32) Art 79 Rn 20: '*Im Wege der Verfassungsauslegung ist daher der unantastbare Grundsatzgehalt der durch Art 79. III geschützten Inhalte herauszuarbeiten*', which roughly translates to: 'By means of interpreting the constitution the untouchable basic substance of the features protected by Art 79 III has to be carved out.'
46 See also the discussion of the decisions of the Indian Supreme Court at Tushnet (n 26) 344 ff.
47 Cf. Arun K Thiruvengadam, *The Constitution of India: A Contextual Analysis* (Hart Publishing 2017) 221.

The interesting part here is the effect entrenching principles of a constitution in a specific way has on the design changes drafters of constitutional amendments might envisage. They reach far beyond the obvious – that the principles themselves cannot be changed, or at least only through a more cumbersome procedure. When it is left to a constitutional court and the constitutional doctrine to establish their scope, the result might be that rather minor design elements are protected from change.

Limits to amendment powers are subject to the individual constitution or the respective constitutional doctrine. However, the constitutional design project is dedicated to the Western-style constitution, which is a result of the philosophical and political theories developed throughout the Renaissance period[48] and the age of enlightenment. It is based on the ideas of popular sovereignty and division of powers,[49] the typical features of a democratic constitution. Popular sovereignty demands sovereignty be equally shared by the members of society, thus providing for equal political rights. Strikingly, the ancient Athenians preferred to address their political system as '*ισονομια*' (= equality of political rights) rather than democracy.[50] Until today, the Australian constitutional doctrine, for example, still emphasises the protection of individual rights through an equal share in political power,[51] thus clearly linking democracy and popular sovereignty with equality in a Rousseauvian sense. The second pillar upon which a democratic constitution rests is the idea of dividing power between different branches of government, usually the legislative, executive and judiciary branches, but also – in a vertical manner – between central and peripheral governments. This idea demands an institutional arrangement and delicately balancing powers in order to prevent one institution from seizing all the power and turning democracy into tyranny.

It can be discussed whether these two principles that form the essence of a democratic government cannot be overturned by amending a democratic constitution and thus by a democratic procedure, as this would run against the theoretical and moral prerequisites of such a procedure. Considerations of that ilk would, of course, not prevent the establishment of an autocratic regime. It would only mean that turning a democracy into tyranny would always be a revolutionary act, even if it came in the disguise of an amendment following all the required procedural steps.

As a new order is always possible, the distinction between 'amendment' and 'new constitution' may be of little value on a cognitive level. It might, nevertheless, be important on a political and/or moral level, as it would deny an authoritarian government democratic legitimation – something, authoritarian governments may still wish for. Denying legitimising an authoritarian government is probably the last, but in the course of history, not the least thing lawyers who are committed to their democratic constitution can do. In any case, authoritarian 'constitutions' would not be recognised under the constitutional design project.

---

48 A comprehensive and excellent account of the philosophical, scientific, political and cultural developments in the Renaissance period is given by Bernd Roeck, *Der Morgen der Welt: Geschichte der Renaissance* (Historische Bibliothek der Gerda Henkel Stiftung, 1st ed, C.H. Beck 2017). Unfortunately, this volume, of over 1,000 pages, seems to be still available only in German.

49 Lutz (n 5) 26 ff, 109 ff.

50 Mogens H Hansen, *The Athenian Democracy in the Age of Demosthenes: Structure, Principles, and Ideology* (University of Oklahoma Press, 2001, reprint of 2nd ed 1999) 69.

51 Cheryl Saunders, *The Constitution of Australia: A Contextual Analysis* (Hart Publishing 2011) 63 f, citing Sir Owen Dixon, 'The Law and the Constitution' (1935) 51 *Law Quarterly Review* 590, 579.

Conclusion

The constitutional design project covers a field of academic research that is based on the observation or suggestion that the features of a specific constitution may be arranged according to a plan, thus the constitution would be 'designed'. Nourished by the experience of the proliferation of Western-style constitutions, it is construed that designers purposefully choose from an array of possible design elements, which can be found in existing constitutions, on cognitive assumptions. The empirical and comparative studies carried out within this research field try to prove or disprove such assumptions aiming at improving design choices.

Drafters of amendments may take advantage of the results such studies might yield, especially when they try to erase imperfections of the constitutions, revealed at later stages, that amendment procedures were originally designed for. Apart from that, drafters of amendments are obviously in a different position to drafters of a new constitution, who may design a constitution from scratch (notwithstanding if that has ever happened). Only in the case of unlimited amendment powers, might it be conceivable that a completely new constitution is drafted and enacted in the disguise of an amendment.

In general (and in practice), however, amendments, although not restricted to erasing imperfections of the constitution, are related to the original design of the constitution. It is suggested that we can distinguish between five types of amendments: design-enhancing, design-adjusting, design-neutral, design-completing and design-changing. Design-changing amendments are sometimes restricted or partly aggravated by a constitution explicitly entrenching particular parts more deeply than others, by either providing for more complex amendment procedures or excluding those parts from change entirely. The same effect may result from a constitutional doctrine and/or the case law of an apex court, when amendment powers are restricted by means of interpretation.

Moreover, on a moral or political level, it can be argued that the defining principles of a democratic constitution, which coincide with the principles of constitutional design, can never be changed by an amendment. Although this would not shield against the establishment of an autocratic government, it would deny such a regime any appearance of being based on democratic legitimation.

References

Boyron S., *The Constitution of France. A Contextual Analysis* (Hart Publishing 2013).

Contiades X. and Fotiadou A., 'Models of Constitutional Change' in X. Contiades (ed), *Engineering Constitutional Change: A Comparative Perspective on Europe Canada and the USA* (Routledge 2013) 417–468.

Dixon O., 'The Law and the Constitution' (1935) 51 *Law Quarterly Review* 590.

Dixon R. and Holden R., 'Constitutional Amendment Rules: The Denominator Problem' in T. Ginsburg (ed), *Comparative Constitutional Design* (Cambridge University Press 2012) 195–218.

Elster J., 'Forces and Mechanisms in the Constitution-Making Process' in S. Voigt (ed), *Design of Constitutions*, Vol. 36 (Edward Elgar Publishing 2013) 67–99.

Ferejohn J. and Pasquino P., 'Constitutional Adjudication, Italian Style' in T. Ginsburg (ed), *Comparative Constitutional Design* (Cambridge University Press 2012) 294–316.

Ferreres Comella V., *The Constitution of Spain. A Contextual Analysis* (Hart Publishing 2013).

Ginsburg T. (ed), *Comparative Constitutional Design* (Cambridge University Press 2012).

Hansen M.H., *The Athenian Democracy in the Age of Demosthenes: Structure*, Principles, and Ideology (University of Oklahoma Press 2001 reprint of 2nd edn 1999).

Haratsch A. in H. Sodan (ed), *Grundgesetz* (C.H. Beck 3rd edn 2015).

Harding A. and Leyland P., *The Constitutional System of Thailand. A Contextual Analysis* (Hart Publishing 2011).

Horowitz D.L., 'Constitutional Design: Proposals Versus Processes' in S. Voigt (ed), *Design of Constitutions*, Vol. 36 (Edward Elgar Publishing 2013) 20–43.

Jacobsohn G.J., 'Theorizing the Constitutional Revolution' (2014) 2(1) *Journal of Law and Courts* 1.

Kelsen H., 'Die Verfassungsreform' (1929) *Juristische Blätter* 445.

Kelsen H., 'Judicial Review of Legislation. A Comparative Study of the Austrian and the American Constitution' (1942) 4 *The Journal of Politics* 183–200.

Leyland P., *The Constitution of the United Kingdom. A Contextual Analysis* (Hart Publishing 3rd edn 2016).

Lutz DS., *Principles of Constitutional Design* (Cambridge University Press 2006).

Madison J., A. Hamilton, and J. Jay, 'Federalist Paper no XLIX' in Isaac Kramnick (ed), *The Federalist Papers* (Penguin 1987) 313.

Montesquieu Charles Louis de Secondat de, *De l'esprit des lois* (Garnier 1941).

Mueller D., 'Constitutional Political Economy in the European Union' in S. Voigt (ed), *Design of Constitutions*, Vol. 36 (Edward Elgar Publishing 2013) 3–19.

Navot S., *The Constitution of Israel. A Contextual Analysis* (Hart Publishing 2014).

Riley A. and Sours P., *Common Law Legal English and Grammar: A Contextual Approach* (Hart Publishing International edition 2014).

Roeck B., *Der Morgen der Welt: Geschichte der Renaissance* (Historische Bibliothek der Gerda Henkel Stiftung 1st edn C.H. Beck 2017).

Saunders C., *The Constitution of Australia. A Contextual Analysis* (Hart Publishing 2011).

Stelzer M., *The Constitution of the Republic of Austria. A Contextual Analysis* (Hart Publishing 2011).

Testa C., 'Bicameralism and Corruption' (2010) 54(2) *European Economic Review* 181.

Thiruvengadam A.K., *The Constitution of India. A Contextual Analysis* (Hart Publishing 2017).

Tushnet M., 'Amendment Theory and Constituent Power' in Jacobsohn G. and M. Schor (eds), *Comparative Constitutional Theory* (Edward Elgar Publishing 2018) 317–333.

Urofsky M.I., *A March of Liberty: A Constitutional History of the United States* (Knopf 2nd edn 2002).

Voigt S. (ed), *Design of Constitutions* Vol. 36 (Edward Elgar Publishing 2013).

Young A.L., *Parliamentary Sovereignty and the Human Rights Act* (Hart Publishing 2009).

9

THE USES AND ABUSES OF CONSTITUTIONAL UNAMENDABILITY

*Yaniv Roznai**

Introduction

Can there be such a thing as 'an unconstitutional constitutional amendment' (UCA)? The idea of the possibility of unconstitutional constitutional norms was famously raised in Germany in the post-Second World War jurisprudence, when in the 1951 *Southwest* case, the Federal Constitutional Court cited with approval a statement of the Bavarian Constitutional Court according to which

> there are fundamental constitutional principles, which are of so elementary a nature and so much the expression of a law that precedes the constitution, that the maker of the constitution himself is bound by them. Other constitutional norms ... can be void because they conflict with them.

By this obiter statement, the court recognized the possibility of an 'unconstitutional constitution'.[1]

The German Constitutional Court, however, has never declared a constitutional provision to be unconstitutional, and until not so long ago, the UCA doctrine was regarded as an extreme peculiarity – a kind of hypothetical scenario constitutional law teachers enjoyed contemplating in classrooms and exams – but a situation deemed unlikely to actually materialize.[2]

However, recently, the UCA doctrine has emerged as a highly successful, albeit still controversial, export in comparative constitutional law, as recent work has demonstrated its migration and growing reception in jurisdictions around the world.[3]

* Earlier versions were presented at The Routledge Handbook of Comparative Constitutional Change Workshop (5 September 2018) and Faculty Seminar, Shaarei Mishpat College of Law and Science (23 October 2018). I would like to thank the participants in these events for their valuable comments.
1 See Gottfried Dietze, 'Unconstitutional Constitutional Norms? Constitutional Development in Postwar Germany' (1956) 42 *Virginia Law Review* 1; Otto Bachof, *Verfassungswidrige Verfassungsnormen?* (JCB Mohr 1951) 15.
2 See, e.g., Gary J Jacobsohn, 'An Unconstitutional Constitution? A Comparative Perspective' (2006) 4 *International Journal of Constitutional Law* 460, 487.
3 Kemal Gözler, *Judicial Review of Constitutional Amendments: A Comparative Study* (Ekin Press 2008); Yaniv Roznai, 'Unconstitutional Constitutional Amendments: The Migration and Success of a Constitutional Idea' (2013) 61(3) *American Journal of Comparative Law* 657; Gábor Halmai, 'Judicial Review of Constitutional

This chapter seeks to provide a broad overview of the recent doctrinal trend in global constitutional law to impose restrictions on the power to amend constitutions, the uses of such a doctrine and its perhaps more recent abuses. The chapter continues in the following manner. First, the two main types of limits to constitutional change – explicit and implicit unamendability – are reviewed. Next, the theory behind constitutional unamendability and its main objection are discussed. Following this, the uses of the doctrine are analysed and its recent abuses described.[4]

Types of constitutional unamendability

Constitutional unamendability refers to the limitations or restrictions imposed upon constitutional amendment powers preventing them from amending certain constitutional rules, values or institutions.[5] An unamendable provision, as Richard Albert describes it, is 'impervious to the constitutional amendment procedures enshrined within a constitutional text and immune to constitutional change even by the most compelling legislative and popular majorities'.[6] This is an explicit form of unamendability, part of the constitutional design. However, as we shall see, unamendability may also be judicially imposed, when a court derives such limitations implicitly from the constitution. These explicit and implicit types of unamendability impose substantive limits on the legal power to amend certain constitutional subjects.[7]

Explicit unamendability

The most famous example of explicit constitutional unamendability comes from Germany where, following the lessons of the Second World War and the horrors of the Holocaust, Article 79(3) of the Basic Law of 1949 (*Grundgesetz*) expressly states that constitutional amendments cannot affect human dignity and the democratic and federal features of the

---

Amendments and New Constitutions in Comparative Perspective' (2015) 50(4) *Wake Forest Law Review* 951. On the continuing rejection, in various jurisdictions, of the doctrine, see Richard Albert, Malkhaz Nakashidze and Tarik Olcay, 'The Formalist Resistance to Unconstitutional Constitutional Amendments' (2019) 70 *Hastings Law Journal* 639 www.hastingslawjournal.org/wp-content/uploads/70.4-Albert.pdf

4 It is important to note that this chapter only provides a general overview of the topic, as the issue of constitutional unamendability is a complex one, perhaps one of the thorniest topics in constitutional theory. For more elaborated studies on the subject see Yaniv Roznai, *Unconstitutional Constitutional Amendments: The Limits of Amendment Powers* (Oxford University Press 2017); Richard Albert and Bertil Emrah Oder (eds), *An Unconstitutional Constitution? Unamendability in Constitutional Democracies* (Springer 2018).

5 See Oran Doyle, 'Constraints on Constitutional Amendment Powers' in Richard Albert, Xenophon Contiades, and Alkmene Fotiadou (eds), *The Foundations and Traditions of Constitutional Amendment* (Hart Publishing 2017) 73.

6 Richard Albert, 'Constitutional Handcuffs' (2010) 42 *Arizona State Law Journal* 663, 666.

7 This chapter does not deal with 'informal unamendability' that may exist when the social or political climate is such that, although legally permissible, it is unimaginable that certain constitutional subjects would be amended. See Richard Albert, 'Constructive Unamendability in Canada and the United States' (2014) 67 *Supreme Court Law Review* 181. It also does not engage with 'covert unamendability' in politically enforced constitutions, where there is a constitutional convention, which may be enforced through disobedience of governmental branches, that certain constitutional arrangements shall not be abolished or significantly altered. See Gert Jan Geertjes and Jefri Uzman, 'Conventions of Unamendability: Unamendable Constitutional Law in Politically Enforced Constitutions' in Albert and Oder (n 4). It also does not deal with banning political parties, a constitutional arrangement that has many similarities with unamendability. On this link see Rivka Weill, 'On the Nexus of Eternity Clauses, Proportional Representation and Banned Political Parties' (2017) 16 *Election Law Journal* 237.

constitutional order.[8] However, explicit unamendability appeared much earlier, already in some of the U.S. states' constitutions in the eighteenth century[9] and in many of the Latin American constitutions of the nineteenth century.[10] For example, the Mexican constitution of 1824 stated that the provisions that establish the 'Liberty and Independence of the Mexican Nation, its Religion, Form of Government, Liberty of the Press, and Division of the Supreme Power of the Confederation, and of the States, shall never be reformed'.[11] Additionally, one of the early European examples of explicit unamendability is Article 112 of the Constitution of the Kingdom of Norway of 1814, according to which amendments 'must never … contradict the principles embodied in this Constitution, but solely relate to modifications of particular provisions which do not alter the spirit of the Constitution'.[12]

Over the years, explicit unamendability has become a popular constitutional design. While between 1789 and 1944, only 17% of world constitutions enacted in this period included unamendable provisions, between 1945 and 1988, already 27% of world constitutions enacted in those years included such provisions (78 out of 286), and out of the constitutions that were enacted between 1989 and 2015, more than half (54%) included unamendable provisions.[13]

The content of explicit unamendability varies.[14] From the protection of the essential requirement for a democratic state governed by the rule of law, as in the Czech Republic's constitution of 1992,[15] to constitutions that declare as unamendable the state religion,[16] the principle of secularism[17] and even the state's territorial integrity.[18] The form and system of government, the structure of government, basic democratic principles such as the rule of law, separation of powers, mode of elections, and values strongly connected to a specific fundamental ideology or identity, can all be found in unamendable provisions. Unamendable provisions thus mostly refer to constitutional values, rules, and institutions that are considered as the constitutional order's core values, in an attempt to preserve the

---

8 See Helmut Goerlich, 'Concept of Special Protection for Certain Elements and Principles of the Constitution Against Amendments and Article 79(3), Basic Law of Germany' (2008) 1 *NUJS Law Review* 397.

9 See e.g., Constitution of New Jersey of 1776, Art. 23; Delaware Constitution of 1776, Art. 30.

10 See Yaniv Roznai, 'Constitutional Unamendability in Latin America Gone Wrong?' in Richard Albert, Justice Carlos Bernal, and Juliano Zaiden Benvindo (eds), *Constitutional Change and Transformation in Latin America* (Hart Publishing 2019) 93–115.

11 Mexican constitution of 1824, Art. 171.

12 See Eivind Smith, 'Old and Protected? On the "Supra- constitutional" Clause in the Constitution of Norway' (2011) 44(3) *Israel Law Review* 369.

13 Roznai (n 4) 20–21. On the origins, differentiation, and migration of unamendable provisions, see Michael Hein, 'Entrenchment Clauses in the History of Modern Constitutionalism' (2018) 86(3–4) *The Legal History Review* 434.

14 Marie-Francoise Rigaux, *La Theorie Des Limites Materielles A L'Exercice De La Fonction Constituante* (Larcier 1985).

15 Ústava České Republiky, Art. 9(2). See Ondřej Preuss, 'The Eternity Clause as a Smart Instrument: Lessons from the Czech Case Law' (2016) 57(3) *Hungarian Journal of Legal Studies* 289.

16 See Richard Albert and Yaniv Roznai, 'Religion, Secularism and Limitations on Constitutional Amendment' in Rex Tauati Ahdar (ed), *Research Handbook on Law and Religion* (Edward Elgar Publishing 2018) 154.

17 See Yaniv Roznai, 'Negotiating the Eternal: The Paradox of Entrenching Secularism in Constitutions' (2017) *Michigan State Law Review* 253.

18 Yaniv Roznai and Silvia Suteu, 'The Eternal Territory? The Crimean Crisis and Ukraine's Territorial Integrity as an Unamendable Constitutional Principle' (2015) 16(3) *German Law Journal* 542.

core of the nation's constitutional identity – or the one that they aspire to.[19] Thus, for example, in post-Soviet states, explicit unamendability was assigned a special role in safeguarding the transition from non-democracy to democracy, by protecting the constitutional order from being replaced by constitutional mechanisms.[20]

Explicit unamendability is not merely declarative. In some countries, such as Brazil,[21] Germany,[22] and the Czech Republic,[23] it is enforced through the exercise of substantive judicial review of constitutional amendments, ensuring their compatibility with the unamendable provisions. When constitutional amendments are deemed incompatible with values, rules, or provisions protected by constitutional unamendability, they can be declared unconstitutional and void. In Turkey, for example, in June 2008, the Constitutional Court invalidated constitutional amendments aiming to abolish the headscarf ban in universities, holding that the amendments infringe upon the constitutionally protected principle of secularism and are therefore unconstitutional.[24] Consequently, the idea of an unconstitutional constitutional norm, once considered factionary has become a reality in some jurisdictions.

Implicit unamendability

Of course, when explicit unamendability exists, judicial review of constitutional amendments would seem a natural mechanism providing 'legal teeth' to the unamendable provisions.[25] But what if the constitution does not include explicit unamendable provisions? Does this mean that the constitutional amendment power is omnipotent?

19 Yaniv Roznai, 'Unamendability and the Genetic Code of the Constitution' (2015) 27(2) *European Review of Public Law* 775; Albert (n 6).
20 Dmitry Shustrov, 'Material'nye predely izmeneniya konstitutsiy postsovetskikh gosudarstv (Material limits of constitutional change in Post-Soviet states)' (2018) 27(2) *Sravnitel'noe konstitutsionnoe obozrenie* 86.
21 See Conrado Hubner Mendes, 'Judicial Review of Constitutional Amendments in the Brazilian Supreme Court' (2005) 17 *Florida Journal of International Law* 449; Yaniv Roznai and Letícia Regina Camargo Kreuz, 'Conventionality Control and Amendment 95/2016: A Brazilian case of Unconstitutional Constitutional Amendment' (2018) 5(2) *Revista de Investigaciones Constitucionales* 35; Juliano Zaiden Benvindo, 'Brazil in the Context of the Debate Over Unamendability in Latin America' in Albert and Oder (n 4) 345; Valentina Rita Scotti, 'Constitutional Amendments and Constitutional Core Values: the Brazilian Case in a Comparative Perspective (2018) 5(3) *Revista de Investigações Constitucionais* 59, 66–71.
22 Ulrich K Preuss, 'The Implications of "Eternity Clauses": The German Experience' (2011) 44(3) *Israel Law Review* 429; Donald P Kommers and Russell A Miller, *The Constitutional Jurisprudence of the Federal Republic of Germany: Third Edition, Revised and Expanded* (Duke University Press 2012) 58–59.
23 See Kieran Williams, 'When a Constitutional Amendment Violates the Substantive Core: The Czech Constitutional Court's September 2009 Early Elections Decision' (2011) 36 *Review of Central and East European Law* 33; Jan Kudrna, 'Cancellation of Early Elections by the Constitutional Court of The Czech Republic: Beginning of a New Concept of "Protection of Constitutionality"' (2010) 4 *Jurisprudencija* 43; Zdeněk Koudelka, 'Abolition of Constitutional Statute by the Constitutional Court of the Czech Republic' (2018) 2 *Russian Law: Theory and Practice* 15–42; Yaniv Roznai, 'Legisprudence Limitations on Constitutional Amendments? Reflections on the Czech Constitutional Court's Declaration of Unconstitutional Constitutional Act' (2014) 8(1) *Vienna Journal of International Constitutional Law* 29.
24 Turkish Constitutional Court Decision of June 5, 2008, No. 2008/16; 2008/116. See, for example, Yaniv Roznai and Serkan Yolcu, 'An Unconstitutional Constitutional Amendment – The Turkish Perspective: A comment on the Turkish Constitutional Court's Headscarf Decision' (2012) 10(1) *International Journal of Constitutional Law* 175. See generally Tarik Olcay, 'The Unamendability of Amendable Clauses: The Case of the Turkish Constitution' in Albert and Oder (n 4) 313.
25 Aharon Barak, 'Unconstitutional Constitutional Amendments' (2011) 44(3) *Israel Law Review* 321, 333.

The fact that a constitution does not include explicit unamendability does not necessarily mean that the constitutional amendment power is absolute and that all the parts of the constitution are amendable. Constitutional courts around the world have recognized a core of basic constitutional principles that should be regarded as implicitly unamendable. Perhaps the most famous example is the Indian one, where in the *Kesavananda Bharati v. State of Kerala* case of 1973, the Indian Supreme Court held that the power of the parliament 'to amend the constitution does not include the power to alter the basic structure, or framework of the constitution so as to change its identity',[26] as it is 'a precious heritage',[27] creating what has come to be known as the 'basic structure doctrine'.[28]

The basic structure doctrine migrated into neighboring and other states, and was accepted and adopted – in various forms and variations – in courts in Bangladesh, Pakistan, Uganda, Kenya, Taiwan, Colombia, Peru, Belize, and Slovakia. In these countries, courts declared that some basic features or principles of the constitution are so imperative to the constitutional order that they are beyond the amendment power even without any explicit limitations.[29]

In Colombia, for example, the constitution of 1991 creates a distinction between amendment (which can be carried out by Congress alone or by referendum) and replacement carried out by constituent assembly. However, it neither establishes any principles determining when each route must be used nor includes any unamendable provisions. It also expressly limits judicial control over constitutional amendments to 'procedural errors' only. Nonetheless, the Constitutional Court gave a wide definition of the concept of 'procedural error', noting, in a line of judicial decisions, that the amendment power does not extend to the replacement of the constitution with a different one. It is only the constituent power, acting through extraordinary mechanisms such as a constituent assembly that can constitute a new constitution. This has come to be known as the 'substitution' or 'replacement' doctrine.[30]

Where courts enforce explicit or implicit unamendability, be it through a 'basic structure' or 'constitutional substitution' doctrine, they regard themselves as 'guardians of the constitution' and its core values.[31]

---

26 *Kesavananda Bharati v. State of Kerala*, AIR 1973 SC 1461.
27 Justice Chandrachud in *Minerva Mills, Ltd. v. Union of India*, AIR 1980 SC 1789, 1798.
28 Much has been written about this doctrine. See e.g., Sudhir Krishnaswamy, *Democracy and Constitutionalism in India: A Study of the Basic Structure Doctrine* (Oxford University Press 2010).
29 See e.g., Yaniv Roznai, 'The Migration of the Indian Basic Structure Doctrine' in Malik Lokendra (ed), *Judicial Activism in India: A Festschrift in Honour of Justice V. R. Krishna Iyer* (Universal Law Publishing Co. Pvt. Ltd 2012) 240; Marcin Józef Szwed, 'S⬚dowa kontrola konstytucyjno⬚ci ustaw zmieniaj⬚cych konstytucj⬚ w Indiach' (Judicial review of the constitutionality of laws amending the constitution in India)' (2016) 3 *Przegląd Sejmowy* 63.
30 See e.g., Carlos Bernal, 'Unconstitutional Constitutional Amendments in the Case Study of Colombia: An Analysis of the Justification and Meaning of the Constitutional Replacement Doctrine' (2013) 11(2) *International Journal of Constitutional Law* 339; Gonzalo Andres Ramirez-Cleves, 'The Unconstitutionality of Constitutional Amendments in Colombia: The Tension Between Majoritarian Democracy and Constitutional Democracy' in Thomas Bustamante and Bernardo Gonçalves Fernandes (eds), *Democratizing Constitutional Law* (Springer 2016) 213; Mario Alberto Cajas-Sarria, 'Judicial Review of Constitutional Amendments in Colombia: A Political and Historical Perspective, 1955–2016' (2017) 5(3) *The Theory and Practice of Legislation* 245.
31 See e.g., Rory O'Connell, 'Guardians of the Constitution: Unconstitutional Constitutional Norms' (1999) 4 *Journal of Civil Liberties* 48; Gábor Halmai, 'Unconstitutional Constitutional Amendments: Constitutional Courts as Guardians of the Constitution?' (2012) 19(2) *Constellations* 182.

The theory and critique of constitutional unamendability

Theory

Scholars have developed a number of defenses of constitutional unamendability.[32] The basic theory behind constitutional unamendability is rooted in the distinction between the people's primary constituent power, which is the absolute power to establish a new legal order, and secondary constituent power or amendment power which is a delegated power that acts within the constitutional framework and is limited under the terms of its mandate.[33] Accordingly, the amendment power must obey those explicit unamendable provisions stipulated in the constitution. In other words, unamendable provisions create a normative hierarchy between constitutional norms. Moreover, the constitutional amendment power cannot be used in order to destroy the constitution from which its authority derives. The amendment process is the internal method that the constitution provides for its self-preservation; by destroying the constitution, the amending power undermines its own *raison d'être*. Similarly, as every constitution consists of a set of basic principles that structure the 'spirit of the constitution' and its identity, and the alteration of the constitution's core results in the collapse of the entire constitution and its replacement by another, consequently, the amendment power cannot be used in order to destroy the basic principles of the constitution. Formal constitutional amendment, Carl Schmitt wrote, can change the text 'only under the presupposition that the identity and continuity of the constitution as an entirety is preserved'.[34]

Constitutional amendment is not constitutional replacement. Replacing the constitution with a new one is the role of the people who retain the primary constituent power; and through its exercise they may shape and reshape the political order and its fundamental principles. The theory of unamendability thus restricts the amending authorities from amending certain constitutional fundamentals. Unamendability does not block all the democratic avenues for constitutional change, but rather merely proclaims that one such avenue, namely the formal amendment process, is unavailable. It makes sure that certain constitutional changes take place through a channel of higher-level democratic deliberations, popular-democratic or consensual rooting. Understood in this way, the theory of unamendability is a safeguard of the people's primary constituent power.[35]

Critique

The doctrine has often been criticized on democratic grounds, for example as creating a kind of super-counter-majoritarian difficulty.[36] Arguments against constitutional unamendability

---

32 For an exploration of the normative arguments for and against the judicial enforcement of implicit substantive constraints on formal constitutional change, see Po Jen Yap, 'The Conundrum of Unconstitutional Constitutional Amendments' (2015) 4(1) *Global Constitutionalism* 114.

33 See Yaniv Roznai, 'Towards a Theory of Constitutional Unamendability: On the Nature and Scope of the Constitutional Amendment Powers' (2017) 18 *Jus Politicum* 5–37.

34 Carl Schmitt, *Constitutional Theory* (Jeffrey Seitzer trans. and ed., Duke University Press 2008) 150.

35 Vicki Jackson, 'Unconstitutional Constitutional Amendments: A Window into Constitutional Theory and Transnational Constitutionalism' in Geburtstag Astrid Wallrabenstein, Philipp Dann, and Michael Bäuerle (eds), *Demokratie- Perspektiven Festschrift für Brun-Otto Bryde zum 70* (Mohr Siebeck 2013) 47, 58–62.

36 For an evaluation and response of critique of the doctrine see Yaniv Roznai, 'Necrocracy or Democracy? Assessing Objections to Constitutional Unamendability' in Albert and Oder (n 4) 29.

and the UCA doctrine tend to focus most heavily on its supposed incommensurable tension with procedural democracy. Since a self-governing people ought to be able to challenge or revise its basic commitments, the ability to amend the constitution seems an essential element of any democratic society. Unamendability positions certain rules or values not only above ordinary politics, but also above constitutional politics and the popular will. By not allowing majorities – even super-majorities – to modify these rules or values, and by neglecting the importance of the present political process as a basic protection for the exercise of democratic self-government, unamendability is in clear tension with democratic principles.[37]

Arguably, it should be the people's decision (directly or through their representatives) whether a certain constitutional element is essential to the constitutional order or not and this decision should not be subject to judicial review. Critics, therefore, argue that unamendability 'betrays one of democracy's most attractive legacies: the ability to modify law',[38] or 'deny citizens the democratic right to amend their own constitution and in so doing divest them for the basic sovereign rights of popular choice and continuing self-definition'.[39]

The challenge of constitutional unamendability is exacerbated when one further considers a common function of constitutional amendment – to act as 'a safety valve' by allowing 'the people' through constitutional politics and heightened majorities to overcome judicial decisions they disagree with.[40] Unamendability coupled with the power of courts to review amendments threatens to cut off this safety valve, leaving 'the people' with no manner by which they can overturn the judicial ruling. The political branches might then turn to more destabilizing or destructive measures, such as undermining or packing a court, or replacing the existing constitution entirely.[41]

Accordingly, constitutional unamendability and the UCA doctrine raise the counter-majoritarian difficulty in its 'most extreme' form.[42]

The uses of constitutional unamendability

Reflecting the people's constitutional identity, constitutional unamendability defines, in many ways, the collective 'self' of the polity – the 'we the people'.[43] When the values regarded as unamendable are not of universal character but rather particular characteristics of a specific – usually the hegemonic – group, then unamendability can be regarded as preserving divisions and exclusions rather than being a unified mechanism.[44]

---

37 Richard Albert, 'The Unamendable Core of the United States Constitution' in András Koltay (ed), *Comparative Perspectives on the Fundamental Freedom of Expression* (Wolters Kluwer 2016) 13.

38 Melissa Schwartzberg, *Democracy and Legal Change* (Cambridge University Press 2009) 2.

39 Albert (n 6) 667. See also Richard Albert, 'Counterconstitutionalism' (2008) 31 *Dalhousie Law Journal* 1, 3.

40 Rosalind Dixon, 'Constitutional Amendment Rules: A Comparative Perspective' in Tom Ginsburg and Rosalind Dixon (eds), *Comparative Constitutional Law* (Edward Elgar Publishing 2011) 96, 98.

41 See Rosalind Dixon and David Landau, 'Tiered Constitutional Design' (2018) 86(2) *George Washington Law Review* 438.

42 See Gary J Jacobsohn, 'The Permeability of Constitutional Borders' (2004) 82 *Texas Law Review* 1763, 1799.

43 Preuss (n 22) 445.

44 See e.g, the unamendable state characteristic of Romania as a 'national state' in Silvia Suteu, 'The Multinational State that Wasn't: The Constitutional Definition of Romania as a National State' (2017) 11(3) *Vienna Journal of International Constitutional Law* 413, or the alleged implicit unamendability of the 'Jewish and Democratic' characteristics of the State of Israel in Mazen Masri, 'Unamendability in Israel: A Critical Perspective' in Albert and Oder (n 4) 169. On this tension between particularistic values and popular sovereignty, see Sharon Weintal,

However, when constitutional unamendability protects core principles of the democratic order, it – together with its judicial enforcement – has a potential utility in guarding against the use of tools of constitutional change to undermine democracy, or what has been called, following David Landau, 'abusive constitutionalism'.[45] Judicial review of constitutional amendments, Claude Klein suggests, was developed precisely because of the fear of abuse of the amendment power:

> what if the 'amending power' would try to bypass the constitution by amending it in order to allow the adoption of problematic laws, such as those that had already been declared unconstitutional? There thus appeared to be a need for 'super-protection' or 'super-entrenchment'.[46]

Especially where the tools of constitutional change are highly flexible the UCA doctrine could be useful in protecting liberal democratic constitutionalism.[47] And particularly in weak democracies, judicial review of amendments might seem valuable for protecting democracies from collapsing into autocratic power.[48]

UCA doctrine was adopted precisely in order to defend democracy, or what courts regard as fundamental values of their constitutional democracy.[49] Indeed, cases from contexts such as India and Colombia suggest that it might be useful to deploy the UCA doctrine when political leaders have the ability to amend the constitution in ways that would damage the democratic order.[50] The use of the UCA doctrine as protector of the constitutional system can be regarded on several levels: as a 'stop sign', a 'speed-bump', a 'warning sign', and as a 'billboard'.

'A stop sign'

The UCA has the capability to completely stop constitutional changes that are deemed as harming, undermining, or dangerous to the constitutional order. Two examples, from Taiwan and Uganda, may illustrate this use.

On September 4, 1999, the Third National Assembly of Taiwan, fearing abolishment, enacted by anonymous balloting the Fifth Amendment to the Constitution, which provides that the Fourth National Assembly shall be appointed from the various political parties

'The Challenge of Reconciling Constitutional Eternity Clauses with Popular Sovereignty: Toward Three-Track Democracy in Israel as a Universal Holistic Constitutional System and Theory' (2011) 44(3) *Israel Law Review* 449, 494.

45 David Landau, 'Abusive Constitutionalism' (2013) 47(1) *UC Davis Law Review* 189, 231–39.
46 Claude Klein, 'An Introduction to the Modernity of a Constitutional Question' (2011) 44(3) *Israel Law Review* 318–19.
47 See Rosalind Dixon and David Landau, 'Transnational Constitutionalism and a Limited Doctrine of Unconstitutional Constitutional Amendment' (2015) 13(3) *International Journal of Constitutional Law* 606; Yaniv Roznai, 'Constituent Powers, Amendment Powers and Popular Sovereignty: Linking Unamendability and Amendment Procedures' in Richard Albert, Xenophon Contiades and Alkmene Fotiadou (eds), *The Foundations and Traditions of Constitutional Amendment* (Hart Publishing 2017) 23, 41–48.
48 Samuel Issacharoff, 'Managing Conflict through Democracy' in Colin Harvey and Alex Schwartz (eds), *Rights in Divided Societies* (Hart Publishing 2012) 33, 45.
49 See Richard Albert, 'How a Court Becomes Supreme: Defending the Constitution from Unconstitutional Amendments' (2017) 77 *Maryland Law Review* 181.
50 See Dixon and Landau (n 47).

according to the ratio of votes each party received in the corresponding Legislative Yuan election. In other words, the amendment turned the National Assembly into an unelected body. It also extended the National Assembly term to two additional years. The amendment was challenged by a group of Legislative Yuan lawmakers. On March 24, 2000, the Council of Grand Justices announced Interpretation No. 499 in which it declared the amendment unconstitutional on the grounds that it violated certain basic unamendable constitutional principles:

> Although the Amendment to the Constitution has equal status with the constitutional provisions, any amendment that alters the existing constitutional provisions concerning the fundamental nature of governing norms and order and, hence, the foundation of the Constitution's very existence destroys the integrity and fabric of the Constitution itself. As a result, such an amendment shall be deemed improper. Among the constitutional provisions, principles such as establishing a democratic republic under Article 1, sovereignty of and by the people under Article 2, protection of the fundamental rights of the people under Chapter Two as well as the check and balance of governmental powers are some of the most critical and fundamental tenets of the Constitution as a whole.[51]

Thus, even in the absence of explicit unamendability, the Council granted itself the power to review and annul constitutional amendments.[52] Scholars claim that this judgment was essential in preserving and stabilizing the democratic constitutional order in Taiwan.[53]

A second example comes from Uganda. On July 26, 2018, the Constitutional Court of Uganda delivered a landmark 814-page judgment embracing and incorporating the Indian 'basic structure doctrine', and holding that parliament has limited amendment powers. The court ruled by 4–1 to uphold provisions of a constitutional amendment that removed presidential age limits. Nevertheless, all judges decided that the amendment's provision extending the term of office for members of parliament from five to seven years is unconstitutional and void. Writing a dissenting view, Justice Kakuru declared the entire amendment to be unconstitutional, holding that the idea that parliament has absolute amendment powers 'is a fiction based on a legal misconception'. If this is the case, the MPs

---

51 An English translation by Andy Y Sun is available at https://cons.judicial.gov.tw/jcc/en-us/jep03/show? expno=499. See also Ming-Sung Kuo and Hui-Wen Chen in 'J.Y. Interpretation No. 499 (March 24, 2000) – Unconstitutional Constitutional Amendments Case' Leading Cases of the Taiwan Constitutional Court (Judicial Yuan 2018) 15–41, http://jirs.judicial.gov.tw/judlib/EBookDownload.asp?pfid=0000231032&showType=1&dlk=X%2C20180912%2C0001

52 Wen-Chen Chang, 'Courts and Judicial Reform in Taiwan: Gradual Transformations towards the Guardian of Constitutionalism and Rule of Law' in Jiunn-rong Yeh and Wen-Chen Chang (eds), *Asian Courts in Context* (Cambridge University Press 2015) 143, 170.

53 See Wu Sheng-Wen, *Popular Sovereignty and Limitations on Constitutional Amendments: Dissertation from Constitutional Interpretation No. 499 of the Grand Justices, Judical Yuan* (Graduate Institution of Political Science, National Sun Yat-Sen University, May 2005); Tzu-Yi Lin, Ming-Sung Kuo, and Hui-Wen Chen, 'Seventy Years On: The Taiwan Constitutional Court and Judicial Activism in a Changing Constitutional Landscape' (2018) 48(3) *Hong Kong Law Journal* 995. Since 2000, however, the court's role in constitutional politics has been curtailed. See Ming-Sung Kuo, 'Towards a Nominal Constitutional Court? Critical Reflections on the Shift from Judicial Activism to Constitutional Irrelevance in Taiwan's Constitutional Politics' (2016) 25(3) *Washington International Law Journal* 597.

can abolish Republic of Uganda or make themselves MPs for life. Parliament can abolish the Republic of Uganda and introduce a monarchy ... the argument that you can vote to amend any article of the Constitution by simple majority is misguided.[54]

In this case, like in Taiwan, the court was able to stop (perhaps only with partial success as it still upheld other problematic provisions of the amendment) what many regarded as an amendment that 'diminishes the spirit of the Ugandan Constitution and to that extent can be viewed as unconstitutional'.[55]

'A speed-bump'

Constitutional unamendability can often act as a stop sign, blocking certain constitutional changes. But then again, can it really stop violent movements aiming to abolish the democratic order? This seems unlikely; as Karl Loewenstein observed, in times of crisis, constitutional unamendability is just a piece of paper that political reality could disregard or ignore.[56] This means that unamendability cannot serve as a complete bar against movements aiming to destroy the core values of societies. However, it can be, especially in normal (i.e. non-crisis) times, a useful red light or a speed-bump, before certain 'unconstitutional' constitutional changes, and stand firm in the normal development of political thrust. Gregory Fox and Georg Nolte remark that the framers of the German Basic Law believed that if an unamendable provision

> had been presented in the Weimar constitution, Hitler would have been forced to violate the constitution openly before assuming virtually dictatorial power. ... [G]iven the traditional orderly and legalistic sentiment of the German people, this might have made the difference.[57]

Even without speculating on alternative histories, constitutional unamendability clearly carries a slow-down character as it mandates public, political and judicial deliberation as to whether or not the change in question is compatible with society's basic principles.

Often, powerful politicians attempt to perpetuate their own power or weaken separation of powers by abusing (commonly flexible) constitutional amendment procedures. When judges invalidate amendments that would significantly harm the democratic constitutional order, these decisions can act – if not as a complete stop sign – as a type of a 'speed-bump', slowing down authoritarian initiatives until different political actors gain power.[58]

---

54 Constitutional Petition No. 49/2017 (delivered on July 26, 2018), https://judiciary.go.ug/.../AgeLimitJudgment_Mbale20180726.pdf; an appeal is currently pending in the Supreme Court of Uganda.

55 Pearl Onyema, 'How Unconstitutional is Uganda's 2018 Constitution Amendment?' (February 28, 2018) *Africa in Development*, https://africaindevelopment.com/2018/02/28/how-unconstitutional-is-ugandas-2018-constitution-amendment/. Consider another example; based upon the unamenable provision prohibiting any amendment concerning presidential term limits, on May 25, 2009, the Constitutional Court of Niger declared as unconstitutional a call for a referendum that would have suspended the constitution and allowed the president to continue in office as an interim president for a period of three years. See Cour Constitutionnelle AVIS n. 02/CC of 26.05.2009, http://cour-constitutionnelle-niger.org/documents/avis/2009/avis_n_002_cc_2009.pdf

56 Karl Loewenstein, 'Constitutions, Constitutional Law' in C.D. Kenig (ed), *Marxism, Communism, and Western Society: A Comparative Encyclopedia* (Herder and Herder 1972) 169, 180–81.

57 Gregory H Fox and Georg Nolte, 'Intolerant Democracies' (1995) 36 *Harvard International Law Journal* 1, 19.

58 Dixon and Landau (n 47).

As an example of such a 'speed-bump', Dixon and Landau cite the use of the Colombian 'constitutional replacement doctrine' in its 2010 decision striking down a referendum that would have allowed President Alvaro Uribe to seek a third consecutive term in office, after the court had earlier allowed Uribe to amend the constitution to seek a second consecutive term.[59] In this case, the court held that a third consecutive presidential term would concentrate executive power, cause severe damage to institutional checks on the president, and force the political opposition to compete on a greatly tilted playing field. After this ruling, Uribe peacefully left power, and scholars have credited the court as playing a potentially key role in protecting against an erosion of democracy in Colombia.[60] This may be regarded as a speed-bump as 'the decision bought time and delayed the anti-democratic effort',[61] or even as a complete stop sign.

'A warning sign'

Even if unamendability cannot act as a complete 'stop sign' or even as a 'speed-bump', it creates a 'chilling effect' leading to hesitation before repealing an unamendable constitutional subject. The mere designation of a certain provision as 'unamendable' raises the political, public, and legal costs of those who wish to change it. This 'chilling effect' may act as a useful warning sign, allowing time for political and public deliberations regarding the protected constitutional subject and placing them at the centre of the public agenda. Such deliberations, then, grant unamendability an important role.

An interesting, and slightly different, example of a 'warning sign' is a 2017 decision by the Israeli High Court of Justice, in which the court issued a nullification notice to a temporary Basic Law that changed the annual budget rule to a biennial one, for the fifth time in a row, by applying a doctrine of 'misuse of constituent power'.[62] Justice Rubinstein, who wrote the main opinion, stated that: 'the repeated use of a temporary order to amend the Basic Law not only overrides the public debate, but also undermines the status of the Basic Laws in a way that justifies a judicial action'.[63] As for judicial remedy, instead of striking down the amendment, Justice Rubinstein issued a 'nullification notice' that allowed the current amendment yet forbade another future amendment of the Basic Law by a temporary order.[64] Through this judgment, the court is issuing a warning sign to the Knesset not to abuse its constituent powers in the future.

---

59 See Decision C-141 of 2010 in Manuel José Cepeda Espinosa and David Landau (eds), *Colombian Constitutional Law: Leading Cases* (Oxford University Press 2017) 352.

60 See e.g., Armin von Bogdandy, 'Ius Constitutionale Commune en América Latina: Observations on Transformative Constitutionalism' in Armin von Bogdandy et al. (eds), *Transformative Constitutionalism in Latin America: The Emergence of a New Ius Commune* (Oxford University Press 2017) ch. 2; Rosalind Dixon and David Landau, 'Democracy and the Constitutional Minimum Core' in Tom Ginsburg and Aziz Huq (eds), *Assessing Constitutional Performance* (Cambridge University Press 2016) 268–76.

61 Dixon and Landau (n 47) 617–18.

62 HCJ 8260/16 *Academic Center of Law and Business v. Knesset* (September 6, 2017). On this case see Yaniv Roznai, 'Constitutional Paternalism: The Israeli Supreme Court as Guardian of the Knesset' (2018–2019) 51(4) *Verfassung und Recht in Übersee* 415–36; Suzie Navot and Yaniv Roznai, 'From Supra-Constitutional Principles to the Misuse of Constituent Power in Israel' (2019) 21(3) *European Journal of Law Reform* 403–23.

63 HCJ 8260/16 (n 59), para 33 of Justice Rubinstein's judgment.

64 Ibid., at para 34.

'A billboard'

Apart from the ability of unamendability to act as a useful stop sign, speed-bump, or warning sing, the mere expression of constitutional unamendability fulfills important educational and symbolic functions.[65] Richard Albert is correct in claiming that just as constitutions carry out expressive functions serving as important symbols for the polity, the unamendability of a principle or an institution conveys its symbolic value. It sends a message both domestically to the citizens and to external observers regarding the state's basic constitutional principles.[66] At the very least, constitutional unamendability 'makes a statement' regarding its importance to and respect for the constitutional order and its constitutive principles.[67] In other words, explicit unamendability is intended not only to protect but also to express deeply cherished values, rules, and institutions, acting as a kind of a billboard for society's core constitutional identity.

The abuses of the doctrine of unconstitutional constitutional amendments

UCA capture

As noted earlier, with reference to the experience in Colombia, the UCA doctrine can be a useful tool against attempts to remove presidential term limits. Indeed, judicial invocation of the UCA doctrine has become a major mode of change on term limits in Latin America in recent years.[68] In a recent set of cases, however, courts have not only paved the way for attempts to ease presidential term limits but have actually rooted out the constitutional term limits themselves by holding them to be UCAs.[69]

Take, for example, the decision of the Supreme Court of Nicaragua in 2009. The incumbent president, Daniel Ortega, sought potential re-election in 2011 after winning the presidency in 2007. However, a constitutional provision, which was added in a 1995 amendment, prohibited consecutive re-election, and limited presidents to serving only two terms in their lifetimes. Ortega had earlier served as president in the 1980s, therefore he ran up against not only the consecutive limit, but also the lifetime limit for presidency. The term limit was not explicitly unamendable, but Ortega lacked the necessary supermajority in Congress to pursue an amendment removing the term limit. In this context, Ortega brought a case in the Constitutional Chamber of the Supreme Court, arguing that the term limit itself, which had been added to the 1987 constitution, was a UCA. The court held that the amendment violated both the core principles of equality, by treating those who had already

---

65 Jon Elster, 'Constitutionalism in Eastern Europe: An Introduction' (1991) 58 *University of Chicago Law Review* 447, 471: 'the purpose of … unamendable clauses is … mainly symbolic'.

66 See Richard Albert, 'The Expressive Function of Constitutional Amendment Rules' (2013) 59(2) *McGill Law Journal* 225.

67 See, generally, Cass R Sunstein, 'On the Expressive Function of Law' (1995–96) 144 *The University of Pennsylvania Law Review* 2021, 2024–25.

68 David Landau, Yaniv Roznai and Rosalind Dixon, 'Term Limits and the Unconstitutional Constitutional Amendment Doctrine: Lessons from Latin America' in Alexander Baturo and Robert Elgie (eds), *Politics of Presidential Term Limits* (Oxford University Press 2019) 53–73.

69 See Roznai (n 10); David Landau, 'Presidential Term Limits in Latin America: A Critical Analysis of the Migration of the Unconstitutional Constitutional Amendment Doctrine' (2018) 12(2) *Law & Ethics of Human Rights* 225.

been elected differently from those who had not, and the rights of 'electoral suffrage' of both voters and those being elected. In particular, the court emphasized the sovereignty of the people, who had the right to make a free choice as to who would represent them. In inserting a term limit, the constitutional amenders had thus violated core principles of the original 1987 constitution and the amendment was void.[70] This was an invalidation of an amendment by using the UCA doctrine. But consider an even more puzzling use of the doctrine for invalidating parts of the original constitution.

In 2017, the Bolivian Constitutional Court issued a decision holding the term limits in its 2009 constitution to be unconstitutional.[71] In particular, the court relied very heavily on the argument that presidential term limits violate international human rights law, an argument that, as we note above, has no real foundation.[72]

A more peculiar case of such judicial intervention, in light of historical circumstances, comes from Honduras. The 1982 constitution limited presidents to only one term in office in their lifetime, prevented any attempt to change the no re-election rule by embedding it in an eternity clause, and provided that anyone attempting to change the term limit would 'cease' to hold office and be barred from doing so for the subsequent ten years. These provisions played a role in the coup that resulted in the removal from power of President Manuel Zelaya in 2009,[73] which points to the use of unamendability as a successful (yet risky) stop sign. But later events shift the focus from the use of the UCA doctrine to its abuse.

In 2015, facing the same limitations on his power, President Juan Orlando Hernandez, thus sought to find another way to relax these requirements. His allies from the now-ruling National Party turned to the Supreme Court and filed a case challenging the relevant provisions of the constitution creating and supporting the term limit. In 2015, the Constitutional Chamber of the Supreme Court responded affirmatively, holding that the one-term limit itself, the eternity clause preventing it from being changed, and the anti-attempt clause must all be held 'inapplicable'. Accordingly, Hernandez subsequently announced plans to run for re-election, and won in 2017. Given the existence of the eternity clause and anti-attempt provision, this judicial decision might have been the only feasible way for Hernandez and his National Party allies to achieve this goal.

The decision was curious for a number of reasons. First, the political context in which the decision was issued raised significant questions of political pressure. The National Party, which dominated elections after Zelaya's removal, had replaced four of the five members of the Constitutional Chamber of the Supreme Court in 2012, after a dispute over decisions the chamber had issued on another matter. The packing of the Constitutional Chamber was likely illegal, since it relied on impeachment powers that the Congress did not possess in the text of the 1982 constitution at the time. It was this newly reconstituted, or 'packed', chamber that issued the unanimous 2015 decision invalidating the relevant limits on re-election and constitutional change.

---

70 Decision 504 of 2009, October 19, 2009.
71 Tribunal Constitucional Plurinacionl, Sentencia Constitucional N. 84 of 2017 November 28, 2017.
72 See S Verdugo, 'How the Bolivian Constitutional Court Helped the Morales Regime to Break the Political Insurance of the Bolivian Constitution' (December 10, 2017) *Blog of the International Journal of Constitutional Law* <www.iconnectblog.com/2017/12/how-the-bolivian-constitutional-court-helped-the-morales-regime-to-break-the-political-insurance-of-the-bolivian-constitution/>.
73 See, on this case, Andrew Friedman, 'Dead Hand Constitutionalism: The Danger of Eternity Clauses in New Democracies' (2011) 4(1) *Mexico Law Review* 77.

Second, the court's reasoning was problematic. The court spoke in the language of the UCA doctrine, but all of the provisions at issue were not amendments, but rather parts of the original 1982 constitution. The distinction between original and derivative constituent power can be used to support the UCA doctrine, but a more difficult set of arguments is needed to support a claim that a part of the original constitution itself (presumably the creation of the original constituent power) can be held unconstitutional. The suggestion of the chamber was that domestic constitutional norms could be set aside if they conflicted with fundamental norms of international or regional human rights law. However, the chamber made little effort to justify this approach or to base it in the Honduran constitutional text.[74]

What is most striking in these cases for our purposes, is that the leaders were able to achieve their goal through judicial decisions that they could not otherwise have attained. It was the UCA doctrine that provided them with the legal tools to override constitutional limitations on their power. Abusing the doctrine allowed them to overcome such legal restrictions.

Judicial self-dealing

Judicial enforcement of unamendability shifts the locus of constitutional change from those authorities entrusted with the amendment power toward the courts, allegedly granting them the last word on constitutional issues.[75] Courts can use unamendability as a strategic trump card, by applying it selectively and generally elevating their powers vis-à-vis other branches.[76] This problem is accentuated in the case of implicit unamendability, where, in contrast to situations in which the textual standard provides guidance and constraints, the judiciary has sweeping power to determine the 'spirit', 'basic structure', or 'basic principles' of the constitution. The UCA doctrine can thus be abused by the judiciary itself to preserve its powers when there are attempts to curtail its competences or change the manner by which judges are appointed.

In Colombia, in 2016, the Constitutional Court – using the 'constitutional substitution doctrine' – invalidated two constitutional amendments reforming the judiciary. In Decision C-285 (June 1, 2016), the court invalidated the 'Judicial Governance Council' that would be responsible for the government and administration of the judiciary; while in Decision C-373 (July 13, 2016) it invalidated the 'Commission of Aforados', responsible for prosecuting criminal and disciplinary offenses by judges. Mario Cajas Sarria writes that in both decisions the use of the UCA doctrine was problematic: 'both seem to confuse the political inconvenience of the constitutional amendment with the substitution of the Constitution'.[77]

---

74 For an elaborated critique of the court's reasoning, see David Landau, Rosalind Dixon and Yaniv Roznai, 'From an Unconstitutional Constitutional Amendment to an Unconstitutional Constitution? Lessons from Honduras' (2019) 8(1) *Global Constitutionalism* 40–70. For different senses of how a constitution may be unconstitutional, see Richard Albert, 'Four Unconstitutional Constitutions and their Democratic Foundations' (2017) 50 *Cornell International Law Journal* 169.

75 Richard Albert, 'Amending Constitutional Amendment Rules' (2015) 13(3) *International Journal of Constitutional Law* 655.

76 Michael Freitas Mohallem, 'Immutable Clauses and Judicial Review in India, Brazil and South Africa: Expanding Constitutional Courts' Authority' (2011) 15(5) *International Journal of Human Rights* 781.

77 Mario Cajas Sarria, 'The Unconstitutional Constitutional Amendment Doctrine and the Reform of the Judiciary in Colombia' (September 1, 2016) *International Journal of Constitutional Law Blog*, www.iconnectblog.com/ 2016/09/the-unconstitutional-constitutional-amendment-doctrine-and-the-reform-of-the-judiciary-in-colombia/

Likewise, in a recent case, the Slovak Constitutional Court invalidated a constitutional amendment regarding 'background check' as a condition to appointment to judicial office. This was the first time the court declared a constitutional amendment as unconstitutional. The court held that the Constitution of Slovakia contains an implicit material core, rooted in principles of democracy, rule of law, division of powers and judicial independence. Even a constitutional act cannot breach this implied material core, and the Constitutional Court has the authority to review constitutional acts and even invalidate a constitutional act that breaches the constitution's implied core.[78] It is, of course, questionable, whether such an amendment violated the core of judicial independence to such an extent that it undermines that constitution's implied core, or was simply a misuse of the doctrine for the protection of the judiciary's own self-interest.

To illustrate this dilemma, let us focus on recent uses of the UCA doctrine in India and Bangladesh, where courts have arguably 'invoked the basic structure doctrine selectively to suit their own substantive and institutional ends'.[79]

Rehan Abeyratne demonstrates how, in some cases, the use of the UCA doctrine by courts in India and Bangladesh had a solid constitutional grounding as it was used against amendments that were incompatible with core democratic principles and assisted in preventing illiberal or authoritarian constitutional changes.

However, two recent judgments demonstrate the court's alleged abuse of the UCA doctrine. The case of *Asaduzzaman Siddiqui v. Bangladesh* (2014) involved a challenge to the constitutionality of the Sixteenth Amendment, which restored a provision that existed in Bangladesh's original 1972 constitution allowing the president to remove Supreme Court judges with the support of a two-thirds majority in parliament. The Bangladesh Supreme Court invalidated the amendment on basic structure grounds, finding that it violated judicial independence. Ridwanul Hoque argues that 'this decision led to the marginalization, indeed defiance, of the founding principles of the Constitution of Bangladesh in regard to judicial removal'.[80]

The Indian Supreme Court confronted a similar issue in Supreme Court *Advocates-on Record Association v. Union of India* case of 2015. In that case, parliament had created a National Judicial Appointments Commission (NJAC) through the Ninety-Ninth Amendment to the Constitution. The NJAC would, among other things, take over appointments to the higher judiciary. Such appointments were originally vested in the President of India, acting on the advice of his cabinet and sitting justices. But over a series of judgments in the 1980s and 90s, the Supreme Court vested final appointment authority in a group of senior justices known as the 'collegium'. The NJAC, therefore, much like the Sixteenth Amendment in Bangladesh, arguably restored the judicial appointments process to something approaching its original form. It vested the appointments power between Supreme Court justices, the Union Minister of Law and Justice, and two 'eminent persons'. However, the Supreme Court held the NJAC unconstitutional for violating judicial independence which is part of the constitution's 'basic structure'.[81] Nonetheless, Abeyratne

---

78 PL. ÚS 21/2014-96, www.ustavnysud.sk/documents/10182/0/PL_+US+21_2014.pdf/233a617c-4dfd-4151-8a6b-16d180b27111; I thank Simon Drugda for directing my attention to this judgment.

79 Rehan Abeyratne, 'Giving Structure to the Basic Structure Doctrine' (2017) 1(2) *Indian Law Review* 182, 187.

80 Ridwanul Hoque, 'Can the Court Invalidate an Original Provision of the Constitution?' (2016) 2 *University of Asia Pacific Journal of Law and Policy* 13, 17.

81 See Rehan Abeyratne, 'Upholding Judicial Supremacy in India: The NJAC Judgment in Comparative Perspective' (2017) 49 *George Washington International Law Review* 101.

argues that this judgment fails to establish how the basic structure of the constitution is violated by a more deliberative, institutionally independent judicial appointments process. Thus, he claims, 'the judgment makes little sense as a matter of law or legal theory and is best explained by the Supreme Court's institutional prerogative to maintain supremacy vis-à-vis the other branches'.[82] Consequently, another form of abuse of the UCA doctrine may be self-dealing by the court for the prevention of modifications in the ways by which judges are elected, i.e., for promoting the judiciary's self-interest.[83]

Conclusion

On August 14, 1884, the French National Assembly revised the Constitutional Law of 1875, which represented the Third Republic and marked the end of monarchism and Bonapartism. As by then, it was apparent that France desired a republican form of government, the Constitutional Law of 1875 was revised and the following statement was added to Article 8(3): 'The republican form of government cannot be made the subject of a proposition for revision'.[84] This formulation repeated itself in the constitution of 1946 (Article 95) and, with different wording, in the constitution of 1958: 'The republican form of government shall not be the object of any amendment' (Article 89).

Claude Klein tells a personal memory on this subject; when he started his law studies in Strasbourg in October 1957, his constitutional law professor was none other than Guy Héraud, who in 1946 published his thesis, defended a year earlier, on the constituent power,[85] and was one of the true specialists of the question. When presenting in class Article 95 of the 1946 constitution still in force, he asked the students: how would it be possible to circumvent this article? Nobody answered and in a great burst of laughter Héraud explained that it was enough to start by repealing Article 95 itself, and then, at a later time, introduce what was desired, for instance, a restoration of the monarchy. Klein then remarks, 'what could we answer, freshmen that we were, impressed by this master so brilliant, if not acquiesce?'[86]

Of course, even if one conceives unamendable provisions that are not self-entrenched to be easily amended through a double amendment procedure as Héraud suggested,[87] this does not render explicit unamendability useless. At the minimum, the unamendability adds a procedural hurdle, and thus better protection for the entrenched value or rule, since the double amendment process is still procedurally more difficult and perhaps more time consuming than a single amendment process.

---

82 Abeyratne (n 79) 187–88.

83 Of course, one may argue that in era of 'constitutional capture' courts must be 'aggressive' in their application of the UCA doctrine precisely against attempts to undermine judicial independence. See Yaniv Roznai and Tamar Hostovsky Brandes, 'Democratic Erosion, Populist Constitutionalism and the Unconstitutional Constitutional Amendments Doctrine' (forthcoming) *Journal of Law & Ethics of Human Rights*.

84 Claude Klein, 'On the Eternal Constitution: Contrasting Kelsen and Schmitt' in Dan Diner and Michael Stolleis (eds), *Hans Kelsen and Carl Schmitt: A Juxtaposition* (Bleicher 1999) 61.

85 Guy Héraud, *L'ordre juridique et le pouvoir originaire* (Sirey 1946).

86 Claude Klein, 'Recension de Yaniv Roznai, *Unconstitutional Constitutional Amendments. The Limits of Amendment Powers*, Oxford Constitutional Theory, 2017' (2017) 18 *Jus Politicum* 39.

87 I object to such an approach, arguing that even non-self-entrenched provisions of unamendability should be implicitly recognized as unamendable. See Roznai, (n 4). For a similar approach see Jason Mazzone, 'Unamendments' (2005) 90 *Iowa Law Review* 1747, 1818.

Unamendability can indeed play various roles. It can be used as a stop sign, completely blocking certain constitutional changes, or as a speed-bump, simply hindering them. It can also create a chilling effect and warn political actors before proposing to amend certain highly valued principles. Finally, unamendability serves as a billboard for the constitutional order, displaying its most cherished values.

The UCA doctrine has been criticized as creating a kind of super-counter-majoritarian difficulty, giving courts a last word in a way that political actors have no way to work around. At the same time, it plays an important role guarding against the use and abuse of constitutional change mechanisms to undermine democracy and the constitutional order and for providing stability to the core identity of the constitution. Accordingly, it has emerged as a successful spread in comparative constitutional law.

This chapter draws on recent cases to show that there is a significant risk that constitutional unamendability with the super-strong version of judicial review carried by the UCA doctrine can be also be abused for distinct ends. The UCA doctrine can by deployed or manipulated for the benefit of incumbents and in defense of generally hegemonic political groups, helping to entrench rather than check their power. When courts are granted the final word over constitutional change, they may also attract political pressure and incentivize their control or capture. Additionally, the UCA doctrine can also be deployed by the judiciary itself in defense of its own institutions and interests, where even innocuous changes to the structure of the judiciary are identified as unamendable core constitutional principles.

While the UCA doctrine is an important constitutional tool, which I believe rests on a solid theoretical ground, its success on a worldwide level, absent some consensus about the situations in which it should be deployed, might not advance constitutionalism and in key circumstances could even undermine it. Thus, more scholarly efforts should move beyond theoretical debates toward more in-depth examinations of how these mechanisms operate in practice in different contexts and more accurate guidelines on its suitable application. This would allow the uses of constitutional unamendability to be maintained while taming its abuses.

10

FEDERALISM AND CONSTITUTIONAL CHANGE

Nathalie Behnke and Arthur Benz

Introduction

Federalism designates a constitutional principle for a polity that joins together autonomous governments to form a compound government. It implies a division of powers between a central government of a federation and governments of the constituent units. How powers are divided and how they enable and constrain the self-rule of central and sub-central governments has to be established in a constitution. Therefore, although federalism has shaped many polities in the history of government, it eventually gained ground as a basic idea in the context of constitutionalism, an idea pointing out a way to moderate the power of a sovereign ruler governing from the centre, but also a way to overcome the weakness of decentralized power (Montesquieu 1989; Hamilton et al. 2008). It is this interpretation of federalism in the history of political thought of Western democracies that lies at the heart of our contribution, thereby limiting its applicability to polities where essentially a constitution is accepted as legitimate by the federation's constituent units. The very establishment of a federal constitution, e.g. in post-conflict societies, the merely formal existence of a constitution without legitimacy, e.g. in autocratic systems, or the contestation of the constitution by parts of society are cases outside the range of applicability of the considerations presented here.

In a compound polity, there is always a tension between officeholders at the centre and at the lower level units, for both tend to expand their power and try to lessen constraints on their self-rule. Therefore, by allocating powers to the different levels, a federal constitution aims at stabilizing the balance of powers. Yet powers are not only resources of rulers, they also define responsibilities for fulfilling public tasks, for solving problems of a society or for achieving the public good. Tasks, problems and perceptions of what the public good means change over time, they are never constant. Accordingly, a federal constitution has to be sufficiently flexible in order to allow adjustments of the division of power to those changes. As we will outline in the next section, we find different solutions of this dilemma between stability and flexibility in federal constitutions.

Another constitutional problem of federalism results from the fact that powers divided in a federation often overlap. Moreover, exerting self-rule in one jurisdiction regularly causes external effects in other jurisdictions. Many public policies have a multilevel character as they concern functions fulfilled at the centre or at lower levels. Hence, a federal constitution can never separate spheres of power into 'watertight compartments' (Aroney & Kincaid 2017: 507). Power is often shared across levels of government, and even if it is separated, governments have to manage interdependence of policies made at the different levels or constituent units. Beyond that, a federal constitution expresses an integration of a demos and diverse demoi in a 'non-centralized' polity (Elazar 1987) and has to accommodate diversity between communities and settle conflicts between them. For this purpose, the division of power in federal systems entails various formal or informal relations between governments. These aims are reconciled in various and highly versatile relations between governments. Legal rules cannot cover these complex interactions, but constitutions can establish institutions and procedures for sharing powers and for making intergovernmental cooperation or competition work. Notwithstanding these rules, intergovernmental relations allow actors in a federation to shift power and shape structures without amending the constitutional law. Thus they are a significant cause of dynamics inherent in a federal system (see below in the section entitled 'Dynamic structures and processes in intergovernmental relations').

In consequence, federalism requires a constitution determining responsibilities of governments and solving conflicts, but constitutional law does not precisely define how powers should be divided. The actual division of powers depends on political reasoning and decisions which often change, and on intergovernmental relations, which cope with overlaps and conflicts. For these reasons federal constitutions have to maintain a balance of power, but at the same time have to be open for change. To preserve the stability of a federal constitution against volatile politics, amendments usually require negotiated agreements among governments and qualified majorities in final decisions. To circumvent these high hurdles, governments can negotiate revised interpretations of constitutional rules or accept emergent practices on matters left in abeyance by constitutional law. Therefore, constitutional change appears in two modes: as constitutional evolution through 'implicit change' and as 'explicit' amendments according to procedures provided for in the federal constitution. As federations are highly dynamic and as constitutional amendments are particularly difficult, both modes are relevant (see section entitled 'Modes of constitutional change').

Society-centred theories emphasize economic developments affecting the fiscal balance or imbalance between governments (Stevenson 2004). The rise of regionalist movements or conflicts in multinational federations with divided societies also shapes constitutional policy. However, in comparative view, parties and courts are most important drivers of constitutional change; parties being essential actors in democracy, and courts, in particular Supreme or Constitutional Courts, being authorized to interpret the meaning of constitutional law and to settle conflicts over power (see section entitled 'Drivers of change: parties and courts').

Federal systems vary in space and time. Accordingly, both the constitutional problems inherent in federalism and the ways to cope with them vary. The following sections illustrate this variety by selected cases. However, instead of providing a systematic comparative analysis, we intend to emphasize the more general aspects, the tension between stability and dynamics inherent in federal constitutions and the typical processes and driving forces of constitutional change.

Basic framework: constitutional rules dividing powers

According to the standard definition, a federal system combines self-rule and shared rule (Elazar 1987). Both types of rule rest on the division of powers between levels, which aims at autonomy of governments or cooperation between them. In those federations that are primarily designed to limit government and to protect individual freedom, the prototype being the US federation, separation seems to prevail, whereas in other federations, pooling of powers and resources are the principal rationales of federalism and shared rule prevails, as is exemplified by the EU or German federation. However, constitutional rules dividing powers are more complex, and often a matter of dispute. Moreover, separation or sharing of powers and, related to this, autonomous or cooperative governing come with various problems and cause unintended consequences. Therefore, constitutional change in federations mostly concerns the vertical division of powers (Karlhofer & Pallaver 2017).

One reason is that the definition of powers by constitutional rules remains abstract and cannot cover all policies falling under the respective categories. In old federations such as the US, the constitution describes powers rather vaguely, and those assigned to the federal and state governments overlap (Robertson 2012). Younger federal constitutions or those having been adjusted by regular amendments to the expansion and differentiation of policies, such as Germany and Switzerland, delineate jurisdictions more precisely, but nonetheless leave room to determine which matter of policy-making falls under which rule. Therefore, constitutional law can never distribute powers in a crystal-clear manner. On the contrary, these rules allow interpretation and provoke dispute. Moreover, in order to facilitate adjustments of federal structures, many constitutions establish concurrent powers. In this case, constitutional rules have to determine under which conditions which government can exert a power and which government's legislation or decision applies in case of conflict.

Federal constitutions enumerate powers. In some federations, catalogues of matters list the powers falling in the jurisdiction of either the federal government or of the constituent units, with the remaining 'residual' powers, i.e. those not listed, falling automatically under the other level's jurisdiction. Only a few constitutions, such as the Canadian, explicitly enumerate both federal and provincial powers. Yet no catalogue can be exhaustive. Therefore, *general clauses* provide for cases where federal power is 'necessary and proper' (article I, section 8 US constitution) or essential to maintain the 'peace, order and good governance' (section 92, Constitution Act of Canada), or where this power results from the 'nature of an issue', as stated by the German Federal Constitutional Court (BVerfGE 3, 407, 423). As a rule, general clauses justify an extension of federal powers and lead to centralization of a federal system, which thus can become imbalanced. The rise of the welfare state and liberalization of market economies have contributed to this trend. Though they did not make federalism obsolete, as Harold Laski had predicted (Laski 2005 [1939]), these developments demonstrate that a division of power can never be fixed by constitutional law and is subject to continuous change.

Two special ways to allocate powers are worth mentioning in this context since they have caused self-enforcing dynamics. One way is to define powers not by circumscribing the matters to be dealt with but by setting goals to be achieved. The treaties of the EU demonstrate this method. As the EU federation demonstrates, the *constitutionalization of policy goals* can justify an extension of powers of a federation, mainly by defining shared powers, at the costs of self-rule at the lower level (Schmidt 2018). Constitutionalized policy goals can also be found in other federations, such as the German 'welfare state principle' (article 20, section 1 Basic Law), which has reinforced a centralist trend. Another highly flexible distribution of powers is enshrined in the Spanish constitution (articles 147, 148), which fostered regionalization. The constitution allows the Autonomous Communities (AC) to expand their power by reforming their statutes, provided that the federal legislature agrees. By extensively exploiting these powers, the AC have contributed to a significant decentralization of the Spanish state (Colino & Hombrado 2017). In this respect, the

Spanish constitution is certainly exceptional. However, some federal constitutions allow constituent governments to opt out or deviate from federal law.

These constitutional principles and rules apply to legislative, executive and fiscal powers. Theories of fiscal federalism recommend concentrating these different state functions at the level and within the boundaries where the government is in charge of the task, i.e. to provide for institutional congruence (Oates 2005; Kropp & Behnke 2016). A government responsible for legislation should also execute the law and bear the expenses. The US constitution divides powers according to this principle of congruence. European federations often divide powers along functional lines. In Germany, the Länder are in general responsible for implementing federal law, and with the centralization of legislative powers, a particular model of administrative federalism emerged (Hueglin & Fenna 2015: 148–155). Other federations follow this method of dividing powers for practical reasons. Irrespective of whether responsibility for expenditure follows legislative or executive power, functional division can cause an imbalance of power. In any event, it increases interdependence between levels of government.

Dynamics of a federal distribution of power can cause instability, as office holders try to expand their power (Riker 1964). To prevent self-enforcing centralization, scholars have suggested institutional safeguards such as subsidiarity checks by courts or parliaments or veto power of constituent governments in federal legislation (Bednar 2009). Against a trend hollowing out the central government, an asymmetric distribution of power seems to provide an option, which is, however, disputed (Watts 2001: 29–30). More often than not, asymmetry results as a compromise of constitutional politics in multinational federations, such as in Canada, India or the EU. Safeguards against centralization and measures preventing disintegration aim at protecting self-rule, but often they increase the need for shared rule which is exerted by intergovernmental relations.

Dynamic structures and processes in intergovernmental relations

While the allocation of powers to territorial units provides a basic structure clarifying who may do what, everyday policy-making requires intense communication, information and coordination between units. Those ongoing communicative processes in intergovernmental relations are the 'lifeblood of federalism in practice' (Poirier & Saunders 2015: 4). They also deal with conflicts when policy decisions cause spill-overs across borders of territorial units, when practical reasons call for uniform implementation, or more generally when the principle of institutional congruity requires a higher-order territorial unit to regulate an issue. For those reasons, formal as well as an informal intergovernmental relations serve to avoid negative externalities, inefficient solutions or disruptive conflict.

Intergovernmental relations are organized in a variety of more or less formalized and institutionalized arenas or processes that make the constitutional power distribution in federal states work in real-life circumstances. While a multiplicity of groups, meetings and the like form in all multilevel states, we outline here the few most typical forms of institutionalized intergovernmental relations that can be compared across federal states – second chambers, intergovernmental councils, joint decision making and intergovernmental agreements.

Some kind of formal representation of constituent units in the federal legislature is provided in many federal constitutions. Federal interest representation in second chambers can follow the Senate or the Council model (Hueglin & Fenna 2015: 206 ff.). In the Senate model, every constituent unit is represented by a number of senators elected by popular vote. In the Council model, the constituent units send government delegates to the second chamber. Popular vote secures direct accountability of the senator to the electorate, motivating them to either pursue pork-barrel politics or to take on an 'elder-statesman' perspective on the entire federation. The government delegation model, on the other hand, secures direct interest representation of the sub-state executives and motivates council members to negotiate territorial interests with their peers. Comparative federalism research suggests thus that the aim of representation of interests of the constituent units is more effectively pursued in a Council than in a Senate model. Although many second chambers fail to effectively check and balance the power of the federal government (Palermo 2018), constitutional change has rarely led to envisaged reforms or abolition of these institutions (Russell & Sandford 2002).

In contrast to second chambers, intergovernmental councils are less formalized arenas for intergovernmental negotiation. Typically, they are not established either constitutionally or by statute, but evolve informally, setting up standing orders that codify ex post the routines that have been established. While second chambers are determined to secure the sub-states' voice in federal legislation, intergovernmental councils typically coordinate interests and decisions in the agenda-setting and in the implementation phase. They can be organized bi- or multilaterally, involving only two, several or all constituent units. And they may be purely horizontal, thus providing a negotiation arena only for sub-state units, or vertical, involving representatives of the federal level as guest, member or in leading positions. Bilateral vertical councils are set up to negotiate individualized agreements between one sub-state unit and the federal state (Petersohn, Behnke & Rhode 2015). This is often the case in asymmetric federal systems. Those vertical bilateral councils weaken, however, the joint position of sub-state units against the federal state (e.g. UK and Spain).

The interlocked system of joint and shared powers in German intrastate federalism, and similarly in the European Union, gives rise to many instances of (compulsory) joint decision making (Scharpf 1988) and to a generally cooperative culture of intergovernmental relations. Joint decision making follows from a general normative attitude that – in spite of the acceptable and expected diversity of policy-making in constituent units – certain economic, social and living standards should be equivalent across a federation's territory. The inclusion of representatives of economically weaker units or of minority nations in such joint decision schemes gives them de facto veto power and considerably raises the bar for arriving at mutually acceptable solutions. Joint decision making has thus often been described as a strong inhibitor of reforms and effective governance. On the other hand, it may serve as a safeguard against centripetal or centrifugal forces inherent in federal architectures, as long as negotiations are not obstructed by confrontation among political parties or divided societies. And they can provide a precious tool for manufacturing incremental adjustment while providing long-term stability.

Finally, intergovernmental agreements can provide a way for solving precise and smaller-scale policy issues on a formal bi- or multilateral foundation. In federations with powerful sub-state units, multilateral intergovernmental agreements are a typical instrument of horizontal self-organization among the sub-states preventing federal involvement. In the US, for example, they are used as a multi-purpose tool to substitute for other weakly elaborated forms of horizontal coordination such as intergovernmental councils (Bowman 2004; Zimmerman 2011). As agreements are typically issue-specific, they are useful for solving issues of financial spill-overs. In Switzerland, the financing of public utilities across Canton boundaries is often subject to intergovernmental agreements. Also, they offer the option of including stepwise further units, enlarging bi- into multilateral agreements if they are successful.

The multiplicity of negotiation fora and the ongoing discussion process provide opportunities for dynamic adaptation of existing power distributions or rules. At the same time they prevent the system from stalemate and disruption because they provide sufficient flexibility in the search and implementation of coordinated policies. Still, the different institutional solutions outlined above vary in their effect on constitutional dynamics. While second chambers are, in a way, the most powerful tool for sub-state interest representation, they are also the most inflexible. Depending on the rules of amendment (see below), they might represent serious obstacles to formal constitutional change. Intergovernmental councils and joint decision making on the other hand are far more flexible and promote ongoing discourse between actors. Not only can they make existing rules work in everyday politics; they can also stretch the activation and interpretation of rules pretty far and thus compensate – at least to a certain degree – for formal constitutional change, as was pointed out by Héritier and Farrell (2007: 47). They observed that sub-constitutional change in the European Union occurred in the intervals between the great treaty reforms in such negotiation systems, a process they called 'interstitial change'. Also, the more informal fora of intergovernmental relations can provide arenas accompanying formal constitutional negotiation processes, contributing to brokering compromises and keeping adversary actors on the negotiation table.

Modes of constitutional change

Generally speaking, constitutional change occurs in federations when actors perceive the need for change, perceive an appropriate opportunity for change, and have the power to enact it. Pressure for change can emerge with respect to the existing power distribution, for example when power constellations shift. That is, one group of actors perceives that it has more real (e.g. economic or ideological) power than is mirrored in the formal power distribution. Then this group will build up pressure to adapt the formal power distribution so that it conforms to the perceived power distribution. Pressure for change may also emerge, in particular in multinational federations, when existing processes are no longer able to accommodate conflicts, when instead deadlock, litigation or even violent conflict prevail. Then actors might try to abolish or change existing processes, struggle for more powerful positions in the process, set up arbiters or establish altogether new processes.

As mentioned above, power distributions between federal and sub-federal governments are a matter of continuous dispute and contestation, because tasks and resources of governments are in flux and because actors try to expand their powers. On the other hand, federal constitutions cannot be altered every other day according to the taste of the government currently in power. To fulfil the precarious task of holding the compound polity together, a federal constitution must signal longevity and predictability in order to allow actors to build stable expectations on the behaviour of others. Thus, while a federal constitution indisputably needs to be flexible and adjustable, it is protected from frequent change by formal amendment rules prescribing a broad majority and consent across different groups of actors to 'explicitly' change a constitution (see 'Amendment rules', below). Whether and how a constitution is actually amended, depends less on amendment rules than on how the agenda for reform is defined, how a proposal is negotiated, how conflicts are managed and how potential vetoes in ratification are taken into account (see 'Explicit constitutional change', below). If, in contrast, rules of procedure in intergovernmental relations or interpretations of formal rules are adapted, these are instances of 'implicit' constitutional change (see 'Implicit constitutional changes', below). 'Implicit' constitutional change might, at first glance, look like a second-best substitute if formal change cannot be achieved for whatever reason (e.g. because the formal rules of amendment set hurdles too high to be achieved by different groups in a deeply divided society). However, if it expresses a broad consent among politicians and citizens, it is a fully acceptable mode of constitutional change on its own, exhibiting democratic merits as much as formal amendments.

Amendment rules

In order to protect a constitution from arbitrary revisions by the executive or parties in power, amendment rules usually establish particular legislative procedures and require qualified majorities for explicit constitutional change. These rules might even exempt certain elements of a constitution from being amended. The various rules, which comparative research has identified in constitutions of the world, make a constitution more or less 'rigid', i.e. difficult to change explicitly (Lorenz 2005). Federal constitutions are not particularly rigid, although they mostly require qualified majorities in amendment legislation.

What is specific about amendment rules in federations is the involvement of sub-federal governments or the '*demoi*' of constituent units (Kemmerzell & Petersohn 2012). From a formal point of view, federal constitutions are changed by federal legislation. If the distribution of power or rights of constituent units to participate in federal legislation are concerned, amendment rules can include special provisions to safeguard a balance of power. Some constitutions of federations (Brazil and Germany) explicitly prohibit the abolishment of federalism, but more common are procedures giving constituent units a voice or vote. In general, constitutional amendments are considered as joint tasks, which are fulfilled in cooperation between federal and sub-federal governments. This is reflected not only in negotiations of amendment proposals, but in most federations also in decision rules which endow representatives of constituent units with veto power.

Yet amendment rules in federations reveal significant variation concerning the actors involved and procedures of joint decision making in constitutional legislation. In general, second chambers have to agree on an amendment with a qualified majority, although not all second chambers represent sub-federal interests (see the discussion on Senates above). These are better protected if sub-federal parliaments participate in the decision. This applies, for instance, in Canada, where in matters of federalism provincial parliaments have to decide on constitutional amendments, and where in fundamental matters, all have to agree to pass an amendment. The US constitution can only be amended if three-quarters of state parliaments or state ratification conventions vote in favour of a proposal submitted by Congress or by a national Convention. In Spain, (sub-federal) parliaments of the AC decide on statute reforms which constitute the most relevant procedure to amend the distribution of power. In South Africa, provincial parliaments have to be consulted. In other federations, sub-federal parliaments have no decision right in constitutional legislation.

Referenda are required by the Australian and Swiss constitutions to ratify constitutional amendments. In both cases, a double majority of voters and states/cantons should ensure that the federal distribution of power remains in balance. Referenda, in particular those requiring qualified majorities, present incalculable obstacles to explicit constitutional change, because actors negotiating an amendment proposal cannot know how people will vote, whereas vetoes of second chambers or parties in parliaments can be anticipated. However, referenda compel negotiating parties or governments to find a broad consensus, which, as the Swiss case demonstrates, can be tested in consultation with civil society and in public discourses. In Australia, party competition often prevented a consensus, and many attempts to amend the constitutions failed.

Referenda usually are required in cases of secession, a rather special case of constitutional amendment, as they de facto alter a country's territory. While federal constitutions may provide rules for internal territorial reorganization, most of them are silent on secession (Doyle 2018). Following the principle of self-determination derived from international law, they usually require a referendum within the territory claiming sovereignty, followed by a negotiated contract on the conditions of secession.

As comparative research has shown, amendment rules are not decisive for success or failure of explicit constitutional change (Lorenz 2008; Closa 2012; Benz 2016). If governments and parties find an agreement, they usually see to it that it will be passed in legislative procedures, and more often than not, 'political parties' agreements may sail through even the most difficult amendment procedures' (Closa 2012: 309). Whether a federal constitution is finally amended or not, depends largely on the ability of participants in constitutional negotiations to anticipate opinions of veto-players. Hence effective processes of agenda-setting and negotiations are decisive for the success or failure of constitutional reform.

Explicit constitutional change: patterns of constitutional reform

Whatever the rules of amendment in a federal polity might be, in order to achieve formal constitutional change, actors need to form a broad majority of supporters of change. That is, different (groups of) actors need to acknowledge the necessity for change, they need to form a consensus on an acceptable direction and substance of change and they need to rally enough support to surmount the hurdles set by the rules of amendment.

Furthermore, incentives for supporting federal constitutional change are unevenly distributed. Changes of the existing power distribution and/or the existing negotiation rules come close to the incentives of a zero-sum game, as giving some groups more power means that other groups will lose influence. Taking into account that there is at least a latent permanent conflict between political actors at the federal level and those at sub-state level, with each trying to expand their sphere of influence, we can readily see that forming a broad majority to enact constitutional change is a challenging task.

Indeed, real-world processes of constitutional change reveal that it is far more likely to initiate constitutional negotiations than to successfully accomplish a reform. If one or several groups of actors claim a re-negotiation of the federal power distribution, they may often have enough power to set the issue on a reform agenda, thus initiating a negotiation process. This does not, however, guarantee the successful enactment of a formal constitutional reform which must surmount the formal hurdles of amendment rules. For example, a region might threaten the federal polity to secede if they are not given more autonomous rights. That is more or less what happened in Catalonia since 2009 and also in Scotland after 2014. If the region is economically powerful, if one or several regionalist parties embark on the secession issue, if politicians and society support the claim, then one single region can enforce a reform debate. Still, it needs to rally a broad support within and also beyond the region's border to successfully accomplish its claim.

Even in constitutional reforms that are less vital than secession processes, the incentives for initiating the process differ from those of accomplishing it. In reform negotiations, it might, under certain circumstances, be possible to establish a discursive actor orientation, an 'arguing' mode among the negotiators (Elster 1998). For example, if the group of negotiators is small and negotiations take place behind closed doors, it is easier to build up mutual trust enabling compromise than in publicly observed debates where politicians need to prove loyalty to their party followers' fundamental ideological lines. Likewise, longer time horizons for negotiation, an initial agreement to discuss only broad lines and no details, or delegating negotiations to experts or special committees can be conducive to a discursive negotiation style (Benz 2016). When it comes to ratification decisions, on the other hand, which are usually taken in votes, pursuit of the rational self-interest becomes prevalent again, thus putting at risk compromises that had been found before.

Furthermore, ratification processes can become hazardous when the rules of amendment provide for groups of actors to ratify a reform that had not been involved in the negotiation process before. That is the case with referenda, for example. If constitutional reforms need to be ratified by referenda, then the negotiation process should be most transparent, encompassing and responsive, offering the citizens the opportunity to familiarize themselves with the issues and arguments at hand and possibly to feed their opinion back into the negotiation process. Or if amendment rules provide for double or triple majorities by different entities (citizens, sub-state units, ethnic groups, etc.) the same argument is true. To the degree that those entities were not involved in the negotiation process, ratification becomes ever more incalculable.

In order to cope with the imponderabilia involved in the multiple-stage process of formal constitutional reform from agenda-setting through negotiation to ratification, it is thus sensible to take precautions to enhance the chances for success. As was mentioned before, two (partially contradictory) measures are important (Benz 2005, 2016). On the one hand, the negotiation process should be organized in a way to elicit the emergence of mutual trust among negotiators, thus facilitating a discursive and argumentative actor orientation. On the other hand, all groups involved in the ratification stage should be informed and heard early on. In order to reconcile those partially contradictory requirements, reform processes are sequenced, alternating between phases of broad contemplation and information and phases of secluded consensus brokering. Also, involving 'neutral' third actors, such as experts or arbiters, might be useful devices for taking the edge off conflict of interest and bringing negotiations back to a rational and discursive mode. Finally, 'buying' consensus through package deals, by offering generous compensation or by threatening even worse solutions is a not uncommon, and usually quite successful, measure to help accomplish a successful reform.

As we can see, formal constitutional change altering the power distribution among the constituent units is a challenging task. Even if groups of actors are powerful enough to initiate reform processes, the negotiation and ratification stages pose numerous obstacles to successful reform. Often, reform processes fail ratification, even if broadly acceptable solutions had been brokered in negotiations, leading subsequently to informal reform processes. But on the other hand, formal constitutional change occurs more frequently than we would expect theoretically. This is the case in particular if processes are structured in a way to promote rationality, neutrality and mutual trust, to involve all ratification agents and to offer something to potential losers of the reform. Yet, it is more likely that constitutional amendments are passed after negotiations on a proposal have ended with a compromise among delegates of governments and parties. Hence a constitution may be changed explicitly, without effectively changing the distribution of power and without effectively solving conflicts. In this instance, deadlock can only be avoided through implicit change.

Implicit constitutional changes: non-constitutional renewal or incremental adjustment

Implicit constitutional change occurs when constitutional power distributions or negotiation processes change without altering the formal text of the constitution. These might be ephemeral phenomena, marking transitional processes in between rounds of formal amendment; or they might follow after failed reform attempts or substitute impossible formal change; finally, while federal constitutional actors prefer formal change, informal change has the potential to provide more flexible solutions among deeply divided negotiation partners, as those solutions are preliminary, tentative, time-limited and potentially revisable (Lerner 2011).

In the case of transitional change, implicit change of federal orders occurs when the existing formal framework is adapted flexibly to new exigencies by the actors. This may come about by judicial sentencing, by sub-constitutional agreements or rule-making or simply by acceptance of all actors involved that formal power distributions are stretched beyond the letter of the law. Such flexible adaptations are useful when a broadly shared understanding about the nature of a constitutional order has changed among politicians and society. The constitutional development of the European Union is a case in point (see Héritier 2007; Héritier & Farrell 2007). For example, when Council and Commission begin to regulate matters that were not yet formally transferred to the European level by the member states, as happened often in the years of crisis between 2009 and 2013; or when the European Central Bank stretches its powers beyond the letter of the law, but with tacit agreement of all European heads of government, this can be interpreted as informal constitutional change which may be formalized in the next round of treaty negotiations.

Another type of informal institutional change can be observed after failed reform attempts. The best illustration for this pattern is Canada in the period of 'Constitutional Fatigue' (Russell 1993: 36) after the failed ratification of the Charlottetown Accord in 1992. When it had turned out that the formal rules of amendment were too high to accomplish formal constitutional change, the federal, provincial and territorial actors in Canada resorted to policy-specific intergovernmental agreements to effectively enact the new schemes of power distribution that had been agreed on in the Charlottetown Accord. In that situation, informal change was possible because the negotiations for formal constitutional change had been successful and only failed ratification (Behnke & Benz 2009: 228 ff.).

This mechanism of intergovernmental agreements is likely to be better suited to the special situation of multinational federations with marked conflict of interest between different territorial groups (Lazar 1998; Lerner 2011; Hueglin 2013). When particular communities strive to emphasize their distinctiveness, when they claim more autonomy and representation, and when they suffer from an unequal distribution of wealth, such deep lines of division make it highly unlikely that an agreement on broad principles of federal power distribution can be reached. Instead, the piecemeal practice of 'treaty federalism' (Hueglin 2013) contributes to societal peace by emphasizing common acceptance of distinct values, thus allowing conflicts of interest on particular issues to be solved.

Drivers of change: parties and courts

In taking an explicitly actor-centred perspective in our account of federal constitutional change, it comes as no surprise that we regard interested actors as the main drivers of constitutional change. Of course, governments of a federation's constituent units are the main actors in constitutional negotiations. They are the ones responsible for brokering and enacting agreements. However, intergovernmental negotiations mark the routine of everyday federal policy-making, where the art of compromise is practised. In such a setting, it is rare that an impulse for changing the existing order emerges. Comparative observation of constitutional change in various federations suggests, however, that two types of actors are particularly influential in triggering processes of constitutional change. These are parties and courts. Parties can induce constitutional change because, by definition, they represent selective interests. If they represent specific regional interests, they can easily become drivers for federal authority migration. Courts, on the other hand, have to interpret constitutional provisions and can promote or hinder amendments of the text in view of perceived value changes in society. In the next two sections, we address those two specific actor groups as main drivers of constitutional change in greater detail.

Parties

Parties can become drivers of constitutional change in three different ways. First, parties as representatives of specific interests can press for changes of the constitutional power distribution in the name of territorially concentrated groups, of specific regions, or of a general political ideology. Research on territorial party politics coined the distinction between statewide parties (SWPs) and non-statewide parties (NSWPs), which is pretty useful in this context (Meguid 2005; Swenden & Maddens 2009; Toubeau & Massetti 2013). NSWPs campaign only in one or several parts of a polity, but not all over the territory. In multinational federations, they typically focus on nationalist, separatist or regionalist ideologies and have a tendency to radicalization (Massetti & Schakel 2016); in other federations, they often make claims for the subsidiarity principle. In election campaigns or in parliamentary debates, they aim at shifting the federal power distribution toward more regional autonomy, i.e. they cause centrifugal tendencies. SWPs, in contrast, campaign all over the territory and at federal level. They might have an ideological preference for or against decentralization, but typically this is not the main issue on which they campaign. In tendency, they act thus as moderators against centrifugal pressures from NSWPs.

Second, the structure of a multilevel party system impacts on dynamics for federal change (Thorlakson 2009). The number and ideology of parties campaigning in a territory can be aggregated to a party system. In federal states, party systems at federal and at sub-federal levels might be the same or they might differ from each other. In strongly regionalized party systems, which usually emerge in multinational federations, the parties campaigning at regional level hardly overlap with parties at federal level. In vertically integrated party systems, parties can moderate territorial conflicts by their integrated vertical power structure. This is true, for example, for the German party system, where party organizations and communication lines provide useful tools for intergovernmental relations, although even there the party system has become slightly more regionalized in the past 20 years.

Third, the congruence or incongruence between coalition governments at different levels of government can be a relevant factor for driving or moderating pressures for federal change. If coalition governments at federal and sub-federal level strongly overlap (which is more often the case in vertically integrated party systems), then strong regionalist tendencies can be balanced by vertical intra-party relationships. If, on the other hand, a coalition at federal level includes as a minor partner a regionalist party which is strong at sub-federal level, then those parties gain influence and can trigger territorial dynamics far beyond their federation-wide political weight. This was the case, for example, during the reform of the Catalan Statute of Autonomy in 2006, with the regionalist-nationalist Esquerra Republicana de Catalunya supporting the socialist minority government at federal level. Another example is the Bavarian Christian Socialist Union in Germany. Due to its permanent joint faction in the federal parliament with the statewide Christian Democratic Union, it gains political influence and promotes Bavarian interests in federal politics far beyond its real electoral power.

We can see that parties promoting regionalist, nationalist or separatist ideologies can be strong drivers for federal constitutional change, even more so if coalition governments at different levels of government overlap, giving NSWPs federation-wide political power. SWPs, on the other hand, typically do not drive change, especially if they are vertically integrated. Rather, they tend to moderate territorial dynamics. Integrated party systems have a stabilizing effect in constitutional change, while regionalized party systems have a centrifugal effect.

Courts

To consider courts as drivers of constitutional change seems to contradict their role as safeguards of an existing constitution. However, Constitutional Courts or Supreme Courts fulfil this function when they decide on conflicts between federal or sub-federal governments concerning the distribution of powers. Since the relevant constitutional rules provide ample room for interpretation and since general clauses allow adjustment of the allocation of power to new policies, courts are regularly called on to decide on issues of federalism. And in response to political and societal developments impacting on federalism, they regularly preserve the constitution by revising its interpretation and thus modifying the effective division of power. In this way, they turn into drivers of implicit constitutional change.

While lower courts rarely deal with disputes concerning federalism, although they may implicitly refer to these matters, only courts with the power for constitutional review have an impact on constitutional change. In federations, where this power is not concentrated in Constitutional Courts, only Supreme Courts actually make authoritative decisions on the constitution. As these are federal institutions, scholars have assumed that they tend to serve the interests of the federal government and support a centralization of power or adopt a unitarist stance. In a recent comparative study including 11 federations, high courts in nine of the countries are characterized as unitarist and favouring centralization, with only the Constitutional Courts in Belgium and Germany being considered as 'balanced' in federal matters (Aroney & Kincaid 2017: 483–486). Single case studies provide less clear results, partly because scholars interpret decisions in different ways, but in particular because courts have changed their doctrines and their understanding of federalism over time.

Scholars suggest various reasons for this trend in court decisions. That courts support centralization and unitarist policies has been explained by their composition and their position in the system of government. Members of high courts are regularly selected by federal institutions, be it governmental or legislative institutions, and their resources come from the federal budget. Accordingly, a more decentralist stance of courts should be found if sub-federal governments can influence the selection of judges or if constituent units are represented in the court (Popelier 2017). Others emphasize the autonomy of courts and explain their impact on constitutional change in federations by their particular doctrines, which can change over time (Baier 2006). A third theory addresses the reasons why courts modify their doctrines. It states that courts are interested in finding support for their decisions in politics and society, and this motivates them to adjust their interpretation of constitutional law whenever they perceive new trends in the mainstream of public discourses (Vanberg 2004).

While this third theory appears particularly relevant to account for implicit constitutional change, it cannot cover cases where courts decide against the will of the federal government or even against the unanimous or majority will of governments in a federation. Courts may also point to issues that a constitution does not provide for, or deny a government legislative power although they declare the content of a law acceptable. In such cases, they turn into drivers for explicit constitutional change as they either provoke or press governments to respond by initiating constitutional amendments. Recent German reforms of federalism clearly demonstrate this role of courts. When the Federal Constitutional Court in several decisions revised its interpretation of the subsidiary clause of the Basic Law, it de facto altered the distribution of power between federal and Länder governments. This led the federal legislature to amend the constitutional law. In a later decision, the court pointed out that provisions for budget crisis of individual Länder are insufficient. It thus influenced the agenda for another constitutional amendment introducing a joint committee supervising budgeting of federal and Länder governments (Benz 2016: 187–189).

In Germany, governments can initiate amendments of constitutional law in order to overrule a court decision, and the legislature usually adopts such amendments. This is much more difficult in federations where parliaments of constituent units or the people have to ratify amendments. Under such conditions of constitutional rigidity, courts can become powerful. The Supreme Court of the US is a case in point, but more powerful is the European Court of Justice (ECJ). Not only is 'primary law' of the EU extremely difficult to change since this requires that treaties are amended with the agreement of all national parliaments. The ECJ has profited also from the 'over-constitutionalization' of EU law (Grimm 2015). The court has interpreted the principles of a free European market extensively and thus invited legal proceedings whenever governments or private actors feel discriminated by national law or policies. In consequence, powers shifted to the European level because the court constrained national policy-making (Schmidt 2018). The ECJ is certainly a unique driver of constitutional change, but the role of other courts in federations should not be underestimated.

Conclusion

Considering amendment rules, difficulties of negotiations and success of reform, the frequency of amendments or the role of parties and courts, constitutional change in federations and in unitary states does not reveal significant differences. The main difference probably lies in the substance, the relevance and the consequences. In federations, it is essential to balance powers between levels and solve conflicts in divided societies. Nonetheless, while it contributes to stabilizing a federation by maintaining its flexibility to adjust to economic, social and political developments in the national and international context, it also bears the risk of creating instability. On the one hand, frequent amendments of constitutional law can undermine its function to establish the basic norms and procedures which are determined to limit the power of governments. On the other hand, implicit change can create a discrepancy between written law and a living constitution, thus undermining the legitimacy of the former.

Therefore, federal constitutions have to cope with a dilemma. They have to guarantee stability of the federal order without turning it into a rigid structure. And they have to provide sufficient room for flexibility in order to adjust the division of power to changing conditions without allowing governments or majority parties to escape the necessary constitutional constraints on their power. Meeting these requirements and finding a balance of power between levels of governments is a demanding task for those designing or revising a constitution and those governing within the framework of a constitution. This challenge is probably not unique for federations, but here it is particularly relevant. All the same, we find reasons to conclude that federalism also provides conditions that make constitutional change a relevant aspect of democratic politics. Moreover, by adjusting the division of powers to changing societal conditions and by addressing the plurality of societies, it contributes to maintaining the integrity of the constitution and the stability of a federation.

References

Aroney, Nicolas & John Kincaid, 'Comparative Observations and Conclusions' in Nicolas Aroney & John Kincaid (eds) *Courts in Federal Countries: Federalists or Unitarists?* (University of Toronto Press 2017) 482–539.

Baier, Gerald, *Courts and Federalism, Judicial Doctrine in the United States, Australia and Canada* (University of British Columbia Press 2006).

Bednar, Jenna, *The Robust Federation: Principles of Design* (Cambridge University Press 2009).

Behnke, Nathalie & Arthur Benz, 'The Politics of Constitutional Change between Reform and Evolution' (2009) 39(2) *Publius* 213–240.

Benz, Arthur, 'Kein Ausweg aus der Politikverflechtung? Warum die Bundesstaatskommission scheiterte, aber nicht scheitern musste' (2005) 46(2) *Politische Vierteljahresschrift* 204–214.

Benz, Arthur, *Constitutional Policy in Multilevel Government: The Art of Keeping the Balance* (Oxford University Press 2016).

Bowman, A.O., 'Horizontal Federalism: Exploring Interstate Interactions' (2004) 14(4) *Journal of Public Administration Research and Theory: J-PART* 535–546.

Closa, Carlos, 'Constitutional Rigidity and Procedures for Ratifying Constitutional Reforms in EU Member States' in Arthur Benz & Felix Knüpling (eds) *Changing Federal Constitutions: Lessons from International Comparison* (Barbara Budrich Publishers 2012) 281–310.

Colino, César & Angustias Hombrado, 'Spain: Complexity, Counteracting Forces and Implicit Change' in Ferdinand Karlhofer & Günther Pallaver (eds) *Federal Power Sharing in Europe* (Nomos Verlagsgesellschaft 2017) 181–206.

Doyle, Oran, 'The Silent Constitution of Territory' (2018) 16(3) *International Journal of Constitutional Law* 887–903.

Elazar, Daniel J., *Exploring Federalism* (University of Alabamba Press 1987).

Elster, Jon, 'Deliberation and Constitution Making' in Jon Elster (ed.) *Deliberative Democracy* (Cambridge University Press 1998) 97–122.

Grimm, Dieter, 'The Democratic Costs of Constitutionalisation: The European Case' (2015) 21(4) *European Law Journal* 460–473.

Hamilton, Alexander, James Madison, John Jay & Lawrence Goldman, *The Federalist Papers* (Oxford University Press 2008).

Héritier, Adrienne, *Explaining Institutional Change in Europe* (Oxford University Press 2007).

Héritier, Adrienne & Henry Farrell (eds), *Interstitial Institutional Change* (Special Issue: West European Politics 2007).

Hueglin, Thomas, 'Treaty Federalism as a Model of Policy Making: Comparing Canada and the European Union' (2013) 56(2) *Canadian Public Administration* 185–202.

Hueglin, Thomas O. & Alan Fenna, *Comparative Federalism: A Systematic Inquiry* (University of Toronto Press 2015).

Karlhofer, Ferdinand & Günther Pallaver (eds), *Federal Power-Sharing in Europe* (Nomos Verlagsgesellschaft 2017).

Kemmerzell, Jörg & Bettina Petersohn, 'Regional Actors' Participation in Constitutional Reform: Opportunities, Limits and Risks' in Arthur Benz & Felix Knüpling (eds) *Changing Federal Constitutions: Lessons from International Comparison* (Barbara Budrich Publishers 2012) 311–329.

Kropp, Sabine & Nathalie Behnke, 'Marble Cake Dreaming of Layer Cake: The Merits and Pitfalls of Disentanglement in German Federalism Reform' (2016) 26(5) *Regional & Federal Studies* 667–686.

Laski, Harold, 'The Obsolence of Federalism' in Dimitrios Karmis & Norman Wayne (eds) *Theories of Federalism: A Reader* (Palgrave Macmillan 2005 [1939]) 193–205.

Lazar, Harvey, 'Non-Constitutional-Renewal: Toward a New Equilibrium in the Federation' in Harvey Lazar (ed.) *Canada: The State of the Federation 1997. Non-Constitutional Renewal* (Institute of Intergovernmental Relations, Queen's University 1998) 3–35.

Lerner, Hanna, *Making Constitutions in Deeply Divided Societies* (Cambridge University Press 2011).

Lorenz, Astrid, 'How to Measure Constitutional Rigidity: Four Concepts and Two Alternatives' (2005) 17(3) *Journal of Theoretical Politics* 339–361.

Lorenz, Astrid, *Verfassungsänderungen in etablierten Demokratien: Motivlagen und Aushandlungsmuster* (Wiesbaden: VS Verlag für Sozialwissenschaften 2008).

Massetti, Emanuele & Arjan H. Schakel, 'Between Autonomy and Secession: Decentralization and Regionalist Party Ideological Radicalism' (2016) 22(1) *Party Politics* 59–79.

Meguid, Bonnie, 'Competition between Unequals: The Role of Mainstream Party Strategy in Niche Party Success' (2005) 99(3) *American Political Science Review* 347–359.

Montesquieu, Charles Louis de Secondat, *The Spirit of the Laws* (Cambridge University Press 1989).

Oates, Wallace E, 'Toward a Second-Generation Theory of Fiscal Federalism' (2005) 12(4) *International Tax and Public Finance* 349–373.

Palermo, Francesco, 'Beyond Second Chambers: Alternative Representation of Territorial Interests and Their Reasons' (2018) 10(2) *Perspectives on Federalism* 49–70.

Petersohn, Bettina, Nathalie Behnke & Eva Maria Rhode, 'Negotiating Territorial Change in Multinational States: Party Preferences, Negotiating Power and the Role of the Negotiation Mode' (2015) 45(4) *Publius: The Journal of Federalism* 626–652.

Poirier, Johanne & Cheryl Saunders, 'Comparing Intergovernmental Relations in Federal Systems: An Introduction' in Johanne Poirier, Cheryl Saunders & John Kincaid (eds) *Intergovernmental Relations in Federal Systems: Comparative Structures and Dynamics* (Oxford University Press 2015) 1–13.

Popelier, Patricia, 'Federalism Disputes and the Behavior of Courts: Explaining Variation in Federal Courts' Support for Centralization' (2017) 47(1) *Publius: The Journal of Federalism* 27–48.

Riker, William H., *Federalism: Origins, Operation, Significance* (Little Brown & Co. 1964).

Robertson, David Brian, *Federalism and the Making of America* (Routledge 2012).

Russell, Mek & Mark Sandford, 'Why Are Second Chambers so Difficult to Reform?' (2002) 8(3) *The Journal of Legislative Studies* 79–89.

Russell, Peter H., 'The End of Mega Constitutional Politics in Canada?' (1993) 26(1) *PS: Political Science and Politics* 33–37.

Scharpf, Fritz W., 'The Joint-Decision Trap: Lessons from German Federalism and European Integration' (1988) 66(3) *Public Administration* 239–278.

Schmidt, Susanne, *The European Court of Justice and the Policy Process* (Oxford University Press 2018).

Stevenson, Garth, *Unfulfilled Union: Canadian Federalism and National Unity* (McGill-Queen's University Press 2004).

Swenden, Wilfried & Bart Maddens, 'Introduction: Territorial Party Politics in Western Europe: A Framework For Analysis' in Wilfried Swenden & Bart Maddens (eds) *Territorial Party Politics in Western Europe* (Palgrave Macmillan 2009) 1–30.

Thorlakson, Lori, 'Patterns of Party Integration, Influence and Autonomy in Seven Federations' (2009) 15(2) *Party Politics* 157–177.

Toubeau, Simon & Emanuele Massetti, 'The Party Politics of Territorial Reforms in Europe' (2013) 36(2) *West European Politics* 297–316.

Vanberg, Georg, *The Politics of Constitutional Review in Germany* (Cambridge University Press 2004).

Watts, Ronald, 'Models of Federal Power Sharing' (2001) 53(167) *International Social Science Journal* 23–32.

Zimmerman, Joseph Francis, *Horizontal Federalism: Interstate Relations* (State University of New York Press 2011).

11

PARTICIPATORY CONSTITUTIONAL CHANGE

Constitutional referendums

Eoin Carolan

The 'referendum revival'

Given the profile and scope for public engagement they offer, referendums are perhaps the paradigm example of participatory constitutional change. As such, they have been a prominent feature of the move in constitutional theory and practice toward participatory devices in the drafting or amendment of domestic constitutions (Wheatley 2017). This 'referendum revival' (Tierney 2012) is demonstrated by the fact that of the 58 functioning electoral democracies with a population of more than three million, 39 conducted at least one national referendum between 1975 and 2000 (LeDuc 2003).

The renaissance in the use of referendums has been attributed to a number of factors. First of all, changes in technology afford increased scope for plebiscitary consultations with the public at local and national level.

Second, the increased use of referendums might relate to broader changes in political and constitutional practices. A greater emphasis on public participation in constitution-making (Guinier & Torres 2014), like the broader deliberative turn in political theory (Dryzek 2000; Gutmann & Thompson 2004), has encouraged interest in the constitutional referendum. That the referendum has been embraced as a principal constitutional good practice was made manifest by its widespread incorporation into the new constitutional arrangements for emerging democracies in Central and Eastern Europe in the 1990s (Auer & Butzer 2001; Blokker 2017). This sense of a link between the referendum revival and broader developments in the political practice is also underscored by the increased use of the referendum in jurisdictions to which it is constitutionally alien. This is the referendum not as constitutional mandate or requirement but as a political choice. While perhaps most obviously exemplified in recent years by the increased recourse in the United Kingdom to referendums on constitutional questions such as devolution, Scottish independence, the electoral voting system, and Brexit, a 'sudden eagerness' to consult the people on constitutional change has also been identified in states from Luxembourg (Gerkrath 2017) to Greece (Fotiadou 2017).

A third potential factor in the popularity of the referendum is that it resonates with trends in political discourse. This might be expected to be most evident in the facultative situation where a referendum is organised for reasons of political calculation rather than constitutional necessity. In that context, it must be assumed that the choice of a referendum is perceived as having a particular political appeal. From that perspective, the shift to the referendum – or indeed other forms of participatory or consultative devices – may have some connection with two identified trends in contemporary politics in many countries: high levels of distrust in traditional politics; and the increased prominence of what is usually described in the literature – not always precisely (Katsambekis 2017) – as populism.

The referendum and contemporary politics I: a populist device?

To look at populism first, it is possible to identify recent examples of voluntary referendums (e.g. Crimea or Brexit), the outcomes of which have been politically presented as a definitive statement of popular will that forecloses all future contestation. This characterisation of the referendum as a monolithic declaration of national policy raises particular concerns for the constitutionalist commitment to limited government. Liberal constitutionalism has long been pre-occupied with the threat posed by the People to values such as legal certainty, generality, equality and fairness (Moellers 2007). One express purpose of the elaborate constitutional machinery of the American republic was the exclusion of the people from active or present participation in national government (Madison 2008). This reflects both the positive and negative dimensions of the People as constituent power. It is the (putative) consent of the People that give life and legitimacy to a constitutional order. Yet it is the People who have traditionally been regarded as the greatest threat to the stability and effectiveness of these constitutional structures – precisely because of their political power as sovereign.

Representative government, by generating multiple institutional claims to speak for the People, has historically been the primary response to this 'paradox of constitutionalism' (Loughlin & Walker 2007). The referendum, however, can be seen as expressing that claim in a purer and more powerful form. In political terms, this may be presented as more than a claim to speak for the people: it *is* the People expressing their views on an issue in a direct and unmediated manner on a question of national importance. This has natural appeal for any populist narrative 'that politics should be an expression of the volonté générale of the people' (Mudde 2004, 543).

Viewed in this light, one difficulty with the referendum as a constitutional device is that, by making present the People as constituent power or sovereign, it creates a situation with the political potential to disturb the constraints of everyday constitutionalism. In principle – and allowing for the various institutional and legal constraints that are available – the presence of an active sovereign in government gives rise to increased risks of unfettered, arbitrary and unpredictable decision making. This has been at the heart of criticisms of direct democracy from the Federalist critique of Athenian government (Madison 2008) through to Arendt's (1963) dismissal of the referendum as 'the unbridled rule of public opinion' (Tierney 2012, 111).

It is also, perhaps, at the root of much of the scepticism that appears evident in the modern literature on the referendum revival. While there has been a revival in the use of referendums, there continues to be considerable focus in both political science and constitutional scholarship on the challenges they pose. The sense of sceptical distrust appears to have been heightened by the number of referendum outcomes in recent years that have diverged from elite preferences. The Brexit referendum has led to much academic and political criticism in the UK of specific aspects of that referendum (Scott et al. 2017; Eleftheriadis 2017) and, more generally, of referendums as a means of determining important political or constitutional changes (Weale 2017). Much of this commentary has centred on the assertion that those who voted in favour of Brexit were misled, misinformed or ill-advised in their actions. Yet it might also be observed that the central question in the Brexit referendum was, by the relative standards of referendum codes of practice, a commendably clear one. Moreover, the question was one that was sufficiently salient for voters to have a view on – something that the relatively high 72 per cent turnout for the vote tends to support.

There is an argument here that elite criticisms of the referendum and of pro-leave voters might be more precisely directed to the objection that voters did not understand the implications – social, political or economic – of the choice they wished to make. In other words, it is not that the decision was ill-informed but that it was a bad one. There are also echoes of this in the political and academic commentary that has previously followed national referendums in which voters rejected proposed European Union treaties (Trechsler 2005; Moravcsik 2008). This kind of commentary can generate the impression of an elitist refusal to countenance or acknowledge the possibility of broad popular support for choices or outcomes outside the scope or the parameters of the elite consensus (Wilkinson 2016) – a feature that perhaps points to another reason for the increased use of referendums in recent decades: the growing disaffection and disenchantment with political institutions and actors. Blokker, for one, has speculated that the re-emergence of referendums in Europe is evidence of a 'counter-tendency towards a "popular constitutionalism"' (Blokker 2017, 32) or counter constitutionalism (Albert 2008) that challenges constitutionalism's 'turn away from the people towards a form of "juristocracy"' (Blokker 2017, 32).

The referendum and contemporary politics II: a response to public distrust?

This disconnect between voters and representatives of institutions creates conditions in which more ostensibly direct forms of public participation – notably the referendum – can appear more attractive, more authentic and more authoritative. On one view, the referendum may provide a method of re-connecting voters with their representative institutions or re-establishing trust in, or the legitimacy of, government. However, these levels of distrust also generate social and political dynamics that must be factored into any assessment of the potential or practice of referendums. It is a curiosity of contemporary constitutional politics that democracies are turning to referendums as participatory conversations on issues of national importance at the same time as there are increasing concerns over the integrity of our democratic and electoral systems, the pollution of public discourse by propaganda and falsehoods, and even the capacity for truly national conversations in an era of online social and cultural fragmentation and highly partisan echo chambers. Referendums might be a response to these social and political challenges – but any referendum will itself be subject to the same social and political conditions that these challenges create. What this might mean for the referendum is considered further below (see section entitled 'Constitutional legality, political legitimacy').

Defining the constitutional referendum

In considering the role of referendums in constitutional change, the first point to note is the importance of precision in identifying what is at issue. Two distinctions appear particularly pertinent to this discussion.

The first is the distinction between the constitutional and non-constitutional referendum. This chapter is concerned with the former category only rather than (for example) the consultative referendum on policy questions or the abrogative or suspensive referendum on legislative acts. This is a distinction that is not always made clear but which is relevant to several of the criticisms of referendums that are most commonly voiced.

The constitutional context means, for example, that the referendum is likely to take place in an established legal and institutional framework in accordance with pre-determined rules and principles. The fact that a referendum is addressed to a constitutional question also means that the question or issue might be expected to be more salient and accessible to voters. The fact that a referendum relates to constitutional norms or structures might be regarded as more appropriate, given the presumptive importance of constitutional questions to the conditions under which public power is exercised. In a similar vein, the constitutional referendum is, arguably, more explicable given the extent to which constitutional texts or norms often connect the legitimacy of the constitution with the consent of the People as the ultimate source of constitutional authority (Tushnet 2010).

The second distinction to bear in mind is the specific role of the referendum as a mechanism for participatory constitutional change. The referendum might have a negative function as a constraint on constitutional change (decision-controlling), or a positive function in providing the impetus for constitutional change (decision-promoting) (Gallagher & Uleri 1996). These are distinct procedures under which the People and the process fulfil quite different constitutional functions. This means that the distinction could have some relevance to the recurring debate in the political and constitutional literature about the legitimacy or utility of the constitutional referendum.

The legitimacy of the constitutional referendum

Arguments in favour

For decades, the conventional scholarly treatment of the referendum was generally negative. In more recent years, authors such as Tierney and Levy have highlighted the potential of referendums as a means of procuring public participation or, more generally, of enhancing the civic democratic or deliberative capacities of modern democracies.

The first and most basic advantage of a referendum is the familiar one; that it provides a direct and very visible means of conferring popular legitimacy on the constitutional change at issue. The existence of a referendum also provides indirect support to the legitimacy and authority of the constitution more generally. This might be expected to apply in particular to jurisdictions with regular experience of constitutional referendums or where the barriers to the constitutional referendum are relatively low. In the latter situation, there is also an argument that the accessibility of the referendum process can enhance the legitimacy or authority of counter-majoritarian institutions, on the basis that measures that are not reversed by referendum can be taken to enjoy presumptive popular permission.

In general, the focus in more recent literature on the benefits of the referendums as a constitutional device has been on their potential to facilitate or encourage debate on questions of national interest or constitutional importance. This work looks beyond traditional notions of direct democracy to emphasise the systemic contribution that a referendum can make to a wider civic or political process. The argument here is that 'the referendum can be a successful constitutional instrument to promote and protect a deliberative environment within which citizen participation can be fostered' (Tierney 2012, 285). It has also been suggested that the referendum may provide an opportunity to educate the public on issues of civic importance (Altman 2011).

By and large, therefore, conceptions of the referendum as a participatory or deliberative mechanism of constitutional change have been at the core of academic and institutional efforts to justify its usage (although it is necessary to bear in mind the distinction between participatory and deliberative justifications (Suteu & Tierney 2018)).

Arguments against

Nevertheless, a number of familiar criticisms of the referendum process continue to be prominent in the scholarship. Most notable perhaps is the long-standing objection to the referendum as a majoritarian tool that may arbitrarily or detrimentally impose adverse or normatively suspect outcomes on minorities (Qvortrup 2013). Examples of this might include the prohibition by referendum of minaret construction in Switzerland or of same-sex marriage in California, Slovenia and Croatia (Josi 2017). This concern for minorities is particularly apposite with a constitutional referendum given that exclusionary or discriminatory measures might attain a level of permanence once incorporated into the constitutional order.

A related concern that has been articulated is the impact the referendum might have on the standing or status of representative institutions of government. In the short term, a referendum result could significantly fetter the autonomy of other governing institutions, be they the courts, executive, parliament or other bodies. In the long term, the holding of regular referendums might weaken the authority of representative actors by institutionalising an alternative mechanism for determining important matters. Conversely, referendums may provide a means for representative actors to limit their accountability (Setala 2006).

Objections have also been expressed about the knowledge or competence of voters to understand constitutional questions. There are a number of reasons that have been identified for this concern. The first and perhaps least sophisticated, is a general scepticism about the capacity or knowledge of voters to deal with political issues (Lupia & Johnston 2001). It has already been observed that this form of criticism appears to be more prominent in the aftermath of a referendum result that diverges from the preferences of the academic or political elite. Given that objections based on voter ignorance are, in principle, applicable to all forms of electoral process, it has been argued that this criticism is, ultimately, a criticism of democracy itself (Bogdanor 2019).

A more nuanced concern has been expressed regarding the suitability of referendums that require voters to make a crude (usually binary) choice on an issue that involves a complex series of trade-offs. It has regularly been suggested, for example, that referendums on lengthy and legalistic European treaties are problematic from the perspective of voter knowledge, comprehension or interest (Mendez & Mendez 2017). More generally, a referendum will frequently oblige voters to make a choice under conditions of significant medium- or long-term uncertainty, and where there is expert or political disagreement over the probable effects of the outcome (Kriesi 2005; Hobolt 2007). In this common scenario, voters must make a decision without knowledge of the consequences. Moreover, the use of a referendum to determine uncertain questions can itself generate institutional or political barriers to revisiting the issue if and when further clarity or information becomes available.

A final and common criticism of referendums is that they are the product of elite strategies to increase or reinforce political power (Lijphart 2012; Boix 1999; Benoit 2004). This is a long-standing charge derived from the reality that political elites have a prominent or determinative role in important procedural or substantive aspects of the referendum process in many states. This can facilitate the use of the referendum as a device to centralise or reinforce the power of incumbents. The 2015 Greek referendum on the Eurozone bailout and 2016 Hungarian referendum on refugee resettlement might be viewed in this light. It has also more recently been pointed out that the risk of manipulation or gaming is not confined to traditional political elites but can also arise from the activities of political entrepreneurs or highly organised interest groups.

Strategies for mitigation

Several measures capable of mitigating these difficulties have been suggested. Principles of good design, such as those outlined in the Venice Commission's *Guidelines on the Holding of Referendums*, might help to avoid difficulties with unduly complex, inaccessible or ambiguous referendums. There is no inherent reason why a referendum question must be difficult to understand. Referendums on social issues such as same-sex marriage or high-profile political debates such as Scottish independence or even Brexit provide examples of situations in which the basic question (if not, perhaps, the complexity of its potential effects) seems to have been generally comprehensible.

In addition, there has been a limited degree of constitutional experimentation with more elaborate referendum designs that aim to avoid the crudity or uncertainty of the binary choice. Options here include the multi-option or 'preferendum' model in which voters are presented with a selection of potential choices; or the multi-stage model where voters have the opportunity to consider the question or questions across more than one vote. New Zealand, for example, used a multi-stage model to consider a change to the electoral system in 1992. Voters were initially asked whether they wished to retain the existing system, and which one of four options they would prefer to replace it. After a large majority voted in favour of change, a second referendum was then held over a year later in which voters were offered a straight choice between the existing system and the option that had received the most votes in the first referendum. While multi-option or multi-stage referendums are relatively unusual, they confirm in principle that the toolkit for constitutional change is more sophisticated than critical commentary sometimes appears to assume.

Efforts have also been made to address the difficulties raised regarding the susceptibility of the referendum process to unfair or elite manipulation by legally regulating aspects of the conduct of the campaign. These include the regulation or prohibition of the use of public funds in a campaign, or the imposition of limits on the levels of permissible expenditure by campaign groups. Principles regulating broadcasting coverage have also been developed in some jurisdictions, such as Ireland. These endeavour to secure a degree of fairness in the allocation of broadcasting time with a view to promoting equality between the campaigns and enhancing levels of public understanding. Other mechanisms that have been adopted or advocated include the provision of independent information, the establishment of official authoritative fact-checking agencies, or, most elaborately, the incorporation of deliberative elements into the referendum process. Levy (2013), for example, has advocated an 'integrated referendum model' involving a structured sequence of distinct opportunities for participation by the public in identifying and refining the options for constitutional change. Under this model, the traditional referendum is one part of a longer process that might also incorporate micro- or macro-deliberative elements.

Limitations to mitigation strategies

Of course, these solutions are not without their own potential difficulties. More elaborate forms of referendum design might offer the prospect of a more sophisticated choice but they equally impose costs in terms of expense, time and potentially public attention or understanding.

Similarly, efforts to regulate the conduct of a referendum campaign or to embed or enhance its deliberative potential are subject to criticism in terms of their effectiveness and their susceptibility to gaming. It is questionable, for example, whether efforts to regulate broadcasting coverage or to ensure equal allocation of airtime on traditional media platforms can be effective given the extra-jurisdictional and highly fragmented character of online political commentary. These efforts to regulate either the conduct or quality of the referendum process may also generate opportunities for manipulation and gaming although they have been criticised for distorting political debate (Barrett 2009; Scott et al. 2017). In Ireland, the requirement for fair or roughly equal coverage has been argued to create a perverse incentive for smaller political parties to oppose any general consensus because of the outsize coverage that will follow during the campaign. Likewise, the obligation to ensure fairness in coverage of the campaign has been argued to encourage a false equivalence or balance under which arguments of limited legal or constitutional merit received undue prominence or relatively uncritical coverage. Alternatively, it might prompt media organisations – fearful of being found to have acted in breach of the legal requirement to treat both sides fairly – to provide only minimal coverage to referendum proposals which attract little or no official opposition.

Questions of effectiveness and unintended consequences can also arise with deliberative measures. Fishkin (2011) has contended that deliberation is most effective in a face-to-face or small group environment. This presents problems of scale and legitimacy (Parkinson 2006) when integrating deliberative mechanisms into a national referendum. Experiences in British Columbia and Australia suggest that it is a challenge to command or sustain public attention during deliberative phases that can precede – sometimes by many months or even years – any referendum vote. Moreover, the design of a deliberative measure itself involves complex decisions over matters such as agenda-setting, composition, inclusiveness and resources (Suteu 2016) which inevitably requires trade-offs between important legitimacy values (Caluwaerts & Reuchamps 2015). Concerns about the potential for the small group deliberative elements to be manipulated by either elites or interest groups have also been articulated (Levy 2018).

Legitimacy as a contextual standard

Overall therefore, the broad and intuitive appeal of the referendum as a participatory process is significantly complicated by considerations of design, structure, process and political dynamics. While the objections that are most frequently articulated in literature are capable of being addressed by specific measures, these methods are, themselves, subject to potential difficulties. This might explain, to some extent, the sense of pessimism in some of the constitutional literature about the potential of the referendum process.

It is also true, however, that scholars have identified several referendums that appear to have provided precisely the kind of engaged, informed, active, respectful and deliberative participation by voters that is central to most recent theoretical defences of the legitimacy of the referendum as a method of constitutional change (see, for example, Tierney (2017) on the Scottish independence referendum) Arguably, what this points to is the necessity for any consideration of constitutional referendums to pay particular attention to the context in which they occur. In considering the potential and the pitfalls of the constitutional referendum, it is important to look beyond the text of the constitution or the conduct of the campaign to those other contextual factors that shape the import and impact of the constitutional referendum: most notably, those relevant to its control, conditions, counterweights and consequences.

Control of the referendum

The issue of control has been the subject of relatively detailed consideration in the literature. It has long been assumed, particularly in political science, that control over a referendum – its initiation; the framing of the question; the length and timing of the campaign – is critical to its outcome. Most commonly, these are matters within the control of an institution of the government or political elite. In some states, the process is one that can be citizen initiated. This is perhaps the purest example of the referendum as a participatory process of constitutional change. It provides a means for citizens to initiate a process under which the people will have the opportunity to express their view on a constitutional question. While this is attractive from a participatory perspective, it has been argued from experience in those Central and Eastern European constitutions that include initiative procedures that these generate difficulties for representative government institutions by diverting political attention to particular issues or, if successful, by introducing constitutional changes that could hamper governance (Podolnjak 2015). At a more conceptual level, this form of citizen initiation and citizen approval might also be queried as coming closest to the image of an unfettered sovereign that liberal constitutionalism has historically associated with arbitrary, majoritarian or abusive exercises of power.

A further complication is that citizen initiative procedures can be used by actors whose primary motivation is rooted in short-term political calculation. Even if referendums resulting from popular initiatives fail, they might succeed insofar as they place an issue on the political agenda (Contiades & Fotiadou 2013). Indeed, in cases such as the Slovakian initiative to prohibit same-sex marriage, these campaigns appear to be as much about elevating the profile or organisational capabilities of a particular interest group as securing constitutional change. Nor, it should be noted, is the possibility of the referendum being employed for political rather than constitutional purpose confined to interest groups. The organisation of an *ad hoc* referendum on Catalonian independence by independence-minded parties was, arguably, as much an exercise in political symbolism as constitutional change. The same might be said of Hungary's referendum on refugee resettlement.

Procedural conditions

The various ways in which the referendum campaign can be subject to procedural regulation have already been briefly alluded to. The overall objective of these procedural conditions is generally to ensure the fairness of the process. This is an important element in securing the legitimacy of the referendum result. However, it is also possible for more substantive forms of condition to apply with a view to assuaging some of the broader normative concerns with constitutional referendums. Insofar as referendums have been argued to be majoritarian, for example, several states make provision for quorum or threshold requirements to guard against the risk of a constitutional change being introduced at the behest of an active or vocal minority group.

Counterweights

The extent to which a constitution contains potential counterweights to the referendum process has received somewhat less attention at the level of general theory or practice. Many of the concerns expressed about referendums assume that they occupy a dominant position in the process of constitutional change. This may, however, overstate the significance or influence of the referendum as a matter of domestic constitutional law. From the point of view of formal legal constraints, there may be a procedural mechanism to challenge or appeal the outcome. A constitution might also make express provision for the involvement of other institutions or actors in the implementation of a referendum result. As the burgeoning literature on unconstitutional constitutional amendments highlights, there is also the possibility of a referendum result being subject to scrutiny, checks or even annulment by reference to implied constitutional values (Albert 2009; Roznai 2017). More formalistically, Josi (2017) has argued for pre- or post-referendum judicial review as a necessary element of a referendum mechanism that engages fundamental rights.

Furthermore, there is also the more general consideration of the extent to which a constitution is amendable – whether expressly or by implication – after a referendum. It may be, for example, that a constitutional change which is introduced by the referendum could, in principle, be removed by the same method within a relatively short period of time. Less dramatically, a referendum might be subject not to reversal but to mediation by other institutions of government. A constitutional change endorsed by referendum might fail to be implemented by legislation, or might be subject to future interpretation by the judiciary in light of other constitutional provisions or values. There is also the possibility of regional or local variations on how a referendum is interpreted or implemented within a federal or devolved jurisdiction.

These are potential counterweights to the referendum result which are relevant to any evaluation of the position or impact of a constitutional referendum in a particular domestic system.

Consequences

A fourth significant factor for any assessment is the consequences of a referendum result. This is most commonly considered by reference to the technical or legal effects of a particular outcome, which is linked to some degree with the presence in the system of potential constitutional counterweights. Are there conditions or situations in which the referendum result can be overturned? Is the referendum subject to further ratification checks or scrutiny by other institutions? What is the likely interpretation or meaning of the text or change if it is introduced?

However, it is also necessary in any examination of the effect of a constitutional referendum to have regard to the political consequences of the result. A referendum could have distinct consequences for what might be described as the legal constitution and political constitutions. In particular, the symbolism and salience of the referendum might have significant political ramifications that are not captured by a legal analysis. These political consequences might include the creation of constitutional pressures that ultimately lead to constitutional change, whether by legal or extra-legal means (for an example, see Choudhry's (2008) account of the Quebec Secession Reference).

Constitutional legality, political legitimacy

It is clear from this overview of the theory and practice of referendums that they inevitably involve a series of complex and context-sensitive trade-offs. At each stage of the referendum process – its design; its organisation; its application to the constitutional order – choices must be made about how to balance its potential for positive benefits and negative costs. At the most general level, this balance is one between the political legitimacy that public participation can confer on a constitutional change and, on the other hand, the risk that might pose to other constitutional values such as legal certainty, equality, fairness or fundamental rights. It is worth recalling, however, that this trade-off between popular legitimacy and constitutional stability is an enduring challenge for constitutionalism as a whole. This points to a possible role for the referendum as one technique for managing these competing constitutional imperatives.

One of the key social functions of a constitution is to provide stable procedures and politically withdrawn principles that can be used to mediate internal contestations within the particular polity (Thornhill 2011). Constitutions typically incorporate various mechanisms with this integrative potential. The constitution itself provides a very visible statement of political identity that defines the boundaries, composition and values of the political entity in question. This visible statement of values has both a definitional and integrative function in that its existence furnishes a focal or coordination point for the reproduction of political legitimacy or power.

Similarly constitutions typically provide fixed procedures and principles by reference to which social and political disputes can be determined. The visibility and public availability of these processes provide a means of shoring up the unifying or integrative functions of a constitution by encouraging parties to resolve these contests within the constitutional structures and by way of an appeal to the expressed constitutional values. In this way, political conflict is internalised within the constitutional order, thereby reducing the risk of it destabilising the system (Loughlin 2003).

These procedures also provide a means for the constitutional order to adjust to social and political pressures. Resolving disputes within the constitutional framework incentivises parties to articulate their claims in the language of existing constitutional norms. This facilitates the capacity of the constitutional system to co-opt emerging social and political narratives where that seems socially or politically necessary.

There are, however, certain limitations of plausibility and legitimacy to any system's capacity to make adjustments within existing constitutional boundaries. There might come a point at which the divergence between emerging social views and the values and norms of the constitutional text or case law is too great for a coherent or legitimate integration. In that case, the referendum has clear potential value as a mechanism for dealing with social or political instability. By offering an opportunity for citizens to participate in discussion on these contested questions, a referendum can confer legitimacy on changes that incorporate new values into the constitutional order or annul established norms. Moreover, it does so in a way that avoids the threat to the legitimacy of other constitutional institutions that can arise when they are obliged to determine or adjudicate upon questions of significant political controversy in the absence of clear or agreed constitutional guidance. The backlash thesis (Rosenberg 2008) posits that constitutional changes that are perceived as the product of institutional activism may have adverse effects for the legitimacy of the change introduced and of the institution involved. For these cases, the referendum has clear potential as an alternative mechanism for addressing contested, controversial or novel constitutional questions that might generally be expected to enjoy greater political legitimacy or acceptance.

The referendum's potential as a source of political legitimacy has been at the core of its scholarly rehabilitation. It is now generally acknowledged that the referendum can in theory provide a democratically and normatively appropriate means of managing constitutional change. The focus of more recent work has largely been on identifying the procedural or regulatory conditions in which this theoretical potential can be realised. This has been allied to a greater willingness on the part of some governments to experiment with novel forms of participatory or deliberative design. These are all necessary and valuable steps in enhancing the referendum's potential as a tool of legitimation.

However, to return to the point made earlier about trade-offs, it is precisely because a referendum can legitimise a constitutional rupture that it can also undermine the stability that is both the purpose and promise of legal constitutionalism. One question that this raises – and which appears so far to have received less attention – is how to deal with referendums that fall short of the democratic, deliberative or republican standards that the scholarship has developed. This is pertinent both because the vast majority of referendums will in some respect fail to meet all of these criteria and, more fundamentally, because a referendum that falls short of deliberative or democratic standards will, nonetheless, remain a highly symbolic political act. In reality, a scholarly diagnosis that a referendum is normatively deficient will likely carry very little political weight.

A key challenge for any account of the referendum as a tool of constitutional change, therefore, is how to address the capacity of the constitutional referendum – including (or perhaps especially) the sub-standard one – to create political facts on the ground. Examples here might include the first Quebec secession referendum, the Brexit referendum or the Hungarian refugee resettlement vote. In each case, the referendum vote had political effects beyond its legal consequences. For example, the Brexit referendum was an advisory vote with no specific or determined constitutional effect. This meant that the referendum, or fact of the referendum, was barely adverted to in the *Miller* litigation that followed in its wake. This led, however, to the slightly curious situation in which the UK Supreme Court delivered a decision on the question of how Brexit-related power should be allocated between the institutions of government without any regard to the single political fact which, in reality, was liable to determine how those powers were exercised. While this was completely correct in a legal sense, it highlights the potential for a degree of myopia in legal accounts of how constitutional referendums relate to their constitutional systems.

It seems necessary, therefore, for constitutional theories and models of the referendum as participatory constitutional change to take due account of the specific political characteristics and dynamics of the constitutional referendum. These are matters that might change from jurisdiction to jurisdiction and which are also likely to evolve over time as political practices and contexts change. In the current political environment, however, there are (at least) two factors that might be worth considering for further investigation.

The first is the likelihood that there are practical limitations to the education or deliberation that may occur within or around a referendum process. The possibility for referendums to provide highly salient focal points for intense public debate or education has been widely discussed in recent literature and arguably exemplified in a number of recent referendums. Even under relatively ideal conditions, however, it seems reasonable to assume that there are natural limits to the interest and the attentiveness of voters. The rational ignorance of voters (Downs 1957) means that there are limits to the amount of time and effort a citizen is likely to commit to discussion or examination of a constitutional question.

This raises particular issues for the more elaborate forms of deliberative design that are increasingly prominent in the literature. While multi-option, multi-stage or integrated options appear more sophisticated at the level of principle, there is a need for more evidence about the extent to which their participatory, pedagogical or deliberative potential might be mitigated by voter apathy, ignorance or fatigue.

A second political consideration that might also merit systematic integration into the study of constitutional referendums is the high level of distrust in traditional elites that seems to have become an established feature of many modern democracies. This is relevant to several long-standing assumptions in the political science field about the pro-elite or the pro-hegemonic potential of the referendum process. That is not to say that referendums are not susceptible to elite control or manipulation under certain political or social conditions. It seems a mistake to assume, however, that this is *always* the case. In a European context, it has been recognised that domestic referendums on treaties have become difficult to win. The same might be true of constitutional referendums more generally. A tendency has been identified across referendums in Ireland (Tonra 2009), Australia (Williams & Hume 2010), the United Kingdom (Whiteley et al. 2016) and elsewhere for voters to apply a presumptive bias against proposals put forward by an incumbent government. In each of these cases a significant minority of voters in surveys after the vote have expressed the view that they were unsure of, or did not understand, the proposal and therefore voted to reject it. This has been the experience even with relatively popular political incumbents. A coalition government elected with over 50 per cent of the vote in Ireland in the 2011 general election lost a constitutional referendum to confer increased powers on parliamentary committees later that year as voters differentiated between their relative satisfaction with government and their willingness to take on trust government proposals to change the constitutional system. This was despite the fact that the proposals attracted high levels of support in opinion polls organised around the time of its initiation. Support for the proposals dropped sharply during the referendum campaign. This phenomenon of voter scepticism and (possibly related) reductions in support once a campaign starts was also evident in Ireland with referendums on European treaties or other constitutional changes such as the abolition of the Seanad (Senate) or the insertion of a section on children's rights into the constitution. Here again, post-referendum surveys indicate a certain portion of the electorate vote No out of a dislike or distrust of incumbents (Tonra 2009; MacCarthaigh & Martin 2015).

This is consistent with an assumption in the political science literature of a status quo bias in constitutional referendums (Nadeau et al. 1999; Clarke et al. 2004). One possibility, however, is that this bias might, in fact, reflect a scepticism regarding the position favoured by political incumbents. From that perspective, an explanation for the status quo bias might be that most constitutional referendums occur in situations where the referendum is a decision-controlling one: i.e. a referendum that is necessary to endorse or approve a proposal advocated by another branch of government. This would also provide a partial explanation of the outcome of the Brexit referendum, given the faith reportedly placed by Remain campaigners in the effects of the status quo bias.

Factoring public disenchantment or mistrust with incumbents into accounts or models of constitutional referendums has several potential implications. From a political science perspective, it might require a re-consideration of the claim that voters in referendums apply a pro-leader or partisan heuristic (Popkin 1991; Sniderman et al. 2006). Perhaps more relevantly for constitutional practice and design, it could also suggest that, contrary to these assumptions, constitutional referendums might, under many conditions, be difficult for incumbents to win. This is in keeping with the views of some domestic constitutional scholars that incumbents – despite the hypothetical advantages sometimes assumed – are, in practice, unlikely 'to exchange the manageable and to a certain extent predictable procedures of representative democracy for the uncontrollable and unpredictable dynamics of referendums' (Reestman 2017, 64). It is also, perhaps tellingly, consistent with the results of Elkins and Hudson's (2019) empirical investigation of referendum success rates which – intriguingly – found much higher failure rates for attempts to amend a constitution by referendum than the pro-elite and pro-hegemonic assumptions of much traditional political science literature would predict.

If this is correct, a further potential consequence may be that voters are actually more likely in a referendum context to trust or at least empathise with positions advocated by persons outside the conventional political elite. This could make referendums particularly appropriate vehicles for 'outsider' campaigns by political entrepreneurs or activist interest groups. This might increase the participatory or deliberative potential of constitutional referendums by highlighting views or positions outside the political mainstream. Equally, however, it could make the referendum potentially susceptible to manipulation or distortion by savvy interest groups. That risk might be particularly present where the referendum framework includes regulatory principles that are designed or intended to counter the presumed – perhaps questionable – bias of the process toward the political elite. Deliberative mechanisms might offer similar opportunities for organised actors to exert increased influence or profile, particularly if they provide preferential access to particular interest groups. That is not to suggest that these risks arise in all cases. What they illustrate, however, is the possibility of unintended consequences under certain political conditions. While evidence is needed about their prevalence or effect, these political considerations highlight aspects of conventional theories or practices of constitutional referendums that might require further refinement.

More positively, if the political dynamics and assumptions that underpin constitutional referendums have changed in some of the ways suggested, this could point to a legitimate role for the referendum as a means of *confirming* rather than *promoting* social, political and constitutional change. If referendums have become more difficult for political incumbents and elites to win (at least under some social and political conditions) then at least some of the traditional pro-hegemonic concerns with their usage might no longer apply with such force. In particular, the presence of an anti-elite or anti-incumbent bias would suggest that a constitutional referendum would be favoured by such actors only if it is constitutionally mandated or where they are seen as very likely to win. Furthermore, if it is the case that an anti-incumbent bias applies, any experienced political leader's calculations of success will factor in the probability that levels of support for a government or elite position will fall as both the constitutional issue and the views of those opposed to the government position become more salient for voters. These strategic disincentives to the calling or conduct of a constitutional referendum on the part of incumbents or elites could go some way to addressing some of the constitutional concerns around the use of referendums. A rational incumbent in these conditions should only hold a constitutional referendum where the support for a change is sufficiently elevated to overcome an anti-incumbent bias and a likely loss of support during the campaign. Support at this level might also be regarded, however, as a strong indication of the presence within that society of a substantial consensus on the change proposed. This returns to the point made earlier about the specific value of the referendum as a means for a constitutional system to balance stability and adaptability. A constitutional referendum under these conditions functions as the final and authoritative confirmation of a process of social or political change. This is a role for referendums which addresses at least some of the concerns about stability while also harnessing its positive potential as a public and participatory mechanism for legitimating a new social, political or collective consensus within that particular polity.

References

Albert, Richard, 'Counterconstitutionalism' (2008) 3 *Dalhousie Law Journal* 1.

Albert, Richard, 'Nonconstitutional Amendments' (2009) 22 *Canadian Journal of Law and Jurisprudence* 5.

Altman, David, *Direct Democracy Worldwide* (Cambridge University Press 2011).

Arendt, Hannah, *On Revolution* (Faber 1963).

Auer, Andreas & Michael Butzer (eds), *Direct Democracy: The Eastern and Central European Experiences* (Routledge 2001).

Barrett, Gavin, 'Building a Swiss Chalet in an Irish Legal Landscape? Referendums on European Union Treaties in Ireland and the Impact of Supreme Court Jurisprudence' (2009) 5 *European Constitutional Law Review* 32.

Benoit, Kenneth, 'Models of Electoral System Change' (2004) 23 *Electoral Studies* 363.

Blokker, Paul, 'Constitutional Reform in Europe and Recourse to the People' in Xenophon Contiades & Alkmene Fotiadou (eds), *Participatory Constitutional Change* (Routledge 2017) 31–51.

Bogdanor, Vernon, *The People and the Party System: The Referendum and Electoral Reform in British Politics* (Cambridge University Press 1981).

Bogdanor, Vernon, *Beyond Brexit: Towards a British Constitution* (Bloomsbury 2019).

Boix, Carlos, 'Setting the Rules of the Game: The Choice of Electoral Systems in Advanced Democracies' (1999) 93 *American Political Science Review* 609.

Caluwaerts, Didier & Min Reuchamps, 'Strengthening Democracy through Bottom-up Deliberation: An Assessment of the Internal Legitimacy of the G1000 Project' (2015) 50 *Acta Politica* 151.

Choudhry, Sujit, 'Ackerman's Higher Lawmaking in Comparative Constitutional Perspective: Constitutional Moments as Constitutional Failures' (2008) 6 *International Journal of Constitutional Law* 193.

Clarke, Harold, Allan Kornberg & Marianne Stewart, 'Referendum Voting as Political Choice: The Case of Quebec' (2004) 34 *British Journal of Political Science* 345.

Contiades, Xenophon & Alkmene Fotiadou 'Models of Constitutional Change' in Xenophon Contiades (ed), *Engineering Constitutional Change* (Routledge 2013) 417–468.

Downs, Anthony, *An Economic Theory of Democracy* (Harper 1957).

Dryzek, John, *Deliberative Democracy and Beyond: Liberals, Critics, Contestations* (Oxford University Press 2000).

Eleftheriadis, Pavlos, 'Constitutional Illegitimacy over Brexit' (2017) 88 *Political Quarterly* 182.

Fishkin, James, *When the People Speak* (Oxford University Press 2011).

Fotiadou, Alkmene, 'The Role of the People in Constitutional Amendment in Greece: Between Narratives and Practice' in Xenophon Contiades & Alkmene Fotiadou (eds), *Participatory Constitutional Change* (Routledge 2017) 156–170.

Gallagher, Michael & Pier Uleri (eds), *The Referendum Experience in Europe* (Palgrave Macmillan 1996).

Gerkrath, Jorg, 'The Sudden Eagerness to Consult the Luxembourgish People on Constitutional Change' in Xenophon Contiades & Alkmene Fotiadou (eds), *Participatory Constitutional Change* (Routledge 2017) 139–155.

Guinier, Lani, 'More Democracy' (1995) 1 *University of Chicago Legal Forum* 2.

Guinier, Lani & Torres, Gerald, *Changing the Wind: Notes towards a demosprudence of law and social movements* (2014) 123 *Yale Law Journal* 2740.

Gutmann, Amy & Dennis Thompson, *Why Deliberative Democracy?* (Princeton University Press 2004).

Hobolt, Sara 'Taking Cues on Europe? Voter Competence and Party Endorsements in Referendums on European Integration' (2007) 46 *European Journal of Political Research* 151.

Hudson, Alexander & Zachary Elkins, 'The Constitutional Referendum in Historical Perspective' in David Landau & Hanna Lerner (eds), *Comparative Constitution Making* (Edward Elgar 2019) 142–164.

Josi, Claudia 'Direct Democracy v Fundamental Rights? A Comparative Analysis of the Mechanisms that Limit the "Will of the People" in Switzerland and California' in Xenophon Contiades & Alkmene Fotiadou (eds), *Participatory Constitutional Change* (Routledge 2017) 82–100.

Katsambekis, Giorgos, 'The Populist Surge in Post-democratic Times: Theoretical and Political Challenges' (2017) 88(2) *Political Quarterly* 202.

Kriesi, Hanspeter, *Direct Democratic Choice: The Swiss Experience* (Lexington 2005).

LeDuc, Lawrence, *The Politics of Direct Democracy: Referendums in Global Perspective* (Broadview Press 2003).

Levy, Ron, 'Deliberative Voting: Realising Constitutional Referendum Democracy' (2013) *Public Law* 555.

Levy, Ron, 'The "Elite Problem" in Deliberative Constitutionalism' in Ron Levy, Hoi Kong, Graeme Orr & Jeff King (eds), *Cambridge Handbook of Deliberative Constitutionalism* (Cambridge University Press 2018) 351–369.

Lijphart, Arend, *Patterns of Democracy* (Yale University Press 2012).

Loughlin, Martin, 'Constitutional Law: The Third Order of the Political' in Nicholas Bamforth & Peter Leyland (eds), *Public Law in a Multi-layered Constitution* (Hart 2003) 27–52.

Loughlin, Martin & Neil Walker (eds), *The Paradox of Constitutionalism: Constituent Power and Constitutional Form* (Oxford University Press 2007).

Lupia, Arthur & Richard Johnston, 'Are Voters to Blame? Voter Competence and Elite Maneuvers in Public Referendums' in Matthew Mendelsohn and Andrew Parkin (eds), *Referendum Democracy: Citizens: Elites, and Deliberation in Referendum Campaigns* (Palgrave 2001) 191–210.

MacCarthaigh, Muiris & Shane Martin, 'The Seanad Abolition Referendum' (2015) 30 *Irish Political Studies* 121.

Madison, James, *Oxford World Classics: The Federalist Papers* Book 63. Lawrence Goldman (ed.) (Oxford University Press 2008).

Mendez, Fernando & Mario Mendez, 'The Promise and Perils of Direct Democracy for the European Union' (2017) 19 *Cambridge Yearbook of European Legal Studies* 48.

Moellers, Christoph, 'We are (Afraid of) the People: Constituent Power in German Constitutionalism' in Martin Loughlin & Neil Walker (eds), *The Paradox of Constitutionalism: Constituent Power and Constitutional Form* (Oxford University Press 2007) 87–105.

Moravcsik, Andrew, 'The European Constitutional Settlement' (2008) 31 *The World Economy* 158.

Mudde, Cas, 'The Populist Zeitgeist' (2004) 39 *Government and Opposition* 541.

Nadeau, Richard, Pierre Martin & Andre Blais, 'Attitude Towards Risk-Taking and Individual Choice in the Quebec Referendum on Sovereignty' (1999) 29 *British Journal of Political Science* 523.

Parkinson, John, *Deliberating in the Real World: Problems of Legitimacy in Deliberative Democracy* (Oxford University Press 2006).

Podolnjak, Robert, 'Constitutional Reforms of Citizen-initiated Referendum' (2015) 26 *Revus* 129–149.

Popkin, Samuel *The Reasoning Voter: Communication and Persuasion in Presidential Campaigns* (University of Chicago Press 1991).

R (Miller) v. *Secretary of State for Exiting the European Union* [2017] UKSC 5.

Qvortrup, Matt, *Direct Democracy: A Comparative Study of the Theory and Practice of Government by the People* (Manchester University Press 2013).

Reestman, Jan-Herman, 'A Future for Referendums in the Fifth French Republic?' in Xenophon Contiades & Alkmene Fotiadou (eds), *Participatory Constitutional Change* (Routledge 2017) 52–64.

Reference Re Secession of Quebec [1998] 2 SCR 217.

Rosenberg, Gerald, *The Hollow Hope: Can Courts Bring About Social Change?* (University of Chicago Press 2nd ed. 2008).

Roznai, Yaniv, *Unconstitutional Constitutional Amendments: The Limits of Amendment Powers* (Oxford University Press 2017).

Scott, Ralph, Charlie Cadywould, Sacha Hilhorst & Louis L. Reynolds, 'It's Who You Know: Exploring the Factors behind the UK's Vote to Leave the EU' in *Mapping and Responding to the Rising Culture and Politics of Fear in the European Union* (Demos 2017) 51–126.

Setala, Maija, 'On the Problems of Responsibility and Accountability in Referendums' (2006) 45(4) *European Journal of Political Research* 699.

Sniderman, Paul, Richard Brody & Philip E. Tetlock, *Reasoning and Choice: Explorations in Political Psychology* (Cambridge University Press 1991).

Suteu, Silvia, 'Developing Democracy through Citizen Engagement: The Advent of Popular Participation in UK Constitution-Making' (2016) 4 *Cambridge Journal of International and Comparative Law* 405.

Suteu, Silvia & Stephen Tierney, 'Squaring the Circle? Bringing Deliberation and Participation Together in Processes of Constitution-Making' in Ron Levy, Hoi Kong, Graeme Orr & Jeff King (eds), *Cambridge Handbook of Deliberative Constitutionalism* (Cambridge University Press 2018) 282–294.

Thornhill, Christopher, *A Sociology of Constitutions: Constitutions and State Legitimacy in Historical-Sociological Perspective* (Cambridge University Press 2011).

Tierney, Stephen, *Constitutional Referendums: The Theory and Practice of Republican Deliberation* (Oxford University Press 2012).

Tierney, Stephen, 'The Scottish Independence Referendum: A Model of Good Practice in Direct Democracy?' in Aileen McHarg, Tom Mullen, Alan Page, & Neil Walker (eds), *The Scottish Independence Referendum: Constitutional and Political Implications* (Oxford University Press 2016) 53–74.

Tonra, Ben, 'The 2009 Irish Referendum on the Lisbon Treaty' (2009) 5 *Journal of Contemporary European Research* 472.

Trechsler, Alexander, 'How to Federalize the European Union … and Why Bother' (2005) 12 *Journal of European Public Policy* 401.

Tushnet, Mark, *Why the Constitution Matters* (Yale University Press 2010).

Weale, Albert, 'The Democratic Duty to Oppose Brexit' (2017) 88 *Political Quarterly* 70.

Wheatley, Jonathan, 'A Problem or a Solution? The Referendum as a Mechanism for Citizens' Participation in Constitution Making' in Saskia Ruth, Yanina Welp & Laurence Whitehead (eds), *Let the People Rule? Direct Democracy in the Twenty-First Century* (European Consortium for Political Research Press 2017) 41–60.

Whiteley, Paul, Harold Clarke, David Sanders & Marianne Stuart, 'Hunting the Snark: A Reply to "Re-Evaluating Valence Models of Political Choice"' (2016) 4(1) *Political Science Research and Methods* 221–240.

Wilkinson, Michael, 'The Brexit Referendum and the Crisis of "Extreme Centrism"' (2016) 17 *German Law Journal* 131.

Williams, George & David Hume, *People Power: The History and Future of the Referendum in Australia* (University of New South Wales Press 2010).

PART III

Informal constitutional change

12

POLITICAL PRACTICE AND CONSTITUTIONAL CHANGE

David Feldman

The meaning of 'political practice and constitutional change'

'The choice of a legal perspective may make it too easy ... to forget that within the European constitutional tradition – not to speak of the so-called socialist one – the constitution had little or no importance as a strictly legal instrument'.[1] Constitutions are made through politics and, sometimes, military and diplomatic action. While making a constitution is an exercise of constituent power unconstrained by any previous constitution,[2] revising or amending occurs through political practices managed in accordance with its own terms, which both reflect and provide a framework for political practice. There might be special, formal practices for proposing and deciding on constitutional change, but changing practices might themselves, without formality, directly change the constitution. The chapter examines these possibilities, beginning by considering the meanings of 'political practice' and 'constitutional change'.

Political practice

'Political practice' encompasses a range of types of behaviour. At one level the term might refer to common behaviours which political actors follow as part of daily political life, including seeking opportunities to influence opinion and raise their public and political profiles. These practices are not peculiar to political actors, but they have little or no normative significance; people follow them to optimise the chance of winning. At another level practices might be followed because political actors feel that it is the right thing to do. An obligation might stem from their position in the constitutional structure. For example, a member of the legislature representing a constituency might write letters to, and lobby, members of the government on behalf of a constituent, and use parliamentary procedures to hold government to account, because he or she accepts that this is part of the responsibility

1 Eivind Smith, 'The constitution between politics and law' in Eivind Smith (ed), *The Constitution as an Instrument of Change* (SNS Förlag 2003) 21–51, 21.
2 See e.g. Antoine Pantélis, *Droit Constitionnel Hellénique* (EPLO/l'Harmattan 2018) 178.

that falls on a representative in a representative democracy. Such practices give effect to and help to reinforce fundamental constitutional norms.

Political practice is concerned with managing sometimes intense disagreement. Political institutions, including parties or factions, allow disagreement to be institutionalised. In a functioning polity, relations between parties are conducted according to accepted procedures; parties have to cooperate in making the procedures work, so there must be agreement on the procedures (including what counts as a decision for the time being) even between groups who may disagree fundamentally with each other. The strain of cooperating to make politics work even when agreed procedures lead to outcomes which one finds deeply upsetting is particularly strong in two circumstances: first, when one espouses absolute standards that affect the matters in dispute, whether on moral, social, religious or ideological grounds; second, when the issue relates to the practices on which principled commitment to political intercourse and institutions depend. To some extent practices must be open to renegotiation and adjustment in order to maintain the commitment of political actors and the population generally to political intercourse, but each change must be justified by considerations of fairness, necessity or mutual advantage which are accepted at least by the most significant actors. But there is no clear line between political practice in general and constitutional politics. To the extent that all politics is shaped by constitutional mechanisms and all effective constitutions, to some degree, reflect political divisions, there is constant interplay between political practice and constitutional requirements, even when the issue under discussion is not itself a proposed change to the constitution.

Constitutional change

Constitutional change is virtually inevitable, because of a tension between three constitutions which co-exist in most, if not all, polities.[3] The 'formal', or strictly legal, constitution is likely to consist to a greater or lesser extent of instruments regarded as having legal force, or at least being judicially cognisable. A real constitution operates alongside and in the interstices of the formal constitution; it consists of the understandings and practices of officials and other actors in the polity, amplifying or adjusting or sometimes ignoring the terms of the formal constitution. Even judges may sometimes respond purposively to political need despite rather than through a purely textual approach to constitutional texts.[4] This preserves the formal constitution by preventing it from becoming a dead letter. Then there is the ideal or aspirational constitution, the constitution as members of the polity like to hope that it can be. This will probably be an idealised vision of the first two constitutions, and may be highly contested with little room for the political compromises that make formal and real constitutions viable. The tensions between these three constitutions, and attempts to manage them, make 'the constitution' dynamic rather than static and demand more than formal adherence to texts.

There is a distinction between two types of constitutional change. Creating a new constitution is entirely political and special processes are likely to be made up for the

---

3 I draw here on Philip Allott, *Eunomia: New Order for a New World* (Oxford University Press 1990) 134–137, paras 9.5–9.12.

4 *Robinson v. Secretary of State for Northern Ireland* [2002] UKHL 32, [2002] N.I. 390, UKHL, considered further below; David Feldman, 'Statutory interpretation and constitutional legislation' (2014) 130 LQR 473–497; *R. (Miller) v. Secretary of State for Exiting the European Union* [2017] UKSC 5, [2018] AC 61, SCUK.

purposes. Another kind of change, on which this chapter concentrates, is constitutional adjustment, amendment or revision. Such change occurs in different ways and for different reasons. Conscious pursuit of change may be driven by a wish to accommodate a reshaping of the state or key values as in Hungary in her post-communist liberalisation of 1989 and also the Fundamental Law of 2011, and in the constitutional revision in Turkey approved in a 2017 referendum to change the system of government and increase the power of President Erdoğan. It may also result from a desire to reverse the effect of earlier constitutional change, as in the USA where the 18th Amendment prohibiting alcohol (ratified in 1919) was repealed by the 21st Amendment, ratified in 1933. Similarly, in Ireland, the Eighth Amendment to the Constitution in 1983 added Article 40.3.3° recognising a right to life of the unborn and effectively making it unlawful to allow abortion except to save the life of the mother, while the 36th Amendment in 2018 reversed this by allowing the state to regulate abortion. Other amendments may be designed to allow an international treaty to have effect as in France's amendment to Title XV of the Constitution of the Fifth Republic and Ireland's 28th Amendment in 2009 to allow them to give effect to the EU's Lisbon Treaty, or in the UK to withdraw from the EU since 2016. Change for any of those purposes is likely to require formal measures to replace or amend the constitution.

Another reason for initiating constitutional change is to provide a road-map for making state structures work more effectively in changing circumstances. This can often be achieved informally or semi-formally, by discussion between officials (or sometimes politicians) in different parts of the system. Sometimes agreements between them are reduced to codified or semi-codified form, as when the working mechanisms for handling relationships between central and devolved institutions in the UK after 1998 were developed and fine-tuned through a series of 'concordats' and 'conventions'.[5] These were free to evolve over time, without the need to resort to law-making. Indeed, the UK's Supreme Court has held that the non-statutory concordats and conventions do not have legal effects and are not judicially enforceable, even when included in an Act of Parliament.[6]

There are at least three reasons why informal political adjustments happen. First, constitutions must provide ways of managing profound disagreement. It is often said that constitutions embody shared values, goals and 'mission statements'.[7] These can be an important element of formal constitutions, but the texts that articulate them are likely to be interpreted very differently by different individuals and political groups. For example, there are deep differences in the USA over the meaning of the Second Amendment of the Constitution (bearing arms) or Fifth and Eighth Amendments (in the contexts of privacy and abortion). Democratic constitutions must provide a framework for allowing debate over those deep divisions without pulling the polity apart or even, as in the USA in the 1860s, provoking civil war. Structures and institutions need to be tough but flexible in order to allow polities and their constitutions to survive. Autocratic constitutions must allow authoritarian measures to control dissent and give ultimate power to an officer or group of

---

5 Richard Rawlings, 'Concordats of the constitution' (2000) 116 *Law Quarterly Review* 257–286. On conventions generally, see David Feldman, 'Constitutional conventions', and Joseph Jaconelli, 'Continuity and change in constitutional conventions' both in Matt Qvortrup (ed), *The British Constitution – Continuity and Change: A Festschrift for Vernon Bogdanor* (Hart Publishing 2013) chs. 6 and 7.

6 *R. (Miller) v. Secretary of State for Exiting the European Union* (n 4).

7 See e.g. Jeff King, 'Constitutions as mission statements' in Denis J. Galligan and Mila Versteeg (eds), *Social and Political Foundations of Constitutions* (Cambridge University Press 2013) 73–102.

officers. This too requires flexibility to allow autocrats a wide range of discretion. Political practice shapes, reflects, and is shaped by the character of the state and its constitution.

Second, constitutions are themselves deeply political. They come into operation through negotiation or imposition. They frame politics and law-making, but are creatures of politics. Martin Loughlin has distinguished three 'orders' of 'the political'. The first is that which informs the foundation of states, defining the realm of politics; the second order is day-to-day political practice which serves to resolve conflicts between aims and ideals in the state. The third order is constitutional law, which helps to confer a sense of the fairness of the state by cultivating 'a belief in the law-governed nature of the state' as 'a means of generating political power and an especially powerful aspect of state-building'. 'Governments obey law – to the extent that they do – essentially because it is a prudential necessity. Law observance is necessary for power maintenance'.[8] Political dictatorships produce constitutions that limit the scope for legitimate disagreement. Democracies tend to produce constitutions that allow non-violent coexistence of deeply held, fundamentally different views. The existence and structure of the state will not usually be controversial, although may be contested, notably at times of attempted secession or following civil war. Below that existential level, however, contention will abound.

Third, tradition – the authority conferred by history – is a significant source of support for institutions alongside morality or democracy, so politicians tend to look backward as well as forward when drafting, operating and adjusting constitutions. Continuity is an asset not to be lightly discarded, so even fundamental changes will often be justified partly by reference to values of past times, as in England in the 1640s. Both King Charles I and the rebels who fought and ultimately executed him appealed to their own conceptions of an 'ancient constitution'; the rebel parliamentarians presented themselves as protecting it against constitutional abuses committed by the king, as did American colonies rebelling against King George III in the 1770s.

We now examine different ways in which political practice creates, facilitates or inhibits change in constitutions.

'Constitutional' and 'non-constitutional' political practice

Constitutional politics may not be clearly differentiated from ordinary, non-constitutional politics. In some respects, constitutional politics might be messier and more difficult to manage than other political processes. Where a proposed amendment relates to a matter that cuts across party-political lines, it could be difficult to use party discipline to channel discussion through normal political processes. Normal political practices, particularly inter-party arrangements, develop to prevent (as far as possible) disagreements from derailing the process of government. When political disagreements relate to constitutional matters, it is likely to put this under pressure, by forcing political actors to confront powerfully opposed and strongly held views and loyalties. Such issues might be difficult or impossible to resolve through political processes, and threaten to fracture the processes and sometimes the institutions of the state or even the state itself, such as slavery in the USA in the 19th century. Where disagreements cut across party lines, they pose a special challenge to

---

8 Loughlin, 'Constitutional law: the third order of the political' in Nicholas Bamforth and Peter Leyland (eds), *Public Law in a Multi-Layered Constitution* (Hart Publishing 2003) 27–51. The quotations are from pp. 31, 41 and 51, respectively.

political practice. This is particularly clear in the UK, where so much of the constitution is composed of political practices that it becomes hard to identify a route toward a constitutional solution to problems that divide and weaken political parties internally, as has happened in relation to the UK's decision to leave the EU. In such situations, strength of feeling overwhelms loyalty to normal, civil political disagreement. Nobody is prepared to accept processes that might leave them on the losing side.

The words 'constitutional amendment' may inspire heightened scrutiny of legislation and principled reflection, but if the governing party controls the legislature and its influence in the country as a whole is strong there are few political constraints on its amending the constitution as it wishes. Only if there is an adjudicator with significant constitutional legitimacy and jurisdiction to review constitutional amendments will there be effective control. This has to some extent been the position in India since 1980, when the Supreme Court held invalid an amendment that sought to prevent judicial review of amendments or purported amendments to the constitution, holding that judicial review for constitutionality was part of the 'basic structure' of the constitution and could not be excluded by amendment.[9] The indeterminacy of the 'basic structure', as well as the appearance that judges were moving into the constitutional space of politicians, made this a highly controversial judgment, but it limits the extent to which certain features of the constitution can be overturned using amendment procedures.

The way in which political practice and constitutional change operate depends in part on the political character of the state concerned, including the extent to which the constitution is seen as requiring public participation as well as elite representation in political decision-making. In South Africa, the popularly elected House of Parliament, the National Assembly, is empowered to amend the constitution (section 44(1)(a)(i) of the constitution) while the other House, the National Council of Provinces (NCOP), representing the interests of the provinces, merely participates in the process (section 44(1)(b)(i)), exercising control only in relation to provincial matters. The African National Congress (ANC), which has governed with a substantial majority both in the National Assembly and in the country at large since the first post-apartheid elections in 1994, thus controls the amendment procedure, although the 17 amendments to the 1996 Constitution passed so far have not been notably partisan in origin or impact. This is in part because of the special majority required in the National Assembly in order to amend the constitution: for most amendments, the Bill must be passed by at least two-thirds of the members of the National Assembly. If the amendment relates to provincial matters it must also be passed by the NCOP with support of at least six of the nine provinces, and the NCOP must not pass it unless it has been approved by the legislatures of the province or provinces affected.[10] The ANC's best performance was in the 2004 general election, when it received almost 70 per cent of the vote and took 279 of the 400 seats in the National Assembly. With this success, it was able to make five constitutional amendments, but at least two ran into considerable political and constitutional difficulties in relation to realigning provincial borders, so that one amendment re-enacted an earlier one which had been held to have been procedurally irregular, while another reversed a change made by an earlier one.

---

9 *Minerva Mills Ltd. and Others v. Union of India and Others* (1980) 2 S.C.C. 591. See Chintan Chandrachud, *The Cases that India Forgot* (Juggernaut 2019) ch. 2.
10 *Ex parte Chairperson of the Constitutional Assembly: In re Certification of the Constitution of the Republic of South Africa* 1996 (4) SA 744 (CC) at para 232.

Thus constitutional law can impinge on politics by changing the nature and amount of political manoeuvring a governing party has to undertake in order to muster sufficient support for amending the constitution. In countries where there is a requirement for public participation and for cooperation between different levels of government, and there is a court that is able to stop changes that have not complied with cooperative procedures or allowed adequate time for consultation, this makes constitutional politics a more complex affair than ordinary politics which operates most of the time in only one dimension of government.

The way in which politics is ideally imagined in a state affects the interpretation of its constitution. All South Africa's legislatures are required to facilitate public involvement in legislation (Constitution, ss. 59(1)(a), 72(1)(a), 118(1)(a)). Constitutional democracy is conceived as participatory as well as representative. It has been held that this entails an obligation on legislatures to allow enough time for public engagement before making a decision.[11] In multi-level and federal states, ideas about democratic politics might have to take account of the fact that there is more than one *demos* whose views are entitled to respect in decision-making. Within states, negotiations between government at different levels and a certain level of consensus might be needed to make central government's actions politically legitimate. In Canada, for example, the Supreme Court has insisted on political negotiation in good faith as a basic (though unarticulated) requirement of the constitution when constitutional issues are at stake.[12] But in the UK, while the political obligation is there, no court will adjudicate on its scope.[13]

States in which politics are dominated by identity face particular problems. If a group's loyalty to the state depends on guarantees that the group's interests will be protected in the political process, it will sometimes lead to constitutional arrangements for power-sharing between groups based on identity, as in Northern Ireland under the Good Friday Agreement and Northern Ireland Act 1998, or in Bosnia and Herzegovina under the Dayton Agreement including the Constitution of 1995. A political system's political and constitutional imperfections might be essential for maintaining sufficient support for the existence of the state itself. We return to this later.

Where groups with competing interests are concentrated in different localities, some form of regionalism with devolution of some governmental powers might offer a way forward. Such limited self-government could be sufficient to maintain the loyalty of political elites and populations to the overall constitutional structure, but it brings its own strains, as regional governments need to be able to agree among themselves and with central government about ways of resolving conflicts and tensions that inevitably arise over the relationship between their exercise of their powers on a day-to-day basis. There will need to be continuous negotiation, the results being reflected in accepted practices, conventions, codes, compacts, memorandums of understanding, or concordats which are unlikely to be formally justiciable but must be followed, by and large, in order to maintain the system of government in working order. Attempts to change the delicate network of interlinked understandings and expectations on which the effectiveness of politics relies are likely to be extremely controversial and dangerous.

---

11 *Minister of Health and Another NO v. New Clicks South Africa (Pty) Ltd and Others (Treatment Action Campaign and Another as Amicus Curiae)* 2006 (2) SA 311 (CC) at paras 118–129; *Matatiele Municipality and Others v. President of the Republic of South Africa and Others (No 2)* 2007 (1) BCLR 47 (CC).

12 *Reference re Secession of Quebec* [1998] 2 SC 217, SCC.

13 *R. (Miller) v. Secretary of State for Exiting the European Union* (n 4).

Political practice as a way of changing the constitution

Political practice can contribute to constitutional change in two ways. First, a constitution might specify that special political procedures are to be followed before any change in the constitution will be formally recognised. Formal, codified constitutional documents are particularly likely to specify procedures for their own amendment. Second, changing political practice might itself be a direct source of constitutional norms. The creation and change of constitutional 'conventions' or practices deriving their authority from general acceptance by constitutional actors may operate in the interstices of formal constitutional law, and can even subvert or disable constitutional rules. There are many examples of governments using powers of appointment and dismissal to prevent the judiciary from acting as a brake on its political programmes or rationing resources for bodies that might hold them to account.

Political processes required to change the 'formal' constitution

'Formal' constitutions typically prescribe the processes to be followed for their amendment. Political elements may include citizens' initiatives, initiation by the legislature itself, initiation by a Bill introduced to the legislature by the government, an assembly summoned to consider a proposed amendment, consultation with the population at large, enactment by the legislature, approval by voters in a plebiscite, approval (or potential invalidation) by a court and, in federal states, approval by a specified number or proportion of provinces or states, either expressed by legislatures or by popular vote. Different combinations of elements might be permitted or required, with the balance of power between political elites (executive and legislative) and the populace, either in the state as a whole or its component parts, varying accordingly.

In the Union of India, a federal union, only the Parliament of the Union has power to add, vary or repeal any provision. It must act in accordance with the terms of section 368 of the constitution. This requires that (i) a Bill is introduced to one of the two Houses of Parliament, effectively giving control to the government of the day if it has a majority, (ii) the Bill is passed in each House by a majority of the total membership of the House and also by a majority of two-thirds of the members present and voting, and (iii) the president has then assented to the Bill. A Bill to amend certain particularly sensitive provisions must, after being duly passed by each House and before being presented to the president, be ratified by resolutions passed in the legislatures of not fewer than half the states. As already noted, there are judge-imposed limits to parliament's power to amend the constitution: the Supreme Court has asserted jurisdiction to rule on the validity of any amendment, not only on procedural grounds but also on the ground that an amendment is inconsistent with the 'basic structure' of the constitution.[14] These apparently demanding requirements have not proved a significant obstacle to change: the constitution has been amended almost 100 times in the 70 years since it was made.

The Commonwealth of Australia's amendment procedure, set out in section 128 of the Commonwealth Constitution, requires approval by both the parliament and voters in a plebiscite through one of two processes. In the first, each House of Parliament must pass a Bill amending the constitution by an absolute majority. In the second, one House must

---

14 *Minerva Mills Ltd. and others v. Union of India and others* (1980) 2 SCC 591, Supreme Court of India.

pass it twice if the other fails or refuses to agree to it. In the former case, the proposed amendment is to be put to the electors for the Commonwealth House of Representatives in each state and territory. If those in a majority of states approve it, and a majority of all those voting approve it, the Bill must be presented to the governor-general for royal assent. In the latter case, the governor-general may submit the Bill to the electors. By comparison with the position in India, it has proved very difficult to persuade Australian electors to approve Bills to amend the Commonwealth Constitution; in 120 years, 44 proposals have been put to the voters and only eight amendments have been passed.

The difference in the frequency of constitutional amendments between India and Australia is explained by political and social factors. In both countries, only the political elite may introduce a Bill for an amendment to the national parliament. In India, political elites remain in control throughout the process; even in the case of amendments requiring approval by resolution of two-thirds of state legislatures, political elites in the states, not the people generally, participate, and it is possible for the national government to exercise significant authority and influence in states and localities, exploiting the ability to confer benefits and protections as well as ties of kinship, clan, religion and caste, even where political parties do not align at union and state levels.[15] In Australia, by contrast, the requirement for a referendum on a Bill to amend the constitution makes it more difficult for political elites to get their way. The referendum is a 'people's veto' allowing the people to 'restrict the unbounded power of a parliamentary majority' which tries to introduce change that the people do not support.[16] It has been said that Australian voters seem to have adequately understood the issues put to them notwithstanding attempts by elite campaigners for change to confuse voters by making exaggerated claims, putting several questions at the same time, or exploiting voters' relative lack of constitutional and political sophistication.[17]

Where an amending procedure is in the hands of members of the ruling party and its supporters, it may be abused to change the constitution for the political benefit of the ruling party. This is particularly likely in states where one party has majority support which is reinforced and embedded for social, nationalist, ethnic or other historical and demographic reasons. In more balanced democracies, some constitutions are drafted to protect against abuse of constitutional amendments to entrench advantageous or disadvantageous positions of particular people, parties or viewpoints, so that constitutional change becomes a party-political tool. For example, in the US state of California an amendment of the state constitution may be proposed by the legislature but must be put to voters at the time of a general election, so cannot benefit members of the current legislature (unless they are re-elected).[18] In Pennsylvania the process is even more demanding. A proposed amendment must be agreed to by a majority of all members of each of the two Houses of the General Assembly (the state legislature), then published three months before the next general

---

15 Paul Brass, 'National power and local politics in India: a twenty-year perspective' in Partha Chatterjee (ed), *State and Politics in India* (Oxford University Press 1997) 303–335.

16 Albert V. Dicey, *Introduction to the Study of the Law of the Constitution* (Macmillan 8th ed. 1914), 'Introduction' pp. xcii, xcix. Dicey was discussing referendums on legislation, but his words apply equally to constitutional amendment on the Australian model.

17 See e.g. Scott Bennett, *The Politics of Constitutional Amendment*, Research Paper No. 11 of 2002–03, Department of the Parliamentary Library, Australian Commonwealth Parliament, available at www.aph.gov.au/About_Par liament/Parliamentary_Departments/Parliamentary_Library/pubs/rp/rp0203/03rp11#top

18 Constitution of California, Art. 18, ss 1, 4.

election. After the election, the proposals must again be agreed by a majority of all members of each House, and must within three months be approved by a majority of electors voting at a referendum. An unsuccessful proposal may not be submitted again for five years.[19]

In Greece, there are alternative amendment procedures, each of which involves a two-stage parliamentary process but without a plebiscite. The parliament first establishes that there is a need for an amendment as proposed by at least 50 members. A three-fifths majority is needed in each of two votes held at least a month apart. The next parliament must then decide on the amendment in its first session by an absolute majority of all its members. Alternatively, the earlier parliament may decide by an absolute majority of its members (but not by a three-fifths majority) that there is a need for the proposed amendment, in which case the next parliament must vote for it by a three-fifths majority if the amendment is to be adopted.[20]

Special political procedures, such as requirements for special majorities in legislatures and preventing a change from coming into force unless and until it has been ratified by a special political process (such as approval by state legislatures, or by conventions summoned in states, or by plebiscites), help to demarcate constitutional politics from ordinary politics. A more radical step is to deprive political elites of control over the initiation, not merely the completion, of formal constitutional change by allowing constitutions to be amended by citizen initiative, allowing voters to lead, not only to respond to, proposals for change. In California, for example, initiatives may be used to change both ordinary law and the state's constitution. Article 2, section 8 of the constitution allows a proposal for constitutional change to be put to a referendum if contained in a petition presented to the secretary of state signed by at least eight per cent of the total votes cast for all candidates at the most recent gubernatorial election. A majority of votes for the proposal changes the constitution accordingly. This takes control over constitutional change out of the hands of political elites. (See also Article 18, sections 3, 4.) It does not, however, differentiate it straightforwardly from ordinary political processes, as citizen initiatives in California can also make ordinary laws or initiate a referendum on a proposal to amend or repeal a law already made, with a petition signed by five per cent of voters at the most recent gubernatorial election needed to initiate it: Article 2, sections 8, 9 and 10.

Changing the formal constitution, however, is not always enough to achieve substantive change. In Ireland, for example, the constitution changes when a majority in a referendum supports a change proposed by the legislature. But sometimes, as for example following the 2018 referendum on the 36th Amendment repealing constitutional prohibition of abortion, further 'ordinary' legislation is needed, in that case to regulate abortion, followed by administrative decisions about resources for abortion services.

Political practices which in themselves amount to constitutional change

Political practices may themselves produce changes in the 'real' or practical constitution. This is most obviously true in those few states that do not have codified constitutional documents containing rules of superior status or force to those contained in other legal instruments. The UK, for instance, did not until recently differentiate between constitutional and non-constitutional legislation, and even now the distinction between

---

19 Constitution of Pennsylvania, Art. XI, s. 1.
20 Constitution of Greece (1975), Art. 110 paras 2, 3 and 4.

them and the significance of the distinction is unclear.[21] Bills that are thought to have constitutional significance take their committee stages in a Committee of the Whole House in each House of Parliament. But much of the UK's constitution is contained not in statutes but in subordinate legal instruments, non-legal agreements and practices, and judicial case-law. Even legislation that appears to give legal effect to a political agreement may be held to be non-justiciable.[22]

The UK's devolution arrangements offer an example. The UK in 1997 embarked on significant devolution of governmental and legislative functions to Scotland, Wales and Northern Ireland, but not to England. This was achieved through Acts of Parliament. In each case, alongside statutory conferral of powers on devolved institutions, arrangements for managing the overlapping competences of UK and devolved authorities were managed by extra-legal discussion at ministerial or official level, producing 'concordats' and other working systems;[23] and UK authorities undertook that the UK Parliament would not normally legislate on devolved matters without the consent of the devolved legislatures (the 'Sewel convention'). Fundamental aspects of the unions that make up the UK were thus managed by bilateral or multilateral discussions which lacked legal status but were necessary to maintain workability and a sense of legitimacy in the system.

Following a referendum in Scotland on independence from the UK in 2014 in which 55 per cent of electors voted against secession, the UK devolved extra powers to Scotland and Wales. Members of the UK House of Commons (MPs) representing constituencies in England objected to MPs from Wales and Scotland being able to affect English law on matters that devolved authorities controlled in Wales and Scotland, respectively. The UK government and House of Commons agreed to change the legislative process in the UK's parliament so that English MPs could always veto provisions in a Bill that applied to England only ('English votes for English laws', or EVEL). England-only provisions in Bills now go to the England Grand Committee, on which only MPs representing English constituencies may vote. This significant constitutional change was achieved by a vote of the House of Commons to change its procedural rules, without public consultation, consideration by the House of Lords or legislation, showing the extent to which a change of political practice can alter the constitutional position of central institutions.

The extent to which devolution depends on political practice as well as law was further demonstrated when electors voted at a referendum in 2016 by about 52 per cent to 48 per cent in favour of the UK's ceasing to be a member state of the EU. Scotland and Northern Ireland voted to remain in the EU, and objected to the UK's government and parliament taking steps that would disadvantage them. Despite the 'Sewel convention' (which had by then been partly embodied in statute), the UK Parliament enacted legislation which closely affected matters devolved to Scotland without the Scottish parliament having passed a consent motion to the legislation. The Scottish Government was effectively side-lined from national planning, but the Supreme Court held that the 'Sewel convention' and its statutory incarnation reflected a political practice that was normally desirable and

---

21 David Feldman, 'The nature and significance of "constitutional" legislation' (2013) 129 *Law Quarterly Review* 343–358.
22 *R. (Miller) v. Secretary of State for Exiting the European Union* (n 4); *Reference by the Attorney General and the Advocate General for Scotland* [2018] UKHL 64, [2019] 2 WLR 1, SCUK.
23 Rawlings (n 5).

constitutionally significant but could not be judicially enforced.[24] As negotiations with the EU continued it became clear that the two main political parties were internally divided on the issue. Normal cooperative practices between them were unable to secure for the government majority support for any plan. In March 2019 the government lost control of the business of the House of Commons, precipitating a constitutional crisis, change of prime minister, unsuccessful attempt to prorogue parliament, and an early general election, leading to the UK's departure from the EU on 31 January 2020. At the time of writing it is not clear what long-term constitutional change will result.

Non-legal constitutional norms reflected in political practice are often matters of convenience or prudence, but must be consistent with the 'ideal' or 'aspirational' constitution as well. As long as political actors recognise their value and abide by them, they provide orderly and predictable mechanisms for governing. In extraordinary times, by contrast, they are amenable to change without notice. This is not, however, peculiar to constitutional politics. It applies also to constitutional 'law'. As Professor Eivind Smith wrote:

> Sociology of law as well as common-sense observations give sufficient ground for calmly stating that legal norms − even when enacted in the formally most unquestionable manner − risk remaining dead letters unless factors like internationalisation by relevant actors, different social mechanisms and self-interest concur in rendering them effective.[25]

Examples abound of political reality, sometimes aided and abetted by constitutional theory, trumping constitutional form. In Australia, section 101 of the Commonwealth Constitution provides,

> There shall be an Inter-State Commission, with such powers of adjudication and administration as the Parliament deems necessary for the execution and maintenance, within the Commonwealth, of the provisions of this Constitution relating to trade and commerce, and of all laws made thereunder.

The commission was envisaged as a 'fourth arm' of the Constitution, partly administrative and partly judicial, sitting alongside legislature, executive and judiciary and partly overlapping the last two. But it became a victim of social realities: first, a sharp political division between supporters of economic liberalism and collectivism relating to regulation of trade and commerce; second, judicial inability to imagine a model of the separation of powers more sophisticated than the US model.[26] Acting pursuant to statute, in 1914 the federal government asked the commission to adjudicate on the validity of a wartime measure introduced by New South Wales to support lower wheat prices for consumers in New South Wales than in other states in time of war. The commission held it to be

---

24 *R. (Miller) v. Secretary of State for Exiting the European Union* (n 4); *Reference by the Attorney General and the Advocate General for Scotland* (n 22); Richard Rawlings, *Brexit and the Territorial Constitution: Devolution, Reregulation and Inter-Governmental Relations* (The Constitution Society 2017).

25 Smith (n 1) 22.

26 Stephen Gageler, 'Chapter IV: The Inter-State Commission and the regulation of trade and commerce under the Australian Constitution' (2017) 28 *Public Law Review* 205–218.

unconstitutional. On appeal, the High Court of Australia held that the commission had lacked jurisdiction, because, despite the express terms of section 101 of the constitution, the parliament could not confer adjudicative functions on the commission. Section 71 of the constitution vested the 'judicial power of the Commonwealth' in courts only, so it was unconstitutional for a statute to confer a judicial function on the commission which also exercised executive functions.[27] The court thereby made the words 'powers of adjudication ... of the provisions of this Constitution relating to trade and commerce, and of all laws made thereunder' in section 101 ineffective. For most of the next century the commission became 'a ghostly presence – a commission without commissioners',[28] its existence mandated by the constitution but with no real role, no resources and a diminishing number of commissioners, a victim of a combination of the economic liberalism of the High Court and the ideological antagonisms of Australian politics.

The US Constitution provides other examples. The original text of Article II, section 1.2, on the election of the president and the vice-president, as it took effect in 1789, was designed as a system in which elite electors appointed in each state voted for candidates of their choice as president, with the runner-up for the presidency becoming vice-president. Parties were not needed to propose candidates or to organise campaigns. Within 14 years politics had moved on; parties were putting forward candidates for election as president and vice-president, so the formal constitution was amended to reflect this.[29] Over the next few years the real practice of presidential elections continued to change, with party candidates being selected through primary elections and increasingly extensive suffrage. Accordingly, a host of political conventions overlaid the formal constitutional provisions so that the constitutional 'electors' in each state were no longer regarded as free to choose which candidate to support. There was also a strong convention that nobody should be re-elected president more than once, derived from President Washington's refusal to stand for a third term. Between 1932 and 1944, however, Franklin D. Roosevelt stood successfully for election in four successive elections, maintaining popular support by his approach to dealing with extraordinary economic, geo-political and military crises. But this proved an ad hominem exception to a popular rule, and after his death in 1944 the convention was strongly reasserted and given formal constitutional status by the 22nd Amendment, passed by Congress in 1947 and ratified in 1951. Political practice, and challenges to it, drove formal constitutional change.

Political practice as a side-constraint on constitutional change

Political practice can make it difficult or impossible to revise a constitution. There is a big difference between politics in societies where political parties espouse different economic or social ideologies and those where parties tend to be formed to protect the interests of a group of people with a defined identity or place of abode. In the former case, the policies advanced by a party might be more likely to benefit members of one social class than another, but they do not exclude from political practices sympathy between members of different classes. Where political practice is based on group identities and loyalties, however, it is more difficult for parties to obtain support from a cross-section of the population. If the

---

27 *New South Wales v. Commonwealth (The Wheat Case)* (1915) 20 CLR 54.
28 Gageler (n 26) 217.
29 US Constitution, Twelfth Amendment (passed by Congress in 1803 and ratified in 1804).

constitution is designed to provide guarantees for the groups against domination by others, it could entrench division by failing to incentivise compromise between different groups. Societies with consociational constitutions provide some examples.

In Northern Ireland, the 1998 Good Friday Agreement halting armed conflict between nationalists and unionists required nationalists and unionists to cooperate in government.[30] Most political parties in Northern Ireland represent the interests of either nationalists or unionists, although there are some cross-community parties such as the Alliance Party. The scheme embodied in the Northern Ireland Act 1998 involves devolving legislative and executive powers to Northern Ireland. Section 16 requires the Northern Ireland Legislative Assembly, following an election or resignation of the first minister or deputy first minister, within six weeks to elect a new first minister and deputy first minister to lead the executive. Only members of parties who self-identify as either nationalist or unionist may vote. If a unionist first minister is elected, the deputy will almost inevitably be nationalist, as the election is required to be supported by majorities of both the unionist and nationalist members of the Assembly. They must work together.

This has not proved easy. In 2001 the first minister resigned and the Assembly failed to elect a first minister within six weeks. Section 32(3) provided that in that event the secretary of state was to 'set a date for the poll for the election of the next Assembly'. The secretary of state set a date in 2005, when the Assembly would have expired in any case. While this was a pragmatic solution, the delay before it happened seemed to breach the requirements of the Northern Ireland Act 1998 and should, on the face of it, have led the Secretary of State for Northern Ireland to dissolve the Assembly and call another election, but the secretary of state decided instead to allow extra time. Yet the Law Lords held it to be lawful.[31] This 'remains an extraordinary decision, in which … the law lords ruled that an unlawful election was lawful, in order to keep Northern Irish devolution afloat and so as to prevent the DUP and Sinn Fein from obtaining office'.[32]

In January 2017, cooperation broke down over nationalists' allegations that the leader of the Democratic Unionist Party had acted inappropriately in the award of a public contract for encouraging commercial and non-domestic premises to move to renewable sources of heat, such as wood pellets. The Assembly which had just been elected was unable to elect first and deputy first ministers, and much executive action became impossible. The Assembly and executive, and in effect the constitution of Northern Ireland, remained inoperative, with the most pressing legislative and executive decisions being taken by the UK government and parliament.[33] Embedded differences, including those relating to religion and language but extending to policy regarding the continuation of Northern Ireland as a constituent part of the UK, bred intransigence, particularly after the UK's 2017

---

30 For a concise history of devolution in Northern Ireland, see David Torrance, *Devolution in Northern Ireland, 1998–2018*, House of Commons Briefing Paper No. 8439, November 2018, available at https://researchbrief ings.parliament.uk/ResearchBriefing/Summary/CBP-8439.

31 *Robinson v. Secretary of State for Northern Ireland* [2002] UKHL 32, [2002] N.I. 390, HL.

32 Adam Tomkins, 'Confusion and retreat: the Supreme Court on devolution', U.K. Const. L. Blog (19 February 2015) (available at: https://ukconstitutionallaw.org/).

33 Northern Ireland (Executive Formation and Exercise of Functions) Act 2018. See also Northern Ireland (Executive Formation etc.) Act 2019, extending the period for re-establishing the Northern Ireland executive. For the official report on the Renewable Heat Incentive affair, see *The Report of the Independent Public Inquiry into the Non-domestic Renewable Heat Incentive (RHI) Scheme* accessible at https://www.rhiinquiry.org/report-independent-public-inquiry-non-domestic-renewable-heat-incentive-rhi-scheme

General Election left the Conservative government dependent on the DUP for its Commons majority. The politics of identity undermined the formal, power-sharing constitution in Northern Ireland for three years, until, following the UK's general election in December 2019 when the DUP lost a great deal of support to the nationalists, an agreement between the DUP and Sinn Fein allowed devolved government to resume in January 2020.

In Bosnia and Herzegovina (BiH), following the war of 1992–5, a constitutional settlement was brokered by the USA and embodied in the Dayton Agreement, Annex IV to which was to become the Constitution of BiH. As in Northern Ireland, most political parties are largely expressions of the separate aspirations of one or other of the three 'constituent peoples', Bosniaks, Croats and Serbs. Parties pursuing non-nationalist goals whose social and economic aims cut across divisions between Constituent Peoples garner less support. The divisive character of BiH politics led to a low turnout in the 2018 General Election (around 54 per cent) and produced a national House of Representatives dominated by ethnic parties. The result was that it proved difficult for the House to elect a Committee of Ministers, hampering political progress on important matters. In the other chamber, the House of Peoples, only the Constituent Peoples are represented, with equal numbers of delegates. Identity-based politics makes it difficult to construct alliances and develop cooperation, making both constitutional change and ordinary politics daunting.

Article X of the Constitution of Bosnia and Herzegovina permits the constitution to be amended by the Parliamentary Assembly including a majority in the House of Representatives consisting of at least two-thirds of those members present and voting.[34] It is generally recognised that changes are needed, but entrenched interests have meant that only one amendment has passed in the years since 1995, a relatively uncontentious change in 2009 to bring the special administrative of Brčko explicitly within the structure of the constitution and under the jurisdiction of the Constitutional Court. Other proposed amendments, for example to remove the international judges from the Constitutional Court or to remove the ethnic privileges of Bosniaks, Serbs and Croats in the political system and state institutions, have predictably stalled, despite having international support. In the case of ethnic privileges, the state was required to amend the constitution in order to give effect to a 2009 judgment of the European Court of Human Rights.[35] Its failure to do so left the country in continuing difficulty with the Council of Europe, but the judgment of the court was arguably doctrinally flawed and pragmatically ill-advised in view of the foreseeable impossibility of giving effect to it given the fractured politics of the state.[36]

Political, legal and administrative elements in constitutional change

Political practice and law interact in maintaining constitutional stability and allowing constitutional change. They are not the only elements effecting or hampering constitutional change. Public administration is part of the operating constitution, and as such can change it through changes in administrative organisation and practice. Administrators, especially when

---

34 Amendments may not derogate from the rights protected by the Constitution: Art. X.2.
35 *Sejdić and Finci v. Bosnia and Herzegovina* (Apps. Nos. 27,996/06 and 34,836/06), judgment of 22 December 2009. See Marko Milanovic, 'Sejdić & Finci *v.* Bosnia and Herzegovina' (2017) 104(4) *The American Journal of International Law* 636–641.
36 For trenchant criticism, see Christopher McCrudden and Brendan O'Leary, *Courts and Consociations: Human Rights versus Power-Sharing* (Oxford University Press 2013) especially chs. 2 and 5 to 8.

they have security of tenure and are insulated against the winds of political change, can do a great deal to maintain respect among politicians for constitutional principles and rules, and provide foundations for the continuance of constitutional government. In the UK, this has long been one of the functions of the Cabinet secretary, and is recognised in the Ministerial Code which requires ministers to treat civil servants with respect for their political impartiality.[37] Economic and fiscal matters also affect the constitution, often in alliance with political practice. In the UK since 1979, the constitution has been politically reshaped under the influence of ideological change. Sovereignty of parliament allowed both Conservative and Labour governments to replace a tradition of state provision of social goods in the public interest with a transfer of responsibilities to, and generation of business for, private-sector businesses as government at different levels moved from the provision of services to the management of contracts for services. What is remarkable is that in the UK this important reshaping of the extent and operation of governmental power required no change to key constitutional rules or beliefs about the proper location of power. As Tony Wright wrote, throughout the 20th century both right and left in British politics were attached to the idea of a strong central state to be used for political purposes; Mrs Thatcher's programme of privatisation and market liberalisation and her undermining of centres of political dissent in local government was far from 19th-century liberalism:

> [I]t was ferociously anti-liberal in its attachment to (and deployment of) the unchecked power of the centralised British state … . It was not detained by the conventional rules of the constitutional game, and certainly did not want to construct any new ones that could inhibit what governments could do.[38]

This trend was continued by Labour's prime minister, Mr Blair, after 1997: he was able to re-shape the constitution by statute while degrading the process of government by making decisions in relatively informal discussions outside the Cabinet, sometimes without a formal record being kept, practices severely criticised by successive inquiry reports as tending to undermine collective government and weaken scrutiny of evidence and ideas.[39]

Formal legal proceedings can sometimes help to shape political action by laying down ground-rules for discussions. Parties might try to circumvent tough political negotiations by referring the issue to a court with constitutional jurisdiction. But where a constitutional reference raises existential issues for a state and its constitution, a wise court will do its best

---

37 *Ministerial Code* (Cabinet Office, August 2019), accessible at https://assets.publishing.service.gov.uk/govern ment/uploads/system/uploads/attachment_data/file/826920/August-2019-MINISTERIAL-CODE-FINAL-FORMATTED-2.pdf, section 5. See Andrew Blick, *The Codes of the Constitution* (Oxford: Hart Publishing, 2016), ch. 6.

38 Tony Wright, *British Politics: A Very Short Introduction* (Oxford University Press 2003) 42. Wright, a political scientist, had become a Labour M.P. in 1992.

39 *Review of Intelligence on Weapons of Mass Destruction* (Chairman: Lord Butler of Brockwell), HC 898 of 2003–04, para. 611: 'We do not suggest that there is or should be an ideal or unchangeable system of collective Government, still less that procedures are in aggregate any less effective now than in earlier times. However, we are concerned that the informality and circumscribed character of the Government's procedures which we saw in the context of policy-making towards Iraq risks reducing the scope for informed collective political judgement. Such risks are particularly significant in a field like the subject of our Review, where hard facts are inherently difficult to come by and the quality of judgement is accordingly all the more important'; *The Iraq Inquiry: Report of a Committee of Privy Councillors* ('the Chilcot report'), HC264 of 2015–16, Section 7, para. 393 et seq., accessible at webarchive .nationalarchives.gov.uk/20171123122743/www.iraqinquiry.org.uk/the-report/.

to push the matter back into political fora and encourage politicians to negotiate while providing broad guidelines on the process they should follow or the level of consensus needed.

The Supreme Court of Canada has from time to time done this. When Canada was drafting a new constitution in the early 1980s with a view to asking the UK Parliament to enact it, a constitutional dispute arose between the federal government and some provinces as to whether there was a convention requiring that the provinces should agree to the federal government's moving to send the draft text and the request for legislation to the UK. The Supreme Court was empowered to give its opinion on a reference to it of this constitutional question. There was no constitutional 'law' determining it, but a majority of the court held that its jurisdiction to opine on constitutional questions included relevant constitutional conventions, and gave as its opinion that a higher level of consensus was required than had then been achieved.[40] This was widely accepted, and federal and provincial governments returned to talks with a view to negotiating a constitution that could command a higher level of consensus. The court later helped to define the terms of engagement for discussion of whether and on what terms the province of Quebec could secede from Canada. The constitution was silent on the issue. The court did not put an absolute prohibition on secession, but pointed out that a democratic solution to the matter would need to take into account the views not only of the electors of Quebec but also of other parts of Canada which would be affected. A clear mandate from a poll in Quebec on a clear question would be necessary, but it would not itself create a right to secede. It would, however, compel the federal government and other provinces to negotiate in good faith to seek an agreed resolution.[41]

These examples are out of the ordinary, but they point to three important facets of the place of political practice in constitutional change. First, change always requires political will. If the will is lacking, the parties are unlikely to achieve anything satisfactory. Second, political will must be reflected in practices that will be shaped and sometimes hindered by the political values and practices making up the 'real' constitution. Third, these practices must be shown to be consistent with a tenable interpretation of the 'ideal' constitution in order to gain legitimacy. Political practice, law and ideals must be able to shape and adapt to each other to make change achievable and sustainable.

---

40 *Reference re Resolution to Amend the Constitution* [1981] 1 S.C. 753, SCC.
41 *Reference re Secession of Quebec* [1998] 2 S.C. 217, SCC.

13

JUDGE-MADE CONSTITUTIONAL CHANGE

Joel I. Colón-Ríos[*]

This chapter is about judge-made constitutional change. Naturally, to address this topic properly one must begin by clarifying what is meant by 'constitutional change' in this context. Lawyers usually distinguish between formal and informal constitutional change, and I will largely adopt that distinction for the purpose of this analysis.

Formal constitutional change is most easily identified in the context of a codified constitution.[1] It refers to modifications to the text of a document according to the procedures prescribed in the document itself. Formal constitutional change is, in that sense, equivalent to what we normally refer to as 'constitutional amendment'. Most codified constitutions are also rigid, which means that their amendment formulas involve requirements that are more difficult to meet than those that apply to the adoption of ordinary laws. This definition of formal constitutional change would nonetheless also apply to a codified, but flexible, constitution (that is, a constitutional text that can be modified through the same procedures that apply to the adoption of ordinary legislation). A fully unwritten constitution (i.e. a constitution *solely* based on custom/conventions – something that does not currently exist in any state), by definition, cannot be subject to formal change: it only changes informally. Of course, if a constitution is partly written, and the written part is, for example, contained in a statute, then a modification of that statute would fall under the definition of formal constitutional change (even though that modification would not be a 'constitutional amendment' in the strict sense of the term).[2] Formal constitutional change, in this respect, is always textual.

Informal constitutional change, on the other hand, takes place outside of the relevant texts. In the context of a codified constitution, it is typically exemplified by changes occurring through constitutional interpretation. That is to say, situations where a text remains untouched, but authoritative interpreters assign to it a new or different meaning,

* Thanks to Luna Arango for her assistance with the preparation of the final draft of this chapter.

1 The terms 'codified' and 'unwritten' are used as analytical tools. In practice, there are no fully codified constitutions. There is always constitutional content outside of the constitutional text. Similarly, there are no fully unwritten constitutions; at least in contemporary legal systems, there will always be constitutional content in a written form. In this chapter, I will use the term 'uncodified' to refer to constitutions, such as those of New Zealand and the United Kingdom, which are largely written but not codified in a single document.

2 Since it does not amount to the change of a formal, or entrenched, constitution, some might prefer to describe it as 'informal'.

with the result that one can say that the content of the constitution has changed.[3] Informal constitutional change may also occur in the context of a codified constitution when certain extra-textual norms (for example, norms related to the standards of interpretation, to tests used by courts to assess the constitutionality of legislation, or to the relationship between the branches of government) suffer a modification. It also includes situations of desuetude, where a constitutional provision loses its force and ceases to be a relevant part of the content of the constitutional order.[4] In the context of a (hypothetical) fully unwritten constitution, informal constitutional change would be the exclusive means of change. The same would apply to the unwritten part of uncodified and codified constitutions.[5] In these cases, informal constitutional change means a change in constitutional custom (broadly understood, that is, as including not only rules of conduct accepted as obligatory by officials – i.e. constitutional conventions – but also unwritten rules constitutive of the constitutional system which might be enforced by courts – e.g. the rules that specify the process that needs to be met in order to produce valid law).

This chapter focuses on instances where judges, not members of the legislature or the executive, change the constitutional order. This notion rests on a broad understanding of constitutional change: constitutional change as any change in constitutional content. Codified constitutions will be central to the analysis, but judge-made constitutional change in the context of uncodified constitutions and decisions by international courts will also be considered.[6] A clarification is in order. As one speaks of constitutional change, formal or informal, one speaks of changes to material constitutional norms. These are changes that relate to the basic structure of government, to the rights of citizens, and to the competences of different public institutions. In the context of a codified and rigid constitution, however, the constitutional text might contain norms that are not constitutional in the material sense. For example, there could be a constitution that contains a provision regulating the enforcement of contracts between foreigners. If that provision became the subject of a formal change, we would be forced to speak of 'constitutional change' even if, in fact, what has taken place is a modification of a rule of private international law. In the context of an uncodified constitution, in contrast, the question of whether a change in a particular norm counts as a constitutional change would turn directly to the question as to whether the norm at issue is materially constitutional (as all constitutional customs/conventions would by definition be).[7]

---

3 It could be argued that all constitutional cases add (or potentially add) new content to the constitutional order (just as all common law cases can potentially affect the ways in which future courts develop the common law). If that is the case, then every time the courts apply a constitution, they informally change it. Whether this idea can be sustained is out of the scope of this chapter.

4 Richard Albert, 'Constitutional Amendment by Constitutional Desuetude' (2014) 62 *The American Journal of Comparative Law* 641.

5 Akhil Amar, *America's Unwritten Constitution: The Precedents and Principles by Which We Live* (Basic Books 2012).

6 As will be seen below, in some cases, judges are able to effect constitutional change by themselves while, in others, they rather trigger (intentionally or unintentionally) a set of events that lead to change. In other cases, however, it will be clear that even though the constitutional order has changed as a direct result of a judicial decision, the change has not been led by judges: they are responding to a wider societal transformation or to another type of external pressure. Put differently, they are simply the final part in a process of constitutional change that has been led by others. I will not consider those external factors in my analysis.

7 Since constitutional conventions (as understood in the English tradition) are not law and cannot be enforced by the courts, they cannot be 'changed' by courts either. However, it is possible that the judicial acknowledgement

Judges as constitution changers

Courts generally recognise that their authority comes from the constitutional order under which they operate. Accordingly, to speak of judges as constitution changers, particularly in the context of codified constitutions, could be seen as a constitutional pathology. Not only judicial authority is derived from the constitution, but an important part of the judges' institutional responsibility is precisely to protect the existing constitutional order. Indeed, when a court operating under a system of strong judicial review invalidates an unconstitutional statute, it is actually preventing the legislature from *changing* the constitution outside of the constitutional amendment procedure. But this very example serves to illustrate one form of judge-made constitutional change.

Let us suppose that a court decides to sustain the validity of an otherwise unconstitutional norm because it concludes that the subject matter of the law raises a political question that the court prefers not to address. That decision could change the content of the constitutional order in two ways. First, to the extent that it creates a new political question doctrine (or alters the scope of an existing one), the court would be altering the relationship between the judicial and the legislative or executive branches of government. Second, by sanctioning a statute that is inconsistent with the constitutional text, the court would be indirectly introducing an exception to a particular constitutional provision. The legally valid but theoretically unconstitutional statute would in that respect become part of the constitution (even if it would not have been codified in the document titled 'constitution'). In this chapter I explore different examples of this type of phenomena. That is to say, instances in which judicial action (or inaction) leads to informal or formal constitutional change. I will focus in the following categories which, needless to say, might sometimes overlap with each other: (1) changes through interpretation; (2) changes in review standards; (3) changes in the relationship between the branches of government; (4) attribution of a new status to certain norms; (5) recognition of new rights; and (6) judicially triggered constitutional change.

The first category, in a certain way, is the most controversial one. If at least some constitutional provisions do not have a fixed meaning, assigning them any meaning would involve a 'change' in the constitutional order. But if that is true, then there are actually very few constitutional cases, if any, that would not result in constitutional change. However, holding that no instances of judicial interpretation can amount to constitutional change

---

of a constitutional convention might actually affect its force or effectivity. As Geoffrey Marshall has noted (*Constitutional Conventions: The Rules and Forms of Political Accountability* (Oxford University Press 1987) 17):

> But what then, one might ask (remembering Dicey's definition of convention), is the status of a non-legal rule that has been declared to exist by a court of law? Does that declaration in any sense change the character or increase the obligation or binding nature of the convention? The answer would seem to be that it does not. In so far as a convention defines duties or obligations they remain morally and politically, but not legally, binding. Nevertheless, in one way a court decision may decisively change the situation since politicians' doubts about what ought to be done may stem not from uncertainty about whether duty-imposing conventions are morally binding but from disagreement as to whether a particular convention does or does not exist. Since opposed politicians are rarely likely to convince each other on this point an advisory jurisdiction, selectively used, seems a useful device in any political system where important constitutional rules are conventional and uncodified. The decision of a court may be accepted as decisively settling a political argument about the existence of a conventional rule.

cannot be right either. There must be a point in which a judicial decision so clearly affects the functioning of the constitutional order, or the relation between citizens and the state, that it becomes impossible to escape the fact that the content of the constitutional order has changed (or put in another way, there are situations where achieving the same result of a court's decision would otherwise require a formal amendment to the constitutional text). The most extreme example would be what Alec Stone Sweet has called a 'juridical coup d'état', a 'fundamental transformation in the normative foundations of a legal system through the constitutional lawmaking of a court'.[8] The examples given under this first category of judge-made constitutional change are not of such a fundamental character but are presented as situations in which the effect of a judicial decision can be understood as producing a (major or minor) change in the constitutional order.

Changes through judicial interpretation[9]

As discussed earlier, every time a court assigns to a constitutional provision a meaning different from what it previously had, one could say that an informal constitutional change has occurred.[10] This includes cases where a court expands or limits the scope of a right or of a constitutional provision (e.g. determining that the right to freedom of expression extends to juridical persons), or situations where the courts sanction legislative content previously declared unconstitutional (or the other way around).[11]

Consider, for example, a recent decision of the Canadian Supreme Court where Section 8 of the Charter of Rights and Freedoms (the right to be secure against unreasonable search or seizure) was understood as allowing senders of electronic messages to claim privacy rights (as long as certain requirements are met, e.g. that their expectation of privacy was objectively reasonable) not only with respect to their own phones, but with respect to the phones of the recipient of the relevant message. This type of decision, by altering the scope of a provision that relates to individual rights in Canada, arguably changed the content of the country's constitution. Or consider the expansion in the legislative power of the U.S. Congress, which can now adopt statutes in areas that were once regarded under the exclusive jurisdiction of the states. That expansion is certainly materially constitutional (it affects the competence of the federal legislature), and it was the result of multiple modifications in the judicial understanding of the Commerce Clause.[12]

There are a number of institutional factors that could affect whether a judicial decision that assigns new meaning to a constitutional provision actually changes the content of the constitution. First, there is the question about whether the decision at issue creates 'general law', understood in this context as a law that goes beyond the parties to a particular case. This depends, on the one hand, on the status of the court at issue. A judgment of a constitutional court, for example, normally applies *erga omnes*. Accordingly, when a constitutional court renders a decision that attributes a new meaning to a constitutional

---

8 A.S. Sweet, 'The Juridical *Coup d'État* and the Problem of Judicial Authority' (2007) 8 *German Law Journal* 915.

9 All judge-made constitutional change can be said to be the result of 'judicial interpretation' broadly understood. This section is about 'judicial interpretation' narrowly understood, that is, about situations where specific provisions found in constitutional text are given novel meanings by courts.

10 David A. Strauss, 'The Irrelevance of Constitutional Amendments' (2001) 114 *Harvard Law Review* 1457.

11 Karl Loewenstein, *Political Power and the Governmental Process* (University of Chicago Press 1965) 139.

12 Article 1, section 8, US Constitution. For a general judicial overview of the evolution in the courts' understanding of the reach of the Commerce Clause, see *United States v. Lopez*, 514 US 549 (1995).

provision, it will be changing the constitution itself. In non-centralised systems of judicial review, the extent to which the decision of a court can alter the content of the constitution would largely depend on the system's adherence to the doctrine of *stare decisis*. Where the doctrine applies, high court decisions that assign a new meaning to constitutional provisions would amount to an informal constitutional change, as they would create new constitutional content that binds lower courts (in contrast, decisions of lower courts would only bind the parties). In a non-centralised system in which no judicial precedents are considered legally binding on later courts (e.g. a 'pure' civil law system with no constitutional court or equivalent institution), the attribution of new constitutional meaning to a constitutional provision by a high court can only result in informal constitutional change indirectly, that is, if the novel interpretation becomes a custom (or, in the alternative, if there is a general custom requiring lower courts to act consistently with decisions of the higher courts even if they are not legally required to do so).

Another illustration of informal constitutional change through judicial interpretation is the endorsement of previously invalidated legislative content or executive action, or the invalidation of a previously sanctioned one. This modality of judge-led constitutional change takes place when the court decides to overrule its previous decision on the constitutionality of particular legislative content (which could be contained in different statutes) or an executive act. A well-known example, directly related to the previously mentioned Commerce Clause of the U.S. Constitution, is that of the U.S. Fair Labor Standards Act of 1937, which was upheld by the Supreme Court in 1941 despite containing provisions that would have been unconstitutional under the court's previous jurisprudence.[13] These provisions specified minimum wages and maximum working hours in certain circumstances (i.e. where the individual produced goods for interstate commerce) and amounted to the federal regulation of local matters such as the manufacture of goods, a power that in *Hammer v. Dagenhart*, 247 U.S. 251 (1918) the court had determined that the U.S. Congress lacked.[14] As David Strauss has explained, these cases were particularly interesting since, in 1924, Congress proposed a constitutional amendment (the Child Labor Amendment) which was rejected by the states and that would have overridden the court's decision in *Hammer*. In other words, the *Darby* court not only altered the content of the U.S. constitutional order but produced a constitutional change that the formal amending power decided not to adopt.[15]

Changes in review standards

When judges assess the constitutionality of a statute or an act of the executive, they generally apply different standards of review. These may take the form of proportionality analysis (as in Germany or Canada) or of various levels of scrutiny (as in the United States). Judicial decisions that alter those review standards or that interpret them in new ways can amount to constitutional changes provided that they affect the potential validity of public acts.[16] That is to say, review standards can (at least in theory) play functions similar to those

---

13 *United States v. Darby* 312 US 100 (1941).
14 See Strauss (n 10) 1475–1476.
15 Ibid.
16 In the English constitutional tradition, the rules of statutory interpretation are generally identified as one of the
    sources of the constitution. These rules have been developed by the courts to include a number of

played by substantive constitutional content. In the United States, the notion that there are different levels of scrutiny applicable to different types of cases was famously expressed in footnote 4 of *U.S. v. Carolene Products Company*.[17] In that case, the court applied what is now known as a rational basis review to economic legislation (in this case, a prohibition against shipping a particular type of milk in interstate commerce) but suggested that a higher level of scrutiny would apply in cases involving statutes that appeared to be prima facie inconsistent with a specific constitution provision.

This type of decision can impact the content of the constitutional order to the extent that it changes the relationship between the constitution – or certain constitutional provisions – and ordinary legislation. In a similar way, further modifications in the requirements of different levels of scrutiny, as well as the addition of new levels (as the addition of intermediate scrutiny in *Craig v. Boren*) would also fall under this category. Needless to say, for changes such as these to actually amount to the alteration of the constitutional order, the relevant standards of review must be doing some work (that is to say, they must limit, in some way, the discretion of judges in terms of the exercise of their review power).

It is also arguable that every time constitutional or supreme courts decide to adopt a structured proportionality test, a change in the constitutional order occurs. For this to be true, the consequence of a structured proportionality analysis must be to make it more difficult (or easier) to sustain the validity of legislation inconsistent with a constitutional right when compared to the previously existing approach. This type of discussion has taken place when scholars compare the U.S. levels of scrutiny approach with structured proportionality. For example, Aharon Barak has maintained that U.S. intermediate and rational basis scrutiny allow for greater limitations of the relevant rights than would proportionality analysis, while it is not entirely clear whether that is or is not the case in terms of strict scrutiny.[18] In contrast (and with respect to the balancing aspect of proportionality), Laurent B. Frantz once maintained that (under the U.S. Constitution), '[t]he balancing test assures us little, if any, more freedom of speech than we should have had if the first amendment had never been adopted'.[19] If any of these views are correct, it would mean that, at least in a system similar to that of the U.S., the adoption by the court of the practice of determining the validity of a law through structured proportionality analysis would alter the content of the constitutional order.

A final example of this category of judge-made constitutional change would be the extension or narrowing of the political question doctrine. The doctrine allows courts to justify a determination of abstaining from hearing a case on the basis that it does not raise legal questions but political ones, and therefore issues that should be decided by the other branches of government. Accordingly, the doctrine has important effects on the

presumptions that protect the rights of individuals, such as the principle of legality. Similar to what happens with changes in review standards, when those rules change, the constitutional order can change with them. For a discussion of the status of the rules of interpretation in the English constitutional tradition, see Philip A. Joseph, *Constitutional and Administrative Law in New Zealand* (Thomson Reuters 2014) 32.

17 304 US 144 (1938).

18 Aharon Barak, 'Proportionality (2)' in Michael Rosenfeld and András Sajó (eds), *The Oxford Handbook of Comparative Constitutional Law* (Oxford University Press 2012) 752–753.

19 Laurent B. Frantz, 'The First Amendment in the Balance' (1962) 71 *Yale Law Journal* 1424, 1448. See also, Stavros Tsakyrakis, 'Proportionality: An Assault on Human Rights?' (2010) 7 *International Journal of Constitutional Law* 468.

enforceability of constitutional provisions. Not surprisingly, it is often used as a tool to 'delineate the boundaries of the courts' scope of authority'.[20] That is to say, every case in which a court determines that a particular subject does not fall under the scope of the political question doctrine, it would be augmenting its own authority vis-à-vis that of the other branches of government.[21] This type of decision amounts to a constitutional change that would perhaps be better captured by the next category. But the doctrine is also closely related to the concept of justiciability, and therefore comes into play every time a court decides to enforce a constitutional provision that was previously considered unenforceable.

This is the case, for example, of the Directive Principles of State Policy (DPSP) in the Constitution of India. According to the constitutional text, these principles (which refer to a number of social and economic rights) are non-justiciable (in the language of the political question doctrine, their enforcement is left to the political branches of government). However, in a number of cases the Supreme Court[22] has moved some of them to the terrain of justiciability by reading them as part of the fundamental right to life.[23]

Changes in the relationship between the branches of government

A central aspect of constitutional regulation is the relationship between the different branches of government. For example, when a court expands the scope of a particular right through interpretation it is potentially restricting the scope of the legislative and executive power on the relevant area (and the other way around as well). The same applies to the judicial alteration of the applicable standards of review. The type of judge-made constitutional change that will be examined in this section, however, is of a more fundamental nature. It is, in the last instance, about the court's power to invalidate legislation and about the legislature's power to override judicial decisions.

The former power does not exist (or at least has never been exercised) in the context of the uncodified (and mostly unentrenched) constitutions of New Zealand and the United Kingdom.[24] In New Zealand, unlike in the United Kingdom, courts have not been explicitly authorised by parliament to declare the inconsistency between a statute and a right recognised in the Bill of Rights Act, 1990. In the recent case of *Attorney General v. Taylor*,[25]

20 Christopher M. Larkins, 'Judicial Independence and Democratization: A Theoretical and Conceptual Analysis' (1996) 44 *The American Journal of Comparative Law* 605, 619. There is a general perception that supreme and constitutional courts are now much more likely to assume jurisdiction to decide issues that, in the past, were thought to raise only political questions. Ran Hirschl, for example, has written that the judicialisation of 'mega-politics' (fundamental political matters that are often highly divisive), 'reflects the demise of the "political question" doctrine and marks a transition to [juristocracy]'. Ran Hirschl, 'The Judicialization of Mega-Politics and the Rise of Political Courts' (2008) 11 *Annual Review of Political Science* 93, 112.

21 *Baker v. Carr* 369 US 186 (1962). In this case, the US Supreme Court decided that redistricting cases fall outside the scope of the political question doctrine.

22 See *Olga Tellis v. Bombay Municipal Corporation* (1985) 3 SCC 545. For critical discussions, see Tarunabh Khaitan and Farrah Ahmed, 'Constitutional Avoidance in Social Rights Adjudication' (2015) 35 *Oxford Journal of Legal Studies* 607; Madhav Khosla, 'Making Social Rights Conditional: Lessons from India' (2010) 8(4) *International Journal of Constitutional Law* 739.

23 This type of constitutional change could also be understood as an example of the fourth or fifth categories – 'Attribution of a New (Higher) Status to Certain Norms'; 'Judicial Recognition of New Rights'.

24 Section 268 of the NZ Electoral Act 1993, entrenches a number of provisions within that Act and provisions of the Constitution Act 1986.

25 [2017] 3 NZLR 24. See also Claudia Geiringer, 'The Constitutional Role of the Courts under the NZ Bill of Rights: Three Narratives from Attorney-General v Taylor' (2017) 48/4 *VUWLR* 547–570.

however, the NZ Court of Appeal determined that courts can indeed formally issue such declarations in certain situations despite the lack of explicit statutory authorisation. The power to issue declarations of inconsistency, understood as remedies in bill of rights cases, alters the relationship between the court and the legislature to the extent that it opens the legislative branch to at least an indirect form of criticism by the judiciary. In that respect, it provides an example of the type of judge-made constitutional change discussed in this section.

A more dramatic change in the relationship between courts and legislatures in this kind of constitutional system would be a judicial assertion of jurisdiction to invalidate parliament-made law (i.e. the transformation of a system of weak judicial review to a strong one via a judicial decision). Some judges, both in New Zealand and the United Kingdom, have expressed (in *obiter*), the existence of such a power, usually associated with the notion of 'common law constitutionalism'. According to common law constitutionalism's proponents, there is a common law constitution that rests on certain principles (such as democracy, the rule of law, or the protection of basic human rights), and judges have the right to identify and enforce these principles against the decisions of parliament. In the United Kingdom, the strongest judicial comments in favour of this approach are probably the ones made by some of the Lords in *Jackson v. Attorney General*.[26] For example, Baroness Hale maintained that courts will 'treat with suspicion (and might even reject) any attempt to subvert the rule of law by removing governmental action affecting the rights of the individual from all judicial scrutiny'.[27]

Notwithstanding the above, the most famous example of judge-made constitutional change in this area remains *Marbury v. Madison*.[28] This case, in addition to defining the boundaries between the executive and the judicial branches of government, ultimately recognised the court's jurisdiction to strike down federal legislation inconsistent with the constitution (even though the constitutional text did not explicitly give it the power to do so). *Marbury* made the Supreme Court (through the operation of the doctrine of precedent), the ultimate arbiter of the validity of ordinary legislation. After *Marbury*, the only means according to which the U.S. Congress could validly act contrary to the court's understanding of the constitution would be through the constitutional amendment procedure.

That is in fact the most common structure of the relationship between courts and legislatures around the world. Nonetheless, some courts, perhaps most famously those of India and Colombia, have changed that type of judiciary–legislature relationship and, with it, carried out a major constitutional transformation. For example, in *Kesavananda Bharati v. Kerala*,[29] a case which dealt with a series of land reforms that affected property rights, the Indian Supreme Court determined that while parliament had the power to amend any constitutional provision, it could not alter the *basic structure* of the constitution (even though the constitution lacked eternity clauses and did not authorise the court to review the

---

26 [2005] UKHL 56.

27 Ibid para 159. For further discussion, see Tom Mullen, 'Reflections on Jackson v Attorney General: Questioning Sovereignty' (2006) 27(1) *Legal Studies* 1. See also Lord Cooke's judgment in *Taylor v. New Zealand Poultry Board* [1984] 1 *New Zealand Law Reports* 394, 398 (CA).

28 5 US 137 (1803). This does not mean that practices of strong judicial review of legislation were unknown in the United States before *Marbury*. For discussion, see William M. Treanor, 'Judicial Review before Marbury' (2005) 58 *Stanford Law Review* 455.

29 1973 (SUP) SCR 0001.

constitutionality of constitutional amendments).[30] In so doing, the court abolished the legislature's ultimate power to override judicial declarations of invalidity through the alteration of the constitutional text. At the same time, it implicitly attributed a special status to certain constitutional principles, a phenomenon that will be discussed further in the next section.

Attribution of a new status to certain norms

A central feature of modern constitutionalism is the attribution of a heightened status to certain norms. This is one of the main legal effects of adopting a formal constitution: the norms contained in the constitution, whatever their content, are given a higher formal status than those adopted through the ordinary law-making process. This status is most clearly reflected in the fact that norms contained in the constitution can only be repealed or changed through a special procedure. Within a particular constitution, of course, there could be a formal hierarchy of constitutional norms expressed, for example, through a tiered amendment process: those norms that are considered particularly important would be subject to the most stringent procedure. Some constitutions may also distinguish between ordinary and organic laws and give the latter a higher level of protection. Attributing to certain norms a constitutional character that places them above other norms would usually require a formal constitutional change. For example, if a government wishes to attribute a higher level of protection to a particular rule, it could include it in the constitutional text through the constitutional amendment process. Among different constitutional provisions, the constitutional amendment process may also be used to give a particular provision a higher status by, for example, making it unamendable.[31]

Courts can also produce a similar type of informal change when they attribute quasi-constitutional status to particular statutes. In the context of an uncodified constitution, quasi-constitutionality means that certain statutes, because of their importance in the legal system, will not be treated by courts as simple ordinary laws. This means, for instance, that they will not be subject to the principle of implied repeal by conflicting (and subsequent) legislation. This is the case in the United Kingdom, where courts have identified certain (formally ordinary) laws as 'constitutional statutes',[32] defined as those norms which '(a) [condition] the legal relationship between citizen and State in some general, overarching manner, or (b) [enlarge] or [diminish] the scope of what we would now regard as fundamental constitutional rights'. These norms include the Magna Carta, the Bill of Rights of 1689, the Human Rights Act 1998, and the European Communities Act 1972.[33] In a similar approach but in the context of a codified constitution, the Canadian Supreme Court has described the Quebec *Charter of Human Rights and Freedoms* as providing 'quasi-constitutional protection' to the right to privacy.[34] Canadian courts have stated that attributing such a status to a law has important effects in terms of its interpretation: a quasi-

---

30 See also Sentencia 55/03, Constitutional Court of Colombia.
31 As mentioned above, courts that operate under the unconstitutional constitutional amendment doctrine can also produce that type of change.
32 *Thoburn v. Sunderland City Council* [2003] QB 151 para 62.
33 Ibid.
34 *Frenette v. Metropolitan Life Insurance Co* [1992] 1 SCR 647, 673.

constitutional statute must be 'interpreted as to advance the broad policy considerations underlying it'.[35]

At the international level, the European Court of Justice's judgment in *Costa v. E.N.E. L.*[36] provides an example of a case falling within this category. In that case, the court determined that European Community law had primacy over national law, national constitutions included. The responses of member states to this decision have been varied but, to the extent that it is followed without having a formal constitutional basis in the country at issue, it would amount to a significant (informal) change in the domestic constitutional order by a court.[37]

Judicially made changes to the constitutional relationship between international and domestic law are also common in other jurisdictions. One manifestation of this phenomenon takes place when the courts attribute a legal effect to unincorporated international treaties that is inconsistent with the prevailing conception of the relationship between international and domestic law in the given jurisdiction. For example, in a country where legislative implementation is necessary to give an international obligation legal effect, a court may determine, as the Supreme Court of Canada did in *Baker v. Canada*, to give consideration to the values and principles reflected in the relevant international instrument.[38] In so doing, it would attribute a new status to a norm that, according to the received constitutional order, should have no impact on the domestic legal system. Finally, we can include under this category the development of the doctrine of the 'constitutionality block' (*bloque de constitucionalidad*), to the extent that it attributes to certain international norms a constitutional hierarchy not recognised in the constitutional text.[39]

Judicial recognition of new rights

Rights regulate in important ways the relationship between states and individuals (and sometimes among individuals themselves): along with the formal structure of government, they are usually seen as one of the main components of a country's material constitution. New rights can be created through the formal amendment process and, in some cases, through ordinary legislation. But new rights may also emerge as a result of judicial decisions. These decisions will usually present themselves not as instances in which new rights are created, but recognised. New rights may be understood, for example, as implicit in the constitution as a whole or as connected in fundamental ways to other constitutional rights (so that, for instance, their lack of protection would be inconsistent with general respect for the constitution). Whether the judicial 'recognition' of new rights is a constitutional change

---

35 *Canada (Attorney-General) v. Viola* [1991] 1 FC 373, 386.

36 Case 6/64 *Flaminio Costa v. ENEL* 1964 ECR 1251.

37 For the examination of the approach followed by different countries, see the essays in Anne Marie Slaughter, Alec Stone Sweet and Joseph Weiler (eds), *The European Court and National Courts Doctrine & Jurisprudence: Legal Change in its Social Context* (Hart Publishing 1998).

38 *Baker v. Canada* [1999] 2 SCR 817 para 70. See also *Tavita v. Minister of Immigration*, [1994] 2 *New Zealand Law Reports* 257; *Teoh v. Minister of Immigration and Ethnic Affairs* (1995) 128 ALR 353. For an in-depth analysis, see Claudia Geiringer, 'Tavita and All That: Confronting the Confusion Surrounding Unincorporated Treaties and Administrative Law' (2004) 21 *New Zealand Universities Law Review* 66.

39 For a dated but useful discussion of the development of the doctrine of *bloque de constitucionalidad* in the jurisprudence of the Colombian Constitutional Court, see Mónica Arango Oyala, 'El Bloque de Constitucionalidad en la Jurisprudencia de la Corte Constitucional Colombiana' (2004) *Precedente* 79. For a history of the doctrine in France, see Charlotte Denizeau, *Existe-t-il un Bloc de Constitutionnalité?* (LGDI 1997).

as important as the creation of a new right by way of a formal constitutional amendment is a complex question that is out of the scope of this chapter (it may depend, for example, on the nature of the new right, on its relationship to the already recognised rights, its place in the history of the constitutional order, whether the drafters of the constitution considered its inclusion in the constitutional text but decided against it, etc.). Nonetheless, to the extent that every time a court determines that there is a new limit to the power of the state over individuals (or to the ways in which individuals may relate to each other), the constitutional order suffers a change. Whether that change is minor or significant is a different question.

The judicial recognition of new rights is perhaps not surprising in situations where there is no formal catalogue of individual rights. Indeed, many individual rights historically protected by the English Constitution (such as the freedom of expression or the freedom from arbitrary arrest or detention) were 'found' by judges in the common law. This is partly why A.V. Dicey once wrote that the constitution 'bears on its face all the features, good and bad, of judge-made law'.[40] Reflecting that approach, the Australian High Court once expressed that: 'The framers of the Constitution ... no doubt considered that the ultimate protection of freedom of expression, along with other important rights, might be found in the common law'.[41] That statement occurred in a case where the court determined that in enshrining a system of representative government, the Australian Constitution, which does not include an express bill of rights, implied a freedom of communication in relation to public affairs and political discussion.[42]

The judicial recognition of rights is not limited to common law jurisdictions; new rights can also be implied by courts operating in very different contexts. For instance, in 1971, the French Constitutional Council recognised freedom of association as 'one of the fundamental principles' of the constitutional order, even though the drafters of the Constitution of 1958 decided that the text would not contain a bill of rights.[43] The Council justified this decision in light of the constitution's preamble, which proclaims the French people's 'attachment' to the Declaration of the Rights of Man and the Citizen of 1789 and the preamble of the Constitution of 1946.

Moreover, the judicial recognition of new rights is not limited to jurisdictions that, at a particular moment in time, lack a bill of rights.[44] In the United States, perhaps the most well-known example is that of *Griswold v. Connecticut*,[45] where Justice Douglas, writing for the majority, maintained that 'specific guarantees in the Bill of Rights have penumbras, formed by emanations from those guarantees that help give them life and substance',[46] and that 'the First Amendment has a penumbra where privacy is protected from governmental intrusion'.[47] The decision effectively read a right to privacy into the constitution, even though such a right was not expressly included in the constitutional text.

---

40 Albert V. Dicey, *Introduction to the Study of the Law of the Constitution* (Macmillan 1959) 196.
41 *Theophanous v. Herald & Weekly Times Ltd* [1994] HCA 46, para 24.
42 Ibid 6. The court emphasised that this was not a general right to freedom of expression, and in later cases called it a 'requirement of freedom of communication' rather than a right. See for example, *Lange v. Australian Broadcasting Corporation* [1997] HCA 25.
43 Decision 71–44, *Conseil Constitutionnel*, July 16, 1971.
44 In Canada, the judicial recognition of implied rights did not stop with the adoption of the Charter of Rights and Freedoms in 1982. For a discussion see, Grant Huscroft, 'Romance, Realism, and the Legitimacy of Implied Rights' (2011) 30 *University of Queensland Law Journal* 35, 39.
45 381 US 479 (1965).
46 Ibid 484.
47 Ibid 483.

The idea that certain rights can be implied from others is also relevant in the judicial application of social and economic rights. It could be argued, for example, that in the *Grootboom*[48] case, the Constitutional Court of South Africa determined (in *obiter*) that a right to electricity can be implied from the constitutional right of access to adequate housing. It could also be argued that when a court determines that a previously non-enforceable principle that regulates the relationship between citizens and the state should be treated as justiciable, a new right emerges. An example of this situation is provided by the Supreme Court of India's decision in *Unni Krishnan v. State of Andhra Pradesh*.[49] In that case, the court determined that an enforceable right to free education until the age of fourteen flowed from Article 21's protection of the right to life and personal liberty. That 'right' was originally contained in the (non-justiciable) Article 45 of the constitution (as part of the previously mentioned DPSP). As we will see below, this judge-made constitutional change eventually led to a formal amendment of the constitution.[50]

Judicially triggered constitutional changes

The categories previously considered refer to situations where the legal effect of a judicial decision was a change in the content of the constitutional order. There are also instances were a judicial decision might not only involve a constitutional change but lead (indirectly or directly) to further alterations of the constitution by the other branches of government. For example, after the previously mentioned decision in *Unni Krishnan* was issued in India, it became possible to apply to the courts for a mandamus directing the authorities to address a situation where a child below the age of fourteen lacked access to free education.[51] Eventually, the decision became an important asset for groups pushing forward reforms in the area of primary education.[52] Partly as a result of this pressure, a constitutional amendment was passed establishing a judicially enforceable right to free education 'to all children of the age of six to fourteen years'.[53] Despite not going as far as the court in *Unni Krishnan*, this formal amendment was indirectly triggered by the decision. The fact that the amendment did not extend the right to education to children below the age of six (which was the subject of criticism), could be understood as an attempt by the legislature to take into account the decision of the court while at the same time asserting its authoritative role as policy-maker.

---

48 *Government of the Republic of South Africa v. Grootboom* 2001 (1) SA 46 (CC) para 37:

> The state's obligation to provide access to adequate housing depends on context, and may differ from province to province, from city to city, from rural to urban areas and from person to person. Some may need access to land and no more; some may need access to land and building materials; some may need access to finance; some may need access to services such as water, sewage, electricity and roads. What might be appropriate in a rural area where people live together in communities engaging in subsistence farming may not be appropriate in the urban area where people are looking for employment and a place to live.

49 AIR 1993 SC 2178. See also *Mohini Jain v. State of Karnataka* AIR 1992 SC 1858.
50 Vijayashri Sripati and Arun K. Thiruvengadam, 'India: Constitutional Amendment Making the Right to Education a Fundamental Right' (2004) 2(1) *International Journal of Constitutional Law* 148, 153.
51 Ibid 153.
52 Ibid.
53 Article 21(a), Constitution of India (1947).

This indirect form of judge-led constitutional change would normally involve different forms and is commonly known as 'constitutional dialogue', broadly understood as situations where 'courts engage in dialogue with societal and political actors over the meaning of the constitution'.[54] In this context, 'dialogue' does not necessarily refer to circumstances where the political branches[55] will seek to reach its policy objectives in a way that avoids a direct clash with a judicial interpretation of a right.[56] It could, rather, take the form of an express disagreement about constitutional meaning that leads to constitutional change. Consider, for example, the aftermath of the Constitutional Court of Uganda's decisions declaring the Referendum Acts of 1999 and 2000 invalid for having been adopted in violation of the applicable legislative procedures.[57] The legislature responded to these decisions by passing a formal constitutional amendment which modified the process by which a bill could be passed into law in order to retrospectively give effect to the Referendum Act of 2000. That Act authorised a referendum that took place after the previously mentioned constitutional amendment.[58]

The Supreme Court (in a Constitutional Appeal) later determined that the aforementioned constitutional amendment was invalid for procedural reasons. This resulted in a further decision of the Constitutional Court declaring once again the Referendum Act 2000 invalid. That decision was then appealed to the Supreme Court, which agreed that the Act of 2000 was unconstitutional, but at the same time validated the result of the referendum that took place under it. The Referendum Acts cases not only indirectly triggered a formal amendment to the Constitution of Uganda (which involved the alteration of several provisions of the constitutional text), but perhaps also altered established then prevailing understandings about the relationship between the legislature and the courts.

There are also examples of courts *directly* triggering formal constitutional change. One of the clearest relates to the involvement of the South African Constitutional Court in the making of the Constitution of 1996. In 1993, an interim constitution was formally adopted by the last apartheid parliament. The interim constitution contained a list of constitutional principles and its Section 71(3) established that 'A decision of the Constitutional Court' shall certify 'that the provisions of the new constitutional text comply with the Constitutional Principles'. The Constitutional Court initially refused to certify the new constitution adopted by a Constitutional Assembly, after concluding that several of its articles were inconsistent with the previously mentioned constitutional principles.[59] This decision effectively required a number of formal changes to be made to the new constitution before it was finally certified by the Constitutional Court.[60]

---

54 Miguel Schor, 'Constitutional Dialogue and Judicial Supremacy' in Gary Jacobsohn and Miguel Schor (eds), *Comparative Constitutional Theory* (Edward Elgar 2018) 86.

55 There could also be dialogue between international and national courts that lead to domestic (formal or informal) constitutional change. For a discussion of the notion of dialogue between international and domestic courts, see René Urueña, 'Luchas Locales, Cortes Internacionales: Una exploración de la protección multinivel de los derechos humanos en América Latina' (2013) 30 *Revista Derecho del Estado* 301.

56 The paradigmatic example here will be Canada, as first thoroughly discussed in Peter Hogg and Allison Bushell, 'The Charter Dialogue between Courts and Legislatures (Or Perhaps the Charter of Rights Isn't Such a Bad Thing after All)' (1997) 35(1) *Osgoode Hall Law Journal* 75.

57 Constitutional Petition No. 3 of 1999 [2000] (Constitutional Court); Constitutional Petition No. 3 of 2000 (Constitutional Court).

58 The discussion of these cases is largely based on Erica Bussey, 'Constitutional Dialogue in Uganda' (2005) 49 *Journal of African Law* 1.

59 *Certification of the Constitution of the Republic of South Africa*, 1996 (4) SA 744 (CC).

60 The order issued by the court, stated: 'We certify that all provisions of the amended constitutional text, the Constitution of the Republic of South Africa, 1996, passed by the Constitutional Assembly on October 11,

A less dramatic example of formal constitutional change directly triggered by courts is found in a 2004 decision of the French Constitutional Council, were it was determined that the French Constitution had to be formally amended before France could ratify the treaty establishing a constitution for the European Union.[61] The Inter-American Court of Human Rights has also ordered states to amend their national constitutions in order to make them consistent with the American Convention. For example, in *Boyce v. Barbados*, the court determined (among other things), that Section 26 of the country's constitution, which prohibited constitutional challenges to ordinary laws enacted prior to the adoption of the constitution was contrary to the American Convention.[62] Barbados later indicated that it would repeal the relevant provision.[63]

Conclusion

This chapter examined six different ways in which judges can change the content of a constitutional order, instances where the direct or indirect effect of a judicial decision is a formal or informal change in a constitution. Courts, it was argued, change the constitution when they attribute a new meaning to a constitutional provision, when they alter the standards they use to review the constitutionality of legislation, when they issue a decision that has the effect of modifying the relationship between the branches of government, when they attribute a special status to certain norms, and when they create or recognise new rights. Courts have also caused other institutions to formally change the constitutional order. The chapter provided examples of decisions that fall under each of these categories from national and international courts, in the context of both codified and uncodified constitutions. The analysis in the chapter was, admittedly, incomplete: the categories are non-exhaustive of the possible manifestations of judge-made constitutional change, their possible overlap was not fully examined, and the very notion of what exactly counts as a 'change in the content of a constitutional order' was inevitably under-theorised. I nevertheless hope that the analysis contributed to our understanding of the involvement of courts in constitutional change, a topic about which there is still much more to write.

1996, comply with the Constitutional Principles contained in schedule 4 to the Constitution of the Republic of South Africa, 1993'. *Certification of the Constitution of South Africa*, CCT 37/96, Constitutional Court, December 4, 1996.

61 Decision 2004–505 DC (November 19, 2004).

62 Judgment of November 20, 2007: 'the State shall adopt, within a reasonable time from the date of notification of the present Judgment, such legislative or other measures necessary to ensure that the Constitution and laws of Barbados are brought into compliance with the American Convention, and, specifically, remove the immunizing effect of section 26 of the Constitution of Barbados in respect of "existing laws", in the terms of paragraphs 127(c) and 128 hereof'.

63 See Case of *Dacosta Cadogan v. Barbados* (September 24, 2009), paras 64–67.

14

GLOBAL VALUES, INTERNATIONAL ORGANIZATIONS AND CONSTITUTIONAL CHANGE

Helle Krunke*

Introduction

This chapter explores whether and how international values and principles guide constitutional change. The rationale is that constitutional change does not happen in a vacuum. International values and principles that have been formed as part of the evolution of global constitutionalism may govern constitutional design and this can play an important role as regards comparative constitutional change.

Method and methodological challenges

The first task will be to discuss what international values and principles are. This is not as simple as it might sound. In particular there might be a certain circularity built into the concept of international values and principles. We shall return to this in the section below.

This will be followed by combined quantitative and qualitative studies. The idea is for the two analyses to supplement each other. The strength of the quantitative study is that it will provide us with an indication of how widespread international values and principles are in constitutions all over the world. The weakness of such a study is that when we search in the constitutional texts for values and principles, we do not know whether they have the same content and meaning in all these jurisdictions and we do not know whether they are actually upheld and enforced. Furthermore, we do not know whether these values and principles have found their way to the constitutional contexts through inspiration from international values and principles or whether they have actually been embedded in the constitutional systems for a very long time. The qualitative study, on the other hand, will allow us to study one or a few case studies in depth. Through the qualitative study we will be able to show more thoroughly how the processes of global values entering into national

* The author wishes to thank Project student Benjamin Vynne Muschinsky for thorough assistance with finding sources and information for this chapter. I would also like to thank my Nordic colleagues Björg Thorarensen, Eirik Holmøyvik and Tuomas Ojanen for assistance with literature.

constitutions play out. This process might even include several steps starting at the global level, moving through a regional level and finally ending up in a constitutional amendment in a nation state. It will be necessary to select some specific case studies. The strength of such a study is that we can trace in detail how international values and principles have affected constitutional change in particular jurisdictions. The weakness is that we cannot necessarily generalize our findings to other jurisdictions. By combining the qualitative and quantitative studies we attempt to extend our insight.

As regards the quantitative study we select some basic international values and principles based on the discussion below of the concept. We then search all the constitutions, which have been translated into English and gathered in the Comparative Constitutions Project database.[1]

In the qualitative study, we select the Nordic countries, Denmark, Finland, Iceland, Norway and Sweden, and study how constitutional change has been impacted by international values and principles in this region. All have signed the UN Declaration of Human Rights. They have all incorporated the European Convention on Human Rights into national law. Three Nordic countries, Denmark, Finland and Sweden, are members of the European Union (EU) and two, Iceland and Norway, are only members of the European Economic Area (EEA). The Nordic countries are interesting because they form a local region within Europe, which is a region in the world. One might say that we apply the most similar criteria when selecting these jurisdictions for our comparative analysis since the Nordic constitutional systems share many characteristics, at least compared to other constitutional systems. One of the most important characteristics, seen from an outside perspective, is of course that the Nordic constitutional systems have strong parliaments and reluctant courts. However, seen from an insider perspective there are slight differences for instance, with Norway at one end of the scale and Denmark at the other, when it comes to how active the courts are regarding constitutional review of legislation. Some differences follow from the traditional Nordic east (Sweden/Finland) and west (Denmark, Norway and Iceland) distinction, which has historic roots. Furthermore, as we shall see, international and European values and principles have also had a different impact in the Nordic countries. Our quantitative study will allow us to examine whether and how international values and principles travel through legal systems at the regional level (Europe) and the local level (the Nordic countries).

What are international values and principles – and where do they come from?

First, one might ask whether such a thing as international values and principles even exist. Starting with an article by Bruce Ackerman (1997), 'The Rise of a World Constitutionalism' in 1997,[2] there has been a trend in constitutional literature claiming that we are approaching a set of common constitutional values. Not only international treaties and documents contribute to this evolution. Constitutional Courts and Supreme Courts inspiring each other and sharing their judgments also contribute to this development. So do international courts. Obviously, globalization and modern technology contributes to making ideas travel across countries and continents.

---

1 Comparative Constitutions Project, *Constitute Project* <www.constituteproject.org> accessed 6 May 2019.
2 Bruce Ackerman, 'The Rise of World Constitutionalism' (1997) 83 *Virginia Law Review* 771.

We need to consider how to define international values and principles. Where do they come from and when does a value/principle turn into an 'international' value/principle? It seems that such values/principles are part of a complex and constant interaction, which includes both bottom-up processes and top-down processes. There is a constant interplay between different levels. Furthermore, values are to a certain extent actor-borne, they travel with the actors between national, regional and international fora, but they can of course also acquire or have a legal or semi-legal character. The many different actors who play a role in creating and spreading global values are, for instance, diplomats, legislators and courts at different levels, scholars and consultants in constitutional design in new democracies. It will not be possible to study this perspective in detail in this chapter. However, it might be worth mentioning that the actor-perspective plays a special role as regards the 'journey' of values and constitutional evolution.

The big question is, of course, whether values/principles become international values/ principles because they are already present legally, politically or morally in an extensive number of nations and regions or whether they are defined and introduced at a global level through, for instance, UN documents and then passed down to the regional and national jurisdictions. Or maybe it happens at the same time nationally, regionally and globally because the world, or at least regions, react to the same experiences such as the Second World War or face the same challenges at a specific point in time such as refugee crises, natural disasters or challenges for democracy. The mentioned possible circularity occurs from the vagueness that surrounds all these processes.

The complex nature of the creation of values and principles makes it somehow difficult to identify precisely when a value or principle is international. We will, therefore, need to simplify things slightly and adopt a definition of international values and principles. The simplest way is to use United Nations documents as a guideline for when a value or principle becomes international.[3] The UN Declaration of Human Rights is not legally binding but it sets out some general values and principles. At a more regional level one might mention the European Convention on Human Rights, which is legally binding. Furthermore, the Venice Commission could be mentioned as a regional forum, which sets out some guidelines as regards general values, principles and good practices. Even regions outside Europe follow judgments from the European Court of Human Rights and Opinions and guidelines from the Venice Commission with great interest. This might be said to contribute to a more general nature of the values and principles expressed in these documents. The EU Charter of Fundamental Rights, general principles and values in the EU treaties and general principles from judgments of the Court of Justice of the European Union (CJEU), which are legally binding on the EU Member States may also be included. In conclusion, we will see international values and principles as some general legal, quasi legal or political expressions found in international documents with a 'global' nature, such as UN documents especially the UN Declaration of Human Rights and some of the UN conventions on women's, children's and disabled people's rights, and regional documents

---

3 The rights mentioned in the UN Declaration of Human Rights are inspired by all existing constitutions and rights instruments, proposals submitted by states, NGOs and individuals. Based on this material, the UN Secretariat drafted 48 Articles that reflected the systems surveyed. See Dennis Davis, Alan Richter, and Cheryl Saunders (eds), *An Inquiry into the Existence of Global Values through the Lens of Comparative Constitutional Law* (Hart Publishing 2015) 6. One might put forward that this means that the Declaration is primarily inspired by the 'old' constitutions of the world. Of the 197 constitutions in 1991 only 20 pre-dated 1950. See Heinz Klug, *Constitutional Democracy: Law, Globalism and South Africa's Political Reconstruction* (Cambridge University Press 2000).

with broader impact such as the European Convention on Human Rights, Opinions and guidelines from the Venice Commission, the EU Charter of Fundamental Rights and general EU principles and values expressed in the treaties or in the case law of the CJEU. Other documents from other regions could be mentioned. However, since we will be studying Europe, the mentioned documents will be especially important.

Finally, a short remark on the distinction between values and principles. Values is a complicated term to work with, especially in a global context.[4] Principles, on the other hand, seems to be a more adequate term to work with in this chapter since it has a resonance with the more familiar term 'legal principles'. Even though the definition of legal principles has also been the object of debate, and even though there is a link between values and legal principles (there are values behind legal principles), it seems to be an easier term to work with for the purpose of this chapter. Therefore, we will only refer to international principles in a broad sense including general/fundamental international norms, soft law norms and legal principles such as democracy, human rights, etc. in the following parts of the chapter (fully aware that behind these principles we find values).

Case studies: quantitative analysis

As mentioned, we selected some samples of international values and principles, which have found an expression in UN documents and/or European documents as described above. Many possibilities exist but we have chosen to focus on some principles, which appear relatively easy to search for in the constitutional texts in the Comparative Constitutions Project database. Quite specific or narrow principles are the easiest to find in a quantitative study. Democracy for instance, is a core principle. However, many constitutions do not use the term democracy and democracy is a quite complex term, which might be reflected in several ways. The presence of democracy is reflected in constitutions through provisions on, for instance, free and open elections, the right to run for office, political freedoms, etc.

We have chosen to search for the following principles: human dignity, freedom of expression and judicial independence. This includes very basic human rights as well as a basic institutional principle. These principles all live up to our definition of 'global principles'. Judicial independence has support in Article 10 of the UN Declaration of Human Rights, Article 6 of the European Convention on Human Rights and Article 47 of the European Union's Charter of Fundamental Human Rights. Human dignity has support in Article 1 of the UN Declaration of Human Rights and Article 1 of the European Union's Charter of Fundamental Human Rights. Furthermore, several provisions of the European Convention on Human Rights, Articles 2, 3 and 4, support the right to human dignity though the term human dignity is not directly mentioned in the Convention. As regards freedom of expression, we find support in Article 19 of the UN Declaration of Human Rights, Article 10 of the European Convention on Human Rights and Article 11 of the European Union's Charter of Fundamental Human Rights. Furthermore, the Venice Commission has adopted several opinions and reports on human dignity, freedom of expression and judicial independence.[5] Support can also be found in the preamble to the Treaty on European Union and in the general values in Article 2.

---

4 As discussed in Davis et al. (n 2).
5 Venice Commission, *The Principle of Respect for Human Dignity* (CDL-STD(1998)026) 1998; Venice Commission, *Report on the Independence of the Judicial System Part I: The Independence of Judges* (CDL-AD(2010)004) 2010;

In our quantitative study we have searched the term itself ('human dignity', 'freedom of expression' and 'judicial independence') but also looked for provisions, which actually describe such a right without using the exact term.

We have reached the following results:

Human dignity: 147
Freedom of expression: 184
Judicial independence: 171

These numbers seem to indicate that at least these three international core principles can be found in a large number of constitutional systems. Furthermore, all three principles are widespread in the sense that they are found in constitutions in regions all over the world. As mentioned earlier we do not know the exact meaning of the provisions, whether they are enforced and the extent of their impact in the individual constitutional systems. Neither does the study show when the provisions were introduced into the constitutions and whether international conventions and documents were the inspiration. However, what we do know is that few constitutions in the world are very old.[6] Therefore, there seems to be a high probability that some of the studied constitutions have been introduced or amended quite recently and that this has involved the introduction of international principles. The study contributes to the impression that international principles actually exist across different regions and jurisdictions and, in this way, seem to spread globally into the national constitutions at least from the point of view of a formal C-comparison (a comparison of the wording of constitutions). In other words, international principles inspire constitutions all over the world. The qualitative study will contribute to this picture at least in one part of the world.

As a last comment to the quantitative study, it can be mentioned that projects such as The World Justice Project try to map principles such as the rule of law globally, through monitoring a number of factors in each country, which reflect whether a country adheres to rule of law in reality and not just formally.[7]

Case studies: qualitative analysis

Introduction: inspiration both ways

We start by addressing the circularity argument mentioned in the section on 'What are international values and principles – and where do they come from?' in a Nordic context. As described, international principles do not come out of the blue. They are inspired by different actors and/or historical events and then they might be codified in an international document and in this way gain a formal label of being international principles. The Nordic context reflects the validity of this argument. First, the Nordic countries have a long

---

Venice Commission, *Report on European Standards as Regards the Independence of the Judicial System: Part II – the Prosecution Service* (CDL-AD(2010)040) 2011; Venice Commission, *Compilation of Venice Commission Opinions and Reports Concerning Courts and Judges* (CDL-PI(2015)001) 2015; Venice Commission, *Compilation of Venice Commission Opinions and Reports Concerning Freedom of Expression and Media* (CDL-PI(2016)011) 2016.

6 As mentioned, out of the 197 constitutions that existed in 1991 only 20 pre-dated 1950. See Klug (n 2).

7 For more information see: World Justice Project <www.worldjusticeproject.org> accessed 6 May 2019.

tradition for rights in their respective constitutions which existed before the European and international treaties and agreements, which express common principles and values, appeared. For instance, the Norwegian constitution dates back to 1814, the Danish constitution dates back to 1849 and the Icelandic constitution dates back to 1874. In Finland rights were protected by the Swedish constitution until the Finnish independence in 1917 and the first Finnish constitution dates back to 1919. All constitutions had provisions on human rights from the beginning. The Danish constitution, among other rights, protected political freedoms, the right to property and social welfare. Furthermore, the Swedish Freedom of the Press Act from 1766 introduced public access to documents of government authorities and a prohibition against censorship. Second, the Nordic countries have been active in promoting rights in European and international political fora, thus contributing to the emergence of European and international treaties and agreements on rights protection. Hence, Denmark, Norway and Sweden were among the founding member states of the Council of Europe in 1949. Furthermore, Denmark, Sweden and Finland are active in promoting the protection of rights in the European Union, for instance as regards the introduction of an EU Ombudsman – the ombudsman institution was originally invented in Sweden – and transparency in the political decision-making processes including public access to documents. Third, in some cases the Nordic constitutions have introduced protection of new rights that are not yet widely recognized, for instance the protection of nature and the environment[8] and the right to good administration.[9] Both rights were introduced in the Finnish constitution in 1995.

However, the Nordic constitutional and legal systems have also developed in several ways under the influence of European and international treaties and agreements. This is reflected in several ways. First, the Nordic countries have ratified a large number of treaties on human rights and in some cases incorporated them. Second, the human rights protection has been strengthened through amendments of the Nordic constitutions in light of international principles. Third, traditionally 'general principles' mentioned directly in the constitutional text have not played an important role in the constitutional culture of the Nordic countries. However, there seems to be a development of the legal culture in this field. Fourth, the role of the courts in constitutional review of legislation has been strengthened in some Nordic countries, as an impact of international treaties. We will focus on the identified developments below.

Ratification and incorporation of international principles

Almost all treaties adopted by the Council of Europe, the United Nations and the International Labour Organization have been signed and ratified by the Nordic countries.[10] Furthermore, very few and minor reservations to these treaties have been made by the Nordic countries.[11] In the 1990s the Nordic countries all incorporated the European Convention on Human Rights into their legal systems. The Convention is legally binding

---

8 Article 20 of the Finnish constitution, Article 112 of the Norwegian constitution and Article 2, Chapter 2, of the Swedish Instrument of Government.

9 The Finnish constitution, Section 21, Part 2.

10 See Tuomas Ojanen, 'Human Rights in the Nordic Countries' in Helle Krunke and Björg Thorarensen (eds), *The Nordic Constitutions: A Comparative and Contextual Study* (Hart Publishing 2018) 136.

11 Ibid 136.

at the legislative level but not as part of the constitutional level through this ratification. While especially Finland but also Norway have been active in incorporating international human rights conventions into their national legal systems, Denmark, Sweden and Iceland have been more reluctant.[12] Denmark and Sweden have not incorporated any other international human rights conventions than the European Convention on Human Rights. Iceland incorporated the UN Convention on the Rights of the Child in 2013. Finally, Denmark, Sweden and Finland are members of the EU, which means that the EU treaties, including the European Charter of Fundamental Rights, apply and according to the EU Principle of Supremacy have supremacy over national law.[13] The Charter has, especially since the 2010s, had an increasing impact on human rights protection in the Nordic EU Member States, for instance in the areas of the *ne bis in idem* principle (no one should be punished twice for the same) and data protection.[14] Norway and Iceland are members of the EEA and this has also had an impact on their human rights protection. For instance, in Iceland rights protection in areas such as social and employment policy and prohibition of discrimination has been strengthened.[15]

Impact of international principles on constitutional amendment

The rights protection in most of the Nordic constitutions has been strengthened in recent times and many of these constitutional amendments seem to be inspired by several international human rights treaties, especially the European Convention on Human Rights. Below we will look at the Finnish, Icelandic and Norwegian constitutions, which have all been revised recently in light of especially the European Convention on Human Rights but also other international treaties within the last 20–25 years. Finally, we will see how the revision of the Danish constitution back in 1953 already had references to international treaties.

As regards Finland, the 1995 reform was primarily inspired by international human rights treaties and especially the European Convention on Human Rights.[16] This led to a comprehensive rights catalogue in the 1999 constitution, which sets out a range of economic, social and cultural rights, in addition to traditional civil and political rights. Furthermore, provisions regarding everyone's responsibility for the environment and environmental rights (Section 20) and the right to good administration (Section 21, Part 2) were introduced.

Iceland amended its constitution in 1995. The European Convention on Human Rights and the UN Covenant on Civil and Political Rights were the main models for the revision of the human right provisions, but the general observations accompanying the Bill also made references to other international treaties such as the European Social Charter, the International Labour Organization Conventions and other UN human rights instruments.[17]

---

12 Ibid 166.
13 Denmark became a member of the EU in 1973 while Sweden and Finland joined in 1995.
14 See Ojanen (n 9) 162.
15 See for instance, Baldur Thorhallsson and Björg Thorarensen, 'Iceland's Democratic Challenges and Human Rights Implications' in Henry F. Carey (ed), *European Institutions, Democratization, and Human Rights Protection, in the European Periphery* (Lexington Books 2014) 233–234.
16 See Juha Lavapuro, Tuomas Ojanen, and Martin Scheinin, 'Rights-based Constitutionalism in Finland and the Development of Pluralist Constitutional Review' (2011) 9 *International Journal of Constitutional Law* 505–531, especially 516.
17 See Thorhallsson and Thorarensen (n 14) 233.

New human rights were drafted and existing rights were modernized. Interestingly the explanatory remarks accompanying the Bill state that the provisions should be based on certain fundamental values and that they should be interpreted in the light of international human rights commitments.[18] While the Supreme Court has, in some cases, followed this recommendation and interpreted constitutional provisions in light of the international conventions, criticism has been raised of the Supreme Court being too dynamic in its interpretations.[19]

The influence of international principles is very visible in the amendment of the Norwegian constitution in 2014.[20] Article 92 states that the state authorities must respect and ensure human rights as they are expressed in the constitution and in treaties on human rights which are binding on Norway. The 2014 revision gathered all the rights in a new Section E of the constitution. The purpose of the 2014 revision was not to define new rights, rather to clarify rights that were established through the international human right treaties to which Norway was a party, or domestic law apart from the constitution, and to provide them with constitutional rank:[21]

> The idea was rather to strengthen the *constitutional protection* of certain rights already protected elsewhere, in order to make them more resistant. The basic legal effect of such transformation of rights into constitutional rights is – generally and simply speaking – that they acquire the status of *lex superior*, in the hierarchy of legal norms that are applicable within the Norwegian jurisdiction, constitutional rights have the highest possible rank.

And furthermore:

> Numerous of the classic civil and political rights as prescribed by the major human rights conventions were taken into the Constitution itself in a new Part E, in addition to certain economic, social and cultural rights and the core rights of the child as prescribed in the UN Convention on the rights of the child.
>
> *(Article 93 to Article 113)*

The intention was that the constitutional rights protection should not be weaker than the international protection, primarily the European Convention on Human Rights, and this has been understood as meaning that the Norwegian constitution should be interpreted in light of the case law of the European Court of Human Rights up until at least 2014. To

---

18 See Björg Thorarensen, 'Judicial Control over the Legislature: Different Trends in Icelandic and Danish Practice' in Michael Hansen Jensen, Søren Højgaard Mørup, and Børge Dahl (eds), *Festskrift til Jens Peter Christensen* (Jurist- og Økonomforbudnets Forlag 2016), Section 4.2.
19 See ibid section 4.2.
20 See Menneskerettighedsutvalget om menneskerettigheter i Grunnloven, *Rapport til Stortingets presidentskap* (December 2011) <www.stortinget.no/globalassets/pdf/dokumentserien/2011-2012/dok16-201112.pdf> accessed 6 May 2019. For a critical approach see Eivind Smith, 'Flere menneskerettigheter i grunnloven?' (2012) 51(6) *Lov og Rett* <www.idunn.no/lor/2012/06/flere_menneskerettigheter_i_grunnloven> accessed 6 May 2019.
21 See Arnfinn Bårdsen, 'Guardians of Human Rights in Norway: Challenging Mandates in a New Era' (speech given at Litteraturhuset, Bergen, 11 May 2016) <www.domstol.no/globalassets/upload/hret/artikler-og-fore drag/guardians-of-human-rights—11052016.pdf> accessed 6 May 2019.

what extent the court's practice after 2014 is relevant when interpreting the constitution has been a matter of discussion.[22]

Interestingly, the impact of the constitutional reform was 'a substantial rise in the use of constitutional provisions in Supreme Court reasoning in 2016', where the average annual number of cases referring to the constitution developed from 0.6% of the total annual case load in period 1990–1999, and 1.2% in 2000–2009, to 2.1% in 2010–2016, and finally 3.6% and 5.2%, respectively, in 2015 and 2016.[23] This shows that the impact of modernizing a constitution in light of international treaties, which are already part of the legal system but only at the legislative level, is that 'new life' is brought to the constitution, which becomes a living constitution:[24] 'Through this constitutional reform, the Parliament affiliated with a true spirit of *sustainable constitutionalism*, inspired by an overarching idea of *revitalizing* the Constitution symbolically, politically and legally'.

In comparison, in Denmark, where the constitution has not been amended since 1953, the European Convention on Human Rights plays a more and more important role, while the constitution slowly loses impact in the field of human rights.

We naturally turn to Denmark, where the last amendment of the constitution took place in the 1950s. The 'new' constitution came into force on 5 June 1953. This means that the last amendment took place right after the Second World War and during a period when the United Nations, the European Council and other international organizations were founded. Therefore, it seems obvious to ask whether the Danish constitution was inspired by European and international principles. As mentioned earlier, the Danish constitution has had provisions on the protection of human rights since its first constitution of 1849, so Denmark was not entirely lacking human rights protection. When the *travaux préparatoires* of the constitution are studied, it appears that few references are actually made to international principles. However, a few references do exist. In the explanatory notes to the new Article 76, Part 1, on the right to work, it is stated that this provision is introduced into the constitution inspired by the United Nations Declaration on Human Rights, several new constitutions and other international conventions.[25] Another reference regards Article 19, Part 2, on the competence to enter into war, where reference is made to the United Nations Pact.[26] A last good example is the fact that Greenland, with the 1953 constitution, became part of the Danish realm and thereby no longer would have status as a colony. The report from the Constitutional Committee has a thorough memorandum written by two professors, Alf Ross and Poul Andersen, on how Denmark's obligations to the United Nations Pact can be fulfilled regarding Greenland's status.[27] This shows that all the new international treaties that blossomed after the Second World War were already having an impact on constitutional amendment back in the 1950s.[28]

---

22 See Jørgen Aall, 'EMKs betydning etter grunnlovsrevisjonen' (2017) 130(05) *Tidsskrift for Rettsvitenskap* <www.idunn.no/tfr/2017/05/emks_betydning_etter_grunnlovsrevisjonen> accessed 6 May 2019.

23 See Anine Kierulf, 'Developments in Norwegian Constitutional Law: The Year 2016 in Review' (19 November 2017) *ICONnect* <www.iconnectblog.com/2017/11/developments-in-norwegian-constitutional-law-the-year-2016-in-review/#_ftn16> accessed 6 May 2019.

24 See Bårdsen (n 20).

25 See Constitutional Committee, *Report* (1953) 40.

26 See ibid.30.

27 See ibid 86–88.

28 Interestingly, a minority in the Constitutional Committee made suggestions with further reference to the UN Declaration on Human Rights as regards a prohibition against discrimination and equal right to education.

General international principles in the constitutional text

Another interesting trend, which shows the impact of European and international principles on constitutional amendment in the Nordic countries, regards the direct reference to such principles in the constitutional text. In order to appreciate the full meaning of the development, one must understand that the Nordic constitutions do not have a tradition for references to 'general principles' in the constitutional texts or to preambles. However, in recent constitutional amendments we see specific international principles inserted in the first provisions of the amended constitutions, thus emphasizing the importance of such principles.

The Finnish constitution has been amended to include a new first provision:[29]

> Finland is a sovereign republic.
> The constitution of Finland is established in this constitutional act. The constitution shall guarantee the inviolability of human dignity and the freedom and rights of the individual and promote justice in society.
> Finland participates in international co-operation for the protection of peace and human rights and for the development of society. Finland is a Member State of the European Union.
>
> *(1112/2011, entry into force 1.3.2012)*

Furthermore, in Section 2 it is stated that Finland has democracy and rule of law.

We find general principles such as human dignity, justice and peace (Section 1) and democracy and rule of law (Section 2) and general references to freedom and rights of individuals and to the development of society. We also find references to international cooperation (for the protection of peace and human rights and for the development of society) and to the EU (Section 1).

If we move on to the Norwegian constitution, a new second provision was inserted in 2012: 'Our values will remain our Christian and humanist heritage. This Constitution shall ensure democracy, a state based on the rule of law and human rights.'[30]

Here we find a specific reference to principles such as democracy, rule of law and human rights. Furthermore, interestingly, we find a confirmation of existing values in the form of the Christian and humanist heritage.

Finally, the Swedish constitution has an even more comprehensive list of basic principles in Article 2:

> Public power shall be exercised with respect for the equal worth of all and the liberty and dignity of the individual. The personal, economic and cultural welfare of the individual shall be fundamental aims of public activity. In particular, the public institutions shall secure the right to employment, housing and education, and shall promote social care and social security, as well as favourable conditions for good health.
> The public institutions shall promote sustainable development leading to a good environment for present and future generations.

They also suggested that Article 2 in the UN Declaration on Human Rights was inserted into the Danish constitution. See ibid 73 ff. and 77.

29 Section 1.
30 Article 2.

The public institutions shall promote the ideals of democracy as guidelines in all sectors of society and protect the private and family lives of the individual.

The public institutions shall promote the opportunity for all to attain participation and equality in society and for the rights of the child to be safeguarded. The public institutions shall combat discrimination of persons on grounds of gender, colour, national or ethnic origin, linguistic or religious affiliation, functional disability, sexual orientation, age or other circumstance affecting the individual.

The opportunities of the Sami people and ethnic, linguistic and religious minorities to preserve and develop a cultural and social life of their own shall be promoted.

Thus, the adoption of 'general legal principles' into the first provisions of the Nordic constitutions reflects a change of legal culture in the Nordic countries, which is closely connected to the international treaties on rights.

The impact of international principles on judicial review of the constitutionality of legislation

Finally, international principles have impacted the Nordic constitutional systems as regards judicial review of the constitutionality of legislation. It might come as a surprise to some readers that the Nordic countries, which are known to have quite high standards as regards the protection of rights, have a tradition of rather reluctant courts and strong parliaments. However, an exception might be Norway, which has a stronger tradition of active courts as regards constitutional review. In the Nordic west, Denmark, Norway and Iceland, courts have had the competence to perform judicial review of legislation for a long time. However, in only one case has the Danish Supreme Court ruled that an Act violated the constitution. Icelandic courts are more active (especially since 1995 when Iceland's constitution was amended toward stronger rights protection) and, as mentioned, the Norwegian courts are traditionally the most active as regards judicial review. In the Nordic east, Sweden and Finland, on the other hand, there has traditionally been a weak tradition as regards judicial review of the constitutionality of legislation. In Finland, the courts have traditionally not had the competence to review the constitutionality of legislation. However, they have had a strong ex ante review of draft legislation in the so-called Constitutional Law Committee. When Finland entered the EU, the courts were provided with the competence to review the constitutionality of legislation (2000). The Finnish courts seem to be highly influenced by international human rights in their judgments, both substantially and as regards interpretation, legal reasoning and legal culture. Legal principles and human rights play a stronger role in Finnish judgments and there seems to be a shift away from a more formalistic positivistic legal approach to more dynamic interpretations with more focus on rights.[31] It seems that international human rights, in general, strengthen the role of the courts in the national separation of powers. Even in Norway, which has traditionally had quite active courts, we see that the courts become more powerful and more dynamic in their interpretations, to an extent where a public and legal discussion of whether Supreme Court judges should be politically nominated in the future has arisen.[32] In conclusion, we

---

31 See Ojanen (n 9).
32 See Eivind Smith, 'Judicial Review of Legislation' in Helle Krunke and Björg Thorarensen (eds), *The Nordic Constitutions: A Comparative and Contextual Study* (Hart Publishing 2018) 107–132.

see strengthened courts in Finland, Sweden, Norway and Iceland and, to a lesser extent, in Denmark, where the traditional separation of powers model with a strong parliament and cautious courts seems to be more upheld than in the other Nordic countries.[33] One major difference between Denmark and the other Nordic countries is, of course, that the constitution has not been amended in light of European and international human rights treaties. Therefore, the Danish courts might be said to be in a weaker position than the other Nordic courts as regards the described development. However, the European Convention on Human Rights de facto plays an important role since the Danish constitution has not been amended since 1953 and, therefore, has a quite old human rights system without protection of more modern rights.

In case the reader wonders how the Nordic countries have traditionally had a high protection of rights even though the courts have been quite cautious as regards review of the constitutionality of legislation, an explanation will be provided. This has to do with the fact that the Nordic political institutions have a tradition for upholding principles such as transparency, rule of law, good governance, human rights and democracy.[34] Corruption is almost non-existent. In the Nordic countries, the citizens have a very strong trust in public institutions. Furthermore, the Nordic countries are quite rich countries with well-functioning welfare systems. This means that there is not as much need for strong courts as there might be in countries in which the political institutions do not adhere to such values and traditions.

Conclusion

The purpose of this chapter was to explore whether and how international values and principles guide constitutional change – the rationale being that constitutional change does not happen in a vacuum.

We have carried out a qualitative study and a quantitative study. Through the quantitative study we have been able to say something about the existence and global spread of international principles. We found a significant existence and global spread of the three international principles we studied: human dignity (147 constitutions), freedom of expression (184 constitutions) and judicial independence (171 constitutions). Even though we do not know when the constitutions that mention these international principles were amended, many of them must obviously have been amended quite recently, since only few constitutions in the world are old constitutions. As mentioned earlier, of the 197 constitutions in 1991 only 20 pre-dated 1950.[35] Therefore, there is also a high probability that some of the constitutions in the study have been inspired by international principles through UN declarations, treaties or other constitutions, which have been used as a model for constitutional change. Whether all the studied countries adhere to the same understanding of the international principles is another question.[36] Whether the principles

---

33 Helle Krunke, 'Impact of the EU/EEA on the Nordic Constitutional Systems' in Helle Krunke and Björg Thorarensen (eds), *The Nordic Constitutions: A Comparative and Contextual Study* (Hart Publishing 2018) 167–202.

34 See Helle Krunke and Björg Thorarensen, 'Concluding Thoughts' in Helle Krunke and Björg Thorarensen (eds), *The Nordic Constitutions: A Comparative and Contextual Study* (Hart Publishing 2018) 204.

35 See Klug (n 2). On the endurance of constitutions, see Zachary Elkins, Tom Ginsburg, and James Melton, *The Endurance of National Constitutions* (Cambridge University Press 2009).

36 On the difficulty of comparing values in different parts of the world, see Dennis Davis et al. (n 2).

are actually being enforced does not follow from the quantitative study either. The quantitative study primarily shows that the three international principles we studied are present in a very large number of constitutions and that the global spread of the principles is significant at least studied through a formal C-comparison lens.

Through the qualitative study we have been able to show more thoroughly how the processes of global principles entering into national constitutions play out. The Nordic countries are good examples of the described journey of international principles. All the Nordic countries have adopted international principles into their constitutions from the European Convention on Human Rights, the EU treaties, UN documents and/or the ILO conventions. In some cases this influence is in the form of the adoption of specific norms and in other cases it is not only an adoption of specific norms but also an adoption of a new, more value- and principle-oriented, legal thinking (change of legal culture) and more active courts. The Danish context differs slightly from the other Nordic countries, among other things, because it is very difficult to amend the constitution. However, this does not mean that Denmark does not have the same international principles. If they are not expressed in the constitution they will be expressed through legislation and legal culture, also bearing in mind that the European Convention on Human Rights is incorporated into Danish law.

Having shown direct links between constitutional amendment and international principles, we have been able to show the impact of international principles on national constitutional change in at least one region of the world, namely the five Nordic countries. It is not possible to draw conclusions for other regions based on our qualitative study. Specific qualitative studies of each region are necessary and fall outside the reach of this chapter. However, as the quantitative study shows there seems to be quite extensive existence and global spread of international principles, at least if we apply a C-comparison and since most constitutions are rather young, there seems to be a quite good probability that constitutional amendment has been inspired by international principles.

References

Aall, Jørgen, 'EMKs betydning etter grunnlovsrevisjonen' (2017) 130(05) *Tidsskrift for Rettsvitenskap* <www.idunn.no/tfr/2017/05/emks_betydning_etter_grunnlovsrevisjonen> accessed 6 May 2019.

Ackerman, Bruce, 'The Rise of World Constitutionalism' (1997) 83 *Virginia Law Review* 771.

Bårdsen, Arnfinn, 'Guardians of Human Rights in Norway: Challenging Mandates in a New Era' (speech given at Litteraturhuset, Bergen, 11 May 2016) <www.domstol.no/globalassets/upload/hret/artikler-og-foredrag/guardians-of-human-rights—11052016.pdf> accessed 6 May 2019.

Betænkning afgivet af Forfatningskommissionen af 1946 (Copenhagen: J. H. Schultz A/S Universitets-Bogtrykkeri 1953).

Comparative Constitutions Project, *Constitute Project* <www.constituteproject.org> accessed 6 May 2019.

Davis, Dennis, Alan Richter & Cheryl Saunders (eds), *An Inquiry into the Existence of Global Values through the Lens of Comparative Constitutional Law* (Hart Publishing 2015).

Davis, Dennis, Alan Richter, and Cheryl Saunders, 'Introduction' in Dennis Davis, Alan Richter, and Cheryl Saunders (eds), *An Inquiry into the Existence of Global Values through the Lens of Comparative Constitutional Law* (Hart Publishing 2015) 1–14.

Elkins, Zachary, Tom Ginsburg, and James Melton, *The Endurance of National Constitutions* (Cambridge University Press 2009).

Kierulf, Anine, 'Developments in Norwegian Constitutional Law: The Year 2016 in Review' (19 November 2017) *ICONnect* <www.iconnectblog.com/2017/11/developments-in-norwegian-constitutional-law-the-year-2016-in-review/#_ftn16> accessed 6 May 2019.

Klug, Heinz, *Constitutional Democracy: Law, Globalism and South Africa's Political Reconstruction* (Cambridge University Press 2000).

Krunke, Helle, 'Impact of the EU/EEA on the Nordic Constitutional Systems' in Helle Krunke and Björg Thorarensen (eds), *The Nordic Constitutions: A Comparative and Contextual Study* (Hart Publishing 2018) 167–202.

Krunke, Helle and Björg Thorarensen, 'Concluding Thoughts' in Helle Krunke and Björg Thorarensen (eds), *The Nordic Constitutions: A Comparative and Contextual Study* (Hart Publishing 2018) 203–218.

Lavapuro Juha,, Tuomas Ojanen, and Martin Scheinin, 'Rights-based Constitutionalism in Finland and the Development of Pluralist Constitutional Review' (2011) 9 *International Journal of Constitutional Law* 505–531.

Menneskerettighedsutvalget om menneskerettigheter i Grunnloven, *Rapport til Stortingets presidentskap* (December 2011) <www.stortinget.no/globalassets/pdf/dokumentserien/2011-2012/dok16-201112. pdf> accessed 6 May 2019.

Ojanen, Tuomas, 'Human Rights in the Nordic Countries' in Helle Krunke and Björg Thorarensen (eds), *The Nordic Constitutions: A Comparative and Contextual Study* (Hart Publishing 2018) 133–166.

Smith, Eivind, 'Flere menneskerettigheter i grunnloven?' (2012) 51(6) *Lov og Rett* <www.idunn.no/lor/ 2012/06/flere_menneskerettigheter_i_grunnloven> accessed 6 May 2019.

Smith, Eivind, 'Judicial Review of Legislation' in Helle Krunke and Björg Thorarensen (eds), *The Nordic Constitutions: A Comparative and Contextual Study* (Hart Publishing 2018) 107–132.

Thorarensen, Björg, 'Judicial Control over the Legislature: Different Trends in Icelandic and Danish Practice' in Michael Hansen Jensen, Søren Højgaard Mørup, and Børge Dahl (eds), *Festskrift til Jens Peter Christensen* (Jurist- og Økonomforbundets Forlag 2016) 709–730.

Thorhallsson, Baldur and Björg Thorarensen, 'Iceland's Democratic Challenges and Human Rights Implications' in Henry F. Carey (ed), *European Institutions, Democratization, and Human Rights Protection, in the European Periphery* (Lexington Books 2014) 178–195.

Venice Commission, *The Principle of Respect for Human Dignity* (CDL-STD(1998)026) 1998.

Venice Commission, *Report on the Independence of the Judicial System Part I: The Independence of Judges* (CDL-AD(2010)004) 2010a.

Venice Commission, *Report on European Standards as Regards the Independence of the Judicial System: Part II – the Prosecution Service* (CDL-AD(2010)040) 2010b.

Venice Commission, *Compilation of Venice Commission Opinions and Reports Concerning Courts and Judges* (CDL-PI(2015)001) 2015.

Venice Commission, *Compilation of Venice Commission Opinions and Reports Concerning Freedom of Expression and Media* (CDL-PI(2016)011) 2016.

World Justice Project, <www.worldjusticeproject.org> accessed 6 May 2019.

15

CRISES, EMERGENCIES AND CONSTITUTIONAL CHANGE

*Giacomo Delledonne**

Setting the scene: states of emergency as a challenge for constitutionalism

The quest for stability is a defining feature of constitutions: in a way, this goal is intimately related to the aspiration, lying at the heart of constitutionalism, to entrench the allocation of powers among the branches of government and to ensure protection of fundamental rights.[1]

Major crises represent occurrences that threaten the stability and potentially the very survival of a given constitutional order: in fact, they may on some occasions culminate in revolutionary upheaval and the establishment of an entirely new constitutional framework. For this reason, handling serious crises might be essential to preserving the basic tenets of the existing constitutional order. Broadly speaking, this typically happens by allowing for temporary derogations from the general constitutional framework. The constitutional treatment of a *state of emergency* ultimately purports to resolve the crisis that has triggered it and to restore the conditions of constitutional normalcy.[2] In this regard, 'emergency powers exhibit, conceptually as well as normatively, a conservative aspect'.[3]

However, even if these requirements are met, states of emergency do not only affect the normal operation of constitutional provisions but may well act as catalysts for constitutional change, whether formalised or informal. The constitutional provisions that regulate states of emergency seek to strike a proper balance between *rigidity*, i.e. the preservation of the basic characteristics of a constitutional order on the one hand, and *flexibility* and *elasticity* on the other.

* I would like to thank Xenophon Contiades and Alkmene Fotiadou for inviting me to contribute to this collective research endeavour. I am also indebted to Richard Albert, Joel Colón-Ríos, Tom Ginsburg, Yaniv Roznai, Chris Thornhill, Francesco Saitto, Giuseppe Martinico, Giovanni Boggero and Edoardo Caterina for their suggestions and comments on earlier drafts of this chapter.

1 Whether or not stability is desirable lies outside the scope of this chapter, but see Zachary Elkins, Tom Ginsburg and James Melton, *The Endurance of National Constitutions* (Cambridge University Press 2009) 33–35.

2 See Giacomo Delledonne, 'History and Concepts of Emergency' in Rainer Grote, Frauke Lachenmann and Rüdiger Wolfrum (eds), *Max Planck Encyclopedia of Comparative Constitutional Law* (Oxford University Press 2017).

3 John Ferejohn and Pasquale Pasquino, 'The Law of the Exception: A Typology of Emergency Powers' (2004) 2 *International Journal of Constitutional Law* 210, 223.

By flexibility I mean that the constitution itself, by regulating states of emergency, facilitates the establishment of a special derogatory regime when extraordinary circumstances occur. By elasticity I mean that the declaration of a state of emergency is not only designed to cope with the challenges posed by a crisis, but ultimately aims to restore the previous state of affairs. In sum, flexibility and elasticity hint at the capacity of a constitutional order to adapt (and hopefully put an end) to a major crisis without relinquishing its core commitments. How flexible should a constitutional order be when a state of emergency is triggered? The possibility of emergency-produced or emergency-related constitutional change is part of this problem. Political and judicial actors might take advantage of serious crises in order to transform the constitutional framework; moreover, and leaving aside the plans of the relevant actors, emergency per se might produce relevant consequences in this respect. In sum, crises and states of emergency pose a formidable challenge to constitutionalism because they challenge the very possibility of constitutional orders facing crises by means of law, as well as providing, where appropriate, for *limited* derogations and exceptions to the ordinary constitutional framework.

The purpose of this chapter is to focus on crises and emergencies as a major factor in initiating constitutional change. In so doing, this chapter will analyse the interaction between three manifold concepts: crises and states of emergency on the one side, and constitutional change on the other.

They will all be used as umbrella concepts. The list of 'crises' and emergency situations that might be considered relevant for the purposes of this chapter has considerably expanded over the last few decades: basically, the notion of 'emergencies' may refer to (a) menaces for the territorial integrity of the state or its internal cohesion, (b) natural disasters, or (c) economic and financial crises. Quite often, this is not reflected in constitutional provisions in very accurate terms: emergency clauses are generally rather vague and refrain from providing precise definitions of what should be meant by national emergency.[4] Furthermore, due to historical reasons a number of different formalised emergency regimes can regularly be found within the same constitutional order, as the French and German cases clearly show.[5] In this chapter, a generic notion of 'state of emergency' will be used. Finally, a number of crises that could trigger a state of emergency combine an internal and an external (or non-exclusively domestic) dimension: this is typically the case of terrorism, economic and financial turmoil, and even of some natural events (e.g. the Indian Ocean tsunami in December 2004). Accordingly, not only is international law – and, most notably, international human rights law – highly relevant for understanding the legal status of states of emergency,[6] but different

---

4 However, recent constitutions and ordinary laws may be more accurate and even provide for differentiated emergency regimes: see e.g. the Canadian Emergencies Act of 1985, which dictates distinct rules in order to cope with public welfare emergency, public order emergency, international emergency, and war emergency. As regards the Canadian model, see Kim Lane Scheppele, 'North American Emergencies: The Use of Emergency Powers in Canada and the United States' (2006) 4 *International Journal of Constitutional Law* 213, 231.

5 See Rainer Arnold, 'Méthodologie et mécanismes institutionnels des états d'urgence et d'exception' (2008) *Annuaire international de justice constitutionnelle* 417, 417–18. In France, three emergency regimes are regulated in the constitution and ordinary legislation: extraordinary presidential powers (Art. 16 of the Constitution of 1958), state of siege (Art. 36 of the Constitution), and state of emergency (*état d'urgence*, law no. 55–385). In turn, the German Basic Law mentions a state of defence (Art. 115a), a state of tension (Art. 80a), internal emergency (Art. 91), and assistance during disasters (Art. 35).

6 See Art. 15 of the European Convention for the Protection of Human Rights and Fundamental Freedoms, Art. 4 of the International Covenant on Civil and Political Rights, and Art. 27 of the American Convention on Human Rights. Among these international instruments for the protection of human rights, the European Commission for Human Rights and the European Court of Human Rights have developed the richest case law

institutional layers are involved in reacting to crises that are not purely 'national'. The Eurozone crisis represents a significant example of this emerging trend.

No less multifaceted is the relevant notion of constitutional change. Comparative enquiries into constitutional change reveal a multiplicity of potential mechanisms and models, both formalised and informal: amending the constitution, either complying with the amending formula or bypassing it, passing ordinary legislation, political practice, judge-made informal change, and informal change resulting from the action of international and supranational actors.[7] The notion of constitutional change may encompass both deliberated and accidental modifications of the constitutional framework.[8] Even more than reactions to terrorist attacks, the economic and financial crisis has necessitated the revision of well-established conceptual categories concerning the relationship between crises and constitutional change.

The research questions underlying a study of the interaction between crises and constitutional change could be presented as such: how does the constitutionalisation of states of emergency affect the dynamics of constitutional change? Does the existence – or the absence – of an entrenched 'emergency constitution' act as a bulwark against arbitrary constitutional change in times of crisis? Do current trends somehow depart from well-established paradigms in this domain? In order to answer these questions, the chapter is structured as follows. The next section discusses the key issues in an analysis of crises, states of emergency, and constitutional change: in so doing, it primarily focuses on turning points in the history of constitutionalism that illustrate the risks of far-reaching constitutional change in times of emergency. Then we look into the constitutionalisation of emergency and its implications for the topic of constitutional change. We then consider recent developments related to the economic and financial crisis, followed by a discussion of the results of the analysis.

What is at stake: lessons from constitutional history

The role of crises in prompting change in the interpretation of constitutions

In his seminal study of constitutional change, Hsü Dau-Lin mentions shifts in the interpretation of constitutional provisions as a typical factor triggering constitutional

---

regarding admissible derogations in times of emergency. Interestingly, in its opinion regarding the so-called Greek case, the European Commission for Human Rights addressed the question of the conservative nature of derogatory measures under Art. 15 ECHR. The applicant governments argued that '[t]o derogate from "democratic rights and human rights and freedoms" was permitted in exceptional cases "for specific purpose only of protecting these very institutions, rights and freedoms". Article 17 excluded derogations which were aimed at the destruction of the rights and freedoms set forth in the Convention'. Having already stated that the main factual conditions of Art. 15 ECHR were not satisfied in that case, the Commission refrained from 'express[ing] a view on the further question whether the respondent Government's derogations under Article 15 were also excluded by Articles 17 and 18 of the Convention' (*Denmark, Norway, Sweden and the Netherlands* v. *Greece*, Applications 3321/67-3323/67 and 3344/67, in *Yearbook of the European Convention on Human Rights: The Greek Case 1969*, Martinus Nijhoff, The Hague, 1972, at 112). See also Emanuele Sommario, *Stati d'emergenza e trattati a tutela dei diritti umani* (Giappichelli, 2018) 34–37.

7 See Xenophon Contiades and Alkmene Fotiadou, 'Models of Constitutional Change' in Xenophon Contiades (ed), *Engineering Constitutional Change: A Comparative Perspective on Europe, Canada and the USA* (Routledge 2013) 417, 435–40.

8 See Andreas Voßkuhle, 'Gibt es und wozu nutzt eine Lehre vom Verfassungswandel?' (2004) *Der Staat* 450, 451–52, emphasising the differences between this farther-reaching approach and Georg Jellinek's distinction between non-deliberated *Verfassungswandlung* and conscious *Verfassungsdurchbrechung*.

change.[9] Major crises such as civil wars and organised terrorism obviously influence political and judicial actors and favour the emergence of interpretations of constitutional provisions that are clearly at odds with previous constitutional practice.

Among the examples mentioned by Hsü Dau-Lin, the American Legal Tender Cases are particularly telling.[10] According to Art. I, Section 8 of the Constitution of the United States, Congress has the power, among other things, to declare war and to borrow money on the credit of the United States. After the outbreak of the Civil War, Congress authorised an issue of paper currency with legal tender – the so-called greenbacks – which was apparently a move that was not authorised under the constitution. At the beginning, many state courts upheld the constitutionality of the Legal Tender Act of 1862, with the order to issue paper currency being interpreted as part of the congressional war powers. Over the course of a hard-fought judicial saga, the Supreme Court ruled that

> [t]he power of issuing bills of credit, and making them at the discretion of the legislature, a tender in payment of private debts ... not being prohibited to Congress by the Constitution ... is included in the power expressly granted to borrow money on the credit of the United States.[11]

The Civil War also played a chief role regarding the suspension of fundamental rights safeguards in a condition of necessity. According to constitutional law scholars and the early case law of the Supreme Court, the president, unlike Congress, did not have the power to suspend the writ of habeas corpus 'when in cases of rebellion and invasion the public safety may require it' (Art. I, Section 9 of the constitution). After President Lincoln suspended the writ on a number of occasions, Chief Justice Taney denied that the president had any such power.[12] However, Lincoln stuck to his own interpretation of the constitution: as Rossiter has argued, '[i]n the end, it was simply a question of this: Taney as Chief Justice was anxious to preserve respect for the law; Lincoln as President was determined to preserve the Union', but '[t]he one great precedent is what Lincoln did, not what Taney said'.[13]

More recently, Italy experienced a long, tragic season of far-left and far-right terrorism. In order to deal with this situation, the legislature adopted a number of extraordinary measures, including a novel regime of pre-trial detention. Some ordinary courts referred these legislative provisions to the Constitutional Court. The court stressed that the whole case had to be considered bearing in mind the exceptional challenge posed by 'terrorism and

---

9 Hsü Dau-Lin, *Die Verfassungswandlung* (Walter de Gruyter, 1932) 35.

10 See Dau-Lin (n 9) 36–38.

11 U.S. Supreme Court, *Juilliard v. Greenman*, 110 U.S. 421 (1884), at 447–48. In his dissenting opinion, Justice Field noted that 'war merely increased the urgency for money; it did not add to the powers of the government nor change their nature; that if the power existed, it might be equally exercised when a loan was made to meet ordinary expenses in time of peace, as when vast sums were needed to support an army or a navy in time of war. The wants of the governments could never be the measure of its powers. But in the excitement and apprehensions of the war, these considerations were unheeded; the measure was passed as one of overruling necessity in a perilous crisis of the country. Now it is no longer advocated as one of necessity, but as one that may be adopted at any time. What was in 1862 called the "medicine of the Constitution" has now become its daily bread. So it always happens that whenever a wrong principle of conduct, political or personal, is adopted on a plea of necessity, it will be afterwards followed on a plea of convenience' (110 U.S. 457–58). See also Kenneth W. Dam, 'The Legal Tender Cases' (1981) *The Supreme Court Review* 367.

12 *Ex parte Merryman*, 17 F. Cas. 144 (C.C.D. Md. 1861), No. 9487.

13 Clinton Rossiter, *The Supreme Court and the Commander in Chief* (Cornell University Press 1976) 25.

subversion' and, correspondingly, 'the need to protect the democratic order and public safety'. Still,

> emergency, in its proper meaning, is admittedly an anomalous and serious condition, but basically it is a temporary one. For this reason, it may well legitimise unusual measures, but these are no longer legitimate if they are unduly protracted in time.[14]

As will be shown later, the notion of suspending the constitutional framework is foreign to the Italian constitutional order, but the Constitutional Court was led to accept it in light of its necessary, temporary character.[15] Nevertheless, critics have highlighted a tendency for those extraordinary measures to persist even beyond the end of the extraordinary circumstances that legitimised them.[16]

Abusive use of states of emergency and constitutional upheaval

Two *loci classici* of the interaction between state of emergency and constitutional change can be identified: the proclamation of a state of siege in 1851 in France, and the downfall of the Weimar Republic in the interwar years. They both serve as negative examples of the risks inherent to legislative or constitutional regulations of states of emergency, as complex as they may be. The abusive use of emergency powers played a crucial role in hastening the subversion of the constitutional order in place.

In the 2nd French Republic, the law of 9 August 1849 laid down the conditions for declaring the state of siege 'in case of imminent danger for internal or external security' (Art. 1). Louis-Napoléon Bonaparte, the Prince-President of France, extensively resorted to this legal tool in the sequence of events that led to the coup of 2 December 1851, the end of the Republic and the establishment of the 2nd Empire.[17]

The German case has been intensively discussed. Art. 48(2) of the Weimar Constitution of 1919 provided the president of the *Reich* with special powers for those situations in which public safety and order were 'seriously disturbed or threatened': under those circumstances, the president was empowered to 'take the necessary measures to restore public safety and order; if necessary, with the aid of armed force'. In order to restore the pre-existing order, the president was given the power to 'temporarily suspend in whole or in part the fundamental rights enumerated in Articles 114, 115, 117, 118, 123, 124 and 153' of the constitution. With regard to this provision, a number of points deserve mention. First, and in spite of the wording of Art. 48(2), resorting to emergency powers was not limited to 'classical' crises such as those related to war and internal turmoil. On the contrary, the *Reich* government used these powers in order to react to the financial and economic crises that plagued the Weimar Republic throughout the course of its existence:[18] 'This extension of emergency powers to the financial and economic domain proved to be momentous: it was the first step towards a general system of emergency government which

---

14 *Corte costituzionale*, judgment no. 15/1982.
15 See Paolo Bonetti, *Terrorismo, emergenza e costituzioni democratiche* (il Mulino 2006) 324–25.
16 See Giovanna De Minico, *Costituzione. Emergenza e terrorismo* (Jovene 2016).
17 See Clinton Rossiter, *Constitutional Dictatorship: Crisis Government in the Modern Democracies* (Princeton University Press 1948) 81.
18 See Rossiter (n 17) 43; Ernst Rudolf Huber, *Deutsche Verfassungsgeschichte seit 1789*, vol. VI, *Die Weimarer Reichsverfassung* (Kohlhammer 1981) 701.

would govern through emergency decrees in other domains as well'.[19] This became particularly evident after 1929, when President von Hindenburg used his own powers under Art. 48(2) in order to bypass the paralysis of the *Reichtstag*, thereby transforming the Weimar Republic, originally a parliamentary democracy, into a presidential dictatorship. This happened well before Adolf Hitler's seizure of power marked the end of the Weimar regime. It is worth mentioning that 'generous' interpretations of the enabling clause of Art. 48(2) gradually gained ground among public law scholars and in the case law of the *Reichsgericht*.[20] Therefore, both scholars and supreme courts ultimately overcame their initial reservations and accepted those transformations of the constitutional order as legitimate.

In theoretical terms, the distinction between 'commissarial dictatorship' and 'sovereign dictatorship', expounded by Carl Schmitt as early as 1921, perfectly illustrates the principal dilemmas underlying the constitutional practice of that time: 'while the commissary dictatorship is authorised by a constituted organ and has an identity in the existing constitution, sovereign dictatorship exists only *quoad exercitium*, and it derives directly from the amorphous *pouvoir constituant*'.[21] As the very same author recognised in a subsequent essay, '[a] sovereign dictatorship is irreconcilable with a constitutional form of government. ... Either sovereign dictatorship or constitution; the one excludes the other'.[22]

Constitutionalising emergency: a never-ending debate

After the end of the Second World War, and in light of widespread reaction against the excesses and horrors of the previous decades, the question often arose of whether or not it was desirable to have a constitutionally entrenched regulation of states of emergency. The question was answered negatively, at least in the immediate aftermath of the war, by the drafters of the post-totalitarian Italian Constitution and German Basic Law.[23] However, a recent quantitative study has shown that nine out of ten constitutions currently in force contain emergency-focused provisions. These could be defined as

> the set of formal legal provisions encoded in the constitution that specify who can declare an emergency, under which conditions an emergency can be declared, who needs to approve the declaration, and which actors have which special powers once it has been declared that the constitution does not assign to them outside emergencies.[24]

19 Marc de Wilde, 'Just Trust Us: A Short History of Emergency Powers and Constitutional Change' (2015) 3 *Comparative Legal History* 110, 122–23.

20 See Giacomo Delledonne, 'Il dibattito dottrinale e l'esperienza di gestione degli stati di crisi economica in Germania' in Eleonora Ceccherini (ed), *Stato di diritto e crisi delle finanze pubbliche* (Editoriale Scientifica 2016) 73, 77–79.

21 Carl Schmitt, *Dictatorship: From the Origin of the Modern Concept of Sovereignty to Proletarian Class Struggle*, translated by Michael Hoelzl and Graham Ward (Polity Press 2014) 127.

22 Schmitt (n 21) 204.

23 Similarly, some liberal constitutions enacted in the 19th century explicitly prohibited the suspension of any constitutional provisions in order to react to the excesses of absolutist rulers (e.g. Art. 187 of the Belgian Constitution of 1831, still in force). As regards the Belgian case, see Francis Delpérée and Marc Verdussen, 'Lutte contre le terrorisme et protection des droits fondamentaux – Belgique' (2002) *Annuaire international de justice constitutionnelle* 91, 98–99; Alicia Pastor y Caramasa, 'Constitution et lutte antiterroriste: le cas belge' (2016) *Annuaire international de justice constitutionnelle* 29, 30–31.

24 Christian Bjørnskov and Stefan Voigt, 'The Architecture of Emergency Constitutions' (2018) 16 *International Journal of Constitutional Law* 101, 103.

Some of these emergency clauses are the product not of constitution-making but of subsequent constitutional amendment. Other 'emergency constitutions' represent part of constitutions that were drafted with an eye to major crises. The former is the case of Germany, where an 'emergency constitution' (*Notstandsverfassung*) was added to the Basic Law in 1968, while the latter is the case of France, with the Constitution of the 5th Republic being drafted and enacted at a time when the Algerian crisis was at its peak.[25] Interestingly, quantitative comparative analyses show that constitutional provisions regulating states of emergency tend to be as exhaustive as possible: more often than not, they do not contain '"by law" clauses that explicitly deem a subject constitutional, but then defer almost all substantive decision-making on the subject to future decision-makers'.[26]

In this respect, the regulation of states of emergency – and, indirectly, the constitutional recognition of special powers for reacting to crises – represents a typical subject for constitutional change. For the purposes of this chapter, a relevant issue is not whether the constitutionalisation of states of emergency is desirable but when (and how) this should take place. Critics have often stressed that such provisions clearly reflect, both in terms of consistency and efficiency, the troubled circumstances under which they were drafted.[27] Bearing this in mind, a wiser precautionary strategy would be to discuss the possible contents of an 'emergency constitution' in good times. For example, this was one of the main arguments used by the West German federal government when it first launched the idea of elaborating an 'emergency constitution' for the Federal Republic: as Interior Minister Schröder stated, 'precaution is necessary' (*Vorsorge tut not*). A popular argument in the ensuing discussion was that it seemed appropriate to regulate states of emergency in the middle of the economic miracle, when the advent of a serious crisis appeared to be a remote occurrence.[28] In the same vein, in the late 1920s Carl Schmitt himself had argued in favour of adopting a law implementing Art. 48 of the Weimar Constitution.[29] By that time, and following a turbulent start, the Weimar regime had apparently vanquished its far-left and far-right opponents and had reached a condition of stabilisation that made it possible to think of a 'normal regulation of exceptional capacities'.[30] Today, the routinisation of crises makes the very idea of taking advantage of 'normal times' in order to regulate states of emergency look like an optimistic, abstract programme of constitutional law-making. In turn, and more realistically, the rationalising function of comprehensive emergency regulations is propounded, especially in common law jurisdictions, by those who cast a doubt on the virtues of a case-by-case approach.[31]

---

25 Law no. 55–385, regulating the *état d'urgence*, was also passed by the French legislature as the Algerian insurrection was escalating and after Prime Minister Mendès France was forced to resign: see Olivier Beaud and Cécile Guérin-Bargues, *L'état d'urgence. Étude constitutionnelle, historique et critique* (LGDJ 2016) 52–54.

26 Rosalind Dixon and Tom Ginsburg, 'Deciding Not to Decide: Deferral in Constitutional Design' (2011) 9 *International Journal of Constitutional Law* 636, 637 and 641.

27 See Roland Drago, 'L'état d'urgence (lois des 3 avril et 7 août 1955) et les libertés publiques' (1955) *Revue du droit public et de la science politique* 670.

28 See Florian Meinel, 'Diktatur der Besiegten? Ein Fragment Carl Schmitts zur Notstandsverfassung der Bundesrepublik' (2013) 52 *Der Staat* 455, 461.

29 Indeed, according to Art. 48(5) of the Weimar Constitution, 'details' regarding presidential emergency powers would be regulated by a federal ordinary law.

30 Schmitt (n 21) 226.

31 See Bruce Ackerman, 'The Emergency Constitution' (2004) 113 *Yale Law Journal* 1029, 1078–79, and counter-arguments by Laurence H. Tribe and Patrick O. Gudridge, 'The Anti-Emergency Constitution' (2004) 113 *Yale Law Journal* 1801.

A distinct question, which has been mentioned in both of the preceding paragraphs, pertains to crises and emergencies as fostering further constitutional change. As mentioned above, emergency clauses authorise a shift in the ordinary balance of powers in order to enable political actors to cope with a major crisis. In this regard, such clauses not only authorise a departure from the general constitutional framework; they also specify how far this can happen. Constitutional change – or at least *formalised* constitutional change – is not foreign to these concerns.

Even in the second half of the 20th century, the rulers of the day have often exploited the triggering of a state of emergency in order to promote extensive modifications of the existing constitution. See, for example, India's Prime Minister Indira Gandhi after a High Court ruling barred her from election. After Mrs Gandhi proclaimed the state of emergency, the Indian Parliament enacted the 38th and 39th Amendments to the Constitution, the first of which immunised from judicial review all laws adopted during that emergency. These events were crucial in stimulating the Indian Supreme Court to elaborate its highly influential Basic Structure doctrine.[32] Under radically different circumstances, after declaring a state of emergency on the whole French territory in November 2015, President Hollande launched a draft constitutional amendment 'for protecting the Nation'. This ultimately unsuccessful *projet de loi constitutionnelle* was sharply criticised by scholars for being either inconsistent or redundant. Still, one of its self-styled goals, as Prime Minister Valls admitted during a hearing before the *Commission des lois* of the National Assembly, was to lay the groundwork to bypass possible judicial objections (*contraintes jurisprudentielles*) against specific emergency measures.[33] A combination of strong presidential law-making powers and frequent resort to the possibility of amending constitutional provisions was a distinctive, recurring character of Latin American emergency regimes prior to the latest wave of democratisation on the continent.[34] Finally, the failed coup in Turkey in July 2016 was instrumental in paving the way for the passing of far-reaching constitutional amendments, including the introduction of presidentialism. As the Venice Commission complained, the declaration of a state of emergency following the unsuccessful coup was at odds with ensuring 'the due democratic setting for a constitutional referendum'.[35] Interestingly, the Turkish constitutional amendments also introduced a new, president-centred regulation of states of emergency, which somehow created unfavourable conditions for restoring the pre-existing state of affairs. Even in the absence of formalised constitutional change by means of amendment, returning to constitutional normalcy is often difficult, as institutional practice in both the United States and Canada in the first half of the 20th century clearly reveals.[36]

In light of this, increasingly sophisticated 'emergency constitutions' strive not to frustrate the purported goal of states of emergency, i.e. dealing with crises and re-establishing the condition of constitutional normalcy. This is all the more true as Schmittian theoretical

---

32 See Yaniv Roznai, *Unconstitutional Constitutional Amendments: The Limits of Amendment Powers* (Oxford University Press 2017) 45–46.

33 See Beaud and Guérin-Bargues (n 25) 165.

34 See José Antonio Cheibub, Zachary Elkins and Tom Ginsburg, 'Latin American Presidentialism in Comparative and Historical Perspective' (2011) 89 *Texas Law Review* 1, 15–18.

35 Venice Commission, *Opinion on the amendments to the Constitution adopted by the Grand National Assembly on 21 January 2017 and to be submitted to a national referendum on 16 April 2017*, CDL-AD(2017)005, 10–11 March 2017, para. 133. See also Valentina Rita Scotti, 'Presidentialism in Turkey. A First Appraisal of 2017 Constitutional Reform' (2017) *DPCE online* 251.

36 See Scheppele (n 4) 221–22.

approaches[37] are generally refuted and 'constitution-centred' theories of emergency prevail, in which '[t]he positive (fixed) constitution always serves as a starting point for argumentation'.[38] According to slightly old-fashioned constitutional jargon, commissarial dictatorships should not transform into sovereign dictatorships: in more familiar terms, states of emergency should not be exploited in order to modify and possibly radically alter the constitutional order. For this reason, formal constitutional change enacted in times of emergency is generally unwelcome or even prohibited. Removing 'the power of formal amendment from political actors' in difficult times is a typical defence mechanism 'codified … within formal amendment rules';[39] in this respect, states of emergency are treated in a similar way to other delicate occurrences, such as foreign occupation, periods of regency and succession to the throne. As the Venice Commission argued in its recent opinion on the Turkish constitutional amendments, such a prohibition

> reflects the importance of protecting the fundamentals of the political system, not-
> ably the Constitution and the electoral system. It stems from the consideration that
> a state of emergency may entail limitations to the normal functioning of parliament
> (especially for the role of the opposition) as well as, very often, limited functioning
> of mass media and limitations on the exercise of political freedoms such as freedom
> of assembly. Under these conditions, the democratic process of constitutional
> amendment may not be fully guaranteed.[40]

In the contemporary constitutional landscape, a number of emergency clauses explicitly limit – or prohibit altogether – the power to amend the constitution in times of emergency.[41] This prohibition may also extend to ordinary laws with clear constitutional

---

37 See e.g. Carl Schmitt, *Political Theology: Four Chapters on the Concept of Sovereignty*, translated by George Schwab (University of Chicago Press, 2005) 5–15. Institutionalist theories according to which necessity is the supreme and extra-legal source of the legal order are also generally refuted: see Santi Romano, 'Sui decreti-legge e lo stato di assedio in occasione del terremoto di Messina e di Reggio-Calabria' in *Scritti minori*, edited by Guido Zanobini, vol. I, *Diritto costituzionale* (Giuffrè 1950) 287, writing in the aftermath of the Messina earthquake and tsunami of 1908.

38 András Jakab, 'German Constitutional Law and Doctrine of State of Emergency: Paradigms and Dilemmas of a Traditional (Continental) Discourse' (2005) 5 *German Law Journal* 453, 471; see also Kim Lane Scheppele, 'Legal and Extralegal Emergencies' in Gregory A. Caldeira, R. Daniel Kelemen and Keith E. Whittington (eds), *The Oxford Handbook of Law and Politics* (Oxford University Press 2008) 165, 165–66.

39 Richard Albert, 'Formal Amendment Rules: Function and Design', Chapter 7 in this volume.

40 Venice Commission, *Opinion on the amendments to the [Turkish] Constitution*, CDL-AD(2017)005, para. 30.

41 See Venelin E. Ganev, 'Emergency Powers and the New East European Constitutions' (1997) 45 *American Journal of Comparative Law* 585, 596; Nicolas Bonbled and Céline Romainville, 'États d'exception et crises humaines aiguës: débats récents autour du terrorisme et des nouvelles formes de crise' (2008) *Annuaire international de justice constitutionnelle* 429, 454–55; Albert (n 39). Among the most important examples, see Art. 115e(2) of the German Basic Law ('This Basic Law may neither be amended nor abrogated nor suspended in whole or in part by a law enacted by the Joint Committee' during a state of defence), Arts 169 and 116 of the Spanish Constitution of 1978 (the process of constitutional amendment may not be initiated in time of war or under any of the states mentioned in Art. 116, i.e. state of alarm, state of emergency, and state of siege or martial law), Art. 60(1) of the Brazilian Constitution of 1988 ('The Constitution cannot be amended during federal intervention, state of defence or state of siege'), Art. 152(3) of the Romanian Constitution of 1991, and Art. 228(6) of the Polish Constitution of 1997 ('During a period of introduction of extraordinary measures, the following shall not be subject to change: the Constitution, the Acts on Elections to the Sejm, the Senate and organs of local government, the Act on Elections to the Presidency, as well as statutes on extraordinary measures').

significance, such as electoral laws or laws governing constitutional courts.[42] Therefore, a substantive notion of constitution – to be protected from self-interested modifications – is often reflected by these emergency clauses. In jurisdictions that have been marked by permanent emergency over the entire course of their history, this effort has focused on the very basic core of the constitutional order. In Israel – which, by the way, has an unwritten constitution – neither Basic Law: The Government nor Basic Law: Human Dignity and Liberty can be amended by emergency regulations: they contain, respectively, 'the constitutional basis for Israeli national security law' and 'the main constitutional provisions on the protection of human rights in Israel'.[43]

In some legal systems, the very same prohibition to amend the constitution during a national emergency may derive from restrictive interpretations of constitutional clauses by constitutional courts. This is the case with France, for example: Arts 89(4) and 7(9) of the constitution of 1958 only state that no amendment procedure can be initiated or continued when the integrity of national territory is placed in jeopardy, thereby meaning war and foreign invasion, or while the presidency of the Republic is vacant. When reviewing the compatibility of the Maastricht Treaty with the constitution, the *Conseil constitutionnel* affirmed that amendment procedures may not be initiated or continued even when resort is made to exceptional presidential powers under Art. 16 of the constitution.[44] Still, these constitutional safeguards are of limited impact if constitutional courts are not entrusted with the power to review constitutional amendments. Again, this is true of France, as the *Conseil constitutionnel* itself clarified in a subsequent decision.[45]

A distinct obligation that may be included in an 'emergency constitution' is to restore the pre-existing legal framework once the crisis that triggered the state of emergency has come to an end. Again, constitutions adopted during post-authoritarian transitions prove to be abundantly aware of the risk of having the legal order durably and ostensibly affected by the implementation of emergency measures.[46]

Finally, a state of emergency is generally conceived as being limited in time, and it can only be renewed subject to the approval of an institution other than the one that declared it. Some scholars have argued in favour of strengthening the counter-majoritarian flavour of these procedures;[47] in any case, they indicate that the focus should be on a 'legislative' or 'executive' model 'for dealing with emergencies' but on 'a normative framework for understanding how, in the light of experience, the grip of constitutional principles can be

---

42 See Art. 115g of the German Basic Law and Art. 228(6) of the Polish Constitution.

43 Daphne Barak-Erez, 'The National Security Constitution and the Israeli Condition' in Gideon Sapir, Daphne Barak-Erez and Aharon Barak (eds), *Israeli Constitutional Law in the Making* (Hart Publishing 2013) 429, 432 and 434.

44 French *Conseil constitutionnel*, Decision no. 92–312 DC of 2 September 1992 (*Traité sur l'Union européenne*), para. 19. See also Kémal Gözler, *Le pouvoir de révision constitutionnelle* (Presses universitaires du Septentrion 1997) 149–152.

45 French *Conseil constitutionnel*, Decision no. 2003–469 DC of 26 March 2003 (*Loi constitutionnelle relative à l'organisation décentralisée de la* République), para. 2. See also Wanda Mastor and Liliane Icher, 'Constitutional Amendment in France' in Xenophon Contiades (ed), *Engineering Constitutional Change: A Comparative Perspective on Europe, Canada and the USA* (Routledge, 2013) 115, 118.

46 See e.g. Art. 228(5) of the Polish Constitution of 1997 ('Actions undertaken as a result of the introduction of any extraordinary measure shall be proportionate to the degree of threat and shall be intended to achieve the swiftest restoration of conditions allowing for the normal functioning of the State').

47 See e.g. Ackerman (n 31), pointing at the South African model.

maintained'.[48] A corollary to the above is a trend that has been brought to the forefront of recent Israeli constitutional practice: the use of temporary constitutional amendments designed to address specific constitutional needs of the moment. Temporary constitutional amendments can be considered part of a wider discussion regarding the merits of experimental legislation and sunset clauses,[49] with some authors even highlighting their positive qualities compared to crisis-pervaded constitution-making processes.[50] In Israel, however, substantial resort to temporary constitutional amendments since 2009 has been described as an example of abusive constitutionalism, whose chief aim is 'the government's intent to entrench its dominant position'.[51]

However, for all the legal sophistication of these constitutional and legislative provisions, which aim to minimise the permanent effects of states of emergency, constitutional developments in the last two decades show that some habits are deeply rooted in institutional practice. Once a state of emergency has been declared, self-perpetuation and the generalisation of extraordinary measures are a typical trend. As Bruce Ackerman claimed in the aftermath of the 9/11 terrorist attacks, '[d]esigning a constitutional regime for a limited state of emergency is a tricky business. Unless careful precautions are taken, emergency measures have a habit of continuing well beyond their time of necessity'.[52] This pessimistic assessment has occasionally been proved correct during recent crises, as the French example aptly shows. As already mentioned, following the terrorist attacks in Paris and Île-de-France in November 2015, a state of emergency (*état d'urgence*) was declared on the whole French territory on 14 November 2015 and subsequently extended six times by the legislature until 30 October 2017.

Critics have highlighted some flaws in this long-lasting emergency regime, on the whole amounting to informal mechanisms of constitutional change. First, the most important anti-terrorist measures that had been available since 14 November 2015 were frequently used in the first weeks after the attacks and became less and less relevant thereafter. Out of 3954 'administrative' search warrants issued by the *préfets* until 11 July 2016, no fewer than 3021 had been ordered prior to 12 January 2016, i.e. in the two months immediately following the attacks.[53] Second, another trend hints at the *normalisation* of the emergency regime: those extraordinary powers that had been authorised to confront terrorism were also deployed in different situations. A key component of the state of emergency declared in France in November 2015 was the power of the minister of the interior to keep individuals under house arrest (*assignation à résidence*) if 'there are serious reasons for thinking that their [behaviour] threatens public safety and order' (Art. 9 of law no. 55–385, as amended by law no. 2015–1501 in November 2015). Although this measure was designed to tackle terrorism

---

48 David Dyzenhaus, 'States of Emergency' in Michel Rosenfeld and András Sajó (eds), *The Oxford Handbook of Comparative Constitutional Law* (Oxford University Press 2012) 442, 460.

49 See Sofia Ranchordás, *Constitutional Sunsets and Experimental Legislation: A Comparative Perspective* (Edward Elgar 2014).

50 See Ozan O. Varol, 'Temporary Constitutions' (2014) 102 *California Law Review* 409, 429–30 and 455 (according to which 'a temporary provision granting emergency powers to the government for use in a post-conflict moment will have little impact on stability if allowed to expire after the societal needs that prompted the adoption of that power have dissipated').

51 Nadav Dishon, 'Temporary Constitutional Amendments as a Means to Undermine the Democratic Order: Insights from the Israeli Experience' (2018) 51 *Israel Law Review* 389, 421.

52 Ackerman (n 31) 1030.

53 See Beaud and Guérin-Bargues (n 25) 145.

and Islamist radicalism, ecologist militants had to serve some days of house arrest as the United Nations Climate Change Conference COP 21 was being held in Paris.[54] Third, some significant rule of law safeguards were informally weakened during the parliamentary debate preceding the enactment of law no. 2015–1501, whose declared goal was to modernise the legal regime of the *état d'urgence*. When Prime Minister Valls addressed the Senate, he explicitly invited its members not to challenge the constitutionality of the law before the *Conseil constitutionnel*, because 'going before the *Conseil constitutionnel* is always risky'.[55] As these episodes in recent French constitutional history suggest, surreptitious constitutional change seems to be intrinsically related to states of emergency, thus triggering institutional dynamics that often transcend the initial purposes of their promoters.

However, the apparently irresistible trend toward the normalisation and generalisation of emergency regimes may well vindicate the reasons for relying on judicial control. States of emergency often create serious embarrassment for courts, which are caught in an unpleasant dilemma between a necessity for deference while crises are hot, and belated intervention in the presence of *fait accompli*.[56] Justice Jackson's dissent in *Korematsu*[57] plainly exemplifies the dilemmas affecting the activity of courts in those circumstances. However, lengthy states of emergency, with extraordinary regimes renewed with no apparent expiry date, somehow modify the pre-existing balance and might induce courts to embrace a stricter approach in order to face *structural* constitutional change.[58] This reading can be confirmed by the recent French vicissitudes. The *Conseil constitutionnel* assumed a clearly cautious approach with regard to the emergency measures in the first months following the terrorist attacks in Paris. However, its attitude changed as time passed, as a judgment issued in March 2017 reveals.[59] The *Conseil* was asked whether or not the extension of house arrest orders beyond twelve months amounted to a deprivation of freedom under Art. 66 of the French Constitution, and ultimately struck down the impugned provisions for their incompatibility with the right to effective legal remedy. In the official commentary attached to the decision of the *Conseil*, reference was made to the moderate case law of the previous months, which had come to the conclusion that house arrest does not produce a deprivation of freedom but a limitation thereof. On the other hand, 'by now, the state of emergency has been in force since November 2015'; according to the wise men in the Parisian rue de Montpensier, this was rendering it necessary to discuss again the soundness of the house arrest regime.[60] In sum, traditional checks and balances might play a stronger role if they have to face long-lasting emergency regimes with an inclination for institutionalisation and self-perpetuation.

---

54 See French *Conseil constitutionnel*, Decision no. 2015–527 QPC of 22 December 2015 (*Cédric D.*). See also Beaud and Guérin-Bargues (n 25) 150.

55 Speech quoted by Beaud and Guérin-Bargues (n 25) 133.

56 See Eric A. Posner and Adrian Vermeule, *The Executive Unbound: After the Madisonian Republic* (Oxford University Press 2010) 52–53.

57 U.S. Supreme Court, *Korematsu v. United States*, 323 U.S. 214 (1944), at 245-46 (dissenting opinion submitted by Justice Jackson).

58 In fact, the same could be argued with regard to other institutions that are supposed to play a monitoring role during states of emergency. For instance, in 2005 the Senate of the United States was crucial – in times of united government – in not allowing for an indefinite prorogation of some provisions of the PATRIOT Act. On a different note, see the sceptical assessment by Scheppele (n 38) 176–77.

59 French *Conseil constitutionnel*, Decision no. 2017–624 QPC of 16 March 2017 (*M. Sofiyan I.*).

60 Official commentary to the Decision available at www.conseil-constitutionnel.fr.

Emerging trends: lessons from the Eurozone crisis

Institutional practice in the European Union has always offered a prime example of informal constitutional change or, as Farrell and Héritier have defined it, interstitial institutional change.[61] This formula has been coined in order to describe a peculiar dynamic in which an alternation of treaty modifications and informal change has played a primary role. Since 2010, reactions to the sovereign debt crisis in the Eurozone have triggered a number of far-reaching changes in the composite European Constitution, thereby meaning both the EU constitution and constitutions in the member states. Apparently, the handling of the Eurozone crisis poses a formidable intellectual challenge for the study of constitutional change. In a nutshell, the main question here is whether a number of significant transformations in the law of the Economic and Monetary Union, which have occurred in the last decade, have triggered a structural constitutional mutation in the composite EU legal order.

At the beginning of the sovereign debt crisis, the main reference in EU primary law was the no-bailout clause in Art. 125 TFEU. Four main 'transformations' have been identified: a shift in the EU's institutional balance toward intergovernmentalism, an erosion of the equality of member states resulting from increased intergovernmentalism, neglect of the existing legal framework to the advantage of genuinely political concerns, and restrictions on the sovereignty of the member states that received financial assistance during the crisis.[62] Many of these transformations were not brought about by EU law instruments but, rather, by making resort to public international law. This was not entirely new, but there was a feeling that the combined impact of these innovations would decisively alter the general legal framework codified in the treaties. Meanwhile, only one provision of EU primary law, i.e. Art. 136 TFEU, has been amended, and the Court of Justice found it to be an unnecessary and somehow redundant change.[63]

The mutation thesis has been extensively discussed, among other scholars, by De Witte, who has warned against the risk of 'extrapolat[ing] too easily overall changes in the EU legal order from the specific changes that occurred within the specific domain of EMU law' and has found no compelling evidence of 'a brutal setting aside of the rule of law in the name of political expediency'.[64] Rather, in the peculiar constitutional arena of the European Union it seems correct to use the notion of increased institutional variation, i.e. the 'variation of decision-making mechanisms and institutional rules across different policy fields'.[65] In this respect, the way in which the Eurozone crisis was tackled does not significantly depart from the traditional patterns of institutional evolution of the European Union and indirectly reveals some peculiar aspects of the process of constitutionalisation of the Union itself.

No less interesting were the reforms triggered at the national level in some member states. Some countries, such as Italy and Spain, hastily modified their own constitutions and

---

61 See Henry Farrell and Adrienne Héritier (eds), *Contested Competences in Europe: Incomplete Contracts and Interstitial Institutional Change* (Routledge 2007).

62 See Bruno De Witte, 'Euro Crisis Responses and the EU Legal Order: Increased Institutional Variation or Constitutional Mutation?' (2015) *European Constitutional Law Review* 434, 448; Giuseppe Martinico, 'EU Crisis and Constitutional Mutations: A Review Article' (2014) 165 *Revista de Estudios Políticos* 247.

63 Court of Justice of the European Union, C-370/12, *Pringle* (2012).

64 De Witte (n 62) 453.

65 De Witte (n 62) 453.

entrenched some kind of 'golden rule' even before the Treaty on Stability, Coordination and Governance in the EMU was signed. They did so in order to face pressure from EU institutions *and* financial markets.[66] Later, the Memorandums of Understanding concluded by virtue of the Treaty Establishing the European Stability Mechanism[67] triggered far-reaching consequences in some of the most heavily indebted member states, especially with regard to standards of protection of social rights. For the purposes of this chapter, the key issue is that such modifications reflect the peculiar conditions of an interconnected legal scenario in which (partial) processes of federalisation and public-private hybridisation have taken place. Extensive reform of the architecture of the Economic and Monetary Union being impossible as of today, imbalances in decision-making power became clearly perceivable in the weakest member states, many of which had to conclude Memorandums of Understanding in order to receive financial assistance.[68] So complex an interaction perfectly illustrates the challenges posed by the economic and financial crisis in an increasingly interdependent world and its impact on the dynamics of constitutional change. Furthermore, the uncertain legal status (both in terms of domestic and EU law) of the emergency measures adopted within the ESM framework has triggered very diverse judicial reactions, at a national and supranational level alike.[69]

A tentative conclusion

The comparative analysis presented in the previous paragraphs lends itself to a contradictory assessment. Crises and emergencies have traditionally represented a serious challenge to the stability of constitutional orders; simultaneously, they are a typical object of constitutional provisions, which strive to limit the undesirable impact of crises on the foundations of the constitution. The success of emergency clauses is part of this narrative, so much so that 'once a country has included emergency provisions into its constitutions, it is unlikely ever to get rid of them'.[70] Like amending formulas, emergency clauses are a typical mechanism used to strike a balance between the persistence of the basic features of the constitutional order and adaptability to difficult circumstances.[71] On the same note, they both form a part

---

66 See Giacomo Delledonne, 'A Legalization of Financial Constitutions in the EU? Reflections on the German, Spanish, Italian and French Experiences' in Maurice Adams, Federico Fabbrini and Pierre Larouche (eds), *The Constitutionalization of European Budgetary Constraints* (Hart Publishing 2014) 181, 185.

67 According to Art. 13(3) of the ESM Treaty, if the Board of Governors of the ESM decides to grant stability support to an ESM member state, it entrusts 'the European Commission – in liaison with the ECB and, wherever possible, together with the IMF – with the task of negotiating, with the ESM Member concerned, a memorandum of understanding detailing the conditionality attached to the financial assistance facility. The content of the MoU [reflects] the severity of the weaknesses to be addressed and the financial assistance instrument chosen'.

68 See Jónatas E.M. Machado, 'The Sovereign Debt Crisis and the Constitution's Negative Outlook: A Portuguese Preliminary Assessment' in Xenophon Contiades (ed), *Constitutions in the Global Financial Crisis: A Comparative Analysis* (Ashgate 2013) 219, 231.

69 See Claire Kilpatrick, 'The EU and its Sovereign Debt Programmes: The Challenges of Liminal Legality', EUI Working Paper LAW 2017/14, at 17; Antonia Baraggia, 'The "Judicialization" of Emergency: The Case of the Eurozone Crisis' (2017) 1(2) *Rivista di Diritti comparati* 1.

70 Bjørnskov and Voigt (n 24) 105.

71 See Xenophon Contiades and Alkmene Fotiadou, 'On Resilience of Constitutions: What Makes Constitutions Resistant to External Shocks?' (2015) 9 *Vienna Journal of International Constitutional Law* 3, 7.

of strategies to introduce a degree of flexibility of constitutional documents.[72] Unlike amending formulas, however, emergency clauses have an intimately conservative inspiration, as they often aim at the restoration of pre-existing (constitutional) 'normalcy', thereby preventing a possible slippery slope toward the stronger concentration of power and the undermining of fundamental rights safeguards. Whereas the idea of 'stability through change' lies at the heart of enquiries into comparative constitutional change,[73] an appropriate formula encompassing the philosophy of institutionalised states of emergency might be, at least at first sight, 'flexibility for the sake of stability'. But this is just one side of the story.

On the one hand, we witness an increasing degree of sophistication in the constitutional regulation of states of emergency. This often occurs through a combination of national and international legal regimes; the latter are particularly relevant when it comes to ensuring that the basic standards of protection of fundamental rights are not abandoned after the declaration of a state of emergency. Some models seem to be particularly suited to escaping the risks of self-perpetuation and abuse, including surreptitious constitutional change.[74] However, the shift toward apparently endless emergency regimes and informal constitutional change has been observed even during recent crises in well-established liberal democracies and appears to be related to a deeply rooted logic underlying emergency itself. In this respect, institutional practice often proves to be more influential than entrenched constitutional or legislative modifications.[75] Furthermore, the practice of emergencies in the last five decades or so shows that countries often bypass their own 'emergency constitutions' in order to deal with any crisis.[76] A hidden risk in all of these developments is the emergence of a 'supra-constitutional emergency law'.[77] On the other hand, long-lasting emergency regimes may revive ordinary constitutional checks and balances, with the judiciary and other branches more willing to block developments that clearly alter the pre-existing constitutional order. The apparent success of enduring emergency regimes might allow courts and other branches to escape the tragic dilemma expounded by Justice Jackson in *Korematsu*.[78]

On the other hand, current crises largely escape traditional regulatory frameworks and pose distinctly new challenges. The most obvious one is the elusive nature of existential threats, which often have a non-exclusively national dimension. This points at the possible flaws of national emergency regimes. This was made evident, to some extent, by the threat

---

72 As empirical analysis has signalled, 'up to certain thresholds, more flexible constitutions that include a wide range of social actors and provide some amount of detail seem to endure longer than those that do not' (Elkins, Ginsburg and Melton, *The Endurance of National Constitutions* [n 1] 10).

73 See Xenophon Contiades and Alkmene Fotiadou, 'The Emergence of Comparative Constitutional Amendment as a New Discipline' in Richard Albert, Xenophon Contiades and Alkmene Fotiadou (eds), *The Foundations and Traditions of Constitutional Amendment* (Hart Publishing 2017) 369.

74 See Ackerman (n 31) 40–41, also mentioning the possible prevalence of a *reassurance* rationale over traditional *existential* rationales in the management of crises.

75 See de Wilde (n 19) 111.

76 See Scheppele (n 38) 174.

77 See Dyzenhaus (n 48) 443; Rainer Grote, 'Regulating the State of Emergency: The German Example' (2003) *Israel Yearbook on Human Rights* 151. A distinct line of thought builds on the legacy of permanent emergency in order to criticise the traditional conception of emergency and war powers as a (hopefully regulated) exception to the ordinary constitutional framework: see Karin Loevy, *Emergencies in Public Law: The Legal Politics of Containment* (Cambridge University Press 2016).

78 See n 57.

of international terrorism and, even more significantly, by the economic and financial crisis in the Eurozone. The necessity of coping with the crisis led to important reform in the EU legal order in the broadest sense: according to some interpretations (see above), these transformations were facilitated by reliance on some well-ingrained aspects of constitutional evolution and adaptation in the supranational order. These were resorted to again in order to face the Eurozone crisis. Furthermore, the constitutional modifications triggered by conditionality programmes represent part of complex negotiations in which the different bargaining positions of the member states and supranational and international institutions involved were a key factor. Again, the outcome was not easily reconcilable with traditional interpretive categories. Instead of flexibility, greater rigidity was introduced in the composite constitutional order, and instead of stability, the basis was laid for further (possibly radical) change. It remains to be seen whether this has only to do with the current traits (and flaws) of the architecture of the Union, or rather with the impending necessity of new paradigms for the interpretation of the law of emergencies.

16

THE MATERIAL STUDY OF CONSTITUTIONAL CHANGE

Marco Goldoni and Tarik Olcay

Introduction

How does political practice impact on constitutional change? Unsurprisingly, while being very much at the forefront of political-science oriented research, the question has often been neglected by constitutional lawyers for at least two reasons. First, a legal and normative conception of the constitutional order has dominated constitutional studies for a long time. The background condition that made this dominance possible is the separation between the two systems (law and politics) or their coupling. If understood in formal terms, such a view implies that the normativity of the constitutional order has to be seen in fundamental legal terms. The second reason is the obsession and the relative narrow focus (visible at least in certain jurisdictions) on the activities of supreme or constitutional courts.[1] Indeed, constitutional studies have focused for the most part on higher courts and their decisions. As we shall see, this focus has limited the capacity of constitutional lawyers and practitioners to grasp fundamental changes of the constitutional order. As a reaction to this type of constitutional analysis, in the last two decades a return to the analysis of the political constitution has been advocated (mostly in Commonwealth countries: see Bellamy 2007; Ewing 2013; Tomkins 2005; Waldron 1999). For this stream of constitutional analysis, political practice is the backbone of the constitutional order and, as a consequence, it is more prone to look into the political system for effectuating constitutional change.

This brief sketch of the state of art in constitutional studies provides the frame for the main models of understanding constitutional change: legal or political. The chapter first unpacks these two models and their roots in different constitutional experiences. It then suggests an integrated view on constitutional change which is defined as 'material' and it relates constitutional change to the formation and development of the undergirding social order. In the last two sections, the chapter introduces three case studies for illustrating the point of a material analysis. In this way, it will be possible to show the limits of an analysis of political practices which reduces it to legal or political constitutionalism either blurs the impact of political practice into a formalism of constitutional change or into a complete overlapping between political practice and constitutional transformation. The case studies discussed in the last section prove that adopting the two classic perspectives, partially blind

---

1 For a denunciation of this narrow view see, classically, Hirschl (2004).

the constitutional observer from noticing the effectiveness of certain constitutional changes while overstating it in other cases.

Constitutional change and legal constitutionalism

The main epistemic problem when addressing the role of political practice in constitutional change concerns the mediation of the legal system. In other words, the issue of the impact of political practice on constitutional change always conjures up an understanding of the relation between law and politics. The risk of a legal colonisation of political practice is concrete, as the dominant model of constitutional ordering is grounded on the premise that the main channel for constitutional change is legal and, in certain contexts, simply judicial. In other words, according to this model of constitutional ordering, constitutional change is not only certified by legal actors (and in particular by courts); it can also be brought about through judicial (or other legally centred) intervention.

First of all, according to the legal constitutionalist model, the law is constitutive of the space and possibilities of politics. Its role is at its most visible when it regulates the political system (e.g., by limiting the political parties, or regulating campaigning). In a sense, this is an intuitive idea as most parts of modern political systems are regulated by law, leaving the impression that without those legal rules, political action would simply be reduced to a series of irrational and unproductive moves. Obviously, constitutional law plays the key role in this narrative. Accordingly, the proponents of this view postulate that it is necessary to tie political practice to fundamental laws (Alexy 2002; Kumm 2004; Sager 1998), usually represented by constitutional rights (as classically advocated, for example, by Dworkin 1977). Often, this view of the constitutive status of law produces the idea that political power shall always be also constrained by law (see the description of the attitude defined as 'legalism' by Shklar 1964). Once located within this framework, political practice might be simply reduced to policy making and, therefore, undignified when confronted with constitutional practices because the latter would assume that form only when constituted by law. In this way, ordinary politics is not only fully institutionalised, but it is also harnessed to the aim of protecting and/or expanding existing constitutional guarantees.

Furthermore, for countries where constitutionality review is centralised, *ex post* and the supreme or constitutional court has the last word on these questions, constitutional change might actually happen directly via litigation in courts. Interestingly, this type of narrative has often found recognition in jurisdictions where constitutional review is strong and coupled with powerful and generally respected highest levels of judicial power. The USA, Germany, Israel and, perhaps only until recent times, Spain, provide important examples of this approach to constitutional change.[2] In these constitutional experiences, it is especially revealing to see how assertive the highest judicial bodies have been even on questions concerning the organisations of the political process. The most important example is given by the case law of the US Supreme Court on electoral funding. In *Buckley v. Valeo* (1976), the US Supreme Court upheld the constitutionality of a limit over campaign expenditures which also strengthened a two-party political system. In the more recent and seminal *Citizens United v. Federal Electoral Commission* (2010), the Supreme Court partially reversed

---

2 For the US, a direct statement of judicial constitutional transformation is represented by Rubenfeld (2005). As for Israel, see Hirschl (2004), Chapter 2; cf. Lerner (2011); on German constitutionalism see Hailbronner 2015; cf. Murkens (2013). For Spain, see Ferreres Comella (2013).

its previous stance and modified its interpretation of the First Amendment by extending the right to free speech to corporations. The court stated that any limitation on financial support for campaigning is equivalent to an unconstitutional interference with free speech. The Supreme Court has come to 'reject [...] the premise that the Government has an interest "in equalizing the relative ability of individuals and groups to influence the outcome of elections"'.[3] The decision contains not only a change in the classic anti-corruption rationale of previous case law, but it also dismisses political practice as cynical representative politics (Teachout 2014, p. 267). This last intervention has the potential of reshaping the form of the political process and the relation between political parties and lobbies. In brief, this type of judgment epitomizes all the virtues and vices of a legalised understanding of the political process and it actually directs the impact of politics on constitutional dynamics.

Another seminal decision which confirms the strictly constitutionalised nature of the political process is given by the famous *Lüth* decision of the German Constitutional Court.[4] The highest German judicial body excluded the reformed neo-Nazi party from the political process by banning it. The same court has also been a decisive protagonist when it comes to the shape of the German electoral law. Until the fall of the wall, the German Constitutional Court would uphold the 5% threshold for accessing proportional representation in the lower house and it has recently decided on the unconstitutionality of the same threshold for the European Parliament elections.

The crux of the relation between legal constitutionalism and political practice shall be seen in the thorny issue represented by the question of the judicial reviewability of constitutional amendments, both in *ex ante* modality (as it happens in Brazil) and in *ex post* (as it happens in a number of jurisdictions such as India and Colombia). Under this approach, constitutional change is always registered as already under the law; in other words, it gets closer to constituted than constituent power. In fact, legal constitutionalists aim to contain the creativity of constitutional amendments both by textual reference to constitutional norms and, most crucially, through judicial review by making reference either to constitutional principles or basic structures. As we shall see below, this viewpoint faces a stark alternative: either it concedes that the law is an objective value whose existence grounds political practice (and, in this way, it legalises constitutional change) or leaves to judges and judicial rationality the task of protecting the legal constitution from potential change. The problem that is highlighted is not so much a question of political or democratic deficit (although this is an important one), but it is rather epistemic. By postulating that law constitutes and constrains political power, legal constitutionalism does not provide enough resources for understanding when a constitutional change is taking place in a substantial manner, not to mention its different scale or impact upon the existing constitutional order. Therefore, from the perspective of legal constitutionalism only formal legal rules, not political practice, can recognise the existence and the magnitude of the constitutional change. Consequently, without accurate legal specifications, there is no criterion for drawing a distinction between constitutional transformation and amendment.

In brief, constitutional change is registered only when it takes a pre-defined legal form. Yet, in the end what we see is a confusion between a change according to a defined legal form and a substantial change. Accordingly, the creativity of political practice (as portrayed

---

3 558 U.S. at 34.
4 BVerfGE 2:1 (1952).

by, e.g., Crick 1962) is hugely underestimated, while the formal aspect of constitutional law is overestimated.

Constitutional change and political constitutionalism

Another important constitutional tradition and stream of thought shall be recognised and studied for the understanding of how political practice acts in and upon the constitutional system. This tradition has developed around the legacy of Commonwealth constitutionalism. In principle, this is a privileged observation point as this constitutional model understands the formation and development of an order as the direct outcome of the political process. Clearly, the basis for this model is provided by the British constitution and the constitutions of some of the countries previously belonging to the British Empire. In a nutshell, the main constitutional tenets of this model are two: parliamentary sovereignty and a flexible constitution (e.g., Loughlin 2011). Of course, there are other important aspects as well (the centrality of the rule of law and a peculiar version of separation of powers which makes the executive an emanation of Parliament), but said two tenets are the most important in order to understand constitutional change from the perspective of what could be called the 'Commonwealth model'. In fact, in this model the constitutional order is conceived as the structure of the political process itself. Most famously, John Griffith (1979) defined the constitution as 'what happens' and, accordingly, 'if nothing happens, that is constitutional as well'. In a sense, this is a pre-revolutionary model as it postulates that ordinary politics exhausts the possibilities of political practice. Therefore, within this constitutional scheme there is no difference between higher and ordinary forms of politics. Bringing Griffith's most famous dictum to its logical consequences, one might state that anything that happens is constitutional change or transformation. It is worth pausing and unpacking further what brings political constitutionalists to a reductionist view of constitutional change. Parliamentary sovereignty is, indeed, conceived in terms of party politics played out in parliament and this is where (in an exclusive manner) political practice happens and unfolds. However, in this way political practice is understood as electoral practice and parliamentary accountability in a way that abstracts it from the undergirding social relations.[5]

Moreover, given the centrality of the political process, this constitutional model has often conceived rights as political elements of the legal order and elevated political structures as the core content of the constitution. Of course, this means that the basic tenets of the political process—meaning, the primacy of parliament and the relevance of the electoral process—constitute the identity of the constitution, but these are rarely described as constitutional essentials. As illustrated by Stephen Gardbaum (2012), even this model might have undergone a constitutional transformation because of the rise of a rights-based legal and political culture, which has partially eroded the purely political nature of this constitutional model. It is worth pausing and unpacking Gardbaum's argument, as it illustrates the dynamics of the constitutional change of the political process in some Commonwealth countries and the impossibility of formalising the change as constitutional. Gardbaum maintains that the constitutional change affected Canada, the UK, New Zealand, and Australian provinces (Victoria), though these jurisdictions were all affected to different degrees. In the last 30 years, a constitutional transformation might have affected these countries but the political process that has brought it about does not seem to have peculiar

---

5 An exception is Bellamy (2007), according to whom the political constitution of the Commonwealth model is a mixed constitution.

traits. Gardbaum notes that these countries now represent a third way between political and legal models of constitutionalism. Canada is the country where the transformation is most visible, and this is because of the relative judicial activism of its Supreme Court. The interpretation of the Canadian Charter has given enough room to the Supreme Court to introduce and develop new rights previously not recognised, and such a change had not been initiated by the political branches. The UK Supreme Court and the New Zealand High Court have been more cautious, exhibiting clear signs of self-restraint. Concretely, the new model translates into the introduction of two peculiar institutions: a bill of rights (note that all these countries did not used to have one) and a legislative review of rights-compliance centrally organised as a parliamentary committee (Gardbaum 2012; Hiebert and Kelly 2015). Is this a constitutional transformation or just an evolution of the previous model?

Ultimately, political constitutionalism lacks any plausible criteria for understanding the status and nature of constitutional change. Anything can be constitutional change because any political practice, in its unfolding, produces some form of constitutional transformation of the content of the constitution. In a nutshell, the risk for political constitutionalism is that it understands constitutional change in terms of a flat living constitution (Strauss 2010) and in this way does not provide any distinctive analysis of the contribution of political practice to the formation of the constitutional order. The meaning of the living constitution changes according to the changes of political practice. The shortcoming of such a view is most visible in the absence of any reflexivity about the assumptions undergirding the political process and the deeper constitutional change that the transformation of one of them would bring about.

Perhaps, within the constellation of political constitutionalism, one might think of an exception that does not come from the Commonwealth context. At the theoretical and historical level of analysis, the most encompassing attempt to capture the dynamic between the political process and the legal system in a balanced way has been provided by Bruce Ackerman, in a series of volumes on the constitutional history of the US (Ackerman 1991, 1998, 2013). Ackerman's effort represents the most encompassing account of constitutional change from a relative political constitutionalist perspective because, unlike classic political constitutionalism, it recognises (1) the difference between higher and ordinary forms of lawmaking, linked to the constitutional recognition of popular sovereignty[6] and (2) that the initiating moment of a constitutional transformation comes from a political impulse in the form of a movement taking over the driver's seat of a political party (Ackerman 2013, ch. 2). Ackerman has tried to understand the development of the American constitutional model by pointing to cycles that unfold by confrontation and/or collaboration among different branches of government. This logic unfolds both at the horizontal level (where the three classic governmental functions interact and conflict) and at the vertical level, between states and central government. In this way, his account actually tries to strike a synthesis between the political and the legal level. The compromise between the two systems is achieved by recognising, on the political side, the initiative of constitutional change, and on the legal side, the recognition and formalisation of the constitutional transformation. In his scheme, this process unfolds in different stages, but what is key is that the final translation of

---

6 In the US context, a similar sensitivity is shared by popular constitutionalism. As shown by Kramer (2004), according to the doctrine of popular constitutionalism political practice becomes constitutionally salient when it instantiates acts of 'the people'.

the impulses coming from the political system happens through judicial means, that is, when the Supreme Court ratifies the transformation and grafts it onto the current constitutional regime. In the case of the New Deal, for example, the 'switch in time' becomes the moment of formalisation that a deep constitutional transformation has occurred. Ultimately, Ackerman's is the most sophisticated and balanced version of a political perspective over constitutional change. However, despite the fact that his theory allows the New Deal and the Civil Rights movement to be seen as constitutional moments, other potential changes are reduced to ordinary politics and remain invisible to his scheme.[7]

Finally, one can find traces of a certain kind of political constitutionalism in those countries where formal constitutional change has to be ratified not by supreme or constitutional courts, but by the political process itself. More specifically, in certain countries referendums can be held in order to instigate or confirm a constitutional change (for an overview, see Tierney 2012). This enlargement of the scope of analysis beyond the political system of parties has to be welcomed. Political parties might have the upper hand on referendums, but there is a number of sufficient cases that prove they are also open to the intervention of other social sectors. The study of referendum (and of popular lawmaking initiatives, for example) is a clear indicator that political practice relevant to constitutional change cannot be limited to a party-based political system, but has to be extended to the wider public and often has to be related to either forms of authoritarianism (the confirmation of the political decisions of an autocrat) or, to the contrary, of social and political movements.

The material study of constitutional change

The juxtaposition between legal and political constitutionalism is based around ideal-types and should not be taken too strictly. As has often been remarked, these two models, though rooted in two different constitutional traditions, help in framing the discourse on comparative constitutional change. They both thematise constitutional change as the outcome of a process that is ultimately sanctioned either politically or legally. The advantages of thinking about constitutional change according to the model of the political constitution are its flexibility, its capacity to adapt to changing circumstances, and the avoidance of an ossified and impoverished political process. The advantages of thinking about constitutional change according to the model of the legal constitution are to be seen in its capacity to control and steer constitutional change and in putting the emphasis on legal and constitutional certainty. The idea of a higher law presiding over political practices is also supposed to deliver a more robust version of the rule of law. Obviously, both models exist ideally only in abstract, while in all constitutional experiences one can find a different mix of both.

However, both approaches are missing an essential aspect of modern constitutional orders when it comes to understanding constitutional change. The model of the political constitution basically portrays the role of the political process as the engine of a living constitution, constantly morphing into an evolving constitutional order. According to this

---

7 The point is that Ackerman's reconstruction is heavily normative as only those changes that expand the constitution are deemed to be constitutional moments, while other political practices potentially reductive of the constitutional order are excluded. This difference might find a normative justification, but in terms of the analysis of constitutional change, it is ineffective.

perspective, the law will have then to register what happens in the political sphere, but the constitution is reduced to a thin procedural fact. The model of the legal constitution, on the other hand, entails that law is constitutive of politics and by changing law one can change politics as well (or, at least, tame it and make it more rational and less interest-based). When, according to legal constitutionalists, political practice is constrained by constitutional law, then arbitrary political change can be severely curbed. Be that as it may, in the case of political constitutionalism, political practice and constitutional order are fundamentally the same. Therefore, any change in political practice entails a change in the constitutional order, no matter the size or the depth of change. The model of the legal constitution suffers from a similar problem. Any change of the constitution is valid and effective as long as (1) it is registered by a certain form and/or procedure of the law and (2) it is adopted according to the proper procedure, be it a constitutional amendment or a decision of the constitutional court, and all of this independently from the magnitude and the substance of the change in society.

In this section, it is assumed that it is possible to avoid the Scylla of legal constitutionalism and the Charybdis of political constitutionalism by adopting a material understanding of the formation and development of the constitutional order. Such an approach has an important and rather dated pedigree (see Heller 1996; Mortati 2019; Romano 2017; Schmitt 2008) which finds its intellectual roots in the first wave of classic legal institutionalism.[8] A key tenet of this theoretical approach is the connection between the development of institutions and the social order. Legal institutionalists emphasised the social origins of the legal order, a link captured by the famous dictum *ubi societas, ibi ius* (Romano 2017, p. 32). Unsurprisingly, they interpreted the constitutional order as deeply intertwined with the political and social nature of the community.

The key constitutional intuition is that there is a crucial distinction between the constitutional order and constitutional law (Schmitt 2008, pp. 70–75; Schupmann 2017, ch. 3). Therefore, a lot of their concerns were directed at the maintenance of homogeneity (Heller and Schmitt) or the integration of social relations and factions into the constitutional order (Romano and Mortati). Be that as it may,[9] the relevant intuition shared by these authors revolves around the juristic idea that social practices have to be selected and harmonised in order to be jurisgenerative. For this reason, the material study reconnects political practice and constitutional change to the underlying social structure and its substantial formation and reproduction. In a nutshell, the material level of constitutional analysis observes and studies the internal connection between societal formation and constitutional ordering. This approach is the opposite of the standard conceptions of how political and legal constitutionalism see the relation between society, political practice and constitutional law. According to the material analysis, political practice is not an instantiation of the autonomy of the political (as celebrated by political constitutionalists). It is rather a way of organising and holding together a certain configuration of social relations, and this assemblage contains seeds of constitutional normativity.

Crucial for the material analysis of constitutional development is to take into account the essential tenets that make up the identity of the constitutional order. First, there must be subjects or bearers capable of imposing and sustaining the order. These subjects are often political parties, but they are not the only ones. Other subjects can also become bearers of

---

8 For a recent reconstruction see Loughlin (2017).
9 This is not the space for a reconstruction of this stream of constitutional thought.

the constitutional order. A classic example is represented by the military or, usually in smaller states, by royal families. Moreover, a plurality of subjects (an alliance) can also become the subjective bearer of the material constitutional order. Organisational capacities are a key requirement for these types of subjects as they have to be able to order important sectors of society. Second, a set of concrete social relations and institutions represent another essential tenet. These are marks of the identity of the constitutional order and are embedded in its materiality. Examples can be provided by the type of property that is regulated and protected, the relation between Church and State, or by the organisation of labour relations. A third core aspect is given by the fundamental political goals that all constitutional orders strive to achieve. Not only is there a teleological element entailed by this assumption, but it is possible to observe a strict continuity between social relations, subjects and fundamental goals. The latter cannot last without the support of subjects and the undergirding base of certain social relations. Once this constellation and its intimate unity are accepted, it is also necessary to recognise that other subjects, other social relations and other political goals are excluded from the constitutional order. Decisively, the consequences of this approach on constitutional knowledge are quite important ones. The material analysis is, at its core, a different way to observe and appreciate constitutional reality. Like legal constitutionalism, the material approach maintains that there is a rigid core at the basis of every constitutional order, but this core is grounded in the material organisation of the social setting. Like political constitutionalism, the material study privileges political subjects as the main bearers of the constitutional orders, but it also includes less formal political actors, institutions and fundamental political aims. When a change in one of the mentioned tenets has a remarkable impact on social relations, then politically driven constitutional transformation has to be recognised.

Finally, all the preceding observations do not drive toward the marginalisation of the formal constitution. To the contrary: the formal constitution represents another important aspect for the material study of the constitutional order. In fact, in the vast majority of cases, the formal constitution is a good indicator of the most important features of a specific constitutional order. However, this is not always the case and one of the epistemic added values of the material study is that it provides a methodology for ascertaining whether changes in the formal constitution do have a substantial impact or are just cosmetic interventions over the material level. The opposite case can be true as well: despite the lack of formal constitutional change, a transformation has occurred at the material level which amounts to a fundamental alteration.

The materiality of constitutional change in practice

Looking at the formal constitutional arrangements and their formal change does not always give the full picture with regard to constitutional change in a given state. There are instances where major constitutional changes occur without any changes to the formal constitution. Likewise, formally major constitutional changes can result in little or no real change to the political system of a state.

In order to demonstrate the merit of adopting a material perspective in making sense of constitutional change, we examine cases in three countries in two groups, where legal and political constitutionalism fail to satisfactorily identify and explain constitutional change. First, we look at the adoption of the 1992 Basic Law of Governance in Saudi Arabia, which is the first comprehensive written constitutional document adopted in the country, and at the adoption of the 1999 Constitution in Switzerland, which replaced the 1874 Swiss Constitution. These two cases are examples where major formal constitutional change did not bring about change to the political system. In those cases, it is necessary to find the proper resources for understanding the constitutional role of political practice. Second, we look at the difficult process through which the ban on wearing religious headscarves by female students on university campuses was lifted in Turkey. The Turkish case demonstrates that it is possible to effect constitutional change without formal constitutional procedures when changes in political arrangements result in changes in political practice, in particular when they have an impact on fundamental social relations. In opposing ways, these two groups of cases show that it is crucial to look at whether there is a major change in political practice or political system in order to identify and understand constitutional change. Only the material study of these experiences can avoid false positives (formal constitutional change without substantial transformation) and negatives (substantial transformation without formal constitutional change).

Formal-immaterial constitutional change

Saudi Arabia

The Kingdom of Saudi Arabia presents a good example to demonstrate the value of the materialist study of the constitution in explaining constitutional change. The adoption of the Basic Law of Governance in 1992 was the first constitutional codification in the country, yet, it introduced virtually no change to the political system of Saudi Arabia. This, therefore, is a good example of a significant formal constitutional change without a material constitutional change.

Until 1992, Saudi Arabia did not have a codified modern constitution or a constitutional document. The Qur'an was regarded as the constitution of the state, and sovereignty belonged to the monarch, who also acted as the religious leader (Al-marayati 1968, p. 293). The teachings of the prophet Muhammad formed the basis of the Saudi jurisprudence and the interpretation of these teachings and the Qur'an were made by qualified Islamic scholars (Al-marayati 1968, p. 293). However, with the king as the ultimate political and religious authority, the Saudi political system operated within a framework of absolute monarchy.

A promise of making a constitution for Saudi Arabia was made by King Abd-al Aziz as early as in 1932 (Al-fahad 2005, pp. 376–377), after the unification of various areas ruled by the Saudis (Brown 2002, p. 59). However, this promise was fulfilled only in the aftermath of the Gulf War with the enactment of the Basic Law of Governance. In the meantime, there have been minor modernisations of the political system, such as the formation of the Council of Ministers in 1953 and a further royal decree in 1958 that formalised the duties and functions of the Council of Ministers and gave it legislative and executive functions, although the ultimate authority continued to rest with the king (Al-marayati 1968, pp. 294–295). Still, until 1992, the political system of Saudi Arabia operated within an informal constitutional framework. The institutional set-up was a derivative of the Qur'an and no separation of powers existed until 1992 (Mallat 2007, p. 160).

The Basic Law of 1992 was drafted in secrecy and with no public debate, and did not have a *constitutive* claim, as it was 'derived from the goodwill of the sovereign' (Al-fahad 2005, pp. 384–385). The Basic Law explicitly states in its first article that the Qur'an and the Sunna (words and acts) of Muhammad are the constitution of Saudi Arabia.[10] It makes no reference to popular sovereignty and provides for no separation of powers in the constitutionalist sense (Al-fahad 2005, p. 385). For these reasons, the adoption of a formal constitutional document in

---

10 Article 1 of the Basic Law of Governance (Saudi Arabia).

Saudi Arabia has been labelled by an observer as an example of 'ornamental constitutionalism' and the whole project as 'the codification of the status quo' (Al-fahad 2005, p. 385). As it introduces no change to the political system of Saudi Arabia and does not even claim to introduce constitutionalist elements to the Saudi political order, unlike many constitutions in the region, it is not regarded as a façade constitution and it is largely followed (Brown 2002, p. 7).

One of the peculiarities of the Saudi Basic Law, therefore, is that its adoption formalised the (already existing) material constitution of Saudi Arabia. In this sense, there is a close overlap between the formal constitution and the material constitution, i.e. the Basic Law is far from being a sham constitution. This is because it is an honest constitution (Al-fahad 2005, p. 389), it is different from façade constitutions (like post-2017 Turkey's, USSR's or Saddam Hussein's constitutions) in that it does not claim to introduce a constitutionalist government. The adoption of the Basic Law in 1992, therefore, is not a constitutional change, but rather the formalisation of the material constitution.

From the perspective of legal constitutionalism, this constitutional change would be said to be a major constitutional change and to have created a new constitutional order for Saudi Arabia. This is due to legal constitutionalism's focus on pre-defined domestic or universal forms as to identify constitutional change. From this perspective, the adoption of a new basic law that institutionalises the political practice in a country previously without a codified constitution is a major constitutional change. However, this approach does not take into account that this is not a change to the constitutional organisation of the state—it is merely a rebranding of it. Legal constitutionalism, therefore, has a limited capacity to identify constitutional change, as it largely ignores the material change to political practice.

A purely political analysis of the Saudi Arabia case would not provide the wrong outcome, as it would be able to detect that it was not a substantial constitutional change. However, one might question whether a purely political analysis would grasp the right reasons behind it, as the inquiry would be limited to the formal political system, which in this case did not change at all.

The point of the material analysis of the constitution is seen here in its capability to explain the merits of what is formally presented as a constitutional change. The material study of the constitution calls the observer to analyse the previous and subsequent political systems in a given constitutional order in order to identify and explain constitutional change. In this example from Saudi Arabia, it identifies no constitutional change, despite the fact that the Basic Law had been presented as a formal constitutional change. Rather, the new constitution is a rationalisation of the undergirding material constitution and it preserves the same bearers of the constitution, its essential institutions, and the fundamental political aims.

Switzerland

Switzerland's total revision of its federal constitution in 1999 is another example of *formal* constitutional change without material constitutional change. Although the 1999 Constitution replaced the previous 1874 Constitution with a complete repackaging, it did not change any of the fundamental underpinnings of the Swiss political system.

The foundations of the Swiss federal political arrangement set by the first federal constitution of 1848 are still in place today even after two total revisions of the constitution (Biaggini 2011, p. 303). Rather than focusing solely on the latest total revision in 1999 itself, in order to understand constitutional change in Switzerland, it is more pertinent to pay attention to what happened between the two constitutional replacements, i.e. between 1874 and 1999 (Biaggini 2011, p. 314). The main constitutional developments in this period are identified as the 'expansion of the instruments of direct democracy, progressive centralisation—still with considerable cantonal autonomy, and the strengthening of *Rechtsstaatlichkeit* (Rule of Law)' (Biaggini 2011, p. 317). The 1999 Constitution represented the consolidation of these developments (Biaggini 2011, pp. 317–324), rather than effecting such changes to the Swiss political system. The total revision in 1999 also served to *codify* the previously unwritten constitutional principles such as the principle of legality, proportionality, good faith (Biaggini 2011, p. 325).

This constitutional reform for total revision was first proposed by the Federal Council and the Parliament with the aim of editing the wording of the Swiss federal constitution (Fleiner 2013, p. 344). Among the goals of adopting a 'new' constitution was to 'ensure that all fundamental rights would be clearly stipulated in an up-to-date text corresponding to the latest jurisprudence of the Supreme Court and to international standards' (Haller 2002, p. 261). It was therefore not presented as a major change to the constitutional system but rather a modernisation of the existing constitutional arrangement of Switzerland.

The 1999 Constitution consequently built upon the reforms made under the 1874 Constitution and limited itself to the reorganisation of the structure of the constitutional text and introduced no major constitutional change (see Barbera 2016, pp. 10–11; Grote 2013). However, as this is a new formal constitution, from the perspective of legal constitutionalism, its adoption created a brand new constitutional order for Switzerland, with a break in the constitutional history of Switzerland.

Given that the 1999 Constitution was also adopted through political means and by respecting the rule of law, it is fair to assume that political constitutionalism would still interpret the change as a fundamental one because it is the outcome of a super-majoritarian political consensus and it produced a whole new constitutional text. However, this would fail to examine that constitutional change from a more reflexive perspective and this is not possible if the political system is taken as a given (as it usually is with political constitutionalism) and its fundamental aims are not at the centre of the analysis.

The point of the material study of the constitution is seen here in its ability to identify where real change to political practice took place. In the Swiss case, it is not the 1999 Constitution that brought about constitutional change. This total revision merely modernised the structure and content of the constitutional text but introduced no significant change to the political system. Therefore, while the adoption of the 1999 Constitution is presented as an important formal constitutional change, it is of little consequence with regard to its effect on the political system of Switzerland. In fact, Switzerland's democratic principles, federalism and main political subjects were not substantially transformed by the 1999 Constitution.

Informal-material constitutional change

Turkey

A relatively more recent example of constitutional change drawn from Turkey demonstrates the relevance and significance of the material study of constitutional change from the opposite perspective. While in Saudi Arabia the adoption of the Basic Law was a major *formal* constitutional change with little material constitutional consequence, Turkey went through a *material* constitutional change despite the failure of a formal constitutional change attempt. In this instance, a constitutional change that could not be achieved through formal constitutional amendment was achieved through a series of ordinary administrative decisions. Consequently, we are faced with a *material* constitutional change by means of legal change at the formally sub-constitutional (even sub-legislation) level. What makes this case peculiar (in contrast with other informal constitutional changes) is that the very same change had been attempted to be made by a formal constitutional amendment and it had caused a major constitutional crisis.

In 2008, the AKP government decided to put an end to the headscarf ban for female students on university campuses. As they did not have the qualified majority required to pass a constitutional amendment, with the support of the ultra-nationalist MHP, the AKP passed an amendment to Articles 10 and 42 of the Constitution, which provide for, respectively, the principle of equality before the law and the right to education.[11] Although the proposed textual changes to the constitution did not mention anything specific to headscarves or Islamic attire in general, the official justifications in the amendment bill stated that the amendment aimed to do away with the headscarf ban.[12] As this was a contentious issue between the religious conservatives and secularists at the time, the ultra-secularist CHP took the amendment to the Constitutional Court for annulment. The Turkish Constitutional Court struck down the amendment on the grounds that it had violated the unamendable principle of secularism.[13] Moreover, this attempt at constitutional change formed the basis of the party closure case against the AKP which resulted in a partial cut to state funding to the party (Bâli 2013, p. 689). This represented the tipping point for the headscarf saga in Turkey. These judgments by the Constitutional Court were preceded by numerous judgments upholding the ban by the administrative judiciary over the past two decades, one of which was unsuccessfully challenged before the European Court of Human Rights.[14]

As a response to this, among other judicial activist challenges to its authority such as the 2007 presidential election crisis and the party closure case, the AKP decided to make major judicial reforms and put these reforms to a referendum in 2010 (Bâli 2013, p. 691). This was a critical turning point in Turkish constitutional history as 58% of the electorate voted in favour of the reforms that allowed a major overhaul of the judicial system especially by reforming the appointments to the Constitutional Court and the High Council of Judges and Prosecutors, which made it possible for AKP to pack and unpack the apex courts (Bâli 2013, pp. 691–692). As a result of these reforms, the power balance in the high judiciary shifted toward more liberal or conservative judges as opposed to the earlier secularist hold in the judiciary. After the 2010 reforms, it became inconceivable for the judiciary to stand in the way of lifting the headscarf ban.

Indeed, the ban was lifted virtually effortlessly, given the magnitude of the 2008 constitutional crisis over the issue. The chairman of the Higher Education Board (YÖK), which oversees universities in Turkey, sent a formal letter to Istanbul University on 27 July 2010 stating that a lecturer could not remove a student from a lecture hall for covering her hair. Although the execution of a similar letter by the YÖK chairman had been suspended in March 2008 by the Council of State,[15] this time the letter stood, and the ban was lifted incrementally across universities in Turkey.

---

11 Law No. 5735, 9 February 2018.
12 General Reasons for this amendment can be reached at <www2.tbmm.gov.tr/d23/2/2-0141.pdf> accessed 6 February 2019.
13 Turkish Constitutional Court, E. 2008/16, K. 2008/116, 5 June 2008, 45/2 AYMKD 1195.
14 *Leyla Şahin v. Turkey* [GC], no. 44,774/98, ECHR 2005-XI.
15 Danıştay 8. Dairesi (8th Chamber of the Council of State of Turkey), E. 2008/1501, 10 March 2008.

Consequently, what could not be achieved through formal constitutional change has been achieved through an ordinary administrative act. This example from Turkey shows the merit of the material study of constitutional change. A formal constitutional amendment failed to bring about the intended outcome of lifting the headscarf ban. This outcome, however, was achieved by a simple administrative act *after* a major overhaul of the political system. The significance of the arrangement of the political system in effecting constitutional change is clear in this example. The lifting was obtained, in the end, by a reorganisation of the political system and the main bearers of the Turkish Constitution.

From the perspective of legal constitutionalism, the lifting of the headscarf ban is not a *constitutional* change as the 2008 constitutional amendment failed and the formal constitution stayed the same. However, this perspective does not account for the change in the political system—the system that did not allow the lifting of the headscarf ban in 2008 with the great resistance yet came to smoothly allow it after 2010.

From the perspective of political constitutionalism, it is difficult to understand the relevance of the headscarf case. In the end, the outcome of that conflict is simply seen as the end result of ordinary politics. The fact that administrative law was the legal tool mobilised to achieve that end strengthens the idea that the whole saga was about ordinary politics. Therefore, political constitutionalism would see in that conflict not a constitutional conflict, but an evolution of the living constitution.

The main takeaway of our study of the Turkish case on the headscarf ban is that in order to understand the dynamics of *constitutional* change, at times it can be futile to look at the formal constitution and the formal amendments to it. As an alternative perspective, the material study of the constitution calls to look at where the political power forms and develops—in this case, not only the change in the composition of the Turkish Constitutional Court and the Council of State, but the new political forces rising within the Turkish political system that effected such change—to make sense of whether a constitutional transformation took place.

References

Ackerman, Bruce, *We the People: Foundations* (Harvard University Press 1991).

Ackerman, Bruce, *We the People: Transformations* (Harvard University Press 1998).

Ackerman, Bruce, *We the People: The Civil Rights Revolution* (Harvard University Press 2013).

Alexy, Robert, *A Theory of Constitutional Rights* (Oxford University Press 2002).

Al-fahad, Abdulaziz H., 'Ornamental Constitutionalism: The Saudi Basic Law of Governance' (2005) 30 *The Yale Journal of International Law* 375–396.

Al-marayati, Abid A., *Middle Eastern Constitutions and Electoral Laws* (Frederick A. Praeger 1968).

Bâli, Aslı, 'Courts and Constitutional Transition: Lessons from the Turkish Case' (2013) 11(3) *International Journal of Constitutional Law* 666–701.

Barbera, Augusto, *La costituzione della Repubblica Italiana* (Giuffré 2016).

Bellamy, Richard, *Political Constitutionalism* (Cambridge University Press 2007).

Biaggini, Giovanni, 'Switzerland' in Oliver Dawn and Fusaro Carlo (eds), *How Constitutions Change: A Comparative Study* (Hart Publishing 2011) 303–327.

Crick, Bernard, *In Defence of Politics* (The University of Chicago Press 1962).

Dworkin, Ronald, *Taking Rights Seriously* (Harvard University Press 1977).

Ewing, Keith, 'The Resilience of the Political Constitution' (2013) 14(12) *German Law Journal* 2111–2136.

Ferreres Comella, Victor, *The Constitution of Spain: A Contextual Analysis* (Hart Publishing 2013).

Fleiner, Thomas, 'Constitutional Revision: The Case of Switzerland' in Contiades Xenophon (ed), *Engineering Constitutional Change: A Comparative Perspective on Europe, Canada and the USA* (Routledge 2013) 337–358.

Gardbaum, Stephen, *The New Commonwealth Model of Constitutionalism* (Cambridge University Press 2012).

Griffith, John, 'The Political Constitution' (1979) 42(1) *Modern Law Review* 1–21.

Grote, Rainer, *The Swiss Confederation: Introductory Note* [online] (Max Planck Institute 2013) [viewed 6 February 2019]. Available from: http://oxcon.ouplaw.com/view/10.1093/law:ocw/law-ocw-cm777.document.1/law-ocw-cm777#law-ocw-cm777-div1-1

Hailbronner, Michaela, *Traditions and Transformations: The Rise of German Constitutionalism* (Oxford University Press 2015).

Haller, Walter, 'The New Swiss Constitution: Foreign and International Influences' (2002) 30(2) *International Journal of Legal Information* 256–264.

Heller, Hermann, 'The Nature and Structure of the State' (1996) 18(3) *Cardozo Law Review* 1139–1227.

Hiebert, Janet and Kelly, James, *Parliamentary Bills of Rights* (Cambridge University Press 2015).

Hirschl, Ran, *Juristocracy* (Harvard University Press 2004).

Kramer, Larry, *The People Themselves* (Oxford University Press 2004).

Kumm, Mattias, 'The Legitimacy of International Law: A Constitutionalist Framework of Analysis' (2004) 15(5) *European Journal of International Law* 907–933.

Lerner, Hannah, *Making Constitutions in Divided Societies* (Cambridge University Press 2011).

Loughlin, Martin, *The British Constitution* (Oxford University Press 2011).

Loughlin, Martin, *Political Jurisprudence* (Oxford University Press 2017).

Mallat, Chibli, *Introduction to Middle Eastern Law* (Oxford University Press 2007).

Mortati, Costantino, *The Constitution in the Material Sense* (Routledge 2019).

Murkens, Jo, *From Empire to Union* (Oxford University Press 2013).

Romano, Santi, *The Legal Order* (Routledge 2017).

Rubenfeld, Jed, *Revolution by Judiciary* (Harvard University Press 2005).

Sager, Lawrence, 'The Domain of Constitutional Justice' in Alexander Larry (ed), *Constitutionalism: Philosophical Foundations* (Cambridge University Press 1998) 235–270.

Schmitt, Carl, *Constitutional Theory* (Duke University Press 2008).

Schupmann, Benjamin, *Carl Schmitt's Constitutional and State Theory* (Oxford University Press 2017).

Shklar, Judith, *Legalism* (Harvard University Press 1964).

Strauss, David A., *The Living Constitution* (Oxford University Press 2010).

Teachout, Zephyr, *Corruption in America* (Harvard University Press 2014).

Tierney, Stephen, *Constitutional Referendums* (Oxford University Press 2012).

Tomkins, Adam, *Our Republican Constitution* (Hart Publishing 2005).

Waldron, Jeremy, *Law and Disagreement* (Oxford University Press 1999).

PART IV

Contemporary challenges in the theory and practice of comparative constitutional change

17

CONSTITUENT POWER AND EUROPEAN CONSTITUTIONALISM

Chris Thornhill

Introduction

This chapter discusses the role of constituent power in European constitutionalism in two senses, and in two perspectives. First, it addresses the classical theory of constituent power, and it examines the linkage between this doctrine and processes of constitution making in national polities in Europe. Second, it addresses the more distinctive application of this doctrine in recent patterns of constitutional formation, focused in particular on the interaction between national polities and the European Union (EU). It therefore analyses the importance of constituent power in European constitutionalism in the broad sense. In both emphases, it sets out a sceptical theory of constituent power, arguing that, if viewed closely, this theory has only limited relevance for our actual understanding of constitutional processes, and, if applied literally, it cannot illuminate constitutional realities in either dimension of European constitutionalism. The chapter concludes by outlining ways in which constituent power might be rephrased so that it can be used more reflexively in contemporary constitutional debate.

The national *pouvoir constituant*: the false translation of facts into norms

The theory of constituent power is broadly conceived as a doctrine of governmental legitimacy, which states that a political system can only legitimately perform its core functions if it reflects founding decisions of a sovereign people, and if the exercise of political power is constrained by constitutional norms established in such decisions. Central to this doctrine is the assumption that, in its original sovereign form, the people stand outside and prior to the political order to which they are subject, and they authorize the constitution of this order by dictating primary legal principles of government, qua constituent power. Central to this doctrine, likewise, is that claim that elected legislative bodies are the most important organs of government, and, within constraints defined by the original acts of constituent power, legislatures are charged with responsibility for translating the will of the people into positive form.[1] In its original formulation, this doctrine was inseparable from

---

1 One account argues that the French Revolution witnessed the birth of a 'unique conception of legislative authority', capable of radically transforming society as a whole: Christophe Achaintre, *L'instance législative dans la pensée*

discourses of nation building and national sovereignty in early modern Europe and in societies outside Europe under European influence. In the European context, this doctrine gave clear expression to the process in which social agents in late feudal societies extricated themselves from private structures of authority and projected themselves, distinctively, as national citizens; this culminated in the revolutionary decades at the end of the eighteenth century. On one hand, the belief that citizens were entitled to insist that the political institutions to which they were subject were accountable to a collectively constituted system of legal norms played a key role in bringing the formation of nation states toward conclusion.[2] On the other hand, early formulations of this doctrine claimed that, if a polity is centred around collective acts of sovereign citizens, broadly linked to the territorial structure of a nation, institutions within the political system have primacy over all other institutions within national society. In these respects, the doctrine of constituent power closely reflected actual sociological processes of structural integration and institution building that characterized early modern societies. Above all, this doctrine articulated and consolidated processes of political centralization and legal positivization, in which institutions connected to the emerging central state acquired a monopoly of power in society, supplanting the patchwork legal orders of pre-modern societies in Europe. In this early period of constitutional reflection, constituent power was invoked as part of a radical process of societal and institutional reshaping, and it served to underpin a legitimational transfer from the monarchical corporations of the *ancien régime* to the more centralized institutions of newly created revolutionary republics.[3] Although in essence a description of sociological process, however, the theory of constituent power subsequently obtained great normative significance. Throughout the subsequent history of modern political and constitutional reflection, the exercise of constituent power has been presented as the condition *sine qua non* of a legitimate national political system, such that law enjoying legitimacy is frequently perceived as a directly authorized constitutional enactment of a national will.[4] Indeed, the presumption in this doctrine that the people can speak in a voice that is prior to, and so overrides, all other law, has held an enduring appeal for constitutionalists, especially those at the more volitional or republican end of the spectrum of constitutional theory.[5]

Despite its early descriptive importance, however, the concept of constituent power played only a limited role in the formation of constitutional systems with real societal force. This concept was not cogently articulated in the revolutionary era, and the core distinction between the *pouvoir constituant* and the *pouvoir constitué* was not cemented at this time, at least in Europe.[6] In

---

constitutionelle révolutionaire (1789–1799) (Dalloz 2008) 21. Accordingly, during the French Revolution, Saint-Just stated that the 'legislative body is like the unmoving light that distinguishes the form of all things …. It is the essence of liberty': Louis Antoine Léon de Saint-Just, *Esprit de la Révolution et de la Constitution de France* (Beuvin 1791) 102.

2 The emergence of this doctrine in revolutionary Europe spelled out both a principle of legitimacy for the national state and a principle of territorial unification for the societies in which national states were located. See discussion in Dieter Gosewinkel, *Einbürgern und Ausschließen: Die Nationalisierung der Staatsangehörigkeit vom Deutschen Bund bis zur Bundesrepublik Deutschland* (Vandenhoeck und Ruprecht 2001).

3 Emmanuel Joseph Sieyès, *Qu'est-ce que le Tiers-Etat?* second edition (Paris 1789).

4 This is illustrated by Dieter Grimm, who considers the 'distinction between *pouvoir constituant* and *pouvoir constitué*' as 'constitutive' of modern constitutionalism. See Dieter Grimm, *Die Zukunft der Verfassung II: Auswirkungen von Europäisierung und Globalisierung* (Suhrkamp 2012) 223. In parallel, see Martin Loughlin, 'The Concept of Constituent Power' (2014) 13(2) *European Journal of Political Theory* 218–237.

5 Antonio Negri, *Insurgencies: Constituent Power and the Modern State*, translated by M. Boscagli (University of Minnesota Press 1999) 2.

6 In revolutionary France after 1789, parliamentary sittings could not easily be divided from constituent assemblies. See Emmanuel Joseph Sieyès, *Collection des écrits* (C. F. Cramer, 17–) 97; Marquis de [Marie-Joseph Paul Yves Roch Gilbert du Motier] Lafayette, *Mémoires, correspondences et manuscrits*, in 12 vols (Hauman et Comp 1839) VII, 50.

revolutionary France after 1789, the polity in which the theory of constituent power first assumed significance in framing conditions of government, constitutions enacted by the exercise of constituent power were short-lived, and from 1799 until 1946 constitutional rule in France was *specifically not based* on constituent power. Indeed, except for the first part of the short-lived Second Republic, the basic order of constitutional democracy in nineteenth-century France was instituted either through Bonapartist or through positivistic patterns of legal norm construction. Outside France, constitutional rule was scarcely consolidated until the 1860s. Although after 1815 some European societies developed systems of representation that allowed members of a thin elite stratum of society to acquire roles in government, the principle that government was originally authorized by the people, and that it was legitimated by the popular participation in political process, found no reflection in reality. No polity in Europe had conducted extensive popular enfranchisement until 1848, when France and Switzerland enacted laws that facilitated some exercise of mass (male) suffrage. Otherwise, broad-based electoral participation was very limited until the 1860s. Moreover, even after the 1860s, constitutions that regulated early democracy were not put into effect by constituent actors. On the contrary, the most important constitutions created in Europe between 1848 and 1914 – for example, the Constitution of unified Italy, the Constitution of unified Germany (1871), and the constitutional laws of the French Third Republic (1875) – were documents that were either simply transferred from already existing polities, or that spelled out brief guidelines to cover the technical functions of state.[7] Overall, there appears a deep disjuncture between the theory of constituent power articulated in and after 1789 and the actual constitution-making processes that first shaped the rise of democracy. The revolutionary concept of constituent power was largely forgotten after 1815, and, of constitutions created by acts of constituent power in revolutionary Europe, none survived.[8]

Despite the fact that constituent power proved irrelevant for the early emergence of states with democratic features, the concept of constituent power long retained a powerful hold on the European constitutional imagination. Eventually, this concept acquired renewed importance in the second period of intensified national formation in Europe – the period following the outbreak of war in 1914. At this time, this concept again coincided with deep processes of accelerated centralization and institution building, and, once more, it projected a description of popular sovereignty to cover and reflect deep-lying patterns of societal transformation. In this period, this concept became a central element in the campaign against positivist constructions of public law in European states, and it formed part of a wide assault on the limited principles of liberal statehood endorsed by much constitutional theory of the later nineteenth century. Between 1914 and 1918, the idea became widespread, especially at extreme positions on the political spectrum, that a constitutional order must derive its legitimacy from a deep and immediate relation to the objective will of the national people, and that all law that deflects from this immediate relation is illegitimate, perhaps even perilous for the stability and security of the polity in question.[9] In its second historical articulation, the concept of constituent power was clearly shaped by the

---

7 The constitution of Italy from unification onwards was the Statuto Albertino, which was created for Piedmont in 1848, and then extended in the 1860s, with no express popular mandate, as the founding document for the united Italian nation state. The German Constitution of 1871 was in essence the temporary constitution of the North German Federation, written by Bismarck while on holiday in late 1866. The Third Republic of France, the major European (male) democracy before 1918, comprised three short pieces of legislation, which eschewed discussion of most fundamental constitutional questions and avoided all mention of popular sovereignty.

8 The only qualified exception is the 1814 Constitution of Norway.

9 See the classic expression in Carl Schmitt, *Verfassungslehre* (Duncker und Humblot 1928).

experience of popular mobilization in the First World War, and it expressed a deeply militarized ideal of constituent participation in government. After 1918, this concept often coalesced with doctrines of commissarial or plebiscitary constitutional legitimation,[10] and it was often cited as a legitimational principle to justify and support political systems that today we would not easily recognize as belonging to the democratic family.

Despite the rebirth of constituent power after 1914, however, it remains difficult to observe this concept as a significant cornerstone of democratic constitutionalism. In different ways, the acute crisis of democracy that was experienced in Europe – and beyond – in the 1920s and 1930s was closely, and probably causally, connected to the common conviction that a political system required legitimation through the exercise of a primary constituent will. Notably, the most salient features of the political systems that underwent democratic collapse in the 1920s were that (a) they assumed hyper-presidential characteristics and (b) they evolved strongly corporatist dimensions. Democratic crisis in European polities of this time was typically triggered either by the fact that presidential executives became excessively powerful and abrogated formal counterweights to their authority, or by the fact that corporatist experiments allowed potent economic groups to obtain immediate access to legislative organs of state, which they then used to serve their own prerogatives. Both crisis-inducing aspects of the constitutional order of European polities in the 1920s were results of the fact that, through the First World War, national polities were pressed into a close integrational relation to their populations, and the expectation that governments should give deep and immediate expression to the popular will was widespread.[11] This expectation of legitimational immediacy was very manifest in theories of presidential power that became widespread after 1918.[12] Likewise, the corporatist elements in many interwar constitutions were designed to ensure that the people could be integrated in government in immediate and comprehensive material form.[13] In both respects, the crisis of democracy resulted from constitutional arrangements designed to incorporate the constituent power as fully as possible in the state. In the first époque of mass-democratic experimentation, in short, the impetus toward full popular-democratic integration linked to constituent power clearly expedited democratic collapse.

Eventually, democracy was consolidated more enduringly after 1945, and the models of democracy promoted at this time were based, fundamentally, in the attempt to avert repetition of the democratic crises of the 1920s and 1930s. This led to the renunciation of the concept of constituent power. The first democracies established after 1945, in the Federal Republic of Germany (FRG), Italy and Japan were created on a pattern that reflected the emergent norms of global law, so that the actual formation of the democratic system was subject to strong pre-political, pre-constituent constraints. Most abidingly stable democracies that emerged after 1945 were defined, quite expressly, by the fact that core normative elements of the democratic system were immediately extracted from an international legal-normative order, attached to the

---

10 See Carl Schmitt, *Volksentscheid und Volksbegehren: Ein Beitrag zur Auslegung der Weimarer Verfassung und zur Lehre von der unmittelbaren Demokratie* (Duncker und Humblot 1927).

11 Chris Thornhill, *A Sociology of Constitutions* (Cambridge University Press 2011) ch. 4.

12 See note 10 above.

13 Much post-1918 corporatism had its origins in emergency laws passed by executives during the First World War, so it always possessed a commissarial element. It has tellingly been observed that the First World War gave rise to a 'precorporatist experience' in many European societies: Franklin Hugh Adler, *Italian Industrialists from Liberalism to Fascism: The Political Development of the Industrial Bourgeoisie, 1906–1934* (Cambridge University Press 1995) 90.

growing corpus of international human rights law.[14] Once created, then, the form of the constitution in most post-1945 polities was defined by the fact that legislative bodies, central to earlier doctrines of constituent power, lost some of their authority, and judicial actors acquired strong countervailing or even co-legislative functions. In some cases, constitutions themselves were progressively elaborated by judicial institutions, often relying on internationally constructed norms, so that the constitution was essentially crafted by institutions holding constituted power.[15] In the first wave of classical constitution making after 1789, judicial organizations had been considered the antithesis of organs of constituent power, and the theory of constituent power had been partly designed to eradicate seemingly non-mandated use of judicial power in the *ancien régime*.[16] After 1945, however, democracy was built around a design in which judicial bodies acquired high salience.

The importance of international human rights law in pre-shaping democracy after 1945 means, simply, that democracy was not primarily the achievement of national sovereign constituencies, and national democratic polities did not ultimately obtain legitimacy through reference to constituent power. It is not accurate to claim, as does Habermas, that all constitutions before the formation of the EU were based in national patterns of self-legislation styled on the constitution-making events in the USA and France in the 1780s.[17] This classical model had been thoroughly revised in the years after 1945. By this time, it was typically not the *primary activation*, but the *material secondarization*, of the constituent power that formed the core legitimational source for the national polity. Constitution making after 1945 involved the deliberate negation of modes of governmental legitimation pioneered around 1918, which had been based in the direct internalization of the popular will in the political system. On this basis, the assumption that constituent power provides a normative construction to evaluate the legitimacy of any democratic polity, especially of any democratic polity in the EU, appears difficult to sustain. The converse is true. Most democracies were specifically *not founded* by undiluted exercise of constituent power.

On balance, the credentials supporting the claim of doctrines of constituent power to support European constitutional democracy are not very strong, and constituent power cannot be realistically presupposed as a criterion of governmental legitimacy. At best, this concept has proven irrelevant for the formation of national democracy. At worst, it has promoted expectations of integrated popular sovereignty that have unsettled democratically legitimated government. In essence, this concept appears as a norm that is extracted from the socio-political processes that typify societies in a state of rapid nationalization, and it articulates a legitimational

14 Constitutionalists in the Parliamentary Council attached to the Social Democratic Party, especially Carlo Schmid and Ludwig Bergsträsser, argued that international human rights law, based in draft instruments of the UN, should be constitutionally entrenched in the legal order of the FRG. This did not quite happen, and international law does not have direct effect. However, it is axiomatic for German public law that human rights, of international origin, are embedded in constitutional jurisprudence, effectively at a higher level than prescribed by international judicial bodies.

15 See the core decision of the Constitutional Court in West Germany, BVerfGE 7, 198. I. Senate (1 BvR 400/51) Lüth-decision. This decision, backed by international norms, stands at the core of the contemporary constitutional order in Germany.

16 See historical analysis in Henri Carré, *La Fin des Parlements* (Hachette 1912). On the conventional status of courts as 'the exact opposite of the constituent subject' see Joel Colón-Ríos, 'Carl Schmitt and Constituent Power in Latin America' (2011) 18(3) *Constellations* 365–388, 365; David Dyzenhaus, 'Constitutionalism in an Old Key: Legality and Constituent Power' (2012) 1(2) *Global Constitutionalism* 229–226, 230.

17 Jürgen Habermas, 'Zur Prinzipienkonkurrenz von Bürgergleichheit und Staatengleichheit im supranationalen Gemeinwesen: Eine Notiz aus Anlass der Frage nach der Legitimität der ungleichen Repräsentation der Bürger im Europäischen Parlament' (2014) 53(2) *Der Staat* 167–192.

principle to link nationalizing societies to their political systems. Yet, the utility of this concept as an actual legitimational premise for government is very dubious.

Constituent power in the EU

Despite its association with the origins of modern nation states, the doctrine of constituent power has begun to occupy an important space in debates about political entities positioned outside the classical confines of nation states and national constitutional law.[18] In such debates, constituent power has partly lost its original status as a concept for describing the founding political acts of sovereign citizens, and it is applied, more generally, as a criterion for measuring the legitimacy of a political system. In this quality, it is widely used either to question, or to re-envision, the constitutional character of the EU as polity, and it figures prominently in reflections addressing the legitimacy of the EU.[19] In some settings, of course, a crude idea of constituent power has been implied to assess this question. This has been catastrophically exemplified by the Brexit referendum and its aftermath in the UK. At a more conceptually refined level, the use of this concept to examine the EU appears in many analyses, typically in the following variations.

First, some analyses of constituent power in the EU simply criticize the EU because it does not possess an origin in acts of an identifiable constituent power.[20] In essence, analyses of this kind largely repeat the classical sovereignty-based theory of political legitimacy, declaring that legitimacy depends on a strong link between national populations and legislative institutions. Second, some analyses deviate from this classical model, arguing that in the EU a distinctive pattern of constituent power has emerged, concentrated especially in institutions of a judicial nature. This view is sometimes expressed critically, to the effect that the exercise of constituent power by judicial bodies, in particular the European Court of Justice, implies an unwarranted transfer of constitution-making force to institutions properly only holding *pouvoir constitué*. Sometimes this view is expressed more affirmatively, suggesting that the judicial order of the EU is legitimated, however remotely, by an original constituent power, as it condenses and re-articulates norms contained in the judicial institutions of the member states.[21] This latter outlook presupposes that

---

18 See Markus Patberg, 'Constituent Power beyond the State: An Emerging Debate in International Political Theory' (2013) 42(1) *Millennium – Journal of International Studies* 1–15.

19 See Peter Niesen, 'Constituent Power in Global Constitutionalism' in Anthony Lang and Antje Wiener (eds), *Handbook on Global Constitutionalism* (Edward Elgar 2017) 222–233.

20 This debate has involved a number of prominent participants, and it can only be sketched here, doubtless in a fashion that omits important interventions. Anxiety about weak constituent power shaped earliest debates about the constitution of the (then) EEC. See Joseph Kaiser, 'Zur gegenwärtigen Differenzierung von Recht und Staat' (1960) 10 *Österreichische Zeitschrift für öffentliches Recht* 413–423. This later became central to sceptical reflection on the EU. In the mid-1990s, for example, Theodor Schilling denied that the EU could claim to derive authority from constituent power, and he used this claim to undermine the legitimacy of EU institutions, notably the ECJ: Theodor Schilling, 'The Autonomy of the Community Legal Order: An Analysis of Possible Foundations' (1996) 37(2) *Harvard International Law Journal* 389–409, 394. This critique also appeared in Ulrich Haltern, *Europarecht und das Politische* (Mohr 2005) 302.

21 For example, one author attributed a collective constituent power to the EU, based in the devolved powers of all citizens of the member states, resulting in the formation of a European Constitution as an 'association of constitutions': Ingolf Pernice, *Das Verhältnis europäischer zu nationalen Gerichten im europäischen Verfassungsverbund* (de Gruyter 2006) 18. One author has argued that in the EU there is 'no scope for creation *ex nihilo* of a distinctive constituent power', but he accounted for the EU nonetheless as a pluralistically authorized legal system: Neil Walker, 'Reframing EU Constitutionalism' in Jeffrey L. Dunoff and Joel P. Trachtman (eds), *Ruling the World? Constitutionalism, International Law, and Global Governance* (Cambridge University Press 2009) 149–176, 172. Other observers echoed this approach, claiming that in the EU constituent power and constituted power cannot be fully separated and the ECJ

all member states are bound by a set of essentially congruent constitutional norms, reflecting a shared constitutional culture, and these norms acquire constitutional effect at the supranational level of the European polity as they are interpreted and implemented by judicial bodies. In both variants of this outlook, the idea is expressed that, in the EU, constituent power is now vested in legal institutions, such that, at the supranational level, norms with constitutional rank are created inner-juridically, without recourse to primary constitution-making acts, or without recourse to collective declarations of popular volition. Third, a step further down this line of reasoning we encounter the assertion that the EU is constitutionally held together by the common reasoning of Constitutional Courts or superior courts located within the member states. On this account, the interactions between Constitutional Courts create a situation in which democratic constitutional expectations established within national societies are translated to, and constitutionalized at, the transnational level, above the member states.[22] In this perspective, Constitutional Courts ensure that the supranational legal order is linked to original constituent acts in the member states, and the interlinked jurisprudence of Constitutional Courts forms a solid foundation for the legitimacy of the EU. This means that the EU appears as the repository of a derived constituent power, assuming derived democratic justification, mediated upwards through courts. The constituent power remains the original source of institutional legitimacy, but it is constructed, preserved, and transmitted in inner-legal form, such that constituted bodies are charged with its supranational construction and expression.

As an extension of this, fourth, perhaps the most refined account of the constituent power supposedly underpinning the EU is found in theories of the *pouvoir constituant mixte*. On this account, the supranational institutions of the EU acquire legitimacy as they extract authorization from institutions in member-state societies, whose own legitimacy is founded in the national *pouvoir constituant*, or at least in the democratic practices and dispositions of populations of individual member states.[23] This means, simply, that institutional formation at the supranational level is subject to the same normative constraints, procedural requirements and democratic expectations as institutional formation within nation states. Constituent power, thus, is *levelled up* to the supranational level, where it acts both as a normative yardstick for assessing the legitimacy of the EU and as a body of constitutional expectations for transfusing its institutions with democratic content.[24] On this account, persons in the EU are always citizens of two distinct but linked polities, one founded at a national level, one founded at the supranational level, both of which are connected by a shared or *co-original* constituent power, which projects the normative demands that define both levels of citizenship.[25] Following Habermas's interventions,

assumes the role of 'permanent *pouvoir constituant*': Anne Peters, *Elemente einer Theorie der Verfassung Europas* (Dunker und Humblot 2001) 410. More recently, Fossum and Menéndez have developed a theory that observes the constituent power of the EU as residing in the synthesis of constitutional arrangements located in the member states: John Erik Fossum and Augustín José Menéndez, *The Constitution's Gift: A Constitutional Theory for a Democratic Union* (Rowman & Littlefield 2011) 53.

22 Andreas Voßkuhle, 'Multilevel Cooperation of the ECCs: Der Europäische Verfassungsgerichtsverbund' (2010) 6 *European Constitutional Law Review* 175–198.

23 Markus Patberg, 'The Levelling Up of Constituent Power in the European Union' (2017) 55(2) *Journal of Common Market Studies* 203–212, 204.

24 Patberg (n 23) 209.

25 Markus Patberg, 'After the Brexit Vote: What's Left of "Split" Popular Sovereignty?' (2018) 40(7) *Journal of European Integration* 1–15, 12; Peter Niesen, Svenja Ahlhaus and Markus Patberg, 'Konstituierende Autorität: Ein Grundbegriff für die internationale Politische Theorie' (2015) 6(2) *Zeitschrift für Politische Theorie* 159–172, 170. For a parallel move see Francis Cheneval and Kalypso Nicolaidis, 'The Social Construction of Democracy in the European Union' (2016) 16(2) *European Journal of Political Theory* 235–260, 244.

proponents of this theory argue that citizens act as bearers of a double sovereignty,[26] containing two congruent sets of normative expectations, and they exercise constituent power at both levels of the EU as polity. As a result, the EU emerges as a set of institutions shaped and bound by original processes of democratic constitutional norm formation.

In these different ways, the concept of the *pouvoir constituant* performs multiple tasks for theories of legitimacy in the EU. It is taken simultaneously as a standard to denigrate, to accentuate and to intensify the legitimacy of EU institutions and polities. Even proponents of the *pouvoir constituant mixte* construct the concept in multivalent fashion. In this theory, the concept functions primarily as a positive term to describe the sources of legitimacy in the EU. Yet, in this context, this concept also acts as a counterfactual principle, implying that constituent power can be treated as a pure normative principle of democratic legitimacy, creating expectations that must be recognized by supranational institutions.

Problems of the supranational *pouvoir constituant*

This recent re-emergence of the concept of the *pouvoir constituant* is rather surprising, and it appears as an oddly chosen instrument for explaining the legitimational substance of the EU. Most obviously, the EU was created as a political entity that was not shaped by classical forms of political agency, so the reason why it should be measured in such terms is not clear. Moreover, each specific use of this concept, either critical or affirmative, to analyse the EU is beset by problems. Much of the discussion resulting from this concept relies on theoretical and empirical distortions, many of which have materially detrimental implications, and much such analysis evaluates the legitimacy of the EU against spurious standards.

First, the concept of constituent power has little value as part of a critique of the EU. The use of this concept as a critical measure of the legitimacy of the EU implies that the (alleged) legitimational deficiency of the EU is due to the fact that its foundations deviate from models of legitimacy typical of more classical (national) political systems. This claim suggests that national polities, especially those eventually locked into the EU, were originally legitimated by the fact that they were constructed through acts of constituent power. As discussed, however, the national polities of post-1945 Europe were not created by acts of constituent power. On one hand, as mentioned, lines of democratic state formation that occurred after 1945 were defined by a reaction against the attachment of political legitimacy to acts of a national constituent power. On the other hand, importantly, a large number of the states that entered the EU after the Treaty of Rome acquired democratic form as a means to acquire EU membership. Many current EU member states – for example, Spain, Portugal, Greece and all states in Eastern Europe – were created as democracies, not least, because democratic institutional form was dictated to them by supranational bodies, linked to the EU, as a model of political organization required for admission to the EU.[27] In many cases, it was not any basic impulsion toward sovereign self-legislation, but

---

26 Habermas (n 17).

27 In Spain under Franco, democratic reform was prescribed externally (by other member states) as a precondition for EU membership. See Daniel C. Thomas, 'Constitutionalization through Enlargement: The Contested Origins of the EU's Democratic Identity' in Berthold Rittberger and Frank Schimmelfenig (eds), *The Constitutionalization of the European Union* (Routledge 2007) 43–63, 58. For the ground rules regarding EU recognition of new post-Communist states see the *EC Guidelines on Recognition of New States in Eastern Europe and in the Soviet Union* (1991). More recently, the impact of the Venice Commission on the promotion of transnational constitutional norms is important and illuminating in this regard. See Maartje de Visser, 'A Critical Assessment of the Role of the Venice Commission in Processes of Democratic Reform' (2015) 63 *The American Journal of*

the aspiration to become a member of the EU that underpinned national processes of democratic constitution making. This meant, in effect, that for many populations the endeavour to accede to the EU was a core component of the constituent power that gave rise to a democratic institutional order. This creates the paradoxical situation that the EU, whose legitimacy is now often seen as undermined by the fact that it does not refer to a constituent power, *actually pre-formed the basic constituent power* for many of the national democracies whose legitimacy, allegedly constructed through constituent power, is now proposed as a yardstick for the legitimacy of the EU.

Second, the concept of constituent power has limited value as a lens for reflecting on the distinctive constitutional features of the EU. In such analyses, as discussed, this concept is normally used to highlight the fact that the exercise of constituent power in the EU has an unusual and characteristic judicial quality. For this outlook, the higher-ranking norms that define the constitutional order of the EU, both as a distinct entity and in the member states themselves, are dictated through acts of judicial interpretation, located within an existing transnational legal system. In principle, however, the process of constitution making in which constitutionalization and judicialization are amalgamated is not an isolated feature of the public-legal order of the EU. Most contemporary democracies have been established through a process in which primary constitutional norms have been defined within a given legal system, so that bodies exercising already constituted power have supplied the normative basis for democracy. As discussed, it is difficult to find any example of a democratic polity created since 1945 in which (a) the prior form of the constitution was not at least partly constructed by external judicial or semi-judicial norm setters, such as supranational courts, international organizations, or human rights bodies;[28] (b) the national judiciary, often applying international norms, has not acquired a key role in establishing the concrete hierarchy of norms within the system of domestic public law. Since 1945, for instance, many states have evolved as political entities that possess only uncertain sovereignty, and their original legitimacy has been determined by an extra-national legal order or extra-national norm providers.[29] There are numerous recent examples in which national constitution making has been promoted by bodies with powers of external territorial administration.[30] More normally, many national constitutions have been rewritten to meet international standards, or to react to grievances expressed by single citizens and brought before supranational courts.[31] On a more day-to-day basis, the transfer of responsibility ideally reserved for constituent actors to judicial bodies is a common phenomenon. The production of legitimacy for legislation through conversations between different courts, especially between courts located at different points in a legal order

---

Comparative Law 963–1008, 1008; Paul Craig, 'Transnational Constitution-Making: The Contribution of the Venice Commission on Law and Democracy' (2017) 2 *UC Irvine Journal of International, Transnational and Comparative Law* 57–86, 58.

28 See Steven Wheatley, *The Democratic Legitimacy of International Law* (Hart Publishing 2010) 245.

29 See Stephen D. Krasner, 'Sharing Sovereignty: New Institutions for Collapsed and Failing States' (2004) 29(2) *International Security* 85–120.

30 Michael Riegner, 'The Two Faces of the Internationalized Pouvoir Constituant: Independence and Constitution-Making under External Influence in Kosovo' (2010) 2(3) *Goettingen Journal of International Law* 1035–1062; Joanne Wallis, *Constitution Making During State Building* (Cambridge University Press 2014) 101, 108.

31 By way of example, far-reaching constitutional reforms in Mexico, which gave higher protection to international human rights law, were conducted against a background marked by censure of the Mexican judicial system in the Inter-American Court of Human Rights (IACtHR). See IACtHR, Case of Radilla-Pacheco v. Mexico, 2 November 2009; Case of Rosendo Cantú et al v. Mexico, 31 August 2010; IACtHR, Case of Fernández Ortega et al v. Mexico, 30 August 2010.

overarching different nation states, is not in any way specific to the EU.[32] In these different instances, the internalization of constituent power within an already existing legal system has now become a standard pattern of constitutional construction, which widely supports the legitimational processes of different national polities. In such processes, both constitutional laws and secondary laws are produced and authorized by reference to norms already articulated within the law. Even the basic sovereignty of nation states, in the construction of which constituent power plays a core role, is typically pre-shaped by a system of norms originating outside national polities, and partly constructed by judicial actors.[33] The reason why, in this regard, the EU should be perceived as anomalous, or as distinctively legitimated, is not clear.

In both these respects, the use of the concept of constituent power to evaluate the EU revolves around a series of historical misconstructions. These misconstructions result, in essence, from the fact that theorists have taken very literally the basic norm of political legitimacy (constituent power), which surfaced in 1789 for contingent reasons, and they have looked within national democracy to find modes of legal-political agency that conform to this norm. In many cases, however, the democratic systems of national societies developed on a pattern that specifically negated this norm. This implies that the attempt to construct the legitimacy of the EU through reference to constituent power is sustained by a deep conflation of theoretical models and factual processes of legitimation. More alarmingly, this also means, in real-world terms, that the legitimacy of the EU is often challenged on untenable grounds, which necessarily leads to the projection of unjustifiably distorted legitimational standards, both within the EU and within the different member states of the EU. Central to the recent use of the concept of constituent power is that it blurs awareness of the fact that, at a legitimational level, the emergence of the EU merely articulates a common sociological phenomenon: namely, that the founding norms of contemporary polities are now quite typically generated *within the existing legal system*.

Third, in this respect, even the more theoretically circumspect assertion, expressed in theories of the *pouvoir constituant mixte*, that there exists an overarching constituent power in the EU, able to translate national constituent power into a normative basis for the supranational legal-political order, relies on very problematic presuppositions.

At one level, such theories indicate that democracy in EU member states was already established in historically stable form before the construction of the EU. In Habermas's counterfactual construction of the double sovereign, for instance, it is clearly assumed that democratic norms were first consolidated outside the EU and legitimation in the EU only becomes problematic because processes for constructing legitimacy need to be extended from national to supranational legal/political entities.[34] As Peter Niesen explains, this

---

32 In some states, large swathes of constitutional law have been constructed through inter-judicial interaction. The classical example of this is Colombia, where the Constitutional Court has used international norms and the jurisprudence of international courts to extend the force of constitutional rights in Colombian society. In fact, owing to its effective internalization of international law, the Colombian Constitutional Court has acquired such wide influence in Latin America that it is a key source of authority in the construction of human rights norms in other superior national courts. In recent years, notably, the Chilean Constitutional Court has cited from the Colombian Constitutional Court to establish protective rights for children (see Rol N° 1683–10 de 4 de enero de 2011).

33 See Dominik Zaum, *The Sovereignty Paradox: The Norms and Politics of International Statebuilding* (Oxford University Press 2007) 166.

34 Habermas (n 17).

approach is designed to ensure that 'levels of justice and individual rights' that are 'historically accomplished' within member states are preserved in the supranational polity.[35] The idea that European societies contained solidified democratic systems that are separate from the EU is thus taken as given. At a different level, some exponents of this theory are keen to qualify the historical claim that European democracy was a historically formed reality that existed before the EU, arguing that the constituent power in the EU ought not to be seen – strictly – as a real power, exercised in primary constituent acts, but rather as a basic formal norm.[36] In such formulations, the idea of constituent power shades closely toward the Kantian idea of constituent power as a transcendental principle: that is, it is observed as a formal normative construction, which underpins the EU as a polity. For Habermas, indicatively, the idea of the double sovereign, in which persons act as citizens on two planes of a quasi-federal polity, is – in essence – a simple 'thought experiment', in which the standard of legitimacy for the EU is extracted from the hypothetical presumption that citizens in member states possess democratic orientations, and that these can be carried over to shape norm construction and public accountability at the supranational level.[37] Other theorists of the *pouvoir constituant mixte* have revised this construction; they have filled out the theoretical abstraction in such approaches with accounts of political life practices able to invigorate and activate constituent power, both in national and supranational settings.[38] Among all theorists of the *pouvoir constituant mixte*, however, the conviction prevails that the liberal democratic systems that exist within member states are *normatively prior* to the EU, and they can be viewed as repositories of constituent power, which express binding legitimational guidelines for the exercise of public functions at the supranational level of the EU. The theory of the *pouvoir constituant mixte* is surely much the most refined of existing positions in reflections on supra-state constituent power. Yet, its core precondition that European democracy has an origin that is decisively external to the EU is deeply problematic. Like other analyses, this approach questions the legitimacy of the EU on constructively fabricated premises.

The presumption that national democracy in Europe decisively pre-existed the EU can be observed as problematic on two separate counts.

First, any presumption that European democracy is *historically external to the EU* is difficult to sustain. The idea that member states possessed democratic systems before their incorporation in the EU is, of course, widely propagated, by theorists on both the political left and the political right. This view is often adopted by theorists who claim that integration in the EU has led to a deterioration of standards of democratic self-determination in national societies.[39] If viewed historically, however, it is difficult to find polities now in the EU in which democracy had reached a higher level of consolidation before the entry of the given polity into the EU than can be found in the same polity at any point subsequent to its entry into the EU. As mentioned, many of the polities that entered the EU after the Treaty of Rome became democracies *in order to obtain EU accession rights*, so that, in such polities, the EU of itself formed part of the democratic constitution-making situation. Similarly, although most societies that signed the original Treaty of

---

35 Niesen (n 19) 229.

36 For example, Patberg agrees with my view that democracy did not pre-exist the EU, but he argues that 'it is not a fiction that the EU consists of democratic nation-states': Patberg (n 25) 7.

37 Habermas (n 17).

38 Markus Patberg, 'Challenging the Masters of the Treaties: Emerging Narratives of Constituent Power in the EU' (2018) 7(2) *Global Constitutionalism* 263–293, 267.

39 This view was at the heart of the pro-Brexit campaign in the UK.

Rome possessed democratic constitutional systems, they were surely not formed as fully evolved democracies before 1958. In 1958, the FRG had not yet emerged as a secure democracy; it was widely questioned whether Adenauer's government could ever become fully democratic. The French Fourth Republic had recently collapsed, and a Gaullist constitution, re-animating military patterns of constitutional formation, was being implemented. Electoral enfranchisement of women in France had only begun fourteen years earlier and was still incomplete. The main polity that falls between these two categories – that is, the main polity that acceded to the EU after the Treaty of Rome, yet which previously possessed an embedded democratic tradition – is the UK. The case of the UK is especially illuminating in this respect, as it underlines the fact that, across Europe, national democracy did not fully pre-date the rise of the EU or the integration of different states in the EU.[40]

In the UK, the idea that accession to the EU somehow undermined a long-standing tradition of consensual national self-legislation is very pervasive and often declared as a simple political fact. Shortly after the Brexit referendum, for instance, *The Telegraph* managed to declare: 'Democratic self-government – parliamentary democracy – is what the modern British nation is founded on'. At the same time, Boris Johnson (later prime minister, educated at Oxford University) stated that democracy is the 'most precious thing' offered by Britain to the world.[41] Of course, the intended implication of both these statements is that the UK is home to a tradition of democracy that was eventually weakened by the legal/political convergence between the UK and the EU. In just reaction to this usurpation, then, democracy had been reclaimed through the dramatic act of national self-legislation, or of national constituent power, expressed in the Brexit referendum. This idea saturates British society, and it is greatly reinforced by the terms of academic debate about the EU.

In fact, however, the UK is an extreme example of the democratic delusion that afflicts much of Western Europe, and the assumption that British democracy was fully consolidated before the UK's entry into the EU underlines the lack of historical knowledge that shapes such discussions. Britain has one of the weakest traditions of electoral integration in Europe, and there is no strong democratic foundation for the British polity that we reasonably could perceive as having been undermined by membership in the EU. To assume the contrary is plainly counterfactual. Prior to 1914, electoral laws in the UK were among the most restrictive in Europe, and, at least in terms of access to voting rights, its political system was substantially less inclusive than those of supposedly authoritarian societies such as Germany and Austria.[42] After 1918, the democratic franchise in Britain was greatly widened, notably in 1918 and 1928. However, Britain could not be accurately classified as a fully evolved democracy until after 1945 – arguably, depending on the strictness of the criteria applied, not until 1950. Before 1945, the UK was only governed for a very short period (1929–1931) by a government elected competitively and under conditions close to equal universal suffrage.[43] The UK only began

---

40 See Chris Thornhill, 'A Tale of Two Constitutions.: Whose Legitimacy? Whose Crisis?' in William Outhwaite (ed), *Brexit: Sociological Responses* (Anthem Press 2017) 77–89, 82.

41 www.telegraph.co.uk/news/2016/06/24/the-european-elite-forgot-that-democracy-is-the-one-thing-britai/ (last accessed 8 January 2019).

42 See excellent analysis in Neal Blewett, 'The Franchise in the United Kingdom 1885–1918' (1965) 32 *Past & Present* 27–56.

43 Before the 1929 elections, most women in the UK could not vote, and those that were allowed to vote obtained this right in part because of the income of their husbands. From 1931 until after the Second World War, elections were not fully competitive and occupancy of government office was not strictly correlated with voting outcomes.

regularly to conduct fully competitive democratic elections after 1945, and the 1950 elections were the first elections held without plural voting – that is, they were the first national elections in which all citizens above a certain age threshold could vote, and all citizens could only vote one time. In consequence, at the beginning of its integration in the EU in the early 1970s the UK could not very plausibly present itself as an example of a historically consolidated political democracy, and its inhabitants could not reasonably imagine that they were heirs to a structurally ingrained history of democratic self-determination. If judged by strict criteria, the UK had been a full democracy for approximately twenty-five years.[44]

All this is simply meant to highlight the fact that the construction of the EU's legitimacy on grounds extracted from the idea that European democracy was institutionalized before 1958, such that democratic institutions in EU member states contain a constituent power that is originally external to the EU, is fictitious. Especially problematic in the presumption that democracy in Europe pre-exists the EU is that it fuels anti-EU sentiment by allowing populations to project themselves as holders of rights of political self-legislation that are somehow independent of the EU. In particular, this presumption encourages populations to identify a clear distinction between political rights that they hold as citizens of nation states and political rights that they hold as members (or even as citizens) of the EU, with the former typically being accorded primacy, and the latter perceived as emanating from the former. Situations in which populations act on this presumed distinction to assert national political rights as rights held separately from rights tied to the EU typically have deeply deleterious consequences both for citizens of the EU and for the citizens of national democracies. Evidently, societies that withdraw from the EU (e.g. the UK) do not find themselves in a situation in which they return to a pristine democratic order. This is no coincidence. In the period before the EU was founded, European democracy was still in a process of consolidation, and, up to the 1990s, no polity became a member of the EU with fully solidified democratic institutions. At best, we can only identify *partial democratization* or *intermittent democratization* as characteristics of European polities before 1945, and these characteristics still determined the form of European democracy up to 1958. National political rights are never fully distinct from rights obtained in the EU.

Second, any presumption that European democracy is *procedurally external to the EU* is also questionable. This conviction also rests on a historical simplification, as it omits to reflect on the degree to which democratic institutions in Europe have been improved by the incorporation of national societies in the EU. In fact, it is rare that political procedures that are specific to national societies form a foundation for democratic polity building that is more reliable than those established at the supranational level, and mechanisms for legitimation and legislation rooted in national political systems in Europe often actively obstruct effective democracy.

Notable in this matter is the fact that in polities with longer-standing traditions of (partial) democratization it is usually the older aspects of constitutional design, which clearly pre-date the EU, that generate the most visibly undemocratic outcomes. To refer to the UK again, the crisis of democratic legitimacy that has recently characterized the British polity was caused in the main by problems resulting from the classical conviction that the polity of the UK obtains legitimacy through *parliamentary sovereignty*. The system of British democracy has been destabilized by the fact that constitutional experts in the Conservative Party decided that the ancient sovereignty of the organs of parliament, which had

---

44 This condenses arguments in Thornhill (n 40) 83.

supposedly been undermined by the direct effect of EU law and regulations, needed to be defended by a plebiscite – i.e. by the exercise of an electoral process, which can only be seen as the antithesis of parliamentary democracy. This decision then created a parliament which, in the defence and assertion of its purported sovereignty, was unable to exercise sovereignty in deciding the question for which its sovereignty had been (purportedly) reclaimed (the question whether or not the UK ought to remain in the EU) because it had accorded hyper-entrenched – i.e. supra-parliamentary – authority to the outcome of a decision reached through a plebiscite. In this, British democracy unsettled itself, as it sought to revert to its own classical form, outside legal procedures attached to the EU. In this case, the attempt to unearth a deeper democratic will beneath the institutions created through integration in the EU resulted in a dramatic weakening of democracy. Quite generally, however, national alternatives to EU membership do not present themselves as very democratic. This is clear enough in the fact that anti-European sentiment is monopolized by parties of the far or populist right, whose commitment to democracy is notional. Moreover, constitutional revisions that diminish the standing of norms that have entered domestic law through normative expectations linked to the EU signally fail to heighten the security of democratic institutions. To illustrate this, we can think of recent processes in Poland and Hungary.[45] Overall, classical democratic procedures show limited capacity for upholding democracy in Europe, and democracy finds its surest hold either in normative systems created by the EU or at least in norms that evolved through the overlapping of national and transnational legal institutions.

In sum, there is very little in the national democratic systems in the EU to indicate that democracy is procedurally stabilized within member-state societies in a form that is external to the EU as a legal/political system. The constituent power that resides in national societies is, most typically, not a constituent power that is strong enough to guide normative expectations in favour of democracy at the supranational level. In fact, it is usually unable to guide normative expectations at the national level. Where allowed free expression, the European constituent power normally urges a return to partial democracy, loosening the normative order of national polities, which only became solidly democratic as they were integrated in the supranational polity of the EU.

However it is conceived, it is not certain that constituent power, seen as a pattern of agency that is originally formative of democracy, can be found in European societies, standing in independence of the EU. The idea that constituent power stands outside the political order that it is intended to legitimate cannot easily be eliminated from the doctrine of constituent power. Transferred to the EU system, this idea inevitably implies that constituent power is located somewhere outside the EU system, either in the democratic histories or the democratic procedures of the member states. In most factual cases, however, we encounter the obverse phenomenon. Democracy is usually secured, not by the *pouvoir constituant*, but by a fine legal mesh that connects national and supranational regulatory structures. In its various historical iterations, the attempt to align governmental systems in Europe to a notion of constituent power has proved deeply deleterious for democracy. This was clearly the case in the 1920s and 1930s. This is clearly the case now, as societies forced,

---

45 In Poland, the shift away from democratic procedure involves a rejection of rule-of-law guarantees established in basic EU treaties. See Robert Grzeszczak and Ireneusz Pawel Karolewski, 'The Rule of Law Crisis in Poland: A New Chapter', at https://verfassungsblog.de/the-rule-of-law-crisis-in-poland-a-new-chapter/ (last accessed 9 August 2018).

in the name of democracy, to disarticulate themselves from the transnational legal form in which they experienced democratization almost invariably weaken their democratic substance. Quite generally, the attempt to reconstruct democracy around norms not already defined *within the transnational legal system* almost invariably creates, not more, but less democracy.

Rephrasing constitutional legitimacy

As mentioned, where it is applied as a positive concept, the concept of constituent power in accounts of the EU is designed to ensure that public offices attached to the EU polity are utilized accountably, and that decisions made at this level can be legitimated by manifest consensus. Above all, it is used to indicate that any expansion of competences vested in the EU needs to be underpinned by strong self-explanatory justifications. Constituent power is thus expected to project a normative order from national society to the supranational level in order to configure standards of legitimacy and accountability for EU institutions. Central to the critique of such views set out above, however, is the claim that national constitutions in Europe, in fact, only established very truncated conditions of political accountability, and they constructed only very partial expressions of democratic consensus for their own societies. To expect national constitutions to extend their norm-generative functions beyond nation states already entails a leap of faith, based in an overestimation of their achievements in national societies. The core implication of the critique proposed above is that it is not sociologically accurate to associate constitutional democracy with national societies. Consequently, the theory of constituent power involves a basic category error, which confuses the normative demands of national constitutions with their factual reality. When we counter-factually identify democracy with national societies, standing separate from the EU, we overstretch the democratic resources of national societies and we rather spuriously undermine the legitimacy of the EU.

The main problem that results from the deficiency of national constituent power as a standard of democracy in Europe is that we lack a robust criterion for measuring the legitimacy of institutions at the supranational level. This is not a trivial problem. It appears perfectly clear that there are variations in the legitimacy of supranational legal and political entities, and it is perfectly reasonable to seek standards to determine their relative validity. At present, we only possess erroneous and ill-constructed criteria, which are often damaging to both tiers of the supranational polity whose legitimacy they are designed to promote.

Below, I sketch some possible alternative approaches to this problem. These approaches indicate ways in which the idea of constituent power might be reconfigured in a form that makes it possible for us to obtain the advantages of a formal legitimational principle for examining supra-state constructions, yet which is also able to avert the pressures and distortions that the concept induces in its current form:

1. One way of formulating the idea of a constituent power in the EU is simply to extend the theory of the *pouvoir constituant mixte* to its logical, at times intrinsically implied, Kantian conclusion. That is, we can extract from this theory a criterion for assessing the legitimacy of supranational organizations by positing a model of democracy based in the principle that democracy is a type of polity that is not constituted by real citizens, but in which the citizen appears as a mere regulatory norm, reflecting the claim that reasonable collective self-legislation is the basic measure of governmental legitimacy. This counterfactual model may have the advantage that it is less likely to exaggerate the degree of democracy in the

member states of the EU, such that the unsettling impulse toward renationalization, stimu-
lated by classical theories of constituent power, will be diminished. In essence, however,
this theory would not be a theory of constituent power, or it would only be a theory of
constituent power to the extent that Kelsen's theory of the *Grundnorm* is a theory of constituent power.[46] In some respects, as mentioned, the doctrine of the *pouvoir constituant
mixte* is itself, at core, little more than a regulatory theory of constituent power.

2. In close relation to this, we may be able to establish a model of constituent power to evaluate the legitimacy of institutions in the EU by translating this theory into a simple theory of
basic human rights. Rephrased in this way, this theory would state that human rights form
the original criterion by which EU institutions are most properly legitimated and their
legitimacy most adequately assessed, and that simple compliance with this criterion demonstrates that political institutions give expression to a democratic constituent power. In the
case of the EU, this theory would diminish the expectation that the EU should reflect (supposedly) classical models of democratic legitimation. It would, accordingly, have the advantage that it would reflect the fact that the legitimacy of the EU needs to be conceived in
a fashion adapted to its position as a sui-generis entity, which is clearly distinct from nation
states. If strictly applied, moreover, this would lead to the hardening of basic rights protections in the EU. Important and relevant historical background to this is contained in the
fact that the EU was initially conceived, by some actors at least, in such terms.[47] However,
if this perspective were followed, the democratic implications of the theory of constituent
power would clearly be weakened. This theory would indicate, in essence, that the EU
polity has to be founded, not in any real democratic procedures, but in a strict system of
constitutional rights, which need not necessarily intensify democratic practices.

3. Alongside this, it is possible to imagine a more sociological perspective for constructing constituent power within the EU. On the basis of the above analysis, it is at least arguable, sociologically, that the concept of constituent power contains a normative claim that is always
inclined to break the parameters of national political institutions. As discussed, it is historically
observable that attempts by national governments to construct their legitimacy as an expression
of constituent power have frequently released an impulsion toward societal integration that
could not be stabilized within the bounds of national society. In such instances, national political institutions usually proved incapable of representing the constituent power as the legitimational centre of democracy. In most polities, the basic subject of constituent power, which is
used as a standard for examining democratic legitimacy, only came into factual and objective
existence as national societies were partly integrated into transnational institutional systems: *the
essential subject of national democracy awaited the emergence of a transnational legal and institutional order
to become effective as the foundation for state legitimacy*. If this view is accepted, a sociologically pro-
portioned debate about constituent power at the supranational level of the EU needs to abandon its focus on the ways in which national constituent power generates legitimacy for
supranational institutions. Instead, analysis of supranational constituent power needs to observe
transnational legal orders as the co-implied precondition for the normative realization of
democratic constituent power. On this basis, such analysis needs to place its focus on ways in
which supranational institutions actually facilitate democracy at the national level, and establish

---

46 On this relation see Hans Heinrich Rupp, 'Europäische "Verfassung" und demokratische Legitimation' (1995)
120(2) *Archiv des öffentlichen Rechts* 269–275, 275.
47 Gráinne de Búrca, 'The Road Not Taken: The European Union as a Global Human Rights Actor' (2011)
105(4) *The American Journal of International Law* 649–693.

manageable forms for the exercise of constituent power within national societies. At the level of normative principle, this outlook necessarily inverts the sequence of norm production underlying most accounts of constituent power in supranational political entities such as the EU, as it views supranational institutions as the bodies that assume the primary responsibility for shaping the actual exercise of constituent power and the resultant consolidation of democracy. Nonetheless, this criterion might provide a valuable perspective from which to observe the legitimacy of the EU. The normative assessment of the EU and its legitimacy in light of the degree to which the EU does or does not facilitate democracy within member states appears both more sociologically reflexive and more politically beneficial than the persistent attempts to construct the legitimacy of the EU by criteria supposedly elaborated within national societies. Use of this criterion would also generate much more robustly sustainable concepts to determine conditions under which the EU loses legitimacy.

Conclusion

Generally, we can observe that the concept of constituent power has limited significance in the analysis of national constitutional states, and it does not allow us to describe the grounds for the legitimacy of a polity.

This chapter argues that the normative account of constituent power cannot be attached without qualification to any factual process within national societies, and the attempt to link constituent power to national institutional forms undermines the practical democracy-enhancing objectives of such theory. Democratic constituent power is almost always constructed from a transnational legal-political source. This is widely observable. Globally, democracy was almost never experienced as a stable and enduring political form until 1945, and it was almost always either comprehensively designed or at least strongly reinforced by institutions in the global domain with responsibility for fostering and enforcing human rights norms. In Europe, the growth of democracy has been concentrated in three temporal waves – the period after 1945, the 1970s, and the 1990s. The relative success of democratization processes in each of these waves is difficult to explain without consideration of the rise of global and regional human rights norms. To argue that the democratic constituent power is primarily located outside national societies is, therefore, not controversial.

In addition, this chapter explains that the concept of constituent power has two uses in debate about the EU, and it claims that in neither of them is it persuasive. At one level, this concept forms a perspective for a simply functional description of the ways in which the system of public law in the EU has been constructed. In this respect, it typically focuses on the role of judicial institutions in framing higher-order norms. In addition, it generates a normative model for identifying sources of norm formation as a means both to challenge, but increasingly also to augment, the legitimacy of the EU. In both respects, however, the theory of constituent power falsely extracts a model of democratic constituent power from national societies, and it does not adequately reflect on the extent to which national societies, on their own, failed to create democracy. The theory of constituent power in the EU needs to be rephrased to acknowledge this essential historical fact. On this basis, we might evaluate the EU itself as the locus of constituent power, legitimated – or otherwise – by its efficacy in promoting democratic constitution making in national societies. The probable upshot of this would be that the EU would be expected to perform functions with greater analogies to those of a human rights organization. But this would be no bad thing.

18

POPULISM AND CONSTITUTIONAL CHANGE

Paul Blokker

Introduction

The widespread view of the relation between populism and constitutionalism is that it forms a negation of liberal constitutionalism and liberal democracy. Mattias Kumm, for one, states in unambiguous terms that 'populists are a greater threat to liberal-democratic constitutionalism than the minority of religiously fundamentalist immigrants ever could be'.[1] In Simone Chambers' recent affirmation, 'both populism and authoritarianism have sometimes been thought to be movements that attempt to bypass, discredit or suspend constitutions'.[2] Rather than buying into the promise of the orderly, universal, rule of law, and power-limiting dimensions of constitutionalism, populism taps into the quintessential modern idea of a society giving itself its own laws. Current 'neo-populisms' re-invoke the idea of constituent power and make strong claims to revitalize popular sovereignty and local, domestic self-government. Populists insist hence on the political dimension of modern constitutional democracy, or more specifically that of *auto-nomos*, but they do this in a distinctively populist manner, defending a pure and undivided or unfragmented form of rule of the people. Evidently, this makes populists wary of liberal constitutional institutions, in particular in their power-limiting, power-dividing, and power-pluralizing dimensions.

One implication of this is that populists often have difficulty with the slowness and mediated nature of democratic, constitutional procedures and the separated while interrelated nature of institutions in liberal democracy. In the populist view, the mediated and deliberative nature of constitutional democracy betrays the popular will.[3] Michael Freeden importantly draws attention to this 'fundamental preoccupation of populists with speed in implementing the "will of the people" before that will can be unpacked as

---

1 See www.wzb.eu/sites/default/files/publikationen/wzb_mitteilungen/s-6-8kummmitteilungen-157.pdf.

2 S. Chambers, 'Afterword: Populist Constitutionalism v. Deliberative Constitutionalism' in R. Levy, H. Kong, G. Orr and J. King (eds), *The Cambridge Handbook of Deliberative Constitutionalism* (Cambridge University Press 2018) 370.

3 Recently, an Italian secretary of state, member of the populist Lega, argued that 'the Parliament has no relevance whatsoever anymore because it is not anymore perceived as such by citizens, who instead perceive it as a primary place of political indecisiveness' and 'if we continue to defend the fetish of representative democracy we are not doing good to democracy as such' (*La Repubblica*, 'Giorgetti: Il parlamento non conta più nulla. Serve l'elezione diretta', 21 August 2018).

consisting of diverse particular components'.[4] Summed up by Jan-Werner Müller, 'populism is inherently hostile to the mechanisms, and ultimately, the values commonly associated with constitutionalism: constraints on the will of the majority, checks and balances, protections for minorities, and even fundamental rights'.[5] Populists are seen as averse to existing procedures and institutions, and as loath of intermediary bodies, as they prefer unmediated, fast relations between the populist ruler and the people. Populists prefer direct, 'natural' or 'pure' forms of politics, in contrast to indirect and artificial ones.[6]

The populist mindset may be related to a form of general 'legal scepticism'[7] toward liberal constitutionalism and the rule of law as impeding or obstructive dimensions of democratic politics. Indeed, it is frequently sustained that populists mostly endorse a negative or reactionary approach toward the existing system, while lacking a substantive and comprehensive 'ideological' programme putting forth an alternative political system.[8] The argument in this chapter is that such observations may be too reductive and that populists tend to make active and constructive use[9] of constitutions and constitutionalism. This can be demonstrated by the fact that populists find themselves increasingly in government, and, once in such a position, frequently engage with political and constitutional reform. As Andrew Arato aptly notes, in fact, it is 'logical for populist governments to reach for the constituent power, and try to produce new documentary constitutions'.[10] And Chambers further argues,

> contemporary populism has often progressed and gained ground through embracing and claiming ownership over national constitutions. Thus, constitutional reform has been the preferred means to consolidate the central authoritarian power in Hungary, Poland, Turkey and Venezuela. European and American populist movements have adopted a similar rhetoric even if they have not had a similar institutional success.[11]

In terms of the main interest of this chapter – the relation between populism and constitutional reform – it is clear that populists frequently engage with constitutionalism as a discourse and practice of power.[12] Populists, in particular once in power, make use of the constitution in a variety of ways, not least in order to safeguard and perpetuate their political power in the name of a 'pure' people (the practical, reform dimension is discussed in the next section of this chapter).

---

4 M. Freeden, 'After the Brexit Referendum: Revisiting Populism as an Ideology' (2017) 22(1) *Journal of Political Ideologies* 1–11, 7.

5 J.W. Müller, *What Is Populism?* (University of Pennsylvania Press 2016) 68; cf. N. Urbinati, *Democracy Disfigured* (Harvard University Press 2014).

6 N. Urbinati, 'Democracy and Populism' (1998) 5(1) *Constellations* 110–124, 111.

7 P. Blokker, 'Populism as a Constitutional Project' (2019) 17(2) *International Journal of Constitutional Law* 536.

8 Freeden (n 4).

9 Populists, in this, are often operating in a constitutional grey zone, using rather aggressive and even unconstitutional means, or at the very least not using formally existing codified amendment procedures, or twisting or abusing such procedures.

10 A. Arato, 'How we got here? Transition Failures, their Causes, and the Populist Interest in the Constitution' (2017). Available at: https://papers.ssrn.com/sol3/papers.cfm?abstract_id=3116219.

11 Chambers (n 2).

12 Cf. Müller (n 5) chapter 2.

Forms of populist constitutionalism in practice are visible in cases of what many see as forms of 'backsliding' or the emergence of 'illiberal' democracy in Central and Eastern Europe, in particular in Hungary and Poland (and to a lesser extent, but evermore visibly so, in Romania too), as well as in emerging forms of authoritarianism, as in Turkey, and now even in so-called established democracies, such as the United States. To the astute observer, however, elaborate populist-constitutional projects had been already extensively present in Latin America (Colombia, Venezuela, Ecuador, Bolivia) since the 1990s. The impact of populism on constitutionalism currently goes even further than this, in that there are ample examples of populist forms of behaviour with regard to constitutionalism beyond populist movements in strict terms.

As observed above, much of the debate in constitutional theory, political science, and political theory appears to be dismissing any positive relation between populism and constitutionalism. Gábor Halmai, for instance, concludes that there is no such thing as 'populist constitutionalism'. He argues,

> [t]he term 'populist constitutionalism' seems to me to be an oxymoron altogether. The same applies to 'authoritarian' or 'illiberal' constitutionalism. If the main characteristic of constitutionalism is the legally limited power of the government, neither authoritarian nor illiberal polities can fulfil the requirements of constitutionalism.[13]

The tendency is hence to identify the relation of populists with constitutionalism as predominantly one of abuse,[14] and as practices that go against the ideas of constitutionalism and the rule of law as such.[15] The stance of many EU scholars and the EU Commission is that the practices of the Hungarian and Polish governments in recent years are threatening or undermining the rule of law and constitutionalism. This chapter wants to argue that the relationship between constitutionalism and populism is, however, more complex than a straightforward dichotomic view would allow for.

First, as noted, in their political projects, populists frequently take recourse to *constitutional reform* and even *constitution-making*. It is clear that populist-constitutional projects cannot be entirely reduced to a mere dismantling of constitutional democracy, but also include forms of constitution-making, for better or worse. Populist projects show significant affinity with constitutions and, in particular, with constituent power.

---

13 G. Halmai, 'Is There Such Thing as "Populist Constitutionalism"? The Case of Hungary' (2018) 11(3) *Fudan Journal of the Humanities and Social Sciences* 1–17.

14 D. Landau, 'Abusive Constitutionalism' (2013) 47 *University of California, Davis, Law Review* 189. Kim Scheppele argues that 'autocrats who hijack constitutions seek to benefit from the superficial appearance of both democracy and legality within their states. They use their democratic mandates to launch legal reforms that remove the checks on executive power, limit the challenges to their rule, and undermine the crucial accountability institutions of a democratic state', see K.L. Scheppele, 'Autocratic Legalism' (2018) 85 *University of Chicago Law Review* 545, 547. Somewhat inconsistent with this clearly realist interpretation, which reduces populism to forms of 'autocratic legalism' in which the main purpose of using constitutions is to hold onto power, in other places, Scheppele writes about how 'counter-constitutions are alternative visions of constitutional order, grounded in different understandings of what a constitution is and should be, understandings that reject the taken-for-granted constitutional vision already in place', K.L. Scheppele, 'The Social Lives of Constitutions' in P. Blokker and C. Thornhill (eds), *Sociological Constitutionalism* (Cambridge University Press 2017) 35. In both writings, Hungary is Scheppele's 'archetypal' case.

15 See, e.g., C. Closa and D. Kochenov (eds), *Reinforcing Rule of Law Oversight in the European Union* (Cambridge University Press 2016).

A second issue regards the fact that (distinctive dimensions of) populist constitutionalism equally emerge in the discourses and actions of political actors, who are not normally or predominantly defined as populist. This indicates a potential *diffusion* of a populist-constitutional mindset into the political mainstream (as is the case in Italy with part of the centre-left[16] or in the UK, where the Conservative Party has embraced populist slogans and claims[17]), which potentially leads to a wider erosion of liberal-constitutional ideals. It also indicates more structural trends of change regarding the relation between democracy and constitutionalism.

A third matter regards the *pertinence of claims* that populists make regarding constitutions. In distinct dimensions, populist claims are radical and unsettling with regard to the existing institutions, and may be said to reflect long-standing debates in constitutional theory over the relation between popular government and constitutionalism (touching upon crucial matters such as judicial review or even the role and nature of constituent power in modern democracy, and the current predicament of liberal democracy).[18] Populist claims and action, even in their rudimentary nature, put into relief complex issues, such as the status of universal human rights in domestic systems as well as the matter of jurisgenerative power.

A final issue is that a more in-depth understanding of the populist-constitutional phenomenon is necessary if one wants to elaborate, and put into practice, valid *democratic alternatives*. This last matter reflects the idea that the manifestation of populism signifies a deep discomfort with, and malfunctioning of, existing democratic institutions. In this regard, Yaron Ezrahi importantly detects the erosion of the collective political imaginaries of modern constitutional democracy.[19] Such structural changes to the perception, imagination, and practice of democratic politics indicate that a mere strengthening of the liberal, constitutional-democratic state or a return to the status quo ex ante might not be sufficient nor effective.

In strict terms, then, the populist approach toward constitutionalism is not entirely negative (in terms of criticizing the establishment and engaging solely with anti-politics). Populist constitutionalism should, in important dimensions, be understood as a constructive constitutional project, as becomes evident not least from ultimately radically different populist projects of constitution-making and constitutional reform, as have emerged in cases in Latin America and East-Central Europe. The actual constitutional practices of populists, but also their constitutional mindset and claims, need to be explored further.

The populist mindset

A variety of rather disparate forms of populist engagement with constitutions is nevertheless grounded in a distinctively populist understanding of the law in general and of constitutional

---

16 See M. Revelli, *Dentro e contro: Quando il populismo è di governo* (Gius. Laterza & Figli Spa 2015).

17 K. Nash, 'Politicising Human Rights in Europe: Challenges to Legal Constitutionalism from the Left and the Right' (2016) 20(8) *The International Journal of Human Rights* 1295–1308.

18 Particularly relevant here is Jeffrey Isaac's argument regarding the state of contemporary democracy, against Jan-Werner Müller's claim that 'illiberal democracy' is an oxymoron. Isaacs argues, in my view rightly so, that 'illiberal democracy' can be a useful label to use, not least because of illiberal tendencies within established democracies themselves, as inter alia visible in 'cartelized political party systems and captured state institutions', rampant social inequalities, and restrictive media oligopolies, see J.C. Isaac, 'Is There Illiberal Democracy? A Problem with No Semantic Solution' (2017) *Public Seminar*. Available at: www.publicseminar.org/wp-content/uploads/2017/07/Isaac-Jeffrey-Is-There-Illiberal-Democracy-Public-Seminar.pdf.

19 Y. Ezrahi, *Imagined Democracies: Necessary Political Fictions* (Cambridge University Press 2012).

law in particular. Populist constitutionalism, in this, needs to be related to distinctively modern understandings and imaginaries of constitutionalism. As recently suggested by Luigi Corrias,[20] populism can be related to a specific – revolutionary and democratic – constitutional tradition, which might be best explored through reference to the work on constitutionalism of radical-democratic thinkers.[21] The revolutionary tradition emphasizes *constituent power*, understood as a founding act of the people, founding the polity anew. As Corrias argues, the understanding of the constituent power of the people in the revolutionary tradition appears as almost absolute, and as potentially being exercised directly in the polity.[22] Populist constitutionalism needs to engage with this radical, constituent dimension, as populists claim that the liberal-democratic version of constitutional democracy is deeply flawed and hence needs to be comprehensively revisited.

What clearly emerges is a *primacy of politics over law* in the revolutionary tradition, in that law is understood as ultimately the outcome or consequence of political action, and cannot claim an independent standing of its own. On this view, constitutions are understood less as higher, universal principles that limit and bind political power, as in legal or liberal constitutionalism, than as positive, political and emancipatory expressions of the rules and norms that a political community wants to give itself.

The revolutionary understanding of constitutionalism is in contrast to a second tradition, the evolutionary tradition, which understands constitutionalism as a negative, limiting instrument, which seeks to create order and stability[23] and to 'tame politics'.[24] As argued by Christoph Möllers, the pedigree of this understanding of constitutionalism is less a democratic one, but rather related to liberal and statist understandings of constitutionalism. The evolutionary approach is endorsing a primacy of the law over politics, displaying a certain distrust of the people and of popular sovereignty, and understanding popular politics as potentially threatening the constitutional order itself. It may be argued that whereas the revolutionary tradition keeps the idea of constituent power alive in the constituted order,[25] in the evolutionary approach, constituent power is seen as absorbed in (the institutions of) constituted power.

The populist understanding of constitutionalism hinges on the revolutionary tradition, but with a specific twist. Populism captures the popular will and claims it as its own, against other social forces, in- or outside society. Populists tend to define the people in strong contrast to some significant Other (elites, foreign forces), and in this turn their (idealized) construction of the people into the only acceptable, non-corrupted one. The people are, in this, equated with a (morally pure) majority, which is understood in contrast to (polluted) minorities. The rule of law and constitutionalism cannot, according to populists, override

---

20 L. Corrias, 'Populism in a Constitutional Key: Constituent Power, Popular Sovereignty and Constitutional Identity' (2016) 12(1) *European Constitutional Law Review* 6.

21 H. Arendt, *On Revolution* (Penguin Books 1990); cf. P. Blokker, 'The Imaginary Constitution of Constitutions' (2017) 3(1) *Social Imaginaries* 167–193; H. Brunkhorst, *Critical Theory of Legal Revolutions: Evolutionary Perspectives* (Bloomsbury 2014); E. Laclau, *On Populist Reason* (Verso 2005); C. Möllers 'Pouvoir Constituant – Constitution – Constitutionalisation' in J. Bast and A. von Bogdandy (eds), *Principles of European Constitutional Law* (Hart Publishing/NOMOS Verlag 2009) 169–204.

22 Corrias (n 20) 16. Cf. Arato (n 10).

23 Blokker (n 21).

24 Corrias (n 20) 15.

25 A. Kalyvas, *Democracy and the Politics of the Extraordinary: Max Weber, Carl Schmitt and Hannah Arendt* (Cambridge and New York 2008).

the popular will. Constitutionalism as such becomes a device in the populist project of rebuilding the state.

Populist constitutionalism seems a rejection of the modern, legal version of constitutionalism and some kind of variant of the revolutionary one. The relation between populism and constitutionalism might be understood by reference to predominantly the revolutionary imaginary, even if with important differences and distortions, as populism strongly rejects the evolutionary, rule-of-law tradition and prioritizes popular sovereignty. Populism rejects the emphasis on the limitation of political power through legal norms and the subjection of power to higher norms as in legal constitutionalism, while it promotes a constitutional order that puts popular sovereignty and constituent power upfront. It denounces the rule of law and the constitutional state as vehicles that promote the interests of minorities (elites) against the well-being of the people and claims to build a new constitutional order that will promote the common good against partial interests.

To what extent is it possible to interpret populism as a manifestation of modern democracy and of modern constitutionalism? There are clear indications that populism threatens established understandings of constitutional democracy and forms an undeniable threat to the institutional status quo. In this, it shares a certain thrust with radical forms of *democratic constitutionalism.*[26] Democratic constitutionalism rejects the preceding order, or the existing order or status quo it agitates against, and wants to create a polity anew, eschewing any of the existing traditions. Democratic constitutionalism puts, in this, the rights of the individual and the idea of equality centre stage, against the corrupting and unequal implications of established traditions based on status and privilege. Democratic constitutionalism targets legal constitutionalism as potentially leading to inequality, as in the lack of possibilities for popular engagement with constitutional politics and norms, and in the emphasis on elitist, higher public reason.

Populist constitutionalism shares this thrust toward denouncing elite rule as detrimental to the common good and as potentially favouring partial interests. It equally denounces the professed neutrality and rationality of the law as potentially resulting in inequality and exclusion. But where the thrust in democratic constitutionalism is the widening and deepening of possibilities of de facto citizen engagement with constitutional politics and norms, in populist constitutionalism the actual engagement of (different groups of) citizens in society is frequently substituted for by the idea of a united People, represented by the populist leader. The main culprit is identified in corrupt elite rule, which simply needs to be replaced by government for the people, but not necessarily by the people.

---

26 It is important to distinguish between democratic constitutionalism and forms of 'abusive' constitutionalism as identified by Landau (I thank Tomek Koncewicz for this observation). Democratic constitutionalism, as theorized in different ways by scholars such as Andrew Arato, James Tully, and Joel Colón-Ríos, strongly emphasizes the inclusiveness of constitution-making processes, the legitimatory potential of civic participation, and a strong recognition of the intrinsic plurality of the political community. In contrast, the concept of abusive constitutionalism rather refers to a political project that uses legal means to dismantle the preceding order and to entrench a new hegemony. The invocation of the political majority (the people-as-one) is to legitimate the populist project, but its exclusivist and Manichaean nature goes clearly against the inclusivist and particularist logic of the democratic-constitutional idea. It should be stressed that abusive constitutionalism is a predominant dimension in populist constitutional projects, but it does not present the whole picture. It has to be acknowledged that abusive constitutionalism is often made possible due to an initially more comprehensive inclusivist and pluralist promise (as for instance in the Latin American cases discussed below). The latter has close affinity to the democratic constitutional idea, but is in many populist projects eventually abandoned for a majoritarian, partisan, and polarizing approach.

Populism therefore, at least in part, criticizes legal constitutionalism on similar grounds as democratic constitutionalism, but its alternative constitutional solution, 'counter-constitution', or 'constitutional counter-revolution' is highly different from the democratic and democratizing idea. This becomes clear in at least some of the 'really existing' examples of populist constitutionalism, such as in Poland and Hungary. Populist constitutionalism rejects the existing order because of its inequalities and injustices, as in democratic constitutionalism, but it does so with the aim to restore (an ideal of) a preceding, historical order. But one can equally identify a Messianic, redemptive dimension, which is future-oriented in that it aims at realizing a pure, non-corrupted polity in the future (in the Polish case, e.g., in the form of a 'Fourth Republic'). Populism – at least in its right-wing, but in some ways also in its left-wing manifestations – understands liberal democracy and the rule of law as a historical interruption and aberration. It rejects the idea of the legal-constitutional order because, according to populists, it produces or favours inequalities (e.g., between the haves and have-nots, between cosmopolitans and locals, or between foreigners and nationals), as well as, more importantly, because it leads to the erosion of the historical nation. The hierarchy of the legal-constitutional order is not to be replaced by an inclusive, more universalistic order, but rather by a return to, or realization of, the past, that is, of a traditional order, based on 'natural' hierarchies related to ethnicity, family, and tradition.

Populist-constitutional reform

The populist imaginary informs the approach of populists to institutions in general, and constitutions in particular. Populists in government frequently take recourse to constitutional means to promote their political projects. Here, I will discuss a number of prominent dimensions to such engagement with constitutions and constitutionalism, which emerge from a variety of experiences with populist-constitutional reform. Populist political projects frequently include dimensions of judicial reform, participatory and direct democracy, the centralization of power and entrenchment of populist rule, and the pursuit of substantive religious-ethical projects.

Judicial reform

A key dimension of populist engagement with constitutional norms and constitutional reform regards the status and independence of the judiciary and of judicial institutions. Populists often attempt to bring the judicial institutions, and most prominently the *sui generis* institutions of constitutional courts, under political control of the majority government. A widely presented populist claim is that judicial institutions are excessively interfering into democratic politics, to defend the status quo of a corrupt, elitist system. As argued by Andrew Arato, there are different reasons for populists to engage with judicial reform, in particular in terms of reforming courts, and different ways of bringing judicial change about (please note that the various modes of reform discussed below contain some overlapping dimensions).[27]

A first and widely used approach is that of structurally changing the *composition of the judiciary*, which may take the form of 'court packing' but can also involve the dismantling of courts. A significant and recent example of a populist government drastically changing the composition

---

27 A. Arato, 'Populism, the Courts and Civil Society' (2017). Available at: https://papers.ssrn.com/sol3/papers.cfm?abstract_id=3082596.

of apex courts is Poland. The Law and Justice party (PiS), in government since 2015, made the Constitutional Tribunal its first main institutional target. PiS started its confrontation with the tribunal by contesting five tribunal judges appointed by the outgoing Civic Platform (PO) government. PiS justified its actions by invoking the need for extensive judicial reform and the development of a different type of constitutionalism. It disregarded a prominent constitutional convention (the oath of the newly appointed judges to be taken by the president), re-amended the Act on the Constitutional Tribunal, denying the legal status of the judges appointed by PO, and rapidly appointed its own judges. The PiS-controlled Sejm, the Polish lower house, subsequently approved amendments of the Act, which changed the necessary quorum for decisions from 9 to 13 judges, out of a total of 15, effectively paralysing the court. On top of this, later rulings by the tribunal, which found the changes unconstitutional, were delayed in publication or failed to be officially published at all. The taking over of the tribunal was complete once, after a year, PiS gained a majority of judges on the tribunal and the presidency was taken up by Julia Przyłębska (installed by means of a newly invented position of 'acting president', replacing the outgoing president Andrzej Rzepliński).[28]

The right-wing populist practices of packing courts in East-Central Europe may have found inspiration in similar methods used in left-wing projects in Latin America, a decade or two earlier. The most striking example is probably that of the coming to power of President Hugo Chávez in Venezuela in 1999. Judicial reform was an urgent and widely popular issue when Chávez came to power, due to issues of profound corruption and politicization of the courts.[29] Initially, the enactment of a new constitution in 1999 led to the establishment of a new apex court and guarantees of judicial independence. By 2004, however, the Chávez government changed its approach drastically. The novel Supreme Tribunal of Justice was taken over politically by means of the enactment of a new law which, inter alia, allowed for the expansion of the court's members from 20 to 32, taken up by Chávez's supporters. Chávez further strongly centralized presidential powers while turning the judiciary into pro-presidential institutions. Through the National Constituent Assembly (ANC) (on which more below), the Supreme Court was put under strict control of a presidential commission, which could remove any judge from office on charges of corruption or otherwise.[30]

A different way of interfering with the composition of the judiciary can be found under Evo Morales in Bolivia. Rather than packing courts, from 2005 onwards the Morales government rather engaged in what has been described as the neutralization or 'dismantling' of courts, based on the 'ability to induce resignations [of judges] without appointments'.[31] By inducing judges to resign or, more explicitly, by engaging in processes of impeachment, courts became dramatically understaffed, even failing at specific points to meet the quora to make decisions.

28 W. Sadurski, 'How Democracy Dies (in Poland): A Case Study of Anti-Constitutional Populist Backsliding' (2018) 18(01) *Sydney Law School Research Paper* 22–23. Available at: https://papers.ssrn.com/sol3/papers.cfm?abstract_id=3103491.

29 Human Rights Watch, *A Decade under Chávez* (2008) 45. Available at: www.hrw.org/sites/default/files/reports/venezuela0908web.pdf

30 F.M. Walsh, 'The Legal Death of the Latin American Democracy: Bolivarian Populism's Model for Centralizing Power, Eliminating Political Opposition, and Undermining the Rule of Law' (2010) 16 *Law and Business Review of the Americas* 241, 247.

31 A. Castagnola and A. Pérez-Linán, 'The Rise (and Fall) of Judicial Review' in G. Helmke and J. Rios-Figueroa (eds), *Courts in Latin America* (Cambridge University Press 2011) 278, 303, 302–304.

Returning to the case of Venezuela, a second, rather different development, which seems now to play out in East-Central Europe too, is the development of *parallel judicial institutions*. The ANC created the Supreme Tribunal of Justice in December 1999 to replace the old Supreme Court, which took over its prerogatives. Over time, this new apex court was itself 'packed' with pro-Chávez judges, while the judges were denied tenure, reducing judicial independence further.[32]

The populist trend toward the creation of parallel institutions is picked up in Europe too and has now become particularly visible in the case of Hungary. Hungary has been spearheading populist constitutionalism in the East-Central European context, and the Fidesz government has engaged in court packing and other measures adding up to a politicization of the judicial system from 2010 onwards, including increasing the number of judges on the Constitutional Court from seven to 15.[33] By the end of 2018, this process had seen a new turn. A new law (Act no. CXXX of 2018) created a separate branch of administrative courts, parallel to the Supreme Court, to operate under the direction of a new Supreme Administrative Court, which itself is under the direction of the ministry of justice.[34] Some observers understand the new law as a pretext that 'essentially enables the packing of the Hungarian judiciary to the degree the 2011 constitutional overhaul could not achieve'.[35]

A second way of populist engagement with judicial reform is by *changing and reducing the jurisdiction of courts* or hindering their effective operation. In Hungary, Fidesz restricted the Constitutional Court's jurisdiction from 2010 onwards, by taking away the court's power over fiscal matters, making it largely impossible for the court to rule on the constitutionality of budgets or taxes.[36] More drastically, with the Fourth Amendment of the new Hungarian Fundamental Law in 2013, review powers of the court were restricted to procedural matters only, while the earlier case law of the court of the 1990–2011 period was annulled.

In Poland, during the 'paralysis' of the Constitutional Tribunal caused by the controversy over the appointed new judges in 2015–16, the PiS government used unconventional measures, as mentioned above, disregarding its constitutional duty to officially publish tribunal judgments, by postponing or even failing to publish altogether, as was the case with the tribunal's judgments on the revised Act on the Constitutional Tribunal, as in December 2015 and March 2016.

A third type of reform is *changing the rules of appointment of judges*, in terms of institutions involved and/or in terms of procedures. The aforementioned adoption of a new law regarding the Supreme Tribunal by the Chávez government in 2004 allowed the National Assembly to select new judges by means of a simple majority vote, which in practice meant that the small governmental majority could be translated into an overwhelming majority of pro-government judges.[37] In addition, as alluded to above, the new law allowed the

---

32 Walsh (n 30) 248–249.

33 A. Vincze, 'Wrestling with Constitutionalism: The Supermajority and the Hungarian Constitutional Court' (2014) 8(1) *Vienna Journal on International Constitutional Law* 86–97.

34 R. Uitz, 'An Advanced Course in Court Packing: Hungary's New Law on Administrative Courts' (2018) *Verf-Blog*, 2019/1/02. Available at: https://verfassungsblog.de/an-advanced-course-in-court-packing-hungarys-new-law-on-administrative-courts/.

35 Uitz (n 34).

36 M. Bánkuti, G. Halmai, and K. Scheppele, 'Hungary's Illiberal Turn: Disabling the Constitution' in P. Krasztev and J. van Til (eds), *The Hungarian Patient: Social Opposition to an Illiberal Democracy* (Central European University Press 2015) 37–47, 38–39.

37 HRW (n 29) 36.

legislature to remove justices from the bench with a simple majority vote, rather than the two-thirds required by the 1999 Constitution.

In Poland, after the capture of the Constitutional Tribunal, the PiS government extended reform to the Supreme Court and the National Council of the Judiciary (KRS). PiS assumed control over the KRS by terminating the terms of existing members and giving parliament the right to appoint a majority of the replacements.[38] In December 2017, PiS adopted a new law which added two new chambers to the Supreme Court, while changing the rules of appointment of Supreme Court judges, forcing all justices of over the age of 65 to retire, unless their terms are extended with presidential approval.[39] In general, PiS changed appointment rules so that it is the parliamentary majority that is now in charge of the appointment of members of both the KRS and the Supreme Court, while the president has gained extensive powers in appointing the president of the court as well as regarding its internal functioning.

A fourth manner is by *changing the rules of operation of courts*, for instance, by changing the voting procedures in judicial review procedures. The example of Poland in the tribunal's 'paralysis' phase is again instructive. The PiS government made the operation of the tribunal more cumbersome by stipulating that judgments should be sequenced on the basis of when a motion reached the tribunal (this was later recalled). Even more problematic was the stipulation that full judgments could be only made with the mandatory participation of 13 out of 15 judges.[40]

A fifth type, related to the diminishment of judicial independence, is the *strengthening of the executive vis-à-vis the judiciary*, for instance, by giving extensive monitoring powers to the executive. In Poland, PiS has, on a more or less on-going basis, tried to strengthen the position of the executive. In the Amendment of 22 December 2015, the president and the ministry of justice were given the power to start disciplinary proceedings against tribunal judges. In a more recent series of attempts to redesign relations between the government and judicial institutions, beginning in the summer and continuing until the end of 2017, the government attempted to importantly strengthen the position of the parliament to appoint members of the KRS. PiS also sought to strengthen the position of the minister of justice in appointing Supreme Court judges and to give the government the power to nominate judges of common courts.[41]

In Latin America, the case of Chávez is conspicuous, starting with an extension of presidential powers in the new constitution and the invocation of the original, untied constituent powers of the National Constituent Assembly, to find its culmination in the successful removal of presidential term limits in 2009.[42]

Participatory and direct democracy

Next to judicial reform, which aims at (re-)politicizing judicial institutions and breaking the power of former ruling elites, much constitutional action of populists relates to the way in which democratic rule and the representation of the popular will are institutionalized. Clearly,

---

38 C. Davies, *Hostile Takeover: How Law and Justice Captured Poland's Courts* (2018) Freedom House: Nations in Transit 5.

39 Davies (n 38). This part of the reform has been challenged by the European Court of Justice and PiS has reversed the retirement of judges.

40 Sadurski (n 28) 26.

41 P. Mikuli, 'The Declining State of the Judiciary in Poland', (2018) *International Journal of Constitutional Law Blog*, May 15. Available at: www.iconnectblog.com/2018/05/the-declining-state-of-the-judiciary-in-poland.

42 D. Landau, 'Constitution-Making Gone Wrong' (2012) 64 *Alabama Law Review* 923.

populism is to be understood as driven by a critique on liberal, representative democracy.[43] Populists claim to be able to present a political alternative to liberal democracy, as expressed in Orbán's 'illiberal democracy' or Poland's 'Fourth Republic'. In many Latin American countries, populists equally claim to pursue 'participatory democracy' or '*verdadera democracia*' ('true democracy') as alternatives to liberal democracy. The broad claim all populists make is that they are able to institutionalize a political regime in which citizens are more fully and more extensively included than in liberal, representative democracy.

In the context of constitutional reform and constitution-making, a significant dimension pertains to, first, how populists pursue constitutional change (which actors and social groups are involved in reform, what kind of procedures and democratic instruments are used), and, second, which objectives and outcomes are achieved through constitutional reform or redesigning the constitution.

The populist critique on liberal, representative democracy, elitism, and elite corruption often translates into the endorsement of a more *direct* involvement of the people in government and rule-making, in some cases including the change of constitutional rules. Many populists, though certainly not all, invoke forms of bottom-up participation as a response to the 'representation deficit' (the lack of representation of the ordinary people or the marginalized in existing democratic regimes). This understanding of participation often pits a unitary people against the old governing elite, promoting in this a form of hyper-representation of highly disparate parts of society.[44] Citizen participation may, however, be realized in very different and even contrasting ways. The populist attitude to citizen involvement seems frequently to take a *plebiscitarian* form, i.e., an appeal to legitimize the populist leader and/or government. It is only in the more radical, left-wing versions of populism that more substantive forms of citizen involvement are endorsed and institutionalized, including forms of *deliberation* and *popular initiative*.

The latter, more substantive forms of citizen involvement have been most pronounced in various constitution-making projects in Latin America since the early 1990s (at least in the earlier stages of these political projects). A particularly conspicuous and relatively unprecedented phenomenon has been the promotion of constituent assemblies in the region.[45] In, for instance, Bolivia, Ecuador, and Venezuela, bottom-up calls for citizen involvement and populist endorsement of 'participatory democracy' resulted in the establishment of constituent assemblies, which were set up to be more inclusive toward marginalized minorities and indigenous peoples.[46] Populist leaders, such as Chávez in Venezuela in the late 1990s and Correa in Ecuador in the later 2000s, endorsed radical change by means of the mobilization of the constituent power of the people. As attested by Angélica M. Bernal, 'these leaders have simultaneously appealed to the constituent power of the people and have sought to expand the people's political protagonism by establishing constituent assemblies selected by popular vote'.[47] In Venezuela, Chávez convened

---

43 Urbinati (n 6).

44 E. De Blasio and M. Sorice, 'Populism between Direct Democracy and the Technological Myth' (2018) 14(5) *Communications* 3.

45 J. Colón-Ríos, *Weak Constitutionalism: Democratic Legitimacy and the Question of Constituent Power* (Routledge 2012).

46 C. de la Torre, 'Populist Citizenship in the Bolivarian Revolutions' (2017) 1(1) *Middle Atlantic Review of Latin American Studies* 4–32, 8.

47 A.M. Bernal, 'The Meaning and Perils of Presidential Refounding in Latin America' (2014) 21(4) *Constellations* 440–456, 443.

a 'constitutional assembly to rewrite the constitution and subsequently submit it to a referendum. The new constitution was then approved by popular vote in 1999 and institutionalized among its articles direct democracy mechanisms and instruments of social control and popular participation'[48] (as in Article 431 which allows for citizens calling for a referendum to propose constitutional changes or Article 348 which allows citizens to call for a constituent assembly). A striking development in Bolivia was the unprecedented introduction of the popular election of high court justices (first exercised in 2011). While the process has shown to be highly cumbersome, the first elections of justices in 2011 proved to be more inclusive of previously excluded indigenous peoples.[49]

Carlos de la Torre describes the processes of drafting of new constitutions in the Latin American countries as participatory and open to social movements, while the final drafts were approved in referenda.[50] But it was not merely the processes that were set up in notably participatory and inclusive ways. The constitutions themselves expanded rights, notably socio-economic ones, but also established a different form of democracy, the aforementioned '*verdadera democracia*', emphasizing more vertical accountability by means of frequent elections, referenda, and plebiscites, whereas horizontal accountability was strongly reduced.[51] The populist political projects in Latin America sought recourse to constitution-making to bring about a 'refounding' of specific states, which meant '*un nuevo comienzo*' (a new beginning), both in terms of a new independence from external, neoliberal powers, and the re-empowerment and inclusion of marginalized groups internally.[52] The Latin American experiences can be understood as radical forms of populism, which both used constitution-making processes 'as a means of channeling civil discontent, mobilizing extensive citizen participation, and representing democratic change',[53] but equally led to 'an alarming expansion of presidential powers'.[54]

In contrast, the Central European experiences with populism in government have seen a largely rhetorical invocation of popular sovereignty and the mobilization of citizens through elections, while actual citizen participation has remained limited and has often been further curbed. In the European context, populist engagement with constitution-making was in important ways spearheaded by the rapid and largely non-participatory and majority-driven drafting of a new Hungarian constitution by the centre-right Fidesz government in 2011.[55] The thrust of much of the Hungarian counter-constitutional process is against the democratic-constitutional order that emerged since 1989, as the leaders 'sensed a fundamental (and in the short term irremediable) disillusionment with the liberal-democratic system across all segments of the Hungarian political community and think they have a long-term solution that will appeal to the masses'.[56] The populist-constitutional project is being justified by means of reference to a different idea of constitutionalism, the

---

48 T. Pogrebinschi, 'The Pragmatic Turn of Democracy in Latin America' (2013) *WZB Berlin* 6.
49 A. Driscoll and M.J. Nelson, 'Judicial Selection and the Democratization of Justice: Lessons from the Bolivian Judicial Elections' (2015) 3(1) *Journal of Law and Courts* 115–148.
50 De la Torre (n 46) 6.
51 De la Torre and Arnson 2013, cited in de la Torre (n 46) 9.
52 Bernal (n 47) 441.
53 Bernal (n 47) 443.
54 Bernal (n 47) 440.
55 R. László, *Dismantling Direct Democracy: Referenda in Hungary* (Friedrich Ebert Stiftung 2016).
56 K. Szombati, 'The Betrayed Republic: Hungary's New Constitution and the "System of National Cooperation"' (Prague: Heinrich Böll Stiftung 2011). Available at: www.cz.boell.org/web/52-972.html.

unwritten 'historical constitution'.[57] In this, the conservative thrust in the Fidesz project can be related to 'communitarian' as well as 'illiberal' views of constitutionalism.[58] What identifies such forms of constitutionalism is the perception of a 'common enemy' in liberal constitutionalism, and a critique of both the 'meta-liberal value of normative individualism' and its understanding of the 'neutral state'. In contrast, illiberal constitutionalism emphasizes community interests and the active promotion of a particular vision of communal life.[59]

In terms of civic engagement and alternative forms of participatory democracy, the 2011 Fundamental Law was adopted in a top-down, majority-driven manner.[60] In the constitution-making process of 2010–11, the populist Fidesz government shunned existing rules that called for inclusive constitutional change. The necessity of consensual constitution-making that was enshrined in a four-fifths rule on the adoption of a new constitution[61] – which imposed collaboration between government and opposition – was eliminated by the Fidesz government by means of an amendment. The actual constitution-writing process was carried out in a highly opaque manner by three members of the Fidesz Party, headed by József Szájer, and rushed through parliament in March and April 2011.[62] Earlier, in 2010, a public consultation procedure had been started, in which the views of the public, NGOs, and opposition parties were solicited, but this procedure did not involve any direct engagement with draft proposals, nor were its results taken into account in the actual drafting in March 2011.

Regarding direct democracy instruments, the New Fundamental Law of Hungary sustained a good part of the institutions of direct democracy in place since 1989. The actual constitutional text did not involve major advancements in terms of participatory democracy, but did abolish some of the existing participatory instruments, such as the *actio popularis* and national popular initiatives.[63] The Fundamental Law further modified the way in which direct democracy can be exercised.[64] This has resulted in restrictions for the opposition and civil society to use referenda (as the quorum for referenda was increased to 50% of eligible voters). Also, as stipulated in Article 8, section 3 of the Fundamental Law, no matters related to constitutional amendment can be put to referendum. In 2013, the Fidesz

---

57 K.L. Scheppele, 'Counter-constitutions: Narrating the Nation in Post-Soviet Hungary' (2004) paper given at George Washington University, Washington DC, 2 April.
58 Cf. L.A. Thio, 'Constitutionalism in Illiberal Polities' in M. Rosenfeld and A. Sajó (eds), *The Oxford Handbook of Comparative Constitutional Law* (Oxford University Press 2012) 133–152.
59 In the Hungarian Fundamental Law, the emphasis on the Hungarian nation and its cultural legacy is more than evident in the elaborate preamble, which starts with 'We, Members of the Hungarian Nation', as well as in such articles as Article D (protection of Hungarians living abroad) or Article L on marriage ('the family as the basis of the nation's survival'), Fundamental Law 2011. The Fundamental Law further makes the enjoying of rights conditional on satisfying duties. In religious terms, the Fundamental Law has been identified as an 'ode to Christianity and a reluctance to separate Church and State', R. Uitz 'Freedom of Religion and Churches: Archeology in a Constitution-making Assembly' in G.A. Toth (ed), *Constitution for a Disunited Nation: On Hungary's 2011 Fundamental Law* (Central European University Press 2011) 197–236, 199.
60 Cf. P. Blokker, *New Democracies in Crisis? A Comparative Constitutional Study of the Czech Republic, Hungary, Poland, Romania and Slovakia* (Routledge 2013).
61 Art. 24(5) of the 1989 Constitution, introduced in 1995.
62 K.L. Scheppele 'Constitutional Coups and Judicial Review: How Transnational Institutions Can Strengthen Peak Courts at Times of Crisis (With Special Reference to Hungary)' (2014) 23 *Transnational Law & Contemporary Problems* 51–197.
63 Cf. Laszlo (n 55) 2.
64 Z. Pozsár-Szentmiklósy, 'Direct Democracy in Hungary (1989–2016): From Popular Sovereignty to Popular Illusion' (2017) 6 *Acta Universitatis Sapientiae Legal Studies* 109, 112.

government adopted a new referendum law that further 'drastically hindered the chance for the certification of referendum questions in topics uncomfortable to the government'.[65] In addition, a new instrument has been introduced, the *national consultations*, invoking a popular participatory dimension, but in practice being government-driven, without any constitutional basis, and remaining highly underregulated, opaque, and inconsequential on the level of policy-making.[66] Observers have argued that direct democracy instruments in Hungary have turned away from counter-democratic logic serving opposition and civil society forces, and turned into an 'instrument of populist majoritarian politics'.[67]

Centralization of power, institutionally entrenching power

A key dimension of many populist political projects is to institutionalize partisan power into the political system, allowing populist forces to retain influence on government even in case of an electoral defeat. As David Landau attests, a key objective of populists is to consolidate power in the hands of the populist leadership by using constitutional reform.[68] Or as Kim Scheppele has argued, populists (or autocrats in her terminology) 'are attacking the basic principles of liberal and democratic constitutionalism because they want to consolidate power and entrench themselves in office for the long haul'.[69] In this, they 'use their democratic mandates to launch legal reforms that remove the checks on executive power, limit the challenges to their rule, and undermine the crucial accountability institutions of a democratic state'.[70] What is conspicuous in such attempts at entrenchment of political power is that 'they use liberal method to achieve their illiberal results' and use as their weapons 'laws, constitutional revision, and institutional reform'.[71]

The entrenchment of political power by populists includes a variety of forms. One significant way is to turn institutions that used to structurally check political power, in particular apex courts, into allies of the majority government or *government enablers*.[72] The aforementioned events in Poland are a case in point. As described in depth by Wojciech Sadurski, the populist PiS government moved quickly after it won the October 2015 elections to paralyse and subsequently capture, first, the Constitutional Tribunal, and in due course (in particular from the summer of 2017 onwards), the larger judiciary, not least the Supreme Court and National Council of the Judiciary. As also stated earlier, key dimensions of this relate to 'packing' the court, putting into place judges loyal to the government while removing judges (for instance through early retirement) hostile to the government, as well as changing the jurisdiction and function of the court in the overall political system. Similar events had taken place years earlier in the Hungarian case, but the Polish case perhaps clearly shows the potential success of such a strategy, i.e., the turning of a counter-democratic (in Rosanvallon's sense) or counter-majoritarian institution into an institution that legitimates government decisions. As Sadurski explains in an apt manner:

---

65 Laszlo (n 55) 3.
66 Pozsár-Szentmiklósy (n 64) 114–115.
67 Pozsár-Szentmiklósy (n 64) 115.
68 D. Landau, 'Populist Constitutions' (2018) 85 *University of Chicago Law Review* 521.
69 K.L. Scheppele, 'Autocratic Legalism' (2018) 85 *University of Chicago Law Review* 545.
70 Scheppele (n 69) 547; cf. Landau (n 68) 8.
71 Scheppele (n 69) 571–573.
72 Cf. Sadurski (n 28); W. Sadurski, 'Polish Constitutional Tribunal under PiS: From an Activist Court, to a Paralysed Tribunal, to a Governmental Enabler' (2018) 11(1) *Hague Journal on the Rule of Law* 1–22.

[T]he Tribunal became an active helper of the parliamentary majority. While the first stage gave reasons for concern that the very existence of the CT [Constitutional Tribunal] was at stake, and that a purely façade body was all that PiS wanted, the second iteration of the Tribunal – as an active collaborator in anti-constitutional assault by PiS – showed that, perhaps contrary to initial attempts at destroying the CT as such, the rulers identified an important function for the CT in their design for democratic backsliding. The fact that PiS does not really consider the prospect of party alternation in power as realistic, and hopes to govern for an indefinite period, explains additionally why it is not interested in having an independent CT.[73]

A further important way of creating enduring influence on national government is by using a classical *liberal-legal tool of entrenchment*, or, in other words, use specific types of law that are very difficult or almost impossible to change by new parliamentary majorities in the future, by using a supermajority rule (two-thirds of parliament).[74] The Hungarian case is particularly instructive here, not least because the Hungarian government on various occasions used constitutional amendment to achieve political goals it could not achieve by ordinary political means. A conspicuous dimension of Fidesz's 'constitutional instrumentalism' is indeed the frequent recourse to constitutional amendment. Since its adoption in 2012, the Fidesz government has already amended the new Hungarian Fundamental Law seven times (as of 2018),[75] while before its entering into force in 2012, and from the moment Fidesz gained its supermajority in 2010, the prior, 1989 Constitution was amended 12 times.[76] A second conspicuous dimension is the usage of so-called 'Cardinal Laws' (or 'organic laws'), which are considered ordinary laws, but due to a qualified majority protection by a two-thirds parliamentary majority (of the parliamentarians present), have (pseudo)-constitutional effects. As criticized not least by the Venice Commission, the extensive usage of such laws prevents a flexible change by parliament of matters that ought to be legislated through ordinary laws, such as issues related to family policy or social and fiscal policy. As the commission argues: 'The more policy issues are transferred beyond the powers of simple majority, the less significance will future elections have and the more possibilities does a two-third majority have of cementing its political preferences and the country's legal order'.[77]

A third way of constitutionally entrenching political power is by *changing the mandate* of important institutional functions, such as that of the president or of the judiciary. The Latin American cases are striking, in that the populist 'constituent Presidents' portrayed themselves as 'constituent agents of change',[78] and in various cases have attempted to remain in power indefinitely, not least by relaxing the term limits for presidential office.[79]

---

73 Sadurski (n 28) 4.
74 M. Bánkuti, G. Halmai, and K. Scheppele, 'From Separation of Powers to a Government without Checks: Hungary's Old and New Constitutions' in G.A. Tóth (ed), *Constitution for a Disunited Nation: On Hungary's 2011 Fundamental Law* (Central European University Press 2012) 237–269.
75 See https://theorangefiles.hu/amendments-to-the-fundamental-law/.
76 Petra Burai, Miklós Ligeti, József Péter Martin, and Ella Salgó, 'Democratic Backsliding and Economic Performance: Building Unity and Support for Democratic and Free Market Values in Central and Eastern Europe' (2017) Country Report on Hungary, *Transparency International* 9.
77 Venice Commission Opinion 621/2011. Cf. M. Bogaards, 'De-democratization in Hungary: Diffusely Defective Democracy' (2018) 25(8) *Democratization* 1481–1489, published online: 25 June 2018.
78 Bernal (n 47) 444.
79 J. Corrales and M. Penfold, 'Manipulating Term Limits in Latin America' (2014) 25(4) *Journal of Democracy* 157–168.

The most radical case is probably that of Hugo Chávez, who by means of a referendum in 2009 managed to mandate the constitution to eliminate constitutional limits on the presidential term so that a presidential figure can potentially remain in power for an indefinite period.[80]

Normative matters (religion, nationalism, ethics)

A fourth, not yet frequently discussed, dimension to populist-constitutional projects is that of the endorsement of a substantive, religious–ethical project of society. This is surely not evident in all populist projects, but in a number of recent experiences, in particular the right-wing projects of Poland and Hungary, it is difficult to deny a collectivist, ethno-national, and religious dimension. The populist projects are about refounding the state on the basis of such understandings, understood as in sharp contrast to the liberal, democratic state that was instituted from 1989 onwards.

As argued by Gábor Halmai, in the case of Hungary, the project of illiberal democracy contains a significant dimension of a nationalist and religious nature. As Halmai claims, the Hungarian Fundamental Law of 2011

> shows the role of religion in national legitimation through characterizing the nation referred to as the subject of the constitution not only as the community of ethnic Hungarians, but also as a Christian community, narrowing even the range of people who can recognize themselves belonging to it.[81]

Indeed, as attested also by Halmai, in particular the Fundamental Law's preamble is littered with religious references, including a reference to the Hungarian Roman Catholic tradition. But equally the actual text of the Fundamental Law reflects clear religious dimensions, for instance in its definition of community and preferred family model, and its provision of the protection of the unborn child.[82]

The populist understanding of the Hungarian people tends to subject individual differences to a collective subject, which finds its origins outside of (the members of) contemporary society strictly speaking and is in this sense pre-political (as in tradition, religion, culture, or identity). The Hungarian collectivist, historical view comes through, for instance, in the 2018 State of the Nation address of the leader of the Hungarian Fidesz Party, Viktor Orbán: 'I believe that we Hungarians have a future if we remain Hungarian: if we cultivate the Hungarian language, defend our Christian and Hungarian culture, and preserve independence and Hungarian freedom'. And, 'Homeland is an anchor needed by everyone in their hearts. And, in spite of attacks and mockery, patriots deserve recognition for again and again lowering this anchor: for telling us to our face, time and again, that the homeland comes before all else'.[83]

---

80 See www.constitutionnet.org/news/term-limits-manipulation-across-latin-america-and-what-constitutional-design-could-do-about-it.

81 G. Halmai, 'Religion and Constitutionalism' (2015) 5 MTA Working Paper 75.

82 Halmai (n 81) 75.

83 See www.kormany.hu/en/the-prime-minister/the-prime-minister-s-speeches/viktor-orban-s-state-of-the-nation-address.

The Hungarian populist project is not merely about symbolic and legitimating ornament, but has clear implications for society.[84] One of these implications was embodied in one of the (aforementioned) Cardinal Laws, which radically changed the status of legally recognized churches, leading to the deregistration of some 200 previously recognized (non-Christian) churches and greatly reducing the freedom to establish new churches in Hungary.[85]

While the Hungarian populist regime does not appear to be a case of theocratic constitutionalism, it does seem clear that the populist project entails 'emerging patterns of politically systemized hegemony of the Catholic Church and religion-centric morality'.[86] A very similar argument could be made for the conservative-populist project of a 'Fourth Republic' in Poland, a project that is equally geared against liberal individualism, and which promotes the Polish Christian nation, and related conceptions of abortion, marriage, and the family.[87]

Concluding remarks

The chapter has argued that the relation between populism and constitutionalism, rather than a merely antithetical one, is more complex and multi-faceted (containing both an abusive/threatening and a democratizing/emancipatory thrust[88]). This is so not least because populists in power extensively use constitutional instruments and engage in at times drastic constitutional reform, including the reform of judicial institutions, the introduction of direct-democratic and participatory instruments, the centralization of power and the promotion of forms of 'leaderism', and the endorsement of distinctive (including conservative) ideological projects. Contemporary 'neo-populisms' are, in this, one-sidedly focused on the modern idea of constituent power and make strong claims to revitalize popular sovereignty and local, domestic self-government (often in strong contrast to external

---

84 In the latest, seventh amendment of the Fundamental Law, the populist and sovereigntist dimension appears to be particularly upfront. Among other things, it aims at the 'protection of Hungary's self-identity' and promotes the idea that Hungary's 'Christian culture is the duty of all state organizations', see https://blogs.eui.eu/constitutionalism-politics-working-group/fidesz-faith-ethno-nationalism-hungary/.

85 Halmai (n 81) 76.

86 Halmai (n 81) 77.

87 Cf. A. Wolff-Powęska, 'Trommler der Revolution Jungkonservative und Polens Rechte' (2018) 3–5 *Osteuropa*. A strongly contrasting example regarding populism and religion can be found in the discourses of Marine Le Pen, the leader of the *Front National*, and in her crusade against 'communautarisme' or the co-habitation of different ethno-religious communities within the secular French Republic. Le Pen opened her programme for the 2017 presidential campaign by stating as her key objective: 'To regain our freedom and control over our destiny by restoring the sovereignty of the French people'. The programme contains various calls for constitutional reform, including the following proposals:

> The defence of national identity, [and] the values and traditions of French civilization. To inscribe into the Constitution, the defence and the promotion of our historical and cultural patrimony … The promotion of secularism and the fight against communitarianism. Inscribe into the Constitution the principle: 'The Republic does not recognize any [ethnic, religious] community'. Restore secularism everywhere, extend it to the entire public sphere, and inscribe it into Labour Law.

See M. Le Pen, '144 Engagements Présidentiels' (2017). Available at: www.marine2017.fr/wp-content/uploads/2017/02/projet-presidentiel-marine-le-pen.pdf: 3, 15.

88 Cf. C. de la Torre and E. Peruzzotti, 'Populism in Power: Between Inclusion and Autocracy' (2018) 1(1) *Populism* 38–58.

interference and universally understood international norms and rights). Populists absolutize the *political* dimension of modern constitutional democracy, or more specifically that of *auto-nomos*, but they do this in a distinctively populist manner, defending a pure and undivided or unfragmented form of rule of the people. The related distinctive populist mindset consists in a form of general 'legal scepticism' toward both liberal constitutionalism and the rule of law (in particular, the idea of self-limitation). But apart from repudiating constraints on political power, populists also seek to promote an alternative, counter-constitutional vision, which allegedly furthers both popular and national sovereignty in the name of a homogeneous, victimized people. While it should nevertheless be recognized that populism comes in different varieties (not least of a left- and right-wing kind), which is also demonstrated by the different approaches of populists to issues of citizen participation and democratic instruments, a generally shared dimension is one of *legal scepticism* toward liberal representation, party and societal pluralism, and power-dividing institutions. This scepticism is frequently translated into at times radical constitutional projects which seek to drastically change, rather than simply undo, liberal-constitutional constellations.

19

THE DEMOCRATIC BACKSLIDING IN THE EUROPEAN UNION AND THE CHALLENGE OF CONSTITUTIONAL DESIGN

*Tomasz Tadeusz Koncewicz**

Explaining and connecting the triad: 'the democratic backsliding – the unconstitutional change – the constitutional design in error'

The democratic backsliding *á la Polonaise* is not an exception.[1] Rather it follows the path already blazed by Hungary.[2] This chapter argues that there are important general constitutional lessons to be learned that go beyond the 'Polish' case. When analyzed together and in a systemic way, the cases of backsliding in Hungary and Poland suggest a new worrying pattern of the erosion of

* The author acknowledges funding received from the European Union's Horizon 2020 Research & Innovation programme under Grant Agreement no. 770142, project RECONNECT – Reconciling Europe with its Citizens through Democracy and Rule of Law. I am happy to recognize my time spent as the 2019 Fernand Braudel Fellow at the European Institute in Florence and many inspirational conversations on topics discussed here that I had with my friend and fellow Braudel Fellow Professor Jeff Dunoff. I am equally grateful to Professor Kim Lane Scheppele for her inspiration and good advice that I can always count on. The usual disclaimer applies.

1 See W. Sadurski, *How Democracy Dies (in Poland): A Case Study of Anti-Constitutional Populist Backsliding*, Sydney Law School Research Paper 18/1. For my earlier iteration on the subject, consult T. T. Koncewicz, *Understanding the Politics of Resentment*, available at https://verfassungsblog.de/understanding-the-politics-of-resentment/; 'Understanding the Politics of Resentment: Of the Principles, Institutions, Counter-strategies, Normative Change and the Habits of Heart' (2019) 26 *Indiana Journal of Global Legal Studies* 501; *The Polish Counter-Revolution Two and a Half Years Later: Where Are We Today?* available at https://verfassungsblog.de/the-polish-counter-revolution-two-and-a-half-years-later-where-are-we-today/; 'The Politics of Resentment and First Principles in the European Court of Justice' in F. Bignami (ed), *EU Law in Populist Times: Crises and Prospects* (Cambridge University Press 2020) 457–476.

2 A. von Bogdandy and P. Sonnevend (eds), *Constitutional Crisis in the European Constitutional Area: Theory, Law and Politics in Hungary and Romania* (Hart Publishing 2015) with further references. M. Bankuti, G. Halmai, K.L. Scheppele, 'Hungary's Illiberal Turn: Disabling the Constitution' (2012) 23 *Journal of Democracy* 138; I. Pogany, 'The Crisis of Democracy in East Central Europe: The "New Constitutionalism" in Europe' (2013) 19 *European Public Law* 341.

constitutional democracies.[3] One may even speak of a recipe for constitutional capture in one state after another that travels in space and in time. This process tends to result in a systemic undermining of the key components of the rule of law such as human rights, independent and impartial courts, free media.[4] It follows a well-organized script and tends to begin with disgruntled citizens voting to break the system by electing a leader who promises radical change, often referring to the 'will of the people' while trashing the pre-existing constitutional framework with cleverly crafted legalistic blueprints borrowed from other 'successful' autocrats.[5] In the context of the European Union (EU) though, the democratic backsliding is much more than just an isolated example of yet another European government going rogue. There is an important international and European dimension to what has transpired in Poland over the last two years: the failure of the supranational order to respond to the danger of democratic backsliding *from within*. Can the EU mount a response to the challenge? Is the EU still able to foster respect for principled commitments that initially brought the member states together? Does it have a safety valve by which it can deflate excessive nationalism and manifestly illiberal practices? Can it preserve the common values that launched the European project – supranationalism among them? More particularly, can domestic constitution-making be constrained from the outside? Thus far these questions have received deflating negative replies as the EU has been reduced to an idle bystander, extending deadlines and assurances of a dialogue, all this while the capture marched on. These questions are vital as they force us to revisit the *raison d'être* of Europe.[6] They challenge the standard story of the EU's origin: that it was founded to bring peace and prosperity to Europe by ending the possibility of war and encouraging the common rebuilding of economies.

The legal order of the EU is defined by openness and flexibility to accommodate the diversity of its components and the ever-changing socio-political circumstances that provide a background against which the EU law operates and strives for the attainment of its objectives. Change runs in the DNA of the EU[7] and different variables played their part in the process: from the incremental and context-sensitive nature of the integration process[8] to open-ended character of the treaties defined as *Traité-cadre*[9] to the constitutional design requiring the unanimity in changing the constitutional document. What has been

---

3 S. Mounk, *The People vs Democracy* (Harvard University Press 2018); D. Runciman, *How Democracy Ends* (Basic Books 2018); A. Huq and T. Ginsburg, 'How to Lose a Constitutional Democracy' (2018) 65 *UCLA Law Review* 78; T. Ginsburg and A. Huq, 'How We Lost Constitutional Democracy' in C. Sunstein (ed), *Can it Happen Here? Authoritarianism in America* (Dey Street Books 2018) 135–156; S. Levitzky and D. Ziblatt, *How Democracies Die* (Crown 2018).

4 D. Landau, 'Abusive Constitutionalism' (2013) 47 *University of California Davis Law Review* 189; O. Varol, 'Stealth Authoritarianism' (2015) 100 *Iowa Law Review* 1673; M. Tushnet, 'Authoritarian Constitutionalism' (2015) 100 *Cornell Law Review* 391. For the United States' flirt with creeping authoritarianism, see C. Sunstein (ed) (n 3); Ginsburg and Huq (n 3) 135–156; T. Daly, 'Enough Complacency: Fighting Democratic Decay in 2017' available at www.iconnectblog.com/2017/01/enough-complacency-fighting-democratic-decay-in-2017-i-connect-column/.

5 K.L. Scheppele and L. Pech, 'Illiberalism Within: Rule of Law Backsliding in the EU' (2017) 1 *Cambridge Yearbook of European Legal Studies* 3.

6 G. de Búrca, 'Europe's raison d'être' (2013) 9/13 *New York University School of Law Public Law and Legal Theory Research Paper Series Working Paper*, available at https://papers.ssrn.com/sol3/papers.cfm?abstract_id=2224310.

7 For classic analysis, see J.H.H. Weiler, 'The Transformation of Europe' (1991) 100 *Yale Law Journal* 555 and also R. Dehousse, *The European Court of Justice: The Politics of Judicial Integration* (Macmillan Press Ltd 1998), in particular Chapter 2.

8 A. Arnull, *The European Union and its Court of Justice* (Oxford 1999) 538–565.

9 R. Lecourt, *L'Europe des Juges* (Bruylant 1976) 235.

a dominant and well-rehearsed trope in the EU studies is how this change affected the institutions[10] and was reflected in their actions.[11] As important as these contributions are, they all deal with a change that is *constitutional*, the result of interplay of the political, legal, supranational and domestic forces and actors.[12] Such change has been a staple of the integration process since its inception. This analysis takes on a different aspect of a change in the polity's fabric. The analysis deals with the pressing aspect of constitutional deficiency at the supranational level: a situation when backsliding creates a situation where not all EU member states share the basic values on which the EU is supposed to be based.

Regime trajectories

In their seminal analysis, J.J. Linz and A. Stepan have argued that no regime should be called a democracy unless its rulers govern democratically. Failing to rule within the bounds of a state of law is not democratic. Only democracies can become consolidated democracies. By consolidated democracy they meant 'a political regime in which democracy as a complex system of institutions, rules and patterned incentives and disincentives' has become 'the only game in town'. Importantly, democratic consolidation combines three levels: behavioral, attitudinal and constitutional.[13] Such consolidation must obtain on three levels. On the *behavioral level*: democracy becomes the only game in town when no significant political group seriously attempts to overthrow the democratic regime or to promote domestic or international violence in order to secede from the state. On the *attitudinal level*: democracy becomes the only game in town when, even in the face of severe political and economic crises, the overwhelming majority of the people believe that any further political change must emerge from within the parameters of democratic procedures. On the *constitutional level*: democracy becomes the only game in town when all of the actors in the polity become habituated to the fact that political conflict within the state will be resolved according to established norms and that violations of these norms are likely to be both ineffective and costly.[14]

Democratic backsliding is important as it shows that even consolidated democracies do break down. As argued by Linz and Stepan, such a breakdown would be related not to the weaknesses or problems specific to the historic process of democratic consolidation, but what they rightly call 'a new dynamic' in which the democratic regime cannot solve a set of problems, a non-democratic alternative gains significant supporters, and former democratic

---

10 Among many analyses consult, for example, Julio Baquero Cruz, 'The Changing Constitutional Role of the European Court of Justice' (2006) 34 *International Journal of Legal Information* 223.

11 M. Dawson, 'The Political Face of Judicial Activism: Europe's Law–Politics Imbalance' in M. Dawson, B. de Witte, and E. Muir (eds), *Judicial Activism at the European Court of Justice* (Edward Elgar 2013) 11–31.

12 It was argued in the literature that the strides that the integration through law has made over the course of the last 60 years helped develop material limitations on the discretion of the member states to modify the treaties at will. R. Bieber famously spoke of 'le noyau dur commun est constitué par deux valeurs fondamentales [...] d'une part des traditions constitutionnelles communes aux États members en tant que principes généraux du droit communautaire et d'autre part de l'identité de l'Union sans cesse plus étroite entre les peuples de l'Europe', 'Les limites matérielles et formelles á la revision des traités établissant la Communauté européenne' (1993) 367(4) *Revue du Marche Commun et de l'Union européenne* 343, 350. The Court of Justice has been credited with (or depending on one's perspectives, accused of) changing the treaties by means of an interpretation.

13 J.J. Linz and A. Stepan, *Toward Consolidated Democracies* in *Consolidating the Third Wave Democracies: Themes and Perspectives* (The Johns Hopkins University Press 1997) 15.

14 *Id.*

regime loyalists begin to behave in a constitutionally disloyal or semi-loyal manner. When the democracy is not the only game in town and liberal narratives are not yet internalized, the law and institutions can do only so much. Without public support and understanding of what these courts do and why they are important for 'our' democracy, democratic breakdown accompanied by attitudes of *disloyal opposition and semi-loyal* behavior occur. The former has been defined by J.J. Linz as a situation in which

> politicians, parties and movements that deny the legitimacy of the democratic system (and its outcomes), that are willing to use force and fraud to achieve their aims, and that are willing to curtail the constitutional rights of their political adversaries, often depicting them as instruments of outside secret and conspirational groups.

On the other hand *semi-loyal* behavior obtains when parties and politicians are willing to 'encourage, tolerate, cover up, treat leniently, excuse or justify the actions of other participants that go beyond the limits of peace legitimate politics in a democracy'.[15] The breakdown is made easier and enabled by the lack of these behavioral safeguards that must go along with the institutional ones. Even the strongest institutions must fall when lacking public support.

Linz's and Stepan's work must be read today in the light of the process whereby the regime trajectory has seen an important shift. Many regimes once deemed democratic or in transition to democracy have veered off the road. The resulting grey area, as aptly coined by Larry Diamond,[16] or 'foggy zone',[17] opens a terra incognita between liberal democracies and outright dictatorships. The politics of resentment does not herald the overnight and dramatic breakdown of democracy. These are (and luckily so) past matters. Rather, they signal slow and incremental erosion of democratic rule and are less spectacular and easy to pinpoint than a *coup d'état*. Just as democratic consolidation is a process rather than a point in time, so is gradual decay and regression. Guillermo O'Donnell anticipated this slow reversion when he spoke about rapid deaths and slow deaths of democracy. The slow death was understood as 'a progressive diminution of existing spaces for the exercise of civilian power and the effectiveness of the classic guarantees of liberal constitutionalism'; it is a slow and opaque 'process of successive authoritarian advances' ultimately leading to a democradura – a repressive façade democracy.[18] The challenge is thus to understand that unconstitutional change does not take place overnight with tanks[19] in the streets and easy-to-detect massive human rights violations. Rather, elected autocrats maintain a veneer of democracy while eviscerating its substance. Today, democracies die slowly in barely visible steps.[20]

---

15 J.J. Linz, *The Breakdown of Democratic Regimes: Crisis, Breakdown & Reequilibrium* (The Johns Hopkins University 1978).

16 L. Diamond, 'Hybrid Regimes' (2002) 13 *Journal of Democracy* 21, 23.

17 A. Schedler, 'Elections without Democracy: The Menu of Manipulation' (2002) 13 *Journal of Democracy* 36, 37.

18 G. O'Donnell, 'Transitions, Continuities, and Paradoxes' in S. Mainwaring, G. O'Donnell, and J.S. Velenzuela (eds), *Issues in Democratic Consolidation: The New South American Democracies in Comparative Perspective* (University of Notre Dame Press 1992) 19, 33.

19 K.L. Scheppele, 'Autocratic Legalism' (2018) 85 *The University of Chicago Law Review* 545. In similar vein, Runciman (n 3) rightly speaks of 'imaginations stuck with outdated images of what democratic failure looks like. We are trapped in the landscape of the twentieth century … tanks in the streets; tin-pot dictators barking out messages of national unity, violence and repression in tow'.

20 S. Levitzky and D. Ziblatt, 'How a Democracy Dies' (7 December 2017) *New Republic*, available at https://new republic.com/article/145916/democracy-dies-donald-trump-contempt-for-american-political-institutions.

> Threats to third wave democracies are likely to come not from generals and revo-
> lutionaries who have nothing but contempt for democracy, but rather from partici-
> pants in the democratic process [...]. With third wave democracies, *the problem is
> not overthrow but erosion*: the intermittent or gradual weakening of democracy by
> those elected to lead it.[21]

What is generically referred to as the democratic backsliding corroborates these fears and
predictions. As understood here the democratic backsliding means

> the process through which elected public authorities deliberately implement gov-
> ernmental blueprints which aim to systematically weaken, annihilate or capture
> internal checks on power with the view of dismantling the liberal democratic state
> and entrenching the long-term rule of the dominant party.[22]

This analysis does not aim to deal comprehensively with the problem of democratic
backsliding in the EU as this has been already done elsewhere. Rather it builds on this
literature and adds constitutional and remedial dimension.[23]

What is behind the democratic backsliding? The concept of the politics of resentment

Resentment is crucial for understanding the rise of illiberal narratives in Europe and
beyond.[24] Although the role of emotion in politics has traditionally been undertheorized as
compared to reason and the rational side of human beings, there is no doubt that in
contemporary politics, emotion has become equally, or indeed, more important. Emotions
are not only a driving force behind the political struggle, they are also a prize to be won.
Crucially, emotions play a performative and constitutive function. They not only express
but help bring subjects into being and constitute identities.[25] And one particularly potent
combination of emotions has become salient in recent times – resentment. Populist leaders
have tapped into a reservoir of anxiety about 'the other'. Anger at the liberal establishment
and the imposition of one correct world view, fear of exclusion, and uncertainty of one's

---

21 S.P. Huntington, 'Democracy for the Long Haul', in L. Diamond, M.F. Plattner, Yun-han Chu, and Hung-
mao Tien (eds), *Consolidating the Third Wave Democracies: Themes and Perspectives* (Johns Hopkins University
Press 1997) 8 (my emphasis).

22 This is the definition adopted by K.L. Scheppele and L. Pech, *What Is Rule of Law Backsliding?* available at
https://verfassungsblog.de/what-is-rule-of-law-backsliding/ Also, Scheppele and Pech (n 5) 3. According to
N. Bermeo, democratic backsliding means the state-led debilitation or elimination of the political institutions
sustaining an existing democracy; N. Bermeo, 'On Democratic Backsliding' (2016) 27(1) *Journal of Democracy*
5–19. Also S. Lindberg, *The Nature of Democratic Backsliding in Europe*, available at https://carnegieeurope.eu/
2018/07/24/nature-of-democratic-backsliding-in-europe-pub76868%20The%20Nature%20of%20Democratic
%20Backsliding%20in%20Europe%20Source:%20Getty%20STAFFAN%20I.%20LINDBERG.

23 In the literature on populism, this remedial aspect of responding to the populist threat is almost lost. While the role
of supranational institutions is acknowledged, the discussion never goes beyond such a general acknowledgement.
C. Mudde and C.R. Kaltwasser, *Populism: A Very Short Introduction* (Oxford University Press 2017) 115.

24 K.J. Cramer, *The Politics of Resentment: Rural Consciousness in Wisconsin and the Rise of Scott Walker* (University of
Chicago Press 2016).

25 M. Holmes, 'Feeling beyond Rules: Politicizing the Sociology of Emotion and Anger in Feminist Politics'
(2004) 7(2) *European Journal of Social Theory* 212–213.

place in the contemporary world. In short, resentment is driving many of the contemporary political developments. To be sure, emotions are a legitimate part of the democratic process and anger and fear are not to be removed from the realm of political discourse as any such attempt would be counterfactual. When, however, populist politicians tap into resentment and create political movements that have distinct implications for the existing institutional order, they take emotion to another level. Resentment is no longer a *feeling* but is *utterance* and *performance*, and it is transformed into 'the politics of resentment'. Resentment is anchored within mainstream politics and is articulated in the public sphere.[26]

The politics of resentment transform our traditional understanding of political conflict. While politicians and political parties in democracies routinely put forward competing visions for society and politics, they always stick to the language of probability in setting out their alternatives to the existing government. They are prepared to test their alternatives through procedures and elections and accept that the constitution is the stage that frames political contestation.[27] As liberal democrats, they share a commitment to the core values of freedom and equality and the formal acknowledgment that their political adversaries have as valid a claim to represent the people as they do. By contrast, resentment-driven populist politicians see their claims as settling most fundamental issues once and for all, and they do not allow room for dissent. Because of the moral dimension of resentment, they do not acknowledge that their claims can be judged as true or false. Rather, their claims are always the best, and not open to further contestation.[28] The emotions of fear, anger and rejection, all under the umbrella of resentment, do not allow for pluralism and the multiplicity of representation and undermine the normative and institutional framework through which populist leaders initially express and advance these sentiments. 'The other' is no longer seen as a legitimate adversary. He becomes an enemy and, as a delegitimized political actor, is hounded and persecuted with the full strength of the law.

With the extreme majoritarianism as one of the cornerstones of the new doctrine, disabling constitutional courts and judicial review is the first order of the day for constitutional capture. All institutions, domestic and supranational, stand in the way and are not part of the new populist constitutionalism.[29] This is no longer gentle constitutional tinkering. This is an all-out constitutional reconquest.[30] Gaining power does not soften populist animus. Quite the contrary, once elected, populist leaders are ready to deliver on their promises and they do so through a constitutional doctrine that competes with the dominant liberal constitutionalism.[31]

---

26 For general discussion, see S. Ahmed, *The Cultural Politics of Emotion* (Edinburgh University Press 2014).

27 I draw here on J.W. Müller, *Populist Constitutionalism: A Contradiction in Terms?* Draft paper, NYU Colloquium (on file with the author) and also at https://verfassungsblog.de/populist-constitutions-a-contradiction-in-terms/.

28 *Id.*

29 See T.T. Koncewicz, 'PIS Takes Its First Step on the Way toward POLEXIT' (13 August 2017) *Gazeta Wyborcza*, available at http://wyborcza.pl/7,75968,22227617,w-puszczy-pis-robi-pierwszy-wielki-krok-do-polexitu.html?disableRedirects=true.

30 Interestingly, while the literature (mostly political science) on populism has been growing beyond imagination, the question of *how* (institutionally and procedurally) to deal with the rise of populist politics has received only scant attention. For a rare exception, see C.R. Kaltwasser, 'Populism and the Question of How to Respond to It' in C. Rovira Kaltwasser, P. Taggart, P.O. Espejo, and P. Ostiguy (eds) *The Oxford Handbook of Populism* (Oxford University Press 2017), 490; For a political science perspective, consult S. Rummens and K. Abts, 'Defending Democracy: The Concentric Containment of Political Extremism' (2010) 58 *Political Studies* 649; and more recently, G. Badano and A. Nuti, 'Under Pressure: Political Liberalism, the Rise of Unreasonableness, and the Complexity of Containment' (2018) 26(2) *The Journal of Political Philosophy* 145–168.

31 For important clarifications, see P. Blokker, 'Populist Constitutionalism' (4 May 2017) *Verfassungsblo*, available at http://verfassungsblog.de/populist-constitutionalism/and his Chapter 18 in the present volume.

This doctrine includes the following, often interrelated, elements: (i) a new understanding of the role of the constitution, no longer as protecting against the state, but as safeguarding the uniqueness of the state; (ii) the constitution ceases to be the supreme law of the land; (iii) the constitutional court is not only incapacitated but also 'weaponized' to be used as a tool against political enemies; (iv) the political dominates the legal; (v) the rule of law is seen as an obstacle to protecting the collectivity; (vi) the rule of law is to facilitate the expression of the will of the people; (vii) political power is no longer subject to checks and balances; (viii) supranational institutions are dismissed as enemies of the people; (ix) collectivity is trumpeted above individual citizens; (x) human rights evolve from the dignitary conception to that of community.

Democratic backsliding and the European Union

While the discussion of the evolution of regimes and actors in response to *social change* (LGBT, euthanasia, abortion) is well documented,[32] the evolution of inter(supra)national law with regard to *political change* (moves from one sort of government to another) is less well documented. The pertinent question is this: When is the constitutional design of any (domestic, international, supranational) polity in error? On the most general level such critical juncture obtains when polity's founding document (treaty, convention, constitution) protects against the dangers that no longer exist or does not protect against the dangers that were not contemplated by the founders. Constitutions not only constitute but should also protect against deconstitution. The claim this chapter makes is that for supranational legal order of the EU[33] to avoid a deadlock of 'being in error' in the above sense, the systemic threats coming from within the polity's component parts must be recognized and constitutional design be changed accordingly. To make it more responsive to threats to democracy, it is crucial to accept that all actors acknowledge their commitment to shared democratic aspirations, core values of dignity, equality and freedom and their embrace of the project as their own. In the end all actors are ready to read their local mandate through a commitment that tramples the momentary desires of the people and their representatives and puts forward the necessity for effective enforcement. Backsliding assumes though that there is a verifiable point at which we might know that, indeed, the process of retreating from the democratic path (backsliding) has just started.

The democratic backsliding within any member state affects not just this state. When using the term 'backsliding', one has to be clear about the values and principles affected by such a retrogressive move in the EU legal order:[34] No less than liberal democracy, rule of law and human rights as the axiological triad of the EU are at stake. Given the interconnectedness and the

---

32 D. McGoldrick, 'The Development and Status of Sexual Orientation Discrimination under International Human Rights Law' (2016) 16 *Human Rights Law Review* 613; J. Scherpe, 'Same-sex Couples Have Family Life' (2010) 69 *The Cambridge Law Journal* 463.

33 The supranationality of the EU is taken as given here. For discussion, see M. Everson and J. Eisner, *The Making of European Constitution: Judges and Law beyond Constitutive Power* (Routledge 2007) 41; A. Vauchez, 'The Transnational Politics of Judicialization: Van Gend en Loos and the Making of EU Polity' (2010) 16 *European Law Journal* 1 and more recently his *L'Union par le droit: L'invention d'un programme institutionelle pour l'Europe* (Les Presses de Sciences Po 2013), in particular 181–223. Also E. Benvenisti and G.W. Downs, 'The Premises, Assumptions, and Implications of Van Gend en Loos: Viewed from the Perspectives of Democracy and Legitimacy of International Institutions' (2014) 25 *European Journal of International Law* 85.

34 On the definition of the legal order, see K. Culver and M. Giudice, 'Not a System but an Order: An Interinstitutional View of the European Union Law' in J. Dickinson and P. Eleftheriadis (eds), *Philosophical Foundations of European Union Law* (Oxford University Press 2012) 54–76.

interdependence of the member states[35] and highly integrated nature of the legal order of the EU, this impacts on the very foundations and values of the community. As rightly argued by K.L. Scheppele and D. Kelemen, the values announced in Art. 2 of the Treaty on the European Union (hereinafter referred to as the 'TEU') allow the European member states to trust each other's governments – and in particular, their judiciaries – to apply EU law fairly and evenly. They add 'much of the legal doctrine built up around the treaties that unites the EU as a common legal space cannot possibly work as announced if the assumptions underlying the system are shattered'.[36] When one member state retreats from the basic values of the EU law, the constitutional profile of this state changes as a result. There is thus an important constitutional pan-European dimension to the democratic backsliding in a member state that will always have a spill-over effect. As important and devastating as Brexit and financial crises are, they are after all crises of governance and institutional structure. The argument presented here is that none of these crises strikes as deadly a blow to the European edifice as the crisis in which one member state tramples the values of democracy, rule of law and human rights; values said to be presumed to be common for the EU and its member states. We are not dealing with yet another rogue government riding roughshod over its treaty obligations (which is not such a rare occurrence after all), but rather we are facing a government that calls into question the very basis of European integration and undermines it from within. We are facing the crisis of the foundational value of the European integration and its constitutional feature – liberal democracy.[37]

While the duty of liberal democracy is rooted in the constraint, rule of law and human rights, democratic backsliding (or retrogression[38]) strikes at the heart of the commitments to live in a liberal democracy and adhere to the human rights and the international rule of law as the founding block of the order. Backsliding is not just another crisis of governance, rather it strikes at the very core of the order of human rights and their protection both at the regional level (liberal democracy, liberty, equality, pluralism and the rule of law), EU law (Art. 2 TEU and the EU Charter) and international law (UN human rights system). Backsliding comes with the constitutional narrative of *capturing* the *domestic* and rejecting *international and supranational*, institutions. Crucially, backsliding changes a constitutional profile of component parts of national legal orders. The states not only fail to respect human rights, but become '*different states*' in terms of their constitutional fabric, the human rights become '*different human rights*' and the liberal rule of law is looked at with contempt. While the global human rights regime stands for individual dignity, the new autocrats propound the idea of communal dignity of the people that must be protected and vindicated. The empowerment, being a staple of liberal constitutionalism, faces a challenge from a rival philosophy of human rights in which the collective wins over the individual. It stands for a systemic weakening of checks and balances and entrenching power by making future changes in power difficult. A core concept of the politics of resentment is constitutional capture.[39] Constitutional capture is power-entrenching mechanism that has an in-built spill-over effect and, as such, the potential of Europe-wide and beyond adverse consequences. Constitutional capture has an inherent spill-over effect, and as such seemingly isolated constitutional capture in Poland and elsewhere risks the potential of

---

35 'Editorial Comments: Membership in Times of Crisis' (2014) 51 *Common Market Law Review* 1.

36 K.L. Scheppele and D. Kelemen, 'Defending Democracy in EU Member State: Beyond Article 7 TEU' in F. Bignami (ed), *EU Law in Populist Times: Crises and Prospects* (Cambridge University Press 2020).

37 For detailed analysis and further references, see Scheppele and Pech (n 5).

38 Ginsburg and Huq (n 3) 135–156.

39 Core concept is defined as referring to the basic unit without which ideologies cannot exist; M. Freeden, *Ideologies and Political Theory: A Conceptual Approach* (Clarendon Press 1996) 77–80.

adverse consequences throughout the entire continent. It travels in time and space, and, just like the politics of resentment, it has its own trajectory.[40] The captures in Turkey, Hungary and Poland show how new authoritarians learn from each other. As there is simply no place for a veto emanating from within the government other than from the majoritarian parliaments, the 'politics of resentment' target institutions that otherwise might be seen as a brake on the power of the people's representatives. Institutions are only accepted as long as they are seen as 'their' institutions and translate only messages that the controlling parties believe to deserve to be in the public sphere. Such an understanding leads to an important tweak to the established narrative: institutions that have been channeling (for populists, 'distorting') the rule of law must be dealt with as expeditiously as possible.

In the context of the EU, the democratic backsliding is not just an emotion-driven backlash against the elites and international legal order. It is a process with its own themes, characters and plots. It rejects rule of law as a constraint, undermines legal compliance as a condition of legality and puts forward illiberal narratives of 'the dangerous Other'. It is impatient with procedures and institutions. It puts forward a competing understanding of the social reality in which *politics* take over law. Liberal human rights are viewed with suspicion as diluting the communication processes between the sovereign ('the people') and the institutions. Importantly these anti-liberal, anti-institutional, intermediary[41] 'outside bodies' are highly suspicious and incompetent to intervene in domestic affairs. More than that, they are the deadliest enemies because of their tainted pedigree that cannot be traced back to the people. Law must be applied by national courts and judges because they are people's institutions.[42] This 'legal' exit, that is, the rejection of the authority and the peremptory jurisdiction of the Court of Justice follows the footsteps of the "values" exit spelled out in art. 2 TEU and attempts to capture the system of international and supranational institutions. This attempt is under way and will intensify, posing an existential threat to the international system of human rights protection. The questions that arise, are how it affects the constitutional and institutional setting of a polity that proclaims to defend the rule of law as one of the tenets of its legal order, and whether the design is ready to contain such 'exits'. Yet, the case law of the Court of Justice shows how the Court, despite the errors in constitutional design, has been closing off the 'exit' strategies for the rogue member states. As a result, we are facing a paradigmatic shift where the values (e.g. Rule of

---

40 On this, see L. Pech and K.L. Scheppele, 'Poland and the European Commission, Part II: Hearing the Siren Song of the Rule of Law' (6 January 2017) *Verfassungsblog*, available at https://verfassungsblog.de/poland-and-the-european-commission-part-ii-hearing-the-siren-song-of-the-rule-of-law/. They argue that first people lose faith in the system and vote to break the system by electing populist autocrats. Securing parliamentary majority is instrumental in going after the institutions. Power, once gained, must be entrenched so the change to election laws follow and make the change in power very unlikely.

41 N. Urbinati, 'A Revolt against Intermediary Bodies' (2015) 22 *Constellations* 477.

42 The disdain for international bodies was on full display in the 'logging case' (C-441/17R – release https://curia.europa.eu/jcms/upload/docs/application/pdf/2017-11/cp170122en.pdf). The case opposed the European Commission and Poland in a dispute over the massive logging activities in the last ancient forest of Europe. The interim injunction of the Court of Justice has been flatly rejected by Poland (first such case in the history of the EU) which prompted the court to threaten the recalcitrant state with a massive penalty payment. For the analysis, see also *infra* and Koncewicz, 2020 (n 1). On the continuing rejection by Poland of the Court of Justice, see also 'Editorial Comments: About Brexit Negotiations and Enforcement Action against Poland: The EU's Own Song of Ice and Fire' (2017) 54 *Common Market Law Review* 1309, 1313–1316 and most recently 'Editorial Comment: 2019 Shaping Up as a Challenging Year for the Union, Not Least as a Community of Values' (2019) 56 *Common Market Law Review* 1.

law) are becoming fully justiciable concepts in their own right. Article 2 TEU is not only political, but imposes legal duties which are enforceable by the Court through Article 19 TEU. We know today that art. 2 TEU is not declaratory but has a substantive dimension. The Court has clearly embraced it as the hard core of EU law and made it justiciable. Crucially, this existential jurisprudence explains that the jurisdiction of the Court is triggered irrespective of any link to substantive EU law other than Article 2 TEU and the duty to respect the values spelled out therein. 'Rule of law' is a legal term and as such within the purview of the Union courts.

The democratic backsliding highlights the errors in the design of the supranational legal order – the EU. Although the EU has faced many crises in recent years, including the ongoing Brexit and the euro crisis, the democratic backsliding in some of its member states is the most serious of all. The backsliders have called into question the shared values of democracy, rule of law and human rights.[43] In doing so, they have called into question the very foundations of European integration and have undermined the European project from within. As such, the 'democratic backsliding' undermines European post-war liberal consensus which has been built around the paradigm of 'never again constitutionalism' and has been reinforced by the legal commitment of the states to make sure that dictatorships would never again arise out of constitutionalism.[44] Political power at the domestic level was to become subject to new international and supranational checks and balances with the legitimacy of the power depending on the continuous adherence to the core values of liberalism; values that transcend the desires of the moment. True institutions (e.g. courts) were given special place in this system of international and supranational checks and constraints imposed on the domestic *pouvoir constituant*. Yet, they were never meant to be alone. The states themselves have recognized that the human rights would work best alongside three complementary safeguards: (i) rule of law and the constitution as the supreme law of the land binding on both the political power *and* the people; (ii) mechanisms of supranational and international control whereby self-governing and sovereign states would hold each other to account according to principles of human rights, guarantees of democracy and openness to the world; and (iii) trust in the binding power of law that would commit the states to the discipline of community.[45] The trust has always been built on the convergence between the fundamental values of member states and their legal orders on the one hand, and the foundations of the Union's legal order, on the other. Indeed, as P. Pescatore emphasized, the supranationality was predicated on the idea of 'an order

---

43 Art. 2 TEU provides:

> The Union is founded on the values of respect for human dignity, freedom, democracy, equality, the rule of law and respect for human rights, including the rights of persons belonging to minorities. These values are common to the Member States in a society in which pluralism, non-discrimination, tolerance, justice, solidarity and equality between women and men prevail.

Art. 7 of the TEU adds a sanctioning mechanism in the case when one of the member states does not respect the values. For discussion, see D. Kochenov and A. Jakab (eds), *The Enforcement of EU Law and Values: Ensuring Member States' Compliance* (Cambridge University Press 2017).

44 C. Dupré, 'The Unconstitutional Constitution: A Timely Concept' in von Bogdandy and Sonnevend (n 2) 364–383.

45 K.L. Scheppele, 'Constitutional Coups and Judicial Review: How Transnational Institutions Can Strengthen Peak Courts at Times of Crisis (with special reference to Hungary)' (2014) 23 *Transnational Law and Contemporary Problems* 51.

determined by the existence of common values and interests'.[46] At the heart of the European project has been a fundamental commitment to a set of First Principles[47] that the member states, institutions and civil society actors bound by the treaties agree to respect, and live by, in their mutual dealings. The rule of law has been among the most essential of these First Principles essential to the post-war consensus as it started transforming 'a political power' into 'political power constrained by law'.[48] And yet, despite all this talk of hope and learning from the past, the EU constitutional system and design have been always in error of 'normative asymmetry': declarations and commitments have never been backed up with the sufficient enforcement tool-kit. Why not? Back in 1951 the authority to ensure that states remained liberal democracies had not been effectively translated into *law* which might have been understandable given the fresh memories of horrors wrought upon the continent by the Second World War. The Founding Fathers must have taken for granted that these memories would always act as a sufficient deterrent against any future backsliding into authoritarianism and the newly created communities would be nothing but a celebration of liberal democracies. History never stops, though, it always moves and today the once unthinkable (an illiberal state *within* the Union) challenges the EU design. The failure of the EU enforcement in Hungary and now in Poland was clearly on display: the EU has been always one step behind the events on the ground, lost in endless and ineffective diplomacy of indignation. The states which are the source of distrust and fear have been called on to sit at trial over one of their fellow (and now backsliding) member states. The European institutions faced dangers for which they were not prepared and then also contributed to the crisis by their own incompetence and lack of political will. As a result, there was no coordinated systemic action. The capture marched on emboldened and strengthened by the lack of credible supranational counter-strategies.

The politics of resentment forcefully illustrates that 'doing Europe' with an overlapping consensus and tolerance might no longer be the dominant European narrative. Instead, the politics of resentment and constitutional capture are pushing Europe to a standstill and an identity crisis. The EU's constitutional design is falling short of the novel challenge that comes along with the politics of resentment. Rethinking the external constraints and limitations imposed on the domestic *pouvoir constituant* in response to constitutional capture of liberal constitutions looms large. As society advances, are we the European peoples ready to continue living together in a constitutional regime, internally divergent, and always ready to respond to the exigencies and demands of new realities? As forcefully argued by Kim Lane Scheppele and Laurent Pech, 'consolidation of majoritarian autocracies […] represents more of an existential threat to the EU's existence and functioning than the exit of any of its Member States'.[49] Constitutional capture plays a pivotal role in disabling checks and

---

46 P. Pescatore, *The Law of Integration: Emergence of a New Phenomenon in International Relations Based on the Experi- ence of the European Communities* (Sijthoff 1974).

47 Term borrowed from D. Edward, *An Appeal to First Principles* (unpublished manuscript on file with the author).

48 'Constrained political power' might be said to be the driving force behind the European consensus and one of the paradigms of post-war constitutional settlement in Europe. Insistence on the element of constraint was, in turn, driven by distrust of popular sovereignty, and fear of backsliding into authoritarianism. On this, see J.W. Müller, 'Beyond Militant Democracy' (2012) 73 *New Left Review* 39. On democracy and the rule of law as the backbone of the European project, see also Scheppele and Kelemen (n 36).

49 L. Pech and K.L. Scheppele, 'Poland and the European Commission, Part I: A Dialogue of the Deaf?' (3 Jan- uary 2017) *Verfassungsblog*, available at http://verfassungsblog.de/poland-and-the-european-commission-part- i-a-dialogue-of-the-deaf/.

balances. Constitutional capture makes a sham of a constitutional document as it strips it of its limiting and constraining function.[50] Separation of powers becomes illusory and opens the gate to unchecked arbitrariness. Yet constitutional capture is not a one-off aberration. It is a novel threat to the rule of law as it is not limited to one moment in time. It is a process of incremental taking over of independent institutions and the liberal state. Hungary is a prototype of a 'captured state' and one would be right in assuming that the European Commission had learned from its passivity and acquiescence toward Orbán's tactics of capturing the state.[51] The lesson was loud and clear and yet missed by the Commission, as the Polish case shows: the only way to derail constitutional capture, or to 'constitutionally recapture unconstitutional capture', is to act preemptively, before capture is complete.[52] Waiting on the sidelines, talking to the perpetrators and hoping for a change of heart, only emboldens and entrenches the regime. Constitutional capture as a process needs time, so it is the time factor that plays a pivotal role in striking back at capture. To thwart capture in the building, counter-action is necessary at the very beginning, not later. The regime knows that and will do anything to buy more time to entrench the capture and make recapture very unlikely. Poland and Hungary show how this has happened, with the EU extending time limits and engaging in a futile dialogue, all the while that constitutional capture has become ever more deeply entrenched and difficult to roll back. Constitutional capture not only calls into question the commonality of values but entails the once startling proposition that constitutions today might be unconstitutional within the EU.

Rethinking the constitutional design: some modest proposals

Today's EU is not equipped to deal with the systemic destruction of democracies and the rule of law at the level of its member states.[53] Elected governments can get away with anything, especially if they are re-elected. The new autocrats of Hungary and Poland know all too well that they cannot engage in mass human rights violations. They figured out other ways to get what they want without any supranational structures interfering. They fiddle with institutional design, media ownership, organizational registration, the electoral process, and more. In short, they are operating in a space for which there are presently no transnational or international institutions or standards in place, and this project would aim at constructing such holistic standards. The supranational law (and international law for that matter) must not sit on the sidelines and watch the slow unraveling of democratic systems and their laws. With the politics of resentment fueling European disintegration, with the exclusion of the other, and with constitutional capture elevated to the status of a new mode of governance, the challenge of 'paddling together' has never been more acute and dramatic. Supranational Europe must be thought of as a safety valve against the excesses of national states and an additional level of supervision over the member states. As much as the Court of Justice might preach 'mutual trust' as one of the paradigms of EU law, distrust drives the EU right now. In light of new phenomena on the rise, such as abusive

---

50 'Sham' or 'façade' constitutions fail to constrain or even describe the powers of the state. On the concept, see D.S. Law and M. Versteeg, 'Sham Constitutions' (2013) 101 *California Law Review* 863.
51 Bankuti, Halmai, and Scheppele (n 2); Pogany (n 2).
52 Pech and Scheppele (n 49).
53 T.T. Koncewicz, *The Democratic Backsliding and the European Constitutional Design in Error: When Will 'How' Meet 'Why'?* available at https://verfassungsblog.de/the-democratic-backsliding-and-the-european-constitu tional-design-in-error-when-how-meets-why/.

constitutionalism,[54] competitive authoritarianism,[55] democracy mutations,[56] hybrid regimes,[57] electoral authoritarianism,[58] democratic decay,[59] backsliding in Central and Eastern Europe, and resurrection of resentment in other parts of Europe,[60] the promise of instituting effective checks on the unfettered freedom of nation-states becomes an existential challenge.

The constitutional capture entrenches power by making future changes in power difficult. This is where the challenge of *rethinking* the constitutional design of the EU comes to the fore. *Rethinking* requires revisiting the *substance* of the EU membership by engaging with the new kinds of regimes within the EU and asking what it means to be a member state of the EU in the twenty-first century. The language and perspectives through which the EU looks at its member states, must be challenged, and changed. Member states must be invested in the legal order and the integration project by repeated acknowledgment that they want to respect the understanding of the EU legality and its First Principles that brought them together. EU legality is understood here as a novel term and a benchmark for review which embraces not only the traditional understanding of the EU law (rules and norms) but also justiciable values enforced throughout courts. The states must speak with one voice that they are ready to defer to the common institutions enforcing these principles in the name of the community. This commitment would then translate into more technical aspects of the tools ('*how*'), and build a remedial framework for the systemic and holistic response to the democratic backsliding. The *rethinking* invites constitutional lawyers to move beyond dangerously over-inclusive and nebulous 'populism talk' and instead focus on, and deal with, the constitutional features of the emerging populist constitutional doctrine that challenges the basic underpinnings of the liberal constitutionalism and calls into question the standard origin story of the EU. The contours of this new doctrine/tradition revolve around a few basic tenets. The politics, rather than being tamed and constrained by law, are increasingly seen as the threat to the constitution. The constitutions are no longer seen as shields against the state, rather they protect the uniqueness of the state and nation understood in ethno-cultural terms. Constitutional courts are transformed

---

54 Landau (n 4) defines abusive constitutionalism as the use of mechanisms of constitutional change in order to make a state significantly less democratic than it was before.

55 S. Levitsky and L.A. Way, *Competitive Authoritarianism: Hybrid Regimes after the Cold War* (Cambridge University Press 2010).

56 See in general Levitsky and Way (n 55); Varol (n 4).

57 Diamond (n 16) 22.

58 A. Schedler, *The Politics of Uncertainty: Sustaining and Subverting Electoral Authoritarianism* (Oxford Scholarship Online 2017).

59 Daly (n 4)

60 At least doctrine is clearly aware of the dangers as attested by the growing number of important voices on the subject. See B. Büller, 'On the Side of Democracy' (3 May 2013) *Eurozine*, available at www.eurozine.com/on-the-side-of-democracy/; J.-W. Müller, 'Should the EU Protect Democracy and the Rule of Law Inside Member States?' (2015) 21(2) *European Law Journal* 141–160 and 'The Failure of European Intellectuals?' (11 April 2012) *Eurozine*, available at www.eurozine.com/the-failure-of-european-intellectuals/; 'What, If Anything, Is Wrong with a Copenhagen Commission?' (July 2013) *Transatlantic Academy Working Paper*, available at www.transatlanticacademy.org/sites/default/files/publications/Mueller_CopenhagenCommission_Jul13.pdf; J. Dawson and S. Hanley, 'What's Wrong with East-Central Europe?' (2016) 27(1) *Journal of Democracy* 20–34; I. Krastev, 'What's Wrong with East-Central Europe? Liberalism's Failure to Deliver' (2016) 27(1) *Journal of Democracy* 35–39; Ch. Walker and L. Way, 'The Authoritarian Threat' (2016) 27(1) *Journal of Democracy* 46–63; von Bogdandy and Sonnevend (n 2); J. Kornai, 'Hungary's U-Turn: Retreating from Democracy' (2015) 26(3) *The Journal of Democracy* 34–38; A. Mungiu-Pippidi, 'The Transformative Power of Europe Revisited' (2014) 25(1) *The Journal of Democracy January* 20–32; see also the contributions to 'Is East-Central Europe Backsliding?' (2007; special edition) 18(4) *Journal of Democracy*.

from counter-majoritarian institutions to government enablers, rule of law becomes rule by law, checks and balances are frowned upon as liberal inventions serving the few, etc.

However, *rethinking* calls for more than retooling the legal register (see analysis *supra*). When dealing with the democratic backsliding, one has to avoid the danger of being trapped in the world of legal expertise and arcane legalistic approaches to the current crisis. The question '*how*' the EU constitutional design should be adapted must go hand in hand with revisiting the '*why*' question. In other words: Changing the ailing constitutional design of the EU in the name of whom? The court's existential jurisprudence aside (see *supra*), one fundamental question looms large: Have we managed to move beyond *ad hoc* patching-up of the sinking ship, and onto more systemic rethinking of the system's ailments? So far, I think, we have not. The crucial '*moral authority for a claim to obedience to the Rule of Law*' is still missing.[61] As long as the union of states does not make a leap toward a community of values shared and enforced in the name of the European peoples, rule of law crises are here to stay with us. J. Weiler is right when he warns that the EU 'should simultaneously hurry up and put its own democratic house in order lest it be reminded again that those living in glass houses should be careful when throwing stones'.[62] In the end, discussion of unconstitutional change that the democratic backsliding entails must weave together high hopes for the counter-strategies, but also concerns, disappointments, healthy skepticism and political constraints. The latter must be as much part of our discussion about the democratic backsliding as the former. As rightly commented by D. Edward, 'our endless discussion of How has caused us to lose sight of Why'.[63]

The problem with the EU-wide response to the democratic backsliding from within boils down not so much to the lack of a common point of reference, but rather to the lack of understanding among the peoples of Europe *why* and *how* the quality of democracy and the rule of law in one of the member states should matter to them all. The EU needs to not only build trust in its member states' adherence to democratic values and the rule of law but, first and foremost, construct a civic narrative and loyalty to these allegedly shared values. Until that happens, even the most ambitious legal proposals for the rule of oversight in the EU will founder on the sands of lack of democratization and apolitical ethos of the European polity, leaving the citizens with the hopeless feeling that this is yet another debate for *aficionados*. Therefore, the EU must be able to defend the narrative and explain at the domestic level not only *what* and *how* the EU is 'doing things', but also *why* it acts to defend voluntary commitments and duties adopted by the states on their accession. Europe needs its own voice and counter-narrative in defence of the rule of law that would be heard in the national capitals. These intangibles go well beyond the (important no doubt) talk of procedures, paragraphs, new institutions, etc. They ask questions about the political will and imagination, readiness and, yes also political courage, to stand up for, and defend, the common project against the domestic idiosyncrasies, fleeting voters' preferences and electorates. True debate about the rule of law oversight needs these intangibles just as much as strong legal mechanisms. As things stand right now, domestic rule of law and independence of courts are of no concern to Dutch, French, etc. people. Without such recalibration of our perspectives and loyalties, rule of law oversight is doomed to be no more than a patching-up process, here and there, rather than a much needed global and principled approach that would look to the causes, not simply cure the symptoms.

---

61 Weiler (n 7) 325.
62 *Id*. at 326.
63 D. Edward, 'Luxembourg in Retrospect: A New Europe in Prospect' (2004) 16 *European Business Journal* 120, 126.

Therefore, the challenge of *rethinking* the EU constitutional design today, faced with the democratic backsliding from within, must be based on two existential pillars: (I) member states must be invested in the legal order and the integration project by repeated acknowledgment that they want to respect the values that brought them together and that they are ready to share these values with others; this will then translate into more technical aspect of the tools ('*how*'); (II) the society of citizens must feel fidelity to values that truly define them as Europeans, rather than mere decorum as a result of their member states' accession. Only the sum of (I) *and* (II) can ensure long-lasting success. We have known for years now that (II) has been missing since the inception of the European project and that the civic register has never been really activated. Unfortunately, as of now, 'the ever closer union' continues to be bound together by the fact of statal membership, with the citizens still lurking in the shadow (despite valiant rhetoric to the contrary from the Court of Justice) of this state-driven narrative. The Union continues to be a union of states and, at best, market-driven and self-interested economic operators. Without (I) *and* (II), EU's rule of law suffers from existential drawbacks. While the EU should continue its efforts to secure observance to the rule of law, it must at the same time show more readiness for critical rethinking of its current mandate and limitations in the rule of law department, and more broadly constitutional design. At some point, treaty changes might indeed be needed to reflect the (un)constitutional change within the polity that faces the democratic backsliding from within.

The challenge of responding to the backsliding and the ensuing change in the constitutional fabric of the Union goes clearly beyond the institutional and procedural dimensions. The *rethinking* advocated here calls on appreciating the interaction between the *legal* dimension of the integration (search for optimal *tools and enforcement competences* to safeguard the EU legality – see *supra*) and its *ethical* face (*narrative and justification that would explain in the name of whom the EU legality is defended*). Only the sum of (I) (commitment of the member states) *and* (II) (constitutional design) *and* (III) (triggering the civic register) can ensure long-lasting credibility and legitimacy of the EU legality. Crucially, as we move forward, the EU legality must be defined before it can be enforced. This term should be understood as a syncretic and overarching concept that encompasses various components: rule of law centered around independence of the judges, checks and balances and human rights. While the EU legality has, thus far, provided a dominant rationale for post-1945 constitutionalism (see *supra*), it is now being challenged by the competing understanding of the legality. The democratic backsliding puts forward a rival reading of the rule of law, democracy, human rights and role of the institutions (e.g. constitutional courts). Only by understanding the main features of, and claims made by, both legalities, will the EU be ready to defend its own narrative built around liberal understanding of the rule of law.

In the end, discussion of unconstitutional domestic change, the supranational resilience and design, must weave together high hopes, concerns, and yes, also disappointments, healthy skepticism and political constraints. *The latter* must be as much part of our rethinking the changing fabric of the European liberal consensus and the ways forward, as *the former*.

Epilogue or a new prologue? Democratic backsliding: moving forward

With the politics of resentment on the rise, the European consensus might be just minutes away from fundamental challenges of mega-politics of identity and self-survival.[64] The gist

---

64 The term 'mega-politics' is taken from R. Hirschl, 'The Judicialization of Politics' in K.E. Whittington, R.D. Keleman, and G.A. Caldeira (eds), *The Oxford Handbook of Law and Politics* (Oxford University Press 2008) 123. He points out that 'the judicialization of mega-politics includes the very definition – or *raison d'être* – of the

of the European overlapping consensus has been the acknowledgment by the parties that they are ready to enter into bargaining process in order to find similar grounds of understanding of the principal commitments. Bargaining presupposes disagreement that will be managed over time to build a common understanding of the basic principles. Parties with unreasonable and irrational doctrines that question liberal democracy as a form of government must be excluded from the consensus because disagreement must not undermine all parties' commitment to support liberal democratic principles under a democratic constitutional regime.[65] The emerging constitutional doctrine of the politics of resentment is anything but reasonable within the consensus's meaning. As such, the politics of resentment pose a mega-politics question of belonging and identity. If other parties' commitment to the consensus continues and their resolve to defend the basic principles on which the consensus is based is genuine, this question must be addressed sooner rather than later. For the EU to have a chance against rising politics of resentment, the language it uses and perspectives through which it looks at the member states must change. In the twenty-first century, 'essential characteristics of EU law' must embrace the rule of law, separation of powers, independence of the judiciary, and enforceability of these mechanisms as part of the ever-evolving consensus in a 'process of creating an ever closer union among the peoples of Europe'.[66]

Make no mistake. The stakes could not be higher: Zorbian[67] wonderful European catastrophe looms large. With this, the time of mega-politics has indeed arrived.

---

polity'. The argument presented in this chapter is that persistent undermining and rejection by one member state of the constitutional essentials behind the consensus belongs to the category of so understood *mega-politics*.

65 J. Rawls, *Political Liberalism* (Columbia University Press 2005) 165.

66 Now art. 1 TEU. Such a union must continue to serve as the overarching and ultimate telos of the European integration. The Preamble to the original Treaty on the European Economic Community already proclaimed "*Déterminés à établir les fondements d'une union sans cesse plus étroite entre les peuples européens*". The memory of this commitment takes on added importance today as the very core of what brought member states together in 1951 is being challenged.

67 'Hey boss, did you ever see a more splendiferous crash?' N. Kazantzakis, *Zorba the Greek* (Simon and Schuster 2014).

20

CONSTITUTION AND SELF-DETERMINATION

*Zoran Oklopcic**

Introduc-*tion*

Rarely discussed in conjunction—let alone against the backdrop of a more general concept such as constitutional change—'constitution' and 'self-determination' speak to a remarkably similar, if not identical set of actions, aspirations, situations, and institutional manifestations. For the most part, we imagine their relationship as politically complementary, if not conceptually co-constitutive. Only once we decide to approach these terms from the perspective of a particular theory—or with the help of a more specialized disciplinary vocabulary—do the conceptual differences between 'constitution' and 'self-determination' start to become clear. At which point their seemingly straightforward relationship will begin to reveal itself as mediated by other norms and ideals. What these norms and ideals are, specifically, will always depend on where we stand as scholars and engaged citizens. For the most part, they include nationalism, subsidiarity, equality, stability, sovereignty, federalism, autonomy, and others which may or may not be enshrined in domestic or international law. In this essay, we set these qualifiers aside. Instead, we begin our enquiry with an interesting morpholinguistic detail. Constitution and self-determination, just as

> [m]ost [other] words ending in 'tion' are ambiguous between process and product, between the way one gets there, and the result. The termination of the contract: that can mean the process of terminating the contract. It can also mean the upshot, the product, the end of the contract. The pattern is not identical for each 'tion' word, because each word nuances the ambiguity in its own way. 'Production' itself can mean the process of producing, or, in other circumstances, the result of producing.[1]

The same is true with constitution and self-determination. 'Constitution' refers not only to a done deed, but also to the activity of constituting. While most of us think of 'constitution' as an outcome of that activity, when confronted with 'self-determination' we tend to think

---

* A meditation on conceptual incisions, sovereign decisions, constitutional transformations, and their relations—beyond disciplinary definitions—but with illustrations.

1 Ian Hacking, *The Social Construction of What?* (Harvard University Press 1999) 36.

otherwise. While it is certainly possible to think of self-determination as an artefact—a state of having been 'self-determined'—we mostly understand it as an activity that a sovereign people may engage in as a matter of right. Even when we think of it as having been 'won', self-determination refers to a state of affairs in which a particular kind of collective, self-determining agency continues to be exercised in an ongoing fashion. Even when we imagine it as having been 'achieved' in a (constitutional) moment—that moment still has an internal duration.

In any event, 'constitution' and 'self-determination' refer to situated configurations—of norms, of boundaries, of jurisdictions, of authority, of power, and so on. They are concretized embodiments of the central concern of modern social theory: the problem of structure and agency. From a particular disciplinary perspective, these configurations exist as compositions: they are integrated assemblages of pre-existing elements: presidents and parliaments, higher and lower norms, supreme and constitutional courts, constituent peoples, and constituted institutions. From a less disciplinarily disciplined perspective, there are no compositions without incisions. Though we take them for granted, the elements in a composition must first be made. Put formulaically: *Every constitution, a configuration. No composition without incisions. The same is true with self-determination.*

Constitution and self-determination: conceptual incisions

Incisions are cuts. To cut is to make an incision into a surface. Without cutting, there is no constituting and no self-determining. What this means, specifically, depends on the situations we imagine. It also depends on the metaphors that we use to reconcile a gap between realistic and idealistic manifestations of popular sovereignty. In some cases, our selection of situations and metaphors will be constrained by specific theoretical preoccupations, or disciplinary vocabularies. In other cases, our metaphors will come from a less disciplinarily disciplined vocabulary. In such cases, we will have more latitude in speculating on the character of cuts that must be made so that we speak of self-determination or constitution in a particular way.

The incisions constitutive of the activity of constituting have three dimensions: literal, planar, and conceptual. In the first case, we speak of the cuts that are made literally: by a shovel that digs a hole for boundary demarcations; or, by a chisel that records in a more permanent medium the content of our constitutional commitments. In the second case, incisions leave their mark upon a surface. Without them there would be no mental schemata, and without these our references to self-determination and constitution would immediately lose their intelligibility: there is no constitution without an inside within which constituted powers rule in the name of a sovereign people, just as there is no point in speaking about a right to self-determination without an outside populated by those who have a corresponding duty to respect it. Metaphors alter this picture in a variety of ways but they cannot displace the mental schemata responsible for its elementary intelligibility.

We confront conceptual incisions once we start recognizing how theoretical concepts relate to each other: nesting within each other at different levels of generality, opposing each other within a dichotomy, or co-existing with each other, non-hierarchically. When it comes to conceptual incisions, we may always choose to cut differently. Performed strategically, such incisions produce 'split topoi'. Following Martti Koskenniemi, a conceptual incision may be seen as 'an analytic device for examining the … mechanisms [that] reveal[s] hidden priorities and principles of political value', which 'increases the scientific rigour of exegesis and expands the range of philosophy', allowing us to focus 'directly on the social construction of selfhood and otherness, [including the] principles of communal identification and separateness'—and in doing so 'reveal the complex strategies whereby social practices "take on" an apparently natural and stable outlook'.[2] In this essay, the incisions are performed not simply on 'constitution' and 'self-determination' as the artefacts of constitutional imagination, but on constitution and self-determination as the members in an under-articulated chain of conceptual equivalences, where

CONSTITUTION ≈ SELF – DETERMINATION ≈ DECISION ≈ TRANSFORMATION

or, more elaborately, where (the act of a) constitution ≈ (the exercise of) self-determination ≈ (a sovereign) decision ≈ (constitutional) transformation. In an era that continues to be shaped by the imaginary of popular sovereignty, our vocabularies of contention hinge on the first and the second link in this chain, while only casually referring to the fourth. In doing so, we mostly tend to take the third link for granted. To be seen as legitimate, constitutional transformations must be the outcome of decisions: a sovereign decision to establish a sovereign state by exercising one's right to self-determination; or a sovereign decision to establish a new constitution by violating existing amending procedures, or some other altogether—but always a sovereign decision nonetheless.

Constitution and self-determination: a re-imagination

Defining the perimeter of imaginable constitutional changes, this chain acts as a theoretical leash. To expand this perimeter, we either need to add new links, make the existing ones more elastic, or break the chain. Through a series of conceptual splits, this essay aims to contribute to the latter. This will require us to look at constitutions beyond foundations, self-determinations beyond the determining selves, and decisions without sovereigns but in specific situations. What awaits us beyond them are two things: (1) a set of new concepts, whose connections are yet to be established; and (2) a new way of looking at constitutional transformations as distinct from more generic constitutional 'changes'. To be transformational, such changes must be material, not *immaterial*. They must change something that *matters*. What matters changes with situations and points of view but is always a matter of practical, polemical and poetic aspiration. Thus far, we accept that the imaginable range of such aspirations must be restricted by the visions of constitutions (as founded); self-determinations (as rightfully exercised), and sovereign decisions (that result in states of exception). This need not, and perhaps should not, be the case—even from the perspective of constitutional theory. The aim of this essay is to show why.

Constituting: beyond foundations

What do we mean by constituting? For the most part, we equate it with 'grounding', 'founding', or 'establishing'. Cuts here are the cuts of shovels and chainsaws. They are to be repeated—over and over again—until we have set the foundations, and have erected a construction that we refer to as the 'constitution'. Most often, we imagine that construction as a dwelling: a defensive endurance-promotion instrument that enhances the capacity of that which is being sheltered inside to withstand threats from the outside.[3] To qualify as 'constituent', the power exercised in

---

2 Martti Koskenniemi, 'Hierarchy in International Law: A Sketch' (1997) 8 *European Journal of International Law* 566, 579.

3 See for example, Xenophon Contiades and Alkmene Fotiadou, 'The Emergence of Comparative Constitutional Amendment as a New Discipline: Towards a Paradigm Shift' in Richard Albert, Xenophon Contiades, and Alkmene Fotiadou (eds), *The Foundations and Traditions of Constitutional Amendment* (Hart Publishing 2017) 370.

the context of dwelling-building must be seen as the power that simultaneously situates constituted powers and makes them capable of acting as powers that shelter constitutional enterprises from what Arendt called 'the ravage of time and circumstances'.[4]

As Andreas Kalyvas rightly points out, the Latin verb *constituere* (as the etymological root of 'constitution' in the English language) is a combination of the prefix con- and the verb statuere [which] comes directly from statuo, which means to cause to stand, to set up, to construct, to put, to place, to erect.[5] How *else* can one cause something to with-stand, apart from the obvious acts of setting the foundations for a (political) home? How else may we imagine a situation in which a structure is caused to endure in a particular place? On earlier occasions, the best image I could think of was a circus act on a high-wire. Though I stand behind this illustration, I have to admit that I could not help but feel mildly embarrassed relying on such a distinctly un-serious example.

The reader will therefore understand how buoyed I felt when I discovered, after the fact, the following emblem in Peter Goodrich's superb *Legal Emblems and the Art of Law*.[6] In his book, Goodrich perceptively notices a variety of details in this emblem, each evoking a particular aspect of sovereignty. Still, he seems to ignore its most striking feature: the fact that *even a sovereign must balance in order to withstand* in this position, given the fickle globe upon which he has erected his sovereignty. Thus, if constituting is causing something to with-stand—a power to balance is a constituent power. As such, it coexists with three other forms of *pouvoir constituant*:

(1) *élan établissant* (establishing enthusiasm),
(2) *force formante* (forming force), and
(3) *capacité accommodante* (situational response-ability).

Notice that our focus on possible manifestations of constituent power undermines not only its unity as a theoretical concept—and not only the sensibility of attributing any of its specific manifestations to a *unified* collectivity—but also the very dichotomy within which the vocabulary of popular constituent power makes sense: a dichotomy between constituent and constituted power. Before we completely set this dichotomy aside, however, we must give another look to its right side and ask a question whose answer contemporary constitutionalists most probably simply take for granted: What are the structural manifestations—the configurations of constituted power?

Constituted: pictures of structures and aspects of agencies

Constituted power is a power that is organized in a particular way. It is *functionally separated*, *horizontally* (between the proverbial 'branches' of government) and *territorially divided*, *vertically* (among at least the two 'levels' of government). Spoken of in the plural, constituted *powers* refer to the successful projection of the force of law through the agency of office-

---

4 Hannah Arendt, *On Revolution* (Penguin 1963) 204.
5 Andreas Kalyvas, 'Popular Sovereignty, Democracy, and the Constituent Power' (2005) 12(2) *Constellations* 223, 238.
6 Peter Goodrich, *Legal Emblems and the Art of Law: Obiter Depicta as the Vision of Governance* (Cambridge University Press 2014). The emblem in question is titled 'Wisdom dominates the stars', and comes from George Wither's eminent *Collection of Emblemes, Ancient and Moderne*.

holders, acting in the name of institutions from which they derive their legal authority. Either way, the meaning of *pouvoir constituée* is not exhausted by its rhetorically inferior position in a binary in which a rhetorically superior position belongs to *pouvoir constituant*. It may also be understood as a shorthand description of the patterns of institutional interactions that—together, over time and within a designated space—radically increase the chances that a constitution, adopted for a certain purpose, will in pursuing it, with-stand.

Most modern constitutions prospectively configure these patterns in light of a structural (as well as ideological) principle that seems to inhere in the very idea of a *constitutional* government: constitutional *supremacy*. To a liberal-democratic constitutionalist, the fertility of this principle manifests itself in three ways: *conceptually*, by making the idea of an efficacious written constitution intelligible; *prudentially*, by setting the conceptual preconditions for the emergence of anti-populist moralizing allegories of constitutional pre-commitment; and *rhetorically*, by contributing to the ideological coherence of judicial review. To a less politically committed constitutionalist, constitutional supremacy will appear in a different light: not as a fertile conceptual assumption, but as an engineering side-constraint.

If so, the totality of constituted powers that conform to this imperative must always be seen as *Janus-faced*. As power-generating, power-limiting, and power-projecting institutions, they are 'constituted' in a particular sense: not simply established, but purposefully organized —functionally separated, spatially divided, and selectively related—with an intention to act as the existential props to a constitutional structure. Without them, no constitution would be able to withstand. At the same time, constituted powers exist not simply within a deliberately designed configuration of interacting institutions, but also within the hierarchy of norms. Within this structure, constituted power is oriented power—positioned somewhere within the ascending chain of constitutional authority. Those who project it, always do so from an ambivalent position of downstream-superiority and upstream-inferiority: as higher-lever norm-makers and, at the same time, lower-level norm-takers.[7]

This picture contains manifold parallel, impregnable surfaces. Ascending toward the top of the pyramid, they are gradually shrinking. We call them levels, and must presume their existence. Without them the ideas of constitutional supremacy and legal unity do not make sense. The constitution that hovers atop them is neither a dwelling, nor a simple text, nor a simple guidebook that codifies the criteria of norm-membership in a legal order. It is a blueprint: it provides templates for institutionalization, the protocols of norm-production, and the procedures for constitution-transformation. In this context, to cut is to determine the boundaries of two kinds of *sets*: of norms and of those who make them. Levels are their pictorial representations. They consist of the members of the same set. To cut out an institutional or normative category is to individuate a level in a constitutional hierarchy.

Here I set aside whether our imagination of constituted powers must refer—however implicitly—to the structuring template of *hierarchy*.[8] Rather than dwell any further on the imaginable structures of institutions and plausible patterns of their interactions, we move on to the question of power itself. What concerns us here is not this or that configuration of norm-makers and norm-takers, but that which allows the former to exercise their authority over the latter across space and over time—*at a distance*. Speaking of the powers of

---

7 See Olivier Beaud, *La puissance de l'Etat* (Presses Universitaires de France 1994). Quoted from the Serbian translation, 2018.
8 Ibid., 201.

constituted institutions will only make sense if those who claim to authoritatively speak in their name somewhere, also succeed—somewhere else—in endowing that speech with the force of law.

We know perfectly well how that occurs in the context of face-to-face exercises of constituted power: A sergeant yells: 'At ease!', and recruits obey. Here, the speech act that ends up having the force of law—confirming the power of the holder of an office in a constituted institution—needs no special assistance to travel between the mouth of a superior and the eardrum of a subordinate. In this case, traversing the distance between norm-maker and norm-taker requires no special vehicle. What travels here, notice, is not simply a particular speech act; what travels is a speech act—one discrete emission of that sergeant's constituted power—*in the form of a wave*.

But how is that power successfully projected at greater distances? Not by means of a sergeant yelling orders at a soldier, but by a court ordering an individual to appear before it in the context of an ongoing litigation? Questions such as these have never really had an opportunity to be taken seriously in an era of increasingly narrow disciplinary inquiries. Simple to the point of sounding naive, these queries reveal an important lacuna in our understanding of power that nudges us to be more specific when we discuss its possible manifestations. And this calls for yet another conceptual incision: one that will allow us to make a distinction between the *modalities* of constitutive action on the one hand, and the *conditions* of its projection on the other. In focusing on the former, we focus on constituting, covenanting, initiative-seizing, irrupting, erupting, acclaiming, deliberating, entrenching, enforcing, founding. In focusing on the latter, we speak of their vehicles.

Put differently, when judge A in place B issues a subpoena to individual C in place D, the speech act that travels from AB to CD is not moving through the air like a wave. What flies across, instead, is a *particle* capable of carrying the *force* of law successfully.[9] Ignored by

---

9 Though one could probably extrapolate this idea from the side-remarks of a number of canonical social theorists —from Marx to Foucault, and beyond—I found the clearest intimation of what may provisionally be called *the particle theory of political power* in Floyd H. Allport, 'The Psychological Nature of Political Structure' (1927) 21(3) *The American Political Science Review* 611, 613–14. Though I cannot develop this line of thought further in this essay, Allport's passage deserves to be quoted in full:

> The actual words of the command do not constitute a political stimulus, since if spoken by another person they might evoke an entirely different response, or, indeed, no response at all. Nothing which could be called 'political' would result from such a situation. On the other hand, it is not the person, the speaker himself, who is the political stimulus; for if he uttered other commands, for example, in the realm of religion or private individual liberties, the response would again be different or totally lacking. It is not even the combination of the person of the ruler and these particular words; because in order to be effective the words must be spoken at the proper time and place, with the proper surroundings, and to his own subjects rather than those of another ruler. This whole set of conditions may be summed up under the original phrase, 'constituted authority speaking within his field of jurisdiction'. But this phrase represents a situation involving not only the stimulus but the individual who reacts. It is a total situation and not a stimulus. As indicated above, the meaning of 'stimulus' is wholly objective [but] ... the facts of 'authority' and 'field of jurisdiction' are not ... They are to be found, rather, in the submissive attitudes of individual citizens whereby they accept a written statement (constitution) that a stated official (the ruler in question) is to be obeyed in certain matters (field of jurisdiction). 'Constituted authority' is an attribute, not of the stimulus, but of the reactors. A king, in brief, is only a man. His kingship lies in the attitudes of individuals who respect and obey him. The same analysis applies to certain stimuli which are, properly speaking, non-social, yet which evoke behavior commonly called political. The 'stars and stripes' carried in a parade is a stimulus which causes the average male American spectator to remove his hat'.

constitutional theorists, the *particles* that carry constituent and constituted powers cannot but challenge the prevailing image of constitutional theory, ever fascinated with its own allegedly theological origins. Traditionally committed to exegesis over empirics, most practitioners see it as an interpretive and historicist, not scientific and experimental endeavor. Once we look beyond these conceptions, constitutional theory emerges in a less flattering light. Its family resemblance is not with theology but with pre-particle theoretical physics of the early nineteenth century, before the discovery of leptons, gluons, W- and Z-boson—the particles that carry the force of law, and project the power of constituent, constituted, and other constitutionally relevant powers.

Constitution and self-determination as unification and pluralization

Constitutions are configurations. In one way or another, their figures must evoke the assemblage of elements, which, when interconnected, form a structure. By using metaphors to imagine such structures in a particular way, they achieve an 'iconic increase', which—on the side of the one who deployed them—results in 'the luminous clearing in which we can compare and contrast motives as different as desires and ethical demands … from professional rules to social customs or to strictly personal values'.[10] Speculating on the profitability of a *deliberate* attempt to picture the structures of our constitutions in a particular way is outside the ambit of this essay. A couple of examples will hopefully be sufficient to illustrate the two points that deserve to be mentioned before we move on.

First: the choice of metaphor—in constitutional theory, as in all other fields of human inquiry—is highly consequential. Taken seriously, the acts of founding evoke constitutions not only as the physical foundations, but also the walls, roofs, and orifices of a built establishment. Such constitutions would, arguably, more likely be seen as a shelter or a dwelling, than the one which we would describe with references to 'checks and balances'. Unlike the latter, which evokes a utilitarian clockwork *mechanism*, the former is more pliable to the nationalist imagery of homes, hearths, and a communal way of life. In cases such as this, constitution-making will not only be seen as an exercise in reflection and choice. Here, architecture serves as a metaphor both for the concrete structures of particular constitutions, as well as for the reflective practice of constitutional design more generally.[11] Elsewhere, such as in Canada, constitutional lawyers will use more 'organic' metaphors, such as 'living tree', to evoke the natural development of constitutional interpretation (within the limits established by the act of foundation).

While it is certainly possible to set aside the pastoral metaphorics of Canadian constitutionalism, and imagine constitutions differently—as ships at open sea, as enchanted castles, or awe-provoking temples, or something else indeed—our attempts to purge metaphors from constitutional reasoning will, in most cases, be only superficially successful. Though we may, for example, refrain from the living tree metaphor in discussing the way in which the Canadian Supreme Court imagined the interaction among the four unwritten

---

10 Paul Ricœur, 'Imagination in Discourse and in Action' in Anna-Teresa Tymieniecka (ed), *The Human Being in Action: The Irreducible Element in Man (Part II)* (Springer-Science+Business Media 1978) 10–12.

11 For the discussion of the metaphor of architecture in modern constitutional theory, the role of metaphors in practical reasoning in general, and the similarities between judges and lawyers on the one hand, and the architects on the other, more specifically, see Kim Lane Scheppele, 'Judges as Architects' (2013) 27(1) *Journal of Law & the Humanities* 345, 382.

principles in the *Secession Reference*, we will soon encounter the passages where they 'breathe life' into constitution, act, in the case of federalism, as its 'lodestar', or 'lie at the root' of the Canadian system of government. Aside from the question of what is a principle that lies *at* the root of that system (but is not *the* root itself) this suggests that metaphors are, if not ineradicable, then at the very least, ubiquitous in constitutional, as well as in legal reasoning in general. What metaphor is not, and cannot possibly be (and here I have to disagree with Vicki Jackson's otherwise magisterial discussion on the subject) is 'only a metaphor'.[12]

In any event, though we oftentimes refer to constitutions as the results of the will of a single, sovereign people, most often we imagine them as the unified structures of diverse elements, the results of the work of political unity, or soon-to-be-unified pre-political plurality. Though always more than the sum of its parts, the figure of a constitution evokes a unity whose parts remain identifiable: whether as metaphorical bricks, or as legal norms. They are the instruments that give birth, or assure the survival of a collective political *unum* while at the same time immemorializing the *pluribus* from which it emerged. In modern constitutional imagination, constitutions are the result of the constitutive effort of two kinds of protagonists: of *multitudes* (the pre-political pluralities that disappear after the act of constitution transforms them into a sovereign unity); or of *peoples* (transparent, already constituted unities whose internal plurality remains on full display). In both cases, however, constitutive pluralities act alone.[13]

The typical environment of a theoretically imagined act of constitution is empty. Constituting occurs nowhere in particular, and with no one around—no one, that is, that would be worthy of being turned into a conceptual problem for a theory of foundational constitutionalism. Whatever plurality exists around those who engage in the act of constitution-making must be treated, from their perspective, as inconsequential. In contrast, self-determination evokes the unity and singularity of the holder of the right to self-determination—an entitlement that can only make sense in a conflictual political environment in which 'external' plurality inevitably generates conflicts that justify a need to address the conflicts over constitution in the language of a *right* to self-determination. In sum, the acts of constitution and self-determination cannot but reconfigure the relationship between plurality and unity. Transforming plurality in a way that gives birth to unity, they also situate that unity in space and time. With constitution, that unity obtains a location. As the rightful claimant of a right to self-determination it also obtains a guaranty of that location's integrity, as well as its duration over time.

Self-determination: in two and three dimensions

Even when we think of it as having been 'won', self-determination refers to a state of affairs in which a particular kind of collective, self-determining agency continues to be exercised in an ongoing fashion. Even when we imagine it as having been 'achieved' in a (constitutional) moment—that moment still has an internal duration. Even when we

---

12 Vicki Jackson, 'Constitutions as "Living Trees"? Comparative Constitutional Law and Interpretive Metaphors' (2006) 75 *Fordham Law Review* 921, 959. For an interesting discussion of the living tree metaphor in the context of Canadian constitutional law, see Hugo Cyr, 'Conceptual Metaphors for an Unfinished Constitution' (2014) 19 *Review of Constitutional Studies* 1.

13 See Neil Walker, 'Constitutionalism and Pluralism: A Conflicted Relationship? In Anthony Lang and Antje Wiener (eds), *Handbook of Global Constitutionalism* (Edward Elgar 2017) 433–444.

become aware of the content of the 'will' of a self-determining people in a single instant—and even if its identification (say through a referendum) is widely expected to have imminent transformative consequences, that 'will' is only possible as the culmination of an effort that is temporally extended: from participating in a long-lasting national-liberation struggle on the one hand, to the mere act of voting, on the other. The conceptual cuts that establish dichotomies between the *civic* and the *ethnic*, and between the internal and the external, define the perimeter of permissible disagreements over the right to self-determination.

Ethnic self-determination occurs in 2D. In asserting its power to decide on its political future independently from the will of other sovereign communities, an ethnic nation exercises its right to be self-determining in a way close to the original meaning of 'determination'. The determination that it makes by itself and for itself is the culmination of de-termining: deciding how far it extends—where the self- of that self-determination ends. The holder of a right to self-determining thus understood goes neither up nor down. It only requires a flat surface on which the struggle for territorial sovereignty unfolds. Demotic self-determination is a bit different. The successful exercise of an 'external' right to self-determination that belongs to a holder defined in reference to a pre-existing territorial unit amounts to a constitutive change in the status of that unit.

The trajectory of that change—from status A to status B—can only be registered by a particular, sideways glance. How else would international lawyers be able to refer to an 'external' right to self-determination as an entitlement of the people of a unit in question to decide on the 'upgrade' in its political status? In other words: the terminology of status upgrades is rendered intelligible by the topology of (higher and lower) levels that can only be observed by imagining two parallel planes—that of international, and that of domestic legal order—and then by observing what happens in the exercise of the right to self-determination, by gazing at that scene askew.

If exercised successfully, external 'self-determination' ends with 'state recognition' when the 'upgraded' entity—that was otherwise constitutionally 'submerged' by an already existing sovereign state—bubbles up, as a new sovereign state, to the surface of the international legal order. Even though the terminology of upgrades provokes us to envision this version of the right to self-determination in 3D, its qualifying adjective—'external'—keeps the scene in which it occurs flat. Two dimensions are all we need to imagine the exercise of collective agency *on the inside*, which results in the authoritative directive to those *on the outside* about how to behave toward that unit in the future.

Beyond the 'self': five (un)popular determinations

A different kind of conceptual cut will lead us not only beyond specific binaries, but beyond 'self-determination' itself. Once we envision self-determination not as a temporally extended—however brief—exercise of collective agency, but rather as its outcome, we'll soon be impelled to confront its analytical blind spots. Those analytical blind spots become obvious once we ask a more pointed question that sets the thorny question of the self-determining 'self', together with the paradoxes that haunt it, aside. Once set aside, we are compelled to confront a more analytically precise, and hopefully more illuminating question: When we speak of self-determination, what exactly do we mean by 'determination'?

Indirectly, our inquiry has already provided us with a fragmentary answer: *localization*—the determination of a boundary that will reconfigure the location of a particular inside and its outside; and *specification*—the determination of a jurisdictional status to be accorded to a particular constituted 'inside'. What is being determined in other words is the *species*—an independent state, an associate state, a member state in a federation, for example—of a spatiotemporally bound polity, that is the implicit but indisputable *genus* of a right to external 'self-determination'.

Localization and specification do not occur, however, in a constitutional vacuum. While early modern constitutional thinkers could afford to imagine it, we do not have the same luxury. In Locke's world, disgruntled subjects could simply take off and establish a new polity somewhere else, far from the reach of existing constitutional authorities. Unlike Locke's, our world is fully saturated with sovereign states, constituted—in our imagination —by self-determining, sovereign peoples. In that case, self-determination must provide not only the normative blueprint of localization and specification, but also the criteria for the determination of the state of affairs that legitimately 'triggers' the transformation of extant constitutional order. What the vocabulary of self-determination conceals in this case—to put it differently—are the criteria that render the initiation of constitutional transformation legitimate in the eyes of international law.

From the perspective of an entity that confronts a demand to be (radically) transformed— initiation is a situation that punctures an ongoing process conventionally known as 'internal' self-determination. Which brings us to our penultimate conceptual cut, which results in the split of the topos of *internal* self-determination into a new conceptual binary—with 'determination' as *institutional structuration* on the one hand, and with *operational adaptation* on the other. The first conforms to what constitutional theorists refer to as an act of constitution-making. The second refers to the totality of interconnected (democratic and non-democratic) determinations usually known under the name of constitutional, collective, or popular self-government. Taken together, what awaits us beneath internal and external 'self-determinations' are (at least) the criteria that ought to guide (at least) five distinct 'determinations' that prospectively define the features of:

(S1) response-provocation,
(S2) boundary-localization,
(S3) relationship-specification,
(S4) institution-structuration, and
(S5) operation-adaptation.

By cutting across the 'determination' that participates in the *topos* of self-determination into five separate moments we seem to have irretrievably undermined the sensibility of the very idea of a sovereign people and its 'will'. If the people do not decide, who will? I have addressed this question at length elsewhere, so my three-part answer here will inevitably be brief: The 'will' that our imagination attributes to a particular imagined community is the name for a signal intended to produce constitutionally relevant consequences. What is important to notice is that the signal emitted by a willing, sovereign 'people' is, perforce, *digital*. Whatever it wills—to be more precise—the 'will' of a sovereign people always affirms one of two possible outcomes: either yes or no, yea or nay, 'in favour' or 'against'— or as in the case of referendum on Brexit—'leave' or 'remain'. We tend not to think of the 'will' of 'the people' in this way. We do not do so, in part, because most constitutional theory encourages us to imagine not one, but two constitutionally relevant surfaces.

The first is the site of localization and specification. This surface establishes the provisional spatiotemporal parameters of a polity whose constitution records the structure of its institutions, setting at the same time further parameters that determine the conditions of their permissible adaptation in operation. Cast over them is the second surface—that of a mask. That mask is the mask of sovereignty. As I have argued elsewhere, we may also imagine it differently: as a blanket, or as a lid, or as something altogether different—such as a shell, a hood, or a case. If so, what awaits us beneath the second surface might be likened to a sophisticated electronic device whose institutional sensors and filters periodically register the analog signals coming from a multitude on the ground, modulating them in conformity with some algorithm of institutional responsiveness. The result is a 0 or a 1: one of two possible digital manifestations of the so-called will of a so-called sovereign people. So, once we have cut that 'self-determination' into five separate determinations, another important question arises: If a sovereign people does not decide, who will? Does it even make sense to continue speaking of a sovereign (people) and its decisions?

From sovereign decisions to situated incisions

To decide, as Henri Lefebvre says, is to 'refuse the risk of immediate failure, but accept the risk of terminal' one. A decision is the biggest cut of them all: it is that which 'transforms instant impossibility into imminent possibility', a cut that 'reduces a complex situation involving the past (which is irreversible and irremediable, but which has allowed for the gaining of a capability or an empowerment), with all its possibilities and impossibilities to two dimensions, to the choice between two possibilities'.[14] And while Lefebvre says that a decision reduces the complexity of a situation, it seems that a decision does much more than that: in deciding, our predicament is not just simplified, it is also (perhaps not always) radically transformed. In deciding, to put it differently, we transition between two radically different existential environments. We exit a situation that is *felt* as a situation by destroying its power to constitute our expectations. *Tick-tock-tick-tock!*[15] *The bomb is about to explode, you must decide which wire to cut!* In making that cut (successfully, for argument's sake) we have not only resolved that particular ticking time-bomb situation, but we have also reintroduced possibility into the field of our expectations.

Sovereign decisions seem different. When we discuss them we turn to Schmitt, not Lefebvre. They are political, not existential, and those who make them are sovereigns, not you and me. When sovereigns de-cide, they decide on the ex-ception; they cut something off in order to take it out. In deciding, a sovereign turns an ano(r)malous situation into the state of exception. Unlike sovereigns, who must take out what they have cut off so they could restore *salus* to their *populus*, decisive cuts of the rest of us non-sovereigns, aim to resolve different kinds of, mostly everyday situations. In some of them we will continue to *de-cide*—cut like sovereigns: cut someone out of the will; have something cut off, so that rest does not get infected; cut off all communication with one side of the family. In many others, however, our decisions will not coincide with de-cisions. In such situations, our decision will not be to cut off, or to cut out. Rather, it will be to cut down to, cut across, or cut through. In those situations, our decisions will be Lefebvrean, not Schmittian.

We can conceptualize a relationship between Schmittian and Lefebvrean decisions in two ways. From the perspective of the former, there is no overlap between the two: the first are

---

14 Henri Lefebvre, *Critique of Everyday Life: Foundations for a Sociology of the Everyday, Volume 2* (first published 1961, John Moore, tr, Verso 2002) 155.
15 www.youtube.com/watch?v=dWfLThXoC8Y

politically existential and of public interest, the second are private, prosaic, and quotidian. From the perspective of the latter, Schmittian decisions are a subset of Lefebvrean decisions, and relate to them conceptually as a *species* to a *genus*. In deciding, a sovereign may always decide not simply *otherwise* but also *differently*—not only different things, but in different ways, with different things in mind. We tend not to look at it that way. With Schmitt, we imagine a sovereign as an actor that cuts (something) out—so that his people may live: freely, orderly, healthily. In our imagination, such cut-outs must always emerge from a situation that can be interpreted as a threat to *salus populi*: only then may we recognize them as being properly 'political'.

Even those who are highly critical of Schmittian decisionism critique it without making an attempt to situate decisions across the diversity of existential environments in which they transform expectations in radically different situations. At best, Schmitt's critics make a conceptual distinction between the decisions that are conservative and order-restorative and those that are creative and constitutive, and which coincide with the exercise of constituent power.[16] Though perhaps ingenious as an attempt to blunt the reactionary edge of Schmitt's decisionism, a distinction between conservative and creative decisions distracts us from appreciating a variety of situations and constitutionally relevant in-cisions that otherwise remain hidden behind the decisionist imagery of popular sovereignty.

Some such situations, for example, will only call for *piercing* incisions: quasi 'decisions' the aim of which is to deflate tension, alleviate pressure, release poison, or restore circulation. Others, however, might invite incisions of a different kind—political cuts that not only pierce, but also *get to the bottom* (of things). With them the aim is something different: to achieve clarification, differentiation, reconfiguration. Finally, there will be situations that might require a political incision where cutting amounts to cutting in. Such incisions could not be further removed from Schmitt's decisions: their political objective is to *interrupt* a trend, or a pattern, or a flow and not *cut out a spatiotemporally distinct state* of exception. What is at stake in each situation is a different kind of *salus*: not the *salvation* of (the health of) the people, but the removal of some non-life-threatening impediment before the successful pursuit of a particular constitutional aspiration.

Beyond Schmittian dramatizations

Could these insights lead to meaningful institutional innovations? In this essay, I leave that question open. Rather, the main objective of these insights has been to cast light on the aspects of deciding that can be captured neither in terms of Schmitt's decisionism, nor in terms set by his anti-decisionist detractors. Missed by both is not only the situational dimension of deciding (i.e., the plurality of ways in which a decision may transform a political situation) but also the templates used in their dramatization. Otherwise completely ignored, the way in which these templates affect *the rich lived experience of popular sovereignty* quickly becomes apparent once we imagine the dramatic scenes of 'deciding' in a variety of possible situations. By way of example, consider the following five.

16 Kalyvas (n 5).

(1) Melodramatic

We've suffered endlessly, but the wicked governors wouldn't listen to our humble cries of pain! Our patience is exhausted, and our hope is depleted. We can endure this humiliating situation no longer. Enough! The time has come for a radical break with the existing order. The time has come for us to exercise our right to self-determination, and begin anew, by adopting a new constitution!

(2) Prosaic

On the basis of available evidence, and taking into account the testimonies of all affected, I've come to the conclusion that only exceptional measures offer an adequate response to a progressively deteriorating situation, one that cannot properly be resolved within the framework of the existing constitution. As a result, I've decided to declare a state of emergency with immediate effect.

(3) Romantic

Countless times over our history we've missed the chance to constitute ourselves as an equal sovereign in the community of nations, because of some clumsy mistake of our inept leaders. Recent dramatic changes that have transformed our political environment have given us an opportunity to do better this time. This is no time to recoil from the sweet call of liberty! The time has come to follow its lead at all costs!

(4) Tragic

My fellow citizens. After protracted battles against an overwhelming enemy, we've been served with an ultimatum that forces us to choose between unconditional capitulation and imminent annihilation—between living in infamy and dying with dignity. In full awareness of this stark choice, our decision can only be one: to remain worthy of our ancestors and their sacred sacrifice!

(5) Heroic

Comrades! The time has come! The Central Committee has decided that we must withdraw from negotiations and show our defiance unequivocally. Let's rise to the occasion! If we don't use this opportunity, there won't be another one. Think about that, and about the lives of all those who have fallen in our struggle against exploitation and tyranny.

While all sovereigns are *dramatis personae*, not all *dramatis personae* are sovereigns. Constitutionally consequential in-cisions are not necessarily sovereign de-cisions on the ex-ception. The one that decides politically is a 'decider' that may or may not bear the mark of sovereignty. At the same time, we would not be speaking of sovereigns who decide on exceptions if we thought that doing so does not somehow alter the fighting chances of worthy causes, or the incidence of serious problems. As long as a sufficient number of us continues to think so, there will be nothing to stop the imaginative hegemony of Schmittian approaches to popular sovereignty. Only once we approach his decisionism pragmatically, and not exegetically, will we stand a chance to imagine those whose decisions alter the course of constitutional conflicts and struggles over self-determination, differently: as melodramatic sufferers, matter-of-fact bureaucrats, reckless troubadours, tragic heroes, or heroic strategists—and not as cardboard figures conjured in the imaginations of Schmittian decisionism.

Constitutional transformations

How is all of this related to the idea of constitutional change? And how is the idea of constitutional change related to a more serious-sounding idea of constitutional transformation? The answer to the first question seems rather straightforward. We constitute and determine our political selves not in the middle of nowhere (as evoked by early modern social contract theorists), but in the world of densely packed, territorially bounded, institutional arrangements. Every act of constitution, every exercise of the right to self-determination cannot but result in constitutional *change*. But what do we mean by change in this particular context? The limbs of a performer demonstrating the evolution of dance over the ages in the eponymous YouTube video are changing their position all the time, yet most of us would be inclined to agree that nothing changed in his *constitution*.[17]

In this essay, I will not try to answer a more general set of questions: Is there a conceptual difference between (mere) constitutional changes and constitutional transformations? And if yes, why does it matter to us that we insist on it? Instead, I will revisit the formula with which we began this essay: (the act of) constitution ≈ (the exercise of) self-determination ≈ (a sovereign) decision ≈ (constitutional) transformation. In thinking about constitutions, self-determinations, and sovereign decisions we think of them as *somehow* transformative, or *frequently* transformative, or *always almost* transformative but we still do not really know how and why. This is the case not only because we usually do not pause to consider how else we might imagine the acts, activities, and situations to which those terms refer, but also because we have not paused to reflect on our implicit understandings of transformation, more generally. Upon reflection, constitutional transformation may refer to a constitutional change that is at least one of the following:

(1) dramatic,
(2) disruptive,
(3) comprehensive,
(4) consequential,
(5) important,
(6) cared for.

What makes an act of constitution transformative in the first case is the suspenseful and unpredictable character of the events that led to a constitutional act. Constituting—or the intensity of engagement of those who took part in them: the width of their participation, the seriousness of their deliberations, the ambitiousness of their aspirations, or the absence of base calculations. Here, the actual changes may actually be trivial—either from a formal, or from a material point of view—but the entire experience of constituting may be transformational.

What makes constitutional changes transformational in the second case is something different: not the experience of sudden intensity (after which nothing will ever be as it was before) but rather the sharpness of a cut that terminated one flow of constitutional time and

17 www.youtube.com/watch?v=dMH0bHeiRNg

which gave birth to another. Here, it is the crudeness of the proverbial constitutional 'moment'—not the actual deviation of the post-constituent trajectory of constitutional time —that subtly encourages us to think of a break between the constitutional 'Before' and constitutional 'After' as transformational. In the third case, a constitutional change will be transformational only if it is comprehensive. What matters here is not constitutional temporality but constitutional substance as it is recorded formally. It is against this formal record that we measure the comprehensiveness of constitutional changes, and evaluate its transformational character.

Now, not all constitutional changes are equally consequential. What follows from this is the difference between the third and the fourth understanding of constitutional transformation. A constitutional change may be comprehensive, but it still might not be consequential. We may transition from a presidential to a parliamentary system of government, from a centralized to a decentralized system of constitutional review, but the daily life of those that notionally authored those changes might not change much, if at all. Needless to say, constitutional theorists do not look at it this way. For them a constitutional change may be consequential, but it still need not be constitutionally important. But what kind of change is important constitutionally? One answer to this question is to reach for the help of the traditional theoretical dichotomy—between formal and material sides of a constitution.

In an important recent article, Marco Goldoni and Michael Wilkinson explain what that means more specifically. Material constitution, they argue, is that which is shaped by the four forces that 'constitute the substance and dynamic of constitutional ordering'—'a political unity; a set of institutions; social relations; and fundamental political objectives'—as well as their 'internal relation with the formal constitution': 'the constitutional texts and unwritten conventions as interpreted by official bodies'. As a result, '[n]ot every formal constitutional change is tantamount to a material transformation of the constitutional order, while constitutional transformations can also occur without any formal modification of the constitution'.

Once they have (rightfully!) relativized the formal–material dichotomy, Goldoni and Wilkinson have no means of preventing the full collapse, however. While they start un-controversially—suggesting that 'the formal constitution is the sum of all constitutional norms and principles that drive the regulation of political and social interactions (constituting the "laws of law-making"), [which] stands in relation to the material constitution'—they end up on a more radical note when 'formal constitution' emerges as 'a feature, an instance, of the material constitution, part of the wider constitutional order'.[18] At this point, however, we are compelled to ask: If formal collapses into material, can we still meaningfully speak of constitutional transformations as the changes of/in the material constitution of a particular constitutional order?

One way to rescue this understanding of constitutional transformation is to reinstate the material–formal dichotomy by specifying the formal constitutional features that participate in the establishment of the four abovementioned forces that 'constitute the substance and dynamic of constitutional ordering'. The benefits of this approach are non-trivial. What it offers is a welcome redistribution of scholarly attention: away from the enduring dichotomies of constitutional thought, and toward the affective, socioeconomic, cultural, and other non-formal(istic) 'conditions which make possible the emergence of a state of affairs as a concrete constitutional order'.

---

18 Marco Goldoni and Michael Wilkinson, 'The Material Constitution' (2018) 81(4) *Modern Law Review* 567.

From the perspective of this essay, however, the cost of this approach is prohibitive. Though welcome as an attempt to politicize contemporary constitutional theory, Goldoni and Wilkinson's conception of a material constitution achieves its objective at the expense of something that is, in the long run, arguably more important: the vitality of our constitutional imagination. In making their material constitution contingent on the existence of collective unities, hierarchical institutions, and macroscopic social relations, they also make an unwitting, if modest contribution to the symbolical efficacy of liberal-democratic, national-capitalist, and compulsively *groupist* constitutionalism.[19]

Elsewhere—such as in the field of nationalism studies—'groupism' has at least been identified as an intellectually naive and methodologically dubious scholarly tendency to presume the existence of categories, which are used in practice (such as nations and peoples, for example) and to use them uncritically as the categories of scholarly analysis. In the field of constitutional theory, however, groupism—with a couple of notable exceptions—reigns supreme. One of them is Paul Kahn. 'Contemporary constitutional theory', says Kahn, 'is largely concerned with the concept of community' existing as nothing but a 'locus of discourse', whose main activity is 'speaking, not governing'.[20] What is behind this 'turn to community'—as Kahn rightly points out—are 'extremely abstract considerations' (which explains the absence of theories focused on a society as 'actually, legally structured', and the dearth of those that evoke communities that are characterized by their members' equality).

Now, one might say that the emphasis on actual political unity is precisely what is needed to alleviate this problem. But is it? Even if we leave the contestability of criteria for identifying political unities on the ground aside, we will still have to start by postulating existence of some form of communal *unity* as one of the forces behind the material constitution unless—*unless*—we need it now (at t1) so that we can put it in a stage later (at t2) and implicate it in the scene in which it will end up exercising its constitutive powers only to transubstantiate itself into another one (at t3). We lose something if we never even pause to put the existence of such unities in question. If you *start*—to put it differently—by unquestioningly postulating a certain political unity, you will probably deprive yourself of an opportunity to reconceive constitutional transformation differently (i.e. by splitting the foundational topoi of popular sovereignty).

What prevents us from doing so is the remarkably resilient binary mode of thought that shapes our political vocabularies, as well as the categorical apparatus of the disciplines that problematize that vocabulary theoretically. In this context, those disciplines offer us an easy way out: to equate the exercise of the right to (external) *self-determination* with identity-destroying and identity-making transformations ((S1), (S2), (S3)) while equating the acts of *constitution* with the identity-preserving transformations (at (S4) and (S5)). Doing so would only beg the question: What are the criteria that would allow us to treat a particular determination—be that response-provocation, boundary-localization, relationship-specification, institution-structuration, or operation-adaptation—transformative?

Conclusion

Only material constitutional changes are transformative. In this essay, the adjective 'material' is meant in a particular way, however: juxtaposed not to formal, but to *immaterial*—the

---

19 Rogers Brubaker, *Ethnicity without Groups* (Harvard University Press 2004) 62.
20 Paul Kahn, *Legitimacy and History: Self-Government in American Constitutional Theory* (Yale University Press 1992).

inconsequential and unimportant. Only those constitutional changes that are consequential *and* important, deserve to be called transformational; only those that *matter* deserve to be called *material*. What matters, however, is a matter of aspiration, orientation, and situation—not objective evaluation: what matters constitutionally can never coincide with what matters from a particular theoretical perspective. Constitutional transformation is a matter of what one cares for sufficiently enough—enough to create institutional structures that help what has undergone transformation survive in place and endure over time.

In seeking to explain why, how, when, and where, scholars must assume, assert, or argue for the superiority of their own conceptualizations: of constitution-making and constitutions, of constituent powers, of rights to self-determination, of states of exception, or of sovereign decisions. This is one way to have a conversation about constitution-making locations, institutional functions, forms of mediation, orientational directions, and constitutive aspirations. All it takes is a new metaphor, a different surface—an additional conceptual cut—to realize that it is not the only one.

21

GENDER IN COMPARATIVE CONSTITUTIONAL CHANGE

Silvia Suteu

Introduction

Despite the significant growth in scholarship on comparative constitutional change in recent years,[1] gender analysis has remained marginal in this literature. Works in this area have often focused on the technical aspects of constitutional amendment, with varying degrees of care to ensure their geographical representativeness. Gender equality, non-discrimination and/or the struggle for women's rights have typically been relegated to passing mentions. We are told of the historical fight for the recognition of women as legal persons in Canada,[2] for example, or of the path to enacting electoral quotas for women in Italy,[3] but little more about the specifics of the struggle for gender equality in either society. The literature on gender and constitutions, feminist constitutionalism, and adjudication of gender equality and non-discrimination has grown at the same time.[4] However, the two bodies of scholarship often remain unhelpfully separate. This chapter seeks to contribute toward bridging this gap and to signal avenues for cross-fertilisation.

The chapter proceeds in two steps. First, I consider the substance of the constitutional change in question. I explore which aspects of the myriad ways gender and constitutional

---

1 See, inter alia, Mads Adenas (ed), *The Creation and Amendment of Constitutional Norms* (British Institute of International 2000); Dawn Oliver and Carlo Fusaro (eds), *How Constitutions Change: A Comparative Study* (Hart Publishing 2011); Xenophon Contiades (ed), *Engineering Constitutional Change: A Comparative Perspective on Europe, Canada and the USA* (Routledge 2013); Richard Albert, et al. (eds), *The Foundations and Traditions of Constitutional Amendment* (Hart Publishing 2017); and Xenophon Contiades and Alkmene Fotiadou (eds), *Participatory Constitutional Change: The People as Amenders of the Constitution* (Routledge 2017).

2 Alan C Hutchinson, 'Constitutional Change and Constitutional Amendment: A Canadian Conundrum' in Contiades, *Engineering Constitutional Change* (n 1) 60.

3 Tania Groppi, 'Constitutional Revision in Italy: A Marginal Instrument for Constitutional Change' in Contiades, *Engineering Constitutional Change* (n 1) 216.

4 See, inter alia, Helen Irving, *Gender and the Constitution: Equity and Agency in Comparative Constitutional Design* (Cambridge University Press 2008); Susan H Williams (ed), *Constituting Equality: Gender Equality and Comparative Constitutional Law* (Cambridge University Press 2009); Beverley Baines, Daphne Barak-Erez and Tsvi Kahana (eds), *Feminist Constitutionalism: Global Perspectives* (Cambridge University Press 2012); Catharine A MacKinnon, 'Gender in Constitutions' in Michel Rosenfeld and Andras Sajo (eds), *Oxford Handbook of Comparative Constitutional Law* (Oxford University Press 2012) 397–416; and Helen Irving (ed), *Constitutions and Gender* (Edward Elgar 2017).

change interact have been most prominent in recent years and why. The two foci I identify are: the fight for basic women's rights, including the continued constitutional debates surrounding abortion and gender quotas, and calls for recognition of the rights of sexual and gender minorities, in particular marriage equality and the rights of transgender and intersex persons. As can be seen, this chapter takes an expansive view of gender, defining it as comprising socially constructed roles, behaviours and attitudes rather than biologically determined characteristics; instead of viewing sex and gender as distinct, however, the chapter understands sex as subsumable to gender, insofar as perceptions of the body are themselves shaped by society.[5] This inclusive approach is itself aimed at bridging gaps between various strands in the literature on engendering constitutions. Second, I look at the procedural aspects of constitutional change and how they interact with gender considerations, including the processes of constitution-making, constitutional reform—be it through legislation, referendum or some other form of participatory mechanism—and judicial review.

Interwoven throughout the study is a different layer that could be applied to an analysis of gender and comparative constitutional change: looking at the constitutional actors involved. When discussing constitution-making, for instance, the people exercising some form of constituent power are likely to be invoked, be it in the form of constituent assemblies or votes in national referendums. Once we look at constitutional amendments passed to advance or restrict the cause of gender equality and non-discrimination, the legislature and courts are bound to be front and centre. It may also be the case that advances in this area will come without formal constitutional amendment, whether in the form of expansive judicial interpretation or progressive government guidelines. Emerging from the various case studies are questions related to who is the legitimate and higher source of authority in deciding these matters. Our preference is likely to depend on how we frame each issue—for example, seeing abortion as a women's rights issue rather than a moral one, or choosing to protect certain rights from majority vote, even during popular referendums or constituent moments. It will also depend on perceptions of each institution and its propensity for progressive or conservative understandings of gender equality. Finally, it will be contingent on our pre-existing disposition toward long-standing debates in constitutional theory—the role of the courts, the direct recourse to the people in constitutional change, issues of rights balancing and definitions of legal personhood, etc.

This chapter cannot propose to solve all these thorny issues. I do hope, however, that it will provide readers with the contours of what a gender analysis of constitutional change entails and with a set of research questions to be further explored in more depth going forward. The chapter concludes with some observations about the nature of gender-related comparative constitutional change. I find that progress in this area has not been linear, neither across time nor space. I also explain how the way issues such as abortion or same-sex marriage are framed plays an important role in campaigns for constitutional change. Finally, I call for more modesty on the part of the constitutional scholar. As the various case studies show, in the area of gender equality and non-discrimination the constitution may be the starting point, but much more work is needed at the legislative and societal level before change becomes truly meaningful.

---

5 This choice follows Linda Nicholson's helpful distinction in her article 'Interpreting Gender' (1994) 20(1) *Signs* 79.

The substance of constitutional change surrounding gender

Before discussing the different mechanisms that can be used to bring about constitutional change in this area, it is helpful to lay out the nature of the constitutional reforms likely to appear on the agenda. The following is not an exhaustive list, but one that captures some of the most visible constitutional battles in recent years, not merely in the West but across the globe. As already stated, I adopt an inclusive understanding of gender analysis, one that comprises the fight for the rights of gender and sexual minorities alongside the rejection of hierarchies of power that systematically discriminate against women.

Women's rights

A wide variety of issues come under this rubric. Depending on the particular national context, the fight for women's rights in the 21st century is about 'old' demands such as equality in the family, marriage and divorce, equal representation in public life and equal citizenship rights, as well as about 'newer' ones such as new reproductive technologies. Battles over women's bodily autonomy and especially over their right to access abortions also continue to be as contentious as ever, whether they are fought at the ballot box or in the courtroom. The reality, however, is that the battle for basic women's rights continues in many countries across the globe, a point sadly illustrated by the 2018 lifting of the ban on women driving in Saudi Arabia alongside the government's continued crackdown on the activists who had demanded the right to drive.[6]

As Rubio-Marin and Chang have aptly termed it, women must be 'read into constitutionalism'.[7] In other words, women must be recognised as full citizens and constitutional law provides the language to do so. Historically, this has meant recognising them as bearers of rights, often starting with the right to vote and to participate in public life. As Rubio-Marin and Chang also note, there was a double impulse behind viewing women's full equality as a consideration of constitutional law: the recognition of sex-based discrimination and the principle of equality in marriage in international human rights instruments post-Second World War.[8] This area may, therefore, be viewed as an early site of the interplay between constitutional and international law, an interplay we have since come to see as both pervasive and inevitable.[9]

Examples in the following section, notably those of Tunisia and Nepal, will show how the fight for basic women's rights still matters, even as they are often taken for granted in scholarship discussing today's fight for gender equality from a largely Western-centric perspective. Constitutionally enshrining full citizenship rights for women, including their ability to retain and pass on their nationality; explicitly recognising gender equality and the principle of non-discrimination, and providing their bearers with access to a court in order to vindicate transgressions; full and equal rights in marriage and in the family; equal political rights, including access to all political offices—these are some of the more prominent examples of basic rights that women are still deprived of in numerous countries. Even unambiguously including women among

---

6 'Saudi Arabia's Ban on Women Driving Officially Ends' (24 June 2018) *BBC News*.
7 Ruth Rubio-Marin and Wen-Chen Chang, 'Sites of Constitutional Struggle for Women's Equality' in Mark Tushnet, Thomas Fleiner and Cheryl Saunders (eds), *Routledge Handbook of Constitutional Law* (Routledge 2012) 302.
8 Ibid.
9 For considerations of the complex ways in which constitutional and inter-/transnational law interact, see, inter alia, Vicki Jackson, *Constitutional Engagement in a Transnational Era* (Oxford University Press 2010) and Christine Bell, 'What We Talk about When We Talk about International Constitutional Law' (2014) 5(2) *Transnational Legal Theory* 241.

the founding parents of the constitution—such as was done in Tunisia's Constitution, whose preamble speaks of the struggle for independence and liberty of 'Tunisian men and women'—has been as rare a move as it could be symbolically powerful.

Two sets of women's rights issues have remained on the agenda across the globe: equal and safe access to abortion and the question of gender quotas in politics. Constitutions tend to be silent on abortion. When they do mention it explicitly, they tend to do so in order to indicate a strong stance against it except in limited circumstances. Thus, Article 26(4) of the Kenyan Constitution, Article 15(5) of the Somali Constitution and Article 15(5) of the Constitution of Swaziland illustrate this, as they each prohibit abortion except under strictly prescribed scenarios. Relatedly, constitutions may recognise the rights of the unborn and on that basis severely restrict a woman's right to bodily integrity and her reproductive freedom. For example, the Chilean Constitution protects the life of the unborn under Article 19(1), whereas Honduras's Constitution stipulates under Article 67 that 'the unborn shall be considered as born for all rights accorded within the limits established by law'. Ireland's Constitution had contained, under Article 40(3)(3), a referendum-inserted provision that affirmed the state's recognition of 'the right to life of the unborn and, with due regard to the equal right to life of the mother, guarantees in its laws to respect, and, as far as practicable, by its laws to defend and vindicate that right'. A popular referendum in May 2018 finally repealed the provision—the culmination of decades of activism and several failed prior attempts.[10]

Electoral gender quotas remain a contested topic, even among feminists. On one side of the debate are arguments about basic fairness and the need to correct the historical underrepresentation of women in politics, the instrumental advantage that appealing to half the electorate will bring, as well as difference-based arguments about giving a voice to women's specific needs and different approach to politics.[11] On the other side, however, are those who oppose quotas as violations of the liberal principle of merit; some feminists also fear that in practice quotas will act as a ceiling rather than a floor of representation, that women are too different to be represented as one group, and that quotas are ultimately not transformative of the structures having led to women's exclusion in the first place.[12] Nevertheless, gender quotas have continued to spread and now come in a variety of forms.[13] The evidence on their efficacy is a more complex matter to assess, made even more complicated when evaluated intersectionally or when looking into whether increased women's representation also translates into reduced bias against women in politics.[14]

When it comes to the actual mechanism for adopting gender quotas, this also varies. Some constitutions explicitly incorporate quotas, such as Rwanda's Constitution requiring a minimum of 30 per cent female representation in decision-making organs (Article 10(4)). Elsewhere, the quota

---

10 Lindsey Earner-Byrne and Diane Urquhart, *The Irish Abortion Journey, 1920–2018* (Palgrave Macmillan 2019).

11 Sarah Childs and Joni Lovenduski, 'Political Representation' in Georgina Waylen, Karen Celis, Johanna Kantola and Laurel Weldon (eds), *The Oxford Handbook of Gender and Politics* (Oxford University Press 2013) 489.

12 See discussion in ibid. and Susan H Williams, 'Equality, Representation, and Challenge to Hierarchy: Justifying Electoral Quotas for Women' in Williams, *Constituting Equality* (n 4) 53.

13 On the global spread of gender quotas, see Melanie M Hughes, Pamela Paxton, Amanda B Clayton and Pär Zetterberg, 'Global Gender Quota Adoption, Implementation, and Reform' (2019) 51(2) *Comparative Politics* 219. For a taxonomy of the different types of gender quotas, see Drude Dahlerup and Lenita Freidenvall, 'Gender Quotas in Politics—A Constitutional Challenge' in Williams, *Constituting Equality* (n 4) 29.

14 Melanie M Hughes, 'Intersectionality, Quotas, and Minority Women's Political Representation Worldwide' (2011) 105(3) *American Political Science Review* 604 and Amanda Clayton, 'Do Gender Quotas Really Reduce Bias? Evidence from a Policy Experiment in Southern Africa' (2018) 5(3) *Journal of Experimental Political Science* 182.

may be stipulated via legislation, usually the electoral law. An example would be Ireland's passing of the Electoral (Amendment) (Political Funding) Act 2012, incentivising political parties to select at least 30 per cent female or male candidates. It may also be the case that legislation needs to be introduced to give effect to an otherwise general constitutional provision. In one-party regimes or monarchies, decrees may bring about the introduction of quotas or, as was the case in Morocco, a gentleman's agreement may set aside a number of reserved seats for women in the face of a constitution that would have prevented formal quotas.[15] Quotas remain understudied so it is difficult to gauge any correlation between the mechanism of adoption and their success. However, we do know that the initial adoption of gender quotas is often followed by further reform wherein legislators tinker with the model and respond to the delayed effects of the quotas.[16]

Gender and sexual minority rights

The fight for gender and sexual minority rights has made incredible gains in recent years. LGBTQ+ (Lesbian, Gay, Bi, Transgender, Queer and others) activists have called for legal recognition, including at the constitutional level, as well as for the adoption of improved rights protections and measures against discrimination. Two arenas of intense constitutional activity are discussed: marriage equality and gender identity recognition.

Marriage equality

The substantive issue that has featured perhaps most prominently in recent LGBTQ+ rights debates has been marriage equality. Whether in the form of legislation and/or popular referendums to legalise (or explicitly ban) same-sex unions or constitutional adjudication around the issue, marriage equality has been front and centre in recent comparative constitutional developments. It is important to note, however, that not all of these initiatives or judgments have been favourable to the recognition of same-sex marriage. Lawmakers and judges in a number of countries have chosen either incremental reform short of full constitutional recognition of marriage equality (such as via the legalisation of same-sex civil partnerships) or outright banning same-sex unions and defining marriage or even family as between men and women.

Framing the issue is important and will be jurisdiction- and context-specific. Most often, the issue is set out as one of equality, with activists in favour of same-sex unions viewing the limitation on access to the institution of marriage as discriminatory in the same way as denying basic rights to any minority group is. While equality arguments are always present, however, they may not always suffice and may require more complex legal argumentation that binds together different rights and principles. It may also be the case that the constitutional text is gender-neutral when invoking marriage and therefore that the institution can be reinterpreted as being open to same-sex unions.[17] Feminist scholars have argued that we should be more critical toward the institution of marriage in general, given its patriarchal and inherently unequal

---

15 Gihan Abou-Zeid, 'The Arab Region: Women's Access to the Decision-making Process across the Arab Nation' in Drude Dahlerup (ed), *Women, Quotas and Politics* (Routledge 2006) 168, 177.

16 Hughes et al., 'Global Gender Quota Adoption, Implementation, and Reform' (n 13).

17 The Romanian Constitution's provision on family may be read as such an example. Article 48 states: 'The family is based on a freely consented marriage by the spouses, their full equality, and the right and duty of the parents to raise, educate, and instruct their children'. In fact, in a decision on the constitutionality of a constitutional amendment initiative redefining Article 48 to explicitly restrict the institution to between a man and a woman, Judge Daniel-Marius Morar of the Romanian Constitutional Court, dissenting, read the

nature.[18] Others have simply subsumed the issue to that of equality within marriage. Catharine MacKinnon, for instance, has noted the discrepancy between finding constitutional guarantees of equality within the family alongside restrictive definitions of marriage as between a man and a woman, 'the simple sex discrimination inherent in dictating one's marital partner by sex apparently overlooked'.[19]

These calls for nuance were largely superseded by facts in places where the constitutional recognition of marriage equality was achieved, particularly where it came at the end of passionate campaigns such as in the United States, via judicial intervention, or in Ireland, via legislation in the aftermath of popular referendum. For all the praise that both these examples, discussed in more detail below, have garnered, there are also those who argue that going through the ordinary legislative process is preferable.[20] They view the traditional legislative route as one more prone to nuance, compromise and incremental changes to the institution of marriage rather than major shifts with unforeseen risks. As will be seen, there are also fears that backlash to legalisation of same-sex unions—especially when achieved through judicial intervention open to accusations of judicial activism—may occur, with other LGBTQ+ rights campaigns bearing the brunt.

Gender identity recognition

Another area of intense constitutional activity in recent years has revolved around questions of gender identity, including the recognition of transgender and intersex rights. Both of these involve moving beyond binary understandings of gender, but they address distinct sets of concerns: the recognition and equal protection of individuals whose gender identity does not correspond to their birth sex and of individuals born with indeterminate gender characteristics or who otherwise do not identify as either 'female' or 'male'.

The fight for transgender rights has picked up pace, often brought to general public attention via the juridification of certain recognition or access issues. In the United States, for example, the debate has centred around questions of whether and how to ensure equal access to school facilities such as bathrooms and locker rooms to transgender students, as well as around the inclusion of transgender servicemen in the military.[21] To these issues we may add legal struggles around recognition on birth certificates, driver's licences and passports, as well as the protection of transgender persons in prisons.[22]

With regard to non-binary notions of gender, the number of systems having engaged in reform has increased. This has come about in different ways: legislative reform, government

---

original provision as allowing for an inclusive, gender-neutral interpretation. See his Separate Opinion to the *Constitutional Court Decision No. 539* of 17 December 2018, 28.

18 See, inter alia, Claudia Card, 'Against Marriage and Motherhood' (1996) 11(3) *Hypatia* 1; Nicola Barker, *Not the Marrying Kind: A Feminist Critique of Same-Sex Marriage* (Palgrave Macmillan 2013); Elizabeth Brake, *Minimizing Marriage: Marriage, Morality, and the Law* (Oxford University Press 2014); and Clare Chambers, *Against Marriage: An Egalitarian Defense of the Marriage-Free State* (Oxford University Press 2017).

19 MacKinnon, 'Gender and Constitutions' (n 4) 405–406.

20 See Justice Scalia's arguments discussed below.

21 The Obama administration had issued guidance on the interpretation of anti-discrimination law aimed at making schools safer for transgender children. See Catherine Jean Archibald, 'Transgender Bathroom Rights' (2016) 24 *Duke Journal of Gender, Law and Policy* 1. However, the Trump administration withdrew that guidance. In January 2019, the Supreme Court issued an order allowing the Trump administration's ban on transgender servicemen to go into effect. See *Trump, President of US, et al. v Karnoski, Ryan, et al.*, Supreme Court of the United States Order, 22 January 2019.

22 Kimberly A Yuracko, *Gender Nonconformity and the Law* (Yale 2016).

policy changes, judicial intervention or a combination thereof. Changes have sometimes covered transgender and intersex persons together and sometimes separately.

India's case is instructive, as rights for intersex and transgender individuals were afforded legal status earlier than elsewhere on account of the long-standing recognition of their presence in society. Already in 2005, Indian passport applications listed a third gender; by 2009, electoral rolls and voter identity cards also did so; and in 2014, the Indian Supreme Court issued a landmark judgment recognising a third gender and requiring government accommodation of this minority on par with others, including access to job and education quotas and healthcare.[23] The Transgender Persons (Protection of Rights) Bill 2016 was later introduced in an effort to implement the judgment, but the legislation has been criticised as inadequately protecting transgender individuals from discrimination.[24] Moreover, India's position is not uniform across gender and sexual minorities: a comparatively progressive stance vis-à-vis the former may be contrasted with conservatism regarding queer sexuality. The Supreme Court's 2013 *Naz* decision had recriminalized homosexuality and, while since overturned, reinforces the special historical status of the third gender in India.[25]

Elsewhere, Australia was a pioneer in this area and illustrates the progressive potential of government and legislative intervention, at both sub-federal and federal level. Already in 2003, Australians had the option of registering gender as 'X' on their passports so long as they could present birth certificates listing their gender as 'indeterminate'. This was expanded in 2011 to include transgender persons and to allow for the 'X' registration upon presentation of a simple letter signed by a medical doctor.[26] In 2013, legislation was amended to prevent discrimination of both intersex and transgender individuals. Thus, the Sex Discrimination Act 1984 was amended explicitly to prohibit discrimination on the grounds of sexual orientation, gender identity and intersex status in many areas of public life.[27] The Australian Government's Guidelines on the Recognition of Sex and Gender further recognise that individuals may identify as a gender other than the sex they were assigned at birth, or may not identify as exclusively male or female, and that this should be reflected in records held by the government; the guidelines also standardise the evidence required for a person to change their sex/gender in personal records held by government departments and agencies.[28]

A further example of judicial intervention triggering legislative change comes from Germany. In October 2017, the German Constitutional Court issued a ruling finding the country's civil status law (the Civil Status Act or *Personenstandsgesetz*) incompatible with the Basic Law.[29] The law in question had required assigning a child's gender as either female or

23 *National Legal Services Authority v Union of India and Others* (Writ Petition No. 400 of 2012 with Writ Petition No. 604 of 2013), Supreme Court of India, 15 April 2014.

24 Devershi Mishra and Komal Khare, 'Deciphering the Reality of the Transgender Persons (Protection of Rights) Bill 2016' (14 April 2017) *Oxford Human Rights Hub* <http://ohrh.law.ox.ac.uk/deciphering-the-reality-of-the-transgender-persons-protection-of-rights-bill-2016/> accessed 31 January 2019.

25 *Suresh Kumar Koushal and Another v NAZ Foundation and Others*, Supreme Court of India, 11 December 2013, subsequently overturned by *Navtej Singh Johar v Union of India*, Supreme Court of India, 6 September 2018. On India's different attitudes toward gender and sexual minorities, see Jennifer Ung Loh, 'Transgender Identity, Sexual Versus Gender "Rights" and the Tools of the Indian State' (2018) 119(1) *Feminist Review* 39 and Bret Boyce, 'Sexuality and Gender Identity under the Constitution of India' (2015) 18(1) *Journal of Gender, Race and Justice* 1.

26 *Sex Files: The Legal Recognition of Sex in Documents and Government Records* (Australian Human Rights Commission 2009).

27 Sex Discrimination Amendment (Sexual Orientation, Gender Identity and Intersex Status) Act 2013.

28 *Australian Government Guidelines on the Recognition of Sex and Gender*, updated 2015.

29 Order of the First Senate of 10 October 2017, 1 BvR 2019/16.

male in the birth register and, where that was not possible, a gender entry was not made.[30] The court found a violation of Article 2(1) (the general right of personality) in conjunction with Articles 1(1) (the inviolability of human dignity) of the Basic Law insofar as the law did not protect the gender identity of those who could not be assigned the status of 'female' or 'male' permanently. Moreover, insofar as the law prevented non-binary gender registrations, the court found it in violation of Article 3(3) of the Basic Law (the ban on discrimination, including on the grounds of sex). Moreover, the Constitutional Court gave the legislature until 31 December 2018 to pass corrective legislation. This led to a law offering a third option on birth certificates, which would indicate gender identity as 'various' ('*divers*' in German), as well as barring surgery on intersex children and allowing later in life decisions to change the birth certificate.[31]

A similar legal challenge in Austria saw that country's Constitutional Court having to determine whether the Civil Register Act was discriminatory. The Austrian court rooted its decision in Article 8 of the European Convention on Human Rights, finding that it afforded individuals the 'right to have their gender variation recognized as a separate gender identity in gender-related provisions; in particular, it protects individuals with alternative gender identities against having their gender assigned by others'.[32] Nevertheless, the court ruled that the Civil Register Act could be read in conformity with these requirements and did not need amendment. Going forward, the child's gender registration would not be limited to 'female' or 'male' but could include alternative gender identities—the court referred to 'diverse', 'inter' or 'open', which had been suggested by the Bioethics Commission of the Federal Chancellor's Office. Thus, in the Austrian case, judicial intervention pushed forward the recognition of non-binary gender identities through creative interpretation, without requiring further legislative or constitutional change from the other branches.

Several conclusions may be drawn from the examples discussed in this section. One is that the fight for gender equality may take several years and, while ideally it will progress toward more protection, this linear development is not guaranteed. As the recurrence of the abortion question in several jurisdictions shows, gains may be contested and even reversed. Moreover, as the gender quotas debate indicates, women's rights advocates may themselves not agree on the best measure to bring about change, which may render reform less straightforward. It is also the case that many of these issues—abortion, but also transgender rights, for example—are prone to politicisation, as has happened in the United States. In such instances, constitutional and legislative reform will be harder to frame as matters of gender equality and instead may be instrumentalised ideologically. India's example vis-à-vis the recognition of a third gender illustrates how much progressive societal views can help push forward legal recognition claims. Finally, several of the examples discussed also illustrate the interplay between domestic advances and supranational or international interventions. For example, in the area of intersex rights, regional and international organisations have adopted

---

30 The option simply not to register the child's gender on the birth certificate had been made available in 2013 to cover intersex children. However, this negative option was criticised as insufficiently protective of the child's choice of gender identity and possibly encouraging surgery. Natalie Muller, 'Third Sex Option on Birth Certificates' (1 November 2013) *Deutsche Welle*.

31 Gesetz zur Änderung der in das Geburtenregister einzutragenden Angaben, 18 December 2018.

32 'Intersex Persons Have the Right to Adequate Entry into Civil Register' (29 June 2018) *Verfassungsgerichtshof Österreich*. The decision was rendered on 15 June 2018 as VfGH 15.06.2018, G 77/2018: *Verfassungskonforme Interpretation: Intersexuelle Menschen haben Recht auf adäquate Bezeichnung im Personenstandsregister*.

declarations and reports aimed at protecting intersex children from surgeries.[33] Austria's example showed how international standards may be invoked to advance the gender equality, though there is also a risk that sovereigntist claims against foreign imposition of values may bar progress.[34]

The fight for legal recognition and the appropriate means for achieving it reflect only parts of the conversation around gender identity and the law. Calls for equal rights and non-discrimination are important, but they also raise deeper structural and philosophical questions about the law's ability to reflect the diversity of gender identities and about the assumptions implicit in gender classifications altogether. For example, the Darlington Statement, adopted in 2017 by Australian and Aotearoa/New Zealand intersex organisations and independent advocates, decried the emphasis on gender classifications instead of how people were treated and denounced such classifications as a form of structural violence. Insofar as the aim remains to fight against the discrimination of those who do not conform to conventional gender norms, having courts and the law themselves take a narrow view of gender identity risks perpetuating the very stereotypes they should be combatting.[35]

The mechanisms of constitutional change surrounding gender

A second axis of analysis of constitutional change surrounding gender is that of the specific mechanism or process used to bring about said reform. Be it in the course of constitution-making, via a process of constitutional amendment, or through judicial review, different paths have been taken by those seeking to engender constitutions. The choice may be strategic or incidental, or it may be predetermined by the features of the constitutional system itself.

Constitution-making

There may be no better opportunity to engender a constitutional text than during a wholly new constitutional moment. Much has been written in recent years about constitution-making from a gender perspective, with authors seeking to identify both guiding principles and case studies that could serve as models.[36] A lot of that literature has understandably

---

33 See, inter alia, Council of Europe Parliamentary Assembly, *Children's Right to Physical Integrity*, Resolution 1952 (2013), 1 October 2013 and Juan E Mendez, *Report of the Special Rapporteur on Torture and Other Cruel, Inhuman or Degrading Treatment or Punishment*, UN Doc A/HRC/22/53, 1 February 2013, paras 76–79.

34 Philip M Ayoub, 'Perils of Success: Backlash and Resistance to LGBT Rights in Domestic and International Politics' in Alison Brysk and Michael Stohl (eds), *Contracting Human Rights: Crisis, Accountability, and Opportunity* (Edward Elgar 2018) 89, 96.

35 Taylor Flynn, '*Transforming the Debate: Why We Need to Include Transgender Rights in the Struggles for Sex and Sexual Orientation Equality*' (2001) 101 *Columbia Law Review* 392.

36 See, inter alia, Alexandra Dobrowolsky and Vivien Hart (eds), *Women Making Constitutions: New Politics and Comparative Perspectives* (Palgrave Macmillan 2004); Dina Francesca Haynes, Fionnuala Ní Aoláin and Naomi Cahn, 'Gendering Constitutional Design in Post-conflict Societies' (2011) 17 *William & Mary Journal of Women and the Law* 509; Helen Irving, 'Drafting, Design and Gender' in Tom Ginsburg and Rosalind Dixon (eds), *Comparative Constitutional Law* (Edward Elgar 2011) 19; Euromed Feminist Initiative IFE-EFI, *ABC for a Gender Sensitive Constitution: Handbook for Engendering Constitution-making* (2015); Aili Mari Tripp, 'Women's Movements and Constitution Making after Civil Unrest and Conflict in Africa: The Cases of Kenya and Somalia' (2016) 12(1) *Politics & Gender* 78; Irving, *Constitutions and Gender* (n 4); Inclusive Security, *How Women Influence Constitution Making after Conflict or Unrest: Lessons from Eight Case Studies* (2017); Helen Irving and Ruth Rubio-Marin (eds), *Women as Constitution-Makers: Case Studies from the New Democratic Era* (Cambridge University Press 2019). For a broader perspective on the role gender plays in democratic transitions, see Georgina Waylen, *Engendering Transitions: Women's Mobilization, Institutions and Gender Outcomes* (Oxford University Press 2007).

focused on conflict-affected states, influenced in no small part by the international community's growing commitment to taking seriously the gendered impact of conflict.[37]

On the one hand, there has been welcome recognition of the fact that the constituent moment is an opportunity to push forward a gender equality agenda, one that should not be wasted. It may be tempting, particularly in the fraught aftermath of conflict, to postpone addressing gender-based discrimination and women's rights until after other, presumably more important, matters have been resolved—power-sharing arrangements, territorial divisions, the electoral system, etc. However, such attitudes risk ignoring not just the role women have played during conflict (supporting their families and increasingly also as combatants in their own right) but also the role they will play during the reconstruction phase. They also risk pushing into the long grass matters related to gender-based discrimination and gender equality, on the ground that they constitute 'divisive issues'.[38] It is true that, during this process, 'everything is a priority' and constitution-making will be only one endeavour among many.[39] Nevertheless, it is difficult to see strong gender equality commitments emerge and be implemented in the absence of a foundational text providing the impetus.

The example of South Africa is instructive here: the strong emphasis on addressing gender-based violence already during constitutional negotiations has been credited with ensuring that the constitution also addresses it. Article 12 of the South African Constitution refers to the freedom and security of the person as including the right to be free from violence, public or private, as well as the right to bodily and psychological integrity, including on reproductive matters. The provision could in turn form the basis for concerted efforts to tackle gender-based violence.

On the other hand, the constitution as a text invariably involves a certain level of abstraction, beyond which implementing legislation and judicial interpretation will be required. This is not to say that constitution-making is irrelevant in the fight for greater gender equality. Quite on the contrary, as many constitutional renewal processes show, activists understand very well that, while not the end of their struggle for gender equality, an engendered constitution can provide them with the symbolic and textual hook to bring forth and legitimise their demands. In the case of South Africa, for instance, despite constitutional engagement, the focus of activists against gender-based violence remained on law reform and services for survivors.[40] However, the level of success at influencing the constitutional text will vary greatly according to, among others, the preparedness of these activists, the political context, and the level of support from the international community.

---

37 Much of this focus has been driven by the United Nations, in particular after the adoption of UN Security Council Resolution 1325 and subsequent resolutions, demanding that gender-based crimes be addressed post-conflict, as well as that women be properly represented in decision-making during peace negotiations and in public life. For an overview and assessment of the impact of the resolution, see UN Women, *Preventing Conflict, Transforming Justice, Securing the Peace: A Global Study on the Implementation of United Nations Security Council Resolution 1325* (2015).

38 For a brief discussion of what might constitute such 'divisive issues' and how constitution-makers can tackle them during negotiations, without undermining the entire process, see Interpeace, *Constitution-making and Reform: Options for the Process* (2011), para 2.5.2.

39 Michele Brandt, *Constitutional Assistance in Post-Conflict Countries: The UN Experience: Cambodia, East Timor & Afghanistan* (UNDP 2005).

40 Catherine Albertyn, 'Women and Constitution-making in South Africa' in Irving, *Constitutions and Gender* (n 4), 71.

All of these have a bearing on how much traction gender equality issues end up carrying during constitution-making.

Perhaps the most visible recent success story in this regard has been Tunisia's 2014 Constitution. The country is increasingly seen as the exception among states involved in the so-called 'Arab Spring', as it is singular in its ability to continue on the path toward a democratic transition.[41] The fight for gender equality played a central role in the constitutional negotiations during 2012–14, reinforcing Tunisia's reputation as the most progressive on these issues in the region.[42] A notable moment occurred in August 2012, when the first draft of the future constitution was published. Its Article 28 contained language that sparked fears among women's rights activists, as it referred to women as 'true partners to men in the building of the nation and as having a role complementary thereto within the family'. Large protests and widespread condemnation followed, although drafters defended their language as aimed at recognition of women's contributions and also blamed shoddy translation.[43] The final text would include clearer language in favour of women's equality with men. It guarantees a general principle of gender equality and non-discrimination in Article 21, as well as making specific references to women—to the duty of the state to guarantee women's representation in elected bodies in Article 34 and to the equality of opportunities between women and men and the state's obligation to eradicate violence against women in Article 46. Such gains, together with the participatory nature of the process, garnered praise for the Tunisian Constitution as a model in the region.[44]

The struggle for gender equality continued after the adoption of the 2014 Tunisian Constitution as well. Electoral law requires gender parity on electoral lists, demanding alternate male and female candidates as well as that at least half of each party list be headed by women (ensuring both horizontal and vertical parity). This has resulted in 47 per cent of the seats in the Tunisian parliament formed after the country's 2018 elections being held by women.[45] Tunisia has reformed some aspects of its personal status law and now allows women to travel unaccompanied by men or to marry non-Muslim men without proof of the latter having converted to Islam. In 2017, Tunisia also adopted a comprehensive law against gender-based violence.[46] These are encouraging signs that the country's transition to democracy will also include a transition toward a more gender-equal society, albeit caveats remain. One refers to the continued hostility to extending equal rights to sexual minorities—for example, the Tunisian criminal code (Article 230) continues to prohibit same-sex conduct and authorities continue to perform forced anal and genital examinations on those suspected of such conduct.[47] Another caveat refers to the protracted process of establishing the Constitutional

---

41 Lakhdar Ghettas, 'The Tunisian Revolution Seven Years On' (14 January 2018) *openDemocracy* www.opendemocracy.net/north-africa-west-asia/lakhdar-ghettas/tunisian-revolution-seven-years-on accessed 31 January 2019.

42 Mounira M Charrad, 'Tunisia at the Forefront of the Arab World: Two Waves of Gender Legislation' in Fatima Sadiqi and Moha Ennaji (eds), *Women in the Middle East and North Africa: Agents of Change* (Routledge 2011) 105.

43 See also discussion in Silvia Suteu, 'Women and Participatory Constitution-making' in Irving, *Constitutions and Gender* (n 4) 19.

44 As a recent comparative study of constitutional reforms in the aftermath of the so-called 'Arab Spring' has shown, gender equality has rarely been a priority. See Euromed Feminist Initiative IFE-EFI, *Comparative Study on Constitutional Processes in the Arab World: A Gender Perspective* (2017).

45 'Historic Leap in Tunisia: Women Make up 47 Per Cent of Local Government' UN Women (27 August 2018) <www.unwomen.org/en/news/stories/2018/8/feature-tunisian-women-in-local-elections>.

46 Loi organique n° 2017–58 du 11 août 2017, rélative à l'élimination de la violence à l'égard des femmes.

47 'Tunisia: Events of 2017' in Human Rights Watch, *World Report 2018*, 2018.

Court—a new institution in the Tunisian legal landscape which has not yet begun its activity despite being mandated by the constitution and special legislation.[48]

Lest one think such issues to be specific to Tunisia or to Muslim-majority states more broadly, Nepal's example comes to show that basic women's rights cannot be taken for granted. The country finally adopted a new constitution in 2015, following a protracted process. The new constitution incorporates language against discrimination on the basis of gender in the preamble, and Article 38 refers specifically to women's rights, which are to include participation in public bodies and affirmative action in certain domains. However, Nepal remains one of 25 countries to discriminate against mothers when it comes to passing on their nationality to their children, and one of over 50 countries that discriminate against women when it comes to them passing on their nationality to non-national spouses or acquiring, changing and retaining their nationality.[49] As Helen Irving has reminded us, the recent past of countries such as Australia, Britain, Canada, Ireland, New Zealand and the United States also contains instances of restrictions of women's citizenship rights and even denaturalisation.[50]

All these examples remind us that the struggle for emancipation is neither linear nor a foregone conclusion. They also serve to show that constitutional protections of women's rights are not the end of the story. They may not suffice to protect women from discrimination via ordinary legislation or simply by omission, when the institutions designed to enforce their rights are ineffective.

Constitutional amendment and the regular legislative process

Whether to pursue constitutional or legislative change to advance a gender equality agenda will depend on the constitutional arrangements and guarantees of individual states. Insofar as the rights of women, sexual and gender minorities can be guaranteed without constitutional amendment, the process for doing so will likely be legislative or judicial. However, often there will be a need for explicit constitutional change—for example, to add gender and sexual minorities among groups guaranteed equality and protection against discrimination or to explicitly constitutionalise gender quotas.

Where amendment is required, pursuing the regular constitutional amendment process may be preferable insofar as it is predictable and less disruptive of the overall system. It is also less likely to trigger accusations of illegitimate change, given that reform happens via the prescribed representative process. However, when the status quo is deeply unequal, taking this course of action will be more difficult. In these situations, change is either redirected toward informal processes such as judicial review[51] or wholesale overhaul of the

48 The reasons for the court not being operational are multiple. Initially, the organic law needed for its establishment had been delayed. Once that was passed, the appointment of judges continued to be delayed, despite the constitution requiring the court to be established no later than one year after the first parliamentary elections, which had been held in late 2014. See more in Nidhal Mekki, 'The Fourth Anniversary of the Tunisian Constitution: The Unfinished Transformation' (19 February 2018) *ConstitutionNet* <http://constitutionnet.org/news/fourth-anniversary-tunisian-constitution-unfinished-transformation> accessed 31 January 2019.

49 See Global Campaign for Equal Nationality Rights, 'The Problem' <https://equalnationalityrights.org/the-issue/the-problem> accessed 31 January 2019.

50 Helen Irving, *Citizenship, Alienage, and the Modern Constitutional State: A Gendered History* (Cambridge University Press 2016).

51 Here, 'informal' is used in opposition to 'formal' change mechanisms, the latter of which will be reflected overtly in the text of the constitution.

constitution, including a new constitution-making process. Nevertheless, many of the gender equality reforms we have seen in recent years have been pursued via the regular amendment process. This has included amendments passed by parliaments, complemented or sometimes substituted by participatory processes such as referendums. A few illustrative examples follow.

One would be forgiven for expecting that constitutional recognition of gender equality as a primordial principle of the fundamental law would result in significant advances for equality in practice. Belgium's example is but one offering some cause for caution. (The examples of Tunisia and Nepal have already been discussed.) In 2002, Belgium amended its constitution to enshrine the principle of parity. Thus, Article 10 was amended to say that: 'Equality between women and men is guaranteed'. A new Article 11bis was inserted, stating that the law 'guarantees that women and men may equally exercise their rights and freedoms, and in particular promotes their equal access to elective and public mandates'; it further stipulated equality of access to certain public functions. A study of the aftermath of these amendments sought to track their impact on the adoption of gender equality legislation and found it wanting.[52] The authors found that constitutional revision was not accompanied by institutional change—whereas the new provisions served as textual hooks to justify the introduction of electoral quotas, they did not have the broader societal and political effects their initiators had hoped for. In other words, though welcome, the constitutionalisation of gender equality guarantees was insufficient, on its own, to shift attitudes or even to emerge as the main frame of reference in the fight for women's rights.

Even deep entrenchment in the form of an unamendable non-retrogression clause extending to the principle of equality may not be sufficient to prevent legislative initiatives potentially harmful to women or sexual minorities. An example is that of Romania, whose Constitutional Court certified a popular initiative to define the family as between a man and a woman as constitutional without addressing any of the gender equality-based objections.[53] The fact that the Romanian Constitution contains an eternity clause in Article 152 barring amendments that would 'result in the elimination of the fundamental rights and freedoms of citizens or of the guarantees of these rights and freedoms' was not seen as an obstacle.

An illuminating case study is that of the United Kingdom. The country's lack of a codified constitution is often seen as underpinning greater flexibility, although in practice, the UK has not always been at the forefront of progressive gender equality legislation. For example, it adopted its Equality Act in 2010, which brought together in a single piece of legislation over 116 Acts previously governing aspects of equality and discrimination law. Already at the time of its adoption, the Act was seen as incomplete insofar as it omitted some axes of discrimination (notably socio-economic status); it has also since been evaluated as doing a poor job of addressing intersectional discrimination.[54] With Brexit negotiations under way, there are fears that gender equality and anti-discrimination protections will be lost in the fray, or weakened through the removal of supranational safeguards.[55]

The UK is comparatively interesting for two reasons. One is the devolution aspect: the country's legal system is multi-layered and asymmetrical, with differing degrees of legislative and judicial autonomy devolved to Northern Ireland, Scotland and Wales. This has meant

---

52 Karen Celis and Petra Meier, 'Guaranteeing Gender Equality: A New Institutional Assessment of Constitutional Reform as Change', Paper presented at the ECPR Joint Sessions, Rennes (April 2008) <https://ecpr.eu/Files tore/PaperProposal/f90230c9-fdf8-442c-a86c-3bcadf963140.pdf> accessed 31 January 2019.

53 See n 17 above.

54 Kate Malleson, 'Equality Law and the Protected Characteristics' (2018) 81(4) *Modern Law Review* 598.

55 See *Ensuring Strong Equalities Legislation after the EU Exit*, Women and Equalities Committee, Seventh Report of Session 2016–17, House of Commons, 22 February 2017.

that gender equality and non-discrimination legislation has varied across the UK's components when addressing devolved matters. For example, marriage is a devolved matter, and the status of same-sex marriage differs across the UK. Recognition came in 2013 in England and Wales, when the Marriage (Same Sex Couples) Act was adopted. It was followed by the Marriage and Civil Partnership (Scotland) Act 2014 in Scotland. Northern Ireland continues to deny recognition to same-sex marriages, with such unions performed elsewhere being recognised as civil partnerships. Abortion has similarly been viewed as a devolved matter, with dire consequences for Northern Irish women. Because Northern Ireland criminalises abortion except in very restricted circumstances, women there have had to travel to other parts of the UK for the procedure. When, in the aftermath of the 2018 Irish abortion referendum, Northern Irish women's rights activists demanded action to ensure access to safe abortions would be extended to the whole Irish island, the UK government invoked devolution as the grounds for its refusal to take action.[56] The UK Supreme Court, asked to review the matter, was split, finding a violation of women's right to family and private life under the European Convention of Human Rights but declining, on procedural grounds of standing, to issue a declaration of incompatibility in the case.[57]

The UK example thus highlights the possibility of unequal diffusion of gender equality norms in a multi-layered constitutional system. The matter may be further exacerbated in federal systems, in which states may have even more autonomy on regulating family law and the recognition of marriage. Depending on whether and to what extent authority over family law is divided between the federal and state levels, reform may be more or less straightforward to advocate for and achieve. A recent study has compared Mexico, where family law is fragmented because of federalism, and Argentina, where it remains a federal matter.[58] The author found this design difference to explain the differences in institutionalisation of the recognition of same-sex marriage, with Mexico showing low levels of institutionalisation despite making it a constitutional right, and Argentina implementing it without obstacles.

A similarly complex question is to what extent the supranational level can drive the fight for gender equality. As the uneven development of gender equality and non-discrimination norms in Central and Eastern Europe has shown, integration into a supranational structure, even one with strong normative commitments in this area such as the European Union, does not guarantee that member states will follow suit. The issue of same-sex marriage is only one example where differences between East and West remain, revealing the limited power of Europeanisation when faced with powerful institutional legacies.[59]

---

56 Peter Walker, 'No Plans to Intervene on Northern Ireland Abortion Law, Says No 10' (29 May 2018) *The Guardian*.

57 *In the matter of an application by the Northern Ireland Human Rights Commission for Judicial Review (Northern Ireland)*, [2018] UKSC 27. In the UK, courts cannot strike down legislation on constitutionality grounds. Under the Human Rights Act 1998 (section 4), they can at most issue declarations of incompatibility when they are unable to read legislation as compatible with European Convention rights as incorporated into UK law. Such declarations must then be addressed by the government, possibly although not necessarily, via new or revised legislation.

58 Jordi Diez, 'Institutionalizing Same-Sex Marriage in Argentina and Mexico: The Role of Federalism' in Bronwyn Winter, Maxime Forest and Réjane Sénac (eds), *Global Perspectives on Same-Sex Marriage: A Neo-Institutional Approach* (Palgrave Macmillan 2018) 19.

59 Maxime Forest, 'Europeanizing vs. Nationalizing the Issue of Same-Sex Marriage in Central Europe: A Comparative Analysis of Framing Processes in Croatia, Hungary, Slovakia, and Slovenia' in Winter et al., *Global Perspectives on Same-Sex Marriage* (n 58) 127.

The UK again illustrates how the fight for gender equality is a long-term process rather than coming to an end with the passing of even seemingly comprehensive legislation. Legislation ensured the recognition of marriage equality irrespective of the partners' genders, at least in England, Wales and Scotland, but left some dissatisfied insofar as it sought to supplant the previous Civil Partnership Act 2004. The latter had recognised to same-sex couples rights akin to those of married ones, including also a formal procedure for dissolution similar to divorce. However, after the passing of the 2013 Act, an opposite-sex couple brought a legal challenge, arguing that their exclusion from civil partnerships amounted to gender-based discrimination and a violation of their human rights.[60]

Even those cases where the recognition of same-sex marriage has been achieved via direct recourse to the people carried their own costs and may not easily be replicated elsewhere. The 2015 Irish same-sex marriage referendum, for instance, resulted in the popular vote endorsing marriage equality and has been much praised as a consequence. The fact that it emerged from a micro-deliberative process, the Irish citizens' assembly, only served to further bolster its democratic credentials. Almost invisible in assessments of the referendum, however, have been studies of the personal and symbolic toll campaigning took on those involved in the referendum, forced to argue in favour of their rights in a way heterosexual individuals never had to.[61] This raises the broader question of whether the rights of minorities should ever be subjected to direct popular vote in the form of a referendum. Examples resulting in recognition of same-sex unions such as Ireland's and Australia's 2017 successful referendums are counterbalanced by those resulting in defeat for legalisation advocates. The Proposition 8 referendum in California, a 2013 one in Croatia and one in 2015 in Slovenia all illustrate that the outcome of referendums on same-sex unions is unpredictable, even where social attitudes may be turning more tolerant overall. This is because success in a referendum campaign depends on mobilisation, resources and how the issue is framed and is not necessarily a mirror of social attitudes (the latter of which may well remain more resistant to change than expected).

The question of social attitudes in the area of gender equality, in particular when it comes to LGBTQ+ rights, is complex. As will be seen, some of the objections to the United States federally recognising same-sex marriage via judicial intervention revolved around the need for incremental, bottom-up change that reflects rather than antagonises societal views on the issue. However, such views are problematic when data shows attitudes to marriage equality are influenced by a whole host of factors, not all of them necessarily to do with the institution of marriage itself.[62] Moreover, data also suggests that, under certain circumstances, policy change in favour of legalisation may actually result in a reduction in anti-gay attitudes over time;[63] a worthy goal in itself.

---

60 See n 79.

61 Brian Tobin has argued the referendum was 'crude' insofar as it placed the rights of a minority in the hands of the majority but nevertheless effective, given lack of political will to advance the issue of marriage equality. See his article, 'Marriage Equality in Ireland: The Politico-Legal Context' (2016) 30(2) *International Journal of Law, Policy and the Family* 115.

62 For an exploration of the multitude of factors influencing heterosexual attitudes to same-sex marriage, see Stephanie Newton Webb and Jill Chonody, 'Heterosexual Attitudes toward Same-Sex Marriage: The Influence of Attitudes toward Same-Sex Parenting' (2014) 10(4) *Journal of GLBT Family Studies* 404. The authors find that attitudes to the family and opposition to same-sex parenthood also play a significant role in opposition to same-sex marriage.

63 Andrew R Flores and Scott Barclay, 'Backlash, Consensus, Legitimacy, or Polarization: The Effect of Same-Sex Marriage Policy on Mass Attitudes' (2016) 69(1) *Political Research Quarterly* 43.

From a constitutional point of view, there is also a case to be made that framing the reactions to the decision in *Obergefell*, and judicial interventions in this area more generally, as 'backlash' may be misleading. Rather than viewing conflict as a negative, Reva Siegel has argued, it should be viewed as a central component of the constitutional culture of the United States, driving societal change and a continuous debate between the people and their institutions, including courts.[64] In her view, '[i]t is not conflict as such that poses a threat to the constitutional order'; instead, 'conflict as well as consent sustain the Constitution's meaning and authority'.[65] Siegel's argument is a nuanced one, holding that it is precisely negotiations around the proper constitutional role of institutions, including courts, which sustain the constitutional order and the allegiance of all groups in society to the constitution. Rather than viewing judicial interventions on same-sex marriage, and abortion or desegregation before them, as illegitimate *tout court*, the constitutional debate they spark should be viewed as a normal component of a healthy democracy. As we will see, such arguments fail to persuade those who believe the separation of powers should constrain courts and leave any official change in understandings of marriage to the legislature.

Judicial review

Engendering the constitutional system will not end with the adoption of a gender-sensitive constitution. While that is a key step, it will not, in and of itself, ensure that the gender equality and non-discrimination guarantees it contains will be implemented. Nor is it possible to cover every policy aspect in the constitution, especially in the needed detail. Oftentimes, matters related to the electoral system, discrimination, gender-based violence, family and marriage and more are relegated to legislation. And it will always be necessary to interpret constitutional provisions, which is where courts come in.

It would be impossible to cover all aspects of gender equality constitutional jurisprudence. There is a growing literature on the matter, with authors seeking to piece together not only gender equality case law but also issues such as representation on the bench, the interplay between interpretive philosophies and judicial approaches to equality and non-discrimination, and the dialogue between domestic and supranational courts.[66] Instead, I will focus on three case studies which illustrate important questions in this area, questions bound to resurface across jurisdictions: (i) who gets to decide that constitutional change is needed, particularly on contentious matters to do with gender equality and non-discrimination; (ii) whether courts should articulate a coherent conception of gender justice when adjudicating; and (iii) whether we can rely on courts as agents of change in this area or whether we should be more distrustful of them. I will address each in turn.

64 Reva B Siegel, 'Community in Conflict: Same-Sex Marriage and Backlash' (2017) 64 *UCLA Law Review* 1728.
65 Ibid., 1766.
66 See, inter alia, Beverley Baines and Ruth Rubio-Marin (eds), *The Gender of Constitutional Jurisprudence* (Cambridge University Press 2005); Ivana Radacic, 'Gender Equality Jurisprudence of the European Court of Human Rights' (2008) 19(4) *European Journal of International Law* 841; Vicki Jackson, 'Conclusion: Gender Equality and the Idea of a Constitution: Entrenchment, Jurisdiction, and Interpretation' in Williams, *Constituting Equality* (n 4) 312–349; and the numerous works emerging from feminist judgments projects in different jurisdictions.

Should courts intervene?

The first question touches on a familiar debate in the literature on judicial review, revolving around the legitimacy of court intervention in a given constitutional debate. Perhaps no case is better to illustrate this in the area of gender equality and non-discrimination than *Obergefell* in the United States.[67] The 2015 judgment read the issue not as a question of whether the US Constitution recognised a right to same-sex marriage, as the states had framed it, but as one of altogether excluding a certain class of people from the institution of marriage. The Supreme Court, in a 5–4 ruling, held that this exclusion could not stand because it violated both the Due Process and the Equal Protection clauses of the Fourteenth Amendment. The result was finding same-sex marriage bans unconstitutional and requiring states to recognise and perform such unions.

All four dissenting opinions in *Obergefell* rejected the textual basis used by the majority to ground their decision, given that the Fourteenth Amendment does not prohibit legislation on the issue. Instead, the dissenters chided the majority for going beyond the constitution and effectively closing off debate on the matter. (Some, such as Chief Justice Roberts, went further and invoked the special nature of the institution of marriage, viewing it as linked to family and childrearing.) Justice Scalia's dissent forcefully highlighted the most important objection for our purposes. He viewed the judgment as an extension of the power of unelected judges over the democratic process, robbing the people of the right to govern themselves.[68] He decried the closing off, by this judicial intervention ('in an opinion lacking even a thin veneer of law'[69]), of passionate democratic debate among the American people, either directly or through their representatives. Because there was no express prohibition in the constitution of bans on same-sex marriages, Scalia argued, the issue should have been left to the electoral process.

While undoubtedly rooted in his originalist interpretive philosophy, Justice Scalia's dissent raises the important question of what the legitimate process for achieving recognition of marriage equality actually is. In other words, when faced with constitutional silence as so many other countries are, should it be for an apex court to intervene in recognition of same-sex unions? What might be the costs of such intervention? In Justice Scalia's eyes, those costs include judicial self-empowerment (a 'judicial putsch'[70]) and the cessation of much-needed democratic debate, the latter of which could backfire in the sense of precluding the cause of marriage equality from garnering societal acceptance. This question continues to resonate in comparative constitutional practice, even when moving beyond the idiosyncrasies of debates around interpreting a constitution three centuries old. As recently as 2018, the Romanian Constitutional Court had to accept a decision of the Court of Justice of the European Union (CJEU) (issued upon the former's referral) that required member states not to deny the right of residence to same-sex spouses of their nationals who had lawfully married abroad.[71] Nevertheless, the Romanian Court emphasised that this did

---

67 *Obergefell v Hodges*, 576 U.S. ___ (2015). Before *Obergefell* there was *United States v Windsor*, 570 U.S. 744 (2013), in which the US Supreme Court invalidated section 3 of the Defense of Marriage Act (DOMA). The latter had restricted federal interpretations of marriage as between a man and a woman and had had the effect of denying federal benefits to same-sex couples. Following *Windsor*, federal authorities were obliged to recognise same-sex marriages concluded in the states that allowed them.

68 *Obergefell v Hodges*, 576 U.S. ___ (2015), Scalia J Dissenting, 2.

69 Ibid., 4.

70 Ibid., 6.

71 The CJEU decision is Case C-673/16 *Coman and Others*, Judgment, 5 June 2018. The Romanian Constitutional Court decision is Decision No. 534 of 18 July 2018.

not mean the recognition, under Romanian law, of same-sex marriages, limiting its ruling to one on the basis of the freedom of movement under European law.

Despite the dissenters' predictions, debate continues in the US as well. Objections to same-sex marriage have been (re)framed in the language of religious freedom and pluralism, with renewed challenges invoking conscientious objections to performing or recognising such unions.[72] In 2018, the Supreme Court upheld a baker's right to refuse to bake a cake celebrating a same-sex couple's marriage on religious grounds.[73] The decision was narrow and grounded on finding discriminatory the decision of the Colorado administrative agency having reviewed the baker's claim. Thus, the question of whether religious-based objections to same-sex marriage deserve constitutional recognition was left for another day.

The UK Supreme Court has had to entertain its own gay wedding cake case. In October 2018, it rendered its decision in a case asking whether a baker's refusal to bake a cake with a slogan in support of same-sex marriage violated UK anti-discrimination law as well as the customer's human rights under the European Convention on human rights.[74] The UK Supreme Court concluded the appellants were entitled to refuse to express a political opinion contrary to their religious beliefs. It found that the bakers had objected to the cake message, not any personal characteristics (including sexual orientation) of the messenger. The European dimension of such questions may well become more salient the more cases reach Strasbourg itself, where the European Court of Human Rights will have to clarify whether and on what grounds gender-based limitations on marriage are justified.[75]

Should courts articulate a conception of gender justice?

The second question I raised is one that requires legislators and judges alike to consider and potentially reconsider the frame of analysis they apply to cases involving gender equality and non-discrimination and to do so in light of changing social understandings of both. The question can also be turned on its head to ask: should judges adjudicate on gender equality *without* a clear conception of gender justice?

An example will prove helpful here. In 2018, the Indian Supreme Court dismissed a public interest litigation petition seeking to replace the gender-specific provisions on rape in the country's penal code with gender-neutral ones (specifically, to change references to the perpetrator from 'man' to 'whoever' or 'person').[76] The court dismissed arguments that the law was discriminatory, instead seeing the gendered language as protective of women. Again, this case is not singular. The US Supreme Court had faced a similar question in 1981, when it too dismissed the claim that gender bias in statutory rape laws was discriminatory.[77] The US

---

72 See discussion in Reva Siegel and Douglas Nejaime, 'Conscience and the Culture Wars' (29 June 2015) *The American Prospect*.

73 *Masterpiece Cakeshop, Ltd. v Colorado Civil Rights Commission*, 584 U. S. ____ (2018).

74 *Lee (Respondent) v Ashers Baking Company Ltd and others (Appellants) (Northern Ireland)* [2018] UKSC 49.

75 While Strasbourg has found that member states are obliged to offer some form of legal recognition to same-sex unions concluded abroad, it still affords a wide margin of appreciation on whether actually to allow same-sex marriages. See *Orlandi and Others v Italy*, Application No. 26431/12, 14 December 2017. For an analysis, holding that Strasbourg would likely have to ground a finding in support of same-sex marriage on multiple Convention rights and growing pan-European consensus, see Frances Hamilton, 'The Case for Same-Sex Marriage before the European Court of Human Rights' (2018) 65(12) *Journal of Homosexuality* 1582.

76 'SC Dismisses Plea for Making Rape Law Gender-neutral' (2 February 2018) *Times of India*.

77 *Michael M. v Superior Court of Sonoma County*, 450 U.S. 464 (1981).

decision was motivated by the higher risks for women involved in sexual intercourse; the Indian one was based on separation of powers considerations. Feminist legal theorists themselves do not agree on the right course of action in this regard. Some have come to accept gender-neutral definitions of rape on the grounds that they better acknowledge the power imbalance, rather than sexuality, involved in the crime, while others view such definitions as the continued effacement of women as legal subjects.[78] Judges can rarely escape taking a stand when faced with cases such as these.

In 2018, the UK Supreme Court handed down its judgment in a case involving civil partnerships.[79] Specifically, the applicants were an opposite-sex couple requesting that they be allowed to register for a civil partnership, a legal institution created for and previously only open to same-sex couples. Despite the adoption of the Marriage (Same Sex Couples) Act 2013, the Civil Partnership Act 2004 was never repealed, thus giving same-sex couples two options when considering formalising their status. The applicants in the case argued that they were discriminated against by the prohibition of opposite-sex couples from civil partnerships, irrespective of the fact that the government was considering legal reform on the matter. The Supreme Court agreed. While the case was fought on anti-discrimination grounds, the applicants made no secret of their views of marriage as a patriarchal and antiquated institution and continue to campaign for equal civil partnerships for all.[80]

Nepal's case is instructive in a different sense. As Mara Malagodi has argued, the country's Supreme Court has played a pivotal role in developing a jurisprudence of equality, even before the adoption of the new constitution in 2015.[81] In an incremental manner, it has given meaning to the constitutional right to gender equality, moving from a formal to a more substantive understanding. Here is, Malagodi argues, a court developing an intersectional understanding of the right to equality, sensitive to the specific needs of its context. Thus, courts *can* get it right, sometimes in spite of rather than in furtherance of a given constitutional text. They can also be aided in their advancement of gender equality by supranational courts, although these too have sometimes stumbled in articulating a progressive, intersectional approach.[82]

Are courts agents of progressive change?

Depending on where you are in the world, the proposition of going through the courts and relying on constitutional adjudication to vindicate your constitutional rights, in particular

---

78 For a discussion, see Yvette Russell, 'Thinking Sexual Difference through the Law of Rape' (2013) 24(3) *Law and Critique* 255. See also Philip NS Rumney, 'In Defence of Gender Neutrality within Rape' (2007) 6(1) *Seattle Journal for Social Justice* 481.

79 *R (on the application of Steinfeld and Keidan) (Appellants) v Secretary of State for International Development (in substitution for the Home Secretary and the Education Secretary) (Respondent)* [2018] UKSC 32.

80 Owen Bowcott, 'Ban on Heterosexual Civil Partnerships in UK Ruled Discriminatory' (27 June 2018) *The Guardian*.

81 Mara Malagodi, 'Challenges and Opportunities of Gender Equality Litigation in Nepal' (2018) 16(2) *International Journal of Constitutional Law* 527.

82 On the European Court of Human Rights developing its sex-based discrimination jurisprudence toward a substantive understanding of equality, see Sandra Fredman, 'Emerging from the Shadows: Substantive Equality and Article 14 of the European Convention on Human Rights' (2016) 16(2) *Human Rights Law Review* 273. For an earlier critique of the court failing to advance the empowerment of women and to address multidimensional discrimination, see Radacic, 'Gender Equality Jurisprudence of the European Court of Human Rights' (n 66).

when it comes to gender, may not seem like a good idea at all. Courts, and the law itself, have long been viewed as generally conservative, in the sense of being slow to change and often reactionary.[83] Courts may have acted as agents of progressive change in very particular historical circumstances in particular places,[84] but should that be reason enough for a broader endorsement of the courtroom for the vindication of gender equality and non-discrimination claims?

Of course, arguing that courts may be and often are regressive in their stances on gender equality does not automatically mean that other branches of government will fare better. One might look with optimism to parliaments such as Ireland's and Chile's[85] legalising abortion, but history abounds with instances in which legislatures and the people voting in referendums have remained opposed to progress in this area. The Polish parliament continues to attempt to impose further limits on the country's already restrictive abortion law. A near-total ban on abortion was rejected in 2016 after mass mobilisation against it, but that did not deter the Polish legislature to begin work on a new initiative in early 2018.[86] Brazil is also mired in a debate surrounding PEC 181, an amendment to the constitution that would ban abortion in all cases and recognise the rights of the unborn child.[87] Even what may at first appear as victories for abortion rights campaigners may swiftly be lost, as demonstrated by Bolivia's switch from legalising abortion (under restrictive conditions) in December 2017 to President Morales repealing the entire penal code that had contained the reform in January 2018.[88] El Salvador remains a particularly depressing example, with one of the world's harshest bans on abortion in effect and regularly enforced, doubled by the constitutional protection of the rights of the unborn.[89]

83 For a classic work on the UK judiciary, see John Aneurin Grey Griffith, *Politics of the Judiciary* (Manchester 1977).

84 A prominent example is the Warren Court in the United States—the Supreme Court responsible for the expansion of civil rights and liberties. However, the increased politicisation of the court and a re-evaluation of the progressive Warren years as the exception rather than the norm has led to serious debates as to whether the court, or the strong judicial review form it practices, should be abolished. See Sean Illing, 'The Case for Abolishing the Supreme Court' (12 October 2018) *Vox*.

85 The Chilean Congress ended a 28-year total ban on abortion in 2017, decriminalising abortion under certain conditions. The law was later upheld by the Constitutional Tribunal. However, subsequent rules adopted by the Chilean government (including allowing conscientious objections to performing abortions to both doctors and private hospitals as a whole) have restricted the reach of the decriminalisation. See Jose Miguel Vivanco, *A Backward Step for Reproductive Rights in Chile*, Human Rights Watch (16 April 2018).

86 Pawel Sobczak, 'Polish Parliament Starts Work on Further Restricting Abortion' (11 January 2018) *Reuters*.

87 Jo Griffin, 'Brazilian Women Braced for Battle Amid Simmering Fears over Abortion' (26 April 2018) *The Guardian*.

88 Ligia De Jesus Castaldi, 'Abolition of Social Grounds for Abortion in Bolivia' (7 March 2018) *Oxford Human Rights Hub* <http://ohrh.law.ox.ac.uk/abolition-of-social-grounds-for-abortion-in-bolivia/> accessed 31 January 2019.

89 Lisa Kowalchuk, 'The Unspeakable Cruelty of El Salvador's Abortion Laws' (12 April 2018) *The Conversation* <http://theconversation.com/the-unspeakable-cruelty-of-el-salvadors-abortion-laws-94004> accessed 31 January 2019.

In lieu of a conclusion: contextualising progress, success and best practices

When it comes to gender and constitutional change, comparative practice instructs a certain degree of caution. The cases discussed above force us to accept that the direction of constitutional change is not linear when it comes to gender equality and non-discrimination. Progress under one aspect will not necessarily bring with it progress across the board. Abortion is perhaps the quintessential issue on which consensus remains elusive. Optimism regarding the wave of countries legalising same-sex marriage has also been replaced by caution when observing the seemingly growing number of countries holding referendums to ban it (Croatia and Slovenia have already been mentioned above; Slovakia and the Bahamas can be added to this list, albeit their referendums were not valid on account of low turnout).

Three further observations are relevant here. The first is that trends or even what might be termed 'best practices' in comparative constitutional reform may work differently when it comes to the pursuit of gender equality and non-discrimination. For example, the strong normative and international push for public participation in constitution-making, justified on grounds of bringing about a more legitimate constitution,[90] may backfire when it comes to delivering a constitution that truly works for women. Tunisia's example may be misleading insofar as it represents a successful instance of designing a participatory constitution-making process and engendering the constitution it produced. However, depending on the political and societal context, the result of a participatory process may well be different and detrimental to women. The degree to which women's rights activists are organised and ready to articulate their demands in constitutional terms will play a role, as will the political will to ensure they actually influence the process. The danger that discriminatory views of women's role in society and the family will prevail has a counterpart in negative societal attitudes toward gender and sexual minorities. As I have written elsewhere, the aim of participatory constitution-making exercises should be to ensure true inclusiveness, which must comprise those affected by the constitutional reform under discussion.[91]

The second insight is that framing matters. Part of why abortion remains so highly contested is because it has been framed as a moral issue and, in places such as the United States, has been constitutionalised. No debate on the merits of legislation either loosening or extending restrictions on abortion can escape constitutional legal language in the US, often to the detriment of the voice and real plight of the women being denied access. In the case of same-sex marriage, the constitutionalisation of the issue may also have unintended consequences, may find rights activists unprepared and may miss the opportunity to rethink the institution of marriage.[92] Moreover, the evidence from places such as Ireland, where a successful and highly participatory referendum brought about constitutional recognition of marriage equality seems to suggest that the personalisation of the debate is what carried the day.[93] In other words, not the legal arguments, but humanising the issue in the eyes of voters.

---

90 Cheryl Saunders, 'Constitution-making in the 21st Century' (2012) 4 *International Review of Law* 1.
91 Silvia Suteu, 'Women and Participatory Constitution-making' (n 43) and Silvia Suteu, 'Constitutional Conventions in the Digital Era: Lessons from Iceland and Ireland' (2014) 38(2) *Boston College International and Comparative Law Review* 251.
92 See n 18 above.
93 Eoin Carolan, 'Some Lessons from Ireland's Marriage Referendum?' (8 December 2015) *UK Constitutional Law Blog* <https://ukconstitutionallaw.org/2015/12/08/eoin-carolan-some-lessons-from-irelands-marriage-referendum/> accessed 31 January 2019.

A certain degree of modesty should therefore be the constitutionalist's approach to these issues. On the one hand, constitutionalising the issue and 'bringing in the courts' risks undermining the chance for progress through more incremental legislative means. As some of the case studies discussed showed, advancements have been possible even—or sometimes because of—the constitution's silence on otherwise divisive views on gender equality. On the other hand, the area of gender equality and non-discrimination is one particularly tied to living instrument understandings of any constitution. It is shifts in societal attitudes, whether pre- or post-dating constitutional reform, that are the true marker of progress.

The third and final observation follows from the above. It is that constitutions are limited in their impact and that both implementing legislation and functioning institutions will be needed to advance the gender equality agenda. It may seem tautological, but many of the examples covered show that this is a lesson still worth emphasising. Basic women's rights, including citizenship and political rights, will typically be regulated via ordinary legislation, as will abortion and, depending on whether there is an explicit constitutional prohibition or not, also same-sex marriage and non-binary gender recognition. Moreover, absent a working apex court ready to intervene and sanction transgressions, as in the case of Tunisia, the fight for gender equality and non-discrimination can only remain incomplete. A commitment to the constant advancement of the gender equality and non-discrimination agenda will be key, as will be collaboration between the different branches of government.

PART V

Case studies
Distinct profiles of constitutional change

22

THE FUTURE OF UK CONSTITUTIONAL LAW

Robert Blackburn

Over the past quarter century, UK governance and its constitutional law has undergone a transformation, with a host of modernising reforms taking place affecting almost all parts of its institutional structure and working.[1] 1997 was a particular watershed in government policy and public attitudes toward reform of the constitution, with the Labour Party elected to office that year with a manifesto promising a radical and wide-ranging programme of constitutional change, and a large overall majority in the House of Commons with which to carry it out.[2] However, despite the major changes that were made, many essential aspects of what was heralded in Labour's programme were left unfinished by the time the party was voted out of government in 2010. Subsequently, the Conservative–Liberal Democrat coalition down to 2015 and the Conservative governments since then have had markedly different preoccupations for shaping Britain's constitutional future, most importantly in the country's relationship with Europe.[3]

Significantly, constitutional reform under both Labour and Conservative governments has been, and continues to be, conducted in an ad hoc rather than coherent or joined-up

---

1 See Vernon Bogdanor, *The New British Constitution* (Hart Publishing 2009); Jeffrey Jowell, Dawn Oliver and Colm O'Cinneide (eds), *The Changing Constitution* (Oxford University Press, 8th ed. 2015).

2 These reforms included devolution to Scotland (Scotland Act 1998), Wales (Government of Wales Act 1998), Northern Ireland (Northern Ireland Act 1998), Greater London (Greater London Act 1999), incorporation of the European Convention on Human Rights into UK law (Human Rights Act 1998), access to official information (Freedom of Information Act 2000), creation of a Supreme Court (Constitutional Reform Act 2005), and statutory recognition and regulation of political parties and campaigning (Political Parties, Elections and Referendums Act 2000). For the policy background see Robert Blackburn and Raymond Plant (eds), *Constitutional Reform: The Labour Government Constitutional Reform Agenda* (Longman 1999). The Labour Party's policy objectives on constitutional reform in their 1997 manifesto were renewed when Gordon Brown succeeded Tony Blair as prime minister in 2007: see *The Governance of Britain* (CM 7170 2007).

3 The reforms since 2010 have included fixed five-year intervals between elections (Fixed-term Parliaments Act 2011) and in terms of constitutional practice the strategic decision to hold three referendums on matters of fundamental political importance, the voting system (Parliamentary Voting System and Constituencies Act 2011, leading to the 2011 poll endorsing the status quo), Scottish independence (Scottish Independence Referendum Act 2013, leading to the 2014 poll endorsing the status quo), and membership of the EU (European Union Referendum Act 2015, leading to the 2016 poll to withdraw from the EU).

manner. This is consistent with one of the most striking features of UK politics and government, which is the paucity of modern theoretical underpinning for the constitution and its component parts, save for the fundamental if rather nebulous concepts of the rule of law and democracy.[4] Not only has the incomplete nature of the parties' earlier modernisation initiatives left the UK constitution in a very unsettled state, but UK governance generally has come under increasing pressures from public discontent with the establishment,[5] especially its handling of the economy, amplified through the new technologies enabling mass communication in mobilising popular opinion.

In addressing the future of UK constitutional law, it is essential to understand the processes and special characteristics of the current arrangements within which it operates. The existing structure of UK government and its constitution is best described as traditional and historical in nature. It is a relic of the 1688–89 settlement, following the Glorious Revolution and forced abdication of King James II.[6] The legal supremacy of parliament over the Crown was accepted by the new monarchs William and Mary and guaranteed in the Bill of Rights 1689. Shortly afterwards, the Act of Settlement 1701 guaranteed the independence of the judiciary, although one in which the courts and the common law performed a subordinate role to Acts of Parliament.[7] Over the subsequent three centuries no further revolutionary moment arose that demanded that the structure and working of government and rights of citizens be set down in documentary form as the fundamental law of state, a written constitution.[8]

The essential elements of the UK constitution therefore have been – and remain – the supremacy of an Act of Parliament as a source of law, and absence of any fundamental law by reference to which the courts can control and declare Acts of Parliament to be unconstitutional;[9] there is extensive reliance upon conventions and political understandings to informally adapt its ancient laws and institutions to modern conditions;[10] and there is no special amendment process by which legislative reforms of the unwritten constitution are conducted.[11]

---

4 The doctrine of separation of powers has never in its strict form corresponded with the facts of UK government, principally because, although the functions and powers of state are largely separated, the personnel of the political executive and parliamentary legislature overlap: see M.J.C. Vile, *Constitutionalism and the Separation of Powers* (Clarendon Press 1967). On a classic exposition of the Rule of Law from a UK perspective, see Tom Bingham, *The Rule of Law* (Allen Lane 2010).

5 The term 'establishment' is commonly used in the UK to signify the matrix of official and social relations within which power is exercised: see Peter Hennessy, *The Great and the Good: An Inquiry into the British Establishment* (Policy Studies Institute 1986).

6 See Ann Lyon, *Constitutional History of the United Kingdom* (Cavendish 2003).

7 In UK law parliamentary statutes may be interpreted by the courts as to their meaning and application, but may not be reviewed as to their constitutional legitimacy: generally, see Neil Duxbury, *Elements of Legislation* (Cambridge University Press 2013).

8 On the proposal for a written UK constitution, see below.

9 This is known as the doctrine of parliamentary sovereignty, on which see A.V. Dicey, *The Law of the Constitution* (Macmillan 1885; 10th ed. 1985); and Jeffrey Goldsworthy, *Parliamentary Sovereignty: Contemporary Debates* (Cambridge University Press 2010). The doctrine also involves the principle that an Act of Parliament may not bind future legislative enactments: *Vauxhall Estates Ltd v Liverpool Corporation* [1932] 1KB 733, *Ellen Street Estates v Minister of Health* [1934] KB 590. A recent qualification to this rule is that where an Act is constitutional in nature its provisions may only be repealed or amended by a later Act containing express words to that effect: *Thoburn v Sunderland City Council* (2003) QB 151; *R (HS2 Action Alliance Ltd) v Secretary of State for Transport* [2014] UKSC 3).

10 See Geoffrey Marshall, *Constitutional Conventions* (Oxford University Press 1984).

11 See Robert Blackburn, 'Constitutional Amendment in the United Kingdom' in Xenophon Contiades (ed), *Engineering Constitutional Change: A Comparative Perspective on Europe, Canada and the USA* (Routledge 2013).

The executive and royal prerogative

There is now a strong movement across the political spectrum to establish greater controls and mechanisms of accountability over executive power. Most of this attention has been focused on the ancient common law prerogative powers of the Crown and how to render their exercise subject to parliamentary scrutiny and consent. The scope of the 'royal prerogative', as these powers are collectively known, goes much further than simply those powers that are vested in the person of the monarch him or herself, and by far the greater part of the prerogative powers that continue in existence today is exercised by ministers and officials acting as Her Majesty's Government. The scope of executive action authorised by the prerogative is very wide indeed and embraces some of the most basic and important tasks of government, extending across the terrain of foreign and international affairs, matters of national security, and into numerous matters at home such as the grant of royal charters, a multitude of public and political appointments, the honours system and the nature and extent of our defence capability. The controversial element of the royal prerogative is that all the powers, privileges and immunities it comprises are in origin common law and extra-parliamentary: in other words, major policies and decisions may be adopted by the government under the authority of the royal prerogative without the need for any formal approval by parliament. Indeed, some such powers may be exercised without any form of parliamentary scrutiny or discussion at all, and in some cases even without parliament's knowledge.[12]

The case for codifying the royal prerogatives and making their exercise subject to parliamentary scrutiny and/or formal approval has continued to gather support in recent decades since Tony Benn's early advocacy on the matter in the 1980s.[13] Whole-scale codification was advocated in the Labour Party's 1993 policy programme, *New Agenda for Democracy: Labour's Proposals for Constitutional Reform*. This objective was subsequently dropped under Tony Blair's leadership of the Labour Party and period in office as prime minister, but taken up by the House of Commons Public Administration Committee in the 2001–05 parliament. The committee's report, *Taming the Prerogative: Strengthening Ministerial Accountability to Parliament*,[14] firmly placed the subject back on the political agenda, and was carried forward by Gordon Brown in his own constitutional policy document, *The Governance of Britain*,[15] published only a few days after he succeeded Tony Blair as prime minister in 2007.

At that time, the case for statutory codification of the prerogative had been strongest in the field of treaty making, the UK being the only country in the EU with no formal procedures to guarantee parliamentary scrutiny for major foreign policy decisions.[16] As one UK parliamentarian had earlier remarked,

---

12 For example, there was no parliamentary debate in 1958 on the agreement reached with the United States for their nuclear weapons to be based on UK territory, a decision taken under the royal prerogatives of defence and treaty making; and no parliamentary debate in 1950 on the UK becoming a contracting party to the European Convention on Human Rights, decided under the royal prerogative of treaty making: historically it seemed the greater the importance of a public policy issue, the less likely parliament has a say in the matter.

13 See for example his Crown Prerogatives (House of Commons Control) Bill (1987–88) HC 117; and for commentary Robert Blackburn, 'The Dissolution of Parliament: the Crown Prerogatives (House of Commons Control) Bill 1988' (1989) *Modern Law Review* 837–840.

14 (2003–04) HC 422.

15 Cabinet Office, CM 7170 (2007).

16 See Lucius Wildhaber, *Treaty-Making Power and Constitution: An International and Comparative Study* (Helbing & Lichtenhahn 1971). In stark contrast to the UK position, the US Constitution requires a treaty to be ratified by two-thirds of the Senate.

We are talking about a remnant of the medieval or at least very early modern British monarchical constitution. It makes nonsense of the principle of the doctrine of parliamentary sovereignty that the Crown retains the right to sign and ratify treaties without having submitted them to Parliament.[17]

Gordon Brown's Constitutional Reform and Governance Act 2010 proceeded to place into statutory form the pre-existing convention known as the Ponsonby rule that a treaty signed by the relevant minister must be laid before parliament for 21 days, and it conferred on the House of Commons a limited form of veto.[18] Otherwise however, apart from placing the civil service on a statutory basis, the 2010 Act failed to address parliamentary control of the royal prerogative more widely, leaving this area of constitutional law ripe for further research and development.

Alongside these parliamentary developments the courts have shaped a judicial role in controlling the arbitrary nature of prerogative decision-making in recent times, departing from their earlier common law position that an exercise of a Crown prerogative power was immune from judicial review.[19] In the landmark case of *Council of Civil Service Unions v Minister for the Civil Service* in 1985, in which a government decision to exclude trade unions from the Government Communications' Headquarters was challenged in the courts, the House of Lords (then the final court of appeal[20]) held that some prerogative powers were now to be justiciable as to the manner of their exercise.[21] More dramatically in 2017, the Supreme Court in the case of *R (Miller) v Secretary of State for Exiting the European Union*[22] held that the government could not initiate a UK withdrawal from the European Union by notification under Article 50 of the Treaty on European Union simply relying on the royal prerogative of treaty making and unmaking, but this action would require the consent and authority of an Act of Parliament.[23]

The prerogative power that has been most extensively debated since the Iraq invasion in 2003 has been that of authorising armed conflict abroad. A number of proposals, including ones embodied in Private Members' Bills presented for debate in parliament, have argued for legislation to require parliamentary approval to military interventions.[24] Gordon Brown's 2007 policy document hesitantly suggested that a resolution of the House of Commons should be required prior to 'significant non-routine' deployment of the armed forces 'without prejudicing the Government's ability to act to protect national security, or undermining operational security of effectiveness',[25] but this proposal was taken no further. In 2013 considerable excitement was aroused in academe after the Conservative Prime Minister David Cameron sought the approval of the House of Commons for air strikes in Syria, and in response to the parliamentary vote opposing such action the air strikes were

---

17 *Lords Hansard*, 28 February 1966, col. 1542.
18 See Part 2: Ratification of Treaties.
19 [1985] AC 374; subsequent case law on the exercise of prerogative powers includes *R v Foreign Secretary, ex p Everett [1989] QB 811; R v Bentley [1994] QB 349; R v Home Secretary, ex p Fire Brigades Union [1995] 2 AC 513*; see also *R (Bancoult) v Foreign Secretary (No. 2)* [2008] 1 AC 453.
20 The Judicial Committee of the House of Lords as final court of appeal was replaced by the Supreme Court by the Constitutional Reform Act 2005, part 3.
21 Generally, see Paul Craig, *Administrative Law* (Sweet & Maxwell, 8th ed. 2016), Part 2.
22 [2017] UKSC 5.
23 European Union (Notification of Withdrawal) Act 2017.
24 For example, Waging War (Parliament's Role and Responsibility) Bill (2005–06) HC 34.
25 Cabinet Office, *The Governance of Britain* (CM 7170, 2007), para. 29.

called off. This led many academic commentators to argue that a new Constitutional Convention had entered into force, one that now required parliamentary approval before armed conflict.[26] Indeed the Cabinet Office's manual prepared in 2011 supported this view, stating that

> the Government acknowledged that a convention had developed in Parliament that before troops were committed the House of Commons should have an opportunity to debate the matter and said that it proposed to observe that convention except where there was an emergency and such action would not be appropriate.[27]

Debates and votes were taken twice shortly afterwards, supporting the government's proposed military action against ISIS in Iraq in September 2014, then for its extension into Syria in December 2015. Earlier in 2011 the then Foreign Secretary William Hague had gone so far as to give a commitment to the House of Commons that the government would legislate for such a rule.[28] However, the present government's attitude has now gone into reversal. In April 2016 the then Defence Secretary Michael Fallon issued a statement that the government had changed its mind and would not be legislating or putting forward a Commons resolution, and the Prime Minister Theresa May was even more emphatic:

> Put simply, making it unlawful for Her Majesty's Government to undertake any such military intervention without a vote would seriously compromise our national security, our national interests and the lives of British citizens at home and abroad – and for as long as I am Prime Minister, that will never be allowed to happen.[29]

This state of affairs serves to illustrate that the principal beneficiary and custodian of the royal prerogative power is not the monarch but the prime minister. In addition to the executive powers in the field of foreign affairs already mentioned, it is under the authority of the Crown that prime ministers make cabinet, ministerial and senior civil service appointments, and that peers as members of the House of Lords are selected and appointed, together with numerous other public appointments. Until Gordon Brown took office in 2007, even the appointment of archbishops and the most senior bishops of the Church of England were in the hands of the prime minister, a power that both Margaret Thatcher and Tony Blair on occasion made use of.[30] Political and academic debates on the future of the

---

26 Cabinet Office, *The Cabinet Manual* (2011), para. 5.38; and see a similar interpretation of the constitutional position given to parliament by the Leader of the House of Commons, Sir George Young, on 10 March 2011: *Commons Hansard*, col. 1066.

27 Para. 5.38.

28 'We will … enshrine in law for the future the necessity of consulting Parliament on military action': *Commons Hansard*, 21 March 2011, col. 799.

29 *Commons Debates*, 17 April 2018, c208–209. For parliamentary select committee inquiries into this subject, see House of Lords Constitution Committee, *Waging War: Parliament's Role and Responsibility* (2005–06) HL 236 (supporting a convention regulating war powers) and *Constitutional Arrangements for the Use of Armed Force* (2013–14) HL 46 (opposing legislation or a parliamentary resolution on the matter); and House of Commons Political and Constitutional Reform Committee, *Parliament's Role in Conflict Decisions* (2010–12) HC 923 (recommending clarity on the arrangements and welcoming the ministerial promise of legislation at that time).

30 See generally, Dominic Grant, 'By Law Established: The Church of England and its Place in the Constitution' in Robert Blackburn (ed), *Constitutional Studies* (Mansell 1992) Ch. 11; R.M. Morris (ed), *Church and State in 21st Century Britain* (Palgrave Macmillan 2009).

royal prerogative are bound up with questions of reform to the office of prime minister itself, and the widely acknowledged presidentialisation of that office. Since the office of prime minister is a pure creature of tradition and convention, and its tenure and powers not provided for in any Act of Parliament, its role and relationship to cabinet and collective ministerial decision-making is whatever the holder of that office chooses to decide.[31] Conversely, others will argue that a prime minister is only as powerful as his or her ministerial colleagues allow him or her to be,[32] though myriad factors are in play in determining this, particularly the force of the personalities involved and the size of the government majority in the House of Commons.

Of far less political importance, but with the potential for considerable disruption in UK constitutional affairs, is some lingering uncertainty surrounding the rules governing the prerogative powers and public conduct of the royal Head of State. The special importance of constitutional conventions,[33] operating as a form of obligatory political morality rather than law, is nowhere more important than in regulating the public role and conduct of the royal Head of State. This is because the occupant of the throne possesses a number of vital legal powers in the royal prerogative that only they can directly exercise, among them prime ministerial (and other ministerial) appointment, the summoning and prorogation of parliament, and the Royal Assent to Acts of Parliament and Orders in Council. Yet there remain doubts and misunderstandings in public and academic life on whether the monarchy is entitled or expected to be personally involved in the exercise of the powers today.

The better view is that these royal powers are purely ceremonial and automatic, leaving no scope or need for personal involvement.[34] On all matters of public conduct the convention is that the monarch is to follow the advice (in other words, direction) of the prime minister, and any difficulties relating to the appointment or dismissal of a prime minister are to be resolved by majority voting in the House of Commons (expressed in no-confidence or confidence motions). The separate issue of the scope for a future monarch to express their personal views in public speeches or advocacy in private to ministers has aroused substantial media speculation in relation to the heir to the throne, Prince Charles, who is well known for strong opinions on a range of public issues ranging across the environment, farming, human rights and occupation of Tibet.[35] However, conduct of this nature operates within the convention of ministerial responsibility, meaning that it is for the prime minister to advise and guide the royal Head of State on the scope of such activities.

Misleading courtesies to the Crown, in the flummery of royal etiquette and use of ancient terminologies about the sovereign, have helped perpetuate the myth of personal and reserve powers of the contemporary monarchy. There is a good case now for codifying the powers, duties and conventions of the royal Head of State, which might be conducted as a separate exercise through an official review and agreed written statement from

---

31 Andrew Blick and George Jones, *Premiership: The Development, Nature and Power of the British Prime Minister* (Imprint Academic 2010); J.P. Mackintosh, *The British Cabinet* (Stevens & Sons, 3rd ed. 1977).

32 For discussion see Anthony King (ed), *The British Prime Minister* (Macmillan, 2nd ed. 1985); Peter Hennessy, *The Prime Minister: The Office and Its Holders since 1945* (Penguin 2000); and for a prime ministerial perspective, Harold Wilson, *The Governance of Britain* (Weidenfeld & Nicolson 1976) Foreword 1–11.

33 Marshall (n 10).

34 See Robert Blackburn, 'Monarchy and the Personal Prerogatives' (2004) *Public Law* 546–563; also Robert Blackburn, 'Queen Elizabeth II and the Evolution of the Monarchy' in M. Qvortrup (ed), *The British Constitution: Continuity and Change* (Hart Publishing 2013) Ch. 10.

35 Robert Blackburn, *King and Country: Monarchy and the Future King Charles III* (Politico 2006).

Buckingham Palace or a Conference on Royal Affairs. Far better however, given the central place in which the Crown fits into the legal structure of the UK's political and constitutional affairs, would be for its rationalisation to form part of a new constitution for the UK, embodied in a written, codified form.[36]

Theory and practice of Parliament

Ever since 1688 the axis of the UK constitution has remained the relationship between the Crown and parliament. The supremacy of an Act of Parliament over the common law and royal prerogative, security for the meeting of parliament, and the accountability of ministers to parliament, together formed the bedrock of the 17th-century constitutional settlement, extended into the Union with Scotland after 1707.[37] Parliament is the heart and soul of the constitution, afforded primacy in the law and politics of the country, and is still shaped by its ancient history and evolution.

It is to the institutions and procedures of the House of Commons, therefore, that one looks for the fundamentals and guarantee of constitutionalism in the UK. As I have written elsewhere on the nature and importance of parliamentary procedure,

> Of all legal subjects parliamentary procedure is the one most often overlooked for its level of importance to the working of politics and the constitution. This is especially the case in respect of the United Kingdom Parliament, since the unwritten nature of the country's constitution means there is no body of entrenched basic law governing and controlling the affairs of the executive and government. Instead the common law doctrine of parliamentary sovereignty provides that Parliament is the supreme and dominant legal and political authority in the state. The consequence of this is that it is within Parliament itself that the primary constitutional architecture exists for controlling and limiting the power and activities of central government and the political executive.[38]

Though the UK's system of parliamentary government, with its executive drawn from the dominant party (or coalition parties) in the House of Commons, is shared with many other countries in Europe and across the world, its special characteristics derived from the unwritten nature of the constitution have led some commentators to describe the UK political system as being one of 'elective dictatorship'.[39] It is true that in the UK the language of checks and balances is misleading because ultimately governments can almost always get their way on its legislative and other policy proposals in the House of Commons,

---

36 See further below.

37 The classic works of UK constitutional history including on the 1688 settlement are F. W. Maitland, *The Constitutional History of England* (Cambridge University Press 1908), and Sir William Anson, *The Law and Custom of the Constitution*, Vol. I: Parliament (Clarendon Press, 5th ed. 1922); Vol. II: The Crown (Clarendon Press, 3rd ed. 1907).

38 Robert Blackburn, 'The Nature and Importance of Parliamentary Procedure' in Robert Blackburn, Arianna Carminati and Lorenzo Spadacini (eds), *Parliament as the Cornerstone of Democracy: Studies on the UK and Italian Parliaments in commemoration of Magna Carta's 800th Anniversary* (King's College London & Brescia University 2018) Ch. 4 45. Under Article 9 of the Bill of Rights 1689 the judiciary may not adjudicate on or inquire into the internal proceedings of parliament ('The freedom of speech and debates or proceedings in Parliament ought not to be impeached or questioned in any court or place out of Parliament').

39 Lord Hailsham, *Elective Dictatorship* (BBC, Richard Dimbleby Lecture 1976).

or at least until the next general election day. A better and more realistic terminology for understanding the parliamentary process is to say that its role and function is not to exercise direct power, command or obstruct government policy and action, but to influence it by generating advice, criticism and scrutiny.[40] Parliament is principally a reactive body, responding to whatever ministers propose or have done, whether in legislative form or as executive action.[41] The parliamentary process, and the procedures that facilitate its workings, is all about pressures, the release and resolution of tensions, and the uninhibited exchange of views.

To facilitate this process, through the ventilation of opinion and holding of government to account for its actions, there has been a succession of major procedural changes in the House of Commons in recent times. Combined, these have greatly strengthened the role of the Commons collectively, as well as members individually. Better resources have been granted to members in their office and working facilities, invigorating their use of the traditional procedures of the House, such as putting Questions to ministers. In 2015–16, for example, there were 4,742 oral Questions tabled for ministers, alongside 35,956 written Questions, a huge increase from earlier times. A significant innovation since 2007 has been that of Topical Questions, allowing 15 minutes in each one hour of Questions to be allocated to matters arising that day or very recently, increasing the relevance of parliamentary business to news and discussions in the media. Two other related innovations have been additional time being created for parliamentary debate through the use of Westminster Hall for parallel sittings of the Commons, and the creation of a Backbench Business Committee on 15 June 2010 for the orderly selection of backbench requests for debates.

Most significant of all has been the success of the government department related Select Committee system, gradually developed and strengthened since being established in 1979, whose formal role under Standing Orders is 'to examine the expenditure, administration and policy of the principal government departments'.[42] Whereas debate in the chamber does not lend itself to scrutiny beyond discussion of general principles of policy, and Questions to ministers do not allow for prolonged interrogation, Select Committees do require ministers, as well as experts or any persons from public life they request to appear before them, to respond to up to two hours of sustained and detailed scrutiny and questioning to assist in the inquiries they decide to pursue. Until recently the composition of a Select Committee, consisting of usually 12 members, was selected and determined by the respective party managers, but pressure developed for greater independence in the appointments, culminating in a major report on the subject by a special Commons committee.[43] The new arrangements since 2010 are for chairpersons to be elected by a cross-party ballot of all members of the Commons, and other committee members chosen by ballot from their party membership in the House. This has substantially enhanced their independence of action and the robustness with which they pursue their inquiries.

A future focus for academic study and research on the House of Commons can be expected to be assessment of the practical impact of these recent procedural changes in

---

40 Blackburn (n 38) 47; Bernard Crick, *The Reform of Parliament* (Weidenfeld and Nicolson 1964), especially at 77.
41 Some limited powers of initiation exist in law-making by way of Private Members' Bills and policy reform proposals from Select Committees, both considered below.
42 HC SO 152.
43 House of Commons Reform of the House of Commons Committee, *Rebuilding the House* (2008–09) HC 748.

terms of influencing government policy and decision-making,[44] and how the role of members is evolving in terms of the relative time they spend on the different categories of political work they perform both at Westminster and in their constituencies. Attention is certain to be focused also on the attempts being made to involve and engage the public more directly in the working of parliament. Greater use of the ancient procedure for public petitions is being made,[45] and a new 'collaborative' e-petition procedure was started in 2015 that allows the public to petition the House of Commons to raise an issue with ministers, and if there are over 100,000 supporters a debate can be held in Westminster Hall.[46] Since 2010 a new 'public reading stage' for government Bills has been trialled on a small number of occasions, inserting an on-line public consultation into the legislative process. These and other attempts at direct popular involvement in parliamentary affairs will continue to be the subject of discussion, proposals and experimentation.

Fresh momentum behind a new voting reform that incorporates a measure of proportional representation (PR) in elections to the House of Commons can be expected to re-emerge in the near future. There has been a cyclical nature to the debate on PR in the UK going back as far as the mid-19th century, with periodic outbreaks of demands for greater proportionality between votes cast and seats won, especially in 1917–18 and 1929–31 and more recently in the periods 1983–87 and 1992–97.[47] The UK First-Past-the-Post (simple plurality) system produces a wide deviation from proportionality in terms of votes cast and seats won for political parties.[48] This was more tolerable in democratic terms under a predominantly two-party system (in the post-1945 era the Conservative and Labour parties). However, in more recent times significant other parties have had substantial electoral support (highest among them being the Scottish National Party and Liberal Democrats) and voting behaviour is now far less tribal, reflecting the changing class structure of UK society and state collectivism no longer being a core ideology dividing the parties. The ill-timed referendum in 2011 offering the Alternative Vote (not a proportional system) may have killed off any prospect of electoral reform for a decade,[49] but the topic can with some certainty be expected to return again before long in forthcoming debates on constitutional reform designed to achieve greater popular representation.

One intractable problem in UK constitutional law has been a democratic settlement for the composition of the House of Lords.[50] UK bicameralism is the product of history rather than contemporary logic, and the existence of the Second Chamber is founded on ancient class representation (the Lords Temporal and Spiritual sitting in the upper chamber of

---

44 An early example of this is Meg Russell and Meghan Benton, *Selective Influence: The Policy Impact of Commons Select Committees* (Constitution Unit 2011).

45 See Erskine May, *Parliamentary Practice* (Butterworths, 24th ed. 2011) 484.

46 See HC SO 145A. A recent case was a petition from 1.8 million people demanding that President Trump did not make a state visit to the UK, subsequently debated on 18 January 2016.

47 See Robert Blackburn, *The Electoral System in Britain* (Macmillan 1995) Ch. 8.

48 Ibid.; also Ron Johnson and Charles Pattie, *From Votes to Seats: The Operation of the UK Electoral System since 1945* (Manchester University Press 2012).

49 At the poll the Alternative Vote was rejected 68:32. The referendum was held as part of a deal struck within the Conservative–Liberal Democrat coalition under which no proportional system was placed on the ballot paper and the Conservative leadership campaigned for keeping First-Past-the-Post. Earlier, an Independent Commission on the Voting System (Cm 4090, 1998) had been established to recommend a proportional alternative to First-Past-the-Post but the Labour government then defaulted on its promise to put this to the electorate in a referendum.

50 See Chris Ballinger, *The House of Lords 1911–2011: A Century of Non-Reform* (Hart Publishing 2014).

parliament, with the gentry sitting separately in a House of Commons). In other countries emulating the Westminster system of parliamentary government, their Second Chamber has usually been afforded one or more special roles in the country's constitutional law, which is commonly to represent the interests of the component states within a federal structure and to approve amendments to a country's written constitution. The House of Lords has no special place or powers in constitutional law in respect of these two vital parliamentary functions at present.[51]

In contrast, a UK government white paper preceding one of the many failed attempts at reform over the course of the past 100 years described the functions of the House of Lords as being the provision of a forum for full and free debate on matters of public interest; the revision of public Bills brought from the House of Commons; the initiation of public legislation, including in particular those government Bills that are less controversial in party political terms and Private Members' Bills; the consideration of subordinate legislation; the scrutiny of the activities of the executive; and the scrutiny of private legislation.[52] These categories of business are precisely what the House of Commons already perform, and there is nothing unique or special stated about the parliamentary role of the Second Chamber. In practice, therefore, the House of Lords performs what is essentially a duplicating function, but without being the chamber on which the life or financial accountability of the government rests. It has minimal power with which to contradict the House of Commons, with its original power of legislative veto being removed in 1911, replaced with a power of one-year delay circumscribed by conventions and rarely exercised in practice.[53] In defence of its position, a theory of it being 'a revising chamber' emerged in the late 19th century, supplementary and useful for second thoughts, but not actually necessary.[54] The weakness of the legislative powers and democratic authority of the Second Chamber has led some to describe the UK parliamentary process as one of 'disguised unicameralism'.[55]

Popular pressure for further reform now largely focuses on a perceived oddity and anachronism in its membership and current arrangements, aggravated by periodic bouts of ridicule in the mass media of misbehaving lordships.[56] The current size of the House has reached 793, the largest Second Chamber in the world, which includes 22 bishops or archbishops and 92 hereditary dukes, earls, viscounts and barons.[57] All these legislators are unpaid, suggesting it is a voluntary activity, which in many respects it is. The frequency and selection of new appointments are matters entirely controlled by the patronage of the prime

---

51 For the author's view on the proper role for the Second Chamber, see Robert Blackburn, 'The House of Lords' in Blackburn and Plant (n 2) Ch. 1.

52 House of Lords Reform (Cmnd 3799, 1968), para. 8. Later government accounts of the Lords functions have been expressed in broadly similar terms.

53 For the history, law and conventions on the legislative powers of the Lords, see Robert Blackburn and Andrew Kennon, *Parliament: Functions, Practice and Procedures* (Sweet & Maxwell, 2nd ed. 2003), Part Four: The Lords.

54 See Walter Bagehot, *The English Constitution* (1867; Fontana 1963) Ch. III.

55 For example, Lord Desai and Lord Kilmarnock, *Destiny Not Defeat: Reforming the House of Lords* (Fabian Society discussion document 29 1997).

56 Oonagh Gay and Patricia Leopold (eds), *Conduct Unbecoming: The Regulation of Parliamentary Behaviour* (Methuen 2004); and for cases Reports of the House of Lords Privileges and Conduct Committee.

57 The number of hereditary peers allowed as members of the House of Lords was reduced to 92 under the terms of the House of Lords Act 1999. For recent debates on the size of the chamber, see *Lords Hansard*, 5 December 2016, cols. 526f; and 19 December 2017, cols. 1965f, 2011f, 2071f.

minister acting under the royal prerogative.[58] Meanwhile in the public eye there is deep confusion as to whether appointments to the House of Lords are made either as an honour or as part of the political process; and if the latter, whether this is to be regarded as a promotion or form of retirement.

In the coming years the future of the Second Chamber will continue to be much debated in academic and political circles, adding to the widespread conviction that something must be done. However, the practical politics of this matter do not bode well for an agreed final settlement reform in the near future. The 2017 manifesto of the Conservative Party referred to Lords reform as 'not a priority'.[59] Nor was there any sense of urgency in the Labour manifesto, which read:

> Our fundamental belief is that the Second Chamber should be democratically elected. In the interim period, we will seek to end the hereditary principle and reduce the size of the current House of Lords as part of a wider package of constitutional reform to address the growing democratic deficit across Britain.[60]

The impetus behind any government initiative suffers from the political reality that any modernising measure is almost certain to confer upon the Second Chamber greater power and authority than it possesses at present, because it will assume greater democratic authority that it may choose to employ to contradict and interfere with government policy and legislation. This is an unattractive proposition to an incumbent prime minister, unless they are strongly ideologically committed. Meanwhile within the House of Lords itself a large majority of peers continues to protect its existing position from any reform involving popular elections,[61] though there is an emerging body of support behind a recent proposal, from a Lords Speaker's Committee on the subject, to change lifetime appointments to non-renewable terms of 15 years.[62]

A prerequisite for a final democratic settlement for the House of Lords will be for a reforming government to manage dissent and disagreement within the governing party to ensure it can command a majority in the Commons. All the serious attempts at reform in modern times were undermined by conflicts of opinion within the governing party leading government proposals to be withdrawn altogether: these included Labour's Parliament Bill

---

58 If and when a prime minister decides that some new peers are to be appointed, by convention he or she offers the leaders of the opposition parties a smaller number of nominations at his or her discretion, usually in proportion to their representation in the Commons.

59 Conservative Party Manifesto, *Forward Together* (2017) at 41.

60 Labour Party Manifesto, *For the Many Not the Few* (2017) at 102.

61 During Labour's failed attempt at reform in 2002–03 the Lords voted in support of retaining a wholly appointed House by 335 to 110: *Lords Hansard*, 4 February 2003, cols. 116–117. See also the debates on the same day in the House of Commons which while voting in favour of an elected Second Chamber failed to approve any particular proportion of elected element from fully elected to 20 per cent: *Commons Hansard*, 4 February 2003, cols. 211–243.

62 A Lord Speaker's Committee report on 31 October 2017 recommended (a) the capping of the size of the House of Lords at 600 (and until this is reached only one new peer should be appointed for every two dying or leaving); (b) members of the Lords should serve a 15-year non-renewable term; and (c) a proportion of seats should continue to be held by crossbenchers (approximately 22 per cent of all seats) with the number allocated to parties determined by the seats and votes won at the preceding general election; and see *Lords Hansard*, 19 December 2017, cols. 1965–2106, on motion to take note of the report, not leading to a vote.

1968–69,[63] Labour's policy proposals in 2001[64] (after a Royal Commission[65]) and in 2003[66] (after a Commons Select Committee inquiry[67]), and the Conservative–Liberal Democrat's Draft House of Lords Reform Bill in 2011.[68] The initiatives in 2001 and 2003 were weakened further by the then Prime Minister Tony Blair's personal opposition to an elected or partially elected Second Chamber,[69] and in 2011 by the proposals coming from the minority Liberal Democrat component in the coalition government. The successful completion of the reforms necessary will require strong leadership from 10 Downing Street and much greater efforts at cross-party cooperation conducted through informal negotiations by the respective parliamentary party managers.

The guarantee of fundamental rights

There has been a long debate in government, parliamentary, policy institute and university circles on the desirability or otherwise of a UK Bill of Rights.[70] For a period after the Human Rights Act 1998 was passed, this debate fell quiet, in large part because although this major piece of legislation was intended to give effect to an international treaty, the European Convention on Human Rights (ECHR), yet it was widely perceived as being a Bill of Rights in all but name, particularly as for the first time it provided for actionable human and civil rights in the courts. However, in 2006 the Bill of Rights debate was reignited by David Cameron, then Opposition leader, in setting out the Conservative case for repeal of the Human Rights Act, which was widely opposed across the Conservative Party for its association with Europe. Mr Cameron proposed a 'modern British Bill of Rights and Responsibilities', arguing that the Human Rights Act undermined national security and the fight against crime and terrorism, and had encouraged a culture of rights without responsibilities.[71]

The long-term objective of the Labour Party in its pre-1997 constitutional reform programme had in fact been for a British Bill of Rights, to be worked toward after the first step of incorporating the ECHR into domestic law.[72] However, until Mr Cameron's intervention in 2006 this had been forgotten, certainly by Prime Minister Tony Blair, and the civil liberties movement in the country was largely content with the working of the Human Rights Act. When Gordon Brown took office in 2007, his reform document *The Governance of Britain* returned to the subject, setting out proposals for a British Bill of Rights and Duties that emphasised its role in shaping notions of citizenship and identity. His green paper *The Governance of Britain* said:

---

63 See Janet Morgan, *The House of Lords and the Labour Government 1964–70* (Oxford University Press 1975).
64 *The House of Lords – Completing the Reform* (Cm 5291, 2001).
65 *A House for the Future* (Cm 4534, 2000).
66 *Constitutional Reform: Next Steps for the House of Lords* (Department for Constitutional Affairs, 2003).
67 Public Administration Committee, *Second Chamber: Continuing the Reform* (2001–02) HC 494.
68 Cm 8077.
69 See for example *Commons Hansard*, 29 January 2003, cols. 877–78.
70 See Robert Blackburn, *Towards a Constitutional Bill of Rights for the United Kingdom* (Pinter 1999).
71 David Cameron, *Balancing Freedom and Security: A Modern British Bill of Rights* (Centre for Policy Studies 2006).
72 'The incorporation of the European Convention on Human Rights is a necessary first step … [but] it is not a substitute for our own written Bill of Rights … There is a good case for drafting our own Bill of Rights' (Labour Party, *A New Agenda for Democracy: Labour's Proposals for Constitutional Reform* (1993); and see Robert Blackburn, 'The Idea of a British Bill of Rights' (2016) 36 *Human Rights Law Journal* 311–323.

It is important to be clearer about what it means to be British, what it means to be part of British society and, crucially, to be resolute in making the point that what comes with that is a set of values which have not just got to be shared but also accepted. There is room to celebrate multiple and different identities, but none of these should take precedence over the core democratic values that define what it means to be British. A British citizen, playing a part in British society, must act in accordance with these values.[73]

As part of this fresh initiative, a Citizenship Review was conducted on ways to promote civic rights and responsibilities,[74] and the Ministry of Justice produced a further discussion paper, *Rights and Responsibilities: Developing our Constitutional Framework*.[75] By the time of the 2010 general election no cabinet agreement had been reached on a Bill of Rights, the major stumbling block being traditional socialist antipathy toward any suggestion that the measure might strengthen the judiciary, still widely thought of as class-ridden and biased against Labour interests.[76]

During the same period the Joint Committee on Human Rights in Parliament took the opportunity of the revived debate in political affairs to conduct its own inquiry, and proposed a Bill of Rights and Freedoms.[77] This would contain a number of rights beyond those in the ECHR including jury trial and children's rights and reject the idea of including duties and responsibilities in the document. On the legal status and priority of the Bill, it recommended requiring common law and statute to be interpreted in a way that is compatible with the Bill of Rights so far as it is possible to do so (similar to the Human Rights Act) and make explicit (in a way that the Human Rights Act does not) that parliament continues to have the power of legislative override by expressly declaring in an Act of Parliament that the Act or any provision in it shall operate notwithstanding anything contained in the Bill of Rights and Freedoms.[78] An independent Commission on a Bill of Rights was set up shortly after the new Conservative–Liberal Democrat government took office, which in its majority report also supported a Bill of Rights unconditional on the exercise of responsibilities, with additional rights beyond those in the ECHR.[79] Like the Joint Committee it rejected a judicial power to strike down legislation on grounds of violation of the Bill of Rights, but preferred adopting the declaration of incompatibility procedure in the Human Rights Act.[80]

---

73 Ministry of Justice, *The Governance of Britain*, Cm. 7170 (2007), paras. 195–196.

74 Published as Citizenship: Our Commons Bond (2008).

75 Cm. 7577 (2009). On the academic debate, see Stephan Parmentier, Hans Werdmolder and Michael Merrigan (eds), *Between Rights and Responsibilities: A Fundamental Debate* (Intersentia Publishers 2016).

76 The classic academic exposition of this view is set out in J.A.G. Griffith, *The Politics of the Judiciary* (Fontana, 5th ed. 1997).

77 Joint Committee on Human Rights, *A Bill of Rights for the UK?* (2007–08) HL 165; and for debate see *Commons Hansard*, 25 June 2009, col. 307WH.

78 Joint Committee on Human Rights, *A Bill of Rights for the UK?* (2007–08) HL 165, 114. The Canadian Charter of Rights and Freedoms has an equivalent provision.

79 Commission on a Bill of Rights, *A UK Bill of Rights: The Choice before Us* (December 2012).

80 Human Rights Act 1998, section 4: a declaration under this section does not affect the validity, continuing operation or enforcement of the provision in respect of which it is given, and is not binding on the parties to the proceedings. Its effect is therefore advisory, putting the Ministry of Justice and parliament on notice of judicial opinion, causing ministers and parliamentarians to review the legislative provision for its amendment or repeal.

Current Conservative government proposals on human rights law are in a state of suspension, with its efforts on implementing withdrawal from membership of the European Union taking primacy over all other constitutional matters. There is a serious possibility that, now the UK has left the EU, the UK might also withdraw from the European Convention and Court on Human Rights, since it will no longer be bound to be a signatory of the ECHR which is a pre-condition of EU membership.[81] An indication of the former Prime Minister Theresa May's antipathy toward the ECHR and European Court of Human Rights was reflected in a speech she made as Home Secretary in early 2016 before the EU referendum had taken place. She expressed her view that,

> [t]he ECHR can bind the hands of parliament, adds nothing to our prosperity, makes us less secure by preventing the deportation of dangerous foreign nationals – and does nothing to change the attitudes of governments like Russia's when it comes to human rights ... So regardless of the EU referendum, my view is this: if we want to reform human rights laws in this country, it isn't the EU we should leave but the ECHR and the jurisdiction of its court.[82]

Subsequently the Conservative election manifesto prepared under her premiership in spring 2017 went on to say:

> We will not repeal or replace the Human Rights Act while the process of Brexit is underway but we will consider our human rights legal framework when the process of leaving the EU concludes. We will remain signatories to the European Convention on Human Rights for the duration of the next Parliament.[83]

The most recent development under Boris Johnson's premiership has been to focus more on the inter-relationship and power balance between judiciary, ministers and parliament, aiming to push back on judicial encroachment on executive decision-making. The 2019 Conservative election manifesto said it wished to 'update' the Human Rights Act and administrative law and ensure that judicial review is 'not abused to conduct politics by another means'. To convert these aims into legislative detail, a Constitution, Democracy and Rights Commission is being established in 2020 to examine the issues involved and bring forward recommendations.

Democratising the constitution

There has been growing pressure from public opinion, and a high degree of agreement across the political spectrum, that government should be brought closer to the people, and new methods found to make the UK system of government at all levels more representative, accountable and inclusive. In this regard, historically it was an accountability failure of European Union governance, leaving a sense of disconnection from EU decision-making and

---

81 See Robert Blackburn and Jörg Polakiewizc (eds), *Fundamental Rights in Europe: The ECRH and Its Member States* (Oxford University Press 2001) 89–100.

82 Reported in the *Guardian* newspaper, 25 April 2016.

83 Conservative and Unionist Party Manifesto, *Forward Together: Our Plan for a Stronger Britain and a Prosperous Future* (Conservative Party 2017) 37.

the benefits of EU membership, which fed directly into the 2016 referendum decision to leave the EU. By contrast, internally within the UK there has been a deepening of national identities, especially in Scotland and Wales brought about by the Scotland Act 1998 and Government of Wales Act 1998, creating a new tier of governance in each of those two areas.[84]

There are now serious dangers that devolution, unless it is embedded in an overarching Act of Union or a newly created federal structure for the UK that settles a form of regional government also in England, may become the first stage of a process that leads to national disintegration and the separation of Scotland and Wales.[85] The UK government's decision to withdraw from the EU has significantly aggravated separatist pressures especially in Scotland which strongly voted in favour of remaining in the EU at the 2016 referendum.[86] In order to find a new, permanent settlement for the four nations of the UK and halt the ambitions of the nationalist parties, a debate in political circles and academe is now under way on how best to frame a final settlement that binds the United Kingdom together in a stronger unit than the complex and asymmetrical series of devolution statutes.[87]

Within the process of national decision-making, various attempts have been made to provide greater consultation or involvement of the public. Use of the referendum has now entered UK political life, though still on a relatively few occasions and only twice on a state-wide basis.[88] Most referendums in the UK have been held within its four nation component parts: in Northern Ireland on staying part of the UK or becoming part of the Irish Republic in 1973 and on the Northern Ireland (Good Friday) Agreement in 1998, in Scotland and Wales on devolution proposals in 1979 and 1998 (and again in Wales in 2011), in London on the Greater London Authority proposals in 1998, and in North East England on a regional assembly proposal in 2004. More controversially, referendums were held in 1975 on continuing membership of the (then) EEC, and since the Conservatives took office in 2010 on the voting system in 2011, Scottish independence in 2014 and membership of the EU in 2016. Popular expectations for referendums on major public policy decisions in the future have therefore been fuelled. Conversely, prime ministers may in the future find it less easy to hold a referendum simply because it suits their internal party differences and political convenience.[89]

---

84 Those two Acts have been subsequently amended, conferring extended powers to the devolved bodies; and for other elements of UK devolution see Northern Ireland Act 1998 (as amended) and Greater London Authority Act 1999. In 2002–04 an attempt was made by the then Labour government to introduce a scheme of regional government in eight areas of England, see Cabinet Office, *Your Region, Your Choice: Revitalising the English Regions* (Cm 5511, 2002): however, this was withdrawn after a failed referendum on 4 November 2004 (78:21 on a 48% turnout) to endorse setting up the first assembly in the north-east of England.

85 For a proposed legislative blueprint, see Act of Union Bill, HL (2017–19) Bill 132. See also Independent Commission of the Bingham Centre, *A Constitutional Crossroads: Ways Forward for the United Kingdom* (British Institute of International and Comparative Law 2015).

86 For parliamentary discussion see Lords Hansard, *Brexit: Stability of the Union*, 17 January 2019, cols. 331–389.

87 See Andrew Blick and George Jones, *A Federal Future for the UK: The Options* (The Federal Trust 2010); Andrew Blick, *Devolution in England: A New Approach* (The Federal Trust 2014); Independent Commission of the Bingham Centre, *A Constitutional Crossroads: Ways Forward for the United Kingdom* (British Institute of International and Comparative Law 2015); Daniel Greenberg, *Discussion Documents: Act of Union and Explanatory Memorandum* (2016).

88 A selective comparison in the period since 1990 of the number of state-wide referendums is: Italy 56, Ireland 27, New Zealand 14, Poland 10, Iceland 8, Denmark 7, France 3, Australia 3, Spain 1, Greece 1: see Independent Commission on Referendums (University College London, Constitution Unit 2018) Ch. 1.

89 It is widely believed that the decision to hold the 2016 referendum on continuing EU membership, which was government policy, was a tactical device of David Cameron the serving prime minister to silence dissent within the governing Conservative Party, rather than a genuine desire or need to consult the electorate, wrongly

There has been widespread criticism of the manner in which some of these referendums have been called and conducted, generating a number of academic studies and parliamentary inquiries and suggested updating revisions to the Political Parties, Elections and Referendums Act 2000. The most important elements to be addressed in any future amendments to the Act are (a) how to ensure a level playing field between the two (or more) options being placed before the electorate in terms of resources and access to the media, and (b) particularly where the policy question raises a complex number of considerations (as in the 2016 referendum on EU membership) whether the Electoral Commission has the resources to provide independent statistical and other factual information on matters at issue during the heat of the campaign. Meanwhile, as the Constitution Committee in the House of Lords concluded in its inquiry into referendums in 2010, while the initiative for calling a referendum remains with the government, the final judgement on whether one should be held or not should be a decision made by parliament.[90] There is a good case for referendums, but care must be taken to ensure they support and do not undermine the UK's institutions of representative democracy.

An important debate is now emerging on the theory and practice of deliberative democracy; in other words, establishing a process for learning and discussion among assemblies representative of the public, at national, regional or local level as the matter or question in issue may involve.[91] In the case of questions of political and constitutional reform, this debate has taken the form of proposals for a Constitutional Convention, alternatively known as a citizens' assembly.

An influential precedent with lessons for the UK has been the convention conducted in the Republic of Ireland in 2012–14, set up by resolution of both Houses of the Oireachtas and paid for out of public funds. A list of issues was referred to the convention for deliberation and recommendation, and these included (among others) reducing the presidential term of office to five years and aligning it with the local and European elections; reducing the voting age to 17; review of the Dáil electoral system; provision for same-sex marriage; increasing the participation of women in politics; and such other relevant constitutional amendments that may be recommended by it. The 100 members of the convention included a chairperson, 66 citizens and 33 elected politicians. The 66 citizen members were randomly selected from the electoral register by an independent polling company so as to be broadly representative of Irish society. The way in which the convention proceeded was to hold at least one weekend-long plenary meeting for each of its inquiries into the issues referred to it. The first day of each meeting featured roundtable discussions supported by facilitators and note-takers, followed by a plenary session during which any emerging themes would be reported. The second day usually began with a roundtable session to reflect on the previous day's discussions and/or a question and answer session with experts. The convention then voted on the matters under discussion, with the results of the vote announced by press release on the same day, and a report subsequently drafted and published. Some recommendations were adopted by government action such as creating an Electoral Commission and extending polling hours; and others were put to

---

calculating that the government would win the referendum (which was lost by the government 48:52): some have described his decision as 'Cameron's catastrophe', especially as it led directly to his resignation from office: see Robert Worcester, Roger Mortimore, Paul Baines and Mark Gill, *Explaining Cameron's Catastrophe* (Indie Books 2017).

90 House of Lords Constitution Committee, *Referendums in the United Kingdom* (2009–10) HL 99, para. 226.

91 See David van Reybrouck, *Against Elections: The Case for Democracy* (Bodley Head 2016) and James Fishkin, *Democracy When the People Are Thinking: Revitalising Our Politics through Public Deliberation* (Oxford University Press 2018).

a referendum including on reducing the minimum age for the presidency (rejected 73:27) and same-sex marriages (supported 62:38).[92]

On the centre-left of politics there is already firm support for a UK Constitutional Convention. The Labour Party's most recent election manifesto pledged it would set one up,[93] and substantial groundwork for how a UK convention might be organised and operate has been conducted by a parliamentary inquiry into the subject.[94] In addition, substantial academic research and writing now exists on the options for the UK, drawing on worldwide precedents of deliberative democracy techniques and practice.[95]

The case for a Constitutional Convention has been linked to the desirability of moving toward the adoption of a written, codified constitution for the UK, since it is no easy task for the ordinary citizen to understand UK constitutional law as it stands, which is a prerequisite to any public debate on how its individual elements and institutions should be modernised and reformed. There is now a growing body of opinion among parliamentarians and university professors, with a converging range of reasons, behind a comprehensive, joined-up documentary constitution of this nature. Some saw the civil service's recent initiative in preparing the Cabinet Manual as the start of such a process, and during Gordon Brown's tenure as prime minister 2007–10 he stated in the House of Commons his personal support for the preparation of a written constitution.[96] Significant progress on this reform proposal was made with the first ever official inquiry into the subject conducted by the House of Commons Political and Constitutional Reform Committee during the 2010–15 Parliament, with its final report containing three illustrative blueprints on how a codified written constitution for the UK could work.[97] Support for a written constitution comes from parliamentarians on all sides of the political spectrum, Conservatives,[98] Liberal Democrats,[99] and Labour.[100]

92 Convention on the Constitution, *Ninth Report of the Convention on the Constitution: Conclusions and Recommendations* (Republic of Ireland, March 2014).

93 Labour Party Manifesto, *For the Many Not the Few* (2017): 'A Labour government will establish a Constitutional Convention to examine and advise on reforming the way Britain works at a fundamental level. We will consult on its form and terms of reference and invite recommendations on extending democracy. This is about where power and sovereignty lies' (at 102).

94 House of Commons Political and Constitutional Reform Committee, *Do We Need a Constitutional Convention for the UK?* (2012–13) HC 371.

95 See Alan Renwick, *After the Referendum: Options for a Constitutional Convention* (Constitution Society 2014), and on the political science of popular deliberation more widely, Ron Levy, 'The Law of Deliberative Democracy: Seeding the Field' (2013) 12 *Election Law Journal* 355 and 'Deliberative Voting: Realising Constitutional Referendum Democracy' (2013) *Public Law* 555.

96 Gordon Brown stated, 'I personally favour a written constitution. I recognise that this change would represent a historic shift in our constitutional arrangements, so any such proposals will be subject to wide public debate and the drafting of such a constitution should ultimately be a matter for the widest possible consultation with the British people themselves'. *Commons Hansard*, 10 June 2009, col. 798.

97 House of Commons Political and Constitutional Reform Committee, *A New Magna Carta?* (2014–15) HC 463. The author served as Special Counsel to this inquiry: see Robert Blackburn, 'Enacting a Written Constitution for the United Kingdom' (2015) 35(1) *Statute Law Review* 1–27.

98 Lord Hailsham (Conservative Party Chairman 1959–60; Lord Chancellor 1970–74 and 1979–83) (n 39) and *The Dilemma of Democracy* (Collins 1978).

99 The 2010 Liberal Democrat election manifesto under Nick Clegg's leadership proposed to 'address the status of England within a federal Britain, through the Constitutional Convention to set up to draft a written constitution for the UK as a whole' at 92.

100 The 2010 Labour election manifesto under Gordon Brown's leadership proposed to set up 'an All Party Commission to chart a course towards a Written Constitution', para. 9:3.

There would be many advantages of writing down UK constitutional law into one documentary constitution. Above all, in support of the UK's political democracy, it would enable people to see and be clear about what the institutions, functions and powers of the political system are together with the constitutional rules that govern them. Professor Vernon Bogdanor, in arguing for a written constitution, compares the current system to a person belonging to a club but not being told what the rules of membership are.[101] This argument for inclusiveness is a powerful one, and there is no doubt that a constitution (especially if it contains a Bill of Rights, the US being a classic example) does perform a powerful educative role in society generally. The report of the House of Commons committee on the subject set out 21 arguments for a written UK constitution, and among these were the desirability of settling in law those constitutional conventions that appear uncertain; distinguishing constitutional law from ordinary law and providing a special legislative process for amendment of the former; using the opportunity to strengthen the checks and balances in the constitution such as settling the position of the House of Lords and including a British Bill of Rights; and enabling the document to serve as an expression of the UK's democracy, identity, future and purpose.[102]

A catalyst will be required that prompts a future prime minister who is already well disposed to the case for a written constitution to set up a commission to prepare a draft document to lay before parliament. A constitutional moment, as this is usually described, is difficult to predict, but a dramatic worsening of the UK's national finances,[103] the impact of the UK's departure from the EU,[104] and demands for Scottish independence, or a combination of such factors, could all stimulate demands for a written constitutional settlement.[105] If a Constitutional Convention as mentioned above is established, especially if set up in the context of a widespread sense of political and economic crisis in the country, as was the situation driving the reform agenda in Ireland,[106] a recommendation from the convention for a written constitution would carry considerable weight and certainly fix this

---

101 'If one joined a tennis club, paid one's subscription, and asked to be shown the rules, one would not be pleased to be told that the rules had never been gathered together in one place, that they were to be found in past decisions of the club's committee over many generations, and that they lay scattered among many different documents; nor would we be pleased to be told that some of the rules – so-called conventions – had not been written down at all, but that we would pick them up as we went along, with the implication that if we had to ask we did not really belong'. Vernon Bogdanor, *The Crisis of the Constitution* (Constitution Society, 2nd ed. 2015) at 46; see also 'Towards a Written Constitution?' in *The New British Constitution* (Hart Publishing 2009).

102 The report, which was neutral in considering the case for a written constitution, also set out 21 reasons against a written constitution (at 24–28), chief among them that it would further politicise the judiciary: Nick Barber, 'Against a Written Constitution' (2008) *Public Law* 11; and Sir John Baker, *Our Unwritten Constitution* (British Academy lecture 2009).

103 The financial crisis in Iceland in 2008 led directly to a major review of the constitution; see also Xenophon Contiades (ed), *Constitutions in the Global Financial Crisis* (Routledge 2013).

104 See Vernon Bogdanor, *Beyond Brexit: Towards a British Constitution* (Bloomsbury Publishing 2019).

105 If the monarchy collapsed for want of a suitable personality on the throne, the legal theory of the Crown as the residual basis of authority in the state would need to be replaced by a written UK constitution serving as the country's fundamental law.

106 Tánaiste Eamon Gilmore in his speech at the launch of the Convention on 1 December 2012 said, 'The idea for a citizen's convention to examine our Constitution came against the backdrop of the most profound crisis our country had ever faced. Caught in a perfect storm, where a world crisis, a European crisis and a domestic crisis met, the very viability of our independent state was in question. Confidence in our institutions – in Government, in the banking system, and, in recent years, the Church – had been shaken to its core'.

proposal on the UK's agenda for reform. A sense of urgency would be needed to drive the measure onto the statute book, especially if it contains a series of reforms to the substance of the law and working of government, parliament or the judiciary, rather than a simple consolidation of existing law and practice.

The pace of social change in the UK at present, driven by new technologies, chronic economic problems and political instabilities, and its impact on public attitudes on political affairs is now so great that the direction of constitutional reform in the foreseeable future cannot be predicted with absolute certainty. Few down to 2016 predicted UK withdrawal from the EU, even during the referendum campaign; still fewer in 2015 envisaged a radical left-wing outsider being selected as Labour Party leader for five years;[107] and the collapse of traditional party politics and political ascendancy of the Scottish National Party in Scotland, agitating for independence from the UK, was never envisaged by the architects of the 1998 devolution arrangements.[108] The 2020 coronavirus pandemic has been an enormous shock, causing emergency laws to be introduced with possible long-term effects to the constitutional balance of the country.[109] The politics of the UK, as across many of the western democracies, has been full of surprises in recent years.

---

107 Jeremy Corbyn, Leader of the Opposition 2015–2020.

108 However, some maintained at the time of the reforms that without devolution being delivered within a federal UK structure, it would serve as the thin end of the wedge toward Scottish independence: see Tam Dalyell, *The Question of Scotland: Devolution and After* (Birlinn 2016).

109 T. Konstadinides and L. Marsons, 'Covid-19 and its Impact on the Constitutional Relationship between Government and Parliament', UK Const. L. Blog, March 2020.

23

CONSTITUTIONAL CHANGE IN AUSTRALIA

The paradox of the frozen continent

Elisa Arcioni and Adrienne Stone[*]

Introduction

The story of constitutional change under the Australian Constitution has several strands. On the one hand, the Constitution is relatively difficult to change with an unusually rigorous amendment procedure. The Constitution's rigidity is buttressed by a strong (though not unbroken) tradition of judicial legalism, characterised in the constitutional context by a commitment to textualism and a moderate form of originalism.[1]

At the same time, there are a number of forces that call into question the significance of the rigidity of the Australian Constitution. If the focus of inquiry is limited to the formal written Constitution, the dominant narrative of Australia as '[c]onstitutionally speaking … a frozen continent' has some force.[2] In this chapter, however, we seek to broaden the lens. We argue that the Constitution's narrowness in fact facilitates political change, some of which rises to the level of informal constitutional change. In particular, we seek to show that judicial legalism has been deployed in ways that call into question the claim that it has stymied constitutional development. Finally, we argue that the social role of the Constitution is slowly, subtly shifting, which indicates a disruption of the orthodox view of the Constitution and which may, in turn, provide increased impetus for constitutional change in Australia.

The picture of constitutional change that the Australian model presents is thus particularly complex, demonstrating the cross-cutting forces of constitutional form, legal tradition and politics. It shows, moreover, that understandings of, and approaches to, constitutional change may themselves change over time.

To present this picture we will start this chapter with an overview of the Constitution before moving to discuss formal and informal change of the Constitution including distinct questions about change posed in the Australian setting.

---

[*] Adrienne Stone's contribution was generously supported by the Australian Research Council pursuant to an Australian Laureate Fellowship.
1 Jeffrey Goldsworthy, 'Australia: Devotion to Legalism' in Jeffrey Goldsworthy (ed), *Interpreting Constitutions: A Comparative Study* (Oxford University Press 2007) 106, 106–159.
2 Geoffrey Sawer, *Australian Federalism in the Courts* (Melbourne University Press 1967) 208.

The Australian Constitution: framing and the path to independence

The Australian Constitution is one of the oldest written constitutions in the world. It was drafted by the members of a series of constitutional conventions held over the 1890s and subsequently adopted by the peoples of the colonies by referenda.[3] Though highly participatory in some respects, the process of Federation took place with the approval of, and subject to the occasional intervention by, the government of the United Kingdom.[4] Moreover, in light of the status of the Australian colonies as British dominions, the formal text was passed (with minor changes) as an Act of the Imperial Parliament in Britain in 1900, coming into effect on 1 January 1901.[5]

The framing of the Constitution was not marked by a sharp political or legal break with the pre-existing legal order. On the contrary, the Constitution was born principally of a desire for federation among the colonies rather than independence from the United Kingdom or in response to any clear or imminent threat – whether internal or external.[6] This context meant that much of the legal framework of the British common law was left in place. The framers supplemented British constitutional arrangements by providing for a federal structure (much influenced by the Constitution of the United States) and an amendment procedure (influenced by the Swiss model). However, the Constitution provided a continued role for British legal institutions. Australian independence was obtained only gradually over the course of the next century[7] and required legislative action by the British parliament (in coordination with Australia). As a result of a series of developments (notably including the Statute of Westminster 1931 (Imp)[8] and the Australia Acts[9]), Australian legislation is no longer constrained in any way by legislation of the parliament of the United Kingdom and the Australian judiciary has complete control over the judge-made law in Australia.[10]

The breaking of ties between the United Kingdom and Australia in relation to executive power, however, has been more complicated, due to the identity of the Australian head of state.

As a matter of substance, the independence of the Australian executive merged through the evolution of constitutional conventions that transformed the constitutional role of the Australian representative of the Queen, the governor-general, so that it is now uncontroversial that the governor-general acts on the advice of Australian ministers in almost all cases (subject only to limited 'reserve powers').[11] As a matter of form, legislation now reinforces the distinct identity of the Australian head of state. At Federation, the Australian head of state was the Queen of the United Kingdom of Great Britain and Ireland. Following changes to the style and title of the monarch, the Australian head of state

---

3 See generally, John M. Williams, *The Australian Constitution: A Documentary History* (Melbourne University Publishing 2005).

4 See, e.g., *Re Canavan* (2017) 91 *Australian Law Journal Reports* 1209, 1217 [33].

5 Commonwealth of Australia Constitution Act 1900 (Imp) 43 & 64 Vict, c 12.

6 Cheryl Saunders, *The Constitution of Australia: A Contextual Analysis* (Hart Publishing 2011) 19.

7 Anne Twomey, '*Sue v Hill* – The Evolution of Australian Independence' in Adrienne Stone and George Williams (eds), *The High Court at the Crossroads: Essays in Constitutional Law* (Federation Press 2000) 77.

8 22 & 23 Geo 5, c 4.

9 Australia Act 1986 (Cth); Australia Act 1986 (UK).

10 See *Sue v Hill* (1999) 199 CLR 462, 492–493; Saunders (n 6) 24–25.

11 Donald Markwell, *Constitutional Conventions and the Headship of State: Australian Experience* (Connor Court Publishing 2016) 49–70.

has become the 'Queen of Australia and Her other Realms and Territories, Head of the Commonwealth'.[12] In a strict legal sense, the two monarchs – the Queen of the United Kingdom and the Queen of Australia – are different, with separate relationships to the United Kingdom and Australia, respectively. Nonetheless, because they are the same person, a link between 'the Crown in right of Australia' and 'the Crown in right of the United Kingdom' remains. This ongoing connection, though largely formal, provides continued impetus for a movement toward an Australia republic.[13]

Written and unwritten constitutionalism in Australia

To speak of constitutional 'change' requires a concept of 'the Constitution', which, in the Australian context is complicated in several ways. First, consistent with the tenor of British constitutionalism at the time of Federation, the Australian Constitution contains little rights protection. Indeed, it is controversial whether any provision or requirement of the Constitution can properly be described as a constitutional 'right', although it is usually accepted that there are rights (or at least, limitations on government power) pertaining to voting, religion, political communication, property and, to some extent, 'due process'.[14] Beyond these cases, rights questions are generally matters for the general law and not the Constitution.

Further, although Australia possesses a written Constitution, it was adopted in the context of a pre-existing Westminster system which, though based on a series of written documents, contains no single consolidated 'Constitution' and depends, in some fundamental respects, on norms or 'conventions' that are 'unwritten'.[15] Australian constitutional law consists, therefore, of the law of the capital–C written 'Constitution' as well as the small-c 'constitution' of conventions and unwritten rules. (These latter rules continue to play an important role in Australian constitutional law)[16] but because they are particularly complex, difficult to crystallise and seemingly non-justiciable, we leave them to one side (for the most part) for the purposes of this chapter.

Formal textual change

The formal process of textual change is provided for by s 128 of the Constitution, titled 'Mode of altering the Constitution'. That section commences:

> This Constitution shall not be altered except in the following manner:
> The proposed law for the alteration thereof must be passed by an absolute majority of each House of the Parliament, and not less than two nor more than six months after its passage through both Houses the proposed law shall be submitted in each

---

12 Royal Style and Titles Act 1973 (Cth).
13 See generally Benjamin T. Jones and Mark McKenna (eds), *Project Republic: Plans and Arguments for a New Australia* (Black Inc 2013).
14 Adrienne Stone, 'Australia's Constitutional Rights and the Problem of Interpretive Disagreement' (2005) 27 *Sydney Law Review* 29.
15 See Robert Blackburn, 'The future of UK constitutional law', Chapter 22 in this volume.
16 Markwell (n 11) 27–48; Gabrielle Appleby, 'Unwritten Rules' in Cheryl Saunders and Adrienne Stone (eds), *The Oxford Handbook of the Australian Constitution* (Oxford University Press 2018) 209.

State and Territory to the electors qualified to vote for the election of members of the House of Representatives.

The section also provides for the possibility of the Houses failing to agree to a proposed change and, in that event, the alteration can be put to the electors if one House passes the proposal twice within a specified time frame.

A proposed alteration is passed if 'in a majority of the States a majority of the electors voting approve the proposed law, and if a majority of all the electors voting also approve the proposed law'.[17] This 'double majority' requirement is an example of the significance of the federal structure of the Australian Commonwealth.[18] Another is the requirement that, if the parliamentary representation of a State, or a State's geographic limits, is affected by a proposal, then a majority of electors in the affected State must approve the change.

The record of formal change

Pursuant to the referendum procedure, the Constitution has been amended in its detail in relation to the timing of elections and replacement of senators; to give electors in the Territories (not just the States) a vote in constitutional referenda; to impose a mandatory retirement age for federal judges; and make some changes to federal legislative powers (for instance by giving the federal parliament a general power to enact welfare benefits).[19] However, no significant structural changes have been made. The most famous successful referendum, in terms of votes in favour of change, occurred in 1967. The referendum was the culmination of a political campaign directed toward equality for the Aboriginal peoples of Australia and is often celebrated as a moment of reconciliation.[20] However, despite its success, this formal change has had only a modest effect on the constitutional status of Aboriginal Australians by including them within federal legislative power regarding 'races' and deleting a section that excluded Aboriginal Australians from being counted as part of the population for some constitutional purposes.[21]

Several referenda succeeded in the 1970s,[22] including a series of amendments concerning issues that arose from a constitutional crisis in 1975.[23] These successes have been followed by a long period without amendment. The more significant unsuccessful referenda since 1977 include an attempt in 1988 to improve rights protection and the failed 'Republic' referendum in 1999 which would have replaced the monarchy with an Australian head of state.[24]

The reasons for the failure are not easy to pinpoint, given the large number of failures and the differences among them. It is clear, however, that the s 128 double majority

---

17 Following the Queen's assent (a formality), the alteration becomes law.
18 See Nathalie Behnke and Arthur Benz, 'Federalism and constitutional change', Chapter 10 in this volume.
19 George Williams and David Hume, *People Power: The History and Future of the Referendum in Australia* (University of New South Wales Press 2010) 88–85.
20 Dylan Lino, *Constitutional Recognition: First Peoples and Australian Settler State* (Federation Press 2018) 135–147.
21 See *Kartinyeri v Commonwealth* (1998) 195 CLR 337.
22 Williams and Hume (n 19) 233–234.
23 There is no room here to discuss the crisis in detail. However, for a thorough analysis, including an argument regarding the significance of the crisis for constitutional change, see Brendan Lim, *Australia's Constitution after Whitlam* (Cambridge University Press 2017).
24 Ibid, 194–231.

requirement is not a significant factor. Of the 36 failed referendum questions, in only five was there a national majority of votes but not a majority of States. That is, the vast majority of failed referendum questions failed at *both* levels.[25] The reasons for the failures considered by scholars of the referendum process include a lack of real dissatisfaction with the Constitution in the Australian population; relatedly, the failure of campaigns for amendment to capture the popular imagination; and the difficulty of communicating the complexity of the proposed amendments to the people.[26] It is also generally accepted that divisive political campaigns surrounding referenda are to blame and it is often pointed out that bipartisan political support is the most significant determinant of success and failure.[27]

The broader political and constitutional context is likely relevant as well. Compounding the difficulty of the amendment process has been the lack of internal crisis or external impetus for change. Australia has not been faced with a serious challenge – such as the threat of secession – of the kind that gripped Canada in the lead up to the 'patriation' of the Canadian Constitution.[28] Australia is not subject to a judicially enforced international human rights treaty (like the European Convention on Human Rights and the American Convention on Human Rights) which might provide an impetus for convergence with other constitutional orders.[29] Nevertheless, some international influence on Australia remains, especially in light of its 'genealogical' relationship[30] with British and American constitutionalism, as well as the migration of constitutional ideas across the globe.[31]

The text of the Australian Constitution remains remarkably unchanged, and rather old-fashioned. There has been considerable pressure toward informal constitutional change. However, change by judicial interpretation has been relatively constrained in Australia by a range of systemic and cultural factors to which we now turn.

Constitutional interpretation and constitutional change

The interpretation and enforcement of the Australian Constitution is the responsibility of the judiciary. Unlike the position in the United States (which is so often an important constitutional model for Australia), the power of constitutional review has never been seriously doubted in Australia and, on occasion, the courts' role has been vigorously reaffirmed. Indeed, the High Court made clear in *Australian Communist Party v Commonwealth*[32] that, as a matter of constitutional law, the courts are the final arbiters of constitutional meaning. And while the Australian system of constitutional review is diffuse, with both federal and State courts possessing the power to decide questions of constitutional

---

25 Helen Irving, 'Referendum on Indigenous Constitutional Recognition: What are the Chances?' (Legal Studies Research Paper No 12/21, *Sydney Law School*, 15 April 2012) 7.
26 Campbell, 'Southey Memorial Lecture 1988: Changing the Constitution – Past and Future' (1989) 17 *Melbourne University Law Review* 1, 12.
27 Ibid, 6; Williams and Hume (n 19) 231–237, 244–246.
28 See generally, Peter W. Hogg, 'Canada: From Privy Council to Supreme Court' in Jeffrey Goldsworthy (ed), *Interpreting Constitutions: A Comparative Study* (Oxford University Press 2007) 55.
29 See Helle Krunke, 'Global values, international organizations and constitutional change', Chapter 14 in this volume.
30 See Nicholas Aroney, 'Comparative Law in Australian Constitutional Jurisprudence' (2007) 26 *University of Queensland Law Journal* 317, 321.
31 Consider the adoption of proportionality analysis by the High Court of Australia in *McCloy v New South Wales* (2015) 257 CLR 178.
32 (1951) 83 CLR 1.

interpretation, the High Court of Australia, itself an institution identified in the Constitution, is at the apex of the judicial hierarchy and consequently the authoritative interpreter of the Constitution.

Interpretation of the Australian Constitution occurs within a common law context. While this affords judges a measure of creativity (discussed below) it also entails some limitations. To begin with, precedent is a clear constraint: lower courts are bound by higher courts and the High Court, as the highest court, while not formally bound by its previous decisions is reluctant to overrule its own decisions without compelling reasons.[33] Further, like other similarly situated courts, the Australian courts tend to avoid constitutional issues if possible, for example by preferring to resolve matters through interpreting a statute in a manner consistent with constitutional requirements.[34] Finally, the Constitution establishes a separation of 'judicial power',[35] which limits the institutional functions of courts. This doctrine is familiar in similar constitutional systems, but it has had distinct effects in the Australian context. In particular, the Australian understanding of 'judicial power' precludes abstract review in federal courts (and thus has prevented a Canadian-style reference power). It also prevents the Australian federal courts from exercising a power to give a 'declaration of inconsistency' under 'dialogic' charter of rights such as the Human Rights Act 1998 (UK), as the power to issue non-binding declarations is, according to the distinctive Australian conception, not a form of 'judicial power'.[36]

A closely related constraint lies in judicial method in constitutional cases. The starting point for this method is found in constraints expounded by the High Court in the seminal *Engineers' Case* of 1920, which emphasise constitutional text and traditional methods of statutory interpretation:

> It is … the manifest duty of this Court to turn its earnest attention to the provisions of the Constitution itself. That instrument is the political compact of the whole of the people of Australia, enacted into binding law by the Imperial Parliament, and it is the chief and special duty of this Court faithfully to expound and give effect to it according to its own terms, finding the intention from the words of the compact, and upholding it throughout precisely as framed.[37]

The *Engineers* method has proved enduring and remains central to Australian constitutional law. Indeed, it is a specific manifestation of a broader set of ideas about judicial method, usually described as Australian 'legalism'. This theory of adjudication is famously associated with Chief Justice Owen Dixon and traced to his statement (on his swearing in as Chief Justice) that 'there is no other safe guide to judicial decisions in great conflicts than a strict and complete legalism'. At the core of Dixon's judicial method is the idea that the law constrains judicial reasoning; that law provides an 'external standard of legal correctness' that governs judicial decision making.[38]

---

33 See *John v Federal Commissioner of Taxation* (1989) 166 CLR 417 at 438–439.
34 See, e.g., *Brown v Tasmania* (2017) 261 CLR 328 at 479–480 (Edelman J).
35 *R v Kirby; Ex parte Boilermakers' Society of Australia* (1956) 95 CLR 254.
36 *Momcilovic v The Queen* (2011) 245 CLR 1.
37 *Amalgamated Society of Engineers v Adelaide Steamship Company Ltd* (1920) 28 CLR 129, 142 (Engineers' Case).
38 Sir Owen Dixon, 'Concerning Judicial Method' in Severin Howard Zichy Woinarski (ed), *Jesting Pilate and Other Papers and Addresses* (W.S. Hein, 2nd ed 1997) 152.

In acknowledging this constraint, we need to provide some context. First, legalism is not endemic to Australia. Indeed, *Engineers* itself involved an adoption of traditional British method of statutory interpretation[39] and that method would no doubt sound familiar to lawyers in many systems. However, the strength of the Australian devotion to legalism is marked. Jeffrey Goldsworthy's study of constitutional interpretation in six jurisdictions (the United States, Canada, Australia, Germany, India and South Africa) concluded that 'of all the national courts, the High Court of Australia has been the most legalist'.[40] Both the conception of judicial power and the techniques of legalism are judicially created. Indeed, it is somewhat ironic that *Engineers* itself is an instance of constitutional change, marking a point of dramatic departure from earlier interpretive approaches pursuant to which the High Court recognised implied limitations on the power of the national government.

Second, even on its own terms legalism does not preclude change altogether and traditional legalists recognise a number of 'legitimate methods of constitutional evolution'.[41] Changes in facts, for instance, can lead to changes in the application of a legal provision of the Constitution.

The concept of a 'foreign power', referred to in s 44 of the Constitution, which would not at Federation have applied to the United Kingdom, now does so given the change in legal and political relations with the United Kingdom;[42] and the concept of 'marriage' is now recognised to encompass same-sex marriage.[43]

Third, the significance of this legalist commitment should not be overstated. Indeed, while dominant, the commitment to legalism has waxed and waned somewhat. There are instances of individual High Court judges who have explicitly rejected legalism, such as Lionel Murphy (Justice 1975–1986) and Michael Kirby (Justice 1996–2009) and others who without explicitly rejecting it have nonetheless shown a capacity to work creatively while appealing to legalist methods.

Indeed, the widely studied 'revolution' of the Mason Court in the 1990s was characterised by a commitment to traditional methods, albeit with a more candid recognition of their limits and the influence of non-legalist methods in reasoning.[44] Moreover, considered overall, constitutional reasoning in the High Court, and the Australian courts in general, is eclectic.[45] Judges deploy a range of accepted methods, including interpretation of the constitutional text in its context, including its historical context, and reliance upon previous case law and inferences drawn from the Constitution as a whole. The choice between these techniques – which are familiar in other systems[46] – itself provides considerable flexibility.

---

39 Jeffrey Goldsworthy, 'Originalism in Constitutional Interpretation' (1997) 25 *Federal Law Review* 1, 14.

40 Jeffrey Goldsworthy, 'Conclusions' in Jeffrey Goldsworthy (ed), *Interpreting Constitutions: A Comparative Study* (Oxford University Press 2007) 321, 329.

41 Goldsworthy (n 39) 30–35.

42 *Sue v Hill* (1999) 199 CLR 462.

43 *Australian Capital Television Pty Ltd v Commonwealth* (1992) 177 CLR 106. See also Jeffrey Goldsworthy, 'Originalism and Interpreting the Constitution in Its Second Century' (2000) 24 *Melbourne University Law Review* 677.

44 See Leslie Zines, 'The Present State of Constitutional Interpretation' in Adrienne Stone and George Williams (eds), *The High Court at the Crossroads: Essays in Constitutional Law* (Federation Press 2000) 224; Jason Louis Pierce, *Inside the Mason Court Revolution* (Carolina Academic Press 2006).

45 Adrienne Stone, 'Judicial Reasoning' in Cheryl Saunders and Adrienne Stone (eds), *The Oxford Handbook of the Australian Constitution* (Oxford University Press 2018) 472.

46 Philip Bobbitt, *Constitutional Fate: Theory of the Constitution* (Oxford University Press 1982).

Nonetheless, the endurance of the *Engineers* method, and the culture of legalism more generally, have been significant counterweights to other forms of change. Perhaps the most important legacy of *Engineers* has been a rather cautious judicial attitude with respect to the recognition of unwritten doctrines of constitutional law. The court will recognise such doctrines only if they meet the standard of 'necessary implication', that is if they are 'logically or practically necessary for the preservation of the integrity of [the Constitution's] structure'.[47] There are three important examples of these 'necessary implications' – the implication protecting the 'essential functions' of the States, which gives rise to principles protecting the States from some federal laws;[48] an implication from representative and responsible government, which gives rise to a freedom of political communication (a limited kind of free speech right)[49] and the implication of a separation of judicial power that gives rise to a range of more specific rules protecting due process and procedural rights.[50]

The latter two doctrines are rather exceptional and, due to the continuing influence of legalism, subject to continuing debate as to their legitimacy.[51] Much further development along these lines is difficult to square with a continuing commitment to legalism. Indeed, under the influence of legalism, the High Court declined to develop a more comprehensive set of constitutional rights, refusing, for instance, to recognise an implication protecting equality, or even requiring equal treatment before the law,[52] or to confer constitutional status upon longstanding rights recognised in the common law.[53] Moreover, in relation to some implications – notably the freedom of political communication – the text and structure method has had adverse effects on the development of the doctrine, with the court tending to take refuge in an apparently textual interpretation of the Constitution and neglecting broader questions of substance and value.[54]

A frozen continent?

The fixed text of the Australian Constitution and the dominance of judicial legalism have been a powerful combination. However, there are a number of elements that work against a simple narrative of rigidity in Australian constitutional law. Indeed, we argue that there are three ways in which the Constitution enables change through ordinary political action.

First, the very limited scope of the Constitution has itself *allowed* for change in many areas that would in other systems require constitutional reform. Despite (or perhaps because of) the High Court's refusal to develop an extensive set of rights, there has been considerable legislative activity with now fairly comprehensive human rights legislation at both the Commonwealth and State levels. However, most rights disputes in the Australian legal system are sub-constitutional. Some rights-protective statutes have become relatively

---

47 *Australian Capital Television Pty Ltd v Commonwealth* (1992) 177 CLR 106, 135.
48 See, e.g., *Melbourne Corporation v Commonwealth* (1947) 74 CLR 1.
49 See, e.g., *Lange v Australian Broadcasting Corporation* (1997) 189 CLR 520; *Coleman v Power* (2004) 220 CLR 1; *McCloy v New South Wales* (2015) 257 CLR 178; *Brown v Tasmania* (2017) 261 CLR 328.
50 Stone (n 14).
51 Ibid.
52 *Leeth v Commonwealth* (1992) 174 CLR 455.
53 For example, the right to receive just compensation for property acquired by a State. See *Durham Holdings Pty Ltd v New South Wales* (2001) 205 CLR 399; Stone (n 14) 35–36.
54 Stone (n 14) 43; Adrienne Stone, 'The Limits of Constitutional Text and Structure Revisited' (2005) 28 *University of New South Wales Law Journal* 842.

entrenched politically, and can have significant impact on the course of legal developments, but it is generally accepted in Australia that they do not rise to the status of constitutional statutes[55] and remain subject to amendment and repeal, including implied repeal, in the ordinary course of legislative activity. The best example is the Racial Discrimination Act 1975 (Cth) which was introduced to implement Australia's international commitments to prevent racial discrimination and which was important in the recognition of native title rights for Australia's Indigenous peoples.[56] Yet, given its sub-constitutional status, the Racial Discrimination Act has been abrogated on several occasions, most recently during a policy known as the 'Northern Territory Emergency Response', or 'the intervention', in which the Act was suspended to allow for legislation – ostensibly directed toward the welfare of Indigenous people – to operate despite its racially discriminatory characteristics.[57]

Second, the Constitution *facilitates* change in other ways – most notably by providing a default position and authorising parliament to take further legislative action. This technique was used, for example, to resolve disagreement among the colonies with respect to the female franchise.[58] At the time of the constitutional drafting debates, only South Australia afforded women the vote, whereas the most populous colonies – New South Wales and Victoria – only enfranchised men and resisted a proposal to entrench adult suffrage in the Constitution. The compromise was to provide, in s 30 of the Constitution, as follows:

> Until the Parliament otherwise provides, the qualification of electors of members of the House of Representatives shall be in each State that which is prescribed by the law of the State as the qualification of electors of the more numerous House of Parliament of the State.[59]

Thus, the question of the female franchise was for local communities to determine, but in a way that would not give a numerical advantage to those communities who were more generous in their political participation rules.[60]

In other instances, the open language of the text allowed for a continuation of particular commitments of the colonial parliaments but did not bind all future federal parliaments to maintain similar commitments. A key example is the issue of race, where the drafters were

---

55 Cf. Farrah Ahmed and Adam Perry, 'Constitutional Statutes' (2017) 37 *Oxford Journal of Legal Studies* 461.

56 *Mabo v Queensland* (1988) 166 CLR 186.

57 Cosima Hay McCrae, 'Suspending the *Racial Discrimination Act, 1975* (Cth): Domestic and International Dimensions' (2012) 13 *Journal of Indigenous Policy* 61.

58 See, e.g., Saunders (n 6) 14. This is also an issue through which one can also understand the impact of gender on the process of constitutional drafting and change in Australia. See Silvia Suteu, 'Gender in comparative constitutional change', Chapter 21 in this volume.

59 Because South Australia enfranchised women (and shortly thereafter Western Australia did so as well), but the other colonies did not, the drafters included in the s 128 formal amendment rule the following condition: 'until the qualification of electors of members of the House of Representatives becomes uniform throughout the Commonwealth, only one-half the electors voting for and against the proposed law shall be counted in any State in which adult suffrage prevails'.

60 Two years after Federation, the parliament extended the federal franchise to women in the Commonwealth Franchise Act 1902 (Cth). The Act however excluded 'any aboriginal native of Australia, Asia, Africa or the Islands of the Pacific, except New Zealand' from Commonwealth franchise unless already enrolled in a State. See 'Electoral Milestones for Indigenous Australians', *Australian Electoral Commission* (web page) <www.aec.gov.au/indigenous/milestones.htm>.

explicitly concerned to allow the new federal parliament to have the power to continue at a national level the pre-existing racially discriminatory policies, particularly with respect to immigration and controls within Australia.[61] While powers over immigration, aliens and race were therefore conferred on the federal parliament, their broad language has meant that those discriminatory policies were not entrenched in the Constitution itself, thus allowing the parliament to move away from them over time.[62]

These are not, themselves, instances of constitutional change as much as instances of legislative change that the Constitution permits or facilitates. However, there is a third category of cases in which legislation has itself *influenced*, even changed, constitutional meaning. Though a development that has been criticised in some quarters,[63] legislation has had an especially significant effect on understandings of the franchise and citizenship. In relation to the franchise, the court has focused on the text in ss 7 and 24 of the Constitution, which requires that members of parliament be 'directly chosen by the people'. That phrase has been used to determine the validity of legislation which affects who a federal elector is – that is, the court assesses whether the legislation leads to the outcome that 'the people' have 'chosen' their representatives. One key question in that context is whether the persons who are enfranchised can be understood as 'the people'. In order to understand the scope of 'the people' acting as electors, the court has looked to legislative patterns regarding the franchise as a source of durable indications of community standards regarding who *should* be included among the electors. Those standards have in turn been constitutionalised as the baseline against which any future restrictions to the franchise will be tested (a ratchet, but one which also allows some backtracking on the basis of proportionate constraints).[64] Thus, the choices of the parliament over time – in this instance to gradually expand the franchise over several decades – have led to a change in the content of the constitutional phrase 'the people'.[65]

Regarding citizenship, the story is more complicated, and the role played by statute implicit. There is no reference to Australian citizenship in the Constitution – at Federation, the relevant status was British 'subject'. There is reference to the exclusionary category of 'alien'. In relation to the categories of both subject and alien, the court has struggled to articulate their precise boundaries or the basis on which a person will be one or the other. What is clear is that central to both is the concept of allegiance. But 'allegiance' is similarly not given any substantive meaning. Instead, the court has relied on statutory concepts of 'citizen' and 'alien' in order to understand the constitutional concepts. In relation to alienage, a person is an alien if they lack Australian citizenship (a statutory status). That is, anyone without the formal status of (statutory) citizen lacks formal allegiance and is therefore an alien subject to exclusion. Implicitly, a person with statutory citizenship is a subject because they have the requisite allegiance.[66]

61 See, e.g., *Official Report National Australasian Convention Debates*, Sydney, 8 April 1891, 703 (Sir Samuel Griffith).

62 Elisa Arcioni, 'Tracing the Ethno-cultural or Racial Identity of the Australian Constitutional People' (2016) 15 *Oxford University Commonwealth Journal* 173.

63 Anne Twomey, '*Rowe v Electoral Commissioner*: Evolution or Creationism?' (2012) 31 *University of Queensland Law Journal* 181.

64 *Roach v Electoral Commissioner* (2010) 243 CLR 1.

65 Elisa Arcioni, 'The Core of the Australian Constitutional People: "The People" as "The Electors"' (2016) 39 *University of New South Wales Law Journal* 421.

66 Elisa Arcioni, 'Citizenship' in Cheryl Saunders and Adrienne Stone (eds), *The Oxford Handbook of the Australian Constitution* (Oxford University Press 2018) 339.

Finally, there is a fourth category of case in which the use of power conferred by the Constitution on political actors profoundly alters the pre-existing structural settings of the Constitution. The Commonwealth has taken advantage of some of the legislative powers in the Constitution to achieve fiscal dominance over the States in a way that strikes at the core of federalism established by the Constitution. At Federation, there was a deliberate decision to limit the legislative power of the new federal parliament by specifying a series of 'heads of power', while allowing the States to retain their general pre-Federation legislative powers. In practice, however, the federal parliament now has the ability to legislate in areas which at Federation would never have been within the contemplation of the framers. For instance, the federal legislative power in relation to 'external affairs' was limited in scope at Federation as Australia did not at that time possess full independent international legal personality. In modern times however, the court has interpreted that power to extend, among other things, to the making of laws implementing international conventions to which Australia is a party which – given the scope of modern international law – gives federal legislative power potentially unlimited reach.

More significant is the change in relative fiscal power between the States and the Commonwealth since Federation.[67] Money was one of the key points of contention in drafting the Constitution – how would the framers achieve a free trade zone throughout the Commonwealth? How were the States to maintain their income? What expenditure would be covered by the Commonwealth? How would the Commonwealth raise income? A key component to the constitutional answer was income tax. The States retained their ability to levy income tax, but the Commonwealth also received legislative power over tax. Over time, the Commonwealth sought to enter the field of income tax and then become the dominant player in that field by requiring Commonwealth income tax to be paid before any State income tax. The Commonwealth was successful in defending its use of its tax power to oust the States from the field. As a consequence, the States lost one of their main sources of income and are now reliant on Commonwealth distribution of tax income through annual agreements.[68]

The judicial opinions in these cases are argued in legalist terms. Specifically, they deploy traditional techniques of statutory interpretation which have been understood to exclude relying on the notion that some powers or spheres of activity are reserved to the States.[69] Moreover, in some cases at least, Australian legalism brings with it a deliberate blindness to its consequences. For instance, in *South Australia v Commonwealth* ('*First Uniform Tax Case*'),[70] which upheld a scheme of four Commonwealth Acts which together ensured that only the Commonwealth could tax income, the court was insistent that each Act be considered in isolation and that the cumulative effects of the scheme were not relevant to the question of validity. Similarly, in *Commonwealth v Tasmania* ('*Tasmanian Dam Case*')[71] which upheld a broad reading of the Commonwealth's external affairs power, the court was unwilling to give much weight to the effect of its decisions on the States (despite strong dissenting opinions invoking the idea of 'federal balance').

---

67 See Saunders (n 6) 237–243.
68 See, e.g., Anne Twomey and Glenn Withers, *Australia's Federal Future: A Report for the Council of the Australian Federation* (Council for the Australian Federation, April 2007) 34–35.
69 James Allan and Nicholas Aroney, 'An Uncommon Court: How the High Court of Australia has Undermined Australian Federalism' (2008) 30 *Sydney Law Review* 245.
70 (1942) 65 CLR 373.
71 (1983) 158 CLR 1.

However, we would defend these as instances of constitutional change. In part we rely upon the profundity of the change they inflict and the fact that the change is structural in nature. Whereas the relegation of rights to the political sphere can be seen simply as the consequence of the Constitution's deliberate silence with respect to rights, it is more difficult to see the growth in the Commonwealth's dominance as anything but an alteration over time of the very matters with which the Constitution is centrally concerned: the balance of powers between the States and the federal government. For this reason, the High Court's federalism jurisprudence is often roundly criticised by constitutional traditionalists.[72]

The paradox of this aspect of Australian constitutional law is that it is precisely by adhering to orthodox interpretive methods that the Constitution has been transformed.[73] Indeed, the depth of change that Australian legalism has allowed with respect to federalism calls into question whether legalism is truly a counterweight to change. Indeed, the propensity for legalism to drive this kind of change has led some to question whether the *Engineers* method was legalist at all. The suggestion is usually traced to Justice Windeyer in *Victoria v Commonwealth* ('*Payroll Tax Case*')[74] who attributed the turn taken in the *Engineers' Case* to social forces, namely 'a growing realization that Australians were now one people and Australia one country and that national laws might meet national needs'. Though this claim is contested,[75] Windeyer's approach has, somewhat remarkably, received judicial approval in the High Court.[76]

Contested roles of the Constitution

Last, we see a disruption of a rigid narrative in relation to the nature of the role of the Constitution itself. As we have written elsewhere,[77] there is a traditional view that the Constitution is a 'small brown bird',[78] lacking in inspirational language or content, unconcerned with identifying the constitutional people or values. That view underestimates both the complexity and the significance of the Australian Constitution and is challenged today by forces both within the legal system and without. Internally, as we have shown, there is a complex and developing jurisprudence regarding the identity of 'the people' under the Constitution and of their political values. The external forces include the ongoing calls, from across the political spectrum, for the constitutional recognition of Australia's Indigenous peoples in order to redress historic silences and discrimination and to better reflect Australian history and current identity.[79]

These calls have led to a political movement for change that culminated in 2017 with the 'Uluru Statement from the Heart', a call for change issued by Indigenous peoples, following

---

72 Nicholas Aroney, 'The Ghost in the Machine: Exorcising *Engineers*' (*Paper presented at Proceedings of the Fourteenth Conference of the Samuel Griffith Society*, Sydney, 14–16 June 2002).

73 Allan and Aroney (n 69).

74 (1971) 122 CLR 353.

75 Jeffrey Goldsworthy, 'Justice Windeyer on the *Engineers' Case*' (2009) 37 *Federal Law Review* 363.

76 *New South Wales v Commonwealth* (2006) 229 CLR 1, 119 ('*Work Choices Case*').

77 Elisa Arcioni and Adrienne Stone, 'The Small Brown Bird: Values and Aspirations in the Australian Constitution' (2016) 14 *International Journal of Constitutional Law* 60.

78 Patrick Keane, 'In Celebration of the Constitution' www.austlii.edu.au/au/journals/QldJSchol/2008/64.pdf/.

79 See generally Megan Davis and Marcia Langton, *It's Our Country: Indigenous Arguments for Meaningful Constitutional Recognition and Reform* (Melbourne University Press 2016); Damien Freeman and Shireen Morris (eds), *The Forgotten People: Liberal and Conservative Approaches to Recognising Indigenous Peoples* (Melbourne University Publishing 2016).

a long and highly participatory 'dialogue' process overseen by a government-appointed Referendum Council. The statement calls for a range of responses to the dispossession and oppression of Indigenous peoples, the most constitutionally significant of which is the call for an Indigenous Advisory Body ('the Voice') to be created and constitutionally entrenched. The statement also calls for ongoing processes of agreement-making between Indigenous peoples and Australian governments as well as a 'truth-telling' process to address overlooked (even suppressed) aspects of Indigenous history and Indigenous-settler relations.

An interesting and significant aspect of this movement is the insistence that 'recognition' for Indigenous peoples requires some form of constitutional reform and the firm and widespread rejection by Indigenous peoples of the suggestion that reform be legislative only. This determination for constitutional change as part of the process of reconciliation belies the suggestion that the Constitution is a 'small brown bird' without significance in the broader political culture. On the contrary, the movement for recognition appears motivated by a strong understanding that the Constitution plays a significant role in constructing or reflecting the identity of the polity.

Conclusion

The idea of an Australian 'frozen continent' does not capture the whole story with respect to constitutional change in Australia. Formal textual amendment is rare and judicial interpretation – perhaps the classic form of informal change – is constrained by Australian legalism. However, the political branches have managed to produce considerable structural change within these constraints, most especially to federal–State relations. Indeed, the courts – with their apparent legalist indifference to outcome – have been critically important to the form of constitutional change. Finally, there remains the possibility, only emerging but potentially significant, that the very nature of the Constitution may come to assume a much more significant role in the broader political culture.

Bibliography

A. Articles/Books/Reports

Ahmed, Farrah and Adam Perry, 'Constitutional Statutes' (2017) 37 *Oxford Journal of Legal Studies* 461.

Allan, James and Nicholas Aroney, 'An Uncommon Court: How the High Court of Australia Has Undermined Australian Federalism' (2008) 30 *Sydney Law Review* 245.

Appleby, Gabrielle, 'Unwritten Rules' in Cheryl Saunders and Adrienne Stone (eds), *The Oxford Handbook of the Australian Constitution* (Oxford University Press 2018) 209.

Arcioni, Elisa, 'The Core of the Australian Constitutional People: "The People" as "The Electors"' (2016) 39 *University of New South Wales Law Journal* 421.

Arcioni, Elisa, 'Tracing the Ethno-Cultural or Racial Identity of the Australian Constitutional People' (2016) 15 *Oxford University Commonwealth Journal* 173.

Arcioni, Elisa and Adrienne Stone, 'The Small Brown Bird: Values and Aspirations in the Australian Constitution' (2016) 14 *International Journal of Constitutional Law* 60.

Arcioni, Elisa, 'Citizenship' in Cheryl Saunders and Adrienne Stone (eds), *The Oxford Handbook of the Australian Constitution* (Oxford University Press 2018) 339.

Aroney, Nicholas, 'Comparative Law in Australian Constitutional Jurisprudence' (2007) 26 *University of Queensland Law Journal* 317, 321.

Aroney, Nicholas, 'The Ghost in the Machine: Exorcising Engineers' (*Paper presented at Proceedings of the Fourteenth Conference of the Samuel Griffith Society*, Sydney, 14–16 June 2002).

Bobbitt, Philip, *Constitutional Fate: Theory of the Constitution* (Oxford University Press 1982).

Campbell, Enid, 'Southey Memorial Lecture 1988: Changing the Constitution – Past and Future' (1989) 17 *Melbourne University Law Review* 1.

Davis, Megan and Marcia Langton, *It's Our Country: Indigenous Arguments for Meaningful Constitutional Recognition and Reform* (Melbourne University Press 2016).

Dixon, Sir Owen, 'Concerning Judicial Method' in Severin Howard Zichy Woinarski (ed), *Jesting Pilate and Other Papers and Addresses* (W.S. Hein, 2nd ed. 1997) 152.

Freeman, Damien and Shireen Morris (eds), *The Forgotten People: Liberal and Conservative Approaches to Recognising Indigenous Peoples* (Melbourne University Publishing 2016).

Goldsworthy, Jeffrey, 'Originalism in Constitutional Interpretation' (1997) 25 *Federal Law Review* 1.

Goldsworthy, Jeffrey, 'Originalism and Interpreting the Constitution in its Second Century' (2000) 24 *Melbourne University Law Review* 677.

Goldsworthy, Jeffrey, 'Australia: Devotion to Legalism' in Jeffrey Goldsworthy (ed), *Interpreting Constitutions: A Comparative Study* (Oxford University Press 2007) 106.

Goldsworthy, Jeffrey, 'Conclusions' in Jeffrey Goldsworthy (ed), *Interpreting Constitutions: A Comparative Study* (Oxford University Press 2007) 321.

Goldsworthy, Jeffrey, 'Justice Windeyer on the *Engineers' Case*' (2009) 37 *Federal Law Review* 363.

Hogg, Peter W, 'Canada: From Privy Council to Supreme Court' in Jeffrey Goldsworthy (ed), *Interpreting Constitutions: A Comparative Study* (Oxford University Press 2007) 55.

Irving, Helen, 'Referendum on Indigenous Constitutional Recognition: What are the Chances?' (Legal Studies Research Paper No 12/51, *Sydney Law School*, 15 April 2012).

Jones, Benjamin T. and Mark McKenna (eds), *Project Republic: Plans and Arguments for a New Australia* (Black Inc 2013).

Lim, Brendan, *Australia's Constitution after Whitlam* (Cambridge University Press 2017).

Lino, Dylan, *Constitutional Recognition: First Peoples and Australian Settler State* (Federation Press 2018).

Markwell, Donald, *Constitutional Conventions and the Headship of State: Australian Experience* (Connor Court Publishing 2016).

McCrae, Cosima Hay, 'Suspending the *Racial Discrimination Act, 1975* (Cth): Domestic and International Dimensions' (2012) 13 *Journal of Indigenous Policy* 61.

Pierce, Jason Louis, *Inside the Mason Court Revolution* (Carolina Academic Press 2006).

Saunders, Cheryl, *The Constitution of Australia: A Contextual Analysis* (Hart Publishing 2011).

Sawer, Geoffrey, *Australian Federalism in the Courts* (Melbourne University Press 1967).

Stone, Adrienne, 'Australia's Constitutional Rights and the Problem of Interpretive Disagreement' (2005) 27 *Sydney Law Review* 29.

Stone, Adrienne, 'The Limits of Constitutional Text and Structure Revisited' (2005) 28 *University of New South Wales Law Journal* 842.

Stone, Adrienne, 'Judicial Reasoning' in Cheryl Saunders and Adrienne Stone (eds), *The Oxford Handbook of the Australian Constitution* (Oxford University Press 2018) 472.

Twomey, Anne, '*Rowe v Electoral Commissioner* – Evolution or Creationism?' (2012) 31 *University of Queensland Law Journal* 181.

Twomey, Anne, '*Sue v Hill*: The Evolution of Australian Independence' in Adrienne Stone and George Williams (eds), *The High Court at the Crossroads: Essays in Constitutional Law* (Federation Press 2000) 77.

Twomey, Anne and Glenn Withers, *Australia's Federal Future: A Report for the Council of the Australian Federation* (Council for the Australian Federation, April 2007).

Williams, George and David Hume, *People Power: The History and Future of the Referendum in Australia* (University of New South Wales Press 2010).

Williams, John M., *The Australian Constitution: A Documentary History* (Melbourne University Publishing 2005).

Zines, Leslie, 'The Present State of Constitutional Interpretation' in Adrienne Stone and George Williams (eds), *The High Court at the Crossroads: Essays in Constitutional Law* (Federation Press 2000) 224.

B. Cases

Amalgamated Society of Engineers v Adelaide Steamship Co Ltd (1920) 28 CLR 129 ('*Engineers' Case*').

Australian Capital Television Pty Ltd v Commonwealth (1992) 177 CLR 106.

Australian Communist Party v Commonwealth (1951) 83 CLR 1.

Brown v Tasmania (2017) 261 CLR 328.
Coleman v Power (2004) 220 CLR 1.
Commonwealth v Tasmania (1983) 158 CLR 1 ('*Tasmanian Dam Case*').
Durham Holdings Pty Ltd v New South Wales (2001) 205 CLR 399.
John v Federal Commissioner of Taxation (1989) 166 CLR 417.
Kartinyeri v Commonwealth (1998) 195 CLR 337.
Lange v Australian Broadcasting Corporation (1997) 189 CLR 520.
Leeth v Commonwealth (1992) 174 CLR 455.
Mabo v Queensland (1988) 166 CLR 186.
McCloy v New South Wales (2015) 257 CLR 178.
Melbourne Corporation v Commonwealth (1947) 74 CLR 1.
Momcilovic v The Queen (2011) 245 CLR 1.
New South Wales v Commonwealth (2006) 229 CLR 1 ('*Work Choices Case*').
R v Kirby; Ex parte Boilermakers' Society of Australia (1956) 95 CLR 254.
Re Canavan (2017) 91 ALJR 1209.
Roach v Electoral Commissioner (2010) 243 CLR 1.
South Australia v Commonwealth (1942) 65 CLR 373 ('*First Uniform Tax Case*').
Sue v Hill (1999) 199 CLR 462.
Victoria v Commonwealth (1971) 122 CLR 353 ('*Payroll Tax Case*').

C. Legislation

Australia Act 1986 (Cth).
Australia Act 1986 (UK).
Commonwealth Franchise Act 1902 (Cth).
Commonwealth of Australia Constitution Act 1900 (Imp) 43 & 64 Vict, c 12.
Human Rights Act 1998 (UK).
Racial Discrimination Act 1975 (Cth).
Royal Style and Titles Act 1973 (Cth).
Statute of Westminster 1931 (Imp) 22 & 23 Geo 5, c 4.

D. Other

'Electoral Milestones for Indigenous Australians', *Australian Electoral Commission* (Web Page)
    <<www.aec.gov.au/indigenous/milestones.htm>>
Official Report National Australasian Convention Debates, Sydney, 8 April 1891.

24

PRESERVATIONIST CONSTITUTIONAL CHANGE IN LATIN AMERICA

The cases of Chile and Brazil

Juliano Zaiden Benvindo

Introduction

Stability and preservationist constitutional change in Latin America: a second-best democratic scenario?

Whenever Latin America is a central topic, it is automatic to associate the region with economic crises, political instabilities, and coups d'état. The same reasoning is prevalent in the literature on Latin America, following the trend that the region is nowhere close to the stability found in the most developed parts of the globe. An institutional deficiency prevails in various of its countries and the capacity to deal with longstanding problems, such as social inequality, widespread corruption, political clientelism and economic mismanagement, has proven rather limited. Yet a visible shift in understanding Latin America is found in recent works, which, more than emphasizing the so-called 'dilemmas of democratization'[1] – a topic that gained momentum in the aftermath of the transitions to democracy in the region – focuses on interpreting the paradox of democratic endurance, on the one hand, and recurring instabilities, on the other.

For example, Steven Levitsky and Gretchen Helmke point out that political representation, democratic accountability, democratic governance, the exercise of citizenship and the functioning of the rule of law are deficient in the region,[2] but, at the same time, a set of informal institutions play a fundamental role 'in structuring the "rules of the game"' and bringing about a certain stability in the region.[3] Even a strong presidential system,

---

1 See T.L. Karl, 'Dilemmas of Democratization in Latin America' (1990) 23 *Comparative Politics* 1, 1–22. See also G. O'Donnell, P.C. Schmitter and L. Whitehead, *Transitions from Authoritarian Rule* (Johns Hopkins University Press 1986) 256, 256.
2 See S. Levitsky and G. Helmke, *Informal Institutions and Democracy: Lessons from Latin America* (Johns Hopkins University Press 2006) 8–13.
3 Ibid 5 (defining informal institutions as 'social shared rules, usually unwritten, that are created, communicated, and enforced outside officially sanctioned channels').

which has long been portrayed as a central cause for instabilities,[4] has been interpreted as not necessarily incompatible with the gradual consolidation of democracy in many Latin American countries,[5] though some instability has occurred as presidential impeachments have become more common.[6] Latin American constitutionalism has proven more heterogeneous than normally depicted,[7] with various degrees of democratic achievements and institutional stability among its countries,[8] and such a configuration has challenged common wisdom and raised new challenges for comparative constitutional studies.

Latin America has indeed become more democratic over the years despite persisting instabilities in some countries. Yet this positive outcome, marked by more sustainable institutional frameworks, has proven interestingly adaptive to particular circumstances of practices that are far from ideal for a democratic environment. A reality that is not easily translatable into practices that are seen elsewhere as typical standards or even determinants of what one could call a democracy, but which, in the end, may paradoxically help to keep it relatively functional. Gretchen Helmke and Steven Levitsky's findings, though pointing out that many of the so-called informal institutions are indeed harmful, sustain that some 'may enhance the performance and stability of democracy'.[9] A similar reasoning may be connected to Pérez-Liñán's argument that there is a correlation between democratic endurance and mechanisms to channel political tensions such as impeachments, however unsettling they might be. It is as if Latin America finds in such practices and mechanisms a type of second-best solution: they are not ideally democratic but may help democracy to stand against more radical movements that could eventually undermine it or even make it recede to authoritarianism.

Those analyses are, however, mostly focused on political behavior, not on constitutional change. They are evidently an inspiration for extending the investigation to the constitutional realm and offer essential premises and data that may help explain other practices that also seem to challenge such democratic ideals. Yet they do not go much further in explaining other current phenomena that are directly connected to the mechanisms of constitutional change. A narrow margin of appreciation that leads to second-best solutions, however, also applies to this case. When we think of constitutional change, for example, it is ideal that it meet society's expectations, but, at the same time, it is also ideal that it be the outcome of thorough, reasonable and careful decision-making. Evidently, political decisions as such are normally far from following those democratic guidelines,[10] but

---

4 See R. Gargarella, *La Dificultad de Defender el Control Judicial de las Leyes* (Isonomía 1997) 55–70.
5 See J.A. Cheibub, Z. Elkins and T. Ginsburg, 'Latin American Presidentialism in Comparative and Historical Perspective' (2011) 89 *Texas Law Review* 1730 (arguing that 'prima facie ... democracy is not incompatible with expanded executive lawmaking' [of presidents]).
6 See A. Pérez-Liñán, *Presidential Impeachment and the New Political Instability in Latin America* (Cambridge University Press 2007) xiv (arguing that 'Latin American democracies proved to be simultaneously enduring and unstable, willing to punish presidential corruption but unable to prevent it, and responsive to popular demands only in the context of massive protests and widespread frustration').
7 See J.Z. Benvindo, C. Bernal and R. Albert, 'Introduction' in R. Albert, C. Bernal and J.Z. Benvindo (eds), *Constitutional Change and Transformation in Latin America* (Hart Publishing 2019) 1–18.
8 See S. Mainwaring and A. Pérez-Liñán, 'Cross-Currents in Latin America' (2015) 26 *Journal of Democracy* 114, 114–27.
9 Levitsky and Helmke (n 2) 8.
10 See J. Elster, 'Forces and Mechanisms in the Constitution-Making Process' (1995) 45 *Duke Law Journal* 370 (arguing that 'by and large, however, the link between crisis and constitution-making is quite robust').

some signs may help identify that a certain practice deviates from what is usually expected from a democratic society in matters of constitutional change.

For example, Latin America has been historically associated with instability, and one of the factors that might have helped see the region as such is the 'long tradition of constitutional replacement and amendment during the twentieth century'.[11] Though the most recent data reveal that 'the frequency of constitutional change there [Latin America] does not differ much from that in other world regions, including Europe',[12] there are some clear outliers in a comparative perspective. As regards constitutional replacement, some countries differ radically from the average in the subcontinent, such as the Dominican Republic (34 constitutions), Venezuela (26 constitutions), and Ecuador (20 constitutions). The reasons for this behavior vary, but they are undeniably associated with political instability and institutional frailty.

More striking, however, is the second phenomenon, which is related to constitutional amendments. In this regard, Brazil has had, up until now, an average of approximately 3.5 constitutional amendments per year since the promulgation of its 1988 Constitution, possibly the fastest pace in the world. Mexico, in turn, has already amended its 1917 Constitution more than 700 times, a hyper-reformism that has been related to Mexico's difficulty in consolidating its democracy[13] and also as a 'tool for *hegemonic preservation*'.[14] Unlike the examples of constitutional replacement above, Brazil and Mexico are particularly interesting as their constitutional changes, more than the outcome of institutional breakdowns, are preservationist of the very constitutional framework. This preservationist behavior, nonetheless, can take place through distinct means. Chile is an interesting case of a country where constitutional amendments have also meant to stabilize the constitutional framework, but, unlike Brazil, this has happened through gradual and cautious changes to a constitution drafted during a dictatorial period. There is also here a *preservationist strategy*, since such changes, though advancing in some cases a democratic agenda, are also aimed at fending off more radical moves to Chilean constitutionalism.

This chapter aims to address the question of whether such constitutional *preservationist strategies*, carried out through constitutional amendments, could be interpreted as a second-best solution for democratic stability. Similarly to those political movements mentioned above, they would be deemed second-best solutions, because, though carried out through standard mechanisms of constitutional change, they are also based on the fear that, to a certain extent, more democracy would also mean disrupting elites' longstanding privileges and benefits. Especially in unequal societies, as is the rule in most Latin American countries, constitutional change may be motivated by the perception that, in order to avoid deeper democratizing moves, it is better to control the constitutional change and, more specifically, the democratic reach of such constitutional changes. It would also be justified by the argument that, in doing so, such changes would operate in favor of preserving the country's

---

11 D. Nolte and A. Schilling-Vacaflor, 'Introduction: The Times They Are a Changin': Constitutional Trans-formations in Latin America since the 1990s' in A. Schilling-Vacaflor and D. Nolte (eds), *New Constitutionalism in Latin America: Promises and Practices* (Routledge 2012) 5.

12 Ibid 4.

13 F. Por-Giménez and A. Pozas-Loyo, 'The Paradox of Mexican Constitutional Hyper-Reformism: Enabling Peaceful Transition while Blocking Democratic Consolidation' in Albert, Bernal and Benvindo (n 7) 221–42.

14 M. Velasco Rivera, 'Mexico's Constitutional Entrenchment Mirage: The Political Sources of Constitutional Hyper-Reformism' in Albert, Bernal and Benvindo (n 7) 243–67.

stability and governability. These changes may, in some circumstances, paradoxically be a channel for more democracy but at the price of keeping many other conflicting parts that are detrimental to this very democracy virtually untouched. They may paradoxically help democracy be more resilient to a certain extent, but they also open up the horizon for increasing social and political dissatisfactions that may erupt even more radically in a certain moment.

For such a purpose, this chapter will focus on two Latin American countries whose *preservationist constitutional changes*, as second-best solutions, might seem at odds one with the other: Chile and Brazil. Both are central countries in the region, representing, the latter, the biggest economy and the largest population, and the former, one of the countries whose democratic credentials have placed it among the so-called 'high-quality democracies'.[15] These two countries have a common history of dictatorships afflicting their realities during the 1970s and 80s, yet the aftermaths of their transitions to democracy have been rather distinct. They have particularities of many kinds that are not naturally immediately translated to other Latin American countries, but the particularity of both being so similar and so distinct at the same time, especially when it comes to the adoption of these *preservationist constitutional changes*, makes them paramount examples of how constitutional change can mean change to avoid deeper changes.

Chile transitioned to democracy in 1989, but its 1980 Constitution, drafted under the auspices of General Augusto Pinochet, is still in force. It has been strongly amended, and important democratic gains have been brought to its text through such mechanism. In Brazil, as has been its behavior all over its history, regime transitions mean constitutional transitions,[16] and the transition to democracy in 1985 was no different, leading thereby to the drafting of the 1988 Constitution. The Constituent Assembly of 1987/1988 was marked by the direct presence of distinct groups of the organized civil society, and the 1988 Constitution is praised as the most legitimate and democratic ever in Brazilian history. It has since been amended more than 100 times, though, and the attempts to reverse some of the democratic achievements through constitutional amendments have been notorious. It seems, at first sight, that, in Chile, a constitution drafted under an authoritarian regime has been amended to make it more democratic. In Brazil, in turn, a democratic constitution appears to have been amended to reverse democratic achievements inscribed in the original constitutional text. In both cases, changes have also meant stabilization of conflicting interests. The strategies vary, but, beneath what seems opposing moves, there is a common ground where *preservationist constitutional amendments* have worked quite efficiently.

This chapter will discuss this phenomenon and draw some conclusions on how, as second-best solutions, such strategies may appease conflicts and stabilize constitutionalism. Yet, as second-best solutions, such strategies come with a price of a legitimacy gap that may reveal itself to be, in the long run, very destabilizing. The question is whether such potential instability is itself a problem or even a solution to the democratic deficits that those *preservationist constitutional changes* have, as second-best solutions, fostered over the histories of both countries.

---

15 Mainwaring and Pérez-Liñán (n 8) 121.

16 See Benvindo, Bernal and Albert (n 7) (arguing that 'history has proven that Brazilians interpret constitutional transitions as the natural outcome of regime transitions') 7.

Constitutional change as both a democratizing and preservationist process: the 1980 Chilean Constitution

The 1980 Constitution of Chile is, in some ways, a paradox in itself. Unlike Brazil, the democratic transition was not followed by a constitutional transition with the drafting of a new democratic document. Though largely amended, Chile, up until the current moment, still adopts the same constitution that was drafted during the military dictatorship (1973–1990) under the auspices of the dictator Augusto Pinochet. This constitution is one of the most successful products of a very well thought out strategy to preserve the *status quo* even in a transition from a dictatorship to a democracy. It is also a document that was originally strongly based on the authoritarian premise that the Chilean society was not yet able to face the inevitable changes that a democracy entails. Still, it has changed and, in some respects, substantively changed also to face the challenges of a democratic reality. Its adaptive behavior is possibly one of the most successful in Latin America to the point that, even though originally from a violent dictatorial period[17] and despite attempts to replace it,[18] its resilience is remarkable.

Such adaptive behavior that has accommodated conflicting interests since the transitions is a paramount example of how formal constitutional change can serve as a catalyst of democratic stability, though with some costs. Even before the transition to democracy, that constitutional document had already undergone structural reforms that were able to eliminate some of its authoritarian enclaves[19] and this pattern has been repeated over and over along with the democratizing process Chile has, by some accounts, successfully carried out. Many of these changes illustrate much of a political strategy that has favored stability over structural reforms that would foster a movement toward greater democratic achievements. It looks like Chile has accommodated interests in a conservative and cautious way to avoid challenging some of the conflicting interests that were left unresolved during the transition to democracy, while, at the same time, allowing for some gradual progress in this area.

The literature is vast when it comes to examining such a stabilizing behavior, but it also argues that such an avenue comes with a price. Fredrik Uggla, for instance, says 'before democratization, the constitution underwent a process of reform that did away with some of its most blatantly authoritarian provisions but preserved a set of institutions that would characterize and constrain the regained Chilean democracy'.[20] Peter Siavelis, by the same token, contends that 'the post-authoritarian model of politics was deeply constrained by institutions and practices inherited by democratic authorities and reinforced by the model of transitional politics and its series of informal institutions, which first facilitated, but then hindered democratic performance'.[21] Sergio Verdugo and Jorge Contesse recently diagnosed

---

17 See J. Valenzuela and A. Valenzuela, *Military Rule in Chile: Dictatorship and Oppositions* (Johns Hopkins University Press 1987); C. Huneeus, *The Pinochet Regime* (Lynne Rienner Publishers 2006).

18 See S. Verdugo and J. Contesse, 'The Rise and Fall of a Constitutional Moment Lessons from the Chilean Experiment and the Failure of Bachelet's Project' (March 13, 2018) *Blog of the International Journal of Constitutional Law* <www.iconnectblog.com/2018/03/the-rise-and-fall-of-a-constitutional-moment-lessons-from-the-chilean-experiment-and-the-failure-of-bachelets-project> accessed 3 January 2019.

19 See F. Uggla, '"For a Few Senators More?" Negotiating Constitutional Changes during Chile Transition to Democracy' (2008) 47 *Latin American Politics and Society* 51, 51–75.

20 Ibid 51.

21 P. Siavelis, 'Crisis of Representation in Chile? The Institutional Connection' (2016) 8 *Journal of Politics in Latin America* 61, 61.

what has been common practice in the country: 'So far, political consensus without public participation had been the norm for constitutional change in Chile', pointing out that the failure of the attempt to draft a new constitution may lie in that 'Bachelet aimed to change it [such practice], but the pendulum swung too far'.[22]

It is commonly argued that, though reaching democratic stability and a rather competitive political system, Chile will not fully redeem itself from its authoritarian legacy while the 1980 Constitution is still in force. 'These accomplishments were made in the shadow of an authoritarian constitutional framework', contends Javier Couso.[23] The particularity of the 1980 Constitution is telling of such a feeling. It was drafted visibly aiming to preserve a set of institutions and practices, while hindering structural changes to its text, as if it were able to control the future.[24] It is a top-down document drafted by the so-called *Ortúzar Committee* or, more precisely, *Comisión de Estudios de la Nueva Constitución Política*, under the leadership of Jaime Guzmán, who saw in democracy a dangerous, though inevitable, regime that is easily captured by a populist agenda.[25] It was a fiercely antimajoritarian project with a premise that democracy should be protected (*democracia protegida*) from actions against, especially, private property rights.[26] Guzmán, as Javier Couse argues, 'thought that the only model of constitutionalism consistent with it [*democracia protegida*] would prevent contingent majorities from changing the fundamental aspects of the political regime designed during the authoritarian period (a moment of technical rationality in Guzmán's view)'.[27]

It is possibly one of the world's best-planned preservationist strategies of how to design a constitutional framework, during an authoritarian regime, which would regularly operate under democratic rule. It is the typical example of what Tom Ginsburg calls *transformational authoritarian constitutions*, which, according to him, '(1) are explicitly framed as helping to structure a return to electoral democracy after a period of time; (2) reflect certain policy goals designed to be permanent; and (3) contain an enforcement mechanism to ensure that both these goals are met'.[28] In principle, they do not substantially differ from democratically drafted constitutions, but, since they are based on a deep mistrust in majoritarian politics, these constitutions set out effective constraints on these majorities.[29]

A controlled – or protected – democracy as envisaged during a dictatorship is naturally deeply paradoxical, but it was quite successful despite the many amendments it has since undergone. The authoritarian enclaves reached matters such as: (1) life-tenured senators; (2) a National Security Council responsible for overseeing matters of national security; (3) an exclusionary electoral system through proportional representation which diminished minorities' powers; (4) a hyper-presidential system;[30] (5) a powerful military with the role of

---

22 Verdugo and Contesse (n 18).

23 J. Couso, 'Trying Democracy in the Shadow of an Authoritarian Legality: Chile's Transition to Democracy and Pinochet's Constitution of 1980' (2013) 29 *Wisconsin International Law Journal* 393, 393.

24 C. Paixão, 'Past and Future of Authoritarian Regimes: Constitution, Transition to Democracy and Amnesty in Brazil and Chile' (2015) 30 *Journal of Constitutional History* 95.

25 See R. Cristi, *El Pensamiento Político de Jaime Guzmán* (Lom Ediciones 2011).

26 See J. Couso, 'Models of Democracy and Models of Constitutionalism: The Case of Chile's Constitutional Court, 1970–2010' (2010) 89 *Texas Law Review* 1531.

27 Ibid 1532.

28 T. Ginsburg, '¿Fruto de la Parra Envenenada? Algunas Observaciones Comparadas sobre la Constitución Chilena' (2014) 133 *Estudios Públicos* 2, 1–36.

29 Ibid 5.

30 See 1980 Constitución of the Republic of Chile, Articles 62, 70, 71.

overseeing the state and the constitution[31] while being favored with many privileges;[32] (6) a weakened parliament whose 'electoral rules virtually [prevented] the formation of a consistent majority';[33] (7) a powerful Constitutional Court aimed at 'insulating policy-making from democratic control';[34] and (8) mechanisms that would constrain popular participation as an instrument to 'prevent the reemergence of the dynamics of polarization and instability of the early 1970s' and keep safe the economic legacy of the Pinochet era. The fundamental purpose was to effectively design a system that could handicap qualified majorities' ability to change the structural core of the constitution once democracy was reinstated.[35] The consequence, in this scenario, would be a serious crisis of representation, or, as Kamel Cazor Aliste correctly argues, a constitution that 'contains severe – and almost unsolvable – legitimacy gaps, both of origin and content, which makes truly difficult the avenue towards a democratic Charter'.[36]

Pinochet left power following the defeat in a plebiscite set to take place in 1988 according to the 1980 Constitution,[37] when the 'no' campaign gained momentum as popular mobilizations spread across the country. Yet, as the 1980 Constitution was drafted already envisaging a transition to a democracy – the *democracia protegida* – a consensual movement was rapidly met that would lead not to a constitutional transition, but rather to some reforms. The calculation was that, since the constitution already provided some democratic gains, better not to go much further and risk Pinochet's and the military's attempt to regain power.[38] Furthermore, these reforms would serve as a barrier for more radical changes, especially when the opposition was getting stronger and could obtain relevant electoral victories. On the other hand, the right-wing parties needed to offer some concessions as they were directly associated with the authoritarian years. There were, as a consequence, a series of negotiations and bargains that fostered two strong coalitions representing these two sides: *Concertación*, from the Left, and *Alianza por Chile*, from the Right. Those negotiations provided some democratic achievements, such as the four-year term for presidents, and a substantial overhaul of Chapter 14, which addresses the rules for constitutional amendment.[39] On the other hand, however, the military could keep many of their benefits and much of their tutelage over the government, some senators could still be appointed by the president, and the electoral system, although slightly changed, kept being largely exclusionary. As Frederik Uggla would posit, 'more than any other democracy, Chile would remain characterized by the institutions inherited from the previous regime'.[40]

The first years of the civilian governments reflected much of these constraints on majoritarian actions for change and the consequence was that more structural reforms were

---

31 Couso (n 23) 398.

32 See J. Samuel Valenzuela, 'La Constitución de 1980 y el Inicio de la Redemocratización' (2007) *Kellog Institute, Working Paper* 242 <https://kellogg.nd.edu/sites/default/files/oldfiles/documents/2420.pdf>.

33 Paixão (n 24) 97; Siavelis (n 21) 65 ('the design of a new legislative election system that aimed to transform the party system and reduce the power and influence of the left').

34 Couso (n 23) 398.

35 See Couso (n 26) 1532; Siavelis (n 21) 64 ('while the Constitution undoubtedly enhanced stability, it did so at the cost of other important dimension of democracy like representation, accountability, and legitimacy').

36 K.C. Aliste, 'Democracia y Constitución en Chile' (2000) XI *Revista de Derecho* 28, 32.

37 See 1980 Chilean Constitution, 28th Transitory Provision.

38 See C. Fuentes, 'Constitutional Debate in Chile: Replacement through Amendment?' (2018) XXV *Politica y Gobierno* 249 (arguing that, at that time, there was a 'fear of provoking a strong military reaction').

39 Valenzuela (n 32) 25.

40 Uggla (n 19) 55.

barred from going much further in Congress. Instead, the prevailing mindset was that, better than challenging such constraints, the Chilean democracy should place emphasis on assuring a peaceful future, even if the rules of the games crafted during the dictatorship would impair the achievement of even stronger democratic ideals. This authoritarian constitutional architecture was, however, very much spread across the institutional life in the country. It was not only the inherited enclaves that were the problem, but, as Garretón argues, 'many of the formulas and institutions established as a result of the bargaining between the democratic opposition and the dictatorship in 1989 and, subsequently, between the first democratic governments and the rightist opposition'.[41] Moreover, informal institutions[42] also have exerted an important role in the political system, transforming its cumbersome framework into one of the most stable in Latin America despite its strong presidentialism and multiparty system.[43]

In the following years, a progressive agenda aimed at democratizing even further the institutions and practices took place. Chile's Constitution became one of the most amended in Latin America, following a pattern that, though for different reasons and at a slower pace, has been also observed in Brazil and Mexico.[44] Already in 1989, before the transition to democracy, the first amendment was approved by the population in a popular consultation,[45] modifying then many parts of the original text, such as removing the president's power to dissolve the Chamber of Deputies, changing the presidential term from eight to four years, and reducing the qualified majority thresholds for constitutional amendments.[46]

This agenda of progressively democratizing the constitution would gain strength in a major reform in 2005 covering 59 fundamental topics[47] after five years of negotiation.[48] This more democratic move was somehow influenced by the arrest of General Pinochet in 2000 and the establishment of a commission on torture and imprisonment to review the atrocities perpetrated during the dictatorship, which fostered the debate over human rights and the role of the military in Chilean society.[49] Progressively, therefore, a movement toward more democracy gained momentum, in an adaptive behavior that has been regarded as more adequate than entirely replacing the constitution. Every amendment would, in

---

41 M.A. Garretón, *Incomplete Democracy* (University of North Carolina Press 2003) 151.
42 Siavelis (n 21) 34 ('informal institutions are most likely to be found where political actors face difficulty operating within formal institutions, or where there is a lack of congruence between political reality and formal institutional arrangements').
43 See L. Tedesco and J.R. Barton, *The State of Democracy in Latin America: Post-Transitional Conflicts in Argentina and Chile* (Routledge 2004) 145 ('over the last three decades, Chile has been widely regarded as the most successful Latin America [country]', although 'it remains one of the most inequitable societies in Latin America'); Couso (n 26) 1522 (arguing that Chile 'has long been considered one where legality and constitutionalism have reached relatively high degrees of consolidation').
44 See Nolte and Schilling-Vacaflor (n 11) 7 ('The Chilean constitution was amended on average once a year in the 1990s, for example, and then overhauled in 2005); See G. Tsebelis, 'The Time Inconsistency of Long Constitutions: Evidence from the World' (2017) 56 *European Journal of Political Research* 820, 820–45 (arguing that the Chilean constitution 'changes very often, despite the locking mechanisms include in it').
45 See Law 18.825, of 15 June 1989.
46 See Fuentes (n 38) 248.
47 Tsebelis (n 44) 820–45.
48 See Fuentes (n 38) 250 (providing a very detailed analysis of the 2005 reform); S. Correa Sutil, 'Los Procesos Constituyentes en la Historia de Chile: Lecciones para el Presente' (2015) 137 *Estudios Públicos* 62.
49 Fuentes (n 38) 251.

a growing movement, lay the groundwork for an even more significant amendment, and concessions that were difficult to obtain in the beginning started to happen as the political environment gradually democratized the constitutional system. The Chilean experience would thus be a 'good example of how constitutional change can evolve in a sequential manner'.[50]

Chile's transition to democracy, unlike what happened in Brazil, did not mean a transition to a new constitution. Yet the progressive movement of constitutional amendments toward democratizing institution and practices, though still insufficient for some,[51] has provided a constitutional framework and a political system that has been regarded as successfully stable and functional. However, such stability and governability have still to come to grips with the 'legitimacy gaps'[52] that are kept largely unresolved despite the democratic constitutional changes over the years. It is no wonder that, already in 2006, protests across the country, especially headed by students, called for changes, and a set of corruption scandals have since led to a crisis of governance and a decline in support for the political system and the institutional framework.[53]

It is as if what has somehow favored the relative success of Chilean post-authoritarian years has also become the reason for the crisis of legitimacy that has directly affected how Chileans support their institutions and practices.[54] The 'protected democracy' still plays a role in Chilean democracy and the need for a new constitution comes from the perception that it is impossible to become a fruitful democracy with the shadow of that past. Even if a relative progress comes about through amendments aimed at gradually democratizing the constitutional framework, there is something of that authoritarian founding moment that challenges any commitment to a learning process that would, over time, legitimize that constitution. It has an original sin of clearly placing citizenship as the enemy of such 'protected democracy'.

The new constitutional moment that Chile has recently been experiencing is paradigmatic of the perception that citizenship needs to be at the forefront of the decisions for Chile's future. A movement to draft a new constitution already gained momentum during President Michelle Bachelet's government, but, in the end, her attempt to foster such constitutional moment from the bottom up with strong participation seemed too radical for a system that has long functioned in a defensive position from society. As Sergio Verdugo and Jorge Contesse claimed at the time, 'uncoupled with an active role for political parties, a "bottom-up" rhetoric for public participation is not sufficient to successfully bring about serious constitutional change'.[55]

Such a reality would be strongly affected in 2019 as over one million people thronged the streets in various mass protests in the country demanding social reform and a new

50 Nolte and Schilling-Vacaflor (n 11) 9.
51 See Sutil (n 48) 73 (arguing that the 2005 reforms were immediately regarded as insufficient).
52 Aliste (n 36) 32.
53 See Siavelis (n 21) 75.
54 Ibid 79; Couso (n 23) 415 (arguing that 'the crisis of representation engendered by the latter [the 1980 Constitution] could end in another violent struggle).
55 Verdugo and Contesse (n 18).

constitution. A new constitutional moment is currently on the horizon. A defensive right-leaning president, Sebastián Piñera, and a fragmented Congress[56] are being challenged to draft a new constitutional document, and a plebiscite was scheduled to decide whether and how to draft the new constitution.[57] There is a growing support of the Chilean society and a broader consensus among distinct sectors seems to have been reached.[58] Although the signs of the sought-after constitutional change are more real than ever, the risks of failure are still high. The agreement for such a plebiscite features some important gaps, and negotiations on structural matters are still ongoing. There is also the risk of increasing polarization and radicalization, which could lead preservationist strategies to regain strength.[59]

The stronger participation of society and the consequent drafting of a document that aims to finally challenge that past have yet to prove capable of overcoming the institutional thresholds still in force. After all, that 'bottom-up' movement is very confrontational with the institutional framework that has longed operated 'top-down', and it is not unreasonable to think that the resistance to more radical constitutional change may still prevail in the end. Chile may experience a very fascinating constitutional moment but it may also not replace its 1980 Constitution, and the shadow of those authoritarian years will keep being a key motive for movements for even more democracy.

Constitutional change, in Chile, has moved the country toward more democracy, but it has also paradoxically moved the country to accept that too much democracy is not feasible in such an unequal country.[60] A model of *preservationist constitutional change*, which changes but does not replace the constitutional text, has thus been deemed a type of second-best solution for the dilemmas of a society that has still to expiate some its sins. It may have worked until the present moment and may still work for some time, despite – or, intriguingly, even because of – the high levels of social inequality. However, the crisis of legitimacy[61] it has brought about raises the question of whether the model of democracy Chile has experienced is really to be praised or, on the contrary, serves as a cautionary tale of the limits of constitutionalism when a political system, from top-down, defines the level of democracy apparently acceptable for its citizens.[62]

56 S. Verdugo, 'On the Protests and Riots in Chile: Why Chile Should Modify its Presidential System' (Oct. 29, 2019) *Blog of the International Journal of Constitutional Law*. www.iconnectblog.com/2019/10/on-the-protests-and-riots-in-chile-why-chile-should-modify-its-presidential-system/ accessed 28 March 2020.

57 L. Hilbink, 'New Constitution or Nothing! The Promise and Pitfalls of Chile's Constitutional Moment' (Nov. 24, 2019) *Blog of the International Journal of Constitutional Law*. www.iconnectblog.com/2019/11/new-constitution-or-nothing-the-promise-and-pitfalls-of-chiles-constitutional-moment/ accessed 28 March 2020.

58 Hilbink (n 57).

59 S. Verdugo, 'Between Constitutional Romance and Real-World Politics: The Incomplete and Fragile Chilean Agreement for a new Constitution' (Dec. 2, 2019) *Verfassungsblog*. https://verfassungsblog.de/between-constitutional-romance-and-real-world-politics/, DOI: https://doi.org/10.17176/20191202-180535-0.

60 See R. López and S.J. Miller, 'Chile: The Unbearable Burden of Inequality' (2008) 36 *World Development* 2679–95.

61 See Siavelis (n 21) 61–93.

62 See L. Thomassen, 'A Bizarre, Even Opaque Practice: Habermas on Constitutionalism and Democracy' in L. Thomassen (ed), *The Derrida-Habermas Reader* (The University of Chicago Press 2006) 179 (saying that 'were it not constitutional, it would not be democratic, because constitutionalism and democracy are not only mutually enabling but also *presuppose* one another').

An 'overly democratic constitution' and the movements for *preservationist constitutional changes* in Brazil

In December 2019, Brazil passed its Constitutional Amendment n. 105, the last as yet to the 1988 Constitution, a document that celebrated its 30th anniversary on October 5, 2018. Along with the six revision amendments passed in 1994,[63] the 1988 Brazilian Constitution has already been amended 111 times. The pace of change is striking, reaching an average of approximately 3.5 amendments/year between 1988 and 2019. Naturally, there are important variables – such as the size of the constitution, the nature and the extension of the amendment, etc. – but, still, those numbers reveal that at least the political system has regularly moved toward constitutional changes at a pace that is visibly faster than most established democracies.[64]

More striking, such a phenomenon was not observed in previous constitutions. Indeed, when compared to the previous constitutional texts, there was a substantial increase in the number of amendments, as can be seen in Table 24.1:

Table 24.1 Rate of constitutional amendments/lifespan of Brazilian constitutions

Year of the constitution	End of the constitution	Duration (years)	Number of amendments	Amendment rate (per year)
1891	1930	40	1	0.025
1934	1937	3	1	0.333
1937	1945	8	21	2.625
1946	1967	21	27	1.285
1967/1969	1988	21	26	1.238
1988	–	31	111	3.5

The reasons for the change in the political behavior that has led to this significant rise in the number of constitutional amendments are naturally complex and not easily consensual among scholars. For some, culture may be the best explanation. Tom Ginsburg and John Melton place Brazil among the 'ultra-flexible' countries, which has a very strong amendment and judicial review culture.[65] As they argue, 'such changes can be explained by cultural factors surrounding the degree of veneration of the constitution that will affect either the number of proposals or the likelihood that proposals will be approved'.[66] Their conclusion is also based on the significant increase in the number of constitutional amendments after the 1988 Constitution: 'Something obviously changed in Brazil, and neither the formal amendment procedure nor the political configuration of the state can explain the change, as both became more restrictive after the promulgation of the 1988 Constitution'.[67] Yet, although stressing culture as a viable explanation for such a behavior, they also pointed out an important phenomenon found in countries with an 'ultra-flexible amendment culture': the capacity of the constitutional

---

63 See 1988 Brazilian constitution, Art. 3 of the Temporary Constitutional Provisions Act.
64 See A. Lorenz, 'How to Measure Constitutional Rigidity' (2016) 17 *Journal of Theoretical Politics* 349.
65 T. Ginsburg and J. Melton, 'Does the Constitutional Amendment Rule Matter at All? Amendment Cultures and the Challenges of Measuring Amendment Difficulty' (2015) 13 *International Journal of Constitutional Law* 689, 686–713.
66 Ibid 701.
67 Ibid.

framework to appease, through constitution-making, tensions in order to avoid a total constitutional replacement: 'Such constitutions have the virtue of being frequently changed through internal mechanisms, avoiding the more costly route of a total replacement'.[68]

This last sentence might explain the adaptive behavior of Brazilian constitutionalism to face the natural dilemmas of a society still marked by some entrenched interests and an authoritarian legacy. The constitution changes frequently because, when it was drafted, there was a fundamental clash between the past and the future that would, in every new circumstance in time, reopen the discussion of some of its clauses. Though culture plays a role – indeed, Brazilians do not venerate their constitution in a way that would necessarily make amendments substantially more difficult – the context of a constitution drafted in the aftermath of a transition to a democracy may offer a more accurate explanation.

The very drafting process of the 1988 Constitution is itself telling. As I argued elsewhere,[69] the best description of the Brazilian transition to democracy and also of its constitutional moment was of a zigzag, where both the traditional elites partly controlled the process, but, at the same time, an effective rupture stemming from a new configuration of citizenship and intense popular participation took place. Therefore, although those traditional groups could keep untouched many of their privileges in the constitutional text through pact-makings and bargains, there was also some pluralism from the direct participation of the organized civil society and many fragmented political and ideological projects. The constitution that came out of this paradox is therefore also itself very paradoxical: it fosters pluralism, public policies and a vast array of individual and social rights, but it also sets out mechanisms and privileges representing the extractive institutions that have historically disrupted Brazil's development. There is an original catalyst for change in the constitutional project resulting from that clash between continuity and rupture, and it is no wonder that in the following years such clash would somehow reflect on the political struggles leading to constitutional change.

The Brazilian political literature has somehow supported this thesis. Celina Souza, for instance, considers the very uncertainties of that constitutional moment, when subjects such as the economic model, the fiscal policy and social policies had to be decided, to be the institutional driver of two aspects of constitutional design that would favor constitutional change. First, the drafters delegated to the federal government and legislative branch future relevant decisions on social rights and policies, and, second, the changes in the economic and political environment over the years led to the need to review some of the decisions on the economic model and public policies, which impacted a constitution characterized by covering such matters in its own text in a very detail-oriented fashion.[70] Other factors also play a role, such as the relative flexibility of the constitution, which requires only the approval of 60% of the members of the two houses, in two readings, with no extra-legislative constraint (referenda, deliberation gap between legislatures, etc.),[71] and the centralization of federative Brazilian model, which places the states and the municipalities in a subsidiary role in defining the central constitutional matters.[72]

---

68 Ibid 689.

69 J.Z. Benvindo, 'The Forgotten People in Brazilian Constitutionalism: Revisiting Behavior Strategic Analyses of Regime Transitions' (2017) 15 *International Journal of Constitutional Law* 356.

70 C. Souza, 'Regras e Contexto: As Reformas da Constituição de 1988' (2008) 51 *Dados* 792, 798, 814–15.

71 See 1988 Brazilian Constitution, Art. 60.

72 D.C. Ferreira and J.Z. Benvindo, 'Brazilian Experience with Subnational Constitutions: What Went Wrong?' in R. Albert and L. Sirota (eds), *A Constitution for Quebec: Challenges and Prospects* (Hart Publishing 2020, forthcoming).

Since the transition to democracy, the clash between continuity and rupture has taken place in distinct proposals for constitutional change aimed at 'correcting the excesses' of the 'overly democratic' document that came out of the debates in the Constituent Assembly of 1987/1988 and which featured a broad participation of diverse sectors of civil society. A strategy that has appeared quite frequently has been the attempt to pass a constitutional amendment that would set up a type of fast-track mechanism of constitutional change, lowering the threshold, which is already low, for the approval of modifications of specific parts of the constitution, many based on the claim for governability.[73] Some of these so-called 'constitutional revisions' were clearly focused on reversing some of those democratic features of the 1988 Constitution. Yet no proposal for 'constitutional revision' has so far succeeded in Congress. All changes to the constitution up to the present stemmed from the regular procedures for constitutional change and even the constitutional revision of 1993, which was originally set out in the constitution[74] and was visibly moving toward reversing some of those democratic achievements, failed in such purpose in the end.[75]

Moreover, as for the standard constitutional amendments, though there have been many attempts to reverse those democratic gains, most of those that succeeded in Congress were not as radical as to disrupt the democratic core of the 1988 Constitution. In fact, the 1988 Constitution has proven particularly resilient against formal changes to its core framework, that is, to the system of government and the bill of rights. The number of amendments is indeed high, but it does not mean that Brazil is deeply unstable when it comes to its constitutional text. An empirical analysis of their contents reveals that most constitutional amendments cover subjects that are not related to the core of the Constitution, with few exceptions such as the possibility of reelection of the members of the Executive and some constraints on the Executive's power to enact executive temporal ordinances.[76]

Moreover, in matters of individual rights and guarantees, federalism, universal suffrage, and separation of powers, the constitution forbids any proposal for constitutional amendments, thereby treating those subjects as unamendable clauses. No formal change has taken place on these subjects, and even social rights – which are not included in this exception and are very broadly provided for in the constitutional text[77] – have been rather protected. True, in 2016 Congress passed a very controversial constitutional amendment aimed at freezing public spending for a period of 20 years,[78] which economically impairs the enforcement of many social rights, in a clear sign of a preservationist constitutional amendment recalling some right-leaning strategies undertaken since the Constituent

---

73 See the Proposals for Constitutional Amendment n. 25/1995 (DCN, 11 May 1995, p. 8026), 30/1995 (DCN, 19 May 1995, p. 8480), 62/1995 (DCN, Seção 1, 7 June 1995, p. 12404), 463/1997 (DCD, 4 May 1997, p. 14561), 469/1997 (DCD 4 June 1997, p. 14579), 478/1997 (DCD, 23 October 1997, p. 24819), 554/1997 (DCD, 13 December 1997, p. 41684), 71/2003 (DSF 4 September 2003, p. 26040), 157/2003 (DCD, 26 September 2003, p. 50457), 193/2007 (DCD, 11 December 2007, p. 65361).

74 See 1988 Brazilian Constitution, Art. 3 of the Temporary Constitutional Provisions Act of the Constitution.

75 See J.Z. Benvindo, 'Constitutional Moments and Constitutional Thresholds in Brazil: Mass Protests and the "Performative Meaning" of Constitutionalism' in Albert, Bernal and Benvindo (n 7) 71–92.

76 See J.Z. Benvindo, 'The Brazilian Constitutional Amendment Rate: A Culture of Change?' (August 10, 2016) *Blog of the International Journal of Constitutional Law* <www.iconnectblog.com/2016/08/the-brazilian-constitu tional-amendment-rate-a-culture-of-change/> accessed 3 January 2019.

77 See J.Z. Benvindo, 'Brazil in the Context of the Debate over Unamendability in Latin America' in Richard Albert and Bert Oder (eds), *An Unamendable Constitution?* (Springer 2018) 345–64.

78 Emenda Constitucional n. 95, de 15 de Dezembro de 2016, DOU 12/15/2016.

Assembly.[79] Despite that, the conclusion that it will fundamentally subvert the core of the Brazilian Constitution is still to be seen in the coming years and the odds that it may be softened, as it proves unfeasible, are high. The Supreme Court, though still sparingly, has also progressively interpreted such unamendable clauses in a broader perspective, and has positioned itself as a legitimate player to strike down constitutional amendments that violate the 'core principle' of the constitution.[80] It has not behaved as an effective guardian of the constitution – its dysfunctionalities[81] and its protection of the *status quo*[82] are still astonishing – but some important decisions,[83] especially in matters of individual rights, point, to a greater or lesser degree, to the defense of Brazilian democratic credentials.

Virgílio Afonso da Silva, in a provocative text written in 2013 titled *Constitution: 50 Years, 150 Amendments, and So What?*,[84] confirms this diagnosis. He attacked the clichés that have usually followed the 1988 Constitution and which are connected to a preservationist strategy and a conservative reaction to the democratic credentials of the constitutional document. At the time of its promulgation, then President José Sarney was visibly disturbed by some of the achievements that sectors of civil society, intervening closely in the works of the Constituent Assembly, could inscribe in the constitutional text, and claimed, in a nationwide TV broadcast, that the constitution would make the country ungovernable.[85] The argument that the constitution would lead the country to a state of ungovernability has since gained many supporters, and the fact that the constitution has undergone many changes over the years would prove such a thesis. However, as Silva stresses, 'the number of amendments does not mean anything in itself … the number of amendments does not necessarily express how much the Constitution was substantively changed'.[86] In fact, similarly to the reasoning above, 'even though this might astonish many people, it is worth noticing that, in general terms, the Constitution that we have today is practically the same we had 25 years ago'.[87] Quality does not mean quantity, after all.[88] He goes even further: If we compare the Brazilian Constitution with the American one, though the latter had only 27 amendments in its more than 200 years in force, 'those 27 amendments have perhaps

---

79 See J.Z. Benvindo, 'Preservationist Constitutional Amendments and the Rise of Antipolitics in Brazil' (October 26, 2016) *Blog of the International Journal of Constitutional Law* <www.iconnectblog.com/2016/10/preserva tionist-constitutional-amendments-and-the-rise-of-antipolitics-in-brazil/> accessed 3 January 2019; R. Albert, 'Constitutional Amendment and Dismemberment' (2018) 43 *Yale Journal of International Law* 39 (calling this amendment in Brazil an example of 'constitutional dismemberment'); Y. Roznai, and L.R.C. Kreuz, 'Conventionality Control and Amendment 95/2016: A Brazilian Case of Unconstitutional Constitutional Amendment' (2018) 5 *Journal of Constitutional Research* 35–56.

80 See Benvindo (n 77).

81 D.W. Arguelhes and I.A. Hartmann, 'Timing Control without Docket Control' (2017) 5 *Journal of Law and Courts* 105, 105–40.

82 A.A. Costa and J.Z. Benvindo, 'A Quem Interessa o Controle Concentrado de Constitucionalidade? O Descompasso entre Teoria e Prática na Defesa dos Direitos Fundamentais' (2014) <http://dx.doi.org/10.2139/ssrn.2509541> accessed 3 January 2019.

83 L.R. Barroso, J.Z. Benvindo and A. Osorio, 'Developments in Brazilian Constitutional Law: The Year 2016 in Review' (2017) 15 *International Journal of Constitutional Law* 495, 495–505.

84 V.A. da Silva, *Constituição: 50 Anos, 150 Emendas, e Daí?* (October 18, 2013) *Valor Econômico* <www.valor.com.br/politica/3308908/constituicao-50-anos-150-emendas-e-dai> accessed 3 January 2019.

85 See J. Bosco, 'Sarney: Constituição tornará País ingovernável' (Nov. 25, 1987), *O Globo*, p. 6. https://www2.senado.leg.br/bdsf/handle/id/133954?show=full.

86 Silva (n 84).

87 Ibid.

88 Ibid.

transformed the original text of the American Constitution in a much more emphatic way than the 74 amendments to the Brazilian Constitution'.[89]

Therefore, the number of constitutional amendments in Brazil does not appear to be a problem in itself, though common wisdom normally points to the hectic pace of changes as a serious concern for governability and as an evidence of the difficulties of a constitution that may have gone too far in opening itself to that democratic moment of 1987/1988. As seen, beneath such an argument lies much of the authoritarian legacy that has accompanied the democratization process and played a fundamental role in fending off more radical modifications in the Brazilian constitutional experience.

The Brazilian model of constitutional change is thereby an interesting example of the adaptive behavior of constitutionalism whose hectic pace of change is not necessarily problematic and can be, rather, beneficial for the stability of the country. It keeps alive some of the promises of the very constitutional text which could not find a more enforceable definition during the Constituent Assembly and adapts them according to the circumstances of the moment, sometimes leading to further constitutional changes. 'The relative easiness of the amendment process made possible the adaptation to new contexts.'[90] As a matter of constitutional design, a relatively flexible system would normally entail the risks of transforming the constitution into a malleable instrument that could undermine some of the democratic values originally inscribed in the constitutional text. Such changes could thus be 'used to promote distinctly antidemocratic ends',[91] or to mold the constitution according to illiberal principles that would deconstruct 'the old institutional order'.[92] In particular, they could result in the reversal of those democratic achievements set out in the constitutional text, especially due to the stubborn authoritarian legacy still playing a role in Brazilian constitutionalism.

Nevertheless, history has proven that such a fear of constitutional change, at least up until now, does not find much ground in the Brazilian experience. Attempts to more structurally change the constitution, in a typical preservationist strategy, have not generally progressed much further in Congress despite the various threats to the integrity of Brazilian institutions,[93] and, even when they succeed – as did the constitutional amendment freezing public spending mentioned above – the odds are that they also suffer further changes as they reveal themselves strongly detrimental to the very functioning of basic activities of the government and the accomplishment of some of those social rights.[94] Naturally, other strategies, such as changes at the infra-constitutional level or the non-enforcement of many of the constitutional clauses, have also played a substantial role in preserving many interests untouched. Still, with ups and downs, at least formal constitutional change in Brazil has not meant the disruption of the democratic achievements – or promises – set out during the Constituent Assembly in 1987/1988. Despite the hectic pace of constitutional amendments, the constitutional text seems rather resilient. It sounds paradoxical, but it might be exactly

---

89 Ibid.

90 Souza (n 70) 815.

91 D. Landau and R. Dixon, 'Constraining Constitutional Change' (2015) 50 *Wake Forest Law Review* 859.

92 D. Landau, 'Populist Constitutions' (2018) 85 *University of Chicago Law Review* 521.

93 See Benvindo (n 77).

94 Indeed, currently, there is an interesting debate over whether such amendment could be more flexible for areas such as education. See *Temer recua e aceita reajustar Orçamento da educação com base na inflação* (August 14, 2018) *O Globo* <https://oglobo.globo.com/economia/temer-recua-aceita-reajustar-orcamento-da-educacao-com-base-na-inflacao-22978999> accessed 3 January 2019.

this capacity of changing without structurally changing that helps explain why the 1988 Constitution is the most changed and the most permanent of all constitutions in Brazilian history.

Conclusion

Chile and Brazil have historically been haunted by an authoritarian legacy which, through diverse strategies, has hampered the achievement of their democratic ideals. In Chile, an authoritarian constitution, gradually democratized through constitutional amendments over the years, has 'protected' their democracy from so-called radical movements by its citizenry. Though this movement has brought stability – indeed, one of the most praised stabilities in Latin America – the price Chile's democracy has paid is an increasing legitimacy gap and the maintenance of an authoritarian shadow over its constitutionalism. It represents a very well-structured system whereby constitutional change means reaching some democratic breakthroughs and overcoming some of the legacies that years of violent dictatorship and economic and political micromanagement have caused in the daily life of Chileans. There is change, but also change to preserve continuity, even though, in a sequential manner, each new change lays the groundwork for even further changes.

On the other hand, in Brazil, the transition to democracy meant the transition to a democratic constitution. The Constituent Assembly of 1987/1988 was the symbol of a constitutional moment where the attempt to control the process by those who supported the dictatorship turned out to be relatively unsuccessful, as various segments of the organized civil society directly participated in – and contributed to – the debates.[95] Yet the 1988 Constitution has since been directly attacked by various conservative sectors of society which left the Constituent Assembly, unsatisfied and frustrated with the original text, deemed 'overly democratic' and a danger for governability. The hectic pace of constitutional amendments that followed that moment would then prove, according to this viewpoint, how impractical and problematic the 1988 Constitution is. It is no wonder that a set of typical *preservationist constitutional amendments* aimed at reversing some of those democratic achievements in the original constitutional text would gain ground in the following years. Interestingly enough, however, most have not succeeded in Congress. In fact, the 1988 Constitution, with its 111 amendments so far, is not very different from the original text, especially in regard to its core principles, rights and institutional framework. Naturally, some *preservationist constitutional amendments* passed in Congress, such as the one freezing public spending for 20 years and which will affect the enforcement of social rights.[96] It is also true that other strategies, such as changes in ordinary legislation and the

---

95 See Benvindo (n 69) 332–57 L.A.D.A. Barbosa, *História Constitucional Brasileira: Mudança Constitucional, Autoritarismo e Democracia no Brasil Pós-1964* (Biblioteca Digital da Câmara dos Deputados 2012); Cristiano Paixão, 'Autonomia, Democracia e Poder Constituinte: Disputas Conceituais na Experiência Constitucional Brasileira (1964–2014)' (2014) 43 *Quaderni Fiorentini* 415.

96 See B.M. Bertotti, '(Un)Constitutional Amendment No. 95/2016 and the Limit for Public Expenses in Brazil: Amendment or Dismemberment?' (August 24, 2018) *Blog of the International Journal of Constitutional Law* <www.iconnectblog.com/2018/08/unconstitutional-amendment-no-95-2016-and-the-limit-for-public-expenses-in-brazil-amendment-or-dismemberment> accessed 3 January; Y. Roznai and L.R. Camargo Kreuz, 'Conventionality Control and Amendment 95/2016: A Brazilian Case of Unconstitutional Constitutional Amendment' in A.C. Santano, E. Gabardo and B.M. Lorenzetto (eds), *Direitos Fundamentais na Nova Ordem Mundial* (Ithala 2018).

non-enforcement of constitutional rights are also commonly adopted as a way to curb those democratic achievements. Yet, as a matter of constitutional design, the resilience of the 1988 Constitution is striking: it has been regularly changed while being kept quite the same.

Chile and Brazil represent only a portion of Latin American constitutionalism, though an important one. Yet their constitutional histories, with their similarities and differences, reveal much of a pattern in the region. Even in those countries where democratic achievements have been brought either through constitutional amendments (as in Chile) or constitutional replacement (as in Brazil), the political system strategically moves forward through a *preservationist behavior* that is deeply telling of a stubbornly and influential authoritarian legacy. At the constitutional level, the adoption of *preservationist constitutional amendments* has been a viable mechanism to gradually change while not thoroughly disrupting the political and economic systems that have long benefitted from informal and formal institutions of the past.

As a matter of constitutional design, however, perhaps replacing an originally authoritarian constitution with a democratic one may bring some dividends, at least symbolic. True, there is no necessary correlation between regime and constitutional change,[97] and, in fact, a *transformational authoritarian constitution* like the Chilean looks more similar to typical democratically drafted constitutions than the word 'authoritarian' suggests.[98] Yet the symbolism of a democratic constitution matters as it connects with the country's constitutional identity, which, as Tom Ginsburg argues, may see in the project of democratically drafting the constitution a way to 'help a nation to concretize the meaning of itself'.[99] In this regard, the resilience of the Brazilian Constitution despite its many amendments may say something of the 'performative meaning' the very symbol of that constitutional transition provides. Formally, it has been continuously challenged by such *preservationist strategies*, such as proposals for constitutional amendment or revision that severely affect its core. Most have not succeeded, notwithstanding many constitutional amendments already passed in Congress.

The first irony is that the Chilean institutional background, despite the 1980 Constitution, has apparently been regarded as more stable and functional than the Brazilian one. The legitimacy gap has visibly been a serious and damaging side-effect of this authoritarian legacy that, though less pronounced nowadays, is still very much embedded in Chilean constitutionalism. The gradual, cautious and preservationist democratizing process has pushed for increasingly further democratization, in a domino effect that has provided visible gains in a sequence. These gains, nonetheless, seem to be largely the result of 'top-down' resolutions that see the people as actors not yet capable of finding the best solutions for their country. The attempt to draft a new constitution during Michelle Bachelet's and, currently, Sebastian Piñera's presidency is revealing of how preservation is still at odds with the construction of 'bottom-up' decisions, and the consequences of a crisis of representation in the middle and long run are already envisaged as the new fundamental challenge of the next years in Chilean constitutionalism.

The second irony is that, even with its democratically drafted constitution, Brazil is not in a much better situation when it comes to a crisis of representation, and the recent political crisis that paved the way for the election of the far-right President Jair Bolsonaro is

---

97 Ginsburg (n 28) 6.
98 Ibid.
99 Ibid 20.

evidence of this phenomenon.[100] The Constituent Assembly of 1987/1988 was indeed a milestone in the country's recent history, a moment where some decisions, despite various compromises, were the result of a typical 'bottom-up' movement. The question lies, though, in how constitutionalism has since affected the Brazilians' daily lives. It has certainly brought important democratic breakthroughs, institutional improvements and social gains. Yet it has also kept some *preservationist strategies* that have impaired the achievement of an even greater and more inclusive democracy. They do not show the same mindful and strategic plan found in the 1980 Chilean Constitution for such a purpose. Still, they were also there, and it is no wonder that many potential democratic gains rely on clauses requiring ordinary legislation, many of which have never come to life. In the legal realm, preservation in Brazil means both this movement at the infra-constitutional level and attempts to amend the constitution. Curiously, at least for this last feature and despite the hectic pace of constitutional change, preservation has been less successful.

In both cases, the difficulty is to grasp how this two-sided movement of more democracy, on the one hand, and preservation, on the other, has been beneficial or detrimental to the development of both countries. Some could argue that this is the 'possible democracy' of countries still plagued by high levels of inequality and privileges among those in charge of the desideratum of their countries. According to this viewpoint, better to go slow and effective, gradual and safe. Those *preservationist strategies* would then be necessary to fend off a radical rupture with practices which, in one way or another, are nevertheless working. They would be a second-best solution for democratic purposes.

This argument apparently has some appeal, but it carries the message the authoritarian legacy aims to instill in the society as a way to preserve its strength in the future. It is also the argument some strategic behavioral analyses have pointed out as a way for development.[101] The legitimacy gap that follows this argument is, nonetheless, increasingly gaining the form of a social backlash whose outcomes may prove uncontrollable. It can come in the form of more democracy, but it can also come in the form of an authoritarian regress. Hopefully, democracy will prevail, but, at least for Brazil, which is now enduring a government that is challenging its democratic credentials, such a prognosis still needs more time – despite the democratic constitution Brazilians have lived with.

---

100 See J.Z. Benvindo, *Brazil's 'False Consciousness of Time': The Rise of Jair Bolsonaro* (November 10, 2018) *Blog of the International Journal of Constitutional Law* <www.iconnectblog.com/2018/11/brazils-false-consciousness-of-time-the-rise-of-jair-bolsonaro/> accessed 3 January 2019.

101 See Benvindo (n 69) 336–47.

25

INFORMAL CONSTITUTIONAL CHANGE IN UNLIKELY PLACES

The case of South Africa

James Fowkes[*]

Introduction

At first glance, and indeed perhaps at second, post-apartheid South Africa presents quite an ordinary picture of constitutional change. The formal constitutional amendment rules, most of the time, are not notably demanding. They have been used to pass a number of mostly uncontroversial amendments. And partly because these formal channels of constitutional change are demonstrably not blocked, South Africa may appear, at first glance and at second, an unlikely site for a discussion of *in*formal constitutional change.

This in itself has something to tell us about informal constitutional change. But if we press further, we will find that looking for informal constitutional change in an apparently unpromising case such as South Africa can be revealing. I argue here that informal constitutional change does matter to understand parts of South Africa's emerging constitutionalism – to date, small parts, but far from unimportant ones. I argue that the clearest examples are a handful of Constitutional Court cases: two concerning the institutional response to corruption, and two recognizing rights not included in the text. I will also discuss a third, much less clear set of cases, which concern the constitutional amendment rules themselves. The South African Constitution does not contain any absolute limits on amendment as a matter of explicit text, and the court has stated that there is 'little if any' scope for something like a basic structure doctrine. But the court has declined to rule it out entirely, and it has also subsequently seemed to review amendments on substantive grounds. This uncertain trend is doubly interesting for present purposes, since it concerns a potential informal constitutional change in the rules for constitutional change themselves.

Understanding these three sets of cases has something interesting to tell us about the dynamics of constitutionalism in dominant party systems, and about the relationship between informal constitutional change and constitutional interpretation by courts. But before I turn to discuss them, I prepare the ground by briefly introducing constitutional

* I am grateful to the editors and other conference participants for their comments on this piece.

amendment in the South African system and the reasons why, these limited exceptions notwithstanding, it is as yet an unpromising site for informal constitutional change.

Constitutional amendment in South Africa: a sketch

For those unfamiliar with the South African case, the basic picture of constitutional amendment can be quickly stated. Most parts of the 1996 Constitution can be amended by two-thirds of the National Assembly. Amendments must also be approved by six of the nine provinces in the National Council of Provinces (NCOP), the second, federal chamber of parliament, if they concern the Bill of Rights or provincial matters. If an amendment specifically affects particular provinces, the relevant provincial legislatures must also give their assent (by an ordinary majority). A special super-entrenchment rule, to be discussed in more detail below, applies to the 'founding values' set out in section 1.[1] As noted, the text does not purport to place any part of itself beyond amendment.

These rules have been used to pass seventeen amendments to the 1996 Constitution to date. If we are compiling a post-apartheid count, we also need to add two amendments made to the 1993 interim constitution during its intentionally short life. South Africa is therefore averaging about one amendment a year in the post-apartheid era.

Some of these amendments have been significant, but most have not been controversial. (I discuss the main exception, concerning floor-crossing, below; the current debates over amending the constitutional right to property are certainly highly contentious, but the outcome remains to be seen.) The most important change to date has concerned the Constitutional Court and the constitutional jurisdiction of the rest of the upper judiciary. The post-apartheid judicial structure started out along the lines of the German model, but with big carve-outs: that is, a system with a Constitutional Court of ostensibly exclusive constitutional jurisdiction, but with constitutional jurisdiction over several significant issues nonetheless being allocated to the High Courts. Over the course of twenty years, culminating in 2013 with the Constitution Seventeenth Amendment Act, this structure evolved into a US-style system of almost fully decentralized constitutional review, with only a narrow set of especially sensitive questions still reserved for the Constitutional Court's exclusive jurisdiction. While the Constitutional Court retains its name, it has become a general highest appeal court for both constitutional and non-constitutional matters. But while this is a significant change, it was expected, has been generally welcomed, and did not give rise to the sort of high stakes constitutional battle in which judges and others might consider deploying more dramatic limits on amendment like the basic structure doctrine.[2]

This, then, is the basic picture of South African constitutional amendment to date: apparently quite routine, and apparently quite routinely using the *formal* channels for amendment to pursue the changes that have been thought necessary in its relatively short constitutional life to date. It is this that makes South Africa appear an unlikely place for a discussion of informal constitutional change – for at least four reasons.

First, the question of informal constitutional change tends to arise, logically enough, only when there is some significant obstacle to making changes via formal constitutional

---

1 Constitution of the Republic of South Africa, 1996, s 74.
2 I discuss these developments in James Fowkes, 'Constitutional Review in South Africa: Features, Changes and Controversies' in Charles Fombad (ed), *Stellenbosch Handbooks in African Constitutional Law*, vol. 2 (Oxford University Press 2017) 162–66.

amendment rules. But South Africa is far from a system where the formal amendment channels are blocked. Its amendment rules are not particularly forbidding, and – much more importantly – South Africa has been a dominant party democracy since 1994. The electoral dominance of the African National Congress (ANC) has meant that a single party has had the votes, unilaterally or with minor allies, to make amendments to the constitution ever since it came into force.[3] As we have seen, amendment through formal channels is routine.

Second, the issue of informal constitutional change tends to matter only when a constitution gets out of step with society in some way. There has to be an important imperative or need to which the written text is not adequate before anyone will have a reason to insist on the constitutional status of developments not reflected in the text. But South Africa has a modern text that has only just entered its third decade in force. It has not yet had time to get out of step. It also has a large number of open-ended value provisions, resulting in plenty of intra-textual flexibility. In addition, South Africa's two-stage drafting process meant that drafters effectively got a trial run. Writing the 1996 Constitution so soon after the 1993 interim constitution allowed the drafters to correct things learned from the first years of post-apartheid constitutional life.[4] This made it even less likely that important changes would need to be made to the 1996 Constitution in its first decades.

Third, a change that acquires constitutional status despite not following the formal amendment rules often does so based on the passage of time: by becoming a settled, broadly accepted element of the system whose abrogation is hard to contemplate. In South Africa, however, old things are apartheid-era things, and so their vintage discredits rather than elevates them. *Post*-apartheid things, meanwhile, are probably still too young to be more than potential candidates for this sort of status in the future.

Finally – and this is in many ways the combined effect of the points already made – while a good deal of development has occurred since 1994, it is often hard to conceptualize it as *constitutional change*. When important legislation is enacted, or important institutions develop themselves, this is usually seen as a matter of *giving effect* to the constitution, not changing it. There may be a sense in which informal change can happen only when a certain set of understandings become settled under a constitution and *then* some different understandings or pressures intrude, such that one can speak of change from one to the other. But if so, South Africa is still establishing that first set of understandings. It is still largely acting out something close to the original thinking, in something close to the original context. The unchanged nature of its governing party since 1994 no doubt contributes to this sense that South Africa is still in its first post-apartheid constitutional regime.[5] At some point, of course, that will change. Current events may signal the beginning of that shift. But as yet, constitutional activity tends to look like implementation, not informal amendment.

---

3 The ANC has won between 62% and 67% of the vote in five national elections from 1994.
4 On the drafting process, see Hassan Ebrahim, *The Soul of a Nation: Constitution-Making in South Africa* (Oxford University Press 1999); Richard Spitz with Matthew Chaskalson, *The Politics of Transition: A Hidden History* (Witwatersrand University Press 2000).
5 On constitutional regimes, see e.g. Bruce A Ackerman, *We the People: Foundations* (Harvard University Press 1991) 58 and the further sources there cited.

Informal constitutional change in a dominant party system

So why, in the face of all these reasons why students of informal constitutional change might pass over South Africa, do I nevertheless think the case is of interest?

The answer is that informal constitutional change arises when there is some effective obstacle to an important change by formal channels – and in South Africa, there is such an obstacle, in the shape of the dominant ANC party. No executive or legislative change can happen in South Africa at the national level if the ANC does not support it. Of course, in one very important sense, this is not an 'obstacle'. There is a deep principled reason why constitutional changes should not happen when the duly elected representatives of the majority are against them. That is popular sovereignty and constitutional democracy in action. But in a dominant party system, two things can complicate this argument.

The first is that the dominant party may abuse its position. It may do things that its supporters do not actually want or which do not serve their interests, without facing an electoral penalty because of the weakness of the opposition and/or the dominant party's abilities to use its position to tilt the political playing field in its favour.[6] The dominant party's control over formal amendment channels can therefore include an ability to block changes aimed at making it accountable, so these can only happen informally.

Since dominant party democracy is often written about in the context of the threat that it poses or could pose, this first point is the obvious one. But a second point is also important. A dominant party may also lack an incentive to constitutionalize its own *good* policies (and I have argued elsewhere that the ANC government has had an under-appreciated number of constitutionally good policies, among others).[7] A dominant party may prefer to pursue these ideas in legislation or simply as a matter of its own practices in government, maintaining flexibility and avoiding imposing constitutional limits on itself or inviting the involvement of the courts. The result is that important things can be expressed in a sub-constitutional way not because the formal amendment rules could not be followed, but simply because the dominant party has lacked any particular incentive to follow that route. As long as that is the case, such policies, too, can only acquire constitutional status informally.

Neither of these points necessarily entails the need for *a lot* of informal constitutional change. If the concern is with the dominant party as a threat, the 1996 Constitution already contains plenty of resources for resisting, as and if it comes to that. The text is packed with rights and value terms and broadly framed grants of power to the courts and the other independent institutions protecting democracy set out in Chapter 9. Checking a dominant party can be difficult, of course, but in South Africa the sources of difficulty do not usually include a gap in the text that cries out for a constitutional amendment whose passage will be blocked by the dominant party. As we will see, however, usually is not never. Insofar as the dominant party is pursuing good policies, it does not necessarily matter if these are expressed as a matter of formal constitutional amendments or not. But sometimes it can, for example when there are conflicts with other legislation or when the government does not live up to its own policies and individuals wish to challenge this constitutionally.

---

6 On electoral manipulation of this sort, see e.g. Lucan Way and Steven Levitsky, *Competitive Authoritarianism: Hybrid Regimes after the Cold War* (Cambridge University Press 2010).

7 James Fowkes, *Building the Constitution: The Practice of Constitutional Interpretation in Post-Apartheid South Africa* (Cambridge University Press 2016).

The dominant party context also accounts for the fact that all the informal constitutional changes I discuss in this chapter come from decisions of the Constitutional Court. This is unsurprising in light of the four reasons I gave why South Africa might appear to be an unlikely place for informal constitutional change to occur. The dominant party controls many constitutional institutions, but the court is the most obvious constitutional authority that is significantly independent of that control. It is therefore a natural site to look for the constitutional expression of changes that the dominant party, for one reason or another, has not chosen to constitutionalize formally. And the court's interpretative authority means that it has the ability to declare that something has constitutional status, as it were, overnight, in a way that is not true for other constitutional institutions. That does not mean a unilateral judicial claim settles the matter. I will argue that it was crucial that the ANC government accepted the cases I will discuss. But because of the judiciary's interpretative authority, court-declared changes are less affected by the obstacle that informal constitutional status may take more time to acquire than has yet occurred in South Africa's relatively young post-apartheid system. Court centrism is not the reason why the search for examples of informal constitutional change, to date, leads us to the doors of the Constitutional Court.

Informal constitutional changes in response to high-level corruption

My first examples of informal court-led constitutional change arise out of institutional responses to corruption. As it turns out, the constitutional text has some design flaws in this regard, and there has been a need to plug some holes in the dyke. The dominant ANC party could not be counted on to fix these problems, because the corruption problems arose at the highest level. They have particularly concerned corruption allegations against Jacob Zuma during the time that he was President of South Africa and of the ANC. In two cases, the Constitutional Court stepped in to supplement the textual protections.

Glenister II was part of a series of judgments on legal challenges to a decision by the ANC government, under President Zuma, to merge a specialized law enforcement agency called the Directorate of Special Operations (DSO) with the main police force.[8] Corruption was part of the DSO's remit, and the move was widely interpreted as a reprisal for the agency's involvement in the prosecution of Zuma before he became president. But this was not something the litigants were able to prove. The challenge, therefore, became about the more abstract issue of a general constitutional obligation to ensure the independence of a corruption-fighting body such as the DSO. And on its face, the 1996 Constitution does not say much about this. Since corruption negatively effects a range of state activities that serve rights and other important constitutional imperatives, one can certainly mount an argument that corruption is constitutionally evil. But it does not follow from this that one may not in principle merge a specialist anti-corruption entity with the main force (remembering that the challengers were unable to prove that the merger had malicious intent). Some other constitutional institutions in this context have specific provisions on their independence. The auditor general and the public protector, for example, are included among the Chapter 9 democracy-protecting institutions whose independence is explicitly protected.[9] If *Glenister II* had concerned a body like these, it would have been a much easier constitutional case. But there is no equivalent provision for a body like the DSO that

---

8 *Glenister v President of the Republic of South Africa* [2011] ZACC 6.
9 Constitution of South Africa, 1996, s 181.

does the vital part of corruption-fighting that involves criminal investigation and prosecution. It is not, therefore, hard to see why the four-judge minority rejected the challenge.

The majority, however, reached the conclusion that there is a specific constitutional obligation to take steps to safeguard the independence of anti-corruption institutions. That obligation did not preclude a merger in principle, but it did require more protections for the independence of the DSO than were included in the proposed post-merger structure. In order to reach this result, the majority relied on a novel use of international law, drawing on treaties that South Africa has ratified but which had not been incorporated into South African domestic law. (South Africa is a dualist system when it comes to treaties.)[10] Obligations to ensure the independence of corruption-fighting bodies that the government had assumed on the international plane became constitutional obligations that the *Glenister II* majority could enforce against the government on the domestic plane.[11] The actual textual hook for this argument was the state's very general s 7 obligation to protect, respect, promote and fulfil the rights in the Bill of Rights. That grounds the duty to fight corruption, while the international law argument is the source of the detailed content about institutional independence that the majority holds that obligation to include.

We could understand this as merely an act of interpretation, albeit a highly creative one in tense political circumstances. But it is more appealing to understand it as an informal constitutional change. The court is not merely using the international treaties to interpret a provision on government corruption or the police force in an expansive way. That the decision is rooted in no provision more specific than the hugely general s 7 shows the extent to which the judges are not interpreting an existing textual obligation, so much as creating a new one. The same thing is suggested by the way a competent minority using more conventional approaches found that no such obligation exists. On more ordinary rules of construction, the fact that the drafters included specific protections for the independence of some institutions, such as the auditor general or the public protector, but had not made a similar explicit provision for a body like the DSO, would be a strong point against reading the constitution to include such an obligation. The sense of filling-in is strong in *Glenister II* precisely because the majority does exactly the opposite of what this argument would imply, and extends protections to a body such as the DSO in a way the drafters did not.

Glenister II is very unusual. But it has at least one possible counterpart in the decision five years later in *EFF v Speaker of the National Assembly*, which concerned the public protector.[12] As noted, the independence of the public protector does receive specific textual protection in the constitution. But *EFF* was not about independence. The public protector had prepared a report on government spending on President Zuma's private residence at Nkandla. The report concluded that state money had been mis-spent and that Zuma should be required to pay back the portion of the spending that did not concern state needs such as security measures. Parliament had noted the report but then not implemented its findings, essentially treating it as advisory rather than in any way binding. This move, too, was

---

10 On monism and dualism in the South African system in the wake of the 1996 Constitution, see John Dugard, *International Law: A South African Perspective*, 4th ed. (Juta & Co. 2013).

11 For the technical questions raised by the court's approach, see e.g. Juha Tuovinen, 'The Role of International Law in Constitutional Adjudication: *Glenister v President of the Republic of South Africa*' (2013) 130 *South African Law Journal* 661.

12 *Economic Freedom Fighters v Speaker of the National Assembly* [2016] ZACC 11.

widely viewed as shielding President Zuma from liability, in a still more obvious way than in the DSO saga. But the constitutional text does not take an explicit position on either the legal status of a public protector's report or the relationship of the public protector to parliament or to the presidency in this respect.

So here was another constitutional gap, as in *Glenister II*. Furthermore, also as in *Glenister II*, unless that gap was filled with definite content, it would not be possible for the court to challenge the president's impunity. Unless the public protector's report was binding on parliament, parliament was under no constitutional obligation to do anything more than consider the report, which it had done. It is this gap that *EFF* moved to fill, ruling that parliament and the president were constitutionally obliged to either follow a report of the public protector or to appeal its findings to a court. The result shares with *Glenister II* the sense of inserting something important into the constitutional structure that was not there before, as opposed to reading something that is there in an expansively purposive manner.

Some may reasonably see this sense as weaker in *EFF*. The public protector, unlike the DSO, is explicitly mentioned in the text, and so there is a greater sense in which the court is making a structural argument about the status public protector reports must have for the office to fulfil its constitutional role. There is, therefore, a greater sense in which this is a matter of giving effect to the constitution. To my mind, however, the same impression of amending, of filling in something the drafters neglected to provide for, is present in both cases.

Finally, in both cases, the ANC government accepted the outcome. The government made efforts to amend the relevant legislation to comply with *Glenister II* (and then made further amendments after a follow-up litigation successfully challenged some aspects of the re-draft).[13] It complied with the court's order in *EFF* and acted on the public protector's report. It also moved to appoint a more pliant figure to that office when the incumbent's term ended, but that does not detract from its acceptance of the constitutional authority of public protector reports; indeed, it rather tends to confirm it. In any case, it did not challenge the court's findings or attack them as illegitimately creative. The government's acquiescence in both decisions is a final powerful part of the argument that they represent informal constitutional change. In my view, such acquiescence should be seen as necessary to this conclusion. If the ANC had openly resisted these decisions, then it would be accurate only to speak of a constitutional contest. The court would have asserted the need for a change, but whether the change could actually be said to have happened would have been dependent on the outcome of the contest.

Rights-based relationships with government institutions

The second area I consider here is less concerned with the sort of nefarious government conduct that observers usually have in mind when they talk about the role of the court in a dominant party democracy. It is a subtler scenario, still narrowly involving a failure on the part of the government, but in the context of a much more constitutionally positive stance.

The globally famous case of *Doctors for Life* concerned public participation in the legislative process.[14] As a matter of ordinary textual interpretation, the relevant

---

13 *Helen Suzman Foundation v President of the Republic of South Africa* [2014] ZACC 32.

14 *Doctors for Life International v Speaker of the National Assembly* [2006] ZACC 11. I and co-authors have discussed the decision previously elsewhere, and I draw on some of those conclusions here. See Fowkes (n 7) 190ff; Susan Rose-Ackerman, Stefanie Egidy and James Fowkes, *Due Process of Lawmaking: The United States, South Africa, Germany and the European Union* (Cambridge University Press 2015) 118ff.

constitutional provision seemed only to require that legislative bodies facilitate public participation as a general matter. On this interpretation, provided there is some sort of policy in place to this effect (and there was), the constitution is satisfied. The drawback of this approach was that, in the case at hand, the conduct of some of the (provincial) legislative bodies in question had been blatantly unsatisfactory. One legislature had stated that it was important to hold a public hearing on a piece of legislation, but then had simply failed to do so. Another had managed to hold a hearing, but had given the public just one day's notice of its intention to do so. Since these provincial activities were part of national processes involving other provincial legislatures, and since some of the other legislatures had conducted much more satisfactory processes, it was also hard to argue that this sort of cursory conduct had been unavoidable due to something like time pressure.

But for the court, after the fact, there was nothing to be done that would offer any relief to those who felt they had been deprived of any fair opportunity to be heard – unless the legislatures' failures meant that the specific legislation in question was invalid because of the defects of the public participation processes. Instead of a general obligation to have a public participation policy, this would turn public participation into a specific requirement for the passage of valid legislation. And since the text on public participation itself does not establish nearly such a specific obligation on its face, the court had to reach for less textual arguments. *Doctors for Life* articulates a richly participatory notion of democracy, on the way to finding that there is an implied individual fundamental right to public participation in democratic processes. This is a far more specific entitlement than one could arrive at by a more conventional reading of the constitution's textual political rights provisions.

This may look like a highly creative act of interpretation intruding deeply into parliamentary procedures. But it matters that a key basis for this argument is the ANC's own deep commitment to the ideas of participatory democracy *Doctors for Life* sets out, including in the specific context of public participation in the legislative process. The judgment could refer to the ANC government's own principled position on the issue, which some of the provincial legislatures it controlled had simply failed to live up to in the particular instances at hand. And while a minority of the court again felt the constitution did not ground a sufficiently definite obligation for this failure to constitute a violation, the majority reached the opposite result by importing the government's own principles into the constitution. While it is again possible to understand this as a mere act of interpretation, we can again see the degree to which the court is inserting something not already there. In *Doctors for Life*, almost uniquely, the court speaks of creating a new fundamental right, not just interpreting one.

I say *almost* uniquely, because the court has done the same thing on one other occasion, in the 2009 decision in *Joseph v City of Johannesburg*.[15] The problem *Joseph* presented was that residents of a building in Johannesburg had been duly paying their landlord for electricity, but he in turn had not been paying the city. It therefore came as an unpleasant surprise to the tenants when the city ultimately cut off the power. The city's position was that its legal relationship was with the landlord, meaning that it was only the landlord that it had to notify beforehand. As a matter of contract law and ordinary municipal practice, this was true. The residents, however, argued that since this was a matter of the delivery of a crucial service, they too should be entitled to notice and to have an opportunity to make representations – especially since, in this case, the situation was not their fault.

---

15 *Joseph v City of Johannesburg* [2009] ZACC 30.

As in *Doctors for Life*, however, it was only possible to do something for the residents if they could be said to have been in a legal relationship with the city, notwithstanding that their contractual relationship was with their landlord. If the case had concerned water, for example, this would have been easy, because there is a fundamental right to water in the 1996 Constitution. But the drafters did not include a corresponding fundamental right to electricity. *Joseph*'s response, therefore, was to create a fundamental right to service delivery. As in *Doctors for Life*, the key practical basis of this right was the government's policies: in this case, policy documents that spoke about just such a relationship between state and people in the context of service delivery, but did not enact it as a matter of formal law.[16] The court's move was to elevate this policy position to constitutional status. *Joseph* is another very unusual case in which the court is effectively inserting something into the text that was not there before, in order to deal with a constitutional gap and establish a constitutional relationship that did not previously exist as a formal legal matter.

Once again, the final element in the process of informal constitutional change is that both *Doctors for Life* and *Joseph* were accepted by the government. Since they involved the government's own stated positions, and the ideas involved had a deep public status prior to the court's decisions, this may not be surprising. But it nevertheless matters that the ANC government accepted the elevation of both these policy ideas to the status of constitutional obligations. Both are remarkably settled constitutional ideas despite their relatively recent articulation, rather than being provocative or outlandish assertions of constitutional power by a court acting unilaterally where we might be reluctant to conclude too quickly that an informal constitutional change had been successfully completed.

Constraints on formal constitutional amendment powers?

In many systems, there are constraints on formal amendment that are themselves a matter of formal constitutional text, in the form of un-amendability or eternity clauses.[17] The 1996 Constitution is not among them. But there is the possibility that such limits might be developed by the courts. While the doctrinal developments to date certainly could not be included in a list of successful informal constitutional changes like those considered under the previous two headings, there are some trace elements that may matter in the future.

We can use the public participation doctrine already discussed as a starting point. *Doctors for Life* concerned ordinary legislation. But its sister decision, handed down the same day, concerned a similar challenge to a constitutional amendment. *Matatiele (2)* held explicitly that the public participation doctrine applies to all bills, including those that purport to amend the constitution, and it invalidated a constitutional amendment on this basis.[18]

On its own, *Matatiele (2)* is just an extension of the familiar and not usually controversial idea that courts can at least check whether constitutional amendments have been passed in accordance with the prescribed procedures. Indeed, the precise basis for the decision is a failure to comply with the s 74(8) procedural requirement that provincial legislatures must approve constitutional amendments that specifically affect them. (The amendment here

---

16 Fowkes (n 7) 249–51.

17 See further Yaniv Roznai, *Unconstitutional Constitutional Amendments: The Limits of Amendment Powers* (Oxford University Press 2017).

18 *Matatiele Municipality v President of the Republic of South Africa (2)* [2006] ZACC 12, invalidating the Constitution Twelfth Amendment Act; for the explicit language, see esp. [48], [88].

altered a province's boundaries.) Because the provincial legislature concerned had failed to facilitate adequate public participation when considering the constitutional amendment, the province's attempt to give the assent required by s 74(8) was invalid, and so the amendment was invalid for failure to comply with the procedural requirements of s 74(8).

But would the court be willing to apply other, more substantive doctrines to constitutional amendments, in the way it was willing to apply its procedural public participation doctrine to them in *Matatiele (2)*? What little the court has said on this issue does not easily match up with what it has subsequently done.

The court's explicit comments on the possibility of reviewing constitutional amendments on substantive grounds are, to date, both limited and sceptical. Its most definitive (but passing) comment came in the context of a constitutional challenge to the introduction of floor-crossing. I noted earlier that most amendments to the 1996 Constitution have been uncontroversial, but the 2002 floor-crossing amendments are the important exception.

Floor-crossing was viewed with concern because it was seen as a strategic bid by the ANC to entrench its dominant party status. The fear was that the party's control over government patronage would allow it to tempt away minority party MPs and weaken the opposition, particularly the smallest parties. In fact, as I have argued, this view misunderstands both the history of floor-crossing's introduction and how it actually worked in practice.[19] But if one sees floor-crossing in this light, it is natural to think of it as a subversion of democracy, or something that threatened to have this effect. The amendments therefore prompted calls for a basic structure doctrine or some other robust democracy-protecting check.

Those making this argument picked up on a stray comment in an early Constitutional Court judgment, *Premier of KwaZulu-Natal*, about a challenge to an amendment to the 1993 interim constitution. In that case, it was argued that 'amendments to the Constitution had to be made within the "spirit" of the Constitution'.[20] The judgment replied as follows:

> The reliance upon the 'spirit' of the Constitution is, in my view, misconceived. There is a procedure which is prescribed for amendments to the Constitution and this procedure has been followed. If that is properly done, the amendment is con-stitutionally unassailable.[21]

But while moving to close the door, the court left it open a crack:

> It may perhaps be that a purported amendment to the Constitution, following the formal procedures prescribed by the Constitution, but radically and fundamentally restructuring and re-organizing the fundamental premises of the Constitution, might not qualify as an 'amendment' at all.[22]

The judgment then briefly discussed the Indian basic structure doctrine before concluding that, 'even if there is this kind of implied limitation to what can properly be the subject

---

19 Fowkes (n 7) 216–32.
20 *Premier of KwaZulu-Natal v President of the Republic of South Africa* [1995] ZACC 10 [45].
21 Ibid 47.
22 Ibid.

matter of an amendment', the amendment in dispute in the case could not conceivably fall under such a doctrine because it did not concern something sufficiently fundamental.[23]

Seven years later, in *UDM (2)*, those challenging the floor-crossing amendments tried to argue that, this time, fundamentals really were at a stake. But the court again disagreed: 'Here too [as in *Premier KwaZulu-Natal*] it is not necessary to address problems of amendments that would undermine democracy itself, and in effect abrogate or destroy the Constitution.'[24]

Since many democracies permit floor-crossing, went the court's argument, it could not be said that floor-crossing was so inconsistent with democracy as to subvert the very idea of it.[25] This implies that something else might, and might not be an 'amendment' as a result. But *UDM (2)* again appeared very sceptical of this possibility, while again not quite ruling it out:

> Amendments to the Constitution passed in accordance with the requirements of section 74 of the Constitution become part of the Constitution. Once part of the Constitution, they cannot be challenged on the grounds of inconsistency with other provisions of the Constitution. The Constitution, as amended, must be read as a whole and its provisions must be interpreted in harmony with one another. It follows that *there is little if any scope* for challenging the constitutionality of amendments that are passed in accordance with the prescribed procedures and majorities[26] (emphasis added).

The court has not said anything more about the possibility since, and so the doctrinal argument for a substantive limit on constitutional amendment remains extremely thin.

But what complicates matters is that, on three subsequent occasions, the court has been willing to test the rationality of constitutional amendments. It has never actually invalidated a purported constitutional amendment on this basis. Two of the challenges were rejected unanimously, and the third, in *Merafong*, by a majority.[27] But the reason in each case was the substantive finding that the amendment was found to be substantively rational, not a jurisdictional finding that the court was not competent to test the amendments against a substantive rationality standard. In *Merafong*, several minority judgments were written concluding that the constitutional amendment in question did not meet the rationality standard. None of them, however, considers how this substantive review relates to the court's earlier doubt that there was any constitutional space for it.

The resulting doctrinal puzzles are complicated, and many of the complexities are only of local, technical interest.[28] For present purposes, I confine my attention to asking how the court's decisions on the issue to date might add up to an informal constitutional change

---

23 Ibid 46, 49.
24 *United Democratic Movement v President of the Republic of South Africa* [2002] ZACC 21 [17].
25 Ibid, esp. 23–35.
26 Ibid 12.
27 *Merafong Demarcation Forum v President of the Republic of South Africa* [2008] ZACC 10, [62]-[115], [166]-[192], [201], [260]-[286], [306]-[310]; *Poverty Alleviation Network v President of the Republic of South Africa* [2010] ZACC 5 [64]-[76]; *Moutse Demarcation Forum v President of the Republic of South Africa* [2011] ZACC 27 [31]-[43].
28 See further James Fowkes, 'Founding Provisions' in Stuart Woolman and Michael Bishop (eds), *Constitutional Law of South Africa*, 2 ed. (Juta & Co. 2014 service), on which I draw in the discussion that follows here.

limiting the power of amendment on substantive grounds. This has to be considered a possible future change: there is far too much uncertainty to argue that any change has yet occurred. But what it might amount to is the only form of basic structure doctrine that is really possible under the 1996 Constitution. It is this possibility that *Premier of KwaZulu-Natal* and *UDM (2)* were not willing to foreclose entirely, and the court's actions in reviewing amendments for rationality are at least consistent with this possibility.

The foremost obstacle to basic structure arguments in the South African case, aside from the fact that the text itself does not mention substantive limits on amendment, is s 1 of the constitution. Section 1 sets out 'founding values', including human dignity, constitutional supremacy, and multi-party democracy. It is hard to think of more constitutionally fundamental ideas than these: these are the sorts of things a basic structure doctrine should be about, if it is to be about anything at all. But s 74(1) of the constitution explicitly permits the amendment of s 1, albeit subject to an especially high threshold of 75% of the National Assembly, and six of the nine provinces in the NCOP. So, if s 1 can be amended, as s 74(1) says, does that mean even these most basic values are amendable – and, therefore, that a meaningful South African basic structure doctrine cannot get off the ground?

As I have argued elsewhere, this conclusion is not entirely inescapable. One can argue that s 74(1) is there to allow minor amendments, or to permit values to be *added* to the super-entrenched section. One can assign a meaningful role to s 74(1) and the amendment power it indubitably creates without having to concede that it can be used to delete basic values. But how does one draw this line, and how does one locate that line-drawing in the text?

The most plausible answer is the one *Premier of KwaZulu-Natal* mentions: that some changes subvert the Constitution to the extent that they destroy the constitutional order or replace it with a different order. Such changes are not 'amendments', because that word implies that the thing being changed survives the change. This approach would explain why s 1 can be amended, as 74(1) says, but also why there are limits to that power: the s 74(1) power to amend is only a power to amend, not a power to destroy or replace.

This answer can explain the three cases in which the court has tested the rationality of constitutional amendments, although something less than this answer can also fit, too. If this answer is correct, then what the court was testing in those three cases was whether the amendment was irrational, such that it would not amount to an 'amendment', and so would not be constitutionally permissible because s 74 only permits amendments. Read that way, this would potentially be the beginnings of a basic structure doctrine, because something else similar contrary to basic values would similarly exceed the bounds of 'amendment'.

But there are other possibilities, and because in none of the three cases do the judges explain what they understand themselves to be doing, these remain at least equally valid interpretations. For example, it might be that introducing an irrational amendment offends the founding values in s 1, but that this only means that if parliament wants to pass such an amendment, it is effectively amending s 1 and so has to follow that special procedure with its especially high thresholds (which the legislature had not purported to do in any of the three cases). Since this interpretation permits founding values to be altered, it would ground no basic structure doctrine, but it provides a perfectly plausible explanation of the basis for the court's three exercises of rationality review of amendments.

Until the court says more, this argument can be taken no further. But it is worth seeing the traces of what might be developing. Furthermore, provided the court does not disavow its past willingness to consider rationality objections to constitutional amendments, this area will represent a further candidate for an informal constitutional change. Whether the three cases are explained on the basis of a basic structure doctrine or not, they do stand to be explained – and in the absence of much text to go on, whatever explanation is adopted may well represent a development of meaning comparable to the other examples I considered.

Conclusion: judgments as informal constitutional change

In one sense, anything a court does is an act of interpretation. In this sense, all the cases I have discussed are just exercises in interpretation, in giving effect to the constitution. As interpretations go, they are expansive and creative, certainly. But many more of the court's interpretations could be described as expansive and creative. So, what exactly is it about the two cases on implied rights and the two on anti-corruption mechanisms that, in my view, separates them from the court's many decisions that could be called creative or expansive?

It cannot merely be their importance. If we were trying to select cases based on their significance as landmarks of South African constitutional law – if we were trying to select a South African canon – it is not clear that all the cases I have picked out would make the cut, and most of the list would consist of cases I have not discussed. The mere degree of their importance as precedents or the significance of their consequences is not what distinguishes these four cases. By way of analogy, a statute might be labelled as a super-statute or said to have small 'c' constitutional status because of its extraordinary significance in a given legal system.[29] But we would want more before we would conclude that the statute concerned represented an informal constitutional change: that it was actually an *amendment* to the constitution and was really part of the *large 'C'* Constitution.

Instead, the key factors in the four cases I have described as informal constitutional changes is the sense of an insertion, of introducing something that was not there before. Consider *Doctors for Life*. The idea of democracy is present in the constitutional text. If *Doctors for Life* had merely advanced a participatory notion of democracy, it would have been creative and expansive and important, but we would probably conclude that it was simply offering an interpretation of the constitutional idea of democracy. It is the fact that the court, in addition, creates a new right to public participation, which does not appear in the text in the way that the concept of democracy does, that I see as the reason to talk of informal constitutional change. Such claims will always be debatable. Any defensible judicial act of informal constitutional change will proceed by interpretation, and any defensible interpretation will have at least some link to what is already in the text. It will accordingly always be possible to argue that nothing more than interpretation is going on. It is certainly possible to claim that *Doctors for Life* is just a reading of the constitutional idea of democracy and to leave it at that. But the sense of filling-in is strong. There is a sense in which, if one confronted a hypothetical constitutional drafter with the problem, the response would not be to explain what the words in the text were meant to mean, but to see the gap and scribble in an insertion. This is certainly a matter of degree, and certainly debatable, but it is still a line worth trying to draw, and these four cases fall within it.

This should be seen as an objective test, rather than a matter of taking a court at its word. Certainly, when judges talk openly of implied fundamental rights and similar things,

---

29 See Ackerman (n 5) 90–91; William N Eskridge and John Ferejohn 'Super-Statutes' (2001–2002) 50 *Duke Law Journal* 1215; Bruce A Ackerman, 'Holmes Lectures: The Living Constitution' (2007) 120 *Harvard Law Review* 1737; William N Eskridge and John Ferejohn, *Republic of Statutes: The New American Constitution* (Yale University Press 2010).

it is easier to conclude that something new and not previously in the text is being created. But judges will often have reasons not to say that they are engaged in amendment. The South African Court was certainly freer with that sort of candour in *Doctors for Life* and *Joseph* than it was in the more politically antagonistic anti-corruption cases of *Glenister II* and *EFF*. It is also easy to see how a judge trying to establish a basic structure doctrine, a doctrine about the deepest principles of the text and the constitutional system, may have a strong reason to say that she is doing the very opposite of creating something new. In truth, what she will be doing is not creating new values, but a new amendment rule in relation to them. But in the fraught political conditions in which such questions often arise the judge may well prefer not to say even that. Therefore, in a putative case of court-led informal constitutional change, we should ultimately judge the court by what it does rather than what it says. The use of the interpretative power to the degree that it effectively amounts to a new insertion into the constitutional text is an expansive exercise of judicial authority indeed. The cases considered here in a dominant party system show why there might be cause for its use. But it should be subject to close scrutiny, and the first step in that is to call it for what it is. When judges create, rather than merely being creative, it is both more honest and more legally satisfying to describe the result as a judicial act of informal constitutional change.

26

CONSTITUTIONAL CHANGES IN JAPAN

Yasuo Hasebe*

Introduction

Modern Japan has experienced two radical constitutional changes: the enactment of the Constitution of the Empire of Japan of 1889 and the creation of the Constitution of Japan of 1946.

The Tokugawa Shogunate implemented the so-called national seclusion policy (*Sakoku*), limiting Japan's diplomatic partners to Korea and Ryukyu (today's Okinawa), and its trade partners to China and the Netherlands. The arrival of the American squadron—led by Commodore Matthew Perry—to Japan in June 1853[1] triggered a tremendous shockwave throughout the country. The United States threatened to wage war if Japan refused to abandon its seclusion policy. Given the overwhelming power of the United States' modern technologies and military, the Shogunate had no choice but to initiate negotiations for the opening of Japan's ports and market to the United States. In 1854, Japan and the United States concluded their Treaty of Peace and Amity, and subsequently concluded their Commercial Treaty in 1858. Other Western powers, such as Britain, France, the Netherlands, and Russia, followed suit.

Since the only source of the Shogunate's authority was its military strength over *daimyos*,[2] its weak-kneed attitude toward the West's gunboat diplomacy as well as its willingness to consult with both *daimyos* and lower ranking subjects regarding such diplomacy eroded its authority tremendously. People felt that the autocratic regime was crumbling. While conservative *daimyos* and intellectuals advocated for maintaining the 'ancestral' seclusion policy and preventing foreign advances, most of the elite class came to the conclusion that without instituting a modernised and centralised government Japan would be subjugated to and colonised by

---

* The author wishes to thank the editors, Alkmene Fotiadou and Xenophon Contiades for their helpful suggestions and comments.

1 In December 1872, the Meiji government changed the official calendar from lunar to solar. I indicate the dates and months based on the lunar calendar until 1872.

2 The Tokugawa Shogunate made little effort to legitimise its authority with noble-looking doctrines. There was no established church. Those in power thought that any religion that made people revere the next world was dangerous to the authority in this world. Accordingly, Christian faiths were banned. To uphold this ban by preventing religious infiltration, the country adopted the seclusion policy. In place of religion, the Shogunate tried to demonstrate its authority with solemn and spectacular ceremonies. See, on this point, Hiroshi Watanabe, *A History of Japanese Political Thought, 1600–1901*, trans. David Noble (International House of Japan 2012) Chapter 3.

Western countries. Prosperous *daimyos* and their vassals in the western part of the country, such as Shimazu and Môri, allied together to overthrow the Shogunate and establish a new government in order to sustain Japan's independence and development.[3]

In October 1867, to outmanoeuvre the anti-shogunal move, the last Shogun Yoshinobu decided to return his government authority to the emperor (*Taisei-Hôkan*). He expected that he could then organise a federal government composed of all the *daimyos* under the auspices of the imperial court. However, anti-Tokugawa clans engineered a *coup d'état* in Kyoto on 9 December 1867 to establish a new government under the emperor. On the same day, Emperor Mutsuhito declared that the imperial government be restored (*Ôsei-Fukko*). Although Yoshinobu tried to recapture Kyoto, his military forces, which were four times larger than his opponents', were defeated by the new government in the suburbs of Kyoto on 3 and 4 January 1868. After several months of turmoil,[4] on 18 May 1869, Hakodate in Hokkaido, the last bastion of the pro-shogunal forces, capitulated.

The newly established Meiji government was burdened by the enormity of tasks it undertook. It moved the capital from Kyoto to Tokyo in 1869, adopted the military conscription system, suppressed rebellions in various parts of the country,[5] achieved the centralisation of political power,[6] changed the object of people's loyalty from local lords to the emperor, and introduced modern technologies and industries from abroad. Moreover, another significant undertaking of the newly installed government was to renegotiate the so-called 'unequal' commercial treaties entered into by the Tokugawa Shogunate and Western countries in 1858–1860 under the latter's overwhelming military pressures.

These treaties did not give Japan the rights to set tariffs; instead tariffs were to be decided by agreement between Japan and the exporting country. Another result of these treaties was that foreigners were privileged via exemptions from Japanese jurisdiction; for example, judicial cases involving American citizens were tried and decided exclusively by American consuls. In the renegotiation process initiated by the new Meiji government, Western countries demanded as a *sine qua non* that Japan introduce a Western legal system. Thus, with considerable effort, between 1880 and 1904, a modern Western-style legal system was constructed based on numerous institutions and ideas borrowed mainly from France and Germany.[7] As a necessary element of this Westernisation of the legal system, the Constitution of the Empire of Japan was enacted.

---

3 These *daimyos* were supported by Britain (and imported arms mainly from British dealers), while the Shogunate was supported by France.

4 While the political and business centre of the Shogunate, Edo city (today's Tokyo), was relinquished to the new government without serious military conflict, the resistance of pro-shogunal *daimyos* of the north-eastern region was brutally suppressed by the new government forces, including those from the Shimazu, Môri, and Yamanouchi clans. The casualties of this war from January 1868 to May 1869 numbered around 8,200, which is relatively low compared to the American Civil War (1861–1865) that claimed nearly 620,000 lives.

5 The most serious rebellion that erupted in 1877 was led by Takamori Saigô (1828–1877), the son of a low-ranking samurai of the Shimazu clan and one of the main protagonists of the Shimazu-Môri alliance to overthrow the Shogunate. He had resigned his government post in 1873 after his defeat in a political struggle within the new government.

6 In 1869, the government made all *daimyos* return their government authorities to the emperor (*Hanseki-Hôkan*) to create a centralised state. These former *daimyos* were immediately designated as governors of their former fiefs; thus, their statuses did not change in substance initially. In 1871, however, the government demanded that these former *daimyos* abdicate their governorships (*Haihan-Chiken*). This radical reform was implemented without any tumult, partly because the majority of the former *daimyos* suffered severe financial difficulties.

7 After its military victory over Russia in 1905, Japan fully renegotiated the treaties. In 1911, Japan attained the rights to set tariffs.

Another factor that necessitated the enactment of a constitution was that in order to modernise the country, the energy of the people had to be mobilised in the political sphere. In 1875, the Meiji government declared that it intended to establish a constitutional regime (*Rikken-no-Seitai*) gradually. However, due to the growth of the popular movement for the creation of a national parliament,[8] the government declared in 1881 that the parliament would be established in 1890. Following this declaration, it was essential that a constitution be enacted in order to organise and authorise the parliament and other state organs.

The Constitution of the Empire of Japan and the monarchical principle

In 1882, Emperor Mutsuhito ordered Hirobumi Itô[9] to research the constitutional systems of European countries.[10] Itô visited various constitutional scholars in Europe, including Lorenz von Stein and Rudolf von Gneist, and after returning to Japan, he prepared a draft constitution with the help of Kowashi Inoue,[11] Miyoji Itô, Kentarô Kaneko, and Karl Hermann Roesler.[12] Although there was significant support among the populace for a British-style parliamentary system, the draft constitution they designed was based on the German constitutional system. On 11 February 1889, the Constitution of the Empire of Japan (Meiji Constitution) was made public. As it was drafted without public participation, it was a typical imposed constitution.[13] The preamble, originally drafted by Roesler, states that:

8 This is called 'the movement for people's rights (*Minken-Undô*)', which advocated that tax-paying people should be granted the rights to participate in national politics, and later advocated for a constitution-building by the people or through an agreement between the people and the emperor.

9 Hirobumi Itô (1841–1909) was the biological son of a farmer in the Yamaguchi region, which was ruled by the Môri clan, and was later adopted by a low-ranking samurai. After studying in Britain, he played an active part in overthrowing the Shogunate. He became the first prime minister in 1885. Under the Meiji Constitution, he organised the first Cabinet supported by a political party (*Seitô Naikaku*) in 1900. Because of his contribution to the creation of the Meiji Constitution, he was nicknamed *Kenpô-Kô* (Lord Constitution). In 1909, he was assassinated by a Korean activist in Harbin.

10 The Japanese term '*Kenpô*' originally meant 'law' in general. However, because Emperor Mutsuhito used this term in the sense of constitutional law in his proclamation that sent Itô to examine the constitutions of European countries, *Kenpô* came to mean constitutional law specifically.

11 Kowashi Inoue (1843–1895) was born in the Kumamoto region. After helping Itô draft the Meiji Constitution, he successively held various government posts including the Chief of the Cabinet Legislation Bureau and the Minister of Education.

12 Karl Hermann Roesler (1834–1894) studied at the Universities of Munich and Tübingen, taught public law at the University of Rostock, and assisted Itô and his subordinates in his capacity as an official advisor to the Cabinet. For more information on Roesler, see Michael Stolleis, *Public Law in Germany, 1800–1914*, trans. Pamela Biel (Berghahn Books 2001) 383–84.

13 After 1880, the government enacted several edicts regulating assemblies, newspapers, and other political activities. These edicts were used to suppress the people's rights' movement (n 8), which advocated for a constitution reflecting the popular will. After the proclamation of the Meiji Constitution, most of those who had joined the movement still accepted it as one granted by the emperor who cared sincerely about the welfare of the people, not as an artefact concocted by Itô and his underlings and imposed upon the people. The constitution established a popularly elected house of parliament and gave the people an avenue through which it could participate in national politics. The first general election took place in July 1890. For more on these points see, Akihiro Kawaguchi, *Meiji-Kenpô Kintei-shi (A History of the Making of the Meiji Constitution)* (Hokkaido University Press 2007) 433 ff.

The right of sovereignty of the State, We have inherited from Our ancestors, and We shall bequeath them to Our descendants. Neither We nor they shall in [the] future fail to wield them, in accordance with the provisions of the Constitution hereby granted.

Similarly, Article 4 of the constitution states that 'the Emperor is the head of the Empire, combining in Himself the rights of sovereignty, and exercises them, according to the provisions of the present Constitution'. Based on this, it is clear that the monarchical principle (*monarchisches Prinzip*) was adapted from the German system and faithfully respected.[14]

The constitutions of Southern German states enacted in 1818–1820 were based on the idea that the prince alone monopolised the state's power in its entirety, including constituent power.[15] The Constitution of Bavaria of 26 May 1818 clearly stated that 'the king is the head of state. He retains all the sovereign powers and exercises them in accordance with the provisions established by him in this constitution'.[16] The constitution is regarded as a result of a voluntary concession on the part of the prince, even where its contents are actually negotiated with his subjects.[17]

These constitutions opposed the idea that the people as a whole could be represented in the assembly, because to permit such representation was incompatible with the monarchical principle. Under this principle, the prince was the sole representative of the body politic, and the 'plenitude of the state power' was united in his hands.[18] Only the *exercise* of legislative power was shared between the sovereign and the *Landtag*, particularly when new laws affected the liberties or property of the subjects. A constitution was regarded as a self-binding of princely power—not the foundation of but merely a limitation on the power. Given that princely power was not derived from a constitution but rather was voluntarily limited by it, competences not clearly attributed to some of the state organs were generally presumed to have pertained to the prince.[19]

Under the Imperial Constitution of Japan, though the emperor exercised legislative power with the collaboration of the Imperial Diet (Art. 5), he convened, closed, and adjourned the Imperial Diet, and had the power to dissolve the House of Deputies (Art. 7). He sanctioned laws and ordered them to be executed (Art. 6), and issued orders to implement laws and maintain public order and peace (Art. 9). The emperor nominated and dismissed ministers, who were individually responsible to him alone (Art. 55). He also possessed supreme command of the Army and Navy (Art. 11).

The new constitution meticulously reproduced the French and German model of limited monarchy.[20] A limited monarchy is one in which the prince's powers are limited by the prince himself. In principle, it is not much different from an absolute monarchy. The quasi-

14 Masatsugu Inada points out that Kowashi Inoue learned the monarchical principle from writings by Hermann Schulze (Masatsugu Inada, *Meiji Kenpō Seiritsu-Shi (History of the Making of the Meiji Constitution)*, vol. 1 (Yûhi-kaku 1960) 537–42). As to Schulze, see Stolleis (n 12) 314–15.

15 Ernst-Wolfgang Böckenförde, *State, Society and Liberty*, trans. J.A. Underwood (Berg 1991) 91.

16 Article 1 in the Second Title. This article was included in the constitution on the initiative of Georg Friedrich von Zentner, a member of the ministerial conference that drafted the constitution. See Markus Prutsch, *Making Sense of Constitutional Monarchism in Post-Napoleonic France and Germany* (Palgrave 2013) 92–93.

17 Jacky Hummel, *Le constitutionnalisme allemand (1815–1918)* (Presses Universitaires de France 2002) 54.

18 Carl Schmitt, *Constitutional Theory*, trans. Jeffrey Seitzer (Duke University Press 2008) 104.

19 Hummel (n 17) 81. This doctrine is called the *paesumptio pro rege*.

20 The German constitutions of 1818–1820 were themselves modelled on the French Charter of 1814. See on this point Schmitt (n 18) 104 and Hummel (n 17) 55.

official commentary on the constitution, *Kenpō Gige*, made public in 1889 in the name of Hirobumi Itô (but written mainly by Kowashi Inoue), states with respect to Article 4 that the 'substance of sovereignty is retained by the Emperor, but it is exercised in accordance with the provisions of the constitution'. The monarchical principle, referred to in Japan as the principle of imperial sovereignty, was upheld until 1945, when Japan accepted the Potsdam Declaration and surrendered to the allied nations.[21]

The monarchical principle and the state=corporation doctrine

It should be noted that constitutional scholarship of Tatsukichi Minobe, who developed the mainstream doctrines under the Constitution of the Empire of Japan, was not founded on the monarchical principle. In his standard textbook on constitutional law, *Kenpô Satsuyô*, Minobe asserts that the state is a corporation constituted by the people and denies the idea that the emperor retains the state power in its entirety above the constitution.[22] Instead, Minobe contends that the emperor merely derives his powers from the constitution as one of the organs of the state. While Article 4 stipulates that 'the Emperor is the head of state, combining in Himself the rights of sovereignty, and exercises them in accordance with the provisions of the present Constitution', Minobe argues that 'we cannot attain the true nature of the state, drawing on the languages the constitution uses'.[23]

Minobe borrowed his theoretical framework from German public law theory of the late 19th century. During that era, the German public law theory attempted to establish itself as a legal science by conceptualising the state as a corporation, and viewing various legal phenomena surrounding the state as delegations of legal powers, interrelationships between state organs, or creations of state will and its implementation, etc. Every legal effect in public law is, thus, to be attributed to the state as a corporation. According to Carl Friedrich von Gerber:[24]

> The public law (*Staatsrecht*) is a science of state power and deals with such questions as: what a state can will; what organ can and should express state wills in what forms and procedures. The starting point and core of public law resides in the legal personhood (*Persönlichkeit*) of the state.

Therefore, if concepts or languages that cannot be explained in terms of this state=corporation doctrine appear in the texts of the constitution, they should be excluded from the domain of public law and cast away as merely the expression of 'political' ideas. Public law theory should be purified as a science 'above all from non-legal but also from the consideration of ethical and political material'.[25] According to Minobe, the text of

---

21 It should be noted that this principle contained a theoretical dilemma; that is, can a sovereign prince equipped with the plenitude of state power validly limit his own power? On this point, see Yasuo Hasebe, 'Constitutional Borrowing: The Case of Monarchical Principle' in Iulia Motoc, Paulo Pinto de Albuquerque, and Krzysztof Wojtyczek (eds), *New Developments in Constitutional Law: Essays in Honour of András Sajó* (Eleven International 2018) 182–83.

22 Tatsukichi Minobe, *Kenpô Satsuyô (Elements of Constitutional Law)* (Yûhikaku 5th ed. 1932) 15 and 23. Tatsuki-chi Minobe (1873–1948) was Professor of Public Law at the University of Tokyo from 1902 to 1934.

23 Minobe (n 22) 23.

24 Carl Friedrich von Gerber, *Grundzüge des deutschen Staatsrechts* (Bernhard Tauchnitz 3rd ed. 1880) 3–4.

25 Gerber (n 24) 237; Cf. Stolleis (n 12), 318 and Yan Thomas, *Mommsen et 'L'Isolierung' du droit* (Boccard 1984) 32.

Article 4 is a typical instance of an expression of such a 'political' or 'mythical' concept that does not belong within the realm of constitutional scholarship.[26]

At least until the early 1930s, Minobe tried to replace the monarchical principle with the state=corporation doctrine while promoting a British-style parliamentary democracy in Japan.[27] The concept of a sovereign who can create as well as destroy a constitutional system was, for him, an incoherent oxymoronic idea. If sovereign power belonged to the emperor as an individual person, 'war should be regarded as his private fighting, taxes as his private income, and the national railway as his private enterprise', he sarcastically pointed out.[28] His theory, however, was denounced as foreign, treasonable, and inconsistent with the principle of imperial sovereignty, as he faced ferocious political as well as physical attacks. The government publicly condemned his doctrine in 1935 and prohibited publication of his books, including *Kenpô Satsuyô*.[29]

The unique state-form (*Kokutai*) doctrine

One of the scholars who fiercely attacked Minobe was Shinkichi Uesugi.[30] As a professor of constitutional law, he started his career as a supporter of the state=corporation doctrine. However, during his three-year stay in Germany, beginning in 1906, he transformed into a fervent nationalist thinker, asserting that Japan was a unique state—unlike any other (*Banpô-Muhi*).[31] His constitutional theory was not simply a positivistic one that accepted the literal meaning of Article 4.

According to Uesugi, all Western countries originated as democratic republics constructed on social contracts which sought to secure participants' private interests.[32] It was later in the development of these republics that greedy lords began ruling people as their own private property, and the strongest and most avaricious lords became kings in their respective countries. In the modern era, some of these countries have become republics, while others have become parliamentary democracies, in which their princes were substantially the same as presidents of republics. These countries merely returned to their original state-forms.[33] In Uesugi's view, although Japan imported the monarchical principle

---

26 Tatsukichi Minobe, *Chikujô Kenpô Seigi (Article by Article Commentary of the Meiji Constitution)* (Yûhikaku 1927) 73. The 'political' here signifies the 'non-legal' and should be excluded from legal science.

27 The first Cabinet which was based on the support of a political party was organised in 1900. Since 1924 until the *coup d'état* by naval officers on 15 May 1932 (the 5.15 incident), politicians, who were essentially supported by the largest party in the lower house, organised Cabinets. This convention was called the 'usual way of constitutional politics (*Kensei no Jôdô*)'.

28 Minobe (n 22) 22.

29 The series of events is called the 'Tennô-Kikan-setsu (Emperor=Organ Doctrine)' incident. Even Emperor Hirohito was reported to be in favour of Minobe's doctrine. See *Honjô Nikki (Memoire by Shigeru Honjô)* (Hara-Shobô 2005) 203–11. General Honjô (1876–1945) was a military officer in attendance to Emperor Hirohito from 1932 to 1936.

30 Shinkichi Uesugi (1878–1929) taught constitutional law at the University of Tokyo.

31 This episode may remind one of radical Islamist thinkers, such as Sayyid Qutb or Anwar al-Awlaki, who transformed themselves during their stays in Western countries.

32 Thomas Hobbes would agree with Uesugi on the point that every commonwealth was at its foundation a democracy. See, for example, Thomas Hobbes, *On the Citizen* (Richard Tuck and Michael Silverthorne (eds), Cambridge University Press 1998) 94–101. It is not certain whether Uesugi read Hobbes.

33 Shinkichi Uesugi, *Kenpô Dokuhon (Constitutional Law Reader)* (Nihon-Hyôron-Sha 15th ed. 1940) 38–39.

from European countries, all European monarchies are crypt republics which are based not on the monarchical principle but on the popular sovereignty principle.

In contrast, regarding Japan, the original governing regime derived from the emperor's power and only later did the state emerge. The emperor, without considering any of his private concerns, ruled the subjects, and the subjects obeyed the emperor as devoted children obey their loving father. This unique state-form (*Kokutai*) of Japan has existed since time immemorial and will continue into the unforeseeable future. Uesugi asserted that describing and explaining this state-form by making recourse to the foreign state=corporation doctrine, which presupposes that every state is in its essence a democratic republic, is pointless.[34] According to Uesugi, the state=corporation doctrine is simply a smoke screen used to cover up the irreconcilable conflict between the princely sovereignty principle and the popular sovereignty principle. Advocates for this doctrine avoid this conflict by asserting that the holder of state power is the state.[35]

Such a way of thinking can be traced back to the *Kokugaku*, the school of ancient Japanese thought and culture, which arose in the Tokugawa era. Moto'ori Norinaga (1730–1801), a prominent scholar in the *Kokugaku* tradition, argued that Chinese thinkers have propagated noble-looking ideas, such as justice (*gi*), virtue (*toku*), benevolence (*jin*), and civility (*rei*), because the Chinese people are an intrinsically wicked and sly people who would fight among themselves incessantly without the constraint of such artificial norms.[36] Norinaga believed evidence of this could be found in the frequency with which they violently upended their dynasties, noting that 'even the meanest rascal of low birth can, if fortunate, suddenly become an emperor in China'.[37] From Noringa's point of view, Ancient Chinese sages (*seijin*) were revered simply because they successfully invented artificial ideas as tactical means to rule wicked people.

Norinaga held that the Japanese people, in contrast, have lived peacefully and obediently without such artificial, alien ideas or *karagokoro*. In his view, the descendants of the Sun God have continuously reigned over Japan, where people are intrinsically good and obedient.[38] People lived in accordance with their genuine, honest feelings, among which the deepest and strongest was that of love between men and women.[39]

34 Uesugi (n 33) 33 and 40.
35 Shinkichi Uesugi, *Shinkô Kenpô Jutsugi (Newly Written Explanation of Constitutional Law)* (Yûhikaku 10th ed. 1929) 104–08.
36 Uesugi was familiar with Norinaga's books. Cf. Ryûichi Nagao, 'Uesugi Shinkichi Den (A Biography of Shinkichi Uesugi)' in Ryûichi Nagao, *Nihon Kenpô Shisôshi (A History of Japanese Constitutional Thought)* (Kôdansha 1996) 120–21.
37 Moto'ori Norinaga, *Naobinomitama (The Spirit of Re-purification)* [originally published in 1825] (Iwanami Shoten 1936) 17.
38 See Moto'ori Norinaga, *Tamakushige (The Beautiful Comb-Box)* [originally published in 1789] (Iwanami Shoten 1934) 35–36 and his *Naobinomitama* (n 37) 17–21. See also Watanabe (n 2) Chapter 13.
39 According to Norinaga, wanting to eat good food, wear good clothes, dwell in a comfortable house, and be respected are genuine and honest human feelings. Those who claim they do not value beautiful women are merely lying, covering up their true human emotions. Japanese people, including the emperor, have expressed such honest love toward beautiful women by composing short sonnets (*waka*). See Moto'ori Norinaga, *Tamakatsuma (The Beautiful Bamboo Basket)* [originally published in 1795–1812], vol. 4 (Iwanami Shoten 1934) 176 and Moto'ori Norinaga, *Isonokami-sasamegoto (Private Talks on the Ancient)* [originally published in 1816], vol. 2 (Iwanami Shoten 2003) 273–74.

The making of the Constitution of Japan

The Constitution of Japan of 1946 was imposed on the Japanese government by the occupying forces after the Second World War.[40] Immediately after the war, the Japanese government was placed under the authority of General Douglas MacArthur, the Supreme Commander for the Allied Powers. At the beginning of the occupation, the Japanese government maintained that despite the surrender, the basic state-form—the monarchical principle—was still intact and there was no need to revise the Constitution of the Empire of Japan.

MacArthur, however, repeatedly urged that the constitution be revised as a crucial step toward implementing the terms of Japan's surrender as stipulated in the Potsdam Declaration. The government reacted by establishing a committee, chaired by Jôji Matsumoto, an eminent commercial law professor, to consider the need for amending the constitution. After several months of deliberation, the Matsumoto committee produced a draft proposal, the conservative contents of which were regarded as unresponsive to the international climate of hostility toward the imperial regime.[41] Accordingly, under orders from MacArthur, the General Headquarters of the Supreme Commander (GHQ) produced its own version of a draft constitution and urged the Japanese government to revise the Meiji Constitution on the basis of this document.[42] The GHQ draft was drawn up in two weeks and delivered to representatives of the Japanese government on 13 February 1946.

Although stunned by the unexpected presentation of the GHQ draft, the Japanese government reluctantly agreed to amend the constitution on the basis of this document. The amendment process adhered strictly to the procedure stipulated under the Meiji Constitution: the draft proposal by the government, which drew heavily on the American draft, was first presented to the House of Deputies, then reviewed by the House of Peers. Finally, with the consent of the Privy Council, the Constitution of Japan was promulgated by the emperor on 3 November 1946, as an amendment to the Meiji Constitution.[43]

The reaction of constitutional scholars to the new constitution was overwhelmingly favourable. Toshiyoshi Miyazawa,[44] who was a key member of the conservative Matsumoto committee, admitted later that upon reading the GHQ draft, he was filled with joy and became its fervent supporter. Prior to reading the GHQ draft, Japanese scholars could not

---

40 For the facts surrounding its adoption, see Ray Moore and Donald Robinson, *Partners for Democracy: Crafting the New Japanese State under MacArthur* (Oxford University Press 2002), and Chaihark Hahm and Sung Ho Kim, *Making We the People: Democratic Constitutional Founding in Postwar Japan and South Korea* (Cambridge University Press 2015) 130–54.

41 One of the draft proposals deliberated at the Matsumoto committee was exposed by the *Mainichi Shimbun* Newspaper on 1 February 1946. The GHQ staff were surprised by its conservative content. See Kenzô Takayanagi, Ichirô Ôtomo, and Hideo Tanaka (eds), *Nihon-Koku Kenpô Seitei no Katei (The Making of the Constitution of Japan)*, vol. I (Yûhikaku 1972) 41–75.

42 A memorandum written on 1 February 1946 by Courtney Whitney, Chief of the Government Section of the GHQ, stated that: 'In my opinion, in the absence of any policy decision by the Far Eastern Commission on the subject (which would, of course, be controlling), you have the same authority with reference to constitutional reform as you have with reference to any other matter of substance in the occupation and control of Japan' (Takayanagi, et al. (n 41) 91–93). See also Moore and Robinson (n 40) 119.

43 Article 74 of the Meiji Constitution stipulates that to amend the constitution, both houses of the parliament should, by two-thirds or more of the members present, pass the proposition sponsored by the emperor, on the condition that in each house two-thirds or more of total membership is present.

44 Toshiyoshi Miyazawa (1899–1976) taught constitutional law at the University of Tokyo from 1925 to 1959. He was a disciple of Tatsukichi Minobe.

imagine that their country might adopt such a liberal and democratic constitution. The resulting constitutional bill of rights is quite similar to those standard in Western constitutions. Equipped with an American-style judicial review system (Art. 81), post-war Japan was reborn as a normal constitutional democracy.

Although we may say that this constitution was imposed upon the government,[45] it is not true that it was imposed against the will of the Japanese people. One of the reasons that the Japanese government agreed to amend the Meiji Constitution on the basis of the GHQ draft was that the GHQ threatened to make its draft public if the government refused to do so.[46] If the Constitution of Japan was null and void because it had been imposed, the Japanese people would have to continue living under the Meiji Constitution, which had itself been imposed upon them by Emperor Mutsuhito and his government. In short, the contention that the Constitution of Japan is void because it was forced upon the Japanese people is incoherent and untenable.

The August revolution thesis: did the basic norm change?

One theoretical difficulty remains with regard to explaining the validity of the new constitution: can one say that this constitution is valid as an amendment of the old constitution? The amendment procedure stipulated in the Meiji Constitution was strictly adhered to when the new constitution was established, but is it possible to coherently establish a new constitution based on the principle of popular sovereignty as an amendment to the old constitution based on the monarchical principle?[47]

This discrepancy is glaringly obvious when comparing the emperor's proclamation and the text of the preamble of the Constitution of Japan. The emperor's proclamation states that:

> We, the Emperor, profoundly pleased that the foundation of the new Japan has been established, approve the amendment to the Constitution of the Empire of

---

45 There were various negotiations between the GHQ and the Japanese government or parliament over the content of the new constitution from February to November 1946. For example, the GHQ accepted the proposal by the Japanese government that the parliament should be composed of two houses. On the initiative of the Japanese parliament, Article 25 on the right to maintain the minimum standards of wholesome and cultured living was added, and to the beginning of the second clause of Article 9 the phrase 'In order to accomplish the aim of the preceding paragraph' was added. The latter modification was proposed by Hitoshi Ashida (1887–1959), the chairperson of the ad hoc committee on constitutional issues of the House of Representatives. He claimed that this modification made it clear that the maintenance of the self-defence forces was possible under Article 9. See Secretariat of the Research Committee on Constitutional Law, *Kenpô Seitei no Keii ni kansuru Shô-Iinkai Hôkokusho (Sub-Committee Report on the Process of the Making of the Constitution)* (Printing House of the Ministry of Finance 1961) 503–04.

46 Takayanagi, et al. (n 41), 328–29.

47 If that were the case, the emperor would be able to retrieve the sovereignty from the people. If we may borrow the expression of Alf Ross: '[T]he assumption that the basic norm may be amended in accordance with its own rules involves contradictions' (Alf Ross, 'On Self-Reference and a Puzzle in Constitutional Law' (1969) 78(309) *Mind* 4. Similarly, regarding the 'well-behaved dominions' of Australia, Canada, and New Zealand, whose constitutions were originally enacted by the UK Parliament, H.L.A. Hart points out that their ultimate rules of recognition have now shifted and new legal system emerged, such that the UK Parliament's legal competence to legislate for these former colonies is no longer recognised [H.L.A. Hart, *The Concept of Law* (Oxford University Press 3rd ed. 2012) 120]. In either view, one ultimate legal authority cannot be a foundation of another ultimate legal authority.

Japan, which the Imperial Diet adopted in accordance with Article 73, with the consent of the Privy Council, and let it publicised.

This proclamation, faithful to the monarchical principle, presupposes that the emperor holds the constituent power. On the other hand, the preamble declares that the sovereign Japanese people established the new constitution, stating that:

> We, the Japanese people, acting through our duly elected representatives in the National Diet, determined that we shall secure for ourselves and our posterity the fruits of peaceful cooperation with all nations and the blessings of liberty throughout this land, and resolved that never again shall we be visited with the horrors of war through the action of government, do proclaim that sovereign power resides with the people and do firmly establish this Constitution.

Miyazawa suggested that when the Japanese government accepted the Potsdam Declaration in August 1945, which demanded the implementation of popular sovereignty, the legal foundation of the Japanese constitutional system was revolutionised,[48] and the monarchical principle was abandoned. The basis of the Meiji Constitution itself then shifted to popular sovereignty. This fundamentally transformed constitution could function as the basis to support the legal validity of the new constitution, which could then be validated as an amendment to the transformed former constitution. This theory, called the August Revolution thesis, is the dominant view used to explain the validity of the Constitution of Japan.[49]

Tomo'o Otaka,[50] Miyazawa's colleague at the University of Tokyo, criticised the thesis, arguing that the sovereignty of Japan resided, both before and after 1945, in the supreme principle of law, that is, *Nomos*. He stated that the difference between imperial sovereignty and popular sovereignty should not be exaggerated because sovereignty should not be understood to be an unlimited, omnipotent power. It should never be exercised in whatever way its holder likes, whether it is the emperor or the people. The so-called sovereign should always govern the state in accordance with the *Nomos*, the supreme principle of law. The genuine sovereign, the highest authority in the state, can be said to be neither the emperor nor the people, but the *Nomos*. Therefore, Otaka asserted, no revolution in the legal sense occurred.[51]

In opposition, Miyazawa retorted that to state that the sovereignty resides in the supreme principle of law does not resolve the question of who will decide the concrete content of that principle. Otaka's thesis simply evades this core question: the answer should be either

---

48 In his textbook on the Meiji Constitution, *Kenpô Ryakusetsu (An Outline of Constitutional Law)* (Iwanami Shoten 1942) 73–75, Miyazawa argued that the monarchical principle was the foundation of the state of Japan, which could not be changed even through the amendment process stipulated in the Meiji Constitution.

49 Toshiyoshi Miyazawa, 'Nihon-Koku Kenpô Seitan no Hôri (The Legal Doctrine on the Birth of the Constitution of Japan)' in his *Kenpô no Genri (Principles of Constitutional Law)* (Iwanami Shoten 1967); Cf. Yasuo Hasebe, 'The August Revolution Thesis and the Making of the Constitution of Japan' (1997) *Rechtstheorie*, Beiheft 17, 335; Hahm and Kim (n 40) 145–57.

50 Tomo'o Otaka (1899–1956) taught legal philosophy at the University of Tokyo from 1944 to 1956.

51 Tomo'o Otaka, *Kokumin-Shuken to Tennô-sei (Popular Sovereignty and the Imperial Regime)* (Seirin-Shoin 1954). While Otaka did not clarify what the contents of the *Nomos* were during the debate with Miyazawa, later in his textbook, *Hô-Tetsugaku-Gairon (Outline of Jurisprudence)* (Gakusei-Sha 1953), he stated that the *Nomos* was nothing other than the ideal of equal welfare of all the people, explicitly referring to the utilitarian principle of the greatest happiness of the greatest number (ibid 284).

the emperor or the people. Miyazawa contended that avoiding this question merely conceals the damage inflicted upon the imperial regime.[52]

It should be noted that Miyazawa's argument here curiously resembles that employed by Uesugi to criticise Minobe's state=corporation doctrine (see above). Once the principle of popular sovereignty has been established and the state-form (*Kokutai*) changed, there is no need to evade the question of who the sovereign is. However, the popular sovereignty principle is obviously contaminated with the same vicious self-reference as the monarchical principle.[53] Moreover, the 'August Revolution' is a theoretical artefact; neither charismatic leaders nor popular movements appeared in this 'revolution'.

As the August Revolution thesis is the dominant view, not a few scholars think that Miyazawa prevailed over Otaka. But the question is not so simple. Miyazawa's thesis is a transcendental exercise trying to make explicit the theoretical presuppositions, which can coherently explain the radical discrepancy between the two constitutions. Miyazawa's thesis is no better than Otaka's thesis in terms of science of law, though some scholars assert otherwise. The question to be asked is which interpretation better explains the historical facts and justifies the current constitution. The answer to that question would vary depending upon what political morality one is committed to.[54]

It should be noted that there is another thesis possible which is different both from Miyazawa's and Otaka's; the acceptance of the Potsdam Declaration was not only a legal revolution shifting the location of sovereignty, but also a starting point of a moral revolution that radically changed basic moral principles uniting the Japanese people. Purely juristic explanations cannot plausibly describe the radical changes that occurred in the Japanese society after the Second World War. And the new moral principles, which correspond to modern constitutionalism, have been firmly entrenched in the current Constitution of Japan. Contrary to Otaka's thesis, the *Nomos* of Japan has been fundamentally modified.[55]

A constitutional change without a constitutional amendment?

Since its adoption in 1946, the Constitution of Japan has yet to be amended. However, there was a debate over whether the meaning of Article 9 changed without undergoing the formal amendment process stipulated in the constitution.[56]

Article 11 of the Meiji Constitution states that 'the emperor has the supreme command of the Army and Navy'. Military forces asserted that this article meant that they were under the direct command of the emperor; in other words, they were not controlled by the Cabinet or the Imperial Diet. When the Hamaguchi Cabinet concluded the London Naval Treaty in 1930 that limited naval shipbuilding, the navy alleged that this treaty infringed on

---

52 Toshiyoshi Miyazawa, 'Kokumin-Shuken to Tennô-sei (Popular Sovereignty and the Imperial Regime)' in Miyazawa, *Kenpô no Genri* (n 49) 281–344.

53 See (n 21).

54 See Hasebe (n 49).

55 I am grateful to Bruce Ackerman for some discussion on the idea described in this paragraph.

56 Article 96 of the Constitution of Japan stipulates that: 'Amendments to this Constitution shall be initiated by the Diet, through a concurring vote of two-thirds or more of all the members of each House and shall thereupon be submitted to the people for ratification, which shall require the affirmative vote of a majority of all votes cast thereon'. While not a few scholars argue that the basic principles of the current constitution, including the popular sovereignty principle, the guarantee of fundamental rights, and the principle of pacifism, are unamendable [see, for example, Yoshinobu Ashibe, *Kenpô (Constitutional Law)* (Iwanami-Shoten 6th ed. 2015) 396–99], no serious scholar ever contends that Article 9 itself cannot be revised at all.

the imperial right of commanding the army and navy. Objecting to this, Minobe argued that the right to command the army and navy should be distinguished from the emperor's right to determine 'the organisation of the army and navy', which the Cabinet could control in accordance with Article 12 of the constitution.[57] Such a way of thinking on the part of the military forces supported the army's adventurous moves on the continent and *coups d'état* before the Second World War.

The Constitution of Japan, however, is based on a contrasting ideal that its contents should not legitimate the waging of war. Article 9 of the Constitution of Japan states that: 'the Japanese people forever renounce war as a sovereign right of the nation and the threat or use of force as means of settling international disputes' and that: 'In order to accomplish the aim of the preceding paragraph, land, sea, and air forces, as well as other war potential, will never be maintained'.

The idea of renunciation of war 'as means of settling international dispute' derives from the Kellogg-Briand Pact of 1928. This treaty endeavoured to terminate the Grotian idea of war as a means to settle international disputes. The founder of this idea, Hugo Grotius, was a just war theorist. His theory was quite peculiar—determining whether a state has a just cause to resort to war by whether it wins the war. Since there was no common judicial court in the international society, states had no choice but to use war as a means to resolve disputes. Therefore, the outcome of war should be accepted as 'right' by all its participants, as a decision of the court would be accepted as 'right' by all its parties.[58]

This Grotian idea was negated by the Pact of 1928, and war 'as means of settling international dispute' was outlawed. Leaders who dragged Japan into the Second World War were condemned as war criminals on the grounds that their use of war contravened the Pact. Article 9, Clause 1 confirmed the principle of outlawry of war 'as means of settling international dispute'. Accordingly, Clause 2 of Article 9 should be understood to prohibit Japan from maintaining instruments to wage war 'as means of settling international dispute'. In other words, the Pact as well as Article 9 permit Japan to exercise the individual right of self-defence.[59] Following such an understanding, successive governments of Japan have taken the view that to use force for the purpose of self-defence is constitutional, and therefore, to maintain self-defence forces (SDF) is permissible under Article 9.

Some constitutional scholars in Japan have argued that the meaning of Article 9 has changed without any formal amendment of the constitution. As a result, they claim, maintaining the SDF is now constitutional though it was unconstitutional under the original meaning of Article 9. This argument is based on the following two arguments: (i) Article 9 prohibits the government from maintaining any military forces, including even those for the purpose of individual self-defence; and (ii) the meaning of a rigid constitution may change in a manner not prescribed by the constitution.[60] Both arguments have faced criticism.

---

57 This dispute was a preliminary stage of the 'Emperor=Organ Doctrine' incident in 1935. See (n 29) and the accompanying text.

58 Oona Hathaway and Scott Shapiro, *The Internationalists: And Their Plan to Outlaw War* (Allen Lane 2017). The authors call this Grotian idea the 'Might is Right' principle (ibid 23).

59 Many signatory states of the Pact including the United States made it clear that they understood that the treaty did not outlaw defensive wars. See the testimony of Frank Kellogg, Secretary of the State, before the Senate Committee on Foreign Relations on 7 and 11 December 1928. See also Hathaway and Shapiro (n 58) 126–27.

60 Kiminobu Hashimoto, *Nihon-Koku Kenpô (The Constitution of Japan)* (Yûhikaku 1980) 432. As to the second point, Hashimoto refers to the German concept of *Verfassungswandlung*, which is discussed in Georg Jellinek, *Allgemeine Staatslehre* (Athenäum 3rd ed. 1976 [1914]) 536–39. Jellinek argues that even a rigid constitution cannot completely prevent the emergence and consolidation of unconstitutional legal norms.

First, as mentioned above, the government has argued that Article 9 allows use of force to defend the lives and property of the Japanese people. It may be conceded that this article sets the baseline about using force and maintaining military forces; that is, on both points, no allowance is the baseline. Article 9 says nothing about the possibility of maintaining the SDF. Therefore, if the government deviates from this baseline, it should provide sufficient reasons for doing so. To the extent that the government successfully justifies the deviation, it is not unconstitutional. From such a view, it is not necessary to argue that the meaning of Article 9 has been changed.

This view is supported not only by the historical background described above but also by the following argument. Since it is unrealistic to protect the people's lives and property without any use of force, to insist that the constitution prohibits the government from maintaining even the SDF would amount to advocating that such a national policy is the realisation that pure pacifism is the only 'good' way of living (or dying). However, such an idea is incompatible with modern constitutionalism which purports to realise a fair co-existence of people who embrace plural worldviews that are often incommensurate with each other.[61]

Second, one of the reasons for establishing a rigid constitution is to effectively constrain the government's actions. To recognise a possibility that the meaning of a rigid constitution, in particular, its principal provision, may change in a manner not prescribed by the constitution is to undermine its *raison d'être*, amounting to an admission that the constitution can be changed by the government's unconstitutional actions.[62]

Under the government's reading of Article 9, constitutional constraints are set by the authoritative interpretations of relevant organs. If these authoritative interpretations are manipulated by incumbent administrations in power, constitutional constraints will evaporate. When the independent judiciary issues authoritative interpretations, we may expect that some checks-and-balances would work and that the incumbent administration cannot change them at will.

However, regarding Article 9, the Supreme Court, which is endowed with 'the power to determine the constitutionality of any law, order, regulation or official act' (Article 81 of the Constitution) has been quite reticent, and the Cabinet Legislation Bureau, which is—formally speaking—just a bureau under the Cabinet, has worked as the authoritative interpreter. The risk of according such a significant task to one cabinet bureau became manifest when, in July 2014, the Abe administration, without providing sufficient ground, changed the long-held government view that only the exercise of the individual right of self-defence is permitted under Article 9.[63]

On 3 May 2017, the 70th anniversary of the effective date of the Constitution of Japan, Prime Minister Shinzô Abe made public his intention to revise Article 9 of the Constitution in a video-message broadcast at a pro-amendment meeting in Tokyo. One of his proposals was to add a new sentence to Article 9, which will clarify that the government can keep the

---

61 See, for example, Yasuo Hasebe, 'Constitutional Borrowing and Political Theory' (2003) 1 *International Journal of Constitutional Law* 224, 242–43.

62 Yôichi Higuchi, *Kenpô (Constitutional Law)* (Sôbun-sha 3rd ed. 2007) 85–86.

63 The Abe Administration declared the use of the right of collective self-defence, which was considered unconstitutional by previous administrations, to be constitutional within certain limits, namely, when the rights to life, liberty, and the pursuit of happiness of the Japanese people are jeopardised by military attacks against foreign countries with which Japan has close relationship. On this issue, see, for example, Yasuo Hasebe, 'The End of Constitutional Pacifism?' (2017) 26 *Washington International Law Journal* 125.

SDF while maintaining the present Clauses 1 and 2. This can be seen as the latest instance of the long-running effort to amend the constitution by right-wing political forces. However, it remains to be seen whether such a revision will soon materialise.[64]

Conclusion

The peculiar idea that there are values specific to Japanese culture which all Japanese people should embrace sustained the national seclusion policy in the Edo era as well as the unique state-form doctrine under the Meiji Constitution. It also supported expansionism via military means before the Second World War. It was argued that because the emperor is a loving monarch who rules his subjects without considering his private interests, that all people, not just the Japanese people should obey him like his children. Under this ideology, foreigners who did not obey the emperor were not compliant enough, and, therefore, had to be punished; such an ideology was a very troublesome idea for neighbouring nations.

Under the current constitution, right-wing politicians in the Liberal Democratic Party (LDP) have often claimed that liberal constitutionalism is an idea foreign to Japan. As such, some allege that Japan would become a much better country if it was purified of this foreign idea, or if, at least, the specifically Japanese values, which they recognise, were balanced against the Western, 'universal' values. We can detect such a line of thinking in the draft constitution made public by the LDP in April 2012.[65] Amending any part of the constitution may become the first step of this purification; the next step would be transforming Japan's regime into an autocratic, illiberal democracy.

The accepted opinion is that the constitution should not be hastily revised when people are familiar with its meanings and practices. However, we cannot expect that the persistent right-wing attacks against liberal constitutionalism will dissipate soon. For the foreseeable future, constitutional scholarship in Japan must not only conduct typical tasks of expounding constitutional developments and providing legal advice but also conduct additional tasks of defending liberal constitutionalism itself.

---

64 If Mr Abe's proposal to amend the constitution were solidly supported by persuasive reasons, it would not be difficult for him to acquire necessary majorities in both houses. In fact, at the time of writing (December 2018), the current government coalition has secured the necessary two-thirds seats in the Lower House and more than 60% seats in the Upper House. The reality is that even MPs of the government coalition are not sure whether it is necessary to change the constitution according to Mr Abe's proposal. According to the opinion poll conducted by NHK (Japan Broadcasting Corporation) in May 2018, only 19% of those polled answered that amending the constitution was the political issue to be prioritised over other issues.

65 https://jimin.jp-east-2.storage.api.nifcloud.com/pdf/news/policy/130250_1.pdf, last visited on 24 March 2020.

INDEX

Page numbers in **bold** refer to content in **figures**; page numbers in *italics* refer to content in *tables*.

Printed and bound by CPI Group (UK) Ltd, Croydon, CR0 4YY

17/07/2024

01019171-0007